BUSINESS REVIEW BOOKS

Marketing

THIRD EDITION

Richard L. Sandhusen

BARRON'S

All inquiries should be addressed to:
Barron's Educational Series, Inc.
250 Wireless Boulevard
Hauppauge, New York 11788
http://www.barronseduc.com

International Standard Book No. 0-7641-1277-5

Library of Congress Catalog Card No. 99-16325

Library of Congress Cataloging-in-Publication Data

Sandhusen, Richard.
    Marketing / by Richard L. Sandhusen.—3rd ed.
        p.   cm.—(Barron's business review series)
    Includes bibliographical references and index.
    ISBN 0-7641-1277-5
    1. Marketing. I. Title. II. Series.
HF5415.S272   2000
658.8—dc21
                                        99-16325
                                        CIP

PRINTED IN THE UNITED STATES OF AMERICA
9 8 7 6 5 4 3 2 1

CONTENTS

PREFACE

This third edition of *Marketing* is designed for students and businesspeople who need a clear, concise understanding of marketing concepts, processes, problems, and applications. Like the first two editions, this third edition provides comprehensive coverage of a standard marketing curriculum, updated to reflect twenty-first century changes in markets and marketing practices. Emphasis is on the marketing planning process whereby environments are analyzed, missions and objectives established, and strategies and controls formulated to bring together target markets and marketing mixes. Also covered are modern tools and techniques for segmenting markets, forecasting sales, and building product-place-price-promotion-marketing mixes. Each chapter begins with an overview summary of chapter content, and concludes with a chapter perspective summary of key concepts covered.

However, this third edition expands on and enhances this coverage of the basic marketing curriculum in five ways.

1. A Single Case Focus: A single master case is the focus of each chapter, involving the reader in the trials and triumphs of the fictitious Merton Electronics Company, as it formulates and implements strategic marketing plans for its line of "Mighty Mind" electronic training systems. These plans involve the assessment of threats and opportunities, and the implementation of strategies for developing, pricing, promoting, and distributing Mighty Mind systems in global and domestic markets. Included are modern tools and techniques for automating the sales function and exploiting the Internet.

2. International Market Coverage: In addition to extensive coverage of marketing in the U.S. marketplace, *Marketing* extensively covers international markets and marketing. This global coverage includes two chapters on environmental threats and opportunities in global markets, and an "International Perspective" section in every chapter that translates marketing concepts and practices from domestic to global markets.

3. Market Focus Features: Every chapter of *Marketing* includes "Market Focus" and "Global Focus" features that integrate and illustrate chapter concepts in real-life contexts, as diverse companies—ranging from corporate giants like Ford and AT&T to single proprietorships like Judith Sans Inc.—tackle marketing problems and exploit marketing opportunities in domestic and international markets.

4. A special chapter on Internet marketing: This chapter focuses on how Internet access levels the competitive playing field and helps companies create and market products and services through all stages of the strategic marketing planning process. Featured are the specifics of Merton Electronics' commitment to a total Internet marketing strategy, with brand, sales, and service Web sites that help penetrate the European marketplace by dramatically improving the way suppliers and distributors are

selected; marketing research is conducted; target markets are defined; products are designed, produced, priced, and promoted; logistics functions are streamlined; and performance is measured and controlled.

5. A new end-of-chapter feature, "Matchup Exercises," that complements interesting, involving, case-based, short-answer exercises as an unusually effective way to review chapter content and test student learning.

As with previous editions, this third edition of *Marketing* is written in a tight, narrative style that avoids redundant puffery and facilitates the extensive new coverage of global and Internet marketing.

CHAPTER CONTENT AND SEQUENCE

Chapter content is sequenced in terms of the logic of the strategic marketing planning process, as follows:

The first five chapters lay a foundation for what is to come by defining basic marketing concepts and processes (Chapter 1), examining the role of the marketing manager in formulating and implementing strategic marketing plans (Chapter 3), and exploring environmental forces, threats, and opportunities in domestic and global markets (Chapters 2, 4, and 5).

The next three chapters focus on integrated company systems through which marketing plans and programs are carried out, including systems for organizing, planning, and controlling marketing programs (Chapter 6), and the marketing information system, with its marketing research input, that underpins the strategic marketing planning process (Chapters 7 and 8).

The next four chapters look out into the marketplace, defining the nature and scope of consumer markets and consumer behavior (Chapter 9), with emphasis on the steps of the buying decision process. Chapter 10 examines organizational markets, with emphasis on characteristics that distinguish them from consumer markets, and defines *buyer behavior*. Chapter 11 examines approaches and techniques for segmenting consumer and organizational markets, and positioning products in these markets; Chapter 12 focuses on approaches and techniques for forecasting market and sales potential.

Chapters 13 through 20 focus on the four components of the marketing mix designed to meet target market needs and achieve company business and marketing objectives. Chapters 13 and 14 examine product management decisions, including branding, packaging, labeling, developing new products and services, and using product life cycles to formulate product/market strategies.

Chapters 15 and 16 focus on pricing problems, objectives, strategies, and tactics; and Chapters 17 and 18 on indirect and direct aspects of promotion, including advertising, sales promotion, publicity, and direct selling in domestic and global markets. Chapters 19 and 20 focus on the place element of the marketing mix, including channel types, functions and flows, and logistics concepts pertaining to transporting, storing, and distributing products in domestic and international markets. Chapter 21, on Internet marketing, highlights the many ways Internet access can help companies create and market products and services through all stages of the strategic planning process.

Richard Sandhusen
April 2000

1
THE MARKETING PROCESS: BASIC CONCEPTS

OVERVIEW

This chapter introduces marketing functions, values, philosophies, and perspectives that inform the strategic marketing planning (SMP) process discussed throughout this book. Also introduced is the Merton Electronics case, which provides examples to clarify the nature and dynamics of the SMP process.

INTRODUCING MERTON ELECTRONICS

In this and subsequent chapters, we focus on activities of marketing managers in formulating strategic marketing plans that create fits among a firm's goals, resources, and changing opportunities. Throughout this text, we will use the following case, based on the fictitious Merton Electronics Company, to illustrate this strategic marketing planning process.

The Merton Electronics Company is a large manufacturer of chip circuits and other electronic components, which it markets to firms in the consumer electronics segment of the organizational market. In the early 1990s, Merton's research and development department, working with its engineering and product design departments, developed a line of lightweight computers, featuring the new-generation Merton Moonchip and infrared ports that connect, remotely if necessary, to desktop computers, facsimile, and telecommunication units. Called the Merton Mighty Mind (MM) line, these advanced computers performed admirably in diverse applications, including interpersonal conferencing, spreadsheets, electronic mail, and word processing. The fact that introducing the MM line of laptop and notebook computers into the consumer market meant competing with their own best customers did not especially concern Merton's management. In the freewheeling, highly competitive consumer electronics market, this was hardly unprecedented. What did concern them was the nature of this competition. With faster, smarter, smaller computers appearing practically overnight, Merton management realized it would take large, established competitors (like IBM and Apple) little time to catch up with, and rush past, Merton's MM line of notebook and laptop computers.

By way of insulating themselves against this likelihood, Merton did two things that facilitated a successful launch of MM systems into the domestic market:

1. Retained Lora Moore as Merton's marketing manager. Moore, a marketing consultant who specialized in developing and commercializing new products, was retained when Merton first devised the MM concept and developed prototype products. Her mission was to fully develop these prototypes into marketable products, identify markets for these products, formulate marketing programs to penetrate these markets, and implement these programs. She was also responsible for organizing the new division of Merton Electronics that she would be managing, called the MM systems division, and developing the marketing systems (such as marketing information and control systems) needed for it to achieve its strategic objectives.

2. Entrenched the MM line in a strong niche market. One of Moore's main initiatives was to focus the MM's marketing efforts on the professional niche market segment (accountants, lawyers, engineers, architects, doctors, and the like). Although members of these professions could purchase individual products from Merton (for example, a personal computer or fax machine), they would be encouraged to purchase packaged systems composed of software and hardware components that addressed problems and opportunities in three areas: communication, training and development, and administration.

   For example, the MM systems designed for an architectural practice could include programs for training practice members, keeping them abreast of new trends and developments in the field, and profitably administering the practice. Advantages Moore envisioned for this packaged systems strategy included insulation against competitors selling hardware or software alone, the affluence of the professional market segment, and the higher profit margins possible as a result of selling entire systems versus system components alone.

   In promoting these systems, Merton emphasized the quality and timeliness of its software, the performance features of MM hardware (computers, faxes, cellular phones, and so on), and—a key point—that all MM systems are customized to the needs of individual customers.

In the rest of this book, we focus on Moore's ideas and actions in defining domestic—and, later, global—markets for MM systems, building a productive marketing team to penetrate these markets, and providing team members with the strategic and practical resources to carry out this mission.

MARKETING CONCEPTS THAT SUPPORT MARKETING PLANS

Underpinning Moore's planning activities are a number of marketing concepts, including needs, demands, exchange, markets, marketing mixes, marketing environments, competition, and marketing itself. Definitions of these concepts will lead, later in this chapter, to a discussion of marketing processes, historical perspectives on marketing, and marketing philosophies. In Chapter 3, we examine how all these concepts come together in the strategic marketing planning process.

Needs are states of physical or mental deprivation. In more advanced economies, needs become more numerous and arise on different levels. For example, needs satisfied by enrolling in a diet program in the United States might simultaneously be functional (to lose weight), psychological (to feel better about your appearance), and social (to attract a mate). An important job of marketing managers is to determine what product-related needs predominate among various customer groups and then to turn these needs into **wants** by focusing on the need-satisfying benefits of the products they are marketing.

Demands are wants backed by purchasing power. In Merton's domestic market, for example, all the money spent by, or for, managers in tax accounting firms who want MM systems to help them better serve clients comprises the demand for these programs in this single target market. Purchases by all groups comprising Merton's market represent total demand for MM systems.

Exchange is the process by which two or more parties give something of value to one another to satisfy wants. As such, exchange is both the objective and common denominator of all marketing activity and, in addition to the exchange of money for tangible products, can take such diverse forms as exchange of tuition for an education, votes for political action, and skills for a job. A tax accountant who pays $3000 for a Merton MM system illustrates conditions required for a voluntary exchange to take place:

1. At least two parties, each with something of value to the other party;

2. Each party capable of communication and delivery;

3. Each party free to accept or reject the other's offer;

4. Each party believing it appropriate and desirable to deal with the other party;

5. Legal authority, such as a law of contracts, to protect the agreement.

In domestic markets, all these conditions apply in most situations where things of value are exchanged: a price that represents appropriate value to both willing parties is agreed upon, and the product is purchased and delivered. If either party is later dissatisfied, legal agreements provide recourse, such as returning the product for a refund or suing for damages.

Markets are groups of actual or potential buyers who can afford to buy the product, have the needed authority to buy the product, desire the product, and will respond similarly to a marketing mix appeal. The acronym MAD-R—for money, authority, desire, and response—will help you remember these characteristics. Groups of people who possess these MAD-R attributes in greater abundance are called target markets. For example, in Merton's domestic market, tax accountants represented an excellent target market for MM systems in that their firms could afford to invest heavily in their continued education, they had the "authority" (that is, they were professionals) to use MM programs, they desired these programs to keep abreast of tax changes affecting client firms, and they generally responded similarly, and favorably, to appeals that stressed how MM systems would help accountants address client needs.

Markets are broadly categorized in terms of what they do and what they buy; the consumer market is composed of people and groups who buy products for personal, family, or household use; the organizational market is composed of people and groups who buy products for further production, use in operating the organization, or resale to consumers. Consumer markets, both domestic and foreign, are covered in Chapter 9; organizational markets are covered in Chapter 10.

Marketing mixes are combinations of marketing tools that marketing managers orchestrate to satisfy customers and company objectives. Called "the offering" from the customer's perspective, the marketing mix is usually associated with the four Ps: **product, price, promotion,** and **place**.

- The **product,** in marketing terms, is defined as anything, tangible or intangible, offered for attention, acquisition, use, or consumption that is capable of satisfying needs. Included can be objects, people, places, services, and ideas. The satisfaction people get from products can derive from any aspect of the product, such as its quality, brand name, service warranty, package, supplementary use, or symbolic value. Product management is covered in Chapters 13 and 14.

- The **price** that customers pay for a product influences the product's image and likelihood of purchase. It is the only revenue-generating element of the marketing mix and the easiest to change. Price, covered in Chapters 15 and 16, is usually based on analyses of costs, customer needs, competitive prices, and government regulatory and political mandates.

- **Promotion** programs, designed to persuade customers to buy the product, include personal selling, advertising (paid messages carried by the media), publicity (unpaid messages carried by the media), and sales promotion (marketing activities, other than those already mentioned, designed to stimulate customer purchasing and dealer effectiveness). Indirect and direct promotion strategies are covered in Chapters 17 and 18.

- **Place** refers to where the product is made available to market members and covers two areas: (1) channels of distribution, such as wholesalers or retailers handling products between producers and consumers, and (2) physical distribution, such as transportation, warehousing, and inventory control facilities designed to make products available at appropriate times and places in marketing channels. Distribution channels and physical distribution are covered in Chapters 19 and 20.

One of the main keys to the success of any marketing program is the ability of a marketing manager like Lora Moore to work effectively with other team members to shape marketing mixes that meet the nature and needs of specific target markets. Market Focus 1-1 illustrates how creative shaping and timing of marketing mix elements led to history's highest grossing motion picture.

MARKET FOCUS 1-1

Titanic: The Amazing Movie

The movie *Titanic* opened in 1997 as the most expensive motion picture ever made; it was so expensive that it would have to gross more than $500 million simply to break even.

That history's most expensive motion picture easily surpassed this figure to become history's highest grossing film is a strong testament to a well-crafted marketing mix, whose product-promotion-place-price components were brilliantly timed and integrated.

The product, a film based on the 1912 sinking of the "unsinkable" liner, *Titanic*, had elements attractive to practically every target market—men, women, teens, seniors—and included spectacular special effects, historical verisimilitude, action/adventure, heroes, villains, and a wonderful love story. Attesting to the film's quality and impact were the astonishing eleven Oscars it won at the 1998 Academy Award ceremonies. Leveraging the film's revenues were the many formats and venues in which it was marketed, including soundtrack recordings, licensed products, a best-selling paperback, and theater and rental markets in domestic and global markets.

Promotion for *Titanic* began with lengthy publicity and public relations campaigns, much of which capitalized on the news that the
movie was running months behind schedule (and tens of thousands
of dollars over budget) to increase awareness and anticipation well before the release date. Just before the release date, promotional support
included talk show appearances by James Cameron, the film's director,
and Kate Winslet and Leonardo DiCaprio, its two stars, and was supplemented by a massive campaign of radio and TV ads as well as a Web
site devoted to the picture.

Key distribution decisions pertained to when and where to release the
film. Since the film had already missed its summer release date, the
studio decided to release *Titanic* in December 1997, when it would
be eligible for Oscar consideration and would not conflict with any of
the studio's other major releases. The movie ran simultaneously in
more than 3000 theaters in the United States, showing worldwide two
weeks later.

Thanks largely to the combined impact of the first three marketing mix
Ps, ticket prices usually sold in the premium $7 to $9 range and were
purchased by a large number of repeat attendees.

Marketing environments are forces that influence marketing managers'
abilities to create and carry out plans that satisfy organizational objectives
and target market needs. The marketing **microenvironment** is composed
of forces close to the company that affect its ability to serve customers, including company strengths and weaknesses, as well as company suppliers,
publics, and competitors. The **macroenvironment** is composed of larger
political, legal, economic, cultural, and technological forces that influence
the microenvironment. Both macro- and microenvironments are covered
in Chapters 4 and 5.

Competition is defined as direct and indirect ways customers can satisfy
needs apart from making an exchange for a particular offering. For example,
a prospective buyer might purchase an MM education system, or purchase
a competitive brand, or spend the money, indirectly, on other ways to
achieve the same educational objectives, such as through a correspondence
course or at a local college. Direct and indirect competition are covered as
a macroenvironmental force in Chapter 4.

The American Marketing Association (AMA) recently broadened its definition of **marketing** to stress what the process achieves as well as what it
does:

Marketing is the process of planning and executing the conception,
pricing, promotion and distribution of ideas, goods, services, organi-

zations and events to create and maintain relationships that satisfy individual and organizational objectives.

Like most quick definitions of complex phenomena, this one leaves a lot of questions unanswered. For example, what is "planning and executing" in marketing terms? How are "ideas, goods, services" conceived, priced, promoted, and distributed? What "individual and organizational objectives" are satisfied through marketing relationships? How do these concepts differ in international and domestic markets? These and related questions will be addressed in the rest of this chapter and book. For our present purposes, we focus on the following assumptions regarding marketing processes that Lora Moore took into account in charting the path of Merton's MM systems division.

Marketing processes close gaps and create utilities. To the extent that marketing processes create satisfying relationships, they also help to close market gaps and create utilities for sellers and buyers.

To illustrate these marketing benefits to individuals, organizations, and entire societies, consider some characteristics of a typical transaction. A staff member in a very small accounting firm spent $3000 to purchase a Merton MM system from a local retailer of electronic equipment and supplies. You will see that several gaps were closed.

- A **spatial gap** was closed by arranging transportation of the system to a location convenient to the buyer.

- A **knowledge gap** was closed by providing the buyer with information about the competitive features and benefits of the system.

- A **value gap** was closed when a final price was agreed upon; it represented a compromise between the buyer's and seller's notions of what the system was worth.

- A **temporal gap** was closed in that the MM system was made available when the accountant wanted it.

- Finally, an **ownership gap** was closed when the new owner took title to the MM system.

In closing these gaps, the marketing process also creates four utilities—place, time, possession, and form—beneficial to individuals, organizations, and societies. To illustrate, the MM system was where the accountant wanted it to be, so place utility was created. The accountant had the system when he wanted it, so time utility was created. When title for the system passed over to him, possession utility was created; form utility was created when system components were tailored to meet his needs.

THE EIGHT BASIC MARKETING FUNCTIONS

Earlier, we noted that the major focus of this book would be on the marketing manager's role in formulating strategic marketing plans that bring together target markets and marketing mixes. In carrying out this role, the marketing manager also deals with eight basic marketing functions that are essential and cannot be eliminated; someone must perform them for satisfactory exchanges to take place.

• *EXCHANGE FUNCTIONS*

First, to create worthwhile exchanges, a seller needs something of value, so the **buying function** is important: searching for and buying products that will prove attractive to prospective customers. Then, to consummate these exchanges, prospective customers must be informed about and persuaded to buy these products, so the **selling function** is important. These two functions—buying and selling—are called **exchange functions**.

• *PHYSICAL DISTRIBUTION FUNCTIONS*

Once products have been purchased for sale or resale, they must be transported from producer to buyer and, perhaps, be maintained in inventory until they are purchased. These two functions—**transportation** and **storage**—are called **physical distribution functions**.

• *FACILITATING FUNCTIONS*

Finally the marketing manager would deal with four **facilitating functions** in building satisfactory exchanges.

- **Grading**—Products for resale are sorted into different quality and quantity categories for more efficient storage and display.

- **Financing**—Arrangements are made for the firm to pay suppliers and for customers to pay the firm for purchased products and services.

- **Risk taking**—The firm assumes a number of risks associated with buying, selling, storing, and financing products. These risks include the risk that people won't buy or pay for the products and the risk that these products will be made obsolete by newer products.

- **Developing marketing information**—Underlying all the other functions is this extremely important function that helps reduce risk by providing the marketing manager with intelligence required to make better decisions. For example, marketing information helps the marketing manager find buyers, identify buyer needs that the firm is capable of profitably satisfying, create effective marketing mix offerings that satisfy company objectives and customer needs, and monitor the progress and results of marketing plans toward objectives.

WHY STUDY MARKETING?

As a field of study, marketing is important to people, companies, and society at large.

• *IMPORTANCE TO PEOPLE*

An individual responds to marketing every time he or she buys a product. The fact that this product meets this person's needs, is effectively promoted, and is available at a convenient time and place attests to the effectiveness of the marketing system. The marketing field also offers career opportunities that are less affected by cyclical and economic fluctuations, and offers better opportunities than many other career paths for growth and advancement based on personal merit (Table 1-1). Salaries in marketing positions rank high among all occupational fields (Table 1-2) and offer excellent prospects for future growth (Table 1-3).

Table 1–1. Female and Minority Employment in Selected Marketing Occupations

Occupation	Percentage of Total Employees		
	Female	African-American	Hispanic
Purchasing managers	41.5	6.6	3.1
Marketing, advertising, public relations managers	35.7	2.2	3.3
Sales occupations	49.5	7.8	6.9
Supervisors/proprietors	38.9	5.6	5.6
Sales representatives:			
Advertising sales	52.9	4.2	4.7
Insurance sales	37.1	5.8	4.6
Real estate sales	50.7	3.4	4.5
Retail/personal services	65.6	11.4	8.9
Securities/financial services	31.3	5.7	5.0

Source: U.S. Bureau of the Census, *Statistical Abstract of the United States,* 116th edition (Washington, DC: U.S. Government Printing Office, 1996), pp. 405–406.

Table 1–2. Median Salaries for Marketing-Management Positions

Marketing assistant	$ 24,000
Advertising manager	44,000
Sales promotion manager	45,000
Brand manager	61,000
Direct-marketing manager	66,000
Regional sales manager	69,000
VP for marketing	146,050

Sources: Justin Martin, "How Does Your Pay Really Stack Up?" *Fortune*, June 26, 1995, pp. 79–86; and U.S. Department of Labor, Bureau of Labor Statistics, *Occupational Outlook Handbook* (Washington, DC: U.S. Government Printing Office, 1996), p. 60.

Table 1–3. Employment Projections for Selected Marketing Positions Through 2005

Occupation	Recent Employment	Projected Growth Through 2005 (%)
Insurance sales workers	418,000	14–24
Manufacturer's and wholesale sales representatives	1,503,000	14–24
Marketing, advertising, and public-relations managers	461,000	over 35
Purchasing agents and managers	621,000	14–24
Real estate agents, brokers, and appraisers	374,000	14–24
Retail sales workers	4,261,000	25–34
Securities and financial services sales representatives	246,000	over 35
Service sales representatives	612,000	over 35
Wholesale and retail buyers	621,000	14–24

Source: U.S. Department of Labor, *Occupational Outlook Handbook*, Bureau of Labor Statistics (Washington, DC: U.S. Government Printing Office, 1996), pp. 61, 69–71, 236–239.

• *IMPORTANCE TO COMPANIES*

As the firm's sole revenue-producing system (the two other major systems—accounting-finance and production—apply revenues to operations), marketing generates income that is managed by financial people to generate profits. By expanding sales and sales revenues, marketing helps to spread fixed costs over more units, thereby enhancing profit return throughout the firm.

• *IMPORTANCE TO SOCIETY*

In free-enterprise, market-driven economies, the marketing process, as the major force in creating mass markets, mass production, and mass distribution, also helps create high levels of business activity, increased investment opportunities, and high employment. These statistics attest to marketing's productive role:

- More than 50 percent of every consumer dollar spent supports such marketing activities as advertising, personal selling, retailing, packaging, and transportation.

- About 45 percent of family expenditures is spent on services (health care, education, recreation, and the like) where the emphasis is on marketing rather than production activities.

- About 30 to 40 percent of people employed in the United States have jobs directly or indirectly related to marketing functions.

The dramatic conversion of command economies to free-market economies, beginning with the fall of communist-bloc states in the late 1980s, dramatizes the increasingly important role marketing will play in the twenty-first century. In less-developed Third World countries, marketing institutions will represent a dynamic element for breaking poverty cycles.

EVOLUTION OF MARKETING: SELF-SUFFICIENCY TO CENTRALIZATION

To illustrate the stages of development of marketing processes, and the philosophies associated with each stage, envision a community consisting of only four families.

EARLY STAGES: SELF-SUFFICIENT, DECENTRALIZED

During the early, self-sufficiency stage of the marketing process—around the Middle Ages—each family provided completely for its own needs: sewing garments, hunting game, making furniture, and so on. Then, during the next, decentralized market stage, each family began specializing in an activity at which its members were most proficient: one family made clothing, another built shelters, another provided food, and so on.

Along with these specialized efforts came (1) **division of labor,** as each family member performed activities he or she was best at, and (2) **standardization,** as each family member developed routinized parts and procedures in producing his or her output.

THE CENTRALIZED MARKET STAGE

As production became more efficient, so did methods for distributing output. In our four-family community, as specialization, standardization, and division of labor took hold, each family could satisfy its needs by purchasing products from each of the other families. This required a total of twelve separate trips—three by each family—to fulfill the needs of all the families.

Then, as each family became more efficient and productive, each found it could produce more of the specialized products it made than was required to satisfy the needs of all four families. To eliminate this surplus, each family set up a booth in a centralized marketplace to exchange its surplus products for the surplus products of other families in other communities. During this centralized market stage of the marketing process, each family in the original community had to make only one trip, to a centralized market, to fulfill its needs, making exchange—the essence of the marketing process—much more efficient.

ENTER MONEY AND INTERMEDIARIES

Although transactional efficiency was enhanced by these early centralized markets, they still contained inefficiencies. For one thing, while members of each family were tending the family booth, they couldn't be specializing their efforts to produce surplus products to sell. For another, the bartering process of exchanging their surpluses for surplus products produced by other families tended to get cumbersome and complex: just how many chairs were three pigs worth, and who was going to lug them home?

Both of these problems were solved with the advent of money and intermediaries. Money became the common unit of value that replaced products that families exchanged to meet their needs, further enhancing transactional efficiency. Intermediaries, who specialized in arranging exchanges between buyers and sellers, took over the family booths to sell family surpluses, making it possible for these families to spend more time at their specialties.

Then, during the next 300 years, sufficient surpluses accumulated to justify trade beyond local barriers, and large wholesalers came into being. As surpluses were distributed over greater distances and centralized markets became more complex, they also became more varied. Modern markets can grow around anything of value, including labor, money, real estate, charities, and ideas.

Today, in modern, market-driven societies, producers and intermediaries are given the role of satisfying customer wants, and customers are free to make their own decisions pertaining to the exchange of values in various markets. Governments, acting for the community at large, make rules to regulate exchange processes and, in exchange for taxes and votes, provide certain necessary services—such as a standing army—that can't be provided efficiently by the private segment. In general, markets are permitted to grow or decline, according to supply/demand dictates, without unnecessary bureaucratic interference.

EVOLUTION OF MARKETING PHILOSOPHIES: PRODUCTION TO SOCIETAL

As marketing evolved from its self-sufficient beginnings to today's diverse, complex, dynamic institutions, four distinct marketing philosophies also evolved to meet the needs of parties to the exchange process, including buyers, sellers, and society at large. These philosophies include the production, sales, marketing concept, and societal marketing concept. They also guided Lora Moore's efforts to meld marketing concepts into strategic marketing plans to enter and grow the Merton Mighty Mind line in domestic and global markets.

• *THE PRODUCTION PHILOSOPHY*

Dating back to the Industrial Revolution, when major manufacturing centers and distribution networks were established, the production philosophy focused on making and distributing products in sufficient quantities to meet burgeoning demand. The prevailing philosophy, "a good product will sell itself," implied emphasis on production rather than sales.

• *THE SALES PHILOSOPHY*

The production philosophy was replaced by the sales philosophy in the early 1920s, when mass production technology, spawned by the Industrial Revolution, produced more products than markets could effectively absorb. This product glut, combined with dramatic increases in consumer discretionary income, led to an emphasis on sales forces and advertising campaigns to find new customers and persuade resistant customers to buy. As in the production philosophy era, however, there was rarely a unifying force within the organization to integrate these sales-oriented activities in terms of defining and satisfying customer needs: communication with customers was unilateral, and the sales function was generally subordinate to finance, production, and engineering.

• *THE MARKETING CONCEPT PHILOSOPHY*

Defined as an integrated customer- and profit-oriented philosophy of business, the marketing concept philosophy differs from predecessor philosophies that emphasized products ("a good product will sell itself") and selling ("don't sell the steak, sell the sizzle") in a number of significant ways:

- The marketing concept defines the firm's mission in terms of the benefits and satisfactions it offers customers, rather than the products it makes and sells.

- It emphasizes two-way communication to identify customer needs and then develops and markets products to satisfy these needs. Gone is the emphasis on one-way communication to persuade people to buy products already made.

- It emphasizes both long- and short-range planning to achieve profits by meeting customer needs. Gone is an exclusive focus on short-range planning to achieve sales volume objectives.

- It emphasizes a total systems integration of all departments to achieve profit goals. Gone is the exclusive focus on the efforts of individual departments and sales forces.

In recent years, the marketing concept philosophy of working back from defined customer needs to marketing mix offerings calculated to profitably satisfy these needs has come under increasing attack from critics who claim that this "customer knows best" pandering to diverse needs is wasteful, inefficient, and inconsistent with an era of shortages and concerns for the environment.

• *THE SOCIETAL MARKETING CONCEPT PHILOSOPHY*

This marketing philosophy, which responds to critics of the marketing concept philosophy, doesn't oppose the free-enterprise notion of determining needs of target market members and delivering desired satisfactions more efficiently and effectively than competitors. It does maintain, however, that these satisfactions should be delivered in a way that also enhances the well-being of society. In short, marketing managers should balance three interests in setting policies and formulating marketing plans: the buyer, the seller, and society at large. The bottle laws that mandate a concern for the environment in the supercompetitive wars among soft drink companies is a good example.

In its domestic market Merton, a good neighbor, had adopted the societal marketing concept philosophy as a guide to its strategic planning efforts.

INTERNATIONAL PERSPECTIVE

In previous sections of this chapter, the emphasis has been on marketing concepts, perspectives, and philosophies as they apply in domestic markets. Now, in this final chapter section, we examine how they might be defined and applied in international markets. For illustrative purposes, we will continue to refer to the Merton Electronics case, and these additional points.

Entrenched in strong market niches consisting of different professional groups (accountants, lawyers, engineers, doctors, and the like), and aided, in the late 1990s, by the development of software that converted ordinary human speech into text with remarkable speed and accuracy, the Merton line of Mighty Mind systems achieved steady, highly profitable growth into the next century, when strong competitive pressures began to squeeze market share and bring profits down. These pressures also alerted Lora Moore to the need to develop profitable new markets for the MM line to offset these anticipated losses. In carrying out this mandate, Moore explored questions like: Did profitable markets exist in the international sphere for Merton's products and services? If so, could these markets be reached with products, prices, promotional campaigns, and distribution channels? How would differing cultural, demographic, technological, competitive, and economic conditions combine to support or thwart market planning? What would be the most effective strategy for entering and growing in the international marketplace?

GLOBAL MARKETS DIFFER FROM DOMESTIC MARKETS

Among the more focused considerations Moore had to account for in charting Merton's path from domestic to global status were these assumptions regarding the nature of marketing processes in international markets:

Marketing processes are generally similar regardless of circumstances. Whether a firm is large or small, markets a tangible or intangible product, aspires to profit or nonprofit objectives, or sells in domestic or international markets, basic marketing processes will be the same. Buyers must be found; products must be conceived, priced, promoted, and distributed; and uncontrollable factors, such as differing economic and competitive conditions, must be taken into account in bringing buyers and products together. These basics are called the technical universals of marketing.

Also similar in domestic and international markets are the basic functions performed by marketing processes, such as researching markets and planning, buying, pricing, promoting, transporting, storing, and selling products. Benefits created by marketing processes are also similar, including bringing together the right products at the right prices for the right people at the right time in the right place.

International marketing is generally riskier, but potentially more rewarding, than domestic marketing. If activities, functions, and benefits characterizing domestic and international marketing are similar, carrying out these activities is generally riskier and more difficult in the global marketplace, where the marketer is subject to a new set of constraints deriving from cultural, technological, economic, demographic, political, and competitive differences among nations that must be accounted for in the strategic planning effort. Another constraint is the frequent lack of information about markets in foreign countries and the difficulties encountered in getting this information. Global Focus 1-1 illustrates how these differences between domestic and global markets were turned into plusses by one innovative domestic marketer who succeeded dramatically in a foreign market.

GLOBAL FOCUS 1-1

Domino's Pizza Changes Its Mix

When Ernest Higa, a Japanese-American, considered franchising Domino's, he found the history of pizza in Japan to be dismal. Faced with the research conclusion that pizza and Japan do not mix, Higa set out to prove otherwise. He believed that the key was to make alterations appropriate for the market.

In Japan, the changes began with the size of the pizza. In Higa's words, "The Japanese aren't big eaters, especially women." So he trimmed the product from 12 to 10 inches. Food delivery in Japan, "demae," is usually expected. Faced with such obstacles as crowded and limited parking, Higa provided his employees with newly designed scooters to help them deliver the pizzas. Higa discovered that the Japanese consumer associates delivery businesses with small-scale operations and limited service capacity. Therefore, he upgraded the marketing materials provided by U.S. headquarters by producing four-color advertisements and handbills. And, of course, new pizza flavors were introduced, so appealing that customers clamored for bowls of rice to go with them.

Today, Higa owns 98 franchises in Japan, runs the most successful Domino's operation abroad, and his franchises average more than double the volume of a typical American Domino's.

Source: Greg Matusky, "Going Global: Franchisors Crack New Overseas Markets," *Success*, April 1993, pp. 59–63.

In spite of these constraints, international marketing offers many potential rewards, as will be discussed in Chapter 2, such as increasing sales and profits and avoiding marketing downturns in the U.S. market.

Marketing mixes that succeed in international markets usually differ from those that succeed in domestic markets. In building marketing mixes for MM systems sold in international markets, Moore realized that she would face problems not faced in the domestic marketplace. In terms of product, for example, MM systems would have to be developed that accounted for differences in language and customs; in terms of place, means would have to be found to transport, store, and distribute MM systems to customers, possibly in countries where few such means presently existed. In pricing the systems, a whole spectrum of problems would arise, including the effect on MM prices of different exchange and inflation rates, differing dealer discount schedules, and escalating costs of exporting MM systems. Promotion problems would include consumer attitudes and governmental constraints regarding information sources; the ability of the distribution system to get promoted products to customers; the translation of appeals into different languages and the cost; and the availability of media to carry these appeals.

Overarching all these problems was the big problem of developing information to solve them: to determine the real product needs of prospective customers, or the competitive environment in different markets, or the relative effectiveness of different promotional appeals. This information would be critical in devising each marketing mix element and in determining the relative emphasis each should receive in Moore's strategic plan for global entry and growth.

Concepts basic to marketing often have to be reinterpreted when applied in global markets. In particular, Moore realized that there would be significant differences in the way needs, competition, and exchange would be reinterpreted from Merton's domestic to its global market.

Needs: Moore recognized that the job of identifying needs satisfied by MM products and services would be considerably more difficult in the diverse, difficult global marketplace, conditioned by different social, cultural, economic, and technological factors, than in the more familiar, comfortable domestic marketplace.

Competition: Products introduced into international markets generally face a broader, more diverse range of competition than exists in their domestic market. Initially, the product usually faces more indirect competition than in its domestic market; then, as it gains market share, it faces more direct brand competition, although not necessarily of the sort faced in its domestic market. For example, in the U.S. market, Gillette is the sales leader for disposable razors, with BIC a distant runner-up; in Europe, these roles are reversed.

Given the complexity of competitive environments and the dramatically quickening pace with which products are introduced, upgraded, and distributed in international markets, Moore recognized that an important part of any MM marketing program would be to continually monitor the nature and scope of competition in each entry market, track competitive initiatives, and assess and respond to these initiatives.

Exchange: In domestic markets, all conditions for successful exchange apply in most situations where things of value are exchanged: a price that represents appropriate value to both willing parties is agreed upon, and a product is purchased and delivered. If either party is later dissatisfied, legal agreements provide recourse, such as returning the product for a refund or suing for damages.

Moore realized, however, that the likelihood of these conditions prevailing in international markets would be considerably less than in the domestic marketplace. For example, the "value" of an MM system would be difficult to agree on in a country where exchange or inflation rates change the daily value of a local currency. Also, "legal authority," as defined in U.S. courts, might have a completely different, and unacceptable, meaning in foreign courts. In some former Eastern-bloc countries, for example, concepts like personal property, ownership, and liability—all key in consummating and protecting exchanges—are still being interpreted.

Marketing philosophies that guide marketing processes in domestic markets may not apply in international markets. In its domestic market, Merton, a good neighbor, had adopted the societal marketing philosophy as a guide to its strategic planning efforts. In other countries with different environments and outlooks, however, Moore recognized that different marketing philosophies, such as the production or sales philosophy, might be more appropriate. Of particular interest was a piece Moore had just read concerning the approach a Merton competitor had taken to penetrate foreign markets successfully.

> The Dell Computer Company, which began European operations in 1987, had sales of $260 million in 1994, or 30 percent of total Dell sales, and two percent of all personal computer (PC) sales in the European market. (During the same period, IBM's European PC sales dropped from 21 to 17 percent of total sales.) Central to Dell's success was a direct mail discount campaign that observers said couldn't possibly work: computer buyers never purchase big ticket items like PCs through the mail, and tend to equate discounted prices with shoddy merchandise. Dell management disagreed. Research showed that PC prices in Europe, set by firms like Groupe Bull's Zenith Data Systems and Olivetti, were about twice that charged in the United States, and that European dealer networks were sluggish and expensive. Dell began its campaign with an intense education program, featuring a series of ads in computer magazines and direct mailings throughout Britain and the continent, stressing Dell's reputation for high quality, fast service, and lowest price. Future plans: institute a single price throughout its Western European market, with a guarantee of 5-day delivery and 2-day service.

Thus, with a minimum of research, and a sales-oriented approach more characteristic of an inexpensive consumer product than a high-ticket business product, Dell scored a quick, solid success in the foreign market.

CHAPTER PERSPECTIVE

Marketing creates opportunities for exchange by harmonizing the elements of the marketing mix in a manner that satisfies individual and organizational objectives. In creating these opportunities, marketing also creates utilities and closes gaps to bring products to customers when, where, and how they want them. Basic to an understanding of marketing processes is an understanding of basic concepts like needs, competition, exchange, marketing environments, and marketing mixes. Also important is an understanding of marketing philosophies associated with various stages of the evolution of marketing processes, including the production, sales, marketing concept, and societal marketing concept philosophies. As with basic marketing concepts, these philosophies must usually be reinterpreted in light of differing cultural, demographic, economic, political, and technological differences in foreign markets. Whether viewed from the micro perspective of the individual firm or the macro perspective of the entire economy, the study of marketing is worthwhile from an individual perspective, the perspective of companies, and the perspective of the entire economy.

KNOW THE CONCEPTS
TERMS FOR STUDY

Buying function
Centralized markets
Competition
Consumer market
Decentralized markets
Demand
Exchange
Form utility
Global markets
MAD-R
Markets
Marketing
Marketing concept
Marketing environment

Marketing evolution
Marketing functions
Marketing mix
Marketing philosophies
Marketing utilities
Needs
Organizational market
Physical distribution
Societal marketing concept
Standardization
Target markets
Technical universals
Uncontrollables

MATCHUP EXERCISES

1. Match the marketing mix element in the first column with the descriptor in the second column.

1. product   a. stimulates customer spending and dealer effectiveness

2. price   b. anything that satisfies needs

3. distribution   c. most difficult to standardize

4. promotion   d. easiest to change

2. Relate the marketing philosophy in the first column with the descriptor in the second column.

1. sales   a. the customer must be sold

2. marketing concept   b. the customer knows best

3. societal marketing   c. a good product sells itself

4. production   d. three parties to the transaction

3. Match the concepts in the first column with the second column descriptors pertaining to various elements of an encyclopedia salesperson's sales plan.

1. MAD-R   a. satisfaction derived from getting straight As

2. target market   b. parents of overachievers

3. indirect competition   c. the reference desk at the library

4. needs   d. members of your target market

QUESTIONS FOR REVIEW AND DISCUSSION

1. Discuss similarities and differences between marketing processes carried out in domestic and international markets.

2. From the perspective of a manufacturer of a new model bicycle, give examples of the different needs this product might satisfy and of the different kinds of competitive products a consumer might purchase to satisfy these needs. Why would these considerations be important to a marketing manager?

3. Briefly argue either side of these criticisms of marketing:
   Marketing does/doesn't waste resources.
   Marketing does/doesn't create monopolies.
   Marketing does/doesn't deceive people.

4. A homeowner buys supplies at a local lumberyard to build a children's playhouse in the back yard. Explain how the marketing process closed four gaps and created four utilities during this single exchange.

5. Explain how two different market aggregates—consumer and organizational—could be customers for the same MM system. What are the marketing mix implications of the different natures and needs of these markets?

6. What is the main difference between the marketing concept philosophy on the one hand and the sales and production philosophies on the

other? Between the marketing concept philosophy and the societal marketing concept philosophy?

7. Give two reasons why you might be interested in the study of marketing as (a) an individual looking for that first job after college; (b) the president of the firm that hires you; and (c) the president of the country where the firm is located.

8. Explain how all four components of the marketing mix might interact in preparing a plan to market Domino Pizza's new package that keeps pizzas hot until after they are delivered. For example, how would the take-out menu (the distribution, or place, component) affect the other three marketing mix elements?

ANSWERS
MATCHUP EXERCISES

1. 1b, 2d, 3c, 4a
2. 1a, 2b, 3d, 4c
3. 1d, 2b, 3c, 4a

QUESTIONS FOR REVIEW AND DISCUSSION

1. Marketing processes carried out in domestic and international markets are similar with respect to the specific activities encompassed (for example, products and services must be developed, priced, distributed, and promoted to meet the needs of defined target markets and company objectives). Also, they both account for marketplace threats and opportunities as well as company strengths and weaknesses. Differences in marketing processes between domestic and international markets derive mainly from environmental differences. For example, differences in language, cultural values, state of economic development, currency stability, infrastructure development, legal systems, and political orientation can all combine to scuttle the most aggressive market entry strategy. Well-planned and implemented global marketing strategies that succeed, however, often generate more profits than their domestic counterparts.

2. The bicycle might satisfy such needs as exercise, recreation, socialization, and status—all of which could conceivably be met by joining a biking club. Other kinds of competitive products to address some, or all, of these needs include other similar bicycles; other different bicycles (a five-speed, for example, instead of a ten-speed); other ways of satisfying a need for socialization, recreation, and exercise, such as joining a health club; or other ways of enhancing the individual's status, such as joining a prestigious country club. From the marketing manager's perspective, it is frequently important to understand all forms of direct and indirect competition for the satisfaction of prospective customers and to take them into account in developing plans for marketing products.

3. **Marketing does/doesn't waste resources:** To the extent that marketing panders to consumer needs that might be considered frivolous or unnecessary, while diverting resources that might help achieve more important social goals, it might be considered wasteful. On the other hand, who is to say that pandering to the needs of enlightened customers in a market-driven economy isn't the most productive way to allocate resources? And, even if it isn't, the societal marketing concept is designed to address these shortcomings.

   Marketing does/doesn't create monopolies: Using the domestic automobile industry as one of many possible examples, one might argue that intensive marketing efforts over the decades have made entry into this industry exceedingly difficult. One might also argue that other factors, such as the capital-intensive nature of this industry, are the main causes for this difficulty, or that marketing made it possible for foreign competitors to gain a strong market share in this country.

   Marketing does/doesn't deceive people: Examples of highly publicized marketing deceits abound (for example, bait-and-switch advertising and mail fraud), but it can also be argued that deceiving the public is a suicidal long-run policy that reputable firms shun. Even if a firm decided to embark on such a course, a broad diversity of watchdog agencies, representing a broad diversity of constituencies (consumer, government, advertisers) make success unlikely.

4. By making these supplies available where the buyer wanted them, instead of having the buyer travel to the factory to purchase the supplies, a spatial gap was closed, and a place utility was created. By making the supplies available when the buyer wanted them, a temporal gap was closed, and a time utility was created. By handling details of the exchange, an ownership gap was closed, and a possession gap created. The price the homeowner paid for the supplies represents a compromise between the price the homeowner was willing to pay and the price the manufacturer would have liked to get, so a value gap was closed. Later, the form of some of these supplies was changed based on the response of this homeowner and other buyers to their present form.

5. In the organizational market, MM systems would most likely be purchased in bulk for training groups of associates (for example, in law firms, accounting firms, and medical centers), whereas, in the consumer market, individual professionals would purchase individual MM systems for home-study purposes. There are several possible marketing mix implications. In each market, MM systems would be priced differently, reflecting quantity and other discounts organizations get that in-

dividuals don't. MM systems would also be distributed differently, through outlets peculiar to each market (for example, wholesalers to the trade and retailers to consumers). Additionally, they would probably be promoted with different appeals and media. For example, in the organizational market, ads in professional journals might stress savings to companies that used MM systems. In the consumer market, systems might be promoted through direct mail, stressing the career advancement benefits of using information and training provided through MM software.

6. The most significant difference between the marketing concept philosophy and the sales and production philosophies has to do with the customer orientation associated with the marketing concept philosophy. Unlike the sales/production philosophies, which start with products and focus on unilateral ways to get these products to customers, the marketing concept philosophy starts with customers and focuses on multilateral ways to develop product/price/place/promotion offerings that will meet their identified needs. The societal marketing concept philosophy differs from the marketing philosophy in that it includes another partner in the exchange process—the welfare of the society in which the exchange takes place.

7. (a) Marketing jobs tend to pay more, and offer more opportunities for advancement, than do other jobs. (b) Marketing is the only company subsystem that raises revenues and has a significant impact on profits (for example, by generating mass-market economies of scale that reduce costs associated with each unit produced). (c) The health and growth of the economy are largely dependent on macromarketing activities (for example, the remarkable strength of the U.S. economy in the 1990s fueled largely by domestic and global corporate sales and profits).

8. The plan might promote the fact that Domino's Pizza delivers orders from its take-out menu (place) with only a small additional charge (price). The plan might also promote the fact that the order is guaranteed to be hot when it arrives.

2

THE INTERNATIONAL MARKET: FORCES AND OPPORTUNITIES

OVERVIEW

This chapter examines reasons for the burgeoning growth of world trade, the general lack of U.S. participation in this growth, the benefits and drawbacks of participating in world trade, the trends that will shape global market threats and opportunities, and where in the world these threats and opportunities exist.

WHY INTERNATIONAL TRADE GROWS

Beginning in the second half of the twentieth century, international trade—the exchange of goods and services among countries—became the fastest growing sector of the world economy, increasing from less than $200 billion to more than $5 trillion between 1975 and 1999. The following interrelated conditions facilitated this growth:

- ### *LONG PERIODS OF GLOBAL PEACE*
  In contrast to the first half of the twentieth century, when much of the substance of advanced countries was diverted toward military adventures, the second half was largely characterized by localized conflicts among less-developed countries, leaving a stable foundation for healthy, rapid growth of the global economy. Global economic growth, in turn, is a potent imperative to peace, as countries, through open trading relationships, create the wealth, productivity, and living standards that substitute for the goals of aggression.

- ### *TECHNOLOGICAL BREAKTHROUGHS*
  Ironically, the wars that diverted resources from peaceful trading pursuits before mid-century were largely responsible for technological breakthroughs that fueled trade after mid-century. Particularly in the fields of

power, communication, and transportation (for example, jet aircraft, electronic data transmission, television), these breakthroughs created products to trade, processes to make them, and the means to market them in geographically dispersed areas. To quote Levitt:

> Technology has created a new commercial reality . . . the emergence of global markets for standardized consumer products on a previously unimagined scale. . . . Almost everyone, everywhere, wants all the things they've heard about, seen, or experienced via the new technology.[1]

• *INTERNATIONAL TRADING AGREEMENTS*

If peace and technology were largely responsible for creating an environment in which international trade could flourish, a common commitment among nations to avoid restrictive trade practices and foster global economic growth was largely responsible for creating agreements to enhance the free flow of goods and services among nations. Examples of these agreements include the **General Agreement on Tariffs and Trade (GATT),** replaced in 1995 by the **World Trade Organization (WTO),** the **International Monetary Fund (IMF),** and the **World Bank.** WTO provides principles and procedures for reducing tariffs and liberalizing trade, such as the Most-Favored-Nation principle, whereby each signatory country extends to all countries its most favorable trade terms. The IMF creates multinational reserve assets that member nations can draw upon for financial support. These assets are usually drawn upon by developing countries with severe balance-of-payments problems, in return for which they are usually expected to make politically unpopular concessions. For example, when the exchange value of the Mexican peso fell by almost half in 1995—reducing living standards and leaving many businesses near ruin—the price of a new line of credit from the U.S. Treasury and the IMF was a draconian economic program guaranteed to ensure recessive conditions.

The World Bank, initially formed in 1944 to aid countries suffering from the destruction of war, tends to take a more active role than the IMF in helping countries modify basic economic policies in return for aid. This aid usually focuses on infrastructure development, such as transportation, communication, and power. More recently, the World Bank has worked with the IMF to resolve debt problems in the developing world, including taking an active role in bringing market economies to former communist-bloc countries.

---

1 Theodore Levitt, "The Globalization of Markets," *Harvard Business Review,* May–June 1983, p. 92.

THE ROLE OF THE UNITED STATES IN INTERNATIONAL TRADE

As the main initiator of technological innovation and agreements to enhance free trade among nations, the role of the United States as a player in international markets hardly seems to have approached its potential.

Figure 2-1 and Tables 2-1, 2-2, and 2-3 focus on the U.S. role in international markets in the context of past trends and future prospects.

Figure 2-1 compares the relative share of world exports and imports of key trading countries. Note that, among these countries, the United States imported about 16 percent of all the world's goods and services, while exporting about 12 percent, leaving a **trade deficit**—the amount by which imports exceed exports—of about $130 billion. At the other extreme, Japan, which exported about 10 percent of the world's goods and services while importing only about 7 percent, generated a **trade surplus** of about $100 billion. The United States has the lowest exports per capita ($1816) among major industrialized nations, amounting to about one–third of Germany's per-capita figure ($5334) and considerably less than figures for Canada ($4898), France ($4111), the United Kingdom ($3284), and Japan ($2734). Although U.S. imports per capita ($2270) were also relatively low, they exceed exports, thus creating the trade deficit.

Measured as a share of its Gross Domestic Product (GDP), U.S. exports, at 7.3 percent (Table 2-1) pale in comparison to countries like Canada (26 percent), Germany (20 percent), the United Kingdom (19 percent), and France (17 percent). Japan, often maligned as the problem child of international trade, exported only 8.3 percent of its GDP in 1994.

HOW WE GROW OUR DEFICITS

Table 2-2 depicts trade patterns among the United States and its major trading partners. Note Japan's contribution to the total U.S. trade deficit of $104 billion: $60 billion, or more than half, on imports to us of $112 billion versus exports from us of only $52 billion. Other countries contributing to this outsized deficit include China ($21 billion), Canada ($11 billion), Germany ($9 billion), and newly emerging East Asian countries ($8 billion). Among these major trading partners, the only countries with which the United States had a trade surplus in 1994 were the United Kingdom and Mexico. (In 1995, the surplus with Mexico became another deficit as the peso plummeted.)

Table 2-3 examines the U.S. trade deficit in terms of major end-use categories. Note that three of these categories—consumer goods, automotive, and industrial materials—generated a $168 billion deficit, which is one-and-a-half

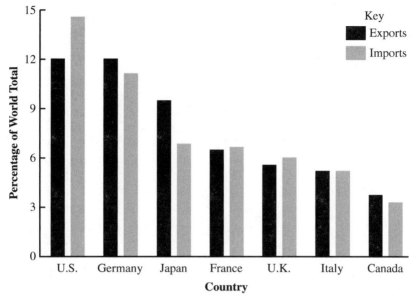

Source: Industrial Marketing Data and Statistics, 1995, Euromonitor Plc, London ECIM SNA.

Figure 2–1. Merchandise exports and imports as a percentage of world total.

Table 2–1. Merchandise Exports as a Percentage of Gross National Product

Period	United States	France	Germany	Italy	Nether-lands	United Kingdom	Japan	Canada
1980	8.1	17.5	23.6	17.1	43.7	20.5	12.2	24.6
1981	7.7	18.2	25.7	18.4	48.5	19.8	13.0	23.5
1982	6.7	17.5	26.8	18.2	48.0	20.0	12.8	22.6
1983	5.9	18.0	25.7	17.5	48.3	19.9	12.4	22.3
1984	5.8	19.5	27.6	17.7	52.4	21.6	13.5	27.1
1985	5.3	19.3	29.1	18.4	53.7	22.0	13.2	26.5
1986	5.1	17.2	27.1	16.1	45.4	18.8	10.7	25.7
1987	5.4	16.8	26.3	15.4	43.7	18.8	9.5	24.3
1988	6.6	17.4	26.9	15.3	45.6	17.3	9.1	24.5
1989	7.0	18.6	28.6	16.3	48.0	18.2	9.5	22.7
1990	7.2	18.2	27.2	15.8	47.0	18.8	9.7	22.8
1991	7.4	18.1	23.6	14.7	45.6	18.3	9.3	21.5
1992	7.4	17.8	22.2	14.5	43.7	18.2	9.2	23.6
1993	7.2	16.4	19.9	16.4	n.a.	19.4	8.6	25.9
1994	7.3	17.0	20.0	16.4	n.a.	19.0	8.3	26.0

Sources: Various 1994 editions of OECD Main Economic Indicators, January 1994; Deutsche Bundesbank; Wirtschaft und Statistik; Information Rapides; U.S. Bureau of the Census; and London Telegram.

**Table 2–2. Trade Patterns Among the United States
and Major Trading Partners**

	Exports to			Imports from			Balance		
	1992	1993	1994	1992	1993	1994	1992	1993	1994
Canada	91	100	104	98	111	115	–7	–11	–11
Japan	48	48	52	97	107	112	–49	–59	–60
European Union	103	97	103	94	98	101	9	–1	2
Germany	21	19	19	29	29	28	–8	–10	–9
United Kingdom	23	26	30	20	22	22	3	4	8
Mexico	41	42	47	35	40	45	6	2	2
East Asia	49	53	55	62	65	63	–13	–12	–8
Taiwan	15	16	17	25	25	24	–10	–9	–7
China	7	9	9	26	32	30	–19	–23	–21

Source: U.S. Bureau of the Census, *Statistical Abstract of the United States: 1995* (115th edition), Washington, DC, 1995.

times as large as the actual deficit. Major categories counterbalancing this deficit included capital goods, with a $24 billion surplus; foods and beverages, producing a $10 billion surplus; and, largest of all, services, which generated a surplus of exports over imports of $55 billion.

Table 2–3. Trade Balances by End-Use Category

	Exports			Imports			Balance		
	1992	1993	1994	1992	1993	1994	1992	1993	1994
Foods and beverages	40	40	40	28	28	30	12	12	10
Industrial materials	109	112	113	138	145	146	–29	–33	–33
Capital goods	177	183	195	134	153	171	43	30	24
Automotive	47	52	55	92	102	108	–45	–51	–53
Consumer goods	50	53	55	123	134	138	–73	–81	–82
Services	180	187	191	123	131	136	56	56	55

Source: U.S. Bureau of the Census, *Statistical Abstract of the United States: 1995* (115th edition) Washington, DC, 1995.

HOW WE LOSE COMPETITIVE EDGE

Viewing the current U.S. role in world trade in its historical context highlights a country that is losing its competitive edge to most of our developed-nation trading partners, who import much less from us than we import from them. This loss is the culmination of a long-time trend, which saw the U.S. share of world exports decline from 25 percent in the mid-1950s to 12 percent today. During the last decade, the U.S. trade deficit passed the $1 trillion mark, transforming history's largest creditor nation into its largest debtor nation. This shift in financial flows, and the subsequent buildup of U.S. debt, has had a variety of adverse effects, such as weakening the international value of the dollar, and triggering many foreign direct investment activities. For example, currently, more than a third of U.S. employees in the chemical industry work for foreign owners, many of the office buildings Americans work in are owned by foreign landlords, and countries like Japan and Germany now hold a sufficient amount of our debt to influence both debt structure and American firms' capability to expand.

Reducing the U.S. trade deficit through increased participation in export markets can have a direct, positive influence on the U.S. economy. In 1994, merchandise exports accounted for more than seven million jobs in the United States, and every $1 billion increase in exports creates about 20,000 new jobs, which, on average, pay more than domestic jobs.

That the United States is capable of greater participation in international markets is documented by Commerce Department figures. These figures show that more than 100,000 U.S. firms were engaged in some level of exporting in 1998, but fewer than 300 of them—led by global giants like General Motors, IBM, Ford, Boeing, and General Electric—accounted for about 85 percent of U.S. exports.

Statistics from the General Accounting Office further document the comparative lack of participation by U.S. firms in international markets. During the entire decade of the 1980s, for example, while foreign direct investment in the United States soared 616 percent, U.S. outbound investment rose just 9.9 percent; only one in five U.S. companies positioned to export actually did so.

One reason for this dramatic imbalance in international investment derives from differences in opportunities among nations. For example, the United States, with its relative affluence, stable political climate, and strong commitment to free trade, represents a much more attractive opportunity for foreign investment than many other countries represent for us. Many developing nations, with more than half the world's population, simply don't have the capacity to absorb enough of our output to qualify as profitable markets.

Other reasons for the comparative lack of U.S. participation in international markets include tariff barriers; high labor costs that often make U.S. products less competitive; the decision of U.S. firms to virtually abdicate such markets as televisions and VCRs; and an overall mindset among American policymakers that the United States, as the leading country in world power and world trade, should assist other countries with their trade performance, with less attention paid to cultivating export markets for U.S. firms. For example, the U.S. budget for nonagricultural export assistance, at 0.03¢ per $1000 of GDP, is exceeded by all its major trading partners.

Perhaps the main reason, however, derives from a complacent satisfaction with the depth and size of the domestic market, which is capable of satisfying consumer wants and national needs with a minimum of reliance on foreign trade. This perception keeps many U.S. managers blissfully ignorant of foreign markets, while the U.S. education establishment generally assigns low priority to knowledge of global environments, languages, and cultures, or of approaches for exploiting international business opportunities.

BENEFITS OF ENTERING FOREIGN MARKETS

Conditions favoring growth of world trade have combined to reinforce among nations the realization that trade holds the promise of better societies, improved living standards, and even a more peaceful world. These conditions also help individual companies realize the following more focused benefits of participation in international markets.

• *EXPLOIT COMPARATIVE ADVANTAGE*

One reason why companies—and countries—frequently gain from trade in foreign markets has to do with the theory of **comparative advantage,** meaning that they exchange goods and services in which they have a relative advantage (for example, better resources, specialization, mechanization, or climate) for those in which they are at a relative disadvantage. For example, some foreign producers have a comparative advantage vis-à-vis U.S. firms in producing footwear, which involves labor-intensive processes that favor low-wage countries. The United States, on the other hand, has a comparative advantage in the production of goods that have a high ratio of capital to labor, such as jet airliners, health-care services, communication satellites, and power generation equipment. The availability of inexpensive imports (for example, shoes and clothing), the theory states, enhances living standards of U.S. citizens and shifts capital and labor used in these labor-intensive industries to produce products (for example, cars, computers, housing) we are good at producing. Global Focus 2-1 illustrates, in practical terms, the dynamics and benefits of comparative advantage.

GLOBAL FOCUS 2-1

The Free Market at Work: From Dirty Hands to Skilled Hands

With low wages and productive workers, South Korea snatched up the global athletic shoe market during the 1980s. The Kukje Corporation's factory in Pusan, South Korea, ran 24 lines and employed 20,000 workers at its peak, making it the largest shoe factory in the world. Korean conglomerate HS Corporation's shoe factory employed 9000 people by the late 1980s and made hundreds of thousands of shoes for such giants as Nike, Inc. and Reebok International Ltd.

An interesting thing happened to the industry since reaching the top. Both of these huge shoe factories are now closed and are waiting to be converted into apartments. Factories like these are shutting down all over Korea, as well as economically similar Taiwan. The reason? As Taiwan and Korea, once low-wage countries themselves, open up trade and investment links to China, hundreds of thousands of jobs have vanished over the past three years in the shoe industry and others, including apparel and toys. Rising wages have simply priced the products out of much of the world market.

"This is the free market at work," proclaims a Hong Kong economist. "Labor is being released from low-wage, low-productivity industries . . . and it's moving into higher value-added, higher-productivity industries and into services." This transition is occurring so fast that those jobs lost in such industries as shoes barely show up in the unemployment statistics. "People are moving from dirty-hand work to skilled-hand work—this is what drives the region's growth."

Source: Paul Blustein, "Asia's Dragons Accept Trade's Pain and Gains," *The Washington Post,* November 7, 1993.

Taken at face value, the notion of comparative advantage might suggest that dissimilarities among countries would lead to more trade among them (for example, capital-intensive producers exchanging products with labor-intensive producers). In actual fact, most world trade occurs among similar countries (for example, industrialized nations with highly educated populations located in temperate zones). The theory of acquired advantage helps explain this phenomenon: specifically, having developed a product in response to observed needs in its domestic market, a producer will turn to foreign markets perceived to be most similar to these markets. However, even though countries that trade most with each other tend to be similar in terms of economic, political, and technological sophistication, they differ in how they specialize to gain acquired advantage. As examples, the British have an advantage in biochemistry, the French have one in pharmacology, and the Germans have one in synthetics, all acquired through technology rather than natural resources.

• *INCREASED SALES*

Because there are more people with greater total purchasing power in the world as a whole than in a single domestic market, companies can increase sales by successfully penetrating international markets. And, often, these markets are more receptive to the product than the domestic market. For example, during downturns in the domestic business cycle, foreign markets are often unaffected because of time lags. They offer excellent outlets for excess inventories and opportunities to utilize productive capacity fully. Global Focus 2-2 shows how three small domestic firms capitalized on these balancing advantages of global markets.

GLOBAL FOCUS 2-2

Exports as a Hedge Against Flat U.S. Market

Exports enable many U.S. firms to maintain and increase their overall sales when the American market is flat.

- "In the late 1980s, we made a decision to expand into the international marketplace as a hedge against the domestic economic downturn," says Harold Adams, president of RTKL Associates, Inc., of Baltimore. The architectural/engineering company cranked up to export its services six years ago. Since that time it has performed work in more than forty countries.

- Finding the U.S. domestic housing market slow, New England Homes, Inc., of Hamden, Connecticut, began exporting homes. Peter M. Hart, the company's senior vice president, said, "Home builders and manufacturers of home elements who want to break out of the housing doldrums should consider building and exporting residences to areas of the world experiencing a housing crisis." The firm is off to a good start in Israel and Japan and is exploring additional foreign markets.

- A company official of C.R. Onsrud, Inc., of Troutman, North Carolina, a manufacturer of woodworking machinery, told the Commerce Department: "One very important lesson we have learned; the broader your sales base the less a recession in the United States will affect you." In a recent year, increased ex-

---

ports enabled the firm to show a profit even though U.S. sales volume was down one third.

Source: Business America, U.S. Department of Commerce, Washington, DC; *World Trade Week,* Vol. 114, No. 9, 1993, p.7.

Furthermore, the fact that most fixed costs can be captured in the domestic market often means that the firm can penetrate a foreign market with a competitive pricing policy that focuses mainly on variable costs. (The behavior of costs in formulating pricing strategies, as well as risks and opportunities implicit in these strategies, are covered in more detail in Chapter 16.)

• *LEVERAGE STRENGTHS*

As companies successfully enter foreign markets, "leverage" benefits accrue from company resources and market resources. Thus, larger international markets multiply the effectiveness of whatever company resources— a unique product, management expertise, access to natural resources, exclusive marketing information, and the like—helped the firm succeed in the domestic marketplace. And, once the company successfully penetrates international markets, it can apply strategies, systems, sources of labor, materials, or funds that prove successful in one country's market to other countries. For example, a global manufacturer of consumer electronics planning the development of a new product line might find that low interest rates and a stable currency suggest the United States as the best source of financing; technological expertise might suggest India as the locale for engineering these products, and wage rates and worker skills might suggest Mexico as the ideal location for assembling these products. Some indication of the extent to which expanded international operations can enhance a firm's competitive posture in all markets is offered in a study by the Boston Consulting Group, which found that economies of scale and shortened learning curves that result when production is doubled through global expansion can reduce production costs up to 30 percent. This, in turn, can create cost and price reductions that can be passed on to customers in all markets.

• *ACHIEVE A COMPETITIVE EDGE*

A firm that successfully penetrates international markets poses two competitive threats to firms left behind: (1) these stay-at-homes will lose market share to leverage benefits generated by the firm's international marketing activities, and (2) these stay-at-homes will lose a future opportunity to enter and grow in foreign markets now occupied by early-bird competitors.

For example, in spite of its recognized technological expertise, the United States has become noncompetitive in its own domestic market against Pacific Rim countries that got a head start in marketing video recorders, television sets, and other consumer electronics products in global markets.

• *ACHIEVE TAX ADVANTAGES*

Many countries entice businesses by offering incentives in the form of reduced property, import, and income taxes for an initial time period. Multinational firms may also adjust revenue reports, or operations, so the largest profits are recorded in countries with low tax rates (often a risky strategy, as discussed in Chapter 15).

In the United States, a tax mechanism called the **Foreign Sales Corporation (FSC)** has been set up, according to strict guidelines of the Internal Revenue Service (IRS) and in conformity with international agreements, to make international marketing activities potentially more profitable by providing firms with certain tax deferrals. For example, if a firm's foreign subsidiary qualifies for an FSC, a portion of its income is exempt from U.S. corporate income tax.

• *PROLONG PRODUCT LIFE*

Often, exporting provides a second life to products and services that are no longer competitive in home markets. For example, Asia represents a booming market for vintage U.S. "B" motion pictures.

• *INCREASE PROFITS*

Through leverage, tax, and competitive advantages, the overseas strategies of American companies can produce profits well in excess of domestic markets. For example, whereas American automobile firms suffered huge profit losses in the domestic market in the mid-1980s, their European operations remained largely profitable. In 1999, Coca-Cola's Japanese market, alone, accounted for 20 percent of the company's profits—about $1 billion—on just 5 percent of its overall sales volume. Other large firms whose profits from overseas markets exceed those of domestic markets include Michelin from France, Sony from Japan, Philips from the Netherlands, and BASF from Germany.

DIFFICULTIES IN ENTERING FOREIGN MARKETS

Offsetting these prospective advantages, a company also faces a number of environmental hurdles in attempting to enter and grow in international markets. Summarized below (and elaborated in Chapter 4), these hurdles follow.

• *POLITICAL AND LEGAL INFLUENCES*

Hostile attitudes by host country governments toward foreign firms that can stifle any chance of successful entry include confiscatory taxes and tariffs, quotas that limit the amount of imports accepted, and "local content" regulations requiring use of host country products, personnel, funds, and facilities.

• *ECONOMIC/DEMOGRAPHIC INFLUENCES*

Measures of economic viability—such as the population's standard of living and the country's stage of economic development and currency stability—are often insufficient to justify the expense and risk of attempting to enter a foreign market. Unfriendly demographic environments might include a lack of people in age, income, or occupational groups likely to buy the company's products.

• *SOCIAL/CULTURAL FACTORS*

Personal beliefs, aspirations, languages, interpersonal relationships, and social structures differ among countries and can adversely affect not only the way a product offering is perceived and received, but also the cost and risk associated with overcoming these negatives.

• *TECHNOLOGY*

Underdeveloped infrastructures to facilitate transportation and communication can make it prohibitively expensive to market product offerings in foreign countries.

• *CONTROL PROBLEMS*

Most firms that achieve multinational or global status find it considerably more difficult to coordinate and control manufacturing and marketing activities—and monitor competitors—in dispersed markets, with different customs, languages, transportation, and communication media.

THE GROWTH OF GLOBAL MARKETS

Since the mid-1980s, an eclectic series of revolutions, including the fall of communist command economies and the wildfire spread of democracies and free-market economies, has dramatically expanded and altered international markets and produced a mixed bag of outcomes: dislocation and consolidation, growth and decline, new alliances and old alienations, and many new competitive opportunities and threats.

Another key outcome was an acceleration of the race to create global and regional economic communities among the nations of the world, with more than 90 percent of the world's nations belonging to economic communities by 1999. Reasons for this integration invariably entail the freeing up of trade among nations by reducing or eliminating political, legal, financial, technological, and competitive barriers.

APEC, WTO, NAFTA, AND THE EU

This race among nations to affiliate in economic communities culminated, within a five-year period, in four agreements that effectively integrate most of the world's production, population, and buying power.

In 1989, the Asia Pacific Economic Cooperation Group (APEC) was created to gradually dismantle trade barriers among fifteen Pacific nations. In 1993, the ratification of the Maastricht Treaty created the European Union (EU), with a commitment to a common European currency, the Euro, by 1999. Also in 1993, the North American Free Trade Agreement (NAFTA) passed Congress, linking Canada, the United States, and Mexico into a trade zone of 360 million people and a Gross National Product (GNP) of $6 trillion.

Finally, in 1993, 117 member countries agreed to provisions of GATT that reduced tariff barriers and fostered free trade. In 1995, the World Trade Organization (WTO) replaced the GATT as the major body overseeing international trade.

In the remainder of this chapter, we examine countries comprising these economic communities, focusing on their present state of development, future prospects, and the opportunities for trade they represent. We begin with our own continent and then circle the globe from west (the Pacific Rim and East Asia) to east (Western Europe). Figure 2-2 shows the regions covered in this analysis and an index of the relative stage of development of countries comprising each region (i.e., number of data transmission devices per 10,000 population).

THE AMERICAS, NORTH AND SOUTH

From north to south, this market is composed of Canada, the United States, Mexico, Belize, Guatemala, El Salvador, Honduras, Nicaragua, Costa Rica, Panama, Colombia, Venezuela, Ecuador, Peru, Brazil, Bolivia, Paraguay, Uruguay, Argentina, and Chile. We begin our discussion of this market with the three northernmost counties, brought together economically by NAFTA, and then focus on the economic revolution in the nations to their south.

CANADA AND THE UNITED STATES: CAUTIOUS FRIENDS

Although Canada's population is only one-tenth that of the United States, the two countries are quite similar in a number of respects. Per-capita GNP is roughly the same (about $20,000), as are consumer spending categories. Both Canadians and Americans spend similar percentages of income for

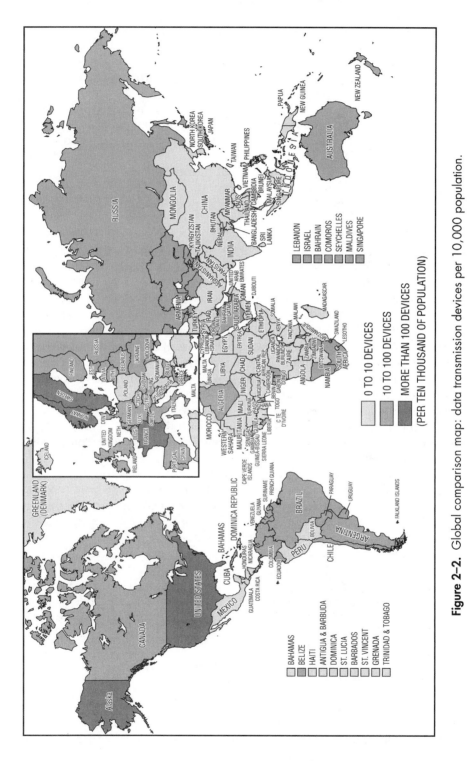

Figure 2–2. Global comparison map: data transmission devices per 10,000 population.

transportation and communication, leisure and education, and clothing, footwear, and textiles. Canadians, with universal health care, spend significantly less for health, and Americans spend somewhat less for housing. In 1996, both countries had about the same GDP growth rate (2.6 percent) and low rates of inflation and unemployment.

In one statistical respect, however, Canada differs markedly from the U.S.: as one of the world's preeminent exporting countries, Canada generated a trade balance surplus of $18 billion in 1996, as compared to a concommitant U.S. deficit of $176 billion. This huge U.S. trade deficit accumulated despite the generally weak dollar that would normally favor exports over imports and despite an increase in U.S. exports from 7.2 to 10.2 percent of GDP between 1985 and 1995. Demand for imports generated by the growth of the U.S. economy simply overwhelmed these considerations.

A significant cultural difference between Canada and the United States pertains to language and lifestyle variables that effectively divide Canada into two countries: French and English Canada. In 1980, French separatists lost in a sovereignty referendum by a 60 to 40 percent margin. In 1995, the vote for an independent, French-speaking Canada was much closer: 49 to 51 percent. From a marketer's perspective, the fact of these two distinct cultures— the staid, efficient, uprightness of English Canada and the exuberant, creative spirit of French Quebec—must be addressed in dealing with Canada. For example, separate communication programs are needed to reach each market because neither group watches or reads the other's TV, books, or newspapers. Rational promotional appeals are said to work more effectively in English Canada, whereas emotive appeals work more effectively in Quebec. Quebeckers also tend to identify more with the United States, support free trade agreements, and feel less threatened by American culture than do English Canadians.

In 1989, after three failed attempts in this century, the United States and Canada signed a free trade agreement that created a single $5 trillion economy—10 percent larger than the United States' own economy and 15 percent larger than that of the EU. A large part of the problem in finally getting this agreement signed derived from Canada's desire to preserve its cultural identity alongside the colossus to its south that dominates broadcast, film, publishing, and similar industries in Canada. The agreement that was finally signed aims to preserve Canada's cultural industries, with free trade arrangements for less-sensitive sectoral areas (for example, automobiles) implemented immediately and then gradually broadened to include more sensitive sectors (such as textiles and steel).

MEXICO: BOOM AND BUST

After the U.S.-Canadian free trade agreement was expanded in 1994 to include Mexico in the NAFTA agreement, U.S. trade with Mexico surged to over $100 billion in the first year, thrusting Mexico ahead of Japan as the

United States' second largest export market behind Canada. During this period, U.S. exports to Mexico—mainly consisting of automobiles, agricultural products, consumer electronics, iron, steel, and other metals—increased by over 20 percent, as did imports from Mexico. In dollar terms, however, this increase in trade further exacerbated a Mexican trade deficit that began in 1987, when Mexico, along with most of its South American neighbors, implemented a mix of free-market initiatives that opened its economy to a flood of formerly restricted imports that helped generate a $30 billion trade imbalance within six years. With domestic savings low, the only way to cover this imbalance was with foreign investments, usually raised through the sale of Mexican treasury bonds and notes. To entice investors, Mexico guaranteed that the peso would not be devalued and backed this promise with a policy of buying pesos that traded outside the parameters of a rigidly controlled range.

Then, a series of political and economic shocks—political intrigues and assassinations, a peasant revolt in Chiapis, higher interest rates in the United States and other developed and emerging countries—stimulated a flow of investment funds out of Mexico to other investment opportunities. Meanwhile, Mexico's Central Bank was spending billions a month to support the peso, now trading outside its controlled range, while failing to prevent the surging growth of the domestic money supply. The dam burst when the bank ran out of foreign currency to buy back the pesos it had been pumping into the economy to keep interest rates low and the economy booming. In desperation, the Mexican government devalued the peso from its precrisis exchange rate of 3.5 pesos to the dollar to a rate of around 6 pesos to the dollar. The predictable results of this devaluation were widespread. In Mexico, living standards—already low by developed-nation standards—dropped further, as did the value of personal savings. Investor confidence in the government, and its ability to negotiate free markets, was diluted, leading to a further flight of capital. Many businesses that owed money in dollars were ruined. Inflation began an upward spiral to 52 percent in 1995.

On the positive side, Mexico's products, produced by workers whose already low wages declined 50 percent after devaluation, were suddenly much more competitive in world markets, transforming Mexico's $18 billion trade deficit of 1994 into a $7.4 billion trade surplus in 1995, and releasing Mexico from the deficit drag that had been slowing economic growth. This new competitiveness also benefited companies and consumers in other countries, who now paid less for Mexican goods. However, the fact that Mexican consumers could no longer afford American products quickly turned the U.S. trade surplus with Mexico into a deficit of $8.6 billion in 1996, which, by the rule of thumb that 17,000 jobs are lost for each $1 billion of negative trade balance, translates into 146,000 additional jobs lost to Mexico.

These economic plusses for the Mexican economy, combined with a draconian economic plan involving frozen prices and wages, spending cutbacks, and enforced savings, began to turn the economy around perceptibly beginning in 1995 and made Mexican securities again attractive to foreign investors. As evidence of this turnaround, by 1998 Mexico had paid back, well ahead of schedule, most of the $10 billion it borrowed from the United States to help weather its financial crisis.

THE REMARKABLE LATIN AMERICAN ECONOMIC MIRACLE

From the mid-1940s to the mid-1980s, the Latin American component of the hemispheric market was statist, protectionist, and anti-United States. By the mid-1980s, all of Latin America was close to economic collapse. Hundreds of billions of dollars, lent by banks and international lending organizations to governments and state-owned businesses, were used to cover budget deficits and to finance projects plagued by bureaucratic tangles, corruption, and mismanagement. Constant defaults on these debt payments threatened the stability of the international banking system. Dealing with dictatorships on the right and left, foreign companies encountered attempts at nationalization, protectionist policies favoring local companies, and spiraling inflation rates. High tariff barriers discouraged trade, and economic cooperation among Latin American nations was minimal.

Then, preceding the fall of communism in Eastern Europe, a political revolution swept Latin America, led by Chile, which lowered or removed tariffs, got rid of import licensing, and generally integrated its economy into the global economy. By 1993, most Latin American nations had followed suit to the point where all governments were free-market democracies. Economic approaches embraced by most Latin governments—emphasizing open markets, low inflation, and balanced budgets—enabled them to reduce once-onerous debt levels. Tariffs were reduced, exports were increased, taxes were cut, capital markets were modernized, small business growth was encouraged, business red tape and regulations were reduced, and judicial processes were changed to ensure equal protection for foreign investors. Entire industries were privatized to relate output to market needs and to face the discipline of competition.

• *MANY PROBLEMS REMAIN*

Maldistribution of wealth and income still oppresses Latin America's burgeoning underclass. And throughout the region there is an acute shortage of banking services, computerization, telecommunications, shopping centers, supermarkets, hotels, insurance, and a host of other services. Many of the new democracies are fragile. To keep investment dollars coming, central banks have kept interest rates high, a drag on growth. There is pressure on governments to follow the Mexican lead and devalue currencies to make exports more competitive.

Judging from the response of the rest of the world, however, it would seem that the plusses of Latin America's dynamic new economic look easily outweigh the minuses. Led by consumer products, technology, and service sectors, businesses in the United States, Japan, and Europe quintupled their investment in Latin America between 1991 and 1996, from $30 billion to over $150 billion. In 1994, Latin American countries raised over $20 billion in bond and stock offerings in the international marketplace, up from an annual average of under $1 billion through the 1980s. According to projections by the World Bank and the IMF, Latin America and Asia will be the primary world growth areas in the twenty-first century.

Led by countries like Chile and Peru, Latin America's economies grew dramatically in the early 1990s, reaching a 4.6 percent increase in GDP in 1994, when the financial crisis in Mexico, combined with another in Argentina, were largely responsible for a GDP growth increase of only 0.6 in 1995. In 1996, however, the growth curve again tilted upward.

THE ASIA PACIFIC MARKET

Today the Asia Pacific countries—Japan, China, South Korea, Hong Kong, Taiwan, Singapore, Thailand, Indonesia, Malaysia, Brunei, the Philippines, Vietnam, Cambodia, Australia, and New Zealand—represent the most powerful economic region in the world, with a staggering GNP of $14 trillion. During an almost unbroken growth period from the early 1960s, the Asia Pacific region saw its collective percentage of global output increase sixfold, from 4 to 25 percent. In 1993, the Asia Pacific share of total world trade of $7 trillion was almost 35 percent, $2.3 trillion. In 1989, the United States and Canada joined these Asian nations to form APEC, which envisions the gradual dismantling of trade barriers, and an eventual free trade area, among member countries.

Another index of the region's economic growth, and the importance of a resurgent China in this equation, is the figures on the growth of each nation's GDP in 1995: China, 11 percent; Malaysia, 9 percent; Thailand, 9 percent; Taiwan, 6 percent; Singapore, 9 percent; Indonesia, 7 percent; Hong Kong, 5 percent; and South Korea, 10 percent. Only Japan, mired in a seemingly endless recession, experienced negative growth figures.

Profiles of key Asia Pacific countries follow.

JAPAN: A HUMBLED GIANT

The Japanese economy has proven to be a phoenix, rising from the ashes of World War II to unparalleled heights. Some of Japan's growth is attributable to its role as a supplier and staging area for U.S. forces during hot and cold war engagements in Korea and Vietnam. Most of it is attributable to hard, smart work, based on a culture that fosters discipline; a government industrial policy that takes the long view in supporting and subsidizing growth industries; a highly educated workforce able to move easily to these growth industries from declining, phased-out industries; a unique ability to import, integrate, and improve technology; and interlocking systems of businesses, financial institutions, and trading companies (*kieretsu*) that effectively bar unwelcome offshore competitors. Japan also has the high savings rate needed to capitalize growth industries, with a population that saves 14 percent of disposable income, compared to 5 percent in the United States.

Today, Japan has the world's most technologically advanced manufacturing plant and the largest pool of investment capital. Japan is also the world's richest creditor nation, with a 1996 trade surplus of $135.4 billion. (The United States, with a 1996 deficit of $176 billion, is history's largest debtor nation.)

As the world's largest creditor nation, Japan is also the world's largest investor nation, with a 17:1 ratio of investment in other countries versus their investment in Japan (similar ratios for the United States and the United Kingdom are 1.05:1 and 1.19:1, respectively). Japan's investments in other countries have largely financed the U.S. debt since the late 1970s (as long as interest rates were attractively high) and represent the largest source of investment funds in Southeast Asia. As Japan uses its strong yen to buy, at bargain prices, more and more factories in cheap labor markets, it is also lowering its labor costs at home and offsetting the effects of a higher yen on its exports.

Yet, with all these financial, cultural, political, technological, and economic strengths, Japan has been mired in a recession since 1992, thanks largely to a cumbersome, inefficient financial system, a strong yen, and a series of crises (political corruption scandals, earthquakes, dysfunctional protectionist policies, nerve gas attacks) that distracted the country from its competitive mission.

Japan's recession continues, only managing to reach a 1 percent growth rate in one year between 1991 and 1996. Unemployment remains high, wages and earnings are flat, and property values are depressed (saddling financial institutions with at least $400 billion in bad real estate loans). Economic deregulation and revamping, necessary for sustained, broad-based vitality in other countries, have had little impact in Japan.

To understand the impact of Japan's malaise on its relations with the United States and other countries, consider the Japanese domestic automobile monopoly, which is representative of many other product monopolies in Japan's protected markets. In 1953, the U.S. share of the Japanese automobile market was 60 percent; by 1960, it was less than 1 percent and has remained there since. (Eighty percent of U.S. dealers sell foreign cars alongside domestic cars; only 7 percent of Japanese dealers sell foreign and domestic cars, and they are usually not American cars.)

The fact that Japanese cars generate more than a 25 percent share of the huge U.S. automobile market has resulted in a trade imbalance that is the single largest component of the United States' worldwide trade deficit. However, the fact that the yen, since 1985, has been soaring in value against the dollar means that Japanese cars made in Japan (in 1996, almost 60 percent of Japanese cars sold in the United States were made in America with American-made parts) are harder to sell in the United States, and generate much smaller profits. These profits lost in the United States are recouped by profits made on Japanese cars sold in the protected Japanese market, at the expense of Japanese consumers, who can't shop in a competitive, free-market environment.

In an attempt to redress this imbalance and persuade the Japanese to open their markets for automobiles and other American products, the United States, periodically since the 1970s, has been threatening and, occasionally, implementing trade sanctions (tariffs, quotas, licensing requirements, and the like) against Japanese products. The results of these initiatives have generally been unproductive. Typically, commitments to open their markets are ignored or otherwise evaded by the Japanese, or retaliatory measures are taken against American products that leave our current account (the trade deficit), and employment picture, unchanged. In recent years, there has also emerged among the world's nations a general feeling that the United States is using the wrong tactics in dealing directly with Japan, instead of using the offices of the WTO, which was set up to resolve international trade disputes.

However, with the world's second largest economy and an embarrassment of export wealth, Japan is likely to grow out of its doldrums and dominate new technologies like biotechnology, superconductivity, and microelectronics.

FOUR GROWING, GROWLING TIGERS

South Korea, Taiwan, Hong Kong, and Singapore, Asia's "four tigers," are effectively following the Japanese model, with hard-working, well-educated labor forces, strong government aid to business, and an aggressive emphasis on moving into new fields (such as automobiles and computers) and regions. Like Japan, they are not averse to protecting their markets, to the point where they accounted for more that 20 percent of the U.S. trade deficit in 1995.

A large part of the growth of these economies relates to the explosive growth in demand by the Chinese and Indonesian economies for high-technology and heavy-industry products including steel, machinery, petrochemicals, consumer electronics, and automobiles (in 1995, for example, the Chinese bought 22 percent of South Korea's auto exports).

As labor moves from low-wage, low-productivity industries into services and higher value-added industries, it is quickly closing the gap between industrialized and post-industrialized status. This transition is occurring so rapidly that it doesn't show up in the statistics, with unemployment under 3 percent in all four economies between 1992 and 1996.

CHINA'S ECONOMIC MIRACLE

Part of China's extraordinary economic growth over the past decade, which has seen urban incomes increase 400 percent and rural incomes increase 300 percent, can be explained by the relatively low productivity base from which it made its great leap upward.

Even now, China's per capita income of under $2000 is but a fraction of most of its Asian neighbors, although, with China's 1.1 billion population, its economy is the third largest in the world, behind that of the United States and Japan. At its present growth rate, China, with Taiwan and Hong Kong (annexed in 1997), will be the world's largest economy in this century.

Some reasons to expect that China's economy will continue to grow follow.

- It is an economy moving tentatively away from the cumbersome communist command model toward free-market institutions.

- It supports a culture that values hard work, education, savings, and investment.

- It requires significant outside assistance. In spite of its present size and future growth prospects, China's economy is still backward; it has huge infrastructure needs—roads, railroads, communication networks—and its antiquated, labor-intensive manufacturing industries require modernization.

- It receives a steady supply of investment dollars to finance growth and modernization from the likes of Japan, the United States, and overseas Chinese.

Opportunities for American companies in China's resurgent economy are reflected in the following examples: Coca-Cola sales have grown an average of 54 percent a year in China since 1985, making China Coke's fastest-growing market; sales of Motorola pagers leaped from 100,000 in 1991 to 4 million in 1995; Kentucky Fried Chicken franchises opened in 31 cities in 1996; Apple, IBM, Hewlett Packard, and Compaq formed a joint venture to build and distribute 30,000 personal computers a year (with only one computer for every 4000 people in China in 1999, the market for computers is expected to grow by 30 percent per year in this century). Heavy demand is also expected to grow in the fields of financial services, heavy industry, transportation, jet technology, automobiles, cellular telephones, agriculture, power plants, and brand-name consumer products to feed increasingly affluent tastes. Overall, the United States is expected to get more than 60 percent of the sales in these fields.

Behind these success stories, however, many building blocks of a successful market economy are still missing in China. Its currency is not yet convertible, its banking system is antiquated and unsound, financial regulation is absent, corruption is rampant, and commercial law is arbitrarily enforced (in 1994, the world's largest McDonald's was unceremoniously evicted from a prime location in Beijing despite a twenty-year lease). Also, its communist government, in spite of the roaring success of its free-market experiments, still insists on churning out laborious five-year plans and subsidizing a huge network of unprofitable, poorly managed state enterprises (of seventeen China-based companies listed on the Hong Kong stock exchange in 1991, only one—Shanghai Petrochemical—was trading at more than its original price in 1996).

Companies planning to do business in China have to expect government meddling and red tape at all stages of entry and development. Approvals to open plants are required on numerous governmental levels; operational constraints can be onerous, governing things like joint ventures, expansion plans, and markets to target; and tax policies can be capricious (in 1995, Beijing cancelled $6 billion in tax rebates promised to export businesses). This difficulty of doing business in China, as compared to the relative ease of entering the U.S. market, is at least partially responsible for China's growing trade surplus with the United States, which grew 30 percent in 1994 to $30 billion. (China's ratio of quantities exported versus quantities imported is 4:1, which is larger than Japan's trade imbalance ever was with the United States.)

Problems affecting trade between the United States and China go well beyond the operational level to encompass human rights violations, arms sales to unfriendly countries, nuclear proliferation, aggressive behavior toward Taiwan, and the piracy of American software, music, and movies. In 1995, the United States and China negotiated an agreement on piracy under which China, among other things, agreed to take immediate steps to curtail infringements on intellectual property. In 1996, a new agreement was negotiated, under threat of such sanctions as tariffs, removal of Most-Favored-Nation status, and entry into the WTO, but it became obvious that the first agreement was being largely ignored.

INDIA: AN AWAKENING GIANT

Since 1991, when, after 40 years of socialist economic policies, India implemented a radical economic overhaul program that embraced market forces and foreign investment, American firms have been the leading investors in many diverse sectors, including breakfast cereals, computers, soft drinks, power plants, and telephone systems. The main attraction of the Indian market is its sheer size: 890 million people with a middle class almost as large as the entire U.S. population. Other attractions include India's democratic form of government, with an independent court system capable of settling disputes, and the widespread use of English. Also, India seems partial to U.S. investment, which accounted for 40 percent of all proposals accepted by India's watchdog agencies between 1991 and 1996, and increased from $350 million to $800 million between 1985 and 1995.

Against these positives, investors in India encounter many of the same obstacles they face in China and Vietnam: bureaucratic interference in all aspects of doing business, a vast network of loss-ridden, state-owned industries, bans and punitive tariffs on many foreign-made consumer goods and equipment for new projects, a crumbling infrastructure, and backward living standards for the vast majority, who have a 60 percent illiteracy rate. Other negatives include a history of nationalizing industries and draconian labor laws that mandate, for example, that no Indian worker can be laid off.

These negatives have combined to help hold India's growth rate since 1991 to only 3.5 percent, about half of what it needs to catch up with fast-track East Asian neighbors like Malaysia, Thailand, Singapore, and South Korea, all of which have annual per-capita incomes many times higher than India's $350.

THE SLUGGISH EUROPEAN UNION

Between 1960 and 1996, what began as the European Free Trade Area (EFTA) evolved into the European Community (EC) and, finally, the EU, uniting fifteen countries into an economic union. As such, member countries are committed to allowing the free movement of people, products, services, and capital, and to surrendering large measures of national sovereignty to supranational authorities, such as the European Parliament in Strasbourg and the European Commission in Brussels.

Beginning in 1999, member nations were expected to harmonize government spending, taxation, and monetary policies, with a common currency, and fixed exchange rates.

In 1996, growth among EU countries was sluggish, at about half the level of growth in the United States, and a third that of the average Pacific Rim country (for example, 1.6 percent for France and Germany and 2.1 percent for Sweden, Britain, Holland, and Austria); unemployment levels were about twice that of the United States and three times that of Pacific Rim countries (for example, 14 percent in Belgium, 12 percent in France, 11 percent in Germany, 12 percent in Italy, and 24 percent in Spain). Deficits among EU countries averaged 5.5 percent of GDP, as opposed to 2 percent in the United States. These recessive conditions began to reverse themselves in 1998, with the discipline imposed on EU countries in anticipation of the introduction of the Euro, a common currency with fixed exchange rates.

By January 1, 1999, 11 of the 15 EU countries participating in the new single monetary policy had harmonized government spending, taxation, and monetary policies to accommodate the Euro. The full changeover culminates in 2002, when Euro bank notes and coins will replace the currencies of participating countries.

In spite of healthy economic growth going into the twenty-first century, EU countries, collectively and individually, still face nagging problems, including the following:

- More aggressive global competition. Going into the twenty-first century, EU countries continue to experience competitive pressures from Asian countries, with their more productive economies, and a United States that has grown more competitive largely in response to aggressive Asian trade initiatives. Today, European technology is behind that of Asia and the United States in a number of critical areas, with high wages and inflexible labor laws further dulling Europe's once keen competitive edge.

- An extensive social welfare system that the Europeans can no longer afford in the competitive global economy, including expensive systems of health care, pensions, unemployment insurance, and family aid that have defined European social and economic policies since World War II. In Germany, for example, 37-hour work weeks, fully paid maternity leaves, and 40 days off each year are mandated. In France, the four-day work week is becoming a mandated reality. These social payments help keep deficits high and, with no broad consensus to change the welfare systems, are difficult to cut. Since World War II, Britain is the only government elected on a plank to reduce the size of government; in France, labor protests paralyzed parts of France at the prospect of minor cuts in social payments in 1996.

- An immigrant tide into West European countries from West and North Africa, Eastern Europe, Asia, and Turkey that is further straining welfare systems and economies. Germany, whose generous asylum laws have been tightened in response to this influx, is particularly hard-hit; of the millions seeking asylum in Western Europe, two thirds try to enter Germany.

- The enormous burden of German unification. Germany, traditionally the engine of European economic recovery and growth, finds its economy stagnating under the load of reunification, and it is dragging down other continental economies in the process. East Germany, with unemployment hovering around 30 percent, a decrepit infrastructure that will cost trillions of marks to modernize, and no training in democracy or free-market enterprise, is proving to be more an albatross than an asset. Largely as a result of the cost of unification and emigration, Germany has a huge budget deficit that puts continual pressure on the central bank to raise interest rates—

increases that radiate throughout Europe to further stifle productivity and exacerbate the recession.

- The end of the cold war and, with it, the end of a unifying force that held European countries together in a common cooperative purpose. Since the fall of the Berlin Wall in 1989, European confidence in U.S. leadership has been eroded by a number of cautions and crises, including the reduction of NATO's influence as a strong unifying force and conflicting strategies for dealing with conflicts in Bosnia and Kosovo. Trust in the United States has been further eroded by what many Europeans perceive to be economic opportunism, using the weak dollar to penetrate European and other world markets. Many also perceive that the United States can no longer be relied on as the main guarantor of Europe's security, with all its other interests in Asia and the Western Hemisphere.

- A big-company mentality. Another prospective damper on European competitiveness that isn't being affected by EU agreements is the dominance of European economies by big companies that are less flexible and creative than smaller companies, from which most technological breakthroughs emerge.

- A protectionist tradition, which extends across the continent, notably in France (which insists on protection for its subsidized farmers even in the face of strong pressures from WTO and EU trading partners), Germany, and the Benelux countries. One manifestation of this tradition is a growing notion among Europeans that they can maintain satisfactorily high incomes and living standards without depending on the global economy. Presently, 80 percent of Europe's trade is internal—about twice that among Pacific rim countries—and the EU is often perceived as a shield behind which to maintain this situation, making Europe a much less attractive trading partner than was envisioned when the Berlin Wall came tumbling down.

Measures taken to address problems enervating the European economy are earnest, if generally ad hoc and insufficient. For example, Germany cut coal subsidies by $7 billion and is making some effort to cut spending, reduce welfare state largesse, and raise taxes (however, when taxpayers are already paying 45 percent of GDP in taxes—49 percent in France—there isn't much wiggle room). Italy pushed through welfare changes in 1995 aimed at saving $60 billion through 2005, Sweden made big cuts in its social safety net, and France raised its value-added tax to 20.9 percent.

However, even though the slumping European economy stands in sharp contrast to the dynamic, vigorous economies of Asia and the Americas, there is little talk of broad-based initiatives of the sort that are dramatically invigorating these economies—such as the extensive privatization of industry, the reduction of social benefits, and tax reforms—to meet globally competitive standards.

CHAPTER PERSPECTIVE

The reasons why four of five U.S. firms in a position to do so don't enter foreign markets—including lack of potential in many markets and barriers to entry in others—are becoming less valid in this new century of all-out global competition. The disadvantages of entering international markets are increasingly being offset by profit-enhancing advantages, including tax savings, less competition, and opportunities to leverage global marketplace strengths. Typically, a firm entering the international marketplace achieves, sequentially, international, multinational, and global status. Underpinning global entry strategies is a strategic marketing plan based on a researched understanding of marketplace threats and opportunities, the nature and needs of customers, and product/place/price/promotion marketing mixes best calculated to meet these needs. Countries belonging to WTO, NAFTA, the EU, and APEC have most benefited from toppling trade barriers and the efficient flow of capital, labor, and expertise resulting from the worldwide spread of free-market, free-enterprise economies. Collectively, they represent America's major markets, but they also present threats as well as opportunities for future growth.

KNOW THE CONCEPTS
TERMS FOR STUDY

Acquired advantage
Comparative advantage
Currency stability
Economic communities
Financial flows
Foreign Sales Corporation
International Monetary Fund
Legal/political factors

Leverage
Most-Favored-Nation principle
Tax advantage
Trade deficit
Trade surplus
World Bank
WTO

MATCHUP EXERCISES

1. Match the organizations in the first column with the descriptor in the second column.

1. IMF

2. WTO
3. World Bank

4. FSC

a. provides tax deferrals for qualified firms
b. Most-Favored-Nation principle
c. assists growth of fledgling economies
d. member nations draw upon reserve assets

2. Match the country in the first column with the descriptor in the second column.

1. Canada

2. United States

3. Germany

4. Japan

a. largest contributor to U.S. trade deficit
b. lowest exports per capita among industrialized countries
c. largest exporter in absolute terms
d. largest exporter as a share of GDP

3. Match the global trading stage in the first column with the characteristic listed in the second column.

1. international

a. achieves major synergies based largely on exploitation of comparative advantage; integrated, interactive management

2. multinational

      b. focuses on the domestic market while pursuing international objectives; top-down management

3. global

      c. recognizes that differences in global markets require adaptation of the marketing mix (product, price, place, promotion) in order to succeed; bottom-up management

4. Match the regional economic community in the first column with the descriptor in the second column.

1. APEC

      a. Mexico becomes the United States' second largest trading partner

2. NAFTA

      b. dismantles trade barriers among 15 Pacific nations

3. EU

      c. issued a common currency in 1999

QUESTIONS FOR REVIEW AND DISCUSSION

1. France and Germany, traditional enemies during previous centuries, are now each other's largest trading partners. Discuss the role of trading agreements, peace, and technological breakthroughs in bringing about this situation.

2. Give examples of natural advantage and acquired advantage that illustrate the differences between these concepts, and explain why most world trade takes place among developed countries.

3. What is a trade deficit? List three reasons why it would be advantageous for the United States to transform its trade deficit into a trade surplus.

4. Assume that the United States implements a policy of reducing its trade deficit by increasing sales in categories where we have acquired advantages to countries with which we presently have our largest balance-of-payment deficits. Does this policy make sense? If so, which product groups would be promoted to which countries?

5. How will the following trends help a company engaged in the manufacture of consumer electronics products compete more effectively in the global market: economic cooperation among nations; reduction in differences among nations; competition from newly emerging nations.

6. Although hemispheres apart, China and Chile are representative of countries that have maintained double-digit growth rates from the mid-1980s to the mid-1990s. What factors common to both economies explain these growth rates?

ANSWERS

MATCHUP EXERCISES

1. 1d, 2b, 3c, 4a

2. 1d, 2b, 3c, 4a

3. 1b, 2c, 3a

4. 1b, 2a, 3c

QUESTIONS FOR REVIEW AND DISCUSSION

1. Both France and Germany are strong, supportive members of the European Union, which facilitates trade among its fifteen member countries by prohibiting import/export duties and improving the mobility of labor, capital, and technology among member states. The absence during the past half-century of large-scale wars on the European continent encouraged trade between France and Germany by diverting resources away from military adventures and toward healthy, rapid economic growth, which not only was fueled by but also helped to fuel global trade. Particularly in the fields of communication and transportation, technological breakthroughs created products to trade, processes to make them, and the means to market them more efficiently and economically.

2. The term *natural advantage* refers to an endowment based on climatic conditions or access to certain natural resources that give a country or region an advantage to the extent that other countries desire this endowment but don't have it. For example, climatic conditions give some countries the wherewithal to produce fruits (pineapples, bananas) demanded by, but not produced in, other countries. By trading these fruits to these other countries, the naturally endowed country creates a larger market for its products and income to purchase products that it needs but doesn't produce. The term *acquired advantage* generally refers to a product or process resource, also in great demand, that a country has created through technological sophistication and specialization (for example, computers). Because most of these acquired-advantage resources are produced and purchased by developed countries and because they cost more than natural-advantage commodities, the percentage of total global trade is much greater among developed countries than among less-developed countries or among developed and less-developed countries.

3. A trade deficit is the amount by which a country's imports exceed its exports. In June 1999, for example, U.S. imports (oil, automobiles, coffee, and so on) exceeded its exports (services, grains, computers, and so on) by $20 billion. Such deficit levels are unsustainable in the long run: they indicate that a country, in its international activities, is consuming more than it is producing, which affects domestic employment by transferring jobs to exporting countries. Conversely, a trade surplus generates jobs; according to Commerce Department figures, $1 billion worth of exports creates, on average, 22,000 jobs. (The levering influence of exports on economic growth was apparent during the economic slowdown of the early 1990s, when export growth accounted for practically all domestic growth and new employment.) From the perspective of individual firms, exporting, by broadening market reach, can achieve economies of scale that help lead to lower costs and higher profits both domestically and abroad. Exporting also helps firms gain stability by not being dependent on a single market and prove their ability to survive in less-familiar environments, in spite of higher transaction costs and different demand structures and cultural dimensions.

4. This policy makes sense to the extent that countries with whom the United States has the largest trade deficits—such as Japan, China, Germany, and Taiwan—are also our largest customers, particularly for products in which we have a comparative advantage (for example, lumber products to Japan). These countries are developed or fast-developing; hence, they have a greater ability to consume and pay for these imports. Given this potential, such a strategy might focus on marketing services (the category in which we have our largest trade surplus), capital goods (such as turnkey processing plants), and foods and beverages to Japan, China, and Germany.

5. Economic cooperation among nations, in the form of regional economic communities like NAFTA and the EU, effectively transform many smaller markets into single large markets, with many fewer trade constraints and the fast, flexible flow of human and financial resources. Together with the reduction of differences among nations, this means that the manufacturer, in dealing with these market aggregates, will be able to reach a much larger market with the same market mix: much less will have to be done to adapt product features, price, distribution, and promotion strategies to many different individual countries. Competition from newly emerging nations implies that they are making the overall pie bigger—just as, for example, competition among many computer producers in the United States benefits all by vastly expanding the market—and that they, themselves, are developing to the point of being worthwhile customers for the firm's products.

6. First, both countries started their growth spurts from relatively low productivity bases, so even slight improvements would tend to be magnified as a percentage of overall GDP. More significantly, both countries have adopted policies designed to increase trade. These policies include lowering tariff barriers; encouraging foreign investment with tax,

licensing, and other incentives; privatizing industry (to a lesser extent in China); encouraging entrepreneurship; working to modernize banking, investment, and judicial processes to stimulate and direct growth; and joining economic communities (APEC for China and Mercosur for Chile) to achieve benefits of leverage and comparative advantage.

3
MARKETING MANAGEMENT AND STRATEGIC MARKETING PLANNING

OVERVIEW

This chapter focuses on the marketing management process and the role of the marketing manager in working with other managers to formulate strategic marketing plans. These plans evolve through a systematic process that analyzes external and internal environments, devises purposeful vision and mission statements, and formulates goals, strategies, tactics, and controls that bring together marketing mixes and target markets.

MARKETING MANAGEMENT CREATES SATISFACTORY EXCHANGES

As defined by the AMA, marketing management involves "planning and executing the conception, pricing, promotion and distribution of goods, services and ideas that create exchanges with target groups that satisfy customer and organizational objectives." In successfully implementing this marketing management process, marketing managers typically engage in a sequence of activities, called strategic marketing planning, involving mission statements, environmental analyses, and the establishment of goals, strategies, programs, and controls.

In the rest of this chapter, we focus on how marketing managers work through the stages of the SMP process to set and achieve company and customer goals. In Chapters 6 through 8, we examine the interconnected systems that organize, inform, and control the process.

WHAT MARKETING MANAGERS DO

In carrying out SMP activities designed to harmonize a firm's objectives and resources with changing market opportunities, a marketing manager works with other managers, above and below, who share similar purposes and goals.

At Merton, for example, the marketing vice president for the entire company, to whom Lora Moore reports, sets overall marketing policy, with the assistance of other managers (finance, production, and the like) from consumer and organizational market divisions. Consistent with these overall policies, Moore works with managers in her department to develop and implement detailed strategic marketing plans. For example, she works with product development and marketing research managers to develop products in the Mighty Mind line that profitably meet customer needs. Her sales manager is responsible for establishing sales goals, assigning territories, training salespeople to sell the MM line, and supervising this effort. Her advertising manager, working with Merton's advertising agency, is responsible for creating and placing advertising and other promotional materials supporting the sales effort. In the organizational systems section of Chapter 6, we examine various organizational structures that facilitate this productive, harmonious melding of ideas and activities.

In working together to create, implement, and control strategic marketing plans, managers on all organizational levels analyze, plan, organize, implement, and control.

For example, analysis of quantitative and qualitative research data might identify a potentially profitable new target market for Merton MM systems. Based on this analysis, Lora Moore's strategic plan for successfully penetrating this market would specify how MM products, prices, distribution, and promotional strategies would meet the defined needs of target market members while achieving company profit objectives. This plan would also specify organizational changes needed to prepare for the plan's execution.

Implementation activities involved in actually carrying out the plan would be based on an assessment of Merton's fit in this new market, while accounting for unforeseen environmental changes and allowing for corresponding changes in the original plan. Concurrently with implementation activities, control mechanisms would lock into place, monitoring environmental forces, competitors, channel participants, and customer receptiveness, indicating areas where planned activities were not achieving desired goals, and providing input to ensure that future plans did achieve these goals. Market Focus 3-1 illustrates this strategic planning process at work.

MARKET FOCUS 3-1

Strategic Planning at Wainwright Industries Earns the Baldrige Award

The message from General Motors was somber: largely because of pressures from foreign competitors, GM would have to cut its number of major suppliers from 400 to 200 and demand higher quality products from the suppliers it kept.

For Don Wainwright, chairman of Wainwright Industries—a Missouri-based contract manufacturer of precision components and subassemblies for the automotive, aerospace, and information-processing industries—this directive from one of the firm's largest customers became the impetus for a strategic planning initiative that began with a compelling mission: to become "a world-class supplier" to firms like GM.

Consistent with this mission, Wainwright set a major business objective: to achieve the Malcolm Baldrige National Quality Award in small business for "excellence in quality management." Criteria required to achieve this goal, pertaining to quality, customer satisfaction, and self-assessment also became objectives that Don Wainwright set for the company to achieve.

To achieve these objectives, Wainwright implemented a program designed to motivate employees to work together to satisfy customers' needs. Among other things, this program:

- Empowered employees to make decisions about improving their jobs and the quality of Wainwright products, with the assurance that management would support them and share information with them. A formal suggestion program was implemented to achieve this goal of making more productive use of human resources.

- Launched training programs in such areas as mathematics, vocabulary skills, problem solving, and interpersonal skills to help employees achieve the firm's higher expectations of them.

- Set up a benchmarking program whereby employees met with previous Baldrige Award winners from other firms to learn about the best practices applicable to Wainwright.

- Adopted a customer-satisfaction measurement system requesting customers to grade Wainwright performance in such areas as quality and service. Another measurement system asked employees to grade the performance of managers and internal supplier departments. Results of these evaluations, along with strategic indicators pertaining to safety, customer satisfaction, quality, and business performance, were posted in a conference room open to all employees.

Tangible results of Wainwright's program for motivating, coordinating, and controlling performance to improve customer satisfaction were winning the Baldrige Award in 1994 and retaining GM as a valued customer. Other tangible results in the years since include dramatically reduced customer reject rates, scrap and rework costs, and operating expenses.

Less tangible results include a sense of ownership and increased job satisfaction among employees and more time for managers to spend on planning for the future, developing relationships with major customers, and identifying new business opportunities.

By combining the marketing concept and strategic planning, Wainwright profits its customers and itself, with consistent growth in market share and profits.

CREATING AND MAINTAINING DEMAND LEVELS

In working with others to create and carry out strategic marketing plans designed to relate marketing mix offerings to target market needs, Moore is viewing the range of products and services making up the MM line as an investment portfolio and devising strategies appropriate to the situation of each, based on demand and profit prospects. In this sense, SMP can be broadly perceived as a process of creating or maintaining various states of demand consistent with the firm's objectives.

Kotler[1] identifies eight **demand states** that marketing managers must recognize and respond to.

- **Negative demand,** where a significant segment of the market dislikes the product and may pay to avoid it. This was the situation that concerned the leisure/travel industry in 1999 when the Y2K threat—imagined or not—persuaded many travelers to cancel travel plans

---

1 Philip Kotler, *Marketing Management,* 8th ed. (Englewood Cliffs, NJ: Prentice-Hall, 1994), pp. 14–15.

in the early months of the millennium. Here, the marketing manager's task is to define reasons for this demand state and take measures to counteract them. Discount fares, extra security measures, and advertised assurances of safety were examples of such measures.

- **No demand** occurs when target market customers are unmotivated or indifferent to the product, like a Broadway play that opens to lukewarm reviews. The job of the marketing manager, then, is to connect potential product benefits to the needs and interests of prospective customers.

- **Latent demand** occurs when many prospective customers share a strong desire for a satisfaction that can't be provided by existing products. Hair restoratives and painless diets are examples of such satisfactions. Here, the job of the marketing manager is to measure the size of potential demand and develop products to meet this demand.

- **Falling demand** is illustrated by problems facing Merton as competitive firms make inroads in its domestic market share. Here, the job of the marketing manager—Lora Moore in this case—is to analyze causes and plan marketing strategies to counter the trend.

- **Irregular demand** occurs when seasonal, daily, or even hourly demand fluctuations cause significant differences in product usage. This problem faces most mass transit systems, with rush hour peak demand occurring only a few hours each day. Here, the marketing manager attempts to alter demand patterns by altering marketing mix variables, such as flexible pricing or special off-season promotions.

- **Full demand** occurs when the firm has all the business it needs. It becomes the marketing manager's job to monitor changes in customer needs and in the competition to maintain this demand level.

- **Overfull demand** occurs when demand is higher than the organization can or wants to handle. Yellowstone Park, with its annual hordes of campers, is an example of overfull demand, which is discouraged by manipulating marketing mix variables, such as higher prices or fewer product features. Using marketing mix variables to decrease demand is called "demarketing."

- **Unwholesome demand,** for products like cigarettes, alcohol, and pornography, challenges marketers of these products to devise marketing plans and mixes that take into account negative public attitudes toward these products. In international markets, this demand state can also be defined by situations where satisfying demand would not be considered morally or legally acceptable in the U.S. market, such as selling off rain-forest timber.

STRATEGIC MARKETING PLANNING MANAGES DEMAND

Strategic marketing planning is the managerial process of developing and maintaining a strategic fit among the organization's resources and objectives and its changing market opportunities. It relies on a clear company mission, supporting objectives and goals, a sound business portfolio, coordinated functional strategies, and effective controls.

SMP is invariably a top-down process, beginning at the corporate level and, in large companies like Merton, working through division, business, and product levels. Figure 3-1 shows a model for SMP at the business level.

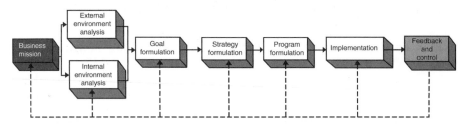

Figure 3–1. The business strategic-planning process.

THE MISSION STATEMENT DEFINES PURPOSE AND DIRECTION

Corporate-level strategic planning begins with a general statement of the company's mission, which serves as a broad statement of organizational direction and addresses such questions as What is our business? Who are our customers? What value do we provide customers? What should our business develop into? Major elements shaping the mission statement include company history and tradition, market threats and opportunities, resources, and distinctive competencies. In reflecting these elements, a good mission statement focuses on a limited number of key goals and defines the main domains in which the firm operates, including markets served; products, applications, and competencies offered; and channels for distributing the firm's products. It is invariably based on a depth analysis of company strengths and weaknesses versus marketplace threats and opportunities and usually emphasizes customer benefits.

The mission statement of International Business Machines (IBM) illustrates these features.

IBM is in the business of applying advanced information technology to solve the problems of business, government, science, space exploration, defense, education, medicine, and other areas of human activity. IBM offers customers solutions that incorporate information processing systems, software, communications systems, and other products and services to address specific needs. These solutions are provided by IBM's worldwide marketing organizations, as well as through the company's business partners, including authorized dealers and remarketers.

In addition to serving as the starting point for overall company policies, goals, and strategies, the mission statement, shared with managers, employees, customers, and other publics, should generate a shared sense of purpose, direction, and opportunity; it should motivate employees and help them work independently, yet collectively, to achieve organizational goals.

BUSINESS-LEVEL STRATEGIC PLANNING

Guided by the corporate mission statement, and the goals and strategies deriving from this statement, Lora Moore's strategic planning at the level of her separate business unit—the Mighty Mind line of products and services—was considerably more focused.

Merton's marketing plan for the MM line, for example, began with this mission statement, which focused on customer benefits:

> The Mighty Mind Systems division of Merton Electronics is in the business of providing state-of-the-art computerized training and communication programs designed to help business executives and professionals become more productive and efficient through the application of modern tools and techniques in areas of general and specialized expertise.

ENVIRONMENTAL ANALYSES PINPOINT THREATS AND OPPORTUNITIES

This mission statement, and the objectives deriving from it, were based on analyses of external and internal environments that helped to identify and define target markets and pinpoint threats and opportunities in penetrating these markets. External environmental analyses covered a broad range of macro- and microenvironmental forces, including competitive initiatives, growth rates for prospective target markets, supplier and distribution problems in reaching these markets, and technological, financial, social, economic, and political influences affecting MM marketing programs.

Internal environmental analyses covered Merton's competencies in functional areas critical to the success of MM marketing programs, including marketing effectiveness (product and service quality; distribution, promotion, and salesforce competence; and the like); financial strength (availability of capital, cash flow, and the like); manufacturing expertise (facilities, work-force dedication, economies of scale, and the like); and organization (leader-ship quality, entrepreneurial orientation, and the like). Chapters 4 and 5 cover these macro- and microenvironmental factors; Chapters 7 and 8 cover marketing information and marketing research systems and procedures designed to gather, process, and interpret this environmental information.

FORMULATING MISSION-RELATED OBJECTIVES

Along with the mission statement, the environmental analyses also helped shape business and marketing objectives that became a key part of Moore's strategic plans. For example, among mission-defined business objectives, Merton would have to attract top-level software engineers to develop state-of-the-art reference materials and training courses for specific professional groups. Marketing objectives would entail identifying and defining target market groups of professionals and preparing marketing mix offerings (for example, designing, distributing, and promoting MM systems attractive to these groups).

Other mission-related goals pertained to profit return, sales growth, market-share improvement, risk avoidance, and innovativeness. All goals were arranged hierarchically, from most to least important (for example, the goal of increased profit return would require the achievement of subgoals in such areas as inventory control, cash flow, revenues, and cost containment). Whenever possible, each goal was quantified so that progress toward its achievement could be measured and was consistent with other goals and the divisional mission statement.

FORMULATING GOAL-RELATED STRATEGIES

Various analyses discussed in the planning systems section of Chapter 6 culminate in marketing strategies for products and services in the firm's portfolio, each strategy designed to satisfy customers in selected target markets through a productive balance of marketing mix elements, and each representing a subset of the overall marketing strategy.

In Lora Moore's division, the firm's portfolio of products was continually assessed against its divisional mission and objectives to identify new product opportunities and strategies appropriate to existing products.

These product portfolio assessments pointed to any one of four broad strategic options: a **hold strategy,** to preserve existing market share; a **harvest strategy,** to increase the product's cash flow regardless of long-term consequences; a **divest strategy,** to liquidate the product and use marketing resources elsewhere; or a **growth strategy,** to increase profits and share of market. Decision criteria for each of these options are discussed in the planning system section of Chapter 6.

MARKET GROWTH STRATEGIES

In Moore's newly formed MM systems division, emphasis was on growth strategies for existing products and new additions to the product portfolio. These strategies were classified as intensive growth, integrative growth, diversification growth, market leader, market challenger, market follower, and market nicher.

Intensive growth strategies stress intensive cultivation of the firm's present markets and are appropriate in situations where existing product/market opportunities have not been fully exploited. They include:

- A **penetration strategy,** which focuses on more aggressive marketing of existing products, typically producing revenues and profits by (1) persuading present customers to use more of the product, (2) attracting customers from competitors, or (3) persuading undecided customers to become prospects.

- A **market development strategy,** which focuses on attracting members of new markets. For example, in the case of MM training systems, these new customers might come from unserved professional market segments, new geographical segments (foreign markets, for example), or new institutional segments (for example, hospital personnel enrolling in electronic administration courses).

- A **product development strategy,** which involves developing new products to attract members of existing markets. In the case of MM systems, additional customers might result from developing new training software for existing target markets, such as courses for tax accountants covering recent decisions of tax courts. New customers might also result from new ways to package and promote existing training programs, such as bonus features offered with systems purchased.

Integrative growth strategies are generally appropriate in situations where the firm's industry is strong and supportive, and the firm can move backward, forward, or horizontally.

- **Backward integration** occurs when the firm increases its control over its supply sources, as when a retailer like Sears or A&P controls its wholesaler supply sources.

- **Forward integration** occurs when the firm increases its control over its distribution system, as when a large refinery owns and controls its network of service stations.

- **Horizontal integration** occurs when the firm increases its control over its competitors. For example, institutions like hospitals and colleges will often negotiate consortium arrangements whereby each member specializes in a single area (for example, heart transplants or accounting doctorate degrees).

Diversification growth strategies, appropriate where few opportunities for growth exist in the firm's own field, generally encompass horizontal diversification, conglomerate diversification, and concentric diversification.

- **Horizontal diversification strategies** entail adding new products to a firm's product line that are unrelated to the firm's existing products but designed to appeal to members of the firm's target markets. For example, Pizza Hut and other fast-food outlets sell toys and other artifacts unrelated to their main product lines.

- **Conglomerative diversification strategies** entail marketing new products unrelated to the existing product line. Unlike horizontal diversification, these strategies are designed to attract new categories of customers. Illustrative of this was the purchase of Universal Film Studios by the Seagram Corporation, a large distillery.

- **Concentric diversification strategies** introduce new products bearing technological or marketing similarities to existing products designed to attract new market segments. For example, when firms like the News Corporation and Viacom purchased 20th Century Fox and Paramount film studios to enhance the value of their cable channels and TV networks and to build lucrative film libraries, they were diversifying concentrically.

Market leader strategies are employed by firms like Coca-Cola, Procter and Gamble, and Gillette, which dominate their market with superior products and/or competitive effectiveness. Leader firms tend to have greater immunity from competitive threats, and hence tend to maintain their leadership positions. For example, when Goodrich competes against leader Goodyear, Goodyear tends to gain much more from Goodrich's marketing efforts than Goodrich gains from Goodyear's efforts. Also, because it has a larger share of the market, Goodyear benefits more from mass-market economies of scale in making and marketing its products. However, leader firms do face the threat of being the main target of all their competitors.

In planning strategic initiatives for the MM line, Moore recognized the value of achieving a position of market leadership. Once this position was achieved, the division would have two strategic options to continue to grow. The first, a cooperative strategy, would increase the overall size of the market for MM systems and competitive systems by finding new users and uses for these systems. The second, a competitive strategy, would gain additional market share by investing heavily to attract customers from competitors. Moore decided her division would employ a version of the first, the cooperative strategy, which would also incorporate a preemptive defense strategy by launching new programs and products to keep competitors from becoming major threats.

Market challenger strategies, adopted by runner-up firms, would take three forms that Moore would have to anticipate when leadership was established:

1. **Frontal attacks** by strong challengers on MM's entire market mix—programs, price, distribution, promotion.

2. **Flank attacks** by weaker challengers, focusing on perceived MM weaknesses, such as the cost of MM systems.

3. **Bypassing strategies,** competing in areas not covered by MM systems, such as electronic educational programs in the government market.

Market follower strategies are employed by runner-up firms not interested in challenging the leader directly or indirectly. Moore perceived that these firms would maintain market share and profits by closely following the MM systems division's product, price, place, and promotion policies.

Market nicher strategies would be adopted by smaller competitors specializing in serving market niches that major competitors overlook or ignore (for example, market segments that the MM division cannot serve profitably).

Moore believed that, ideally, the MM division would grow and prosper best in a competitive climate consisting largely of follower and nicher firms, with a minimum of strong challengers. Its own planned cooperative leader strategy, she hoped, would help to create this climate.

PROGRAM FORMULATION

Missions, environmental analyses, objectives, definitions of target markets, descriptions of marketing mixes, strategies and tactics for bringing markets and products together were all formalized in a written strategic marketing plan. Also included in this plan were descriptions of the means for implementing marketing strategies and the controls, discussed in the control system section of Chapter 6, for monitoring performance to ensure that objectives were being achieved.

INTERNATIONAL PERSPECTIVE

In Merton's domestic market, Moore realized that components of strategic marketing plans—such as environmental analyses, objectives, strategies, implementation programs, and controls—were relatively easy to formulate. It was a stable, well-defined, predictable market with which she and her associates had many years to become familiar.

In international markets, however, strategic marketing plans aren't easy to formulate and implement, for reasons pertaining to environmental differences among nations and the frequent paucity of information about these differences. Entering a foreign market often means dealing with volatile currencies, learning a new language and laws, facing political and legal differences and harassments, and totally redesigning products to meet discrete customer needs. Some of these problems are illustrated in Global Focus 3-1.

GLOBAL FOCUS 3-1

Formulating a Successful Export Strategy

In general, a successful export strategy identifies and correlates at least four factors that jointly determine the most suitable kind of export operation: (1) the firm's export objectives, both immediate and long range; (2) specific tactics the firm will use; (3) scheduling of activities, deadlines, and the like that reflect chosen objectives and tactics; and (4) allocation of resources among scheduled activities.

The marketing plan and schedule of activities should cover a two- to five-year period, depending on the kind of product exported, the strength of competitors, conditions in target markets, and other factors.

Following are three success stories of companies that follow the strategic planning approach for penetrating global markets:

- The SIT String Corporation of Akron, Ohio, emphasizes the high quality of its guitar strings and seeks to develop a reputation for reliability. Robert Hird, vice president, said, "We keep trying to develop better sounding strings. Foreign customers, in particular, want to know a U.S. supplier is dependable and has some longevity. It takes time to develop this kind of reputation, but we think we are doing it, because our exports are growing." SIT sells 40 percent of its products overseas, in thirty-six countries, and Hird says, "We are just getting started!"

- A similar export strategy is used by Purafil, Inc., of Atlanta, Georgia, to show that its air purification equipment is technologically superior. "To get the leading edge, American companies need to offer something that is technologically ahead of the others," says William Weiller, president and CEO. "We find that technology is the key ingredient in differentiating our product offering." To get the word out, the firm takes part in scientific forums around the world and publishes technical articles in international trade/scientific journals.

- Until 1989, Metrologic Instruments of Blackwood, New Jersey, paid little attention to small countries and small customers. In that year, it made a strategic decision to establish relationships with new dealers and resellers worldwide. The refocusing was successful: within two years, the company had added seventy new foreign customers, was selling in twenty-four previously uncovered countries, and saw international sales increase 25 percent.

Source: Business America, Volume 114, Number 9, Spring 1993.

STRATEGIC PLANNING IN GLOBAL MARKETS

Because of environmental differences, when strategic plans evolve to enter or grow in foreign markets, special emphasis is placed on the "environmental analysis" component to address questions like these.

- **Should we enter this market?** Specifically, do the potential rewards of entering a foreign market justify the costs and risks involved? (Reasons for entering foreign markets were discussed in Chapter 2.)

- **Which markets should we enter?** A key decision area for firms seeking to enter and grow in international markets pertains to the number of foreign markets they will enter, the proportion of sales and profits desired from these markets, and characteristics of countries they enter. Answers to these questions are influenced by a number of findings from the environmental analysis, including the general attractiveness of the market in terms of growth potential, competitive advantages, logistical problems, entry barriers, and financial and political stability.

Although there are many approaches—and combinations of approaches—for entry and growth in risky international markets, most firms generally follow a cautious, staged approach designed to minimize risk and cost while maintaining control and flexibility. Such an approach typically encompasses the following stages:

Initially, the firm achieves **international status** by entering one or two host-country (foreign) markets that best match characteristics of home-country (domestic) markets. Canada is overwhelmingly the country of choice for U.S. firms. Firms that achieve international status mainly export or import products or buy and sell products to capitalize on price differentials in different nations. Host-country facilities are used initially to market the firm's products, later supported by home-country personnel, supply sources, finances, and facilities.

Then, learning from a hopefully successful experience, **multinational status** is achieved as additional foreign countries are entered, with greater use made of host-country personnel, supply sources, finances, and facilities. Multinational does not simply imply doing business in many countries; rather, it refers to companies that produce products or have subsidiaries add value in one or more foreign countries, as opposed to merely trading. This is what the Japanese, for example, did in transplanting automobile manufacturing to the United States after years of just marketing their automobiles here.

Conceivably, over time, a firm achieves **global status.** This term refers to firms that take advantage of synergies among their various affiliates, planning strategies according to the comparative advantage of each country location, and using the same production and marketing resources to form a coherent operation spanning several countries so as to achieve economies of scale and scope. Global companies search for global synergies, as opposed to running several parallel but separate multinational operations.

How should we enter this market? While passing through these stages from international to global status, companies engage in one or more entry and growth strategies, depending on such considerations as the firm's strategic objectives, the product being marketed, and political, legal, economic, and competitive threats and opportunities in the host countries. Typically, a firm will begin with an exporting strategy during the first, international stage and then move to joint venture and direct ownership strategies during multinational and global stages. As shown in Figure 3-2, commitment, risk, resource needs, and degree of control all increase with joint venture and direct ownership strategies. Flexibility, or the ability to change or terminate an entry strategy, is highest with joint ventures and lowest with direct ownership.

Following are characteristics, pros, and cons of these entry/growth strategies:

- **Exporting:** Using this strategy, the exporting firm markets products produced in the United States to foreign customers either directly—through the firm's salesforce located in the United States or the host country—or indirectly—through host-country distributors. This low-risk, low-cost approach works best when customers are concentrated and easy to locate. A big drawback is that there is less control over host-country distributors, who may not be knowledgeable enough to market the firm's products.

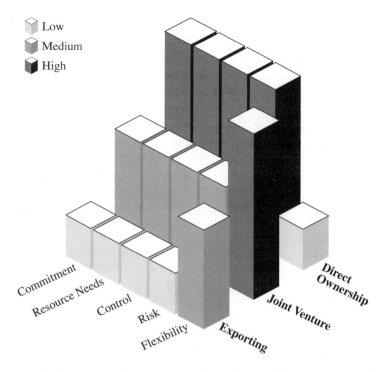

Figure 3–2. Dimensions characterizing alternative global market entry strategies.

- **Joint ventures:** This strategy can assume a number of formats, all of which have in common a partnership arrangement between the exporting firm and a host-country company to combine some aspect of manufacture or marketing in order to share expertise, costs, and/or connections. Potential advantages of joint ventures include lower costs and more favorable trading terms because foreign ownership is established. (Some countries require joint ownership with a local company as an entry condition.)

  Potential disadvantages include losing patents and profits to host-country owners or, if the firm isn't wise enough to maintain a controlling interest in the jointly held company, losing complete control. Also, the possibility exists that a host-country co-owner can become a competitor.

  Joint ownership formats include the following:

  1. **Licensing** occurs when, for a fee or royalty, a host-country company is assigned some rights, such as the use of patents, trademarks, or marketing expertise. Licensing is often an effective way to establish foreign production with minimal capital outlays, prevent free use of assets by foreign firms, and generate income in

markets where exportation or investment is not otherwise feasible.

2. **Franchising** is a form of licensing whereby the exporter (that is, the franchiser) grants an independent entity (the franchisee) the right to do business in a prescribed manner. This right can entail selling the firm's products and/or using its name, and production and marketing techniques. Although there are myriad problems involved in franchising foreign firms—securing good locations, finding franchisees and suppliers, maintaining standards and cost controls, agreeing on contract terms, and the like—the expansion of U.S. franchisers into global markets has been dramatic since the 1960s. Reasons for this expansion include foreign market potential, financial gain, and saturated domestic markets.

3. **Contract manufacturing** entails negotiating contracts under which host-country companies manufacture the exporter's products, with the exporter keeping control of any patented processes. Like management contracting, under which the exporter only contracts to provide management expertise to a host-country manufacturer or marketer, contract manufacturing represents an effective way to generate income through trade with little capital outlay. Both options are most frequently used in start-up operations, in the face of host-country ownership restrictions, and for facilities with operating problems. Although these options avoid most risks of global market participation, they also forfeit many benefits, and are therefore generally seen as a last line of defense.

4. **Turnkey operations** are specialized management contracts in which the exporting company provides complete operating facilities for a host-country client, including all associated equipment, materials, programs, and expertise. This package arrangement assigns responsibility to one source, thereby easing negotiation, supervision, and accountability problems for the host-country client. To the extent that turnkey operations are owned and controlled by the host-country client, they are often perceived by foreign governments as acceptable alternatives to foreign direct investment.

5. **Joint ownership arrangements,** whereby exporters join with foreign investors to create local businesses in which they share ownership and control of manufacturing and marketing programs, are often the best way for a firm to spread geographically at a faster rate and to help spread fixed costs over a larger sales base. Shared ownership also helps firms identify synergies among multiple partners in different countries and assume a

local character to deflect host-country criticism of foreign ownership.

6. **Strategic alliances** are special forms of joint ventures designed to achieve competitive advantages by leveraging capabilities, increasing innovation, and improving flexibility in responding to market threats and opportunities. Firms comprising the alliance, at either the corporate or industry level, have common business objectives that focus on such areas as improved profitability, new technologies, and better organization or management. Penetrating foreign markets, protecting domestic markets, coopting competitors, and spreading cost and risk are all reasons for forming a strategic alliance.

- **Full ownership arrangements:** Under these arrangements, the exporter fully implements and controls global operations, with ownership of production, marketing, and other facilities. This control gives the exporter much greater freedom of action, without having to share profits or policies with local stockholders, who can be very vocal in global markets. Governments are growing increasingly hostile to full ownership, which they perceive as threatening to local ownership arrangements.

CHAPTER PERSPECTIVE

In formulating strategic fits between the organization's goals and resources and its changing market opportunities, marketing managers engage in analysis, planning, implementation, and control activities that culminate in strategic marketing plans. The SMP process begins with effective mission statements that lead to business and marketing objectives that point to strategies, tactics, and controls required to achieve these objectives. Strategies appropriate to different product/market situations are classified as hold, harvest, divest, or growth; growth strategies are classified as integrative, intensive, or diversified. Competitive strategies include leader, challenger, follower, and market nicher strategies. In international markets, marketing plans typically evolve through international, multinational, and global stages and entail exporting, joint venture, and full ownership strategies.

KNOW THE CONCEPTS
TERMS FOR STUDY

Challenger strategies
Contract manufacturing
Demand states
Diversification growth strategies
Divest strategy
Exporting
Follower strategies
Franchising
Global status
Harvest strategy
Hold strategy
Integrative growth strategies
Intensive growth strategies

International status
Joint ownership arrangements
Joint ventures
Licensing
Macroenvironment
Market development strategies
Microenvironment
Mission statement
Multinational status
Nicher strategies
Strategic alliances
Strategic marketing planning
Turnkey operations

MATCHUP EXERCISES

1. Relate the demand state in the first column with the appropriate strategy in the second column.

   1. latent
   2. irregular
   3. negative
   4. overfull

   a. alter marketing mix elements
   b. develop new products
   c. take counteractive measures
   d. demarket

2. Match the strategy in the first column with the descriptor in the second column.

   1. horizontal integration

   2. concentric diversification

   3. market development

   a. Merton Electronics Company implements the Mighty Consumer Electronics Division
   b. Mighty Mind Division seeks to enter foreign markets
   d. four hospitals agree to each specialize in a given field of medicine

3. Match the global trading stage in the first column with the characteristic listed in the second column.

   1. international

   a. achieves major synergies based largely on exploitation of comparative advantage; integrated, interactive management

2. multinational

3. global

    b. focuses on the domestic market while pursuing international objectives; top-down management

    c. recognizes that differences in global markets require adaptation of the marketing mix (product, price, place, promotion) in order to succeed; bottom-up management

QUESTIONS FOR REVIEW AND DISCUSSION

1. Explain how the steps in the strategic marketing planning process are interrelated.

2. What are the benefits of strategic marketing planning to companies? To customers?

3. Using a local department store as an example, distinguish among strategic planning, strategies, and marketing programs.

4. Using the department store in Question 3 as an example, distinguish among intensive, integrative, and diversification growth strategies.

5. Describe how the four marketing management activities might be applied in planning and implementing a job quest strategy for yourself.

6. Come up with a mission statement for yourself that might appear on your job résumé. What characteristics of this statement make it effective?

7. Discuss similarities and differences between marketing processes carried out in domestic and international markets.

8. Excerpts from an article in the *New York Times* entitled "Another Coup for the Fighting Gallos":

> With Bartles & Jaymes, the Gallo brothers have stormed into first place in the booming wine cooler business, one of the few bright spots in an industry suffering from flat sales . . . that coup . . . was only the latest of a remarkable string of successes that allowed the E&J Gallo winery to grow from a shed in the Great Depression into the world's largest winery. And the cooler's success has left its stunned competitors gaping in awe . . . in addition to ranking No. 1 in wine coolers, its E&J Brandy is the best selling brandy in the country. Its Andre champagne is the best selling sparkling wine. It is also the leading supplier of low-priced flavored wines . . . and inexpensive table wines . . . . Even in premium varietal wines, for which it is not known, Gallo sells more than anyone else . . . . Key to Bartles & Jaymes success . . . indeed, the winery's success . . . are Ernest and Julio Gallo, who have perfected a system of clever advertising,

adroit product positioning and brute force sales and marketing, backed up by the most vertically integrated and efficient production process in the industry . . . .

Base your answers to the following questions on these excerpts.

    a. Discuss how the four steps of the strategic marketing planning process might have been used to create the Bartles & Jaymes success story.

    b. Identify and describe the following growth strategies implicit in the Gallo success story: penetration, product development, and market development.

    c. Describe how Gallo might employ the two conflicting leader strategies discussed in this chapter, and how R. Stuart Bewley might employ challenger strategies to compete with Bartles & Jaymes. Bewley is the co-founder and president of California Cooler, "which started the wine cooler craze and until recently was the leading seller."

ANSWERS
MATCHUP EXERCISES

1. 1b, 2a, 3c, 4d
2. 1c, 2a, 3b
3. 1b, 2c, 3a

QUESTIONS FOR REVIEW AND DISCUSSION

1. The mission statement defines the needs of the firm's target markets (domains) and shows how features and benefits of its offerings will satisfy these needs. These definitions, in turn, suggest what objectives the firm can realistically expect to achieve, as well as the product portfolio and other marketing mix elements best calculated to achieve these goals by bringing together offerings and target markets.

2. Strategic marketing planning benefits companies by helping to identify and exploit worthwhile marketing opportunities to achieve worthwhile objectives and make efficient use of resources. SMP benefits customers in that the process typically satisfies an unfulfilled market need, or a fulfilled market need more effectively, resulting in better products or product-related attributes (for example, price and distribution).

3. For a department store, a strategic plan might identify and define worthwhile target markets for the product-price-place-promotion offerings of a given department (housewares, sports equipment, and so on) and then devise a plan relating these offerings to identified needs in this target market. A strategy would encompass the annual plan to bring together the offering and the needs, including initiating special seasonal promotions, supporting markdowns, changing merchandise mixes, and so on. The marketing program for the department store would meld all the plans for all the departments into a single overall plan.

4. Intensive growth strategies, including penetration, market development, and product development strategies, would be used by the department store to better exploit existing product/market opportunities. For example, it might attempt to penetrate more deeply existing target markets with more effective promotions, to attract more members of these markets with new product lines (product development), or seek new markets for its existing lines (for example, provide transportation to the store for senior citizens). Integrative growth strategies might involve the department store in controlling its supply sources (backward), as Sears does, or link it with other department stores in the community for special promotions (horizontal), or controlling smaller, less centralized retail outlets (forward). Diversification growth strategies would be employed by the department store in the event that opportunities in its present market disappear, perhaps through a change in its neighborhood. Horizontal diversification would occur if the store got into other businesses (such as banking), unrelated to its existing business, to attract the remaining members of this existing business, while conglomerate diversification would market these new, unrelated businesses to new categories of customers. Concentric diversification would occur if the store got involved in businesses technologically related to its present business, such as a catalog-buying service, to attract new categories of customers.

5. You might first analyze the situation by listing skills and abilities you could offer a prospective employer, specific fields (accounting, banking, and so forth) where these skills might be applied, and specific employers in these fields. Then, you might devise a plan for conveying information about your skills and abilities to prospective employers, including the preparation of a résumé and cover letter, as well as a schedule of mailings and follow-up calls. Next, you might implement this plan by sending out the letters, making follow-up calls, and going for interviews. Finally, you might exercise control by modifying your original plan (revise résumé, redirect mailings) if performance doesn't meet expectations (if you don't get a job after the first campaign).

6. Such a statement should be a benefit-oriented exposition covering such domains as products, customer groups covered, and customer needs satisfied. Domains in such a statement would be fields in which you are applying for a position; products are the skills you bring to the job; customer groups are prospective employers; and needs are the require-

ments of unfilled jobs. The following statement by an accounting major would meet these criteria:

> To conduct audits for small business clients of a large public accounting firm that will enhance my employer's profitability by enhancing the profitability of its clients.

7. Marketing processes carried out in domestic and international markets are similar with respect to the specific activities encompassed; for example, products and services must be developed, priced, distributed, and promoted to meet the needs of defined target markets and company objectives and to account for marketplace threats and opportunities and company strengths and weaknesses. Differences between marketing processes in relatively homogeneous domestic and heterogeneous international markets derive mainly from environmental differences. For example, differences in language, cultural values, state of economic development, currency stability, infrastructure development, legal systems, and political orientation can combine to scuttle the most effective, aggressive market-entry strategy. Well-planned and well-implemented global marketing strategies that succeed, however, tend to generate more profits than their domestic counterparts.

8. **a.** Here are a few observations, from an infinite number of possibilities, that might be noted in reference to the role of the strategic marketing planning process in the creation of the Bartles & Jaymes success story:

   - *Defining the company mission:* Unlike the statements of many of its competitors, Gallo's mission statement does not restrict it to a narrow product/market focus (for example, only wines for the relatively small wine drinker market). Wine coolers obviously represent a relatively new product entry aimed at a new, and much larger, market than traditional wine drinkers. As the article makes clear, Gallo is an innovator in a broad spectrum of wine-related product areas, from the low-priced to the premium.

   - *Setting company objectives and goals:* The effectiveness of Gallo's positioning and promotional campaigns ("clever advertising," "brute force sales and marketing") suggests realistic, integrated marketing programs that encompass all its product lines and derive from broader business objectives and their sales and cost goals sequenced to achieve these objectives.

   - *Designing the business portfolio:* Gallo's consistent record of growth and profitability, based on a broad spectrum of mission-related product lines, suggests a continuing, systematic appraisal of each product line in terms of its growth and profit potential and an implementation of invest, hold, and harvest strategies consistent with these appraisals. A continual search for new product/market opportunities, like the Bartles & Jaymes wine cooler, is also suggested.

- *Planning marketing and other functional strategies:* The article emphasizes the strong, effective, goal-oriented marketing strategies and tactics that characterize Gallo's marketing program. Not noted, but of signal importance to the winery's growth and profitability, are the other functional strategies in such areas as production, distribution, research and development, and finance, which must be effectively coordinated with its marketing program.

b.

Strategy	Defined	Example
Penetration	persuade present accounts to use more of product, change "undecideds" to customers, attract customers from competition	Bartles & Jaymes wrests market leadership from California Cooler wine coolers
Product Development	new firm develops products of interest to present or prospective customers, or new ways to package or distribute existing products	Andre champagne, an inexpensive sparkling wine, joins Gallo's line of inexpensive wines
Market Development	firm develops products to attract members of new markets (geographic, consumer, institutional)	Bartles & Jaymes wine cooler attracts the "Yuppie" segment not associated with wine drinking

c. From its position of leadership, Gallo might employ either a leader strategy that builds the size of the overall market, for Gallo and its competitors, by introducing new products, and finding new uses, and users, for existing products; or a leader strategy that gains additional market share by attracting customers from competitors. Both strategies are implicit in the facts of the Gallo case: The success of the Bartles & Jaymes wine cooler is effectively creating huge new markets for all cooler producers; meanwhile, Gallo has successfully positioned its cooler against California Coolers, and replaced this product in its leadership position.

R. Stuart Bewley, president of California Coolers, might attempt to regain its lost leadership position by employing *frontal attack, flank attack,* or *follower strategies.* Given Gallo's solid leadership position in a variety of product lines, a frontal attack strategy against this entire product line hardly seems feasible; however, a flank attack strategy against perceived weaknesses in B & J's offering, or a by-passing strategy focusing on market segments not attracted to B & J (a gourmet cooler, for example) might succeed.

4
THE MARKETING ENVIRONMENT

OVERVIEW

External to the strategic planning process are dynamic, interrelated forces that present threats and opportunities, and must be accounted for in bringing together target markets and marketing mixes. On the macroenvironmental level, these forces include demographic, economic, social-cultural, political-legal, competitive, and technological influences; on the microenvironmental level, they include company mission, objectives, suppliers, customers, marketing intermediaries, and diverse publics.

HOW ENVIRONMENTAL VARIABLES INFLUENCE STRATEGIC PLANNING

In the previous chapter, we examined the role of the marketing manager in developing strategic marketing plans and programs designed to reconcile a firm's objectives and resources with changing marketplace opportunities.

As a first step in this planning process, and continuously throughout the process, marketers systematically scan internal and external environments to uncover threats and opportunities important in building and revising marketing strategies. Examples of the importance of environmental scanning abound; considerably more important, as illustrated by Market Focus 4-1, is making productive use of the information that emerges from scanning the environment.

MARKET FOCUS 4-1

AT&T Responds to Full-Scale Environmental Change

The telecommunications industry broadly encompasses telephone companies, cable TV franchises, computer firms, wireless cellular service producers, Internet providers, and publishing and entertainment giants that design, build, manage, and service the information superhighway that links telecommunications and data resources to business-

---

es and individual households. (Chapter 21 examines ways in which marketers can use the information superhighway.)

As a leader in this industry, AT&T faced environmental changes on many fronts as it entered the twenty-first century focused on its goal of turning technology into useful services available at reasonable prices.

On the political-legal front, the global telecommunications industry was continuing the accelerating pace of deregulation and privatization that started in the United States in the 1980s. As part of that trend, the Telecommunications Act of 1996 allowed long-distance companies like AT&T and local-service firms to enter each other's markets.

On the technological front, the life span of a new technology had declined from a five- to a one-year average over the decade of the 1990s, with the Internet and its graphical interface leading the way.

On the economic front, worldwide economic growth, combined with dramatic declines in the cost of technology, was creating huge new markets for telecommunication products, as more and more products and services became affordable. In 1999 alone, for example, Internet usage in North America increased by 20 percent.

On the social-cultural front, many of the products of the telecommunications revolution, such as interactive Internet software, were assuming the role of necessities, as were television sets half a century earlier.

Combined, these environmental influences had a dramatic impact on the competitive environment, with small Internet-related firms like Amazon.com assuming a greater valuation than giants like General Motors.

Initiatives taken by AT&T in response to these environmental changes included:

- Restructuring the firm into three separate global corporations: (1) the new AT&T, offering customers a full range of communications and information services; (2) Lucent Technologies, producing telecommunications equipment and systems, software and products; and (3) NCR, producing transaction-intensive computer systems and services. Each company has its own operational and strategic planning capability and can respond faster than the original AT&T to marketplace threats and opportunities.

- Focusing on five areas that offered AT&T the best potential to realize its mission: long-distance service, local service, wireless communication, online (Internet) services, and access to home entertainment.

- Emphasizing global markets as a major growth opportunity. Toward this end, AT&T is forming partnerships, strategic alliances, and consortiums to market telecommunications services to businesses and consumers worldwide.

Although well-positioned to be a major player on the global information superhighway, AT&T management realizes that continual change in its macro- and microenvironments will mandate continual changes in its response to them.

MACRO/MICROENVIRONMENTS AFFECT MARKETS AND MARKETING MIXES

In formulating marketing plans and programs for products in the newly formed MM systems division, Moore began with analyses of the impact of broad macroenvironmental factors, including demographic, economic, social-cultural, competitive, political-legal, and technological variables.

Then, her focus changed to microenvironmental factors affected by the macroenvironment. These included the company itself, with its missions, objectives, and policies; suppliers of resources to make and market MM systems; customers who would purchase these systems; market intermediaries who would help finance, promote, and distribute products to customers; and various publics that could help or hinder MM marketing efforts.

Figure 4-1 shows the route of Moore's analyses, from macro- to microenvironmental factors, to marketing mix variables, to markets targeted for exposure to these variables.

THE MACROENVIRONMENT: THREATS, OPPORTUNITIES, AND RESPONSES

Starting with the demographic component of the macroenvironment, Moore analyzed, in turn, economic, competitive, social-cultural, legal-

Figure 4–1. Elements of the marketing mix within an environmental framework.

political, and technological environments. Her findings regarding the impact of each component on marketing plans for MM systems follow.

THE DEMOGRAPHIC ENVIRONMENT

Because markets are made up of people, Moore first turned her analytical attentions to the demographic environment, consisting of "state-of-being" variables defining populations, such as age, gender, family size, family life cycle, income, occupation, education, religion, race, and nationality.

POPULATION TRENDS AND DEVELOPMENTS

Of particular importance to the success of MM marketing plans were trends and developments pertaining to population growth rate and age mix.

• *POPULATION GROWTH RATE*
Population growth rate worldwide was a burgeoning 1.6 percent per year, leading to predictions of a world population over 6 billion by the year 2000

and associated problems of overcrowding, pollution, declining resources, and a deteriorating quality of life. Most of this growth, however, would take place in less-developed regions, containing 70 percent of the world's population. In Merton's domestic market and in foreign markets it would be most likely to penetrate, the population growth was actually declining toward zero, which suggested fewer people available to buy MM systems.

• *POPULATION AGE MIX*

Population age mix worldwide ranged from countries with an extremely young (and fast-growing) population, like Mexico, to countries like Japan, with comparatively elderly and slow-growing populations. When Moore analyzed the age mix of Merton's domestic market, it turned out that the potential market for MM systems would actually increase appreciably. Thus, even though the size of the teenage segment, only a marginal market for MM systems, declined, the 20–34 and 34–54 age groups would show appreciable increases, and these were the two most potentially profitable age-group segments. After the 34–54 age group, the over-65 group would experience the second largest growth of all age group segments (20 percent). Moore made a note to develop MM training systems specifically targeted to this group.

KEY DEMOGRAPHIC VARIABLES: POPULATION DISPERSION, ETHNICITY, AND EDUCATION

After analyzing age-group growth patterns, Moore examined the geographic dispersion of the population for market opportunities. Worldwide, the 1990s saw the greatest migration of populations within and between countries in history, resulting from things like the breakup of the Soviet bloc, the formation of regional trading blocs like the EU, and the ethnic turmoil in the Balkans. In the domestic market, as shown in Figure 4-2, the most rapid population growth would occur in South and Southwest regions—mainly of people in prime-market age groups for MM systems.

Other demographic units subjected to Moore's analytical attentions included ethnic groups, whose unique needs suggested marketing mix chacteristics (for example, targeted educational courses and promotional programs) to sell MM systems, and educational groups, whose profiles (illiterate, high-school dropout, college graduate, and the like) suggested unfilled needs for MM systems.

THE ECONOMIC ENVIRONMENT

In analyzing the impact of the economic environment on strategic plans and programs, Moore was primarily concerned with how economic variables af-

U.S. +7.6%

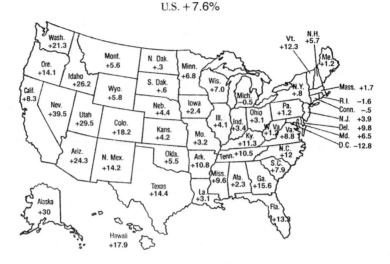

Figure 4–2. Projected population growth rates, 1990–2000.
(*Source:* Bureau of the Census, U.S. Department of Commerce)

fected consumer spending patterns relative to the MM systems product line. In general, analyses of these spending patterns focused on what products and services people bought, when they bought them, and how much they were prepared to pay for them. As related to specific products and services purchased, these spending patterns were defined in terms of three concepts: (1) **disposable income** or what consumers had left to spend after taxes were paid, (2) **discretionary income** or what consumers had left to spend after taxes and necessities were paid for, and (3) **Engel's laws.**

In 1857, Ernst Engel, a Prussian statistician, composed three general statements or laws regarding the impact of changes in household income on consumer spending. According to Engel, as family spendable income increases (that is, as more discretionary income is available), the percentage

- spent on basic necessities like food and clothing decreases,

- spent on housing remains constant (except for utilities like gas and electricity, which decreases),

- spent on other items, such as recreation, education, self-help, and luxury items increases.

In sum, Engel's laws conclude that as the income profile of an economy moves from disposable to discretionary, a greater percentage of it is spent on "other items" like those in the MM systems line of self-help and education products. From Moore's perspective, this meant first defining domestic (and later international) market opportunities in terms of four factors—the business cycle, inflation, unemployment, and income distribution—that combine to generate income profiles favorable to the purchase of MM systems. Then, since strategic marketing plans affected by these factors were forward-looking, she would attempt to project these trends into the future, using techniques discussed in Chapter 12.

BUSINESS CYCLES AFFECT BUYING PATTERNS

Historically, business cycles have followed a fairly predictable pattern of prosperity, recession, depression, and recovery. However, by the late 1990s, after a decade of growth, some economists were beginning to argue that it might be possible to prevent future depressions and maintain economic health indefinitely through a combination of sophisticated fiscal and monetary policies, enlightened global market trade programs, free-enterprise competition and deregulation, and technological revolutions in such areas as transportation and electronic communications.

From Moore's perspective, it was helpful to understand how consumer buying patterns differ from cycle to cycle. During prosperous times, consumers buy at a brisk pace, so marketers expand product lines, increase promotions, expand distribution, and raise prices. During recessions, with less discretionary income, customers buy basic, functional products with low price tags; for example, they are a lot more likely to spend a day's income at Home Depot than at a fancy restaurant. In response, marketers lower prices, eliminate marginal products, increase promotional outlays to gain a competitive edge, and launch value-priced offers (such as Merton's offer of a free personal computer with the purchase of a number of hardware and software accessories).

During recoveries, customers may be able to buy, but they may not necessarily be willing. For example, during the recovery of the early 1990s, customers were more likely to pay down debt than start discretionary spending again. Then, as the recovery gained strength, customer discretionary spending for relatively pricey goods and services accelerated, as did business investment in new construction and equipment. Finally, in the late 1990s, a point was reached where consumer debt actually rose faster than income, and personal bankruptcies reached an all-time high.

INFLATION AFFECTS PURCHASING PATTERNS

Persistent price increases characterizing inflation devalue money by reducing the number of products and services it can buy, and unless income increases keep pace, which they rarely do, consumer purchasing power obviously declines. In the United States, inflation soared to double-digit levels throughout the late 1970s and early 1980s, reaching a high of 13.6 percent in 1980. Then, throughout the 1990s, this trend reversed, averaging less than

3 percent a year during the last years of the decade. Three possible consumer purchasing strategies resulting from inflationary pressures—all of which Moore had to anticipate at various times in assessing domestic and international markets—include (1) buy now in anticipation of increasing prices, (2) alter purchasing patterns to mitigate losses through inflation (for example, lease rather than purchase an automobile), and (3) postpone purchases entirely. From Moore's perspective, the first strategy was obviously preferable, and was stressed in MM promotional materials.

UNEMPLOYMENT AFFECTS CONSUMER SPENDING

After peaking at 8 percent in 1992, the unemployment rate—defined as the percentage of people in the economy who do not have jobs and are actively looking for work—declined steadily to less than 4 percent in 1999. To the extent that unemployment insurance, personal savings, and union benefits offset lost income, the impact of high unemployment on purchasing patterns is lessened. However, broad-based discretionary income is best generated during periods of full, or near full, employment, with income reasonably distributed throughout the economy.

INCOME DISTRIBUTION PATTERNS AFFECT PURCHASING PATTERNS

As the United States enters the twenty-first century, an unprecedented cluster of conditions—a booming economy, low interest rates, and very low unemployment and inflation rates—combine to create unprecedented wealth among the American working population. Moore realized, however, that aggregate wealth alone, as expressed primarily through per-capita income, is not necessarily the best measure of purchasing power, which should also take into account prices, savings, and credit availability.

Raw per-capita income figures also overlook an extremely important measure of national wealth and purchasing power—the way income is distributed among members of a population. For example, per-capita income could be distributed in at least four ways in a country: (1) practically all low per-capita incomes; (2) some high per-capita incomes, many low per-capita incomes; (3) a roughly equal number of low, medium, and high per-capita incomes; or (4) roughly the entire population with medium per-capita incomes.

From Moore's perspective, the second and third options were preferable because they assured at least a segment of the population with the wherewithal to purchase MM systems. Of these two, the third option was preferable because it assured a larger number of affluent prospects with discretionary spending power. In Merton's domestic market, however, the trend was toward the second option—a few high, many low per-capita incomes.

More specifically, real income per capita in the United States remained stagnant between the mid-1970s and the mid-1990s, saved only by the growing number of dual-income households. This was leading to a two-tier U.S. market, with the rich growing richer and buying more expensive goods while the size of the middle class shrank and the poor remained poor. Indeed, workers' earnings showed almost no growth until 1996, when they began to climb steadily upward. In 1998, real pay (adjusted for inflation) was 1.6 percent higher than the year before, the largest increase in more than a decade.

In addition to class, consumers' discretionary income also varies greatly by age group, with older people having significant buying power, even compared to other groups with higher incomes.

THE SOCIAL-CULTURAL ENVIRONMENT

At this point in her analysis, Moore had profiled prospective target markets in terms of demographic and economic forces that defined the nature, scope, and location of demand for MM systems, as well as purchasing patterns characterizing this demand. Now, she focused on social and cultural trends that would shape and direct this demand.

SOCIAL CLASSES SHOW DISTINCT BUYING PATTERNS

Social classes are defined as relatively homogeneous and enduring divisions in a society whose members share similar values, interests, and behavior. A number of studies have shown, among other things, that social classes are hierarchically structured and that similar social class hierarchies exist in all areas, from small towns to large cities. An individual's position in a given hierarchy is not based on income alone but takes into account the type of income, occupation, type of house, and area of residence within a community. Members of a given social class show distinct product and brand preferences in such areas as clothing, home furnishings, and automobiles. In the United States, lines between social classes are not fixed; over their lifetimes, people can move up or down among the hierarchies.

A number of researchers have attempted to categorize social classes in terms of such salient characteristics as income, occupation, attitudes, interests and opinions of members, lifestyle preferences, and purchasing patterns. For example, Engel, Blackwell, and Miniard have identified seven social classes—ranging from upper-upper to lower-lower—in terms of these characteristics. Here is how they define the two social classes of most interest to Moore in targeting the MM systems offering to the nature and needs of target markets:

- **Lower-upper class** (about 2 percent of the population): High income or wealth earned through exceptional ability in business or professions; active in social, civic affairs; buy status-symbol products for selves and children (expensive homes, cars, electronic learning systems, and the like). Include nouveaux riche, whose pattern of ostentation is designed to impress classes above and below them. Main ambition: to be accepted, and have children accepted, by members of upper-upper class.

- **Upper-middle class** (about 12 percent of the population): Professionals, independent business people, and corporate managers who possess neither family status nor unusual wealth; are primarily concerned about careers for selves and children. Highly civic-minded joiners; they like to deal in ideas and "high culture," entertain friends and clients at home. Represent a quality market for good homes, clothes, furniture, appliances, personal computers and software, and vacation amenities.

CULTURES AFFECT HOW PEOPLE BEHAVE AND BUY

Culture is a complex whole, learned and shared by members of a society, encompassing beliefs, values, language, religion, art, morals, law, education, customs, habits, and capabilities.

VALUES GUIDE BEHAVIOR

The "values" component of culture, defined as widely held beliefs that some activities, relationships, feelings, or goals are important to a community's identity or well-being, has the following characteristics of interest to marketers: (1) values guide culturally appropriate behavior; (2) they are difficult to change; (3) they are widely accepted; and (4) they incline people to respond to specific stimuli in standard ways.

To illustrate, a value associated with culture in the United States is humanitarianism—a strong and enduring sense of personal concern for the rights and welfare of others. This shared value produces such standard responses to stimuli as aid in mass disasters and a huge philanthropic system devoting time and money to such organizations as the United Way, the Red Cross, and CARE.

VALUE CATEGORIES THAT HELP RESEARCHERS

Values can be perceived from a number of perspectives helpful to researchers in defining markets and market opportunities:

- **Core and secondary values:** Core values are highly persistent; secondary values are much more likely to change. As examples, persistent core values include getting married and raising families; secondary values include getting married later in life and raising smaller families. Emerging secondary values, such as a new appreciation for low-fat foods, can represent opportunities for marketers who can relate their offerings to these values; disappearing secondary values, such as the communist menace, can lose opportunities for marketers who stay with them too long.

- **Subculture and culture values:** Subcultures are separate segments of a culture organized around such factors as race, nationality, religion, or geographic location. Common values shared by members of discrete subcultures—in food, recreation, politics, religion, child rearing, and so on—frequently represent marketing opportunities not available in the culture at large.

- **Instrumental and terminal values:** Instrumental values focus on modes of conduct; terminal values deal with end-states of existence. For example, a member of our society might believe that ambition and self-discipline (instrumental values) will lead to prosperity and happiness (terminal values).

- **Material and nonmaterial values:** Material values pertain to things, including things people buy ("most store brands are as good as advertised brands") and places where they buy them ("WalMart has the best selections and prices"). Nonmaterial values, which pertain to ideas, customs, and beliefs, can also condition consumer behavior, especially toward less tangible services and religious or political orientations.

VALUES CAN DEFINE NEEDS

Values can also be associated with products. For example, widely held values pertaining to the desirability of getting married and raising families imply spending on a broad range of products, such as matrimonial services, furniture, appliances, clothing, vacations, baby food, toys, and doctors' visits.

THE MARKETER'S TASK: FIND AND USE PREDISPOSING VARIABLES

In accommodating marketing plans to cultural values, the marketer's first task is to identify variables, or combinations of variables, most likely to predispose people to buy the marketed product. The marketer's second task is to then incorporate predisposing variables into such marketing plan aspects as the market targeted and the marketing mix aimed at this market.

IDENTIFYING SIGNIFICANT CULTURAL VARIABLES

Three approaches for identifying significant cultural variables include observational fieldwork, content analysis, and value measurement surveys. Each has supporting assumptions, advantages, and drawbacks.

• *OBSERVATIONAL FIELDWORK*

The observational fieldwork approach typically involves trained researchers observing the behavior of a small sample of people from the culture being studied. For example, Merton researchers might observe responses to Mighty Mind computer models at computer trade shows. Field observation usually takes place in a natural environment, with or without the subject's awareness.

• *CONTENT ANALYSIS*

Using the content analysis approach, researchers make inferences about changing social and cultural values based on the content of verbal and pictorial communications. For example, the way minority groups and females are depicted on television or in newspaper articles could lead to broader inferences about value changes in the entire culture.

Both observational and content analysis approaches for identifying significant cultural variables suffer from limited applicability, the need for expensive trained researchers, and/or difficulties in relating variables to class or brand-specific buying behavior. Value measurement surveys address these shortcomings.

• *VALUE MEASUREMENT SURVEYS*

The value measurement surveys approach involves the direct measurement of values using scaled questionnaires, called value instruments, to show how people feel about various values and related behaviors. Two examples of these direct measurement surveys include the Rokeach Value Survey (RVS) and SRI International's Value and Lifestyle Survey (VALS).

The RVS scale groups and profiles respondents in terms of (1) terminal values designed to measure the relative importance of "end-states" of existence (personal goals), (2) instrumental values designed to measure the relative importance of various approaches an individual might follow to achieve these goals, and (3) related buying behaviors. For example, one RVS identified the following value clusters as defining liberals and traditionals.

	Values	Social Issues	Consumer Products
Liberals	Exciting life Equality Self-respect Intellectual Logical	Air pollution Freedom of the press Housing discrimination	Compact cars Outdoor recreation

Traditionals	National
	  security
	Salvation
	Social recognition
	Family values
		Crime control
		Drug problems
		Pro-life
			Standard-size cars
			Stylish clothes
			Videocassette
			  recorders

The VALS scale combines value and lifestyle information with demographic data to create four general consumer profiles said to predict product purchases: (1) need-driven consumers (11 percent of the domestic population), (2) outer-directed consumers (66 percent), (3) inner-directed consumers (21 percent), and (4) integrated consumers (2 percent). Each group is then defined in terms of value-lifestyle orientations and buying behavior patterns.

THE POLITICAL-LEGAL ENVIRONMENT

Like the social and cultural forces that produce them, political and legal forces tend to change slowly and can yield helpful clues for positioning and promoting products. In analyzing the influence of these forces on the MM systems division, Moore identified five areas where government legislation and policies established by government regulatory agencies would most affect strategic marketing plans:

1. **General monetary and fiscal policies,** which determine how much the government will spend for goods and services, how much money is made available to consumers, and how much discretionary income people will have left after taxes and necessities are paid for.

2. **Broad social legislation and accompanying regulatory agency policies,** such as civil rights and environmental protection laws.

3. **Government relations with individual industries,** such as subsidies for agriculture and shipbuilding, and import quotas on foreign products.

4. **Legislation relating to marketing,** including laws and statutes designed to (1) maintain a competitive environment, (2) regulate competition, (3) protect consumers, and (4) deregulate specific industries. Table 4-1 summarizes major laws in each group, to which will soon be added cyberspace laws to police Internet and online services against fraud, deceptive services, and invasion of privacy. Table 4-2 shows how selected laws to regulate and maintain competition relate to each of the four marketing mix elements.

5. **Information that helps marketers,** such as census information, discussed in Chapter 7, which helps marketers define markets demographically and geographically.

Table 4–1. Major Federal Laws Affecting Marketing

Date	Law	Description
A. LAWS MAINTAINING A COMPETITIVE ENVIRONMENT		
1890	Sherman Antitrust Act	Prohibits restraint of trade and monopolization; identifies a competitive marketing system as national policy goal
1914	Clayton Act	Strengthens the Sherman Act by restricting such practices as price discrimination, exclusive dealing, tying contracts, and interlocking boards of directors where the effect "may be to substantially lessen competition or tend to create a monopoly"
1914	Federal Trade Commission (FTC) Act	Prohibits unfair methods of competition; establishes the Federal Trade Commission, an administrative agency that investigates business practices and enforces the FTC Act
1938	Wheeler-Lea Act	Amends the FTC Act to outlaw additional unfair practices; gives the FTC jurisdiction over false and misleading advertising
1950	Celler-Kefauver Antimerger Act	Amends the Clayton Act to include major asset purchases that will decrease competition in an industry
1975	Consumer Goods Pricing Act	Prohibits pricing maintenance agreements among manufacturers and resellers in interstate commerce

Table 4–1. Major Federal Laws Affecting Marketing

Date	Law	Description
1980	FTC Improvement Act	Gives the Senate and House of Representatives joint veto power over FTC trade regulations; limits FTC power to regulate unfairness issues

B. LAWS REGULATING COMPETITION

Date	Law	Description
1936	Robinson-Patman Act	Prohibits price discrimination in sales to wholesalers, retailers, or other producers; prohibits selling at unreasonably low prices to eliminate competition
1937	Miller-Tydings Resale Price Maintenance Act	Exempts interstate fair trade contracts from compliance with antitrust requirements
1993	North American Free Trade Agreement (NAFTA)	International trade agreement between Canada, Mexico, and the United States designed to facilitate trade by removing tariffs and other trade barriers among the three nations

C. LAWS PROTECTING CONSUMERS

Date	Law	Description
1906	Federal Food and Drug Act	Prohibits adulteration and misbranding of foods and drugs involved in interstate commerce; strengthened by the Food, Drug, and Cosmetic Act (1938) and the Kefauver-Harris Drug Amendment (1962)
1939	Wool Products Labeling Act	Requires identification of the type and percentage of wool used in products
1951	Fur Products Labeling Act	Requires identification of the animal from which a fur product was derived
1953	Flammable Fabrics Act	Prohibits interstate sale of flammable fabrics
1958	National Traffic and Safety Act	Provides for creation of safety standards for automobile tires
1958	Automobile Information Disclosure Act	Prohibits automobile dealers from inflating factory prices of new cars

Table 4–1. Major Federal Laws Affecting Marketing

Date	Law	Description
1966	Child Protection Act	Outlaws sale of hazardous toys; 1969 amendment adds products posing electrical, mechanical, or thermal hazards
1966	Fair Packaging and Labeling Act	Requires disclosure of product identification, name and address of manufacturer or distributor, and information on the quality of contents
1967	Federal Cigarette Labeling and Advertising Act	Requires written health warnings on cigarette packages
1968	Consumer Credit Protection Act	Truth-in-lending law requiring disclosure of annual interest rates on loans and credit purchases
1970	Fair Credit Reporting Act	Gives individuals access to their credit records and allows them to change incorrect information
1970	National Environmental Policy Act	Establishes the Environmental Protection Agency to deal with various types of pollution and organizations that create pollution
1971	Public Health Cigarette Smoking Act	Prohibits tobacco advertising on radio and television
1972	Consumer Product Safety Act	Created the Consumer Product Safety Commission, which has authority to specify safety standards for most products
1975, 1977	Equal Credit Opportunity Act	Bans discrimination in lending practices based on sex and marital status (1975) and race, national origin, religion, age, or receipt of payments from public assistance programs (1977)
1990	Nutrition Labeling and Education Act	Requires food manufacturers and processors to provide detailed information on the labeling of most foods

Table 4–1. Major Federal Laws Affecting Marketing

Date	Law	Description
1990	Children's Television Act	Limits the amount of advertising to be shown during children's television programs to no more than 10.5 minutes per hour on weekends and not more than 12 minutes per hour on weekdays
1991	Americans with Disabilities Act (ADA)	Protects the rights of people with disabilities; makes discrimination against the disabled illegal in public accommodations, transportation, and telecommunications
1993	Brady Law	Imposes a five-day waiting period and a background check before a gun purchaser can take possession of the gun

D. LAWS DEREGULATING SPECIFIC INDUSTRIES

Date	Law	Description
1978	Airline Deregulation Act	Grants considerable freedom to commercial airlines in setting fares and choosing new routes
1980	Motor Carrier Act and Staggers Rail Act	Significantly deregulates trucking and railroad industries by permitting them to negotiate rates and services
1996	Telecommunications Act	Significantly deregulates the telecommunications industry by removing barriers to competition in local and long-distance phone and cable television markets

Table 4–2. Effect of Federal Antimonopoly Laws on the Four Ps

Law	Product	Place	Promotion	Price
Sherman Act (1890) Monopoly or conspiracy in restraint of trade	Monopoly or conspiracy to control a product	Monopoly or conspiracy to control distribution channels		Monopoly or conspiracy to fix or control prices

Table 4–2. Effect of Federal Antimonopoly Laws on the Four Ps

Law	Product	Place	Promotion	Price
Clayton Act (1914) Substantially lessen competition	Forcing sale of some products with others—tying contracts	Exclusive dealing contracts (limiting buyers' sources of supply)		Price discrimination by manufacturers
Federal Trade Commission Act (1914) Unfair methods of competition		Unfair policies	Deceptive ads or selling practices	Deceptive pricing
Robinson-Patman Act (1936) Tends to injure competition		Prohibits paying allowances to "direct" buyers in lieu of intermediaries' costs (brokerage charges)	Prohibits "fake" advertising allowances or discrimination in help offered	Prohibits price discrimination on goods of "like grade and quality" without cost justification, and quantity discounts limited
Wheeler-Lea Amendment (1938) Unfair or deceptive practices	Deceptive packaging or branding		Deceptive ads or selling claims	Deceptive pricing
Anbmerger Act (1950) Lessen competition	Buying competitors	Buying producers or distributors		
Magnuson-Moss Act (1975) Unreasonable practices	Product warranties			

THE TECHNOLOGICAL ENVIRONMENT

In modern economies, a strong technological base, fueled by public and private research and development expenditures, supports competitive strength and a solid growth rate. Technology affects all elements of the marketing mix, creating new goods and services to sell, improving existing products, and reducing prices through cost-efficient manufacturing and distribution processes. As the United States entered the twenty-first century, this impact of technology on marketing was accelerating dramatically, with the Internet transforming the way companies promoted and distributed products, and spawning whole new businesses, such as Web page designers, new types of software firms (like MM systems), interactive advertising agencies, and companies that allowed customers to negotiate business transactions over the Web. Other dramatic technological breakthroughs included industrial and medical use of lasers, superconductor transmission of electricity, molecular computer switches, wireless communication products, biologically enhanced seeds and plants, and genetically engineered proteins that fight disease.

In analyzing the technological environment surrounding MM systems, Moore perceived many opportunities to benefit from such technological advances as telemarketing and TV/computer home shopping, and target market opportunities created by cable television. These opportunities are covered in Chapter 21.

THE COMPETITIVE ENVIRONMENT

Having identified threats and opportunities in the demographic, economic, social-cultural, political-legal, and technological environments, Moore now turned her analytical attentions to threats and opportunities in the competitive environment, where she perceived four kinds of competition for Merton customers: (1) brand competition from other manufacturers of computer-based educational systems; (2) form competition from other forms of MM systems (for example, computerized distance learning courses offered by many state and community colleges); (3) generic competition from producers of products different from MM systems that would perform essentially the same educational function (for example, traditional courses offered by state and community colleges); and (4) desire competition, encompassing all other desires prospective customers might satisfy before purchasing a Merton MM professional education system (such as a new automobile or a home mortgage).

As noted in the Chapter 1 discussion of competition, understanding the kind of competition characterizing a market is key to formulating plans to develop that market. In Merton's domestic market, Moore realized that brand competition would be the main problem; however, after the MM systems line had established itself in domestic markets and aimed to penetrate global markets, she recognized that other kinds of competition would play a larger role.

To identify and respond to competitive threats and opportunities of whatever kind, Moore referred to a matrix (Figure 4-3) that identified characteristics of four competitive situations Merton would most likely face: monopoly, oligopoly, pure competition, and oligopolistic competition. At different stages of development, in different territories, the MM systems line could face any combination of these situations.

Important dimensions / Types of situations	Monopoly	Oligopoly	Pure competition	Monopolistic competition
Uniqueness of each firm's product	Unique	None	None	Some
Number of competitors	None	Few	Many	Few to many
Size of competitors (compared to size of market)	None	Large	Small	Large to small
Elasticity of demand facing firm	Either	Kinked demand curve (elastic and inelastic)	Completely elastic	Either
Elasticity of industry demand	Either	Inelastic	Either	Either
Control of price by firm	Complete	Some (with care)	None	Some

Figure 4-3. Some important dimensions regarding market competitors.

- A **monopoly** exists when a product or service is provided by the government (the U.S. Post Office), a private regulated monopoly (a regulated utility), or a private monopoly (DeBeer's diamonds). During its introductory stage, the MM's unique features and benefits might create a monopoly situation with no brand competition and a generally inelastic demand pattern. Up to a point, revenues would increase as prices were raised, although Merton would have to use some discretion: too high a price could attract unwanted competition or bring on charges of price gouging.

- An **oligopoly** consists of a few large sellers of similar products dominating the market, with many smaller sellers following their lead. In the PC systems field, Moore envisioned that Merton might find itself in an oligopolistic situation, competing with a few large sellers like Apple, IBM, and Microsoft. The fact that each competitor could keep close watch on the others would lead to the **kinked demand curve** phenomenon, illustrated in Figure 4-4, whereby competitors usually quickly match any attempt by one firm to generate additional sales by lowering prices.

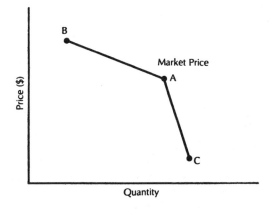

Figure 4-4. Oligopoly: kinked demand curve situation.

Assume that all firms priced their systems at point A. Should Merton decide to increase its price to point B, the other firms, to gain Merton's lost market share, will keep their prices at lower point A, thus assuring a falloff in demand for Merton's higher priced systems. If, on the other hand, Merton lowers its MM systems' price to point C, the other firms, not wanting to lose market share to Merton, will do the same, so Merton's overall sales won't increase much, if at all. In this situation, Moore realized, it is important to find the kink point and stay there.

- **Pure competition** means that many sellers are offering similar products to many buyers, each with fast, full knowledge of market transactions. The commodity market is an example of pure competition, with buyers and sellers aware, via their computer monitors, of the exact price pork bellies and other commodities are fetching at any point in time. In this situation, sellers face an almost flat demand curve. The slightest increase above the bid price for a product will practically eliminate demand for this product. This low-profit situation, shown in Figure 4-5, was one Moore wished to avoid for any products in the MM systems line. Even when these MM products were practically identical to competitive products, she would at least try to get them into the next competitive category, monopolistic competition.

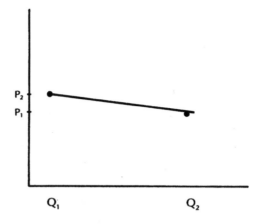

Figure 4–5. Demand curve: pure competition.

- In a **monopolistic competition** situation, few, or many, firms offer products that, at least, are perceived as different by customers. For example, Moore could easily envision a situation in which IBM, Apple, and dozens of other foreign and domestic competitors were offering practically identical versions of MM systems. However, by effectively designing and combining marketing mix elements, Merton might create the perception among target market members that MM systems were somehow unique. Thus, in effect, Merton would have a small monopoly for MM systems in this competitive market.

Knowledge of competitive climates that will confront products in different markets, along with knowledge of company objectives and resources, helped Moore answer two key questions in formulating competitive strategies:

In what markets should MM systems compete?
How should we compete in these markets?

The planning systems section of Chapter 6 addresses the first question; the rest of the book explores the second question.

THE MICROENVIRONMENT: THREATS AND OPPORTUNITIES

After Moore took over as manager of the newly formed MM systems division of Merton Electronics and initiated her assessment of macroenvironmental forces that Merton would have to respond to in formulating strategic marketing plans, she also focused on a group of microenvironmental forces that would be influenced by these macroenvironmental forces. These microenvironmental forces included the company itself, customers for MM systems, suppliers and marketing intermediaries who would help make and market these products, and publics that could influence the success of Merton's marketing efforts. Moore recognized that an understanding of these microenvironmental influences, and how they interacted with each other and with the macroenvironment, would be key to setting up the systems (discussed in Chapters 6 through 8) required to effectively and efficiently devise, implement, and control strategic marketing plans. She also recognized that she would have a much greater degree of control over these microenvironmental forces.

THE COMPANY

Moore realized that the MM systems division, which had full operational and strategic planning capabilities, would encounter a diversity of interdepartmental conflicts, summarized in Figure 4-6. These conflicts would be based largely on differing views as to which publics and company resources were most important in making and marketing MM systems and related products.

For example, marketing's emphasis on sales features, custom components, many models, and frequent model changes would conflict with the emphasis of other departments on things like functional features, few models, and few model changes. Marketing's emphasis was based on the primacy of customer wants and needs, while conflicting viewpoints could work together to accomplish overall company objectives.

Thus, an important task of marketing management would be to get all functional areas to view their activities through the customer's eyes, consistent with the marketing concept mandate of coordinating differing functions toward customer satisfaction. Moore envisioned working closely with other managers and staff in these functional areas and, considering their viewpoints, in setting up systems for organizing her division, developing and disseminating information, and planning, implementing, and controlling marketing strategies.

CUSTOMERS

Although individual professionals would be the primary market for MM systems, Moore did not overlook other market aggregates that could represent target markets for the new division's products, including:

- the producer market, composed of organizations that buy products for use in producing other products (covered in Chapter 10);

- the reseller market, composed of firms that buy products to resell at a profit (covered in Chapters 15 and 16);

Department	Emphasis	Marketing Emphasis
R&D	Basic research Intrinsic quality Functional features	Applied research Perceived quality Sales features
Engineering	Long design lead time Few models Standard components	Short design lead time Many models Custom components
Purchasing	Narrow product line Standard parts Price of material Economical lot sizes Purchasing at infrequent intervals	Broad product line Nonstandard parts Quality of material Large lot sizes to avoid stockouts Immediate purchasing for customer needs
Manufacturing	Long production lead time Long runs with few models No model changes Standard orders Ease of fabrication Average quality control	Short production lead time Short runs with many models Frequent model changes Custom orders Aesthetic appearance Tight quality control
Inventory	Fast-moving items, narrow product line Economical level of stock	Broad product line High level of stock
Finance	Strict rationales for spending Hard and fast budgets Pricing to cover costs	Intuitive arguments for spending Flexible budgets to meet changing needs Pricing to further market development
Accounting	Standard transactions Few reports	Special terms and discounts Many reports
Credit	Full financial disclosures by customers Low credit risks Tough credit terms Tough collection procedures	Minimum credit examination of customers Medium credit risks Easy credit terms Easy collection procedures

Figure 4–6. Point of view differences between marketing and other departments.

- the government market, which could purchase MM systems for use in producing public services or transferring goods and services to others; and

- the international market, composed of customers, producers, resellers, and government market aggregates in other countries.

Each of these market aggregates would have to be evaluated in terms of its potential purchases of MM products and systems and, when worthwhile potential existed, divided into market segments. Each segment would then be defined in terms of unique characteristics affecting the buying decision process (market definition and segmentation techniques are covered in Chapters 11 and 12).

SUPPLIERS

Although the MM systems division was capable of designing and developing many of the products and systems it marketed, Moore realized that the division would find it more economical in certain situations to have other firms make them. Even in situations where the MM systems division decided to make rather than buy, it would have to locate suppliers of products and services needed to produce and market these made products. An important part of Moore's planning efforts would involve first establishing quality control and other standards for selecting the best suppliers and then planning for such contingencies as rising prices and product shortages. (Relations with distributors are discussed in Chapters 19 and 21.)

MARKETING INTERMEDIARIES

In addition to selecting suppliers of products and services needed to produce MM systems product lines, Moore realized that a number of marketing intermediaries would also have to be selected.

- **Financial intermediaries,** such as banks, insurance companies, and credit companies, would help finance the development, production, and marketing of MM systems.

- **Selling intermediaries,** such as agents, brokers, wholesalers, and retailers, would help move MM products through channels to ultimate users, finding customers, closing sales, and creating time, place, and possession utilities.

- **Physical distribution intermediaries,** such as warehouses and rail, truck, and airline transporters, would stock and move MM products through channels to final target market destinations.

- **Marketing service agencies,** such as marketing research firms, advertising agencies, and media consultants, would help identify and define target markets for MM products and develop marketing programs to penetrate these target markets.

As with suppliers, Moore realized that policies and procedures would have to be established to identify intermediaries best able to help the MM systems division achieve its objectives, along with systems to help achieve mutually profitable working relationships with these intermediaries.

PUBLICS

The final microenvironmental forces considered by Moore were publics with actual or potential influence on her division's ability to achieve strategic marketing objectives. Properly handled, these publics could spell opportunity; ignored, they could represent crippling threats.

For example, financial publics, including investment banks, brokers, and stockbrokers, might be key in financing the new MM systems division; media publics might provide publicity needed to ensure marketing success; government and citizen action publics might stimulate legislation (such as truth in advertising and environmental legislation) that could help or hinder product sales. Even local publics in areas where MM products would be produced, internal publics consisting of MM systems division's managers and employees, and the general public, which could help create the "corporate image" of the new division, could help or hinder the division's success.

To help in assessing the potential impact of each public, Moore categorized them as welcome (such as stockholders and venture capitalists), unwelcome (such as negative reviews of MM products in the consumer electronics press), and sought (such as favorable publicity for MM products). Then she assessed the impact of each public and the cumulative impact of all these publics on the MM systems division's plans and made plans herself to communicate with each significant public to help ensure a favorable response to the new division and its products. For example, special press kits would be prepared for members of the sought media public, and newsletters about division products and progress would be sent to stockholders and staff members.

CHAPTER PERSPECTIVE

In formulating strategic marketing plans that reconcile a firm's objectives and resources with changing market opportunities, marketing managers must account for dynamic macro- and microenvironmental forces that affect all components of these plans, including objectives, marketing mixes, and target markets. Macroenvironmental forces, including demographic, economic, technological, social-cultural, and competitive forces, help define target markets and marketing mix appeals in a number of ways, including age group, income, values, and brand and product preferences. Microenvironmental forces, including the company itself (with its mission, objectives, and resources), customers, suppliers, marketing intermediaries, and publics, must be understood in terms of how they are influenced by macroenvironmental forces and can combine to achieve strategic goals.

KNOW THE CONCEPTS
TERMS FOR STUDY

Competitive factors
Content analysis
Core values
Culture
Demographic factors
Discretionary income
Disposable income
Economic factors
Engel's laws
Environmental scanning
Income distribution
Inflation
Kinked demand curve
Legal-political factors
Macroenvironment

Marketing intermediaries
Microenvironment
Middlemen
Monopolistic competition
Monopoly
Observational fieldwork
Oligopoly
Publics
Pure competition
Social-cultural factors
Subcultures
Suppliers
Technological factors
Unemployment
Value measurement surveys

MATCHUP EXERCISES

1. Match up the concept in the first column with the buyer behavior in the second column.

1. inflation
 a. spends more on vacations and self-help programs

2. Engel's laws
 b. just manages to cover expenses for food, rent, and other necessities

3. lower-upper class
 c. postpones purchases

4. disposable income
 d. buys status-symbol products and services for self and family

2. Match up the concept in the first column with the producer behavior in the second column.

1. kinked demand curve
 a. dares not raise price

2. demographics
 b. lowers prices, eliminates marginal products

3. recession
 c. maker of anti-wrinkle elixir, targets over-65 female market

4. prosperity
 d. raises prices, expands product lines

3. Match up the concept in the first column with the descriptor in the second column.

1. content analysis

    a. purchases of consumer electronics products among members of the Asian subculture increasing at a faster rate than among any other ethnic group

2. values

    b. more and more in the media, African-Americans are being portrayed in professional and executive positions

3. purchasing power

    c. must take prices and savings into account

4. income distribution

    d. dual-income families help rectify imbalance

4. Match up the political-legal category in the first column with the descriptor in the second column.

1. regulating competition   a. Telecommunications Act
2. protecting consumers   b. Brady Law
3. deregulating industries   c. Consumer Goods Pricing Act
4. maintaining competition   d. NAFTA

QUESTIONS FOR REVIEW AND DISCUSSION

1. How might Engel's laws apply in predicting sales of the following products in China and Canada: Mercedes Benz automobiles, a Mediterranean cruise, fuel for home heating, cigarettes, rent on an apartment, and health care.

2. Explain why a marketing manager might be more interested in the growth rate of a single population group than in the growth rate of the overall population.

3. The Dugal Corporation of Miami, Florida, exports its complete line of fashion jewelry to countries in Europe, Southeast Asia, the Middle East, and South and Central America. Important to the success of the firm's global marketing efforts is co-founder Joanna Ponimal's attendance at worldwide jewelry trade shows, where she makes contacts and negotiates contracts. Discuss how the following studies might help explain Mrs. Ponimal's success in designing jewelry that meets customer needs: observational fieldwork, value measurement studies, and content analysis.

4. From a buyer's viewpoint, what is the main advantage of pure competition? From a seller's viewpoint, what is the main advantage of oligopolistic competition?

5. According to surveys conducted by the Yankelovich marketing research team, the following are significant secondary cultural values characteriz-

ing the youth and young adult population segments: anti-bigness, living for today, less emphasis on possessions, equality of the sexes, mysticism, and physical fitness. To what extent, and in what ways, do you attribute these values to the trend among the young, described in a *New York Times* article of August 8, 1999, to "backpack into challenging territory well before the big money resorts or tchotchke merchants." What are the marketing implications for commercial firms (such as cruise lines and Club Med) of this cultural trend?

6. Describe how the political-legal environmental influences listed in the left-hand column might influence each of the marketing situations listed in the right-hand column:

general fiscal-monetary policies	renting empty office space in Newark, New Jersey
social legislation and regulatory policies	Daimler-Benz and Chrysler merge to become Daimler Chrysler
government relationships with individual industries	tobacco farmers make plans to market next year's crop
legislation relating to marketing information that helps marketers	Boeing competes with Airbus for a large commercial aircraft order

7. Describe how interdepartmental conflicts interfere with marketing concept precepts.

ANSWERS

MATCHUP EXERCISES

1. 1c, 2a, 3d, 4b
2. 1a, 2c, 3b, 4d
3. 1b, 2a, 3c, 4d
4. 1d, 2b, 3a, 4c

QUESTIONS FOR REVIEW AND DISCUSSION

1. According to Engel's laws, as family income rises, the percentage spent on food declines, the percentage spent on housing remains constant (except for such utilities as gas, electric, and public services, which decrease), and both the percentage spent on other categories and that devoted to savings increase. Given the relative difference in average incomes in China and Canada, Engel's laws would indicate that the aver-

age Canadian citizen would spend a larger percentage of his or her income on the Mercedes Benz, the Mediterranean cruise, and health care,
whereas the Chinese citizen would likely spend a larger proportion of
his or her income on fuel and cigarettes. Each would spend about the
same proportion on rent.

2. The single population age group might consist of a target market whose
   members consume a disproportionate amount of total product output.
   For example, if 80 percent of all cereals sold are consumed by children
   in the 6–16 age group, the marketing manager would be more interested in this group's growth rate than in the rest of the population.

3. Observational fieldwork involves observing the behavior of a sample of
   people from the culture being studied. The worldwide jewelry trade
   shows Mrs. Ponimal attends, which are also attended by members of
   Dugal target markets from around the globe, provide a perfect opportunity to observe, converse, and record information on the nature and
   needs of prospective customers, limited only by the size of the sample
   observed and their ability to interpret this information. Value measurement studies use scaled questionnaires to identify values common to
   known customer groups that relate to the product/service marketed.
   Possibly Mrs. Ponimal could have such questionnaires available at the
   Dugal booth at the worldwide trade shows she attends, with an offer
   of a premium for completing each one. Content analysis involves making inferences about changing social and cultural values based on the
   content of verbal and pictorial communications (for example, newspapers and TV shows). Checking competitive jewelry advertisements in
   fashion magazines in targeted countries illustrates how Mrs. Ponimal
   might use this technique.

4. From a buyer's viewpoint, the main advantage of pure competition is
   the low market price he or she pays, given that marketers lack the pricing protections of other competitive climates. The seller might prefer
   the relatively high market price received by the few competitors comprising an oligopoly, from which there is little incentive to depart. (As
   the kinked demand curve shows, if prices are increased, revenues will
   decline rapidly.)

5. Although the Yankelovich survey findings relate cultural values to the
   youth and young adult population segments, they can probably be assumed to influence other segments of the consumer population as well.
   Indeed, a focus on the values of youth in characterizing American society is a persuasive value in itself.

   The backpacking trend of traveling "light and cheap" into appealing,
   less traveled destinations such as Thailand, Vietnam, and Bolivia reflects
   all the values noted in the survey, especially less emphasis on possessions, equality of the sexes, and living for today. For commercial marketers, these backpackers represent trailblazers of the tourist set who influ-

ence all elements of their marketing mix: destinations, prices, means of travel, and ways their trips and tours are promoted.

6. Following are some ways in which each of the listed political-legal environmental forces might influence each of the listed marketing situations:

- Renting empty office space: Government monetary and fiscal policies, which affect the economy through taxation and interest rate policies, might help explain why the office space is empty and why owning office space is no longer the desirable tax write-off it once was.

- Daimler-Benz and Chrysler merge: Social legislation, pertaining to monopolistic practices in restraint of trade (which also qualifies as legislation relating to marketing) was certainly considered before this merger actually took place.

- Tobacco farmers market crop: Paradoxically, political-legal forces both help and hinder the marketing efforts of tobacco farmers. Hindering these efforts is social legislation designed to discourage consumption of tobacco products; aiding these efforts is the government's relationship with the agricultural segment (often resulting from government fiscal and monetary policies) that mandates subsidy supports for this industry.

- Boeing competes for a large aircraft order: Government legislation relating to marketing might force Boeing to use different ground rules in competing with foreign aircraft manufacturers for this order (for example, no under-the-table bribes); however, government relationships with individual industries—especially defense industries—provide loan subsidies and other assists that make it possible for Boeing to successfully compete.

7. A key precept of the marketing concept is that all the firm's departments and functions should work together cooperatively to profitably satisfy the needs of target market members. For example, if a certain product feature will attract members of a profitable new target market, then such departments as purchasing, production, and marketing should work together to ensure that this feature is incorporated into the product and promoted as such. Interdepartmental conflict, however, might arise because it is difficult for purchasing to procure this feature or for production to retool to build it into the product. Hence, the cross-purposes of individual departments frustrate the profitable purposes of the marketing concept.

5

THE INTERNATIONAL MARKETING ENVIRONMENT

OVERVIEW

Economic, political-legal, and social-cultural environments must differentiate global from domestic markets and must be accounted for in formulating strategic marketing plans and programs for entry and growth in foreign markets. Assessments of economic climates typically focus on the stage of economic development as well as physical, financial, and demographic characteristics contributing to economic well-being. Assessments of social-cultural climates focus on cultural variables (values, language, religious beliefs) that can be used to define target markets and build marketing mixes. Assessments of political-legal climates focus on home and host country government influences that affect trade, for better or worse, by promoting, impeding, or actively competing with imports and exports.

GLOBAL ENVIRONMENTS AFFECT STRATEGIC PLANNING

In prioritizing foreign markets for entry and growth, Moore recognized that there would be three areas of environmental concern—the economic, the social-cultural, and the political-legal—where threats and opportunities would most influence the success or failure of strategic marketing plans for MM systems. Her general approach for assessing a prospective foreign market, then, was to apply criteria in these three areas that compared this market with Merton's domestic market. Sources for this information included World Bank publications, statistical abstracts for individual countries, the Statistical Yearbook of the United Nations, and Department of Commerce sources and services covered in Chapter 7.

ECONOMIC CONSIDERATIONS

By way of simplifying the task of assessing a foreign market for possible entry, Moore first assessed prospective markets against the following model for judging a country's stage of development, under the assumption that only industrialized and post-industrialized countries would represent worthwhile markets for the expensive, technologically sophisticated line of MM systems.

This model classifies countries according to economic variables found to define markets for Merton products in the United States, including population, gross domestic product, manufacturing as a percent of national income, infrastructure, and per-capita income.

- **Preindustrial countries,** with per-capita incomes under $500, are characterized by high birth rates and low literacy rates, political instability, little industrialization, much agriculture and subsistence farming, and heavy reliance on foreign aid. Concentrated mainly in Africa, these countries represent limited markets for most products and are insignificant competitive threats.

- **Less-developed countries,** with per-capita incomes of under $2000, are at the early stages of industrialization, with factories erected to supply growing domestic and export markets. With consumer markets expanding, these countries represent an increasing competitive threat as they mobilize cheap and highly motivated labor. Together with preindustrial nations, these countries, concentrated in Asia, possess two thirds of the world's population but less than 15 percent of world income.

- **Developing countries,** with per-capita incomes averaging about $4000, are moving rapidly from an agricultural to an urbanized industrial base. Good worker skills, high literacy rates, and significantly lower wage costs than in advanced countries make these countries formidable competitors in export markets. Examples include Latin American countries like Uruguay and Peru.

- **Industrialized countries,** with per-capita incomes of about $9000, are major exporters of manufactured goods and investment funds. They trade goods among themselves and also export them to other types of economies (developing, postindustrial) for raw materials and finished goods. High wages, strong infrastructures, a highly educated population, and a large middle class make these countries rich markets for all kinds of goods and formidable competitors in export markets. Taiwan and South Korea are examples of industrialized countries that are poised to leap to postindustrialized status.

- **Postindustrialized countries,** with per-capita incomes in excess of $14,000, are distinguished by an increased emphasis of the service sector (which accounts for more than 70 percent of GNP in the United States); the primacy of information processing and exchange; and the ascendancy of knowledge over capital and intellectual technology over technology. Other distinguishing features include an orientation toward the future, the importance of interpersonal and intergroup relationships, and sources of innovation that are derived increasingly from the codification of theoretic knowledge rather than from random inventions. Japan, Germany, Sweden, and the United States are good examples.

ASSESSING ECONOMIC FACTORS

In assessing the economies of countries selected as entry prospects, Moore focused on the following areas: fiscal and monetary policies, currency stability, income distribution, and infrastructure.

- **Fiscal and monetary policies:** A county's **fiscal policies** pertain to taxation and expenditures; its **monetary policies** pertain to efforts by its central bank to vary the supply of money. Working together, fiscal and monetary policies influence a country's inflation rates, interest rates, and the stability of its currency, all of which are significant in assessing the health and strength of an entry country's economy. High interest rates can have a dampening effect on economic activity by pricing money needed to make, market, and buy products out of the reach of producers and consumers. High inflation rates can have a similarly depressing effect by devaluing currency and creating uncertainty for marketers, who may have to change their offerings by, say, lowering product quality or increasing prices to cope with advancing prices. While stifling productivity and purchasing power, excessively high interest and/or inflation rates also work to cut productivity, corporate profits, employment, and the gross national product, while increasing national indebtedness—all anathema to the economic health of prospective entry markets.

- **Currency stability:** When a foreign currency fluctuates widely in relation to an entering country's currency (for Merton, dollars), sales and profits are affected. For example, from mid-1988 to 1989, the value of the Colombian peso against the U.S. dollar fell from 290 to 361 pesos per dollar. This meant that, in 1989, a Colombian consumer had to spend 361 pesos to buy a $1 U.S. product and that foreign firms, due to these higher prices, had greater difficulty exporting products to Colombia. It also meant that Colombian goods were cheaper in other countries, encouraging Colombian exports.

- **Income distribution:** In turning her attention to the distribution of wealth and income in industrialized and postindustrialized economies, Moore recognized the following considerations:

1. Even though income is a useful index for screening markets, it is not always valid in specific cases. Depending on the product or service purchased, a high per-capita income in one country could be equivalent to a low per-capita income in another country. In Cuba, for example, monthly rent for a subsidized apartment costs one fifth what it does in Washington, D.C.; on the other hand, a color TV set will cost a Cuban resident 22 times what it costs the D.C. resident.

2. Also distorting per-capita income as an index of purchasing power is the consideration that certain products are either not available for purchase in certain countries or received free of charge. In Tanzania, for example, per-capita income under $500 hardly reflects the fact that the sun, the local well, and community healers replace expensive utility and health bills incurred in other countries.

3. For expensive MM systems, affluence of a proportion of the population large enough to constitute a target market was the main consideration. Population composition would also be important; for example, there would probably be more professionals in need of Mighty Mind systems in Singapore (population 2.9 million) than in China (population 1.2 billion).

- **Infrastructure:** The components of a country's infrastructure pinpoint its importance to marketers: communication amenities to tell customers about products; transportation amenities to distribute products to customers; and energy amenities to power production and marketing activities. Indicators of the extent of a country's communication networks include number and quality of telephones, print media, and broadcast media; indicators of the extent of land, rail, air, and waterway transportation services include number of passenger cars and buses, rail freight tons per kilometer, air miles traveled, and pipeline mileage. Per-capita energy consumption is a standard measure of energy capacity.

In addition to sufficiency, other important considerations in assessing a country's infrastructure pertain to quality (for example, are communication and transportation amenities subject to frequent breakdowns?), compatibility (for example, are current and voltage compatible with products marketed?), affordability (can prospective market members afford to tap into infrastructure networks?), and synergy (do the networks mesh together efficiently so that, for example, products can be produced and distributed to people who have been sold on them?).

ASSESSING SUPRANATIONAL ECONOMIC COMMUNITIES

Global and regional economic communities, designed to improve trade among signatory members through cooperative preferential arrangements, range from agreement among two or more nations to reduce trade barriers to the full-scale economic and political integration of many countries. Table 5-1 lists major regional economic communities.

Table 5–1. Major Regional Trade Associations

AFTA	**ASEAN Free Trade Area** Brunei, Indonesia, Malaysia, Philippines, Singapore, Thailand
ANCOM	**Andean Common Market** Bolivia, Colombia, Ecuador, Peru, Venezuela
APEC	**Asia Pacific Economic Cooperation Group** Australia, Brunei, Canada, China, Hong Kong, Indonesia, Japan, Malaysia, New Zealand, Philippines, Singapore, South Korea, Taiwan, Thailand, United States
CACM	**Central American Common Market** Costa Rica, El Salvador, Guatemala, Honduras, Nicaragua
CARICOM	**Caribbean Community** Anguilla, Antigua, Bahamas, Barbados, Belize, Dominica, Grenada, Guyana, Jamaica, Montserrat, St. Kitts-Nevis, St. Lucia, St. Vincent and the Grenadines, Trinidad-Tobago
ECOWAS	**Economic Community of West African States** Benin, Berkina Faso, Cape Verde, Gambia, Ghana, Guinea, Guinea-Bissau, Ivory Coast, Liberia, Mali, Mauritania, Niger, Nigeria, Senegal, Sierra Leone, Togo
EU	**European Union** Austria, Belgium, Denmark, Finland, France, Germany, Greece, Ireland, Italy, Luxembourg, Netherlands, Portugal, Spain, Sweden, United Kingdom
EFTA	**European Free Trade Association** Austria, Finland, Iceland, Liechtenstein, Norway, Sweden, Switzerland
GCC	**Gulf Cooperation Council** Bahrain, Kuwait, Oman, Qatar, Saudi Arabia, United Arab Emirates
LAIA	**Latin American Integration Association** Argentina, Bolivia, Brazil, Chile, Colombia, Ecuador, Mexico, Paraguay, Peru, Uruguay, Venezuela

Mercosur	**Southern Common Market**
	Argentina, Brazil, Paraguay, Uruguay
NAFTA	**North American Free Trade Agreement**
	Canada, Mexico, United States

In assessing the impact of supranational economic communities on plans for globally marketing MM systems, Moore found it helpful to first categorize them. The main criteria defining these categories are the extent to which (1) trade barriers between and among countries participating in the integration effort are reduced and (2) factors of productivity, including goods, services, capital, labor, and technology, are mobile and interchangeable within the integrated nations (that is, factor mobility). Thus, as degree of integration moves from free trade areas, through customs unions and common markets, to full economic union, trade barriers are reduced, and factor mobility is increased, to the point where a fully integrated economic union resembles, conceptually, the political, financial, social, and economic integration of the United States.

Free trade areas, the loosest, least restrictive form of economic integration, remove barriers to the sale of goods and services among member nations to enhance international competitiveness, economic growth, and job creation. However, each member nation maintains barriers against nonmembers. As described in Chapter 2, the four major examples of free trade areas in the world today are the WTO, NAFTA, APEC, and the EU.

POLITICAL-LEGAL CONSIDERATIONS

Moore's examination of political-legal climates in prospective entry markets began with the home country, where the political-legal climate might constrain or support exporting products and services to other countries. Then her examination broadened to encompass political-legal climates in prospective host countries and regions.

HOME-COUNTRY INFLUENCES ON TRADE

Export quotas, export controls, and embargoes are typically the main constraints faced by a home-country company in its efforts to penetrate global markets. Balancing these constraints, most home countries also provide means to support trade.

• *EXPORT QUOTAS*

Export quotas, which limit the quantity of products that may be exported from a country, are established for a number of reasons. For example, quotas on the amount of redwood and other rare-wood lumber that can be exported from the United States are designed to ensure that scarce natural resources are not depleted, and are available to domestic consumers at affordable prices. Export quotas are also established to raise export prices by restricting supplies of the product in foreign markets, as when countries combine to restrict the world supply of commodities like oil and coffee.

• *EXPORT CONTROLS*

Export controls are a more extreme form of export quota designed to deny, rather than delimit, the acquisition of strategically important goods by adversaries. In the United States, the export control system is based on the Export Administration Act and the Munitions Control Act, which combine to control all exports of goods, services, and ideas, usually for reasons of national security, foreign policy, or nuclear nonproliferation. Firms like Merton wishing to export products must first get a license from the Department of Commerce, which has drawn up lists of sensitive products, unreliable countries, and unreliable individual firms (for example, firms that secretly sold sensitive nuclear materials to Iraq prior to the Persian Gulf War).

Nonsensitive products sold to traditional partners may be exported under a general license. Otherwise, especially with high-tech products sold to unfriendly nations, a validated export license is required. The fact that U.S. domestic controls often place domestic firms at a competitive disadvantage vis-à-vis firms from countries with less severe controls is discussed in Global Focus 5-1.

GLOBAL FOCUS 5-1

Export Controls Hurt U.S. Firms

That Japanese trade practices exclude billions of dollars worth of U.S. exports is common knowledge. Not so visible are U.S. rules that forbid U.S. companies from selling abroad and block even more export sales.

Syracuse University economist J. David Richardson's comprehensive study of export disincentives estimates their cost to U.S. companies to be $21 billion to $27 billion a year. By comparison, a study done by the Institute for International Economics puts the annual loss of U.S. exports due to Japanese trade restraints at $9 billion to $18 billion. According to Richardson, the United States is the world's most aggressive controller of exports and Washington has been "unduly nonchalant" about the economic effect.

The U.S. export controls target high-tech industries that are key to economic growth. Among those hit hardest are makers of computers, telecommunication equipment, machine tools, and civilian aircraft.

American Telephone and Telegraph (AT&T) estimates that over the next five years, U.S. restrictions dating from the cold war will cost it $500 million of foreign business. These are sales that probably will go to competitors from Europe or Japan. AT&T chairman Robert E. Allen complained to Congress: "It is unrealistic, perhaps bordering on arrogance, to think that any country would go without advanced information technology just because U.S. companies are forbidden to provide it."

Source: Robert Keatley, "U.S. Rules Dating from the Cold War Block Billions of Dollars in Exports," *The Wall Street Journal,* October 15, 1993, p. A7.

• *EMBARGOES*

An embargo is a specific type of quota that prohibits all trade, either imports or exports, on whole categories of products regardless of destination, on specific products to specific countries, or on all products to given countries. Typically instituted for adversarial or political, not economic, reasons, embargoes invariably raise a number of controversial issues. For example, how effective are embargoes in changing another country's policies? And, perhaps most important to international marketers, how will firms that suffer when embargoes close their markets be compensated? These questions continue to be asked in reference to the embargo the U.S. has maintained against Cuba since 1960, in protest against Fidel Castro's dictatorial policies. In 1996, the controversial Helms-Burton Act attempted to recompense U.S firms affected by the embargo and Castro's policies by allowing these firms to sue foreign companies and their executives that use expropriated U.S. assets to do business in Cuba.

• *TRADE SUPPORTS*

In addition to constraints on trade, home countries also help promote trade in three ways:

- **Financial assists** generally include tax incentives that treat earnings from export activities—such as developing new overseas markets—preferentially, either by applying a lower rate to earnings from these activities or by providing a refund of taxes already paid for income associated with exporting. Other financial assists include allowing accelerated depreciation of export-related assets and outright subsidies to reward export performance. Far Eastern, Latin American, and European trading nations are especially generous in offering these financial assists, often leaving themselves open to retaliatory actions by other nations who feel these assists excessively tip the playing field.

- **State trading companies** engage governments in commercial operations, either directly or through agencies under their control. These companies function either in place of or in addition to private traders. For example, consistent with its recent industrial policy designed to target overseas industries and markets that show high potential for export growth, the Australian government formed the Australian Trade Commission that consolidates various export assistance agencies into a single body and effectively grants the government decision-making powers over imports and exports previously made in the private sector.

  Whether in place of or supplementing private traders, state trading companies, like their private trading company counterparts, present problems for individual companies and entire countries. For example, an exporting company like Merton, dealing with a monolithic state trading company that often doesn't have to show a profit, has little chance to build loyalty relations with specific customers, and is often at the mercy of bureaucratic decisions made with little understanding of marketplace realities. (Functions and benefits of trading companies are discussed in Chapter 19.)

- **Government information services** offer information assistance to importers and exporters, particularly concerning the location of markets and credit risks and the promotion of products in foreign markets. In the United States, for example, more than a dozen federal organizations actively collect information from around the world concerning problems and opportunities for importers and exporters. Much of this information abundance is free or inexpensive, if sometimes bureaucratically slow. These sources of information and assistance are covered, along with illustrative examples of their use, in Chapter 7.

HOST-COUNTRY INFLUENCES ON TRADE

In assessing the impact of political-legal climates in prospective host countries, Moore's main concerns pertained to each country's attitudes toward trade, the stability of its government and currency, and its potential to discourage trade through quantitative and qualitative restrictions.

• *WHAT ARE THE COUNTRY'S ATTITUDES TOWARD FOREIGN TRADE?*

Attitudes toward importing goods from another country range from largely free markets, as exist between the United States and Canada, to a total embargo on the products of another country.

• *HOW STABLE IS THE COUNTRY'S GOVERNMENT?*

There are two key concerns of firms assessing the stability of a prospective host country's government: (1) Are government policies and practices consistent and predictable in such areas as taxes, profits, and ownership rights? (2) Is there an orderly process for selecting and empowering new leaders? Unless both questions can be answered in the affirmative, the entering company will likely face a climate of instability and discontinuity leading to three kinds of political risk: (1) **ownership risk,** exposing property and life; (2) **operating risk,** exposing the firm's ongoing operations to interference; and (3) **transfer risk,** encountered when the firm attempts to shift funds between countries.

Ownership risk generally prevails in countries where civil disturbances, such as coups, guerrilla warfare, and terrorism, take on a strong anti-business bias, with U.S. businesses often the most vulnerable targets. The two most likely manifestations of ownership risk include **confiscation,** or the transfer of ownership to the host country with no compensation (especially affecting mining, energy, public utilities, and banking enterprises), and **expropriation,** or the transfer of ownership to the host country with compensation (rarely sufficient, usually at the book value of the firm and in the local currency).

HOW FIRMS REDUCE POLITICAL RISK

Often, judicious preparation can mitigate political risks endemic in unwelcoming political-legal climates. For example, the U.S. government's Overseas Private Investment Corporation (OPIC) ensures investments in less-developed countries against such perils as currency inconvertibility, expropriation, and physical damage resulting from war or political strife. OPIC also finances manufacturer foreign direct investment, individually or as a joint venture, through direct loans and loan guarantees to U.S. lenders.

• *WHAT TRADE RESTRICTIONS WILL WE FACE?*

A country with a hostile attitude toward importing foreign products and services has at its disposal a broad range of trade restrictions for making it difficult, if not impossible, for a firm like Merton to penetrate its well-protected markets.

Examples of these restrictions, as they apply to imports, include:

- **License requirements:** An import license is a privilege permitting a company to sell goods within defined limits in the country issuing the license. Mexico, for example, requires import licenses limiting the importation of certain products to encourage domestic growth of manufacturers of these products. (Many of these licensing requirements have been phased out under NAFTA, discussed in Chapter 2.)

- **Tariffs:** A tariff is a tax on imports stated as a percent of value (ad valorem) or on a per-unit basis. **Protective tariffs** are designed to protect home industries by reducing imports of protected goods; **revenue tariffs,** usually lower than protective tariffs, are designed to raise money. Different tariff rates may be applied to different countries, or groups of countries, or a single rate may be applied to all countries.

- **Taxes:** Some countries, in addition to standard taxes on foreign companies and imports, levy special taxes to serve special purposes. Examples include **excise** or **processing taxes** on certain products to provide revenues from local sales and **border taxes,** which are levied on imports in European countries to equalize their cost to that of locally manufactured products.

- **Quotas:** Specific provisions that limit the amount of foreign products a host country can import. They may be applied to all countries or on a country-by-country basis.

QUALITATIVE CONTROLS ALSO DISCOURAGE IMPORTS

License requirements, taxes, tariffs, and quotas are all examples of quantitative controls, which specify quantities of goods that can be imported and/or amounts, and kinds, of payments for these goods. In addition, host countries also have a number of qualitative controls in their trade arsenals to restrict or discourage imports. These controls include (1) restrictive customs procedures that promulgate complex rules and regulations for classifying and valuing commodities as a basis for levying import duties, making compliance difficult and expensive, and (2) discriminatory government and private procurement policies, such as "Buy British" or "Buy American" campaigns, which effectively discriminate against imported products.

SUPRANATIONAL INFLUENCES ON TRADE

In addition to acting alone, home and host countries can facilitate imports and exports by joining organizations set up for this purpose. Examples of such organizations include:

1. The **International Monetary Fund,** with a membership of more than 150 countries, was chartered to oversee the management of the international financial system by exercising surveillance over exchange rate policies of members, monitoring developments in the field of international liquidity (for example, the effect of higher German interest rates on cash flows to other countries), providing temporary balance-of-payments assistance to member countries in external difficulties, and offering technical aid to promote cooperation in international financial relationships.

2. **Economic communities,** discussed earlier in this chapter, are designed to improve trade among member nations through cooperative preferential arrangements. The two largest such communities are NAFTA, which links Canada, Mexico, and the United States into a single trade zone encompassing 360 million people, and the EU, which commits fifteen European countries to remove all tariffs and trade restrictions on the movement of goods and services.

GLOBAL LEGAL SYSTEMS AFFECT BUSINESS DECISIONS

In analyzing how legal systems would affect marketing plans, Moore focused on questions that she perceived would be most critical in entering and growing in global markets.

• *WHAT TYPE OF LEGAL SYSTEM IS IN PLACE?*

In general, there are two types of legal systems in place in industrialized countries: the code law system, deriving from old Roman and Napoleonic codes, and the common law system, deriving from English common law. Code law, characterizing most of continental Europe, divides the judicial system into civil, commercial, and criminal law divisions, with separate administrative sections, and all-inclusive, relatively inflexible written statutes for each division. Common law, on the other hand, characterizing British Commonwealth countries and the United States, tends to merge civil, commercial, and criminal law under a single administrative structure, with tradition, past practice, and precedents from previous rulings guiding legal decisions.

A significant recent departure from this tendency is the development of the Uniform Commercial Code in the United States, which, like code law, brings together a body of specifically designed written rules covering only commercial conduct.

• *UNDER WHOSE LAWS WILL MANAGERS FUNCTION?*

Some foreign countries—in Latin America, for example—mandate that foreigners agree to be treated as nationals, forfeiting jurisdiction of their own national laws. This can present real conflicts when a manger's home country mandates this jurisdiction, as is the case with the U.S. Foreign Corrupt Practices Act. This act makes it a crime for U.S. firms to bribe foreign officials for business purposes, with the rationale that business dealings abroad should reflect U.S. moral and ethical leadership and free-market competitive forces. In 1988, the act was revised to clarify conditions under which U.S. managers were expected to know about violations of the act and distinguished between facilitation of routine governmental actions (such as getting licenses and permits) and of policy decisions (such as obtaining or retaining contracts). Still, U.S. firms complain that even the revised act puts them in a difficult position vis-à-vis foreign competitors from Europe and Japan, who have no such legal constraint.

Other situations where U.S. managers are expected by host countries to recognize laws that conflict with general standards of behavior and ethics in the U.S. abound, including meager safety standards in Mexican firms, Brazil's profligate abuse of its rain forests and other natural resources, and China's human rights abuses and use of prison labor to make products for export.

Still another conflict situation involves U.S. laws pertaining to boycotts implemented by other countries. For example, some Arab nations blacklist firms that do business with Israel, but U.S. laws impose fines on and deny export licenses to U.S. firms that comply with these boycotts.

• *WILL PATENTS AND TRADEMARKS BE PROTECTED?*

This question was of vital importance to Merton, which held patents on computer hardware and trademarks on software. Thus, they assessed prospective entry nations in terms of adherence to such patent agreements as the International Convention for the Protection of Industrial Property (honored by forty-five countries), the Patent Cooperation Treaty (honored by thirty-nine countries), and the European Patent Convention (honored by eleven countries). Under these conventions, Merton would no longer have to patent products in every country it entered.

• *TO WHAT EXTENT WILL WE CONTROL OUR COMPANY'S DESTINY?*

A number of countries require entering companies to dilute their equity. For example, under India's Foreign Exchange Regulation Act, foreign equity participation in local projects is reduced to 40 percent. Merton planners recognized that circumstances might make such dilution feasible, but they would rather avoid it.

• *HOW FREE WILL WE BE TO COMPETE?*

Antitrust laws, long a part of the legal environment in the United States, can apply to international operations of a firm as well. For example, when a U.S. company buys or enters into a joint venture with a foreign company, or makes an agreement with a competing firm abroad, the U.S. Department of Justice has the authority to approve or disapprove such an agreement, based on its likely competitive effect on the U.S. market. However, with increasing globalization of business and concerns about our laws infringing on the sovereignty of other nations, disapprovals are rare.

In general, U.S. antitrust laws have not taken root in other countries. For example, although the European Community Commission prohibits agreements and practices that prevent, restrict, or distort competition, it also exempts large categories of "good" cartels to encourage certain businesses to compete effectively with U.S. and Japanese businesses.

Two U.S. laws that address problems faced by U.S. firms competing with foreign oligopolies, monopolies, and cartels are (1) the **Webb Pomerene Act,** which excludes from antitrust prosecution firms that cooperate to develop foreign markets, and (2) the **Export Trading Act,** which permits small to medium-sized firms to join forces in international market development activities.

• *WHAT RECOURSE WILL WE HAVE TO ADJUDICATE DISPUTES?*

Lawsuits in foreign countries can be long, costly, possibly biased, and conducted in unfamiliar surroundings under different rules. For this reason, Merton established as a condition of entry the existence of arbitration proceedings, typically involving a hearing of all parties before a three-member panel and a judgment that all parties agree in advance to abide by. That such proceedings in an entry country would be impartial and professional would be evidenced by membership in such groups as the International Chamber of Commerce, the London Court of Arbitration, and the Inter-American Commercial Arbitration Committee. Also, arbitration clauses would be written into all contracts in entry countries, presuming the possibility of litigation.

INTERNATIONAL LAW

International law, which is composed of the rules and principles that countries consider binding on themselves, faces two severe constraints: (1) the lack of an adequate judicial and administrative framework, or an agreed-upon body of law, to form the basis of a truly comprehensive international legal system, and (2) the reluctance of most nations to relinquish what they perceive to be vital rights to an international tribunal—and there is little other nations can do if one refuses to submit to arbitration or recognize an unfavorable judgment against it.

CULTURAL INFLUENCES ON GLOBAL MARKETS

In assessing foreign countries as worthwhile target markets, Moore was especially sensitive to how cultural differences in such areas as language and religion would affect MM marketing programs.

LANGUAGE COMPETENCE CREATES TRUST

Language, as a cultural variable, includes words used, how they are used, and nonverbal elements of the communication process, such as gestures and eye contact. As a component of the marketing process, language is important to a company like Merton in achieving access to an entry market (and allaying concerns about the firm's intentions); gathering and evaluating information (for example, attitudes and needs regarding products and services); interpreting contexts in which communications will take place; and actually communicating with prospects, customers, staff members, and facilitating personnel. A manager's competence in a foreign language must go well beyond simply understanding and speaking words to include contexts in which communication takes place and idiomatic meanings (in England, for example, "tabling a proposal" means immediate action must be taken and a "bombed" negotiation is a smashing success).

One way to address communication problems, which usually arise through misunderstandings and translation errors, is to retain advertising and marketing research agencies located in unfamiliar entry markets. Another, applicable for promotion and other written communication, is the **back-translating** approach, whereby a message translated into a foreign language such as Chinese is translated back to the original language by a person other than the one who made the first translation.

Nonverbal language is composed of conditions under which communication takes place and cues, other than words, with which people communicate. Of special concern in this area are differences in time and space; in the United States, punctuality is seen as a virtue, whereas the concept of punctuality may be radically different in a foreign country. In many Arab, Latin American, and Asian countries, for example, time is flexible to the point where it is considered discourteous to arrive at an appointment at the invited time.

Another aspect of nonverbal communication is the amount of space people want to separate them from others. For example, South Americans like to sit or stand very close to each other when they talk business—almost nose to nose. The American business executive tends to keep backing away as the South American moves closer, which may be taken as a negative reaction.

Body language is another aspect of nonverbal communication that differs from country to country. For example, the "yes" of a Greek or Turk is indicated by a head movement identical to the negative shake used in the United States, and the thumb and finger sign that connotes success in the United States means "money" in Japan and "I will kill you" in Tunisia. In negotiations, Southern Europeans tend to involve their bodies a lot, whereas Northern Europeans are comparatively stiff and reserved.

RELIGION CREATES COHESION AND CONFORMITY

Religion, which in most cultures is a dominant force toward group cohesion and conformity, is also of interest to global marketers in terms of its formal strictures and protocols. For example, food taboos and holidays can represent opportunities for marketers in meeting local needs such as nonalcoholic beverages in Arab countries and holiday artifacts. On a larger scale, religious strictures often define the relative role of the sexes, with marketing consequences. For example, in Japan and the Middle East, women are prohibited from functioning as they do in the West, with implications for hiring policies among global firms (for example, women may not be employed as managers) and their role as consumers (for example, women may have less input into buying decisions and may be reached only through female sales personnel, direct marketing, and women's specialty shops).

SURVEY LIMITATIONS IN GLOBAL MARKETS

In Chapter 4, we examined a number of approaches—such as content analyses and value measurement surveys—for identifying those cultural variables that help define target markets and marketing mixes for products and services sold in the domestic market. In global markets, where companies face language and attitudinal barriers, findings from these approaches do not necessarily indicate relationships among value systems and buying behavior. Furthermore, they are expensive to conduct and subject to most of the problems and biases endemic to survey research.

Given the limitations of these approaches in global markets, the "Search for Cultural Universals" approach is gaining adherents.

• *SEARCH FOR CULTURAL UNIVERSALS*

Unlike the other approaches covered, which assume that cultural values—and their relationship to behavior patterns—differ with place, time, and situational variables, this approach assumes that there are certain universal cultural values that can be identified and related to behavior patterns.

To the extent that these universal values exist, and can predict product class or brand choice, it is possible for the global marketer to standardize various marketing plan components. For example, assuming similar cultural values predisposing people to purchase Mighty Mind computers in the United States and Taiwan, the same target market(s) in each country could be subject to the same marketing mix, adjusted for language differences, and geared to these universal values. Advantages of standardizing marketing plans in international markets include quicker penetration of markets with a single marketing mix and cost savings from fewer product models, distribution channels, promotional appeals, and media outlets.

Although the notion that such universal values exist across a broad spectrum of products is debatable, there is general agreement that they exist for some products—Coca-Cola for example. There is also general agreement that a diversity of trends, including population mobility, economic integration among countries, computers, and cross-boundary communications are working to increase the number of universal values and move toward cultural convergence, whereby the time required for a culture to adopt an innovation is shortened.

Examples of global marketing approaches that assume measurable universal values include Murdock's list of universals, Kluckholm's value orientations, and Hall's High/Low Context Cultures.

• *MURDOCK'S LIST OF UNIVERSAL VALUES*

Athletic sports, bodily adornment, cleanliness training, cooking, courtship, dancing, division of labor, education, ethics, folklore, food taboos, inheritance rules, kinship, joking, law, medicine, mourning music, nomenclature, population policies, property rights, puberty customs, religious rituals, status differentiation, surgery, toolmaking, trade, weaning, weather control are included in Murdock's list of universals.

Assuming the universality of these values, the role of the international marketer is to identify those deemed important to members of the society studied and to motivate interest in the product class or brand being marketed. For example, in marketing Mighty Mind computers in the domestic market, highly regarded values like education and status differentiation were incorporated into a promotional campaign that stressed the importance of professional education in achieving higher status positions.

• *KLUCKHOLM'S VALUE ORIENTATIONS*

Combine individual values into clusters said to define five basic orientations thought to be universal among nations: human nature, relationship of man to nature, sense of time, activity, and social relationships. Each orientation runs a spectrum of beliefs as shown in Table 5-2.

Table 5–2. Variations in Value Systems

Orientation	Range		
Human nature	*Evil (changeable or unchangeable):* Most people are basically evil and can't be trusted	*Mixture of good and evil (changeable or unchangeable):* There are evil and good people in the world.	*Good (changeable or unchangeable):* Most people are basically good and can be trusted.
Man-nature relationship	*Subjugation-to-nature:* Life is largely controlled by outside forces.	*Harmony-with-nature:* Live in harmony with nature.	*Mastery-over-nature:* Man should challenge and control nature.
Time-sense	*Past-oriented* (tradition bound): Man should learn from and emulate the glorious past.	*Present-oriented* (situational): Make the most of the present moment. Live for today.	*Future-oriented* (goal-oriented): Plan for the future in order to make it better than the past.
Activity	*Being:* The spontaneous expression of impulses and desires. Stress on who you are.	*Being-in-becoming:* Emphasizes self-realization, development of all aspects of the self as an integrated whole.	*Doing:* Stressing action and accomplishment.

Table 5–2. *Continued*

Orientation	Range		
Social relations	*Lineal* (authoritarian): Lines of authority are clearly established with dominant-subordinate relationships clearly defined and respected.	*Collateral* (group-oriented): Man is an individual as well as a group member participating in collective decisions.	*Individualistic:* Man is autonomous and should have equal rights and control over his own destiny.

Source: Adapted from Florence R. Kluckhohn, "Dominant and Variant Value Orientations," in Clyde Kluckhohn and Henry A. Murray, Eds., *Personality in Nature, Society, and Culture,* 2nd ed. (New York: Alfred A. Knopf, 1953), p. 346.

Here, the marketer's task involves understanding what types of value orientations predominate in a given society. In Merton's domestic market, for example, a "future-oriented" time sense, "doing" activity, and "individualistic" social relations were all woven into strategic planning for MM systems.

• *HIGH- AND LOW-CONTEXT CULTURES*

Hall suggests the concept of high- and low-context cultures as a way of identifying and relating to cultural orientations perceived as universal in groups of countries. The universal "language," written and verbal, is the basis for this perception. In a high-context culture—Hall cites Japan and Arab countries as examples—less information is contained in the verbal component of a message because much more is implicit in the context in which the message is sent and received, including the background, associations, and values of the communicators. In low-context cultures—Hall cites the United States and Northern European cultures as examples—the message itself is the focus of negotiations.

Negotiating a business deal illustrates characteristics of high- and low-context styles. As compared to low-context negotiations, in high-context negotiations the words describing terms and conditions are less important than the negotiating context. Shared cultural values, a sense of connection and trust among the negotiators, and a strong sense of honor and personal obligation in fulfilling the conditions of the deal are more important. Time is less important; more important is getting to know one another. Social distance is shorter and more personal; negotiations tend to be lengthier; legal sanctions (and lawyers) are less important than a person's word in consummating the deal; responsibility for errors is taken at highest levels, not pushed to lower levels; and competitive bidding is less frequent. Global Focus 5-2 shows how an understanding of context has helped American marketers succeed in global market negotiations.

GLOBAL FOCUS 5-2

It Helps to Know the Negotiating Context

Illustrative of how an understanding of cultural context can help a business succeed in global markets is the experience of Judith Sans, founder of Judith Sans Internationale of Atlanta, and Henry F. Henderson, Jr., president and CEO of H.F. Henderson Industries of West Caldwell, New Jersey.

- Judith Sans began marketing her natural cosmetics and skin care salons and schools overseas in 1985, when she joined a trade mission in the Far East to meet representatives of foreign businesses. Her firm now sells in more than twenty countries, with exports accounting for 46 percent of total sales volume in 1993. Ms. Sans now regularly attends worldwide specialty trade shows to meet potential customers and check over the competition (a Hong Kong show opened the door for her products in China; an Italian show got her firm's products distributed in Italy and Germany). In her dealings with foreign businessmen, Ms. Sans credits "cultural flexibility," and an understanding of context, from a woman's perspective, as important to her firm's success in global markets. For example, in Saudi Arabia, she never meets alone with a male client, and she knows when it's acceptable to be polite but aggressive (an activity that is acceptable in China but not acceptable in Japan).

- Henry Henderson, who chooses to sell his firm's automatic weighing systems directly to foreign customers rather than through overseas agents or distributors, emphasizes travel and the ability to adapt to language and cultural differences. Henderson and his associates have made dozens of trips to countries like China (including Hong Kong), Australia, South Korea, France, Russia, Switzerland, Austria, Hungary, Italy, Finland, Great Britain, Costa Rica, and Brazil and have adopted their negotiating styles to each. Ben Martyn, a Henderson marketing manager, noted some differences: Americans "force terms and conditions, and insist that all the boilerplate be legally sanctioned and lived up to . . . for the Chinese and Japanese, a handshake is enough; to back down from an agreement would mean to lose face. So they don't need lawyers, but they must have the last word . . . for the English, it's usually sufficient to agree that they'll do the best they can."

Source: Business America, U.S. Department of Commerce, June 1993.

CHAPTER PERSPECTIVE

Analyses of elements of economic, political-legal, and social-cultural environments begin the process of formulating strategic marketing plans for entry and growth in global markets. Generally, these analyses focus on aspects of these environments that are favorable to trade and that are similar to those in the firm's familiar domestic market. Analyses of economic climates focus on the stage of economic development; physical, demographic, and financial attributes conducive to economic health, and the impact on trade of global and regional economic communities. Analyses of the political-legal environment cover assessments of incentives and disincentives to trade, including an examination of specific trade policies and practices, the type of legal system in place, and adherence to the mandates of international law. Analyses of the social/cultural environment examine aspects of cultures, including social structures, values, beliefs, languages, and religions, that influence all aspects of the strategic planning process.

KNOW THE CONCEPTS
TERMS FOR STUDY

Arbitration
Back-translating
Body language
Boycotts
Code law
Common law
Confiscation
Cultural convergence
Cultural universals
Currency stability
Economic communities
Embargoes
Export Administration Act
Export controls
Export Trading Act
Expropriation
Factor mobility
Fiscal policies
Government information
   services
Helms-Burton Act

High- and low-context cultures
Income distribution
Infrastructures
International Monetary Fund
License requirements
Monetary policies
Munitions Control Act
Nonverbal language
OPIC
Per-capita income
Political risk
Qualitative restrictions
Quantitative restrictions
Quotas
Religion
Stages of economic development
Taboos
Tariffs
Trading companies
Webb Pomerene Act

MATCHUP EXERCISES

1. Match the concept in the first column with the descriptor in the second column.

1. less-developed countries

    a. major exporters of manufactured goods and investment funds

2. postindustrialized countries

    b. moving rapidly from agricultural to urbanized industrial bases

3. industrialized countries

    c. although in the early stages of industrialization, the ability to mobilize cheap and highly motivated labor represents an increasing competitive threat to more industrialized countries

    4. developing countries   d. knowledge, technology, and services

2. Match the concept in the first column with the descriptor in the second column.

    1. fiscal policies   a. money value doesn't fluctuate against entering currency

    2. currency stability   b. tax and spend

    3. monetary policies   c. make more money available

    4. price indices   d. money is losing its value

3. Match the concepts in the first column with the definitions in the second column.

    1. export controls   a. an export license is required to sell supercomputers to China

    2. embargo   b. Arab nations blacklist firms that deal with Israel

    3. boycott   c. American firms are forbidden to sell products to Cuba

    4. domestic content law   d. U.S. firms in India buy supplies and parts locally

4. Match the concept in the first column with the description in the second column.

    1. code law   a. jurisprudence based on tradition, past practices, and precedent

    2. common law   b. Webb Pomerene Act protects U.S. firms in foreign markets from prosecution

    3. antitrust law   c. jurisprudence based on relatively inflexible written statutes

    4. International Chamber of Commerce   d. impartial, professional arbitration

5. Match the concepts in the first column with the descriptions in the second column.

    1. core values   a. passing a CPA exam

    2. secondary values   b. belief in God

    3. instrumental values   c. school prayer

    4. terminal values   d. achieving high social status

    5. material values   e. purchasing a BMW automobile

6. Match the concepts in the first column with the descriptions in the second column.

    1. outer-directed consumers   a. people who are driven toward success

    2. RVS scale   b. salvation, pro-life, standard cars

3. religion
4. nonverbal communication

c. late arrival for an appointment
d. food taboos, holidays

QUESTIONS FOR REVIEW AND DISCUSSION

1. Assume that an individual quits a good job selling pneumatic and hydraulic components for a manufacturer to set up shop as an independent sales representative selling these components in the global market for a number of manufacturers. Give examples of how forces in the macro- and microenvironment might work for, or against, the success of this venture.

2. In terms of demographic, economic, political-legal, and technological factors that can work for or against successful entry into the global market, speculate on why a company might decide to reject a country for consideration as an entry market.

3. Discuss why all five criteria defining an effective infrastructure might be important in successfully penetrating a foreign market for Merton MM systems.

4. Assume that two expatriate executives for a large American manufacturer—one stationed in Japan, the other in Australia—earn the same salary in U.S. dollars in 1995. Explain how exchange rates, inflation rates, product requirements, and product costs could markedly change the actual purchasing power of each salary.

5. Panels International, Inc., a small company in the State of Washington, recently negotiated a joint-venture agreement with a large Russian building company and commercial bank to market and build American-style dachas (vacation homes) in Eastern Russia. The company plans to produce several homes per month. Discuss how this firm might face ownership, transfer, and operating risk in implementing this agreement. Which risk (if any) would be most likely to materialize?

6. Discuss how supranational and national supports might have been instrumental in Merton's success in global markets.

7. Explain, with examples, how "language," as a cultural variable, would affect Merton's efforts to identify target markets for MM systems in Germany and to design marketing mixes to penetrate these target markets.

8. Select four universal values from Murdock's list that might be useful in positioning and promoting a new tennis racket developed by the Prince Sports Group of Bordentown, New Jersey. This racket, called the Long Body, will supplement the oversized heads pioneered by the company with longer handles (29 inches vs. the traditional 27 inches) said to impart more power, spin, reach, control, and comfort. Following the racket's success in the United States, Prince plans to introduce the racket into European and Pacific Rim markets and hopes that, by relying on

universal values, the company will be able to use a standardized promotional campaign.

ANSWERS

MATCHUP EXERCISES

1. 1c, 2d, 3a, 4b

2. 1b, 2a, 3c, 4d

3. 1a, 2c, 3b, 4d

4. 1c, 2a, 3b, 4d

5. 1b, 2c, 3a, 4d, 5e

6. 1b, 2a, 3d, 4c

QUESTIONS FOR REVIEW AND DISCUSSION

1. Before setting up in business as an independent sales representative, the individual might arrive at the following optimistic conclusions. Regarding macroenvironmental influences: demographically, the industries involved represent a large and growing global market; economically, these industries have sufficient disposable income to afford these components; technologically, these components will represent the state of the art; and competitively, especially in overseas markets, these products will offer benefits that will give them a strong edge. Regarding microenvironmental influences: the individual has received assurances from a number of previous customers that they will continue to buy products in the new situation; the sales rep has already received commitments from six manufacturers to represent them; a local bank (market intermediary) thinks so well of the sales rep's prospects for success that it will extend a $50,000 line of credit to get started.

2. A company might decide to reject a country for consideration as an entry market for a number of reasons. Demographic: an insufficient number of people in various age and occupational groups are attracted to the offering to justify the risk and expense of an entry strategy. Economic: the stage of development of the country, as reflected in indices like corporate and per-capita income, is not sufficiently advanced to generate profits for the firm's product line. Political-legal: high tariff barriers and "local protection" laws designed to help domestic companies might make it prohibitively expensive for the firm's products to compete in the entry market, regardless of other favorable factors. Technological: insufficiently developed infrastructures, particularly in the areas of transportation and communication, might make it prohibitively expensive for the firm to produce, distribute, and promote its product line even in a country that might otherwise represent an excellent market.

3. The five criteria of an effective infrastructure, from Merton's perspective, encompass sufficiency (there are enough infrastructure amenities, such as telephones, bridges, and power plants), quality (the amenities are reliable, not subject to breakdowns), compatibility (they are compatible with those in Merton's domestic market), affordability (people can buy and use them), and synergy (they operate in harmony with each other). To focus on the promotion aspect of the marketing mix, for example, there would have to be a sufficient number of communication outlets (electronic and print media) to carry Merton's message persuasively; Merton should be able to count on these outlets to work; they should work in a manner compatible with Merton's domestic market media (for example, state-owned media in command economies probably would not); prospective Mighty Mind customers should be able to afford these media (TV sets, magazines, and so on); and the media should work in harmony with other infrastructure amenities (for example, transportation amenities should make MM systems available to customers when they have been "sold" by the communication media).

4. In 1995, the Japanese yen was stronger against the U.S. dollar than was the Australian dollar, meaning that the expatriate would not be able to buy as much in Japan as in Australia. On the other hand, the inflation rate in Japan was about one third of what it was in Australia, meaning that, at the end of the year, the salary of the expatriate in Japan would be worth more in purchasing power than the salary of the expatriate in Australia. In Australia, however, product requirements would probably be less, overall, since the climate is warmer than in Japan, meaning considerable savings on clothing, housing, and utilities. Additionally, products that would be required by U.S. expatriates in these countries—such as apartments, homes, restaurant meals, and most durable goods—are usually less expensive in Australia than in Japan.

5. Ownership risk, which would refer to Panels's exposure of life and property, would most likely take one of two forms if initiated by the Russian government (perhaps at the behest of the firm's joint-venture partners): confiscation—the transfer of property without compensation, or expropriation—the transfer of property with compensation. Domestication is illustrative of operating risk, whereby the Russian government might demand partial transfer of ownership and management responsibility beyond the provisions of the joint-venture agreement with Panels's partners. Transfer risk would be incurred in the event that the Russian government imposed controls on the movement of Panels's profits or investment funds in or out of the country. Such controls could include excessive taxation on such funds and mandatory conversions of dollars into rubles. Assuming that any control would be imposed on Panels,

domestication would probably be the most likely outcome, in that it can achieve the benefits of confiscation and expropriation without the negative legal and public relations consequences.

6. On the supranational level, economic communities such as the WTO and the EU might have been instrumental in Merton's success by actively encouraging and stimulating trade through the creation of large, integrated markets that cross national boundaries and the reduction of trade barriers among member nations. On the national level, Merton might have received various direct and indirect financial assists (for example, an OPIC loan or accelerated depreciation for export-related subsidiaries), as well as assistance in locating markets, gaining distribution, assessing credit risk, and promoting products overseas through the auspices of such government agencies as the Chamber of Commerce and the Small Business Administration.

7. Language would play an important role in identifying and defining German target markets in that much information (computational needs, perceptions of competing computers, and the like) would have to be generated about these markets from these markets using both written and verbal media in which the ability to write and read German would be key. Once target markets have been defined, the task of building marketing mixes attractive to them would also depend mainly on a knowledge of German. For example: (1) The design of software and instruction manuals accompanying Mighty Mind computer models would have to be in proper German (product design). (2) Fluency in German will be required, first, to persuade German distributors to carry the Mighty Mind line and, second, to work with these distributors in implementing such programs as physical distribution, inventory management, training, and motivation (distribution). (3) Whatever form the promotion program assumes (for example, emphasizing publicity, direct marketing, direct selling, advertising and/or sales promotion) will have to be in understandable, persuasive German (promotion). (4) The price paid by German buyers of Mighty Mind computers will have to reflect additional costs incurred for adapting the product to the German market, including costs for communicating to and through distributors to end-users (price).

8. Among presumably universal values Prince might use to build a standardized promotional campaign for the Long Body are sports, status differentiation, courtship, and bodily adornment. For example, the campaign might stress, directly or implicitly, the value of excellence at a prestige sport like tennis for achieving status in life and attracting members of the opposite sex. Building on this message, the campaign would stress the value of the new Long Body racket for achieving these desired outcomes.

6
MARKETING SYSTEMS

OVERVIEW

A marketing system consists of the organization itself, the marketing mix offering, the target market, and marketing intermediaries that facilitate exchange. Activating and directing the marketing system are interacting systems for organizing the enterprise, formulating strategic plans, controlling plan effectiveness, and generating, analyzing, and distributing information. All systems have inputs, flows, and outputs. If they work together efficiently to satisfy target market and company objectives, synergy is created whereby the total effect is greater than that of individual elements acting alone.

MARKETING PROCESSES AND SYSTEMS

In the two previous chapters, we viewed marketing as a process culminating in the formulation of strategic marketing plans designed to reconcile a firm's objectives and resources with changing marketplace opportunities. We also examined marketing concepts and philosophies that comprise and guide the SMP process in domestic and international markets.

In this chapter and Chapter 7, we view marketing processes as a **system** composed of four major systems that facilitate the preparation, implementation, and control of strategic marketing plans. Again, we will use Merton Electronics, and the newly formed MM systems division, as a source of examples.

SYSTEMS THEORY EXPLAINS MARKETING PROCESSES

According to *Webster's New Collegiate Dictionary,* a system is "a regularly interacting or interdependent group of items forming a unified whole." Four concepts define a system: input, flows, output, and synergy. For example, a computer software program, designed to help integrate a multinational firm's international markets, would function as a system: input on marketing performance in a specific country would flow into a database to be matched with similar data from other countries' markets. Analyses of all this data would then be summarized in a report noting areas of subpar performance and possible reasons for this result. This output information would then become input for better managerial decisions for bringing performance up to par in all markets. This cooperative interaction among various agencies—the computer components, the software program, the decision makers—would help produce a total effect greater than the sum of effects taken separately, called **synergy.**

In an efficient marketing system, all functions—sales, marketing research, advertising, and the like—interact synergistically with other internal and external systems, including other departments, customer groups, distributors, and outside agencies, to achieve organizational goals by meeting the needs of target customers. In the process, one department's output becomes input for other departments. Sales reports, for example, fuel activities in accounting, marketing research, and production departments.

As illustrated in Figure 6-1, two sets of flows characterize these interactions: the first set—communications and products—flows between the company and its markets. For example, a businesswoman, responding to a direct-mail promotion, might purchase a Merton MM customized training system. The second set—payments and market information feedback—flows between markets and the company. The businesswoman's payment for the Merton system, and information she provides on how, when, where, and why she purchased it, illustrate these flows.

Multiply this single transaction by all the exchanges with target markets generated by Merton's marketing system, and a picture of the complexity of marketing processes and systems will begin to emerge. Further compli-

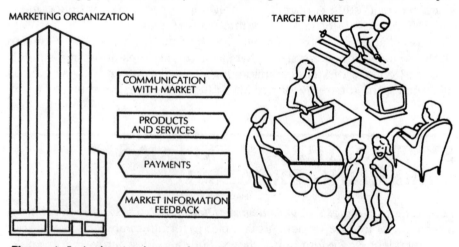

MARKETING ORGANIZATION   TARGET MARKET

COMMUNICATION WITH MARKET

PRODUCTS AND SERVICES

PAYMENTS

MARKET INFORMATION FEEDBACK

Figure 6-1. In the simplest marketing system, the interacting elements—the marketing organization and the target market—are connected by two sets of flows.

cating this complexity are all the functions, activities, and alternate approaches involved in carrying out marketing plans; the differing, often conflicting, objectives these plans seek to achieve; and all the interacting, uncontrollable elements in the macro- and microenvironment that these plans must account for.

SYSTEMS WITHIN THE MARKETING SYSTEM

The marketing system consists of the organization itself, the marketing mix offering, target markets, and marketing intermediaries, such as banks, advertising agencies, retailers, and transport agencies that facilitate exchanges between the marketing organization and its markets.

In designing a marketing system to market Merton products effectively and profitably, Lora Moore focused on four major systems within this system:

- **The organizational system,** which holds together and harmonizes the interacting systems comprising the marketing system.

- **The marketing planning system,** which identifies marketing opportunities and helps generate customer-oriented strategic plans.

- **The marketing control system,** which monitors performance of strategic plans and activates necessary measures to keep performance pointed toward objectives.

- **The marketing information system,** which generates, analyzes, and disseminates decision information needed to fuel the other systems and the overall marketing system.

Working together synergistically, these four systems support each step of the SMP process discussed in Chapter 3 (Figure 6-2).

We will examine the first three of these systems in this chapter and devote Chapters 7 and 8 to the fourth system.

THE ORGANIZATIONAL SYSTEM HARMONIZES MARKETING EFFORTS

In a modern marketing organization, the organizational system provides a structural framework within which marketing analysis, planning, implementation, and control activities are effectively coordinated and carried out. In small firms, such as a job shop or hardware store, one person performs these

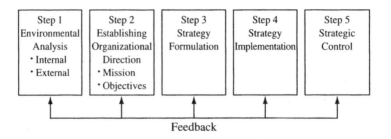

Figure 6–2. The strategic marketing planning process.

activities. Then, as the firm grows larger, the work is divided into functional activities, such as sales and market research, which are assigned to people who specialize in these activities. If the area to which the person is assigned involves responsibility for generating profits by directing, coordinating, motivating, and controlling the activities of other people, it is called a **line position.** Lora Moore, for example, is a line marketing manager. If the area of responsibility is specialized and advisory in nature, with little direct responsibility for profits, it is called a **staff position.** For example, in Figure 6-3, which depicts the organizational structure of Merton's industrial products division, the advertising manager and marketing research manager reporting to the marketing vice president would both hold staff positions. Supplemented by job descriptions, this organizational chart spells out duties of all line and staff personnel and establishes lines of authority and communication through which managers on all levels accomplish their work.

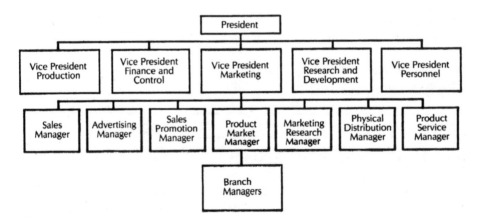

Figure 6–3. Formal line and staff marketing organization.

CHARACTERISTICS OF EFFECTIVE ORGANIZATIONS

To operate at its synergistic peak, an organizational system should exhibit two characteristics that preoccupied Lora Moore as she planned the systems comprising the new MM systems division:

- It should incorporate policies and procedures for effectively selecting, training, directing, motivating, and evaluating line and staff people.

- It should reflect the strategic objectives and approaches of the organization it integrates.

In terms of the strategic objectives and approaches of Merton's industrial products division, the organizational structure depicted in Figure 6-3 did its job well. Each staff member understood his or her responsibilities and was delegated sufficient authority to fulfill these responsibilities. Activities required to fulfill these responsibilities were clearly defined and specialized in terms of what each staff member, from the newly hired salesperson to the company president, did best.

From Moore's perspective, however, this structure was not an effective long-range model for generating and carrying out strategic plans for the new MM systems division.

SUCCESSFUL COMPANIES TEND TO THINK SMALL ORGANIZATIONALLY

Moore had in mind an organizational structure that tended to characterize successful firms in high-tech environments, such as Merton's MM systems division. For one thing, these firms tended to think small organizationally. Instead of one centralized authority, as in Merton's industrial products division, authority and responsibility tended to be decentralized and dispersed. Flexibility was important, with temporary task forces forming and reforming to address different problems.

Even relatively permanent components of the organization tended to be lean and simple and designed around a single entity, such as a single product or group of related products. In these small, flexible groups, authority was delegated at as low a level as possible to encourage an entrepreneurial spirit. Communication within and among these groups tended to be informal, roles were less specialized, and intragroup competition was encouraged and rewarded.

With their emphasis on motivation and innovation, these small, dynamic entrepreneurial groups would permit the new division to adapt quickly to threats and opportunities in the high-tech professional consumer marketplace.

GE'S SBUs: SMALL BUSINESSES WITHIN BIG BUSINESSES

The organizational model Moore had in mind to achieve her new division's strategic objectives was the strategic business unit (SBU) model pioneered by the General Electric Company. Consistent with this model, Merton's MM systems division would be structured around a single business (MM systems) and would have outside competitors (other firms marketing electronic systems) and a distinct mission. This SBU would have strategic and operational planning capabilities, with control over the production of MM units, and profit center responsibility for formulating, implementing, and controlling plans for marketing these units. Coordination between domestic and international operations would be achieved by a joint domestic-international staff that interacted in strategic planning, with plan approval required at senior management levels. Moore believed that this structure would facilitate decentralized, delegated authority and responsibility and encourage an entrepreneurial spirit, with less formalized roles and communication channels to encourage fast, flexible responses to marketplace

As illustrated in Figure 6-1, two sets how the Ford Motor Company's reorganization along SBU lines decentralized operational and strategic capabilities to serve its markets more efficiently and economically.)

MARKET FOCUS 6-1

Ford Reorganizes to Serve Markets Better, Faster, and Cheaper

The Ford Motor Company today announced its most sweeping reorganization in more than 25 years, in a bid to compete better in the coming decades not only in its established European and North American markets but also in the potentially huge car and truck markets developing in Asia.

At the end of the year, Ford's North American Operations and Ford of Europe will vanish, merging into a single operating unit, Ford Automotive Operations, with global reach. Ford's Asian-Pacific and Latin American operations will remain separate until the other, more extensive operations are merged.

Under its new organization plan, Ford plans to establish centers dedicated to developing specific types of vehicles that Ford will sell worldwide. For example, the new center in Europe . . . will develop Ford's small, front-wheel-drive cars, like the Escort, for sale in Europe, Asia, and America.

"We're going to combine the resources of a large and successful company with the speed and responsiveness of a small company," said Alexander Trotman, Ford's British-born chairman and chief executive. "This, of course, will assure a better return for our stockholders, a more certain future for all employees and, we believe, much better product, and a wider array of product, for all our customers around the world."

Source: James Bennet, "Ford Revamps with Eye on the Globe," *The New York Times,* April 22, 1994, p. D1.

THE PLANNING SYSTEM HELPS DEFINE AND EXPLOIT OPPORTUNITIES

The end product of the planning system is a strategic marketing plan that adopts the firm's objectives and resources to its changing opportunities. In formulating marketing plans and programs for the MM systems line, Moore followed a three-stage process involving:

- A SWOT analysis matching Merton strengths and weaknesses to market opportunities and threats;
- A statement of strategic intent;
- Preparation of a formal marketing plan.

SWOT ANALYSES

SWOT analyses of company strengths and weaknesses matched to opportunities and threats were made using planning models integrated into the marketing information system. In particular, Moore relied on the General Electric strategic planning grid, the Boston Consulting Group (BCG) growth share matrix, and Porter's competitive analysis model. The general focus of these models was on internal resources and constraints—such as products, personnel, and financial capabilities—and external marketing conditions—such as competitive, cultural, and political climates—that strategic marketing plans would have to account for.

THE GE STRATEGIC PLANNING GRID

The General Electric strategic planning grid (Figure 6-4) provides a framework for analyzing a prospective new product or business opportunity in terms of the attractiveness of a prospective market and the business strengths of the firm assessing the opportunity. The more attractive the market is and the stronger the business strengths of the company are, the better the prospects of success in entering this market are. As such, the grid helps facilitate SWOT analyses that balance a firm's internal strengths and weaknesses with external opportunities and threats.

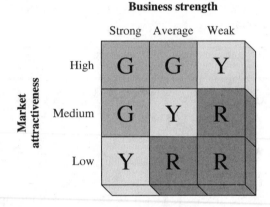

Figure 6–4. The strategic planning grid.

Green light opportunities, in the G boxes in the grid, indicate an invest and grow planning strategy; full marketing resources are appropriate, and profitability is expected to be high. Yellow light opportunities, in the Y boxes, indicate a cautious planning strategy; a product might have a strong position in a weak industry, a moderate position in an attractive industry, or a weak position in an attractive industry. Weaknesses should be strengthened before the new product is launched; otherwise, with an existing product, no additional resources should be committed. Red light opportunities (R boxes) indicate no-go strategies and no new product launches; they indicate the need to harvest or divest existing products.

In using the GE grid to select worthwhile markets for MM systems and to formulate entry and growth strategies in these markets, Moore used these criteria to determine **industry attractiveness:** market size, market growth rate, profit margin potential, strength of potential competition, macroenvironmental constraints, and the role of technology in making and marketing the product. Given these criteria, a product launch for an MM system would probably be successful if there were a large, profitable, growing market for the system, very little competition, and high technological barriers for any competition to overcome.

Criteria used to assess Merton's resources for entering attractive markets included financial resources, relative market share, product quality, price competitiveness, market knowledge, sales effectiveness, and geographical proximity. Given these criteria, and assuming a potentially attractive industry, a product launch of a new product in the MM line would probably succeed when Merton already had a strong share of market with existing MM products, could afford the launch, had the knowledge and expertise to market the new product, and could use existing distribution channels.

BCG GROWTH SHARE MATRIX

The Boston Consulting Group growth-share matrix (Figure 6-5) focuses on portfolios of products and the relationships among them. Using the BCG grid, all company products and businesses are classified according to their positions on two axes: a horizontal axis labeled "Relative market share" and a vertical axis labeled "Market growth rate."

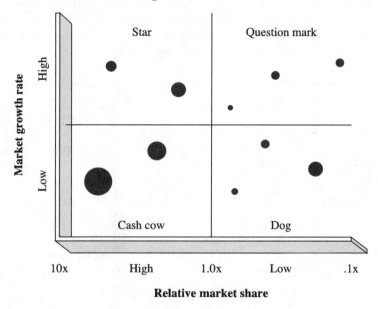

Figure 6–5. The growth-share matrix.

Products in the high-high quadrant, called stars, typically require considerable cash to finance their rapid growth—often in excess of the revenues the product generates. Key sources of this cash are other products, called cash cows, which occupy the lower-left-hand quadrant; although their market isn't growing at nearly the rate of the stars, these products occupy a high-share leadership position that requires less investment and produces positive profits and cash flows. Question mark products in the upper-right-hand quadrant (low market share in a high-growth-rate industry) typically lack consumer support, have unclear differential advantages, and require a lot of cash to hold share. Dog products in the low growth/low share lower-right-hand quadrant are unable to attract customers and lag the competition in sales, image, and operating costs.

The location of a product in the growth-share matrix helps devise strategies relative to other products in a portfolio depicted on the matrix. For example, as a star, Merton's tax accounting MM system was selected to spearhead other professional accounting systems in the MM line. Merton's cash cow products, including its mature line of chip circuits manufactured in the industrial division, would help to finance this effort.

PORTER'S COMPETITIVE ANALYSIS MODEL

A third planning model Moore used to implement SWOT analyses was Michael Porter's competitive analysis model,[1] which is based on an assessment of five competitive factors: (1) the threat of new entrants, (2) the bargaining power of suppliers, (3) the bargaining power of buyers, (4) the threat of substitute products, and (5) rivalry among existing firms.

- **Threat of new entrants:** A good entry market for MM systems would be difficult for competitors other than Merton to enter, for a variety of reasons. For example, MM's strong brand identity, product differences, or cost advantages might deter competitors. Other deterrents could include excessive capital requirements or government policies making entry difficult.

- **Bargaining power of suppliers:** A market entry opportunity should be avoided in situations where suppliers of parts and components for MM systems are so powerful that they could raise prices or reduce quality at will. Determinants of this kind of power include size and concentration of suppliers, the importance of high volume to the supplier, the presence of substitutes for suppliers' products, and the degree of competition among suppliers.

- **Bargaining power of buyers:** Buyers have the potential ability to force MM system prices down, bargain for higher quality or more services, and play competitors off against each other. The likelihood that they will is determined by such considerations as their concentration, the volume of their purchases, the cost to them of switching from Merton to other providers, substitutes for MM systems, the strength of MM's brand identity, and buyer access to information about Merton and its competitors.

---

1 Michael E. Porter, *Competitive Advantage* (New York: The Free Press, 1985), Chapter 1.

- **Threat of substitute products:** How likely would a substitute product in an entry market be to wipe out Merton's strong entry position? Determinants include the technological complexity of the original product, the price and performance superiority of the substitute, and the propensity of buyers to switch to the substitute.

- **Rivalry among existing products:** A high incidence of price competition, advertising battles, new product introductions, and excessive customer service are evidence of a hypercompetitive environment that might undercut entry and growth efforts. Rivalry determinants include product differences, brand identities, and concentration among rival firms.

• *STATEMENTS OF STRATEGIC INTENT AND OBJECTIVES*

The SWOT analysis conducted in step two of the strategic planning process should provide information needed to prepare these statements.

Concerning a marketing strategy for entering, or growing in, one or more markets, the four major options—discussed in more detail in Chapter 3 and summarized in the **product/market opportunity matrix** (Figure 6-6), are each appropriate for specified product/market situations:

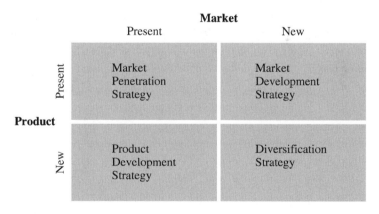

Market

	Present	New
Product Present	Market Penetration Strategy	Market Development Strategy
New	Product Development Strategy	Diversification Strategy

Figure 6–6. Product/market opportunity matrix.

- A **market penetration strategy**—marketing existing products more aggressively in existing markets—is appropriate when the market for a product is growing, or not quite saturated. More aggressive selling of MM systems to members of Merton's tax accountant target market would be an example. Typically, a penetration strategy brings in revenues and profits by attracting nonusers and competitors' customers and raising the usage rate among current customers.

- A **market development strategy,** applicable when a firm seeks to achieve greater sales of present products from new markets, focuses on new geographic or customer segments.

- A **product development strategy,** effective when a firm has a core of strong brands and a sizeable customer following, involves developing new products to attract members of existing markets—for example, new MM courses to meet the training and development needs among members of Merton's accounting and law target markets.

- A **diversification strategy** involves introducing new products into new markets, and is appropriate when more opportunities for growth exist outside the firm's present markets.

Two of these growth strategies—market penetration and product development—essentially involve concentration of marketing efforts in a small number of markets. The other two—market development and diversification—essentially involve diversification into a number of markets.

As indicated in Table 6-1, data from a SWOT analysis can identify which of the two strategies is appropriate to a given target-market situation. Thus, a concentration strategy would be indicated in situations where the following conditions existed in a prospective entry market: high and stable growth rates, rapid responses to marketing efforts, a strong lead over the competition, the expensive need to tailor the product and the promotion campaign to the needs of the market, and program requirements that mandate extensive interaction with clients and intermediaries.

Table 6–1. Factors Affecting the Choice Between Concentration and Diversification Strategies

Factor	Diversification	Concentration
Market growth rate	Low	High
Sales stability	Low	High
Sales response function	Decreasing	Increasing
Competitive lead time	Short	Long
Spillover effects	High	Low
Need for product adaptation	Low	High
Need for communication adaptation	Low	High
Economies of scale in distribution	Low	High
Extent of constraints	Low	High
Program control requirements	Low	High

Sources: Igal Ayal and Jehiel Zif, "Marketing Expansion Strategies in Multinational Marketing," *Journal of Marketing*, Vol. 43, Spring 1979, p. 89. Reprinted from *Journal of Marketing*, published by the American Marketing Association.

On the other hand, in target-market situations where product and promotion campaigns can be standardized for all markets, where demand and competitive conditions are similar, a diversification strategy would probably be indicated.

• *PREPARE A FORMAL MARKETING PLAN*

Key components of this plan, as discussed in Chapter 3, include a situation analysis, objectives and goals, long-term strategies and short-term tactics for bringing together target markets and marketing mixes, an implementation timetable, cost and profit estimates, provision for control, and contingency plans if needed. An important part of this formal marketing plan is provision for a loop between the situation analysis and implementation stages to ensure that decisions are made on the basis of current information. For example, if the control process shows that a particular price or promotional appeal isn't achieving desired results in targeted markets, this information will be incorporated into subsequent SWOT analyses through the marketing information system (discussed in Chapter 7).

THE CONTROL SYSTEM KEEPS PLANS ON TRACK

Having considered organizational and planning systems for Merton's MM systems division, Moore next turned her attention to the control system within the total marketing system.

Control, broadly defined, means making something happen the way it was planned to happen. It requires a clear understanding of the expected results of a particular action (for example, a price change designed to increase sales by 10 percent), a way to measure the extent to which these expected results materialize, and alternatives for corrective action. An effective control system monitors the entire spectrum of environmental variables, including customers, competitors, channel participants, and both controllables (for example, prices, products, promotions) and uncontrollables (for example, political and economic forces). These variables are monitored over both the short (one year or less) and the long term (over one year).

In an SBU like Merton's MM systems division, with operational capability to make MM systems, and strategic capability to market these systems, both operational and strategic control systems would be in place, working to ensure that activities were synergistically coordinated to achieve company and customer objectives.

Operational control involves functions like production control, quality control, and inventory control. Strategic control focuses on monitoring and evaluating the steps of the SMP process, from environmental analysis through strategy implementation. The relationship between operational and strategic control is shown in Figure 6-7.

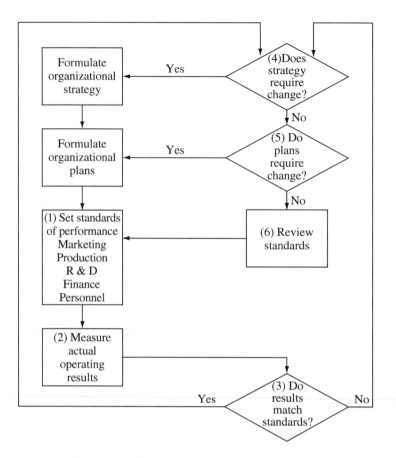

Figure 6-7. Operational/strategic control matrix.

Because the control process encompasses and helps to integrate all the firm's operational and strategic activities, it is typically handled at the headquarters level, although largely autonomous SBU subsidiaries like the MM systems division make inputs into the process. For example, Moore would be responsible for developing, as part of the overall strategic plan, budgets that would anticipate (1) revenues from MM global sales; (2) all costs—production, physical distribution, marketing, and the like—anticipated in generating these sales; and (3) the net profit difference between these figures. The figures in this budget, along with other figures defining strategic performance (for example, sales quotas and net profit per average sale) become standards against which to measure performance.

However, just as Moore's budget encompasses other budgets—for individual customer groups, territories, even individual salespeople—hers must be reconciled with all of Merton's other divisional and group budgets, and appropriate tradeoffs must be made at headquarters level.

Regardless of what kind of control system is being installed, it will probably be made up of the three steps depicted in Figure 6-7, which are designed to measure performance, compare performance with standards, and take corrective action when performance doesn't meet standards.

To illustrate, assume that Moore's strategic plan envisions that use of a particular distribution channel to reach the business/professional market in France will produce so many dollars in sales, at a cost of so many dollars. These "so many dollar" figures become standards against which to measure and assess the actual performance of this distribution channel (steps 1 and 2). If figures come in on target, nothing is done; no control is necessary (step 3). If costs are higher, and sales lower, than planned, some kind of corrective action will be built into the next plan; such controls might include changing the channel, providing incentives for better channel performance, or, perhaps, lowering expectations to more realistic standards (steps 4, 5, and 6). Control will also come into play if channel performance exceeds expectations and costs are lower, and sales higher, than anticipated. Particularly in global markets, this result might be a good reason to try this distribution channel in other areas.

INTERNATIONAL PERSPECTIVE

For firms seeking to enter and grow in international markets, marketing systems used to organize, plan, implement, inform, and control strategic marketing processes differ from those used in domestic markets based on differences in the nature and needs of these international markets.

INTERNATIONAL ORGANIZATIONAL STRUCTURES

Among firms committed to global marketing programs, the nature and shape of organizational structures and reporting systems change over time to reflect a company's increased involvement in foreign activities. Generally, they evolve from integrated to separated international structures and systems based on products, areas, functions, or combinations of these dimensions.

Figure 6-8 shows how these changes might occur over time as a firm evolves through domestic, international, and multinational stages to achieve global status. The firm begins this evolution with a simple export department, perhaps managed by a single individual, responsible for processing orders from abroad through a distributor who takes title to the merchandise and handles all export details. Because title changes hands in home-country currency, the seller has little concern for things like cultural differences, currency valuations, tax and legal considerations, and promotion, price, and distribution strategies. This was the situation when Lora Moore began to develop global markets for products in the MM systems division.

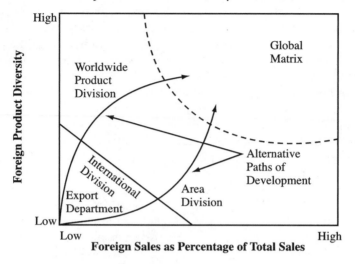

Figure 6–8. Evolution of international organizational structures.

Moore's first initiative was to move the MM systems division to the next organizational level—an international division that centralized international expertise, information flows, authority over international activities, and other functions associated with global operations such as marketing research, sales, export documentation, and foreign government relations. Manufacturing and related functions remained in domestic divisions to achieve economies of scale.

Figure 6-9, a simplified version of the international division structure, suggests a major problem associated with this form: dependence on domestic divisions for needed product, personnel, technology, and other resources. To the extent that domestic division managers are assessed on domestic performance, they may have an incentive to withhold resources from international divisions.

PRODUCT, AREA, AND MATRIX STRUCTURES

An integrated international structure, while characteristic of firms committed to proactive development of a global market presence, does not necessarily suit the needs of firms that have achieved this presence. Typically, when a firm's international market approaches, or achieves, parity with its domestic market in sales and profits, the functions of the international department will be absorbed into domestic divisions of the firm. Now, with status equal to domestic divisions, and equal access to company resources and senior decision makers, the absorbed division will presumably be able

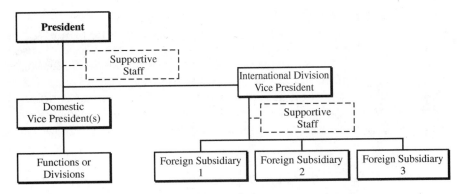

Figure 6–9. The international division structure.

to plan for and respond to market threats and opportunities more efficiently and effectively. Examples include product, area, and matrix structures.

• *PRODUCT STRUCTURE*

The product structure, which is most used by multinational firms like Motorola that market highly diverse product groups, gives worldwide responsibility to SBUs for marketing specific product lines.

Moore envisioned this structure for Merton once its major product lines had achieved a substantial presence in international markets. As shown in Figure 6-10, this structure would create business teams with a global strategic focus for each of these product lines, with status equal to domestic market business teams. The central pool of specialized expertise characterizing the international division would now be fragmented among the divisions, placing a premium on managers with strong international experience. Also emphasized would be coordinating mechanisms to provide expertise in such areas as marketing research and international law and to settle resource allocation problems among the product divisions.

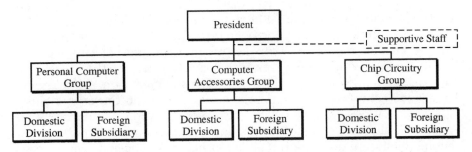

Figure 6–10. The international product structure.

• *AREA STRUCTURE*

The area structure, illustrated in Figure 6-11, organizes the firm in terms of geographic areas served. This structure, the second most frequently used worldwide, characterizes large European multinationals like Nestlé that have large foreign operations not dominated by a single area. It is also used where market conditions affecting product acceptance and operating conditions vary widely. As with product structures, central staffs are responsible for providing coordination support for worldwide planning, implementation, and control activities.

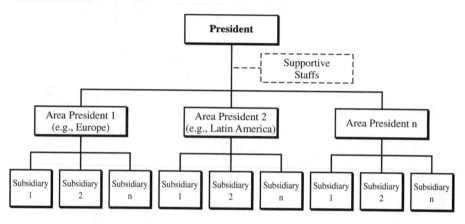

Figure 6–11. The international area structure.

• *MATRIX STRUCTURE*

The matrix organizational structure addresses problems implicit in integrated or separated structures by combining elements of both. For example, as illustrated in Figure 6-12, Merton's three major product divisions intersect with area divisions to provide much closer coordination among country managers and business managers. Conceivably, a three-dimensional matrix structure would include functional managers (for example, marketing, manufacturing, and research) in this mix. The driving force within the matrix structure is the product manager, who builds a team with the other intersecting managers, exchanging information and resources and encouraging a strategic global focus. Competition among product, functional, and area managers to attract resources and build teams presumably creates more productive, creative responses to marketplace threats and opportunities.

This very competition, however, is cited as a drawback to the matrix structure, often resulting in unproductive conflict and confusion. Another drawback is the complexity of the matrix model, which can cause problems in reporting relationships that can actually lower the company's reaction time. Among the alternatives for addressing these problems are rotating managers among the groups and reporting relationships with line and staff oversight groups.

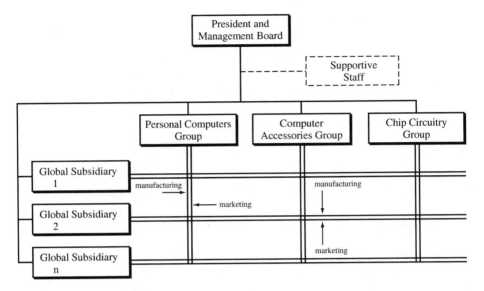

Figure 6–12. The international matrix structure.

INTERNATIONAL PLANNING SYSTEMS

Once product lines comprising Merton's MM systems division reached stages of sales maturity and decline, Moore recognized that future prospects for profitable growth could best be achieved through planned growth in the international marketplace. Her basic models for formulating these strategic plans, incorporated into the divisional planning system, were the same as those used in the domestic market, with some changes to reflect global market realities.

For example, SWOT analyses matching divisional strengths and weaknesses to global market opportunities and threats focused on market conditions in prospective global host countries, such as competitive, cultural, logistical, and political climates that Merton's marketing resources would have to address. These analyses also examined Merton's strengths and weaknesses (for example, sales personnel familiar with foreign culture and language) in relating to these conditions.

Similarly, criteria plugged into the GE strategic planning grid reflected global realities. For example, criteria for industry attractiveness included things like the need for product and communication adaptation and distribution facilities, as well as cultural, political, and environmental constraints marketing initiatives could face. A country or region with favorable scores in these criteria areas would score "high" on the "market attractiveness" dimension of the grid.

Criteria used to assess Merton's resources for entering attractive markets included financial resources (capital availability, ability to transfer funds);

product resources (quality, ability to accept adaptations, transport practicality, production capacity, monopolistic characteristics); price competitiveness (ability to profitably price product under competition); human resources (knowledge of foreign markets and marketing, foreign marketing skills, ability to recruit desired personnel); and environmental effects (ability to respond to adverse changes in such areas as distribution, currency valuation, demand changes, societal attitudes).

In modifying the BCG growth share matrix to international markets, Moore substituted countries for a single country along the "relative market share" axis. For example, in Figure 6-13, company A is seen to be a leader in five of the countries in which it markets its products, with cash cows in the United States and Canada and stars in Great Britain, France, and Germany. Only its Spanish affiliate, a question mark, has not achieved leader status.

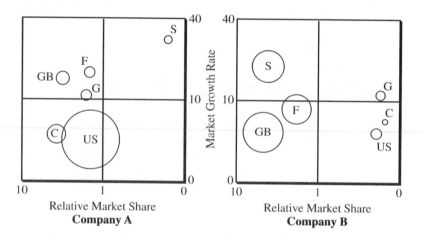

Figure 6–13. International growth-share grid.

At the same time, Company B, A's main competitor, although not a threat in A's major U.S. market, has a commanding lead in three fast-growing markets, Great Britain, Spain, and France. Comparing the firm's portfolio with those of competitors suggests strategies to counter competitive initiatives, as illustrated in Global Focus 6-1, which shows how the Whirlpool Company used global portfolio analyses to position itself in its quest for global status. In addition to helping Moore identify global territories where star products would most likely succeed, this matrix also indicated where question mark and dog products in the domestic market might fare better in foreign markets.

GLOBAL FOCUS 6-1

Whirlpool Succeeds Abroad

Holding the top market position in North America, the number 3 position in Europe, and a leading presence in South America, Whirlpool Corporation is, according to a market analyst, "the best positioned appliance company for the 1990s." U.S. rival companies such as Maytag Corporation have struggled with global strategies, but Whirlpool is making its aggressive expansion work. By moving into Europe and developing nations, the firm aims to tap growth areas to complement its mature, slow-growth business in North America.

After acquiring the European appliance business of Philips Electronics NV, Whirlpool is posting higher profits and bigger market share in Europe, despite the recession and very slow recovery there. . . . In 1993, European shipments rose about 5 percent, even as the overall European appliance business was flat or declining. Further increases are likely over the next few years. Currently, Europe has a collection of 200 appliance brand names, many of them popular in just one country. Whirlpool's strategy is to stand out with strong pan-European brands. President of Whirlpool Europe NV, Hank Bowman, explains that "Research shows that trends, preferences and biases of consumers, country to country, are reducing as opposed to increasing." Although regional preferences will remain, the company sees a chance to profit from the move toward a less-fractured Europe.

When Whirlpool first entered Europe, it used a dual Philips/Whirlpool brand to introduce consumers to its flagship Whirlpool brand. It is now going it alone, silencing skeptics who thought Europeans would not buy the new American name. According to electronics analyst Andrew Haskins, "Philips had a strong brand name, and Whirlpool has been able to build on that quite considerably."

Source: Robert L. Rose, "Whirlpool Is Expanding in Europe Despite the Slump," *The Wall Street Journal,* January 27, 1994, p. B4.

INTERNATIONAL CONTROL PROBLEMS AND PROCEDURES

Establishing standards and measurement tools—necessary control components—is difficult enough in the domestic market, and especially challenging in international markets. Environmental changes, which also change standards, occur at different rates in different countries, and communication problems arise from differences in language and customs and the greater distance between top management and foreign subsidiaries.

To measure performance continuously, Moore incorporated into Merton's Marketing Information System—discussed in the next chapter— standards reflecting conditions in individual countries against which to compare this performance. She also incorporated the means to effectively analyze and distribute emerging information to appropriate decision makers.

CHAPTER PERSPECTIVE

Properly designed and integrated, the four major systems comprising the marketing system generate synergistic output much greater than the sum of their individual components. The organizational system provides a framework for efficient, effective, coordinated activities; the planning system provides a means for generating and implementing strategic marketing plans that achieve mission-related objectives; and the control system provides a means to ensure that proper action is taken when these objectives aren't achieved. The marketing information system, discussed in the next chapter, provides a means of gathering, processing, and disseminating the right information to the right people at the right time in the right form.

KNOW THE CONCEPTS
TERMS FOR STUDY

Budgets
Cash cows
Concentration strategy
Control system
Diversification strategy
Dogs
Export department
Green light opportunity
Growth share matrix
Information system
International division
Market development strategy
Matrix structures
Organizational system

Penetration strategy
Planning system
Product development strategy
Product/market opportunity matrix
Product organizational structure
Question marks
Red light opportunity
Stars
Strategic business unit (SBU)
Strategic planning grid
SWOT analysis
Synergy
Yellow light opportunity

MATCHUP EXERCISES

1. Match the statement in the first column with the section of the marketing plan where it would most likely appear, which is listed in the second column.

1. Initially, distribution will be through agents and brokers in the host country.

    a. strategies and tactics

2. At the end of the first quarter, any necessary changes will be made in the marketing mix elements to bring performance in line with planned expectations.

    b. objectives

3. Budgeted expectations are for a 10 percent return on investment at the end of year 2.

    c. provision for control

4. The promotion campaign will focus, initially, on generating distribution through a "pull" strategy of generating demand among end-users.

    d. marketing mix

2. Match the strategic option in the first column with the descriptor in the second column.

1. diversification

    a. high growth rates, strong competitive lead, unique product

2. concentration

    b. standardized marketing mixes, similar cross-cultural demand

3. product development

    c. greater sales of existing products from new markets

4. market development

    d. development of new products to attract members of existing markets

3. Match the organizational structure in the first column with the appropriate characteristic in the second column.

1. export department

    a. most frequently used, worldwide

2. international division

    b. centralizes internal expertise

3. strategic business unit

    c. has outside competitors, a distinct mission

4. area structure

    d. processes orders for host-country intermediaries who take title to products

5. matrix structure

e. brings together country, product, and functional specialists

QUESTIONS FOR REVIEW AND DISCUSSION

1. Explain how the adaptation of the marketing concept relates to the view of a modern organization as a total system.

2. Explain how the four systems comprising the marketing system work together to facilitate the strategic marketing planning process.

3. A salesman of telecommunications equipment is planning his daily presentations to prospective customers. Would this individual qualify as a system? Why?

4. Distinguish between a traditional line and staff organizational structure and the more fluid, flexible SBU organizational model that characterizes many modern consumer-oriented firms.

5. Speculate on the role of the marketing system in each of the following product/market situations, and explain which of the four flows would be most important in each situation:

   • Quaker Oats wants to increase sales for Gatorade, which it purchased from Stokely VanCamp. Presently, 85 percent of the purchases of the thirst quencher are made by heavy users, mostly in Sunbelt states during the summer months.

   • The Henry Orleib Brewing Company has three profitable years in a row, in spite of competition from the likes of Miller and Budweiser beer in a field that has dwindled from 125 breweries to fewer than 40 in 25 years. The Philadelphia brewer advertises its beer as "more full-bodied . . . maltier . . . ."

6. What is the significance of each letter in the SWOT acronym in terms of Merton's search for the most worthwhile global entry market?

7. Discuss similarities and differences between the GE strategic planning grid and the BCG growth share matrix. Which would be most appropriate for a multinational or global firm seeking to expand its global reach?

8. What is the difference between operational and strategic control, and how are they related?

ANSWERS

MATCHUP EXERCISES

1. 1d, 2c, 3b, 4d

2. 1a, 2b, 3d, 4c

3. 1d, 2a, 3c, 4b, 5e

QUESTIONS FOR REVIEW AND DISCUSSION

1. The marketing concept is based on the notion that profits result when a firm integrates functions to identify and satisfy the needs of target markets more efficiently and effectively than its competitors. The total systems concept is based on the notion that the marketing concept works most efficiently and effectively to identify target markets and develop marketing mixes to satisfy these markets through the synergistic interaction of system components for organizing, planning, controlling, and informing the marketing effort.

2. (1) The organizational system organizes resources so that motivated, specialized people work together effectively to create and carry out marketing plans; (2) the planning system provides the wherewithal to formulate strategic marketing plans that match company strengths with marketplace opportunities to achieve mission-related objectives; (3) the control system provides standards and protocols for comparing actual with planned performance, and taking necessary steps when they deviate excessively; and (4) the marketing information system generates and distributes decision information that fuels all the elements of the strategic planning process.

3. Yes. Input into the system would include the information the salesman absorbs from such sources as past call reports, sales analysis figures, and customer complaints. Flows would be the two-way communication between the salesman and his customers and prospects, based largely on his analysis of information received and the plan he devised for relating his products to his prospects' needs. Output would be the sales and profits generated, and new information cycled back into the system, which would help him plan next month's calls.

4. The traditional line and staff structure can be envisioned as a single, centralized structure, with a number of layers of authority (middle managers, supervisors, and the like) between the uppermost layer and the layer closest to customers. Clearly defined lines of authority mean that each individual knows his or her responsibilities and to whom he or she reports. Tasks are specialized in terms of what each individual does best, and communication routes are relatively fixed. The SBU organizational model, on the other hand, can be envisioned as many smaller structures, each organized around a single product, business, or group of related products. Managers atop each of these structures, with operational and strategic responsibilities, are much closer to the market, and individual authority and responsibilities, along with communication flows, are much less formally defined. People are likely to be involved

in many different activities, often with members of other SBUs. As compared to the more traditional structures, SBUs can frequently respond faster to marketplace problems and opportunities and reform or regroup to address them.

5. Following are possible market system roles and dominant flows in each product/market situation:

- Increasing Gatorade sales: Marketing system roles would probably entail setting up and staffing an organization to market the new product (organizational system); developing profiles of other target market groups, in addition to the heavy-user Sunbelt group (marketing information system); developing marketing plans to profitably penetrate these new target markets (marketing planning system); and monitoring, measuring, and, if needed, modifying plans when actual performance deviates from expectations (control system). Flow emphasized would probably be market information feedback to identify and define new target markets and communication-with-market flow to sell Gatorade in these markets.

- Orleib Brewing Company thrives: Orleib's profitability, which seems to derive from effective positioning and promotion in a highly competitive, dwindling market, suggests an effective marketing information system to identify and define target market needs and competitive initiatives, an effective marketing planning system to convey its promotional message persuasively, and an effective control system to keep the plan on track. Flows emphasized would probably be market information feedback to generate information on changing market needs and products and services to keep delivering its popular product.

6. The letters in the SWOT acronym imply that a firm is matching its Strengths and Weaknesses against Opportunities and Threats in the marketplace, by way of evolving a strategic plan that will effectively utilize company strengths to exploit opportunities and counter threats. In Merton's case, an opportunity would be a global entry market most receptive in terms of such considerations as the nature and needs of professionals comprising target markets, a general lack of competitive activity, transportation and communication networks to distribute MM systems, the economic wherewithal to purchase MM systems, and legal, political, and cultural values (language, attitudes toward modern devices, and so on) similar to those in the domestic market.

7. The GE strategic planning grid and the BCG growth share matrix are similar in that each is designed to help formulate product/market strategies that best match company strengths and weaknesses against threats and opportunities in prospective foreign markets. The significant differ-

ence between these two grids derives from the fact that the GE grid makes these matches on a product-by-product basis in terms of the attractiveness of a prospective market, and the firm's resources for penetrating this market, while the BCG matrix makes these matches in the context of an entire product portfolio, with cash cows, stars, question marks, and dogs all identified by their locations on axes that depict the growth rate of a market and the relative market share of each product. For a global or multinational firm intent on expanding market reach, the BCG matrix would probably be most appropriate in that it helps to define strategies for individual products appropriate to the sweep of products and territories encompassed by the firm's marketing programs. For example, a green light "Go" strategy indicated by a GE grid analysis of market attractiveness and company strengths for an individual product might be a "No Go" strategy when viewed in the context of other products in the firm's portfolio in that entry market.

8. Operational control focuses on operations within the firm concerned with making products for markets, such as production, quality control, finance, research and development, and inventory management; strategic control focuses on strategic plans implemented outside the firm designed to bring together product offerings and target markets. The important role of the control function, in addition to ensuring that performance in operational and strategic areas meets benchmark standards, is to ensure that both areas work together efficiently and economically and that behaviors in different parts of the organization are compatible and support common goals. For example, effective controls will help ensure that production, quality control, and inventory management controls will work with strategic controls to help the ultimate customer get the right product at the right price and place.

7
MARKETING INFORMATION SYSTEMS AND MARKETING RESEARCH

OVERVIEW

In Chapter 6 we examined three of the systems that facilitate the preparation, implementation, and control of strategic marketing plans. Included were the organizational system, the planning system, and the control system, all interacting synergistically to drive the marketing system. In this and the next chapter, we examine the marketing information system and the marketing research process, which combine to fuel the other systems by collecting, recording, analyzing, and distributing information about marketing opportunities, problems, and processes.

MARKETING INFORMATION SYSTEM FUELS OTHER SYSTEMS

A marketing information system (MIS) is an integrated system of data, statistical analysis, modeling, and display formats, relying on computer hardware and software technology, that gathers, sorts, evaluates, stores, and distributes timely and accurate information for use by marketing decision makers to improve planning, organization, implementation, and control.

For Merton's new MM systems division, Moore recognized the critical importance of marketing information in building marketing strategies. She also recognized problems to be faced in generating this information in markets separated by time, space, and cultural and technological differences.

To address these needs and problems, she envisioned an MIS that would encompass the elements depicted in Figure 7-1. This system would work as follows to synthesize information from many sources and convert it into usable form to help her, and other managers involved in strategic planning, to make faster, smarter decisions.

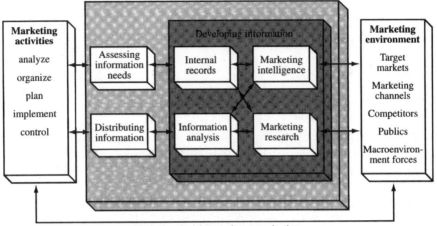

Figure 7–1. A marketing information system.

- From the internal records section, she could access information developed internally, including records of sales, orders, costs, cash flows, production schedules, shipments, inventories, reseller reactions, competitive activities, and customer needs.

- From the marketing intelligence section, she could access information from many sources in the marketing environment, including company personnel, suppliers, resellers, customers, and even competitors. Much of this information would be gathered from online databases or such suppliers as the A.C. Nielsen Company, which sells data on brand shares and retail sales worldwide.

- From the marketing research section, Moore could access information generated through formal and informal studies of specific situations to supplement information from the internal records and marketing intelligence sections. For example, she might want to test pricing or promotion strategies for MM systems in areas where such information wasn't otherwise available.

Information from these sections would then be pulled together in the information analysis section of the MIS and presented to Moore in a form that would facilitate activities—from analysis to control—required of the strategic planning process.

Illustrative of the systematic, continuous nature of these MIS processes is **environmental scanning,** which receives and processes continuous information on trends and developments (for example, changing market needs or competitive environments) that help marketers develop long-term policies, broad strategies, action plans, operating programs, and budgets.

Market Focus 7-1 describes computerized information systems used by two companies to scan environments by way of generating intelligence that aids strategic and tactical decision making and planning.

MARKET FOCUS 7-1

The Global Spyglass

Both Corning and Digital Equipment Corporation are strong believers in global computer networks for gathering and disseminating competitive intelligence.

Corning started its global system, called the Business Information Exchange Network, with a pilot program in early 1989. One key feature is a news search service that lets users inform the system of topics that interest them. The system then automatically clips articles and places them in the user's electronic mailbox.

Digital Equipment launched its Competitive Information System (CIS) in 1984. Initially, it was mainly used to collect and distribute data on domestic competitors, but after four years, it became truly global. CIS contains product descriptions; announcements; internal and external competitive analyses; company strategies, policies, and overviews; market analyses; and a direct feed from an external news wire. "Our data serves both strategic and tactical needs," explains Laura J. B. Hunt, Digital's manager of information access services. Digital's competitive analysts use data from CIS for strategic decision making and planning; its sales representatives use CIS data to formulate sales tactics. The system now has more than 10,000 registered employee users and generates more than 100,000 log-ins worldwide.

Source: Kate Bertrand, "The Global Spyglass," *Annual Editions: International Business,* F. Maidment, Ed. (Guilford, CT: 1992), pp. 90–92.

BUILDING THE MIS DATABASE

Moore had no illusions as to how difficult it would be to build an MIS for the MM systems division. Too much information, too little information, incomplete information, dated information, information served up in the wrong form, and information that cost more than it was worth—all were problems she would face.

To address these problems, and to help ensure the success of the MM systems division's MIS in fulfilling company needs, her needs, and the needs of other Merton managers, Moore first designed and distributed a questionnaire covering the following points: decisions each manager regularly made; information needed to make these decisions; information that each regularly received; special studies each periodically requested; information each would like to have but didn't get; frequency requirements for each type of information (daily, weekly, monthly, and the like); publications or trade reports each would like to receive on a regular basis; specific topics each would like to be kept informed of; types of data analysis each would like made available.

Responses were first edited to eliminate duplicate, irrelevant, or overly expensive information. Information to be used was then integrated into a database to effectively serve the needs of each manager, the division, and the overall organization. In general, information for each manager pertained to the planning, organizing, implementing, and controlling activities that characterized the marketing system as a whole. The sales manager, for example, needed information to plan the most efficient allocation of resources—human and otherwise—to enhance the profitability of Merton's MM systems division sales force. To accomplish this, his primary need was for information pinpointing the relative profitability of products, territories, target markets, and salespeople. With this information, he could direct and control the division salesforce to bring together profitable products and high-potential customers in high-potential territories.

Similarly, the advertising manager received information that would help plan, implement, and control productive promotion campaigns to support the salesforce; the various product managers received information that would help them plan, organize, implement, and control strategies for their product groups; and the marketing manager received information that would help her recognize worthwhile marketplace opportunities, develop productive marketing programs, and monitor the performance of other managers in devising and carrying out these programs.

WHAT MARKETING RESEARCH DOES

Marketing research (MR) is the systematic collection, recording, analysis, and distribution of data and information about marketing problems and opportunities. This information applies to each step of the SMP process: identifying environmental threats and opportunities, comparing the potentials of diverse markets, selecting target markets, establishing realistic missions and goals, formulating and implementing goal-oriented strategic plans, and controlling marketing performance.

WHO DOES MARKETING RESEARCH?

Every firm that markets things needs MR information. Large firms have their own MR departments, using outside firms for special tasks or studies. Smaller firms are more likely to rely on outside MR firms. In 1998, the 50 largest MR firms in the United States generated revenues of more than $4 billion, 30 percent from research in foreign markets.

PRODUCT/MARKET MR APPLICATIONS

A recent survey by the American Marketing Association indicates that the following percentages of U.S. firms conduct, or commission, the following research studies:

- **Sales and market research:** measurement of market potentials (97 percent); market share analysis (97 percent); determination of market characteristics (97 percent); sales analysis (92 percent); sales quotas and territories (80 percent); distribution channels (76 percent).

- **Business economics:** short-range forecasting (up to one year) (89 percent); long-range forecasting (over one year) (87 percent); studies of business trends (87 percent); pricing studies (83 percent).

- **Product research:** competitive product studies (87 percent); testing of existing products (80 percent); new product acceptance and potential (76 percent).

- **Advertising research:** studies of ad effectiveness (76 percent); media research (68 percent).

Moore might easily commission research studies in all these areas in implementing a strategic plan. For example, she might begin with a marketing potential study to identify customer groups most likely to respond favorably to a new MM systems offering. Then, a new product acceptance study might be undertaken to more precisely define the response of targeted groups to this offering in terms of how they would use it and what features they would expect. Pricing and distribution studies would also be conducted to make sure the offering was profitably priced and distributed through cost-efficient channels.

Sales forecast, sales territory, and sales quota MR studies would also be undertaken to provide information for allocating dollars and people to bring in the best return. Once profitable sales were generated in selected territories, sales analysis studies would help control the marketing effort by measuring the extent to which sales performance (revenues and profits generated in different territories by different salespeople) achieved budgeted expectations. Advertising effectiveness studies would provide feedback on how advertising appeals and media strategies were achieving goals.

MR APPLICATIONS DIFFER BY INDUSTRY AND ROLES

The extent to which MR studies are used, and for what purposes, differs within and among organizations. Within organizations, MR applications differ by management level and position. For example, Merton senior management would be more interested in long-range forecasts and information summarizing sales and profitability findings across many products and territories, on which to base decisions for allocating resources to different divisions. Middle- and lower-echelon managers would be more interested in research information reflecting their positions (for example, territory, quota, and sales analysis for the sales manager and advertising effectiveness for the advertising manager).

Among companies, MR scope and emphasis differs by markets served and offerings made in these markets. Consumer-oriented firms place more stress on MR studies designed to identify and profile target markets and build attractive marketing mixes. Firms serving industrial markets will more likely stress MR studies concerning economic trends and developments and distribution, pricing, and selling activities.

These differences in emphasis are reflected in the size of marketing research budgets, which usually range from 0.01 to 3.5 percent of sales, with higher percentages in more competitive, consumer-oriented firms. Between one half and three quarters of this money is spent directly by the marketing research department, with the remainder being used to buy services from three categories of outside firms:

1. Syndicated-service research firms gather and sell consumer and trade information. For example, Nielsen Media Research reports on television audiences and Simmons reports on magazine audiences.

2. Custom marketing research firms carry out specific research projects. Examples would include feasibility studies leading to the creation of Merton's MM systems division.

3. Specialty-line marketing research firms provide specialized services to other marketing firms and company research departments. An example would be firms that conduct store audits or sell field interviewing services to other firms.

KEY MR CONSIDERATIONS: VALIDITY AND RELIABILITY

Depending largely on what they aim to accomplish in what kind of an environment and at what cost, MR studies are subject to a wide range of constraints that should be taken into account in planning research strategies. To understand these constraints requires an understanding of two key concepts related to any kind of research: validity and reliability.

Validity is the extent to which a research study measures what it is supposed to measure. For example, test market research occasionally shows a strong preference for a product, such as "new formula" Coca-Cola, that never materializes in the marketplace. When study findings don't accurately measure what they set out to measure, they are said to be invalid. When findings apply only to the population surveyed (for example, they love new formula Coke in Peoria, but nowhere else), they are said to have **internal validity.**

Reliability is the likelihood that research results can be repeated. Assume, for example, that the new formula Coca-Cola study indicated a strong preference for new formula Coke among residents of Peoria. To be reliable, the study should produce similar preference findings among groups in other cities who are similar in all pertinent respects to the Peoria population (matched populations). Note that it is possible for a study to be reliable (all samples surveyed indicate a preference for new formula Coke) without being valid (the findings don't really measure the preferences they set out to measure).

Validity and reliability are especially important to marketing managers because many MR studies entail considerable cost and risk and can create expensive problems if the information they yield leads to bad decisions. A wrong price, an unpopular product feature, a poorly conceived promotion campaign, an inefficient distribution channel—all can put a firm at a competitive disadvantage from which it may never recover.

KEY MR CONSTRAINTS: SUBJECTS, INSTRUMENTS, AND CONTROLS

To illustrate built-in constraints that limit marketing research validity and reliability, consider two research studies: one in the physical sciences, to measure the boiling point of water at various pressures, and the other a survey of prospective purchasers to measure the likelihood each will purchase an MM system at various prices.

- **Complex subjects:** In the boiling-point study, subjects being studied—water, heat, pressure—tend to be simple, stable, and predictable. With people, however, the researcher is dealing with complex, dynamic variables like intelligence, feelings, attitudes, and beliefs, which are impossible to define and measure precisely.

- **Crude instruments:** In the boiling-point study, finely calibrated instruments measure variables like temperature and pressure with high degrees of precision. The MM survey, on the other hand, must use crude measurement instruments—like questionnaire surveys— that carry a heavy baggage of ambiguities and biases.

- **Poor controls:** In the boiling-point study, experimental conditions—temperature, height, weight, and the like—can be precisely controlled. In the MM survey, conditions, like changing environments in which behavior is studied, are much too complex and diverse to control with exactitude.

- **Time constraints:** In the boiling-point study, there is usually sufficient time to ensure that study findings are valid and reliable. In marketing research studies, competitive pressures and pressures from a changing environment often result in sacrificing validity and reliability for speed.

THE MR PROCESS: FORMULATE, COMPILE, ANALYZE, AND RECOMMEND

Recognizing the critical importance of valid, reliable MR information to the success of Merton's strategic plans to market MM systems, as well as the imposing constraints on generating this information, Moore formulated a systematic protocol for conducting MR studies. This protocol, designed to optimize validity, reliability, efficiency, and economy in the MR process, encompassed seven steps:

1. Define the research problem and objectives.
2. Conduct a situation analysis.
3. Design the research plan.
4. Collect primary data.
5. Analyze data.
6. Make recommendations.
7. Implement recommendations.

We cover the first three of these steps in this chapter; the last four are covered in Chapter 8.

DEFINE RESEARCH PROBLEM AND OBJECTIVES

This was a collaborative effort among Moore, managers whose decisions would be influenced by research findings, representatives of an outside marketing research firm retained by Merton to conduct the study, and the marketing research manager for the MM systems division. Moore had a "big picture" understanding of problems to be addressed by research and information needed to address these problems. Other managers knew what decisions they would have to make and what information they would need to fit into this big picture.

In defining problems, researchers usually distinguish between causative (primary) problems and symptomatic (secondary) problems. For example, the fact that sales of MM systems were below expectations in a given territory might only be a symptom of other causative problems, such as competitive inroads or a decline in economic activity. A good way to begin a research study often is to list as many causative problems as possible; each then becomes a hypothesis to be tested or rejected during later stages of the research process. Once primary problems have been identified, research objectives that define types of research and research methodology required can be established.

Sometimes the objective lends itself to exploratory research—to gather **secondary information** that will further define the problem and suggest solutions. Sometimes it is **conclusive research**—to describe problems statistically or through experimental methods and infer solutions from these descriptions. Frequently, research objectives will change during the course of a study. For example, exploratory research might reveal all the researcher wants to know or suggest the need for additional conclusive research.

CONDUCT A SITUATION ANALYSIS

The main objective of this second step in the research process is to find reasonable explanations, or **hypotheses,** for unexpected events. This exploratory stage is less expensive and less disciplined than later, more conclusive stages of the research process, when hypotheses are evaluated and tested.

Secondary data have already been published or collected for purposes other than those of the researcher. Hence, their usefulness may be suspect and should be carefully assessed in terms of **relevance** to the current research project, **accuracy** in terms of validity and reliability, **timeliness,** and

impartiality. For example, a five-year-old article describing how a training program met the needs of tax accountants in the United States might fail in all criteria areas when applied to training needs in a foreign country.

SURVEYS OF KNOWLEDGEABLE PEOPLE

These informal surveys are often used to supplement secondary data searches during the exploratory research stage. They are usually restricted to executives and others in the company with an informed knowledge of how to achieve MR study objectives. Later, if this inside information isn't sufficient, the research study will seek information from outside sources. Since little was known about international markets among Merton's domestic personnel, "knowledgeable people" surveyed were primarily international contacts familiar with prospective target markets.

REALISTIC OBJECTIVES EMERGE

Exploratory findings from secondary sources and knowledgeable people helped produce a set of research objectives that were relevant, attainable, and specific to the needs of the strategic plan and managers responsible for making the plan work.

These objectives were calculated to answer these questions:

- In terms of cultural, economic, technological, competitive, and political environments, which country would be most receptive to initial entry with MM systems?

- In terms of income level, educational needs, and work activities, which market segment(s) in this country's business/professional segment would be most receptive to the MM offering?

- How would marketing mix aspects of the MM offering (product features, price, distribution, and promotion) have to be modified to ensure a favorable, profitable market entry?

Note that these objectives are prioritized to generate data in a cost-effective manner. For example, if sufficient demand doesn't exist in a foreign market for MM systems, then research addressing the next two objectives is canceled.

DESIGN A RESEARCH PLAN

Frequently, the exploratory phase of the research process is sufficient for the decision maker's purposes. For example, the perceived problem is discovered not to be a problem, or a solution to an actual problem emerges. Alternately, exploratory research might only serve to define the problem more precisely or suggest diverse solutions from which to select a single solution. For example, exploratory research might suggest a number of possible global markets for MM systems, but narrowing them down to the most productive entry market, and further defining target segments and building marketing mixes attractive to these segments, would require conclusive MR studies. Conclusive research, including approaches and techniques for generating primary data, is discussed next.

INTERNATIONAL PERSPECTIVE

In formulating strategic plans to enter and grow MM systems in foreign markets, Moore recognized that she would face problems in generating and processing valid, reliable information considerably different from problems faced in Merton's domestic market. For example, Merton's global MIS and MR programs would have to deal with:

- **Different environments,** including cultures, languages, political systems, societal structures, economies, and infrastructures.

- **Different parameters,** such as currencies, modes of transportation and documentation, port facilities, and business rules and regulations.

- **Different competitors,** including, in addition to direct brand competition that characterized Merton's domestic market, many forms of indirect competition.

Another problem in conducting international MR studies is a general dearth of statistical summary data, especially in less-developed countries with primitive data-gathering and research services. Even in countries that do provide productive data sources, the problem of data comparability often arises. Censuses, output figures, trade statistics, and base-year calculations are published for different periods in different countries. There are also numerous definitional differences among countries. For example, in Germany, consumer expenditures are estimated largely on the basis of tax receipts; in the United Kingdom, they are estimated on the basis of a combination of tax receipts, household surveys, and production sources. Standard age categories for classifying statistical data covering consumer purchases are defined as follows in four different countries:

Venezuela	Germany	Spain	Italy
10–14	14–19	15–24	13–20
15–24	20–29	25–34	21–25
25–34	30–39	35–44	26–35

Suspect data sources are another problem in researching global markets. Countries are often motivated to distort data—for example, to attract investment by exaggerating economic growth—and even without such ulterior motives, data availability and collection techniques are often primitive. As a result of these distorting factors, the margin of error for some international statistics can be as high as 25 percent.

HOW TO SET UP GLOBAL MIS AND MR PROCEDURES

Recognizing the problems Merton would face led Moore to the recognition that special care would be required to set up marketing information systems and marketing research procedures to scan and probe global markets. More specifically, she would need complete answers to these questions in building and implementing these systems and procedures.

WHAT INFORMATION WILL WE NEED?

In international markets, a firm's information needs generally derive from its research objectives, which depend primarily on whether it is engaged in exporting or importing activities.

• *INTERNATIONAL MR OBJECTIVES, EXPORTING*

The most frequent research objectives among exporting firms pertain to foreign market opportunity studies. Typically, these studies begin with a general, low-cost exploration in prospective foreign markets of market variables that will define target markets for the firm's offering. For example, Moore recognized that, to qualify as a market for MM systems, a country would need a certain number of professionals in various fields, earning an average minimum per-capita income. In Merton's case, such cursory studies reduced the number of markets considered for MM entry to a manageable number—eighteen.

Next, Merton's research effort focused on individual markets for further evaluation, applying a new set of qualifying criteria to prioritize each in terms of market size, growth rate, and economic/competitive/political constraints for marketing MM systems, as discussed in Chapter 5.

Once prospective markets had been identified and prioritized, research objectives shifted to define supply-demand patterns, dollar potential, and marketing mix offerings best calculated to realize this potential.

• *INTERNATIONAL MR OBJECTIVES, IMPORTING*

The most frequent market research objectives among firms engaged in importing activities involve identifying sources, or potential sources, of needed supplies or materials. As with the research approach to identifying export markets, objectives include acceptability standards against which markets are assessed, such as standards for reliability, quality, and delivery time. Source-country environment is also investigated, including such concerns as currency stability, source-country export rules, and transportation problems.

Table 7-1 categorizes areas covered in a marketing information system set up to help conduct research studies relating to these research objectives.

Table 7–2. Categories for a Global Marketing Intelligence System

Category	Coverage
I. Market Information	
1. Market Potential	Information indicating potential demand for products, including the status and prospects of existing company products in existing markets.
2. Consumer/customer attitudes and behavior	Information and attitudes, behavior, and needs of consumers and customers of existing and potential company products. Also included in this category are attitudes of investors toward a company's investment merit.
3. Channels of distribution	Availability, effectiveness, attitudes, and preferences of channel agents.
4. Communications media	Media availability, effectiveness, and cost.
5. Market sources	Availability, quality, and cost.
6. New products	Nontechnical information concerning new products for a company (this includes products that are already marketed by other companies).
II. Competitive Information	
7. Competitive business strategy and plans	Goals, objectives. Definition of business: the "design" and rationale of the company.

Category	Coverage
8. Competitive functional strategies, plans, and programs	Marketing: target markets, product, price, place, promotion. Strategy and plan: finance, manufacturing, R&D, and human resource strategy, plans, and programs.
9. Competitive operations	Detailed intelligence on competitor operations. Production, shipments, employee transfers, morale, etc.

III. Foreign Exchange

10. Balance of payments	Government reports.
11. Nominal and real interest rates	Expert estimation.
12. Inflation rate compared to weighted trading partner average	PPP theory.
13. Estimate of international competitiveness	Expert judgment.
14. Attractiveness of country currency and assets to global investors	Currency demand.
15. Government policy re: country competitiveness	Expert assessment.
16. Country monetary and fiscal policy	Expert assessment.
17. Spot and forward market activity	Market reports.
18. Expectations and opinions of analysts, traders, bankers, economists, business people	General assessment.

IV. Prescriptive Information

19. Foreign taxes	Information concerning decisions, intentions, and attitudes of foreign authorities regarding taxes upon earnings, dividends, and interest.

Category	Coverage
20. Other foreign prescriptions and laws	All information concerning local, regional, international authority guidelines, rulings, laws, decrees other than foreign exchange and tax matters affecting the operations, assets, or investments of a company.
21. Home-country prescriptions	Home-country incentives, controls, regulations, restraints, etc., affecting a company.
V. Resource Information	
22. Human resources	Availability of individuals and groups, employment candidates, sources, strikes, etc.
23. Money	Availability and cost of money for company uses.
24. Raw material	Availability and cost.
25. Acquisitions and mergers	Leads or other information concerning potential acquisitions, mergers, or joint ventures.
VI. General Conditions	
26. Economic factors	Macroeconomic information dealing with broad factors, such as capital movements, rates of growth, economic structure, and economic geography.
27. Social factors	Social structure of society, customs, attitudes, and preferences.
28. Political factors	"Investment climate" meaning of elections, political change.
29. Scientific technological factors	Major developments and trends.
30. Management and administrative practices	Management and administrative practices and procedures concerning such matters as employee compensation, report procedure.
31. Other information	Information not assignable to another category.

Source: Warren J. Keegan, *Global Marketing Management,* 5th ed. (Saddle River, NJ: Prentice Hall, 1989), p. 407.

WHO WILL COLLECT THE DATA?

Given the sheer amount of data and information the MM systems division would require to conduct research in the global marketplace and problems associated with this effort, Moore realized that assistance would be needed in addition to Merton's marketing research department and the research capabilities of its domestic advertising agency. Specifically, Merton would require the services of a marketing research agency—or agencies—with specialized knowledge of countries selected for possible entry.

There is no shortage of such firms in the foreign marketplace. For example, more than 500 marketing research agencies in 17 Western European countries offer services, databases, and bibliographies covering such aspects of international marketing as the business environment, population demographics, and economic forecasts.

HOW WILL THE GLOBAL MR EFFORT BE STRUCTURED?

Three options are available to firms in organizing the MIS/MR effort:

- A **centralized structure,** whereby the research design and focus are determined at headquarters and implemented on the local country level;

- A **decentralized approach,** whereby home-country headquarters establishes broad research policies and guidelines and then delegates further design and implementation to local countries;

- A **coordinated approach,** whereby an outside intermediary, such as a marketing research firm, brings headquarters and country operations together.

Centralizing the international research function is generally appropriate when research is intended to influence company policy and strategy, and markets are similar. When markets differ from country to country, firms generally move to a decentralized research format. In the process, they gain closer proximity to markets, the ability to respond more flexibly to challenges and opportunities, and the benefits of interaction among home- and host-country personnel. Global Focus 7-1 shows how the marketing research function at Hewlett-Packard integrates home- and host-country resources to achieve the benefits of centralization and decentralization.

GLOBAL FOCUS 7-1

How Hewlett-Packard Finds Market Opportunities

Hewlett-Packard (H-P), a $16-billion company that produces technical products for business and dominates the high-quality end of the hand calculator market, has organized its marketing information system/marketing research (MIS/MR) functions to benefit from both centralization and decentralization in its global operations.

The nerve center of MIS/MR at Hewlett-Packard is its Market Research & Information Center (MRIC), a shared resource whose library and staff of forty professionals H-P divisions may contract with at the cost of incremental expenses of projects they request. MRIC is divided into three groups, consisting of:

- The Market Information Center that provides background information on industries, markets, and competitors using, mainly, syndicated and secondary data sources.

- Decision Support Teams that provide research counseling to H-P divisions.

- Regional Satellite Groups located strategically throughout H-P's global market that support regional initiatives at the local level.

Supplemented by outside research suppliers of proven quality, MRIC follows a research protocol consisting of gathering information to identify market opportunities and stimulate creative solutions; testing proposals to assess decisions covering such variables as target market characteristics, price changes, product features, and advertising appeals; and tracking results to interpret causal behaviors and generate control data.

• WHAT SECONDARY DATA SOURCES ARE AVAILABLE FOR CONDUCTING GLOBAL RESEARCH?

In the United States, more than a dozen federal organizations actively collect information from around the world concerning problems and opportunities for importers and exporters. Much of this information abundance is inexpensive or free.

For most practical purposes, however, an enterprise like Merton's MM systems division, new to the challenges of the international marketplace, is best advised to begin its search for worthwhile global opportunities with the Commerce Department or the Small Business Administration (SBA), both of which integrate information from all sources and tailor it to the needs of individual small- to medium-sized firms in specific industries.

To illustrate, here are some of the sources that helped Moore formulate and implement Merton's marketing plan for finding and penetrating high-potential target markets for MM systems in international markets. These sources are sequenced as they were used, to (1) identify governmental information sources; (2) get specialized consulting services; (3) find worthwhile target markets, as well as worthwhile customers and distributors in these markets; and (4) promote MM systems to these customers and distributors.

• *IDENTIFYING INFORMATION SOURCES*

Commerce Department Hot Line (1-800-872-8723) runs through all federal export programs.

Commerce Department Trade Information Center is a "one-stop shop" for information on assistance from nineteen federal agencies. It provided Moore with helpful sources of export counseling, international marketing research, leads to distributors and customers abroad, schedules of overseas and domestic trade shows, and export financing and information on documentation and licensing requirements, in addition to state and local programs.

• *SPECIALIZED CONSULTATION SERVICES*

SBA Small Business Development Centers offer export counseling; there are more than 700 such centers.

Commerce Department Counseling, at sixty-eight district offices, provides small companies (under 100 employees) with comprehensive export advice, usually based on the personal experience of trade counselors.

Expert legal assistance network (202-778-3080), cosponsored by the Commerce Department, the SBA, and the Federal Bar Association, brings new exporters and trade attorneys together to discuss legal aspects of entering world markets.

• *FINDING WORTHWHILE TARGET MARKETS/ CUSTOMERS/DISTRIBUTORS*

Matchmaker Missions, co-sponsored by the Commerce Department and the SBA, enable first-time exporters in specific fields like electronics and medicine to attend dozens of prearranged meetings with potential customers abroad. Fees for attending firms like ELI range between $1200 and $2000 (The SBA may pick up $750).

Commercial News, a monthly catalog sent to more than 100,000 buyers in the international market, represents a fast, inexpensive way to generate leads and build a mailing list. Advertisements cost about $250 and are restricted to one product, a photograph, price, company name, address, and phone number.

Commerce Department agent/distributor service provides trade specialists who tap overseas contacts for distributors willing to sell exporter's products. The search costs $125 and can take two months to complete. An additional $100 buys reports on the sales history and credit standing of distributors.

Commerce Department Foreign Buyer Program brings in thousands of overseas buyers to domestic shows sponsored by major trade associations. Signing up is free.

Market Reports taps the Commerce Department trade data bank to detail foreign demand for specific goods. Updated monthly, this newsletter is available free or at a nominal charge at Commerce Department district offices and some 400 federal depository libraries. Subscription cost is $360 a year or $35 for any month.

• *PROMOTING PRODUCTS*

Catalog and Video Shows display a company's catalogs or video demos at "catalog shows" in U.S. consulates and embassies abroad. Shows are often geared to specific industries like marine equipment and consumer electronics. The Commerce Department advertises each show and passes names of interested parties on to exhibitors. Cost: between $100 and $300.

Foreign Trade Shows, sponsored by the Commerce Department, provide small exporting companies with an excellent opportunity to meet buyers and scan the competition. Fees for participating companies average $400, plus travel costs.

CHAPTER PERSPECTIVE

In this chapter, we examined marketing information systems and the marketing research process that work together to help formulate, implement, and control strategic marketing plans. MR applications and needs differ among industries and managerial echelons and can result in higher cost, waste, and misdirection when validity and reliability are sacrificed to poor planning and ineffective measurement tools. A productive research plan directs and sequences exploratory and conclusive research activities for efficiency and economy through the effective, selective use of secondary data sources, including government agencies and knowledgeable people.

KNOW THE CONCEPTS
TERMS FOR STUDY

Advertising research
Business economics
Causative problems
Conclusive research
Environmental scanning
Exporting research objectives
Government information
    sources
Importing research objectives
Internal validity
Marketing information system
Marketing research

MR constraints
Product research
Reliability
Research hypotheses
Research plan
Sales research
Secondary information
Small Business Administration
Surveys of knowledgeable people
Symptomatic problems
Validity

MATCHUP EXERCISES

1. Match the MIS information category in the first column with the appropriate information need in the second column.

1. broad strategic issues

2. foreign market assessment

3. marketing mix selection

a. What are comparative costs of alternative distribution channels?

b. Can we afford the customized product and promotion requirements of this prospective market?

c. To what extent do entry market demographics match those in our domestic market?

2. Match the section of an MIS listed in the first column with the information it would produce, listed in the second column. This information pertains to an environmental scan of two countries, Saudi Arabia and Egypt, that are customers for water purification systems manufactured by the firm doing the research.

1. marketing intelligence

a. Last year, sales of our systems were down by 20 percent in Egypt, while increasing by 11 percent in Saudi Arabia.

2. internal records

    b. Our major competitor increased its share of market by 30 percent in Saudi Arabia and 10 percent in Egypt.

3. information analysis

    c. In countries with a per-capita income of under $3000, price increases of 5 percent reduced sales of our units by 20 percent.

4. marketing research

    d. Our study showed that price sensitivity toward our products is approximately three times as great in Egypt as in Saudi Arabia.

3. Match the titles in the first column with the types of research information each would likely need to help arrive at a decision as to the desirability of entering the Russian market with a line of used medical equipment, which is listed in the second column.

1. president

    a. size and needs of prospective target markets

2. vice president, marketing

    b. sales potential by territory and customer group

3. marketing research manager

    c. how marketing mix elements will have to be adapted to Russian market

4. sales manager

    d. likely return on investment after first and second year in market

QUESTIONS FOR REVIEW AND DISCUSSION

1. Assume that you are a real estate agent selling residential properties in a highly competitive environment. List at least five specific types of information from your firm's MIS that would help you do a more efficient job, and describe an annual marketing research study you would commission.

2. Distinguish between validity and reliability. Give an example of how marketing research shortcomings might limit both in a marketing research study designed to forecast the results of a presidential election.

3. Distinguish between primary and secondary data. Explain how each might be used in selecting a good place to dine in a strange town, and give two reasons why each might prove to be invalid.

4. How might the following components of an MIS combine to produce a prediction that a price increase for MM systems in country B will not decrease sales, even though a similar increase decreased sales in the domestic market: internal records; marketing intelligence; marketing research; information analysis.

5. Two research studies, conducted by the National Industrial Conference Board (NICB) on the South American market, presented findings pertaining to (1) the relationship between changes in currency valuations and productivity, and (2) attitudes of South Americans regarding joining NAFTA. Why would the first study findings tend to be more valid and reliable than the second study findings?

6. List the seven steps of the marketing research process. Why are the first and sixth steps especially important?

7. Why might the following information be suspect in terms of criteria for the acceptability of secondary data?

According to an article in last June's edition of the Commerce Department magazine *Business America,* NAFTA has created unprecedented opportunities for investment in the growth of the Mexican economy. Studies by the Mexican Board of Trade all indicate that GNP will increase by at least 10 percent per year, most import/export trade barriers have been eliminated, and privatization has created welcoming political and economic climates.

8. Referring to the Mexican Board of Trade studies in question 7, how might the following secondary sources have been used: internal secondary sources, external secondary sources, surveys of knowledgeable people.

ANSWERS
MATCHUP EXERCISES

1. 1b, 2c, 3a
2. 1a, 2b, 3c, 4d
3. 1d, 2c, 3a, 4b

QUESTIONS FOR REVIEW AND DISCUSSION

1. Types of information provided by MIS databases that would help the real estate agent do a more effective job include: sales trends of residences in different price and age categories, numbers of new listings by geographic area, interest rate projections, competitors' share of market, and projections of new housing starts. An annual market research study that might be commissioned might develop a statistical profile correlating sales of homes in various age, price, and location categories with variables, such as disposable income or new housing starts, presumed to influence these sales.

2. Validity addresses the question: Does this study measure what it is supposed to measure? Reliability addresses the question: Are we likely to get the same result if we conduct another such study with the same conditions and controls? To illustrate how MR shortcomings might limit both validity and reliability, consider some of the reasons why election forecasts are frequently so far off the mark in terms of validity (they often *don't* measure people's real beliefs or intentions) and reliability (these beliefs and intentions can change with the next debate, producing completely different results from the last survey). People are unpredictable, survey instruments suffer all the imprecisions of our language, time pressures are intense, and—simply judging from differing interpretations of the same results by opposing candidates—the purpose of the research is often subjectively self-serving.

3. Secondary research data are data that were produced by other people for purposes other than that of the present research study. Primary data are data gathered for the specific research purposes at hand. Secondary sources referred to in locating a good restaurant in a strange town might include a directory of restaurants or listings in a telephone book. Primary sources might include the bellhop in your hotel, or the proprietors of restaurants listed in the directory. A restaurant display ad in the local Yellow Pages might prove invalid to the extent that it is probably biased, possibly dated, and not based on sound research. The same comments might be made with respect to the evaluations by the bellhop or the proprietor.

4. Internal records, such as sales analysis reports of dollar sales by territory in the domestic market, might indicate a drop in sales of MM systems in all territories following a price increase, leading to the hypothesis that the price increase was the main cause of the price decline. Marketing intelligence, however, might highlight significant differences between foreign market B and the domestic marketplace that would tend to maintain sales volume levels in spite of a price increase; for example, intelligence pertaining to economic and competitive environments might profile a market where a high level of affluence among professionals permits them to easily afford the increased price, and where there is practically no competition to exploit Merton's higher price. A marketing research study, perhaps summarizing findings and conclusions from focus group meetings of prospective buyers, might tend to confirm this conclusion, which might further be confirmed by actually raising the MM's price in a test segment of the market. All this information regarding demand patterns in these two markets would be organized, analyzed, and translated into useful decision information by the information analysis section of the MIS.

5. In the first study, the research findings were objectively determined using, primarily, mechanical and electronic means that are much less subject to invalidating influences found when dealing with people, such as biases (interviewer, interviewee, self-selection, nonresponse, halo, and the like), poor measuring devices (questionnaires), complex sub-

jects (people), and ineffective controls. To these reasons are added a number of other barriers in global markets (for example, different languages and poor communication media).

6. The seven steps of the marketing research process include (1) define research problem and objectives, (2) conduct a situation analysis, (3) design research plan, (4) collect primary data, (5) analyze data, (6) make recommendations, and (7) implement recommendations.

    While all the steps of the marketing research process are obviously important, the first and sixth steps are especially important in light of their impact on the decision-making process, which is the ultimate purpose of marketing research. The first step has an impact on decision making, as well as all succeeding steps in the process and the cost and time of the research undertaken. An improperly defined problem, or unrealistic research objectives, can lead to unnecessary research (for example, expensive conclusive studies that generate primary data, when secondary data will suffice) or misdirected marketing research (for example, a study based on the hypothesis that promotion is the problem when it's really distribution) that can dramatically increase the cost of the research while negating the value of decisions based on this research. The sixth step of the process—making recommendations—is important because it integrates data generated by the preceding steps and is the basis for decisions made to activate the final, implementation step, without which the best planned study is just so many useless facts and figures.

7. Before acting on this information, an investor planning to enter the Mexican marketplace might wish to verify (1) the timeliness of this piece (What has happened since last June? A lot, if this piece appeared before the problems with the peso); (2) the disinterestedness of the researchers (both the Commerce Department and the Mexican Board of Trade presumably have an interest in encouraging U.S. firms to invest in Mexico); and (3) the methodology of research undertaken to arrive at this optimistic assessment.

8. Internal secondary sources would include the Board's existing records of various indices of economic activity in Mexico, such as growth in GDP, increases in exporting and importing, and profitability of firms entering the Mexican market. External secondary sources would include sources external to the Board's own internal records that provide generally available data and information either free or for a price. Included could be publications of governmental agencies (both from Mexico and the United States), databases, and periodicals published by associations, banks, and commercial sources. Surveys of knowledgeable people could include, for example, groups of U.S. and Mexican company managers who have achieved success importing or exporting goods in the NAFTA aftermath.

8
MARKETING RESEARCH: TOOLS AND TECHNIQUES

OVERVIEW

Effectively designed and implemented, conclusive marketing research studies produce recommendations that marketing decision makers can act on with confidence. To achieve this result in diverse, dynamic, changing market environments requires effective use of tools and techniques for sampling populations, designing survey instruments, analyzing survey responses, and generating conclusions and recommendations from analyzed information.

DIFFERENCES BETWEEN EXPLORATORY AND CONCLUSIVE RESEARCH

In Chapter 7, we examined the nature, scope, and importance of marketing information systems and marketing research processes, and how they work together to formulate, implement, and control strategic marketing plans. We also examined constraints to the generation of valid, reliable, actionable research findings in complex, quixotic markets and introduced a systematic approach for addressing these constraints.

This approach began by defining the problem to be studied and collecting secondary data bearing on this problem that clarify research objectives. Frequently, this **exploratory research stage** of the research process is sufficient to achieve research objectives.

Alternately, exploratory research might suggest a diversity of possible causes and cures, at which point the next four steps of the process—collecting primary data, analyzing data, making recommendations, and implementing findings—will be necessary. This is called the **conclusive research stage.** The end-product of conclusive research is information that helps marketers make better decisions in all areas of the strategic marketing process, from identifying environmental opportunities through defining worthwhile target markets to implementing and controlling attractive marketing mix offerings.

CONCLUSIVE MARKETING RESEARCH GENERATES PRIMARY DATA

Conclusive and exploratory MR differ in the following significant ways:

1. Conclusive MR tests hypotheses rather than seeking to find these hypotheses (for example, it would test the hypothesis that a price decrease of 10 percent will increase sales 20 percent).

2. Conclusive MR applies much more rigorous controls.

3. Conclusive MR deals with larger numbers and leads to mass data analyses covering classes, averages, percentages, and dispersions.

4. Conclusive MR leads to predictions (for example, a price decrease of 10 percent will increase sales by 30 percent).

Conclusive marketing research also differs from exploratory research in producing primary data, which, unlike secondary data, are collected specifically for the purpose of the investigation at hand by known, controlled methods. Primary data are also usually more current and reliable than secondary data.

Sooner or later, most firms engaged in marketing planning require primary data to answer issue-specific questions that can't be answered with secondary data, such as psychographic and behavioristic segmentation variables (for example, lifestyle, attitudes, behavior patterns) that help define target markets and build attractive marketing mixes.

DESIGNING THE RESEARCH PLAN

To illustrate the final four steps of the marketing research process (collecting, analyzing, recommending, implementing), we focus on decisions and actions involved in designing a conclusive research plan to assess a specific group—tax accountants—as a target market for MM systems.

We begin with the assumption that exploratory research has provided sufficient hypotheses about the nature and needs of this market segment to justify the expense and effort of a conclusive research study. For example, hypotheses suggest that members of this market—accounting firms and individual tax accountants—have needs for training and development programs that can best be met with MM software and electronic classroom teaching methods.

COLLECTING, PROCESSING, AND APPLYING PRIMARY DATA

In deciding on which techniques to use, the research team focused primarily on the nature of the information desired and the people who would presumably provide this information. For example, to what extent was the desired information to be objective (such as demographic characteristics in prospective markets) or subjective (such as attitudes and behavior patterns in these markets)? Future-oriented (such as changing information needs) or oriented toward past experience (such as attitudes toward existing methods of generating information)? And what degree of validity and reliability would be required?

With respect to the audience, to what extent would educational, cultural, and social differences influence people's willingness to divulge information, and the selection of information-gathering research techniques?

Given these considerations and constraints, the Merton MR team designed a conclusive research study that stressed observation and survey data-gathering methods.

THE SAMPLING PLAN FOCUSES ON RESEARCH EFFORT

As the first step in designing the research study, the research team formulated a sampling plan designed to ensure the desired degree of reliability for the type of information generated. For some types of information (such as subjective attitudes toward products), high reliability might not be necessary; for other types of information (such as per-capita income figures among prospective customers), it might be. Thus, the sampling plan was concerned with who would be observed or surveyed, the type of information that would be elicited, and techniques used to elicit this information.

SAMPLING PLAN DESIGN CONSIDERATIONS

A sample is defined as "a limited portion of a larger entity." In a statistical study of income and accreditation characteristics of tax accountants, for example, the larger entity consisted of all tax accountants; the limited portion, or sample, could be any number up to one less than the total number comprising the population.

All samples observed or surveyed during marketing research studies are either probability or nonprobability samples. In a probability sample, each member of the population has the same likelihood of being chosen. Thus, if there were 10,000 tax accountants, and the probability sample chosen comprised 100 of them, each member would have exactly one chance in 100 of being chosen.

A nonprobability sample is selected on the basis of criteria that ensure that some members of the population will have a greater chance of being selected than other members. Thus, members of a **judgment nonprobability sample** would be selected on the basis of the researcher's judgment. For example, he or she might feel that tax accountants with a better knowledge of training and development practices should participate in a focus group discussion of how MM systems can improve these practices.

Members of a **convenience nonprobability sample** are chosen because they are conveniently located. For example, tax accountants at a single accounting firm might be selected to participate in the round-table discussion. Or, members of a **quota sample** might be selected based on their representation in the population. For example, if one tenth of tax accountants employed by accounting firms were partners and one quarter were managers, this might be the percentage of each reflected in a quota sample.

Nonprobability samples are more applicable during exploratory research, when problems and opportunities are being defined and hypotheses emerge for further testing. During conclusive research, when accurate information is required, probability sampling offers a number of advantages.

- **Less information needed:** Basically, all that is needed to construct a probability sample is a way to identify each universe element, and knowledge of the total number of universe elements (that is, tax accountants).

- **Measurable accuracy:** Probability sampling is the only sampling method that provides measurable estimates of accuracy. For example, it's possible to come up with a statement like this with a properly selected probability sample: "In 95 cases out of 100 when a sample of 100 accountants is randomly selected from a population of 10,000 accountants, sample members will indicate an intention to purchase a total of between 23 and 27 MM systems when they appear on the market."

Marketing managers who can have this degree of confidence in the accuracy of their research conclusions can also have considerably greater confidence in the accuracy of decisions emerging from these conclusions.

COLLECTING DATA THROUGH OBSERVATION

Observation methods observe and record present behavior or the results of past behavior. In personal observation, the researcher poses as a research subject, such as a customer in a store being observed; mechanical observation records behavior through electronic or other means, such as an electric cord across the highway counting the number of passing cars. Observation can be unobtrusive (with subjects unaware they are being observed) or obtrusive (with subjects aware they are being observed). In the MM study, for example, the research plan entailed unobtrusively observing training sessions conducted for tax accounting personnel, to generate data on terminology, accounting practices, and training needs peculiar to British accounting. A judgment sample of firms presumed to use the most modern methods was selected.

COLLECTING DATA THROUGH SURVEYS

Surveys systematically gather information from respondents by asking them questions, either in person, over the telephone, or by mail. They are particularly applicable for generating specific answers to narrow questions, such as how respondents perceive competitive products or features desired in new products. Because surveys involve communications among people, they are subject to a number of biases, some of which follow:

- **Interviewer and interviewee bias** occurs when the attitudes and actions of either the interviewer or respondent distort questionnaire findings.

- **Nonresponse bias** occurs when people don't respond to a survey, thus potentially biasing findings since the reason they didn't respond might change survey results.

- **Self-selection bias,** the opposite of nonresponse bias, suggests that the reason people volunteer to participate in a survey, such as enthusiasm for a political candidate, might bias survey results.

- **Halo effect bias** is the tendency for respondents to generalize from a favorable part to the whole. For example, responses to a questionnaire measuring attitudes toward a new product might be biased by a favorable experience with existing company products.

A well-trained and supervised staff of field researchers will usually reduce the adverse influences of these biases in survey results.

QUESTIONNAIRE DESIGN: A KEY STEP

The MM study researchers realized that they would be using a number of surveys to explore and define the tax accountant market and that properly designing questionnaires would help mitigate biases while achieving desired degrees of reliability. This design process involved decisions relating to questionnaire objectives; type of questionnaire; mode of questionnaire communication; question content, wording, and format; and question sequence.

• *QUESTIONNAIRE OBJECTIVES*

Since the main purpose of a questionnaire is to translate research objectives into specific questions, a good starting point in designing a questionnaire is to briefly summarize these objectives. For example, an important objective of the MM tax accountant study was to determine the educational needs of various subgroups comprising the tax accountant market, along with dissatisfactions with how these needs were being met, what features these groups would expect in MM systems, what they would expect to pay for these systems, and so on.

• *TYPES OF QUESTIONNAIRES*

In terms of information desired and respondents' ability or willingness to provide this information, questionnaires can range from highly structured to unstructured. A highly structured questionnaire, with unchanging question content and sequence, generally elicits uncomplicated information that the respondent is both willing and able to provide (for example, a job application). An unstructured questionnaire lets the interviewer probe respondents and guide the interview according to their answers, often generating information that respondents were unaware they possessed, or might otherwise have been reluctant to reveal (for example, a "focus group" of accountants discussing problems they faced with existing personal computer software programs).

Focus groups comprise seven to ten people who gather for a few hours to talk about a product, service, or organization. Although focus-group output is not statistically significant, a skilled leader can help encourage participant interaction that generates a substantial amount of information on perceptions, emotions, issues, and ideas that would not emerge during individual interviews. With advances in electronic communication illustrated by MM systems, focus groups can operate over large distances, with participants in different regions interacting as if in a single location.

• *MODES OF COMMUNICATION*

Three methods of communication are available for conducting surveys: personal interviews, telephone interviews, and mail surveys. Table 8-1 profiles the relative merits of each approach in terms of cost, control, flexibility, validity/reliability, and ease of interpretation. Note that, although personal interviews are flexible—questions can be stopped or changed at any time and can generate information not otherwise available—they are the most expensive of the three methods. Telephone surveys are less costly but don't generally provide as much in-depth information as personal surveys, and miss people who hang up or don't have phones. Mail surveys can reach dispersed respondents, have no interviewer bias, and are relatively inexpensive,

Table 8–1. Comparison of Questionnaire Type by Structure/Disguise Characteristics

	Structured/Nondisguised	Nonstructured/Nondisguised	Nonstructured/Disguised	Structured/Disguised
Key Characteristic	Question content and sequence identical on each questionnaire.	Question content and sequence vary at interviewer's discretion.	Study objectives disguised to overcome unwillingness or inability of respondent to answer personal questions.	Questionnaire content fixed, but questionnaire objectives are disguised. Real attitudes are inferred from answers.
Typical Applications	During exploratory research, develop hypotheses to be tested later, during conclusive stages.	"Depth interviews" during exploratory research stage to generate hypotheses and relationships.	Exploratory research probes for subconsciously held attitudes, motivations.	To elicit "private" information (on religion, politics, etc.) respondent would otherwise be reluctant to provide.
Cost Elements	If by phone, line charges and interviewer expenses; if by mail, recipient list and costs for mailing questionnaire, processing responses.	Recruiting, training, administering interviewers, setting-up focus groups.	Essentially the same as for nonstructured/nondisguised type.	Essentially the same as for structured/nondisguised.
Control	Difficult to control accuracy of recipient list, size of response.	Difficult to control questionnaire content, sequence, and quality of responses.	Essentially the same as for nonstructured/nondisguised.	Essentially the same as for structured/nondisguised.
Flexibility	Question content and sequence difficult to change, except by rotating questions and directing respondents to skip irrelevant questions.	Question content and sequence easily changed at discretion of interviewer.	Projective materials (such as word association and picture completion surveys) are difficult to change, but interviewer questions can be changed.	Essentially the same as for structured/nondisguised.

Validity & Reliability	No interviewer or interviewee bias with mail surveys, but possible halo, Hawthorne, self-selection, and nonresponse biases.	Interviewee, interviewer, halo, nonresponse, and self-selection biases all possible.	Disguised nature of questions reduces interviewee bias, although all other biases associated with nonstructured/nondisguised are possible.	Essentially the same as for structured/nondisguised, lessened somewhat because of disguised nature of probe.
Ease of Interpretation	Responses easiest of all to tabulate, organize, and analyze.	Different interviewer styles and subjective responses make responses difficult to tabulate and interpret.	Essentially, same problems as associated with nonstructured/nondisguised.	Generally as easy as structured/nondisguised responses, with some room for error in making subjective inferences from objective answers.

Control refers to the extent to which the questionnaire can be monitored and corrected. For example, the activities of field researchers conducting face-to-face interviews are more difficult to control than those of supervised telephone interviewers.

Flexibility refers to the extent to which questionnaire content and sequence can change in response to answers.

Validity and reliability refer to the likelihood that biasing factors built into the questionnaire will prevent the questionnaire from measuring what it was designed to measure or make it difficult to repeat survey results.

Ease of interpretation refers to the degree of cost and effort involved in processing questionnaire responses after interviews are completed. For example, drawn-out responses elicited during an unstructured, focus-group interview would be much more difficult to organize and analyze than short answers to true of false questions.

but they suffer from nonresponse bias and slow returns. In Merton's study of the tax accountant market, all these modes were used.

CONSTRUCTING THE QUESTIONNAIRE

Once researchers have clearly defined questionnaire objectives and decided on questionnaire type and communication method, the stage is set for preparing the questionnaire. This process involves determining question content, wording, format, and sequence.

• *QUESTION CONTENT*
The Merton research team followed these guidelines:

1. Avoid unnecessary questions.

2. Respondent should be willing to answer the question. For example, potentially embarrassing questions pertaining to personal finances or family life were eliminated or asked in the context of innocuous questions or an explanation of their importance.

3. Respondent should have the information required for an answer. For example, questions should be within the respondent's experience, and shouldn't require respondent to work to get the information.

• *QUESTION WORDING*
The researchers followed these guidelines:

1. **Define the issue.** Check each survey question against the who-what-why-when-where-how questions characterizing an effective news story. For example, a question like What is your income? leaves out an important "what" (What comprises income? Salary alone? Salary and benefits?) and "when" (weekly? monthly? annually?).

2. **Use understandable words.** In any language, many words (such as the word "many") have different meanings to people, and some locutions (such as the word "locution") have no meaning at all to some people. Pretest the questionnaire to find and eliminate problem words.

3. **Avoid leading questions or questions that require generalized answers.** Leading questions lead the respondent to an answer, usually by naming the product in a favorable way. Questions that elicit vague, generalized answers are usually phrased that way (for example, What do you think of professional learning?).

• *QUESTION FORMAT*

Four types of question formats are available for communicating question content, ranging from unstructured open questions to more highly structured multiple-choice, dichotomous, and rating-scale questions.

OPEN QUESTIONS

Open questions do not suggest alternative answers and thus can be answered as the respondent sees fit. This open question, asked during a focus-group discussion of electronic training, illustrates advantages and disadvantages of this format:

> What, in your opinion, are the main advantages and disadvantages of the "electronic classroom" approach to learning accounting principles?

As the first question on a questionnaire, an open question is frequently a good way to familiarize the respondent with the purpose and content of the survey, to interest the respondent in the survey, and to prepare the way for more specific questions. Also, since open questions do not point to possible answers, they can produce unexpected responses, which can help solve problems or identify opportunities or, during exploratory research, suggest hypotheses to be tested during the conclusive research stage. These answers can also help design questions for more structured surveys used during the conclusive research stage.

Disadvantages of open questions include difficulty in recording and tabulating answers (they are three to five times more expensive to process than structured questions), interviewer bias resulting from long, rambling answers, and interviewee bias when better-educated respondents give more articulate answers that weight results.

MULTIPLE-CHOICE QUESTIONS

Multiple-choice questions offer respondents a number of alternatives from which to choose, and address most of the problems of open questions while introducing a few of their own. To illustrate, here is a typical multiple-choice question that might appear on the Merton study questionnaire:

> Which of the following features would you find most useful in a personal notebook computer?
>
> _ Online conferencing capability
>
> _ Memory capacity
>
> _ E-mail capability
>
> _ Software programs
>
> _ Computational speed
>
> _ User-friendly

In addition to the fact that all alternatives listed should be defined more precisely, this excerpt also illustrates the following problems with multiple-choice questions:

- Too many alternatives can cause respondents to lose interest in the entire questionnaire. Four choices are usually considered a reasonable limit. Also, respondent should be informed if more that one alternative can be selected.

- Alternatives may not include all possible categories (so include an "other" category).

- Alternatives may not be mutually exclusive (for example, "user-friendly" might imply the other attributes).

Other problems peculiar to multiple-choice questions are two biases they engender:

- **Position bias,** or the tendency for respondents to select the first alternative in a multiple-choice sequence.

- **Order bias,** or the tendency to select an alternative in the center of a sequence.

Both biases can be mitigated by rotating question sequence on mailed questionnaires.

DICHOTOMOUS QUESTIONS

Dichotomous questions allow a choice of only one of two alternative answers (yes or no, did or did not, and so on) and are the most widely used of all question formats. In general, the same advantages and disadvantages of multiple-choice questions apply: they eliminate interviewer bias and are relatively easy to edit, code, and tabulate, but both alternatives might be true, and other possible answers might be excluded.

SCALING QUESTIONS

Scaling questions are a variant of multiple-choice questions developed mainly to measure subjective variables like motives, attitudes, and perceptions. For example, consumers might be asked to rank various telephone systems in terms of their perceptions of the clarity of each. On the simplest level, an **ordinal scale** would rank the systems with no attempt to measure the degree of favorability of the different systems (Sprint, MCI, AT&T).

A variant of the ordinal scales with marketing applications is the **Likert scale,** which permits respondents to indicate degree of agreement/disagreement with a series of statements reflecting attitudes toward products and product attributes. Consider the following example:

	Strongly Agree	Agree	Undecided	Disagree	Strongly Disagree
Continuing education is very important in my profession	_____	_____	_____	_____	_____
Companies should pay for professional courses employees take	_____	_____	_____	_____	_____

Interval scales carry ordinal scale rankings a step farther by measuring the distance between rank positions in equal units. For example, computer users might be asked to rank personal computer memory capacity along the following interval scale:

	Poor	Average	Excellent
IBM	_____	_____	_____
Apple	_____	_____	_____
Compac	_____	_____	_____

On this scale, the difference between "poor" and "average" is the same as the distance between "average" and "excellent." However, such a scale doesn't permit the conclusion that "excellent" is twice as good as "average," since no zero position has been established.

A variant on interval scales with many marketing applications is the **semantic differential,** in which the respondent selects a point between two bipolar words that best represents the direction and intensity of his or her feelings.

For example, here is how such a scale might profile respondent attitudes toward three personal computers, brands A, B, and C:

	1	2	3	4	5	6	7	
Inexpensive								Expensive
Slow information processing								Fast information processing
Large memory								Small memory
Low quality								High quality

• *QUESTION SEQUENCE*

Here are sequencing guidelines designed to enhance respondent interest and involvement in the survey:

- Place questions that respondent might be reluctant to answer in the body of the questionnaire, to be asked when respondent is at ease with the interviewer or questionnaire content.

- Consider the influence of question placement on succeeding questions; for example, questions that use the product name should appear at the conclusion of the questionnaire.

- Arrange questions in logical order, avoiding sudden topic changes that will confuse respondent.

The questionnaire should follow this basic sequence:

- A **basic information section** is composed of actual questions asked;

- A **classification information section** provides demographic information (such as age, income, and education level) that can be related to respondent's answers.

- An **identification information section** includes identifying data (such as names, addresses, and code numbers) for all questionnaire participants: interviewer, interviewee, editor, and so on.

• *IMPROVING QUESTIONNAIRE RESPONSE*

Research studies suggest a variety of approaches and techniques for improving the quality and quantity of responses to questionnaires communicated by personal interviews or through the mail.

- Number questionnaires serially to verify that all are accounted for. Formerly, a code number on a mailed questionnaire was thought to compromise a promise of anonymity, but research indicates it influences results little, if at all.

- Make sure that the questionnaire is of proper size and length. For a personal interview, the questionnaire should be sufficiently large so that information is not cramped, yet not so large that it is awkward to handle. Mailed questionnaires of more than two pages show an appreciable falloff in returns, as do personal questionnaires of more than two pages. A questionnaire that runs into several pages should be made into a booklet for easier handling and data entry.

- People are more likely to respond to questionnaires that (1) have interesting titles and first pages; (2) include a cover letter explaining the purpose of the mailing and relating this purpose to respondent's self-interest; and (3) are personalized by hand-signing and addressing respondent by name.

- The use of direct incentives, including cash, trading stamps, lottery tickets, and similar premiums, almost invariably improves response rates. With cash incentives, larger amounts included with each letter increase returns up to about one third, beyond which the percentage return levels off. Research findings are ambiguous regarding the optimal amount to include as an incentive; the figure tends to change with respondent groups and inflation rates. However, research strongly indicates that cash incentives are a cheaper way to ensure a desired rate of return than follow-up mailings and phone calls.

- Mechanical and perceptual devices that increase returns include (1) telephone contact with respondents before they receive the questionnaire explaining its purpose and importance; (2) questionnaires sent via special delivery, registered mail, and first-class mail; and (3) stamped, self-addressed envelopes included with each mailing for returning the questionnaire.

• *PRETEST THE QUESTIONNAIRE*

Regardless of questionnaire design or communication approach, it should be pretested to eliminate ambiguous phraseology and distortive biases. Ideally, pretesting should be conducted under the same conditions that will be used in the contact situations. At a minimum, the mailing should be pretested on a group composed of experts and members of the population to receive the mailing.

INTERPRETING DATA WITH STATISTICS AND EXPERIMENTS

Once gathered and organized, primary (and sometimes secondary) data are typically interpreted using statistical or experimental methods.

• *STATISTICAL METHODS*

Statistical (descriptive) methods classify data in such a way that inclusion in one category implies inclusion in one or more other categories, often revealing significant relationships among data categories. These relationships can then lead to predictions about future occurrences. For example, Table 8-2 compares two samples, each composed of 100 tax accountants, in terms of criteria that predict enrollment in self-administered professional education courses of the sort offered by the MM systems division. According to the data in this table, tax accountants making less than $80,000 annually and working for accounting firms, or independently employed, are less likely to be enrolled in such courses than tax accountants making more than $80,000 working for accounting firms, or independently employed.

Table 8–2. Comparison of Tax Accountants in Terms of Criteria Predictive of Professional Course Enrollment (Sample size: 100)

	Income under $80,000		Income over $80,000	
	Enrolled in Programs		Enrolled in Programs	
	Number	Percent	Number	Percent
Employed in accounting firms	60	60	70	70
Independent accountants	55	55	65	65

These findings will help Moore more precisely define the tax accountant segment of the professional market for MM systems, and provide ideas for positioning the division's MM offerings. For example, promotional materials sent to tax accountants making under $80,000 can stress the correlation between professional training and higher incomes.

• *EXPERIMENTAL METHODS*

Although statistical research findings are often sufficiently indicative to act on, they are never conclusive. For example, in the preceding statistical analysis, it cannot be conclusively inferred that taking self-administered training courses causes higher incomes.

Experimental (causal) methods are a more effective (and expensive) research approach for identifying and defining cause-effect relationships. Illustrative is a test market experiment involving selecting matched groups of subjects, giving them different treatments, controlling unrelated factors, and checking for differences in group responses. For example, two groups of tax accountants, closely matched in all significant variables (for example, income and education level), are each exposed to similar MM offerings with only a 20 percent lower price as a significant difference. If, after this test market has run its course, a check for differences reveals that the group exposed to the 20 percent lower price purchased 40 percent more MM systems, then it might be assumed that the lower price produced the sales increase. Other elements that can be manipulated in the experimental format include product features, promotional appeals, and distribution channels.

However, at least four variables can combine to invalidate these findings:

1. **Selection:** Consciously or not, different criteria might have been used to select each group, so they are not truly matched.

2. **Mortality:** Members of one group might desert in greater numbers, so even groups that begin as matched might not stay that way.

3. **Pretest effect:** When members of a group know they are being selected to participate in a test market study, they might behave in an unnatural way (for example, purchase MMs to please the researchers).

4. **History:** Outside events might bias experiment results; for example, a competitor might initiate a campaign promoting its MM systems.

TEST MARKETS AS EXPERIMENTS

These invalidating factors, along with high dollar and time costs associated with test market experiments, have persuaded many marketers to use consumer panels to generate hypotheses and describe situations and opportunities. Panels are cheaper and quicker than test markets and ensure a much higher degree of secrecy—important when a new product, or product concept, is being tested.

CODING AND TABULATING DATA

If appropriate sampling and data-gathering methods have been used, marketing research data will meet established standards of validity and reliability. For these data to be of value to marketing managers in making critical decisions, however, they must be properly processed in a sequence of activities that involve coding, tabulation, and analysis.

- **Coding** is the process of transforming questionnaire responses into interpretable form by assigning responses to categories. Referring to Table 8-2, for example, each response from each subgroup would automatically be assigned to a numbered category indicating such things as income, employment, and enrollment in self-administered training programs.

- **Tabulation** is the process of summarizing responses by categories, with results expressed as totals or percentages.

- **Analysis** involves the use of various statistical techniques to evaluate findings with respect to original research objectives. In the tax accountants' study, for example, statistical tests of significance showed that there was virtually no chance that percentage differences among responses from the different groups studied (income over/under $80,000, enrolled/not enrolled in self-administered courses) would result through sampling error, making them highly significant.

GENERATING CONCLUSIONS AND MAKING RECOMMENDATIONS

After the research plan had been formulated and followed in collecting, coding, tabulating, and analyzing secondary and primary data, a report was prepared that summarized study findings, conclusions, and recommendations.

The "recommendations" step is the most important of the entire marketing research process because recommendations are what decision makers rely on. For example, a wrong decision to enter a market, based on faulty research and recommendations deriving from this research, could cost Merton millions of dollars.

Conclusions and recommendations are generally presented in written (in some cases oral) form to decision makers. Since these presentations are often communicated to both headquarters and local managers, all interests should be represented. Study results should be presented clearly and concisely, avoiding lengthy analyses and demonstrations; just note where information of limited general interest can be found. Also, make sure presentations demonstrate how research results relate to original research objectives and are consistent with overall corporate strategy.

IMPLEMENTATION AND FEEDBACK

Finally, the marketing research process comes full circle as findings, conclusions, and recommendations are programmed into marketing information systems and used in the subsequent creation, implementation, and control of strategic marketing plans.

INTERNATIONAL PERSPECTIVE

Marketing research tools and techniques—such as surveys and statistical analyses required for primary research—that can be applied with valid, reliable results in the domestic market face constraints in global markets that frequently make them much more difficult to apply.

These constraints include poorly functioning postal and telecommunication systems and limited information on dwellings, their location, and their occupants. In some countries, even street maps aren't available. And even if respondents can be reached through mail, telephone, and personal interviews, cultural factors might negatively affect responses. For example, people have different degrees of sensitivity to survey questions pertaining to topics like income, age, and political orientation. Thus, in Japan, it's much easier to generate data on consumer needs and preferences from personal visits to dealers and other channel members than from the type of customer surveys typical of research studies in the United States. In Saudi Arabia, the entire population of women is generally inaccessible for any mode of survey. In some countries, entire populations are motivated to provide incorrect information on surveys (for example, to elude tax collectors or for fear the information will be leaked to the government). And in developing countries, demonstration aids are usually required in conducting surveys among poorly educated people, effectively eliminating mail and telephone surveys.

Personnel issues present other constraints. For example, as noted in Market Focus 8-1, recruiting, training, and activating a staff to conduct survey research can present a number of unexpected problems.

GLOBAL FOCUS 8-1

Adjusting Marketing Research to Market Conditions

Western businesses are on a mission to discover how Ivan shaves and what Olga uses to wash her hair. To find out, some marketers have hit the research trail in Eastern Europe, hoping to gain the upper hand on those waiting for the coast to clear of remaining uncertainties.

In order to carry out research, marketers need to think creatively and work around barriers. One U.S. researcher has developed an interesting system of dispersing questionnaires to interviewers distantly located. The routine is to find a willing traveler, perhaps a train conductor or Aeroflot stewardess, to deliver the package of questionnaires and then call ahead to the destination with a description of the ad hoc courier. Sometimes the plan works, other times it flops—like the time some filled-out questionnaires were stranded for weeks because of fighting in Armenia.

Special attention must be paid to training local interviewers and reviewing their work. One Western researcher recalls a woman in Moscow being trained to be a focus-group moderator. He described her as a drill sergeant while imitating her: "I just asked you a question and you have to respond." Another researcher's experience was with a local interviewer hired in Ukraine. He left the questionnaires with the respondents instead of interviewing them.

Discussion groups can be a good method of finding important information on particular subjects. But unlike in the West, discussions have to be held on the same day as recruitment. Participants cannot be asked to come back in a couple of days because, one researcher comments, "They can't predict what they'll be doing in two days. They may have to stand in some line." Interpretation of data, once they have been collected, has its problems as well. Pepsi-Cola International received results from a survey in Hungary that said drugstores were an outlet for soft drinks. "But drugstores don't exist in Hungary," said the Pepsi marketing director. Apparently, the information obtained had been forced into categories developed in the West.

Source: "Western Firms Poll Eastern Europeans to Discern Tastes of Nascent Consumers," *The Wall Street Journal,* April 27, 1992, p. B1.

IMPROVING GLOBAL RESEARCH RESULTS

Given the need for valid, reliable research findings and conclusions in Merton's efforts to identify and define profitable foreign markets for entry/growth strategies, Moore first retained an international research firm that would be capable of addressing the problems in achieving these results.

Selection criteria stressed the research firm's experience in global markets, especially Asia, Europe, and North and South America, and the quality of information produced in previous engagements. Moore then compared the prospective firm's capabilities with capabilities available in-house and from competing research firms.

Moore also applied rigorous criteria in assessing research plans and findings produced by her research team composed of in-house and support agencies. For example, she wanted to be sure that the right questions were being researched. As suggested in Table 8-3, these global marketing research questions generally parallel the stages of the strategic planning process.

Table 8–3. International Marketing Questions Determining Information Requirements

Broad Strategic Issues
  What objectives should be pursued in the foreign market?
  Which foreign market segments should the firm strive to satisfy?
  Which are the best product, place-distribution, pricing, and promotion strategies for the foreign market?

Table 8-3. *Continued*

What should be the product-market-company mix to take advantage of the available foreign marketing opportunities?

Foreign Market Assessment and Selection

Do opportunities exist in a foreign market for the firm's products and services?

What is the market potential abroad?

What new markets are likely to open up abroad?

What are the major economic, political, legal, social, technological, and other environmental facts and trends in a foreign country?

What impact do these environmental dimensions have on the specific foreign market for the firm's products and services?

Who are the firm's present and potential customers abroad?

What are their needs and desires?

What are their demographic and psychographic characteristics—disposable income, occupation, age, sex, opinions, interests, activities, tastes, values, etc.?

What is their lifestyle?

Who makes the purchase decisions?

Who influences the purchase decisions?

How are the purchase decisions made?

Where are the products purchased?

How are the products used?

What are the purchase and consumption patterns and behaviors?

What is the nature of competition in the foreign market?

Who are major direct and indirect competitors?

What are the major characteristics of the competitors?

What are the firm's competitive strengths and weaknesses in reference to such factors as product quality, product lines, warranties, services, brands, packaging, distribution, salesforce, advertising, prices, experience, technology, capital and human resources, and market share?

What attitudes do different governments (domestic and foreign) have toward foreign trade?

Are there any foreign trade incentives and barriers?

Is there any prejudice against imports or exports?

What are different governments doing specifically to encourage or discourage international trade?

What specific requirements—for example, import or export licenses—have to be met to conduct international trade?

How difficult are certain government regulations for the firm?

How well developed are the foreign mass communication media?

Are the print and electronics media abroad efficient and effective?

Are there adequate transportation and storage or warehouse facilities in the foreign market?

Table 8-3. *Continued*

Does the foreign market offer efficient channels of distribution for the firm's products?

What are the characteristics of the existing domestic and foreign distributors?

How effectively can the distributors perform specific marketing functions?

What is the state of the retailing institutions?

Marketing Mix Assessment and Selection

Product

Which product should the firm offer abroad?

What specific features—design, color, size, packaging, brand, warranty, etc.—should the product have?

What foreign needs does the product satisfy?

Should the firm adapt or modify its domestic market product and sell it abroad?

Should it develop a new product for the foreign market?

Should the firm make or buy the product for the foreign market?

How competitive is or will be the product abroad?

Is there a need to withdraw the product from the foreign market?

At which stage in its life cycle is the product in the foreign market?

What specific services are necessary abroad at the presale and postsale stages?

Are the firm's service and repair facilities adequate?

What is the firm's product and service image abroad?

What patents or trademarks does the firm have that can benefit it abroad? How much legal protection does the firm have concerning patents, trademarks, etc.?

What should be the firm's product mission philosophy in the foreign market?

Are the firm's products socially responsible?

Do the products create a good corporate image?

What effect does the product have on the environment?

Price

At what price should the firm sell its product in the foreign market?

Does the foreign price reflect the product quality?

Is the price competitive?

Should the firm pursue market penetration or market-skimming pricing objectives abroad?

What type of discounts (trade, cash, quantity) and allowances (advertising, tradeoff) should the firm offer its foreign customers?

Should prices differ according to market segment?

What should the firm do about product line pricing?

What pricing options are available if costs increase or decrease?

Table 8-3. *Continued*

Is the demand in the foreign market elastic or inelastic?

How are prices going to be viewed by the foreign government—reasonable, exploitative?

Can differentiated pricing lead to the emergence of a gray market?

Place—Distribution

Which channels of distribution should the firm use to market its products abroad?

Where should the firm produce its products, and how should it distribute them in the foreign market?

What types of agents, brokers, wholesalers, dealers, distributors, retailers, etc., should the firm use?

What are the characteristics and capabilities of the available intermediaries?

Should the assistance of EMCs (export management companies) be acquired?

What forms of transportation should the firm use?

Where should the product be stored?

What is the cost of distribution by channel?

What are the costs of physical distribution?

What type of incentives and assistance should the firm provide its intermediaries to achieve its foreign distribution objectives?

Which channels of distribution are used by the firm's competitors, and how effective are these channels?

Is there a need to develop a reverse distribution system, e.g., recycling?

Promotion—Nonpersonal (Advertising and Sales Promotion)

How should the firm promote its products in the foreign market? Should it advertise? Should it participate in international trade fairs and exhibits?

What are the communication needs of the foreign market?

What communication or promotion objectives should the firm pursue abroad?

What should be the total foreign promotion budget?

What advertising media are available to promote in the foreign market? What are their strengths and limitations? How effective are different domestic and foreign advertising media?

Should the firm use an advertising agency?

How should it be selected?

How effective and competitive are the firm's existing advertising and promotion programs concerning the foreign market?

What are the legal requirements?

Are there foreign laws against competitive advertising?

Promotion—Personal Selling

Is there a need for personal selling to promote the product abroad?

What assistance or services do foreign customers need from the salesforce?

Table 8-3. *Continued*

What should be the nature of personal selling abroad?

How many salespeople should the firm have?

How should the sales personnel be trained, motivated, compensated, assigned sales goals and quotas, and assigned foreign territories?

What should the nature of the foreign sales effort be?

How does the firm's salesforce compare with its competitors'?

What criteria should the firm use to evaluate sales performance?

How should the firm perform sales analysis?

Source: Adapted from Vinay Kothari, "Researching for Export Marketing," in *Export Promotion: The Public and Private Sector Interaction,* M. Czinkota, Ed. (New York: Praeger Publishers, 1983), pp. 169–172. Reprinted with permission of Greenwood Publishing Group, Inc., Westport, CT. Copyright © 1993.

She was also concerned that the proper research methodology was employed in addressing these research questions. In general, face-to-face interviews and observational research are the most common methods of conducting research outside the United States, with experimental research, focus groups, and mail surveys much less common than in the United States. Telephone interviewing is another method that is not always suitable in other countries, especially where large numbers of respondents do not have telephones.

She was also concerned that, when surveys were conducted, question content reflected demographic differences among countries. For example, in an undeveloped country, a white-collar worker would be part of the upper class, whereas in a developed country, he or she would belong to the middle class.

One effective test of the understandability of questions in a foreign language is the **back-translation approach,** which involves first translating the question into the language of the foreign country and then having a translator from this country translate it back into the original language so that the two versions can be compared.

CHAPTER PERSPECTIVE

This chapter examined the last four steps of the marketing research process, involving (1) gathering primary data through surveys and observation; (2) transforming data into decision information using statistical and experimental methods; (3) using the information to generate conclusions and recommendations for further action; and (4) implementing and following up on the recommendations in the strategic planning process. The chapter focused on problems and approaches for generating data in international markets, in addition to effective sampling, questionnaire design, and statistical and experimental approaches that address these problems.

KNOW THE CONCEPTS
TERMS FOR STUDY

Analysis
Bias
Coding
Communication modes
Conclusive research
Confidence levels
Convenience samples
Data collection
Data processing
Decentralized research
Experimental methods
Exploratory research
Focus groups
Hypotheses
Internal scales
Judgment samples
Likert scale
Nonprobability samples
Observation
Ordinal scales

Pretesting questionnaire
Primary data
Probability samples
Questionnaire design
Questionnaire objectives
Questionnaire types
Question content
Question sequence
Quota samples
Report conclusions
Report recommendations
Research plan
Sampling plan
Scaling
Secondary data
Semantic differential
Statistical methods
Surveys
Tabulation
Test markets

MATCHUP EXERCISES

1. Match the questionnaire type in the first column with the information need in the second column (the questionnaire has to do with the needs and attitudes of prospective Russian buyers of expensive dacha-style homes manufactured in the United States and assembled on-site in Russia).

   1. structured/nondisguised

   2. nonstructured/nondisguised

   a. attitudes toward high incomes allowed under new entrepreneurial, free-enterprise Russian environment

   b. design features that would make it easier to sell the dachas in the Russian market

3. nonstructured/disguised   c. reasons for wanting to purchase an expensive dacha-style home

2. A large Eastern wine distributor, intent on improving its shaky competitive position, is planning a series of surveys to determine U.S. preferences in wine. The wine line that will be marketed will be positioned and promoted to reflect these characteristics, and will be aimed at the "heavy user" market segment (that is, the 20 percent of U.S. citizens who consume 85 percent of the wine). Match up the survey type in the first column with the sample selected in the second column.

1. probability   a. One in 5000 members of the entire population will be selected randomly in this sample.

2. judgment   b. Twenty percent of this sample will comprise the heavy user segment.

3. quota   c. One sample will be restricted to editors of food and drink magazines and newsletters.

4. convenience   d. The distributor's advertising agency will conduct taste tests among its staff members.

3. Match the form of research study in the first column with information desired in the second column regarding the nature and needs of target markets for MM systems.

1. exploratory: internal secondary   a. relationships between the profession purchasing MMs and profitability generated

2. exploratory: external secondary   b. consensus as to the most worthwhile professions to focus on in market entry campaign

3. conclusive: statistical   c. the extent to which different incentives offered distributors will encourage them to promote MM systems

4. conclusive: experimental   d. distribution of sales among different professions in domestic market

QUESTIONS FOR REVIEW AND DISCUSSION

1. What is the significance of the word "probability" in defining probability and non-probability samples? Why are nonprobability samples more important during exploratory research and probability samples more important during conclusive research?

2. Describe two circumstances that would work against the use of each of the following survey methods: person-to-person, telephone, mail.

3. Discuss advantages and disadvantages of centralized, decentralized, and coordinated approaches for generating information on emerging global markets. Which would you recommend for Merton (1) during its present state as an exporter and (2) if it eventually achieves multinational status?

4. Distinguish among mechanical, personal, obtrusive, and unobtrusive observation methods. How might mechanical and personal methods be used to test student response to a new MM software training course for doctors featuring "virtual reality" surgery experiences?

5. How might the following biases invalidate survey findings indicating that between 40 and 44 percent of the Indonesian female population between the ages of 24 and 50 would be likely to purchase a line of American dishwashers about to be introduced into this market: interviewer, interviewee, nonresponse, halo effect.

6. Shown here is a semantic differential scale that depicts perceptions toward two brands of laptop computers in terms of the four dimensions presumed to be of most importance to users: reliability (it almost always works, even under adverse conditions), speed (it provides results quickly), portability (it is easy to pack and travel with), and value (it is priced right in terms of utilities provided). What would you conclude from this depiction? What product strategy would you recommend for computer B based on these perceptions?

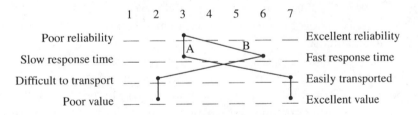

7. As part of its strategy to increase its share of the Canadian market, a U.S. manufacturer of dentifrice products implements a two-city test market for a new kind of dental floss that can simultaneously brush and floss teeth. In each city, 200 randomly selected participants are provided a free three-month supply of the dental floss, with the understanding that, at the end of this period, they will fill out a questionnaire exploring their feelings and attitudes toward the floss. This information will then be used to make any necessary modifications of price, product design, and promotion aspects of the offering. In terms of selection, mortality, and history, why might conclusions deriving from this test market be suspect?

8. Explain how you might engage in the following activities leading up to recommendation that a friend go out on a blind date with another of your friends: coding, tabulating, analysis.

ANSWERS
MATCHUP EXERCISES

1. 1c, 2b, 3a

2. 1a, 2c, 3b, 4d

3. 1d, 2b, 3a, 4c

QUESTIONS FOR REVIEW AND DISCUSSION

1. In sampling, probability means that every member of a population has an equal chance of being selected for a sample. The significance of this characteristic derives from the nature of findings and conclusions emerging from probability samples. Unlike nonprobability samples, these findings and conclusions can be stated with a measurable degree of accuracy. For example, you can make a statement like this: "In 98 of 100 cases where a sample this large is drawn from a population of American males, the average height of sample members will be between 5'8" and 5'9"." Furthermore, it is possible to obtain these valid, reliable confidence levels from comparatively small samples, and at comparatively small cost.

   During exploratory research, the purpose is usually investigative in nature (for example, to investigate attitudes toward products, needs to be met, or possible causes or solutions to problems). Frequently, the best way to generate this information is in small, freewheeling discussion sessions, such as focus groups, in which the researcher has no idea of the outcome and statistical analyses would be irrelevant. However, during the conclusive research stage, when hypotheses generated during exploratory research are tested, much larger samples are desired to generate valid, reliable data in a few areas through analyses covering classes, averages, percentages, and dispersions.

2. **Person-to-person:** When survey questions are simple and uncomplicated, and willingly answered by respondents, then the considerable expense and administrative bother of a person-to-person interview can be avoided by using a telephone or mail survey.

Telephone: If the information desired is complex and subjective, requiring long, in-depth interviews or a group sharing of ideas, or if it can be gathered more efficiently and economically through a mail survey, then these other communication modes would be more effective.

Mail: Lengthy or highly subjective information that cannot be obtained in the relatively short, fixed format of a written questionnaire would be more effectively pursued using other information-gathering approaches.

3. With centralized approaches, research design and focus are decided by headquarters and forwarded to local-country operations for implementation. This approach is generally applicable when research is intended to influence company policy and strategy, and the nature and needs of markets are generally similar. With decentralized approaches, home-country headquarters establishes broad research policies and guidelines; then delegates further design and implement at local-country headquarters. This approach is applicable when markets differ from country to country. It provides closer market proximity, more flexible responses to marketplace threats and opportunities, and the benefits of interaction among home/host-country personnel. With the coordinated approach, an outside intermediary, such as a marketing research firm, brings home- and host-country research operations together, helping to realize the benefits of both.

   As an exporter to a single country, which is Merton's immediate goal, the company, with no host-country personnel in place, must perforce employ essentially a centralized approach. However, it has retained a marketing research firm, which is helping the firm to realize its short-term goal and, later, will help to implement a coordinated approach when Merton reaches international status.

4. Mechanical observation relies on some sort of mechanical or electronic device, such as a radar gun, to observe behavior; personal observation relies on people observing behavior. In obtrusive observation, the observer makes his/her role as an observer known (for example, an immigration officer inspecting the contents of a suitcase); in unobtrusive observation, the observer's role is not revealed to the observed (for example, an FBI infiltrator of a militant hate group).

   Merton could use mechanical observation by having trainees respond electronically to a series of questions about the course; personal observation would occur if one of the students taking the course was also a researcher assigned to monitor reactions of the other students.

5. Interviewer/interviewee bias: Attitudes or actions by either the interviewer or interviewee can distort responses during personal interviews. For example, if the interviewer is perceived by the interviewee to have a higher socioeconomic status, there would possibly be a tendency on the part of the interviewee to verbally equalize this difference by exag-

gerating her responses, and the interviewer's interpretation of her responses might reflect this difference in his or her interpretation of responses.

Nonresponse bias: The reason a large proportion of the sample refused to answer questions regarding purchase intent might bias the results. For example, they might do their wash in the traditional manner, and be too embarrassed to admit unfamiliarity with modern appliances like washing machines.

Halo effect bias: Words used in the questionnaire, or the way these words are sequenced, can distort responses. For example, if the name of the washing machine manufacturer is familiar to the respondent and is used early in the questioning, she might generalize favorable attitudes toward this name into a statement of intent to buy the washing machine.

6. On a scale of 1 to 7 ("excellent" to "poor"), both computers score equally high on reliability (2.2), so this is not an issue in differentiating the two. Significant differences between perceptions occur in the areas of response time and transportability, with B scoring 3 points higher in response time, and A scoring 5 points higher in transportability. Since A is perceived as a better value than B by 5 points ("excellent" vs. "fair"), it can probably be inferred that users place a much higher value on speed than on portability. Given these perceptual differences—and assuming this is a market in which B wishes to compete against A—a product strategy for B might be to redesign its computer to make it at least as fast as A, even at some sacrifice of portability.

7. Among the variables that could invalidate findings from this study:

   - Selection: In spite of efforts to choose samples from similar populations, people in each city might tend to have significantly different attitudes toward dentifrices.

   - Mortality: Many more people might drop out of one group than the other so that they would no longer be matched.

   - History: Outside events bias results. For example, in one of the test cities, a competitor, learning of the test, might seek to "jam" results by manipulating marketing mix variables (for example, a special promotion).

8. Coding: You might, for example, identify certain important attributes (charm, wit, and the like) that both your friend and the prospective blind date have in common. Tabulating: You might then total the extent to which each possesses these attributes (for example, they both score "10" in "good looks" and "loves Bruce Springsteen"). Analysis: You compare these totals in these key categories and conclude they are meant for each other.

9 CONSUMER BEHAVIOR

OVERVIEW

An understanding of consumer behavior is critical during all stages of the strategic planning process, from setting objectives through implementation and control. Key to an understanding of consumer behavior is an understanding of the intra- and interpersonal influences that trigger the buyer decision process and the dynamics of this process.

CONSUMER BEHAVIOR DEFINES TARGET MARKETS AND MARKETING MIXES

This chapter focuses on consumer behavior, which we define as the full range of decisions and activities involved in evaluating, acquiring, using, and disposing of goods or services. For example, referring to Merton's strategy for positioning and promoting MM systems, planners will want to know how buyers in prospective markets learn about MM systems; how they assess these systems against competitive models; who, or what, influences the selection of an MM system over competitive makes; how and when these systems are used; what benefits and features are desired; and what happens to obsolete MM systems.

Answers to these and related questions about the nature and needs of target market members will prove helpful to Merton marketers during all stages of the SMP process. First, it will help them segment broad market aggregates into smaller target markets, each comprising groups of prospective consumers with similar buying behavior favorable to the purchase of MM computers (segmentation concepts are covered in Chapter 11).

This information on consumer markets will also help in setting marketing objectives, measuring and forecasting sales and marketing potential (covered in Chapter 12), preparing budgets, and controlling the effectiveness of sales efforts. Perhaps the most important use of information on consumer behavior is in building marketing mixes calculated to appeal to members of each target market. For example, with an understanding of how, why, from whom, and for what price MMs are purchased by members of a given target market, Merton planners will be in a much better position to reach them with a product positioned, priced, and promoted to meet these criteria.

A MODEL OF CONSUMER BEHAVIOR

The nature of consumer behavior, focusing on when, why, how, and where people do or do not buy products, is illustrated by the "black box" model in Figure 9-1.

To illustrate the decision-making process implicit in this model, consider the process leading up to an architect's purchase of an MM system consisting of a personal computer with associated hardware and software designed to provide a complete training program package customized to her needs.

First, the architect might have been exposed to two kinds of stimuli (from the "Environmental Factors" box in the model): **marketing stimuli,** which are largely under the control of the marketing manager, and **environmental stimuli,** which are largely beyond the marketing manager's control. For instance, the architect might have been impressed with product features and price when a Merton sales representative put on a demonstration/ presentation at the architect's firm. Then, the favorable response of her associates to the MM system might have further persuaded her to investigate a possible purchase.

Helping to define and direct this investigation further are a group of "buyer characteristics" (the "Buyer's Black Box" in the model), including the architect's **perception** of the MM system as compared to competitive systems and the **motivating goals** she feels the MM will help achieve. Many, perhaps all, of these stimuli would then combine to motivate and direct her decision to purchase the MM system (the "Buyer's Response" box).

ENVIRONMENTAL FACTORS		BUYER'S BLACK BOX		BUYER'S RESPONSES
Marketing Stimuli	Environmental Stimuli	Buyer Characteristics	Decision Processes	
Product Price Place Promotion	Economic Technical Political Cultural	Attitudes Motivation Perceptions Personality Lifestyle	Problem recognition Information search Alternative evaluation Purchase decision Post-purchase behavior	Product choice Brand choice ·Dealer choice Purchase timing Purchase amount

Figure 9–1. Black box model shows how stimuli, consumer characteristics, and decision processes interact in eliciting consumer responses.

STIMULI THAT INFLUENCE CONSUMER BEHAVIOR

Stimuli that influence consumer decision-making processes can be classified as interpersonal (between people) or intrapersonal (within people). **Interpersonal influences** include social and cultural groups to which people belong or would like to belong, such as family- and gender-based groups. **Intrapersonal influences** include drives, perceptions, and attitudes that shape consumer behavior. Primarily, Merton planners were searching for strong underlying values and behaviors that were broadly similar among diverse cultures, that tended to differentiate one group, or market, from another, and that predisposed these groups toward Merton products.

The planners used this information on strengths, similarities, and differences to define worthwhile target markets, with similar values and behaviors favorable to MM systems, and to address questions pertaining to the MM's marketing mix strategy. For example, how would MM systems have to be modified to harmonize with current and evolving values and behaviors in different target markets? (If these values and behaviors were sufficiently similar across markets, no modification might be required.) What means of communication (for example, advertising and direct marketing) would apply? What media should be used to deliver these communications?

HOW INTERPERSONAL VARIABLES INFLUENCE CONSUMER BEHAVIOR

In understanding and integrating consumer behavior into MM marketing plans, Merton planners started with an examination of the influence of larger groups, such as cultures, subcultures, and social classes, on consumer behavior, and then narrowed to focus on the influence of smaller peer and reference groups. In general, the smaller the group is, the greater its influence on consumer behavior is.

CULTURES AND SUBCULTURES SHAPE BEHAVIOR

Employing analytical tools and techniques examined in Chapter 4, Merton planners identified cultural and subcultural values relating to consumer behavior toward MM systems in prospective entry markets. Later, these values would shape marketing plans calculated to stimulate favorable buying decisions.

In examining subcultures—separate segments of a culture organized around such factors as race, nationality, religion, or geographic location—the planners focused primarily on (1) subcultures that had grown sufficiently large and affluent to qualify as target markets, and (2) characteristics of these target markets on which Merton could base marketing programs to serve market needs. Examples of such markets follow.

• *AFRICAN-AMERICAN CONSUMERS*

The African-American population of the United States is growing in affluence, with a total annual purchasing power of more than $250 billion realized by the year 2000. Strongly motivated by quality and selection, blacks spend relatively more than whites on clothing, personal care, and home furnishings. They are also more price conscious and brand loyal, and shop more at neighborhood stores. As their buying power and sophistication grow, African-Americans are now emerging as an attractive market for pricier products such as large appliances, life insurance, automobiles, financial services, and computer-associated hardware and software.

• *HISPANIC CONSUMERS*

Numbering more than 40 million by the year 2000, Hispanic consumers—Americans of Mexican, Cuban, and Puerto Rican descent—are the second largest and fastest-growing U.S. minority, with an annual purchasing power exceeding $150 billion. More than half of all Hispanics live in six metropolitan areas—New York, Los Angeles, Miami, San Antonio, San Francisco, and Chicago. Long a target for marketers of food, beverages, and household care products, Hispanics, like African-Americans, are now emerging as an attractive market for upscale products like computers, photography equipment, and financial, recreation, and travel services. Hispanic consumers tend to be brand and quality conscious and are easily reached through growing networks of Spanish-language broadcast and print media.

• *MATURE CONSUMERS*

Composed of people 65 and older, the mature consumer segment of the population, numbering over 40 million by the year 2000, is becoming a very attractive market. Seniors are better off financially, with annual buying power exceeding $200 billion and twice the disposable income, than consumers in the under-35 age group. Although a natural target for products like laxatives and dentures, most seniors are healthy and active, with many of the same needs and wants as younger consumers. And with more time and money, they represent an ideal market for exotic travel, restaurants, high-tech home entertainment products, leisure goods and services, financial services, home physical fitness products, and personal care products.

In analyzing subcultural groups, the planners also recognized that, even in the most homogeneous of groups, there are usually as many differences as similarities within each subculture.

SOCIAL CLASS PREDICTS BUYING BEHAVIOR

As discussed in Chapter 4, a social class is a relatively homogeneous and enduring division of a culture whose members share similar values, interests, and behavior. As documented by researchers like Richard Coleman and James Engel, social classes are hierarchically structured, usually ranging from lower-lower to upper-upper strata, with approximate percentages of the population assigned to each stratum (for example, Coleman's model locates less than 1 percent of the population in the upper-upper stratum, 12 percent in the upper-middle stratum, and 9 percent in the upper-lower stratum). An individual's position as a member of a given social class is based on a number of variables, including amount and type of income, occupation, type of house, and area of residence. Persons within a given social class tend to act more alike than members of different social classes, including having distinct product and brand preferences in such areas as home furnishings, consumer electronics, travel and leisure activities, and automobiles. The fact that they also have distinct preferences in media (for example, *The New York Times* vs. *The National Enquirer*) often suggests the best media strategy for reaching a targeted social class.

HOW REFERENCE GROUPS INFLUENCE CONSUMER BEHAVIOR

Reference groups have a direct (face-to-face) or an indirect influence on consumer attitudes and behavior. Major reference group categories include

- Membership groups the individual already belongs to,

- Aspirational groups the individual would like to join, and

- Disassociative groups whose values the individual rejects.

Membership and aspirational groups influence people in a variety of ways of interest to marketers. They expose people to new products and behaviors, influence an individual's attitudes and self-concept, and create pressures to conform to group norms. The force of this influence depends on

- The cohesiveness of the group, with highly cohesive groups, such as a religious cult, exerting more influence;

- The people being influenced by group norms and values, with "other-directed" people, who adopt values of reference groups, more likely to be influenced than "inner-directed" people, who act more on personal values;

- The product concept, with group influence strongest when products are highly visible and can be seen in use by others, as with MM systems.

Family-, gender-, and age-based reference groups are of particular interest to global marketers in that they differ appreciably in form and substance among markets.

FAMILY-BASED GROUPS

As the smallest reference group with which the consumer interacts, the family is also the most important buying influence in society. Two kinds of family—the family of orientation and the family of procreation—exert this persuasive influence. The **family of orientation,** consisting of the consumer's parents and siblings, imparts behaviors and values toward religion, politics, economics, feelings of personal ambition, and product worth. This family can even influence the buyer's unconscious behavior. The **family of procreation,** comprising the consumer's spouse and children, has a more direct influence on buying behavior than any other group.

Key differences among family-based groups relate to the size, strength, and cohesion of the family unit. From a marketer's perspective, the average size of a household—which is a good measure of family size, although it includes related and nonrelated occupants—in a prospective market often defines the nature and size of a market for such products as appliances and prepared foods. For example, Norway (average household size: 2.1) would likely be a much better customer for single-serving portions of frozen food than Colombia (average household size: 6).

Strength and cohesion of family units are also key indicators of market potential for many products. In ethnic Mediterranean and Latin American communities, for example, the family constitutes the most important membership group, with family membership often exceeding individual accomplishment as a measure of social status. In these communities, families can exert strong leverage in shaping consumer behavior. Also helpful in shaping consumer behavior is family cohesion. For example, in ethnic Greek and Korean communities, strong family cohesion manifests itself in cooperative business ventures (restaurants, retail outlets, and the like) that are customers for diverse products and services.

The family life cycle (FLC), a useful construct for relating family influence to buying behavior (Table 9-1), assumes a number of distinct stages in the life of a typical family, each with different demographic characteristics, values, and product needs and each requiring a different marketing strategy. As a major determinant of buying behavior, the FLC is an effective basis for segmenting markets and is often the best way to account for consumption differences among people of the same age and sex.

Table 9–1. Consumption Patterns During Life Stages

Family Life Cycle Stage	Demographic and Consumption Patterns
1. Bachelor stage. Young, single people	Don't live at home. Few financial burdens. Fashion opinion leaders. Recreation oriented. Buy: basic kitchen equipment, furniture, cars, vacations, "mating game" equipment.
2. Newly married couples	Young, no children. Better off financially than in later stages. Highest purchase rate and highest durables purchases. Buy: cars, refrigerators, stoves, sensible and durable furniture, vacations.
3. Full nest I	Youngest child under age six. Home purchasing peak. Low liquid assets. Dissatisfied with finances. Interested in new, advertised products. Buy: washers, dryers, TV sets, baby food, vitamins, dolls, children's toys.
4. Full nest II	Youngest child age six or over. Better financial position. Some wives work. Less influenced by advertising. Buy: larger sizes, multiple units, many foods, bicycles, music lessons.
5. Full nest III	Older married couples with dependent children. Still better financial position. More wives and children have jobs. Advertising has less influence. High average purchase of durables. Buy: new, more tasteful furniture, auto travel, non-essential appliances, boats, dental services, magazines.
6. Empty nest I	Older married couples, no children living with them, head in labor force. Home ownership at peak. Most satisfied with finances. Interest in travel, recreation, self-education. Make gifts, contributions. Little interest in new products. Buy: vacations, luxuries, home improvements.

Table 9–1. *Continued*

7. Empty nest II	Older married, no children at home, head retired. Drastic income cut. Keep home. Buy: medical appliances, medical-care products that aid health, sleep, digestion.
8. Solitary survivor, in labor force	Income good, likely to sell home.
9. Solitary survivor, retired	Drastic income cut. Special needs for medical products, attention, affection, security.

In the domestic market, the FLC has been faulted for overlooking significant market segments, such as "singles" and "mingles" (unmarried couples of opposite sexes) categories, which more than tripled in size between 1975 and 1999. In global markets, similar modifications should be made to the FLC to reflect demographic and lifestyle characteristics.

GENDER-BASED GROUPS

Country-specific attitudes toward males and females are of interest to global marketers in that they help define the nature and size of markets, and marketing mixes that best meet the needs of these markets. To varying degrees, for example, most Asian and Islamic countries exhibit male preference, manifested in China by the widespread practice of aborting female fetuses, and in Saudi Arabia by the separated, downgraded socioeconomic status of women, who must attend separate schools, are generally restricted from working outside the home (and then mostly in professions with no male contact), and are legally prohibited from driving cars or riding in a taxi without a male escort. Even when women constitute a large portion of the working population, there are dramatic differences in types of jobs regarded as "male" or "female." In Sweden, for example, more than 45 percent of administrative and managerial positions are held by women, compared to less than 5 percent in Spain. Thus, for a company like Merton, an understanding of the relative socioeconomic status of the sexes can help answer a number of questions pertaining to consumer behavior, such as how large each market is, what products each needs, who makes purchasing decisions, and how each market can best be reached.

HOW INTRAPERSONAL VARIABLES INFLUENCE CONSUMER BEHAVIOR

Having identified significant interpersonal variables—such as cultural and social values—that defined target market characteristics and needs as well as marketing mix strategies for reaching target market members, Merton planners next focused on intrapersonal variables predisposing individual target market members toward the purchase of MM systems. For example, what would be the effect of a respondent's age and economic condition on a decision to purchase an MM system? What personal motivations would such a purchase satisfy? How would lifestyle and personality characteristics predispose purchase?

In exploring the nature and impact of these variables on consumer behavior, the planners began with demographic intrapersonal variables—including age, occupation, and economic circumstances—and then explored psychographic intrapersonal variables, including motivation, learning, perception, attitudes, personality, and lifestyle.

DEMOGRAPHIC INTRAPERSONAL VARIABLES

Information on demographic variables, which pertain to such state-of-being characteristics of human populations as size, density, location, age, sex, and race, are relatively easy to come by and frequently correlate well with buyer behavior. Thus, in every market studied, Merton planners found significant relationships among three demographic variables—age, occupation, and income—and interest in purchasing MM systems. They found, for example, that "middle management" in accounting, banking, and insurance fields, primarily in the 30–50 age group, had the strongest interest in purchasing MM systems and sufficient discretionary income and borrowing power to fulfill this interest.

PSYCHOGRAPHIC INTRAPERSONAL VARIABLES

Unlike demographic variables, significant psychographic variables—motives, attitudes, perceptions, and the like—are generally difficult to identify and measure. Often it's worth the effort, however, since these variables can be the most useful of all for segmenting markets and building persuasive marketing mix offerings that relate to potent emotive responses.

Following are brief definitions of motives, perceptions, attitudes, and lifestyles and the Merton planners' conclusions pertaining to the effect of each on consumer responses to MM marketing mix variables.

• *MOTIVATION*

A **motive,** or drive, is a stimulated need that an individual seeks to satisfy. Until it is satisfied—or otherwise eliminated—it will continue to generate an uncomfortable tension. Stimulated needs can be classified as primary buying motives (associated with such broad product categories as computers) or selective buying motives (associated with such specific product brands as MM computers). Marketing activities can be viewed as a way to both stimulate motives (to feel a need for a computer system) and to satisfy motives (to make an offer that meets this need that the buyer can't refuse).

Maslow[1] identifies a hierarchy of five levels of needs, arrayed in the order in which an individual is motivated to gratify them, starting with physiological needs and working up through safety, social, and esteem needs to self-actualization needs atop the hierarchy. Accepting Maslow's hierarchy, Moore would then attempt to identify the need hierarchy level occupied by prospective MM systems buyers, then plan a promotional campaign to reach this target market, based largely on a researched understanding of the nature and needs of this segment.

• *PERCEPTION*

Perception is the process by which people derive meaning from the selection, organization, and interpretation of stimuli from within themselves (such as a feeling of frustration) or from the external environment (such as an advertisement for MM computer systems). Three perception-related concepts are of particular interest to marketing managers. Here is how each might influence a promotional campaign for the Merton MM:

- **Selective exposure** means that people only have the mental capacity to process a small percentage of the millions of stimuli competing to "get through" to our cognitive centers. Stimuli (such as an advertisement or sales presentation) that relate to an anticipated event, show how the audience can satisfy needs, or represent a significant change in intensity from other stimuli have been found more likely to be selected. Thus, a full-page advertisement (intensity change) might announce a free special seminar to learn about MM systems (anticipated event) and explain how this seminar can satisfy needs for increased income and an improved lifestyle (need satisfaction).

- **Selective distortion** means that people change the meaning of dissonant stimuli so that they become consistent with their feelings and beliefs. For the marketer, this means that the offering should be consistent with these feelings and beliefs, or the intended meaning will be lost.

- **Selective retention** means that people are more likely to remember stimuli that support preconceived feelings and beliefs and to forget stimuli that do not. In general, people tend to ignore, or quickly forget, stimuli that they perceive as a functional risk (the product will not perform as claimed) or a psychological risk (the product will not enhance the prospect's self-concept or well-being). For stimuli

---

1 Abraham H. Maslow,*Motivation and Personality,* 2nd ed. (New York: Harper & Row, 1970) pp. 80–106.

promoting the MM, this suggests appeals stressing proofs of performance.

• *ATTITUDES*

Attitudes are relatively stable tendencies to perceive or act in a consistent way toward products or classes of products. They are formed or adjusted by what is learned from families, peers, and other social groups; from information received; and from previous behavior. Although attitudes are second only to intentions as predictors of behavior, they are difficult to define, measure, and relate to product classes (computers) or specific brands (Merton).

To mitigate this difficulty, Merton marketers found it useful to define and measure the influence of attitudes toward product purchases in terms of four product-related functional areas:

- **Utilitarian,** or the ability of the product to help achieve desired goals (a productive career path, for example);

- **Ego-defensive,** or the capability of the product to defend the buyer's self-image against internal or external threats;

- **Value expressive,** or the degree of consistency of the product with the buyer's central values or self-image;

- **Knowledge,** or the ability of the product to give meaning to the individual's beliefs and experiences.

For example, a measurement of these attitudinal dimensions (using rating scales discussed in Chapter 5) among middle managers might show confusion as to how the MM could achieve utilitarian or ego-defensive goals, which could be addressed in MM promotional literature.

• *LIFESTYLE*

Distinguishing combinations of activities, interests, and opinions that lead to relatively consistent and enduring responses to the environment comprise an individual's lifestyle. The usual technique for defining an individual's lifestyle, called **psychographics,** involves measuring attitudes, interests, and opinions (AIO) in diverse areas (work, politics, recreation, and the like) by soliciting agree-disagree responses on lengthy survey instruments. Once distinctive lifestyle groups are revealed through similar AIO response patterns, an attempt is made to relate these groups to demographic and marketing mix variables. Although problems involved in generating and interpreting lifestyle data can be formidable, they often provide multidimensional views of target market segments that suggest new product and product positioning opportunities, improved communications, and generally improved marketing strategies.

HOW BUYERS MAKE DECISIONS

Inter- and intrapersonal variables, along with broader economic, competitive, and legal environmental variables, all come together to influence buyer
decisions to buy or not to buy. To illustrate this decision-making process,
we move to a five-stage model of the buyer decision process (Figure 9-2).

Figure 9–2. Five-stage model of buyer decision process.

UNDERSTANDING THE DECISION-MAKING PROCESS

For marketers, the five segments of the buyer decision process serve as
a reminder that a prospect's decision to purchase a product is only one step
in a process that started before the decision and will have consequences
after. By illustrating the nature and dynamics of decision making, this model
also suggests strategies for leading the prospect through to a final, favorable
purchase decision. Market Focus 9-1 shows how a professional marketing
team followed these steps in launching a new product in the face of strong
environmental constraints.

MARKET FOCUS 9-1

The Consumer Decision Process Guides Rogaine's Promotion

Two specific challenges faced marketers at Pharmacia and Upjohn, Inc.
(P&U), a large pharmaceutical and health care company, when they
initially planned the marketing campaign for the newly developed
product, Rogaine—a prescription drug intended to restore hair
growth.

First, all promotion for the product would have to stay within the strict
regulatory guidelines of the Food & Drug Administration (FDA). This
meant that, until the product was fully approved by the FDA, the name
Rogaine could not appear in any promotional materials and, even after
approval, all claims would have to be totally documented. No puffery
or exaggerated claims are allowed.

Second, the fact that Rogaine was the first hair restorative product for which strong clinical evidence of efficacy existed categorized it as a uniquely new product. Consequently, few precedents existed regarding the nature and needs of prospective markets and how Rogaine should be positioned and promoted.

By way of addressing this second challenge, P&U marketers set about building a solid research base to guide their marketing initiatives. Research studies undertaken included a review of the secondary data on baldness, mail and telephone surveys, personal interviews, and focus-group sessions. They all focused primarily on attitudes toward baldness among men and women and how baldness affected an individual's self-perception.

The results of these studies indicated a broad spectrum of attitudes and opinions toward baldness, ranging from preference to aversion. In general, and despite a growing public acceptance of baldness, P&U's research indicated that society still pays close attention to a person's appearance, and women tend to shy away from balding men.

Analyzing the research data produced profiles of target markets toward which P&U would direct its marketing campaign, as well as promotional appeals and media strategies to reach these target markets.

Guided by the stages of the buyer decision process, the campaign for Rogaine began with promotion relating to the problem recognition step. Specifically, consumers were informed that those concerned with hair loss could contact a physician at a toll-free number to receive information on Rogaine (although the name was not noted) and how to get a prescription for the drug. Simultaneously, promotion was targeted to doctors, nurses, and pharmacists to make them aware of Rogaine's existence and features.

The next phase of the campaign related to the information search stage of the buyer decision process, with a more aggressive promotion strategy that used the Rogaine name (the FDA had approved the drug) and made a direct appeal urging prospective users to call doctors for information on Rogaine and a trial prescription. Helping prospective buyers get and evaluate the information they needed was a free video featuring doctors providing technical information on Rogaine, and men who had tried Rogaine with varying degrees of success.

By way of relating to the purchase decision stage of the process, P&U initiated a broad-based promotional campaign that (1) offered rebates for purchasing Rogaine ($10 toward a first bottle or $20 for sending in the box tops from the first four emptied bottles); (2) targeted hair stylists and barbers with offers of handling fees for displaying Rogaine; and (3) generated considerable publicity in media preferred by targeted groups, stressing the unique characteristics and benefits of Rogaine.

EFFECT OF BUYING SITUATIONS ON DECISION MAKING

To understand the extent to which all five stages of the buyer decision-making process must be accounted for, marketers should first understand something about buying situations in which these decisions get made. These situations are generally defined by (1) the amount of involvement and complexity they entail and (2) the number of individuals who influence the decision. Viewed in these terms, buyer decisions can be categorized as routinized, limited, or extensive problem solving.

- **Routinized problem solving** characteristically involves low-cost, low-risk, low-involvement products purchased impulsively or habitually. A six-pack of Diet Coke, or the latest *TV Guide* are examples of such products. The marketing challenge in response to routinized problem-solving situations is to (1) keep present customers by maintaining a consistent level of quality, service, and availability; and (2) attract new buyers through intensive product development and promotional activities (for example, new versions of Coca-Cola—classic, cherry, and the like—supported by intensive coupon promotions).

- **Limited problem solving** occurs when the buyer encounters unfamiliar brands in a familiar product class. This is the situation that typically awaits firms that export products to foreign markets for the first time, as when South Korea introduced its Hyundai automobile into the American marketplace to compete with familiar American and Japanese brands. To relate to the needs of buyers engaged in limited problem solving, the marketing effort should center around designing communication programs to increase buyer confidence and comprehension, often by positioning the unfamiliar brand against familiar ones.

- **Extensive problem solving** characterizes situations where the product class itself is unfamiliar and few, if any, standards exist on which to base a decision. Such a situation typically prevails with high-involvement products that are comparatively expensive, highly visible, and of enduring interest to the buyer. Such products are also usually associated with a diversity of risks, including **performance risk** (the product won't perform properly), **financial risk** (it will cost more than it's worth), **physical risk** (it might cause injury or threaten health), **psychological risk** (it won't be compatible with buyer self-image), **social risk** (it won't meet approval of peers), and **time-loss risk** (it will take too long to get the system purchased, delivered, repaired, or replaced).

SITUATIONS CONDITION BUYER RESPONSES

Marketers must also understand how the buyer decision-making process differs with different buying situations and what marketing responses are appropriate to each situation. To illustrate, we will examine an extensive problem-solving situation, involving many risks and all the steps of the decision-making process: problem recognition, information search, alternative evaluation, purchase decision, and post-purchase behavior.

PROBLEM RECOGNITION

Regardless of type of buyer decision situation, some combination of internal and external stimuli will first trigger the buying decision process by highlighting an unsatisfied need. For example, a manager in an accounting firm might be motivated to explore the purchase of an MM system by a felt need to enhance career opportunities (internal stimuli), combined with the effect of an associate's endorsement, as well as articles assessing personal computer training systems in accounting journals (external stimuli). In relating marketing plans to the dynamics of this first stage, Merton planners anticipated what kinds of needs or problems would most likely motivate prospects toward a product class (computers) and how these needs could be stimulated.

INFORMATION SEARCH

If the felt need-motivating behavior is strong enough and the product is capable of quickly satisfying this need, the buyer will probably not reach this second stage of the decision process. When it is reached, however, two levels of search activity are possible: (1) some search, during which heightened interest makes the buyer more receptive to product information, and (2) active information search, during which the buyer actively searches for such information.

The extent to which buyers engage in active search depends on a variety of considerations, including degree of motivation toward a product class, amount of information available, ease of obtaining additional information, value placed on this information, and the satisfaction of engaging in the search. In our example, the accounting manager was highly motivated to explore a personal computer (PC) purchase, which he saw as a way to satisfy a frustrated need to advance in his profession. He also perceived that information on PC training programs was readily available from professional journals, associations to which he belonged, and other accountants.

These information sources could be classified as either commercial or personal. **Commercial information sources,** such as an advertisement or article about personalized education programs in an accounting journal, perform information and persuasive functions. **Personal information,** like an endorsement from a respected associate, performs evaluative and legitimizing functions. The task of marketing planners is to determine, through research, the relative influence of commercial and personal information sources in the decision-making process and how this information can be most effectively distributed. In analyzing the accounting target market, for example, Merton planners determined that both sources would be equally important and that commercial information should be disseminated through publicity and advertising in highly regarded accounting trade journals and that personal information would be disseminated through accounting professional associations, at whose conventions Merton would be represented.

EVALUATION OF ALTERNATIVES

During this third stage of the decision-making process, prospective buyers evaluate alternative purchase selections resulting from the information search. Four models illustrate possible approaches buyers might use to arrive at a buying decision, depending on such considerations as the cost of the product, the use to be made of it, and the number of people involved in the decision process.

1. The **expectancy value model** is based on the assumption that buyers consider a number of product attributes in making a decision, assigning weights and values to each attribute, and purchasing the product with the highest score. To illustrate, assume that the manager of human resource development for a large insurance company is considering the purchase of MM computers and considers speed, memory, and portability to be the three most important attributes. Figure 9-3 illustrates the expectancy value model of his/her decision processes to select from among the three competing firms—Dell, Compac, and Merton—that emerged from her active information search.

   The Compac model is perceived as a 10 for speed, as compared to an 8 for the Dell model and a 7 for the Merton MM. Because speed and memory are each considered twice as important as transportability as desired product attributes, each is assigned a weight of 0.4, as against a weight of only 0.2 for transportability. Totaling the products of weights and values produces a tie, at 7.8, for the Dell and Merton models, with Compac the preferred choice with a score of 8.

BRAND	SPEED		MEMORY		PORTABILITY		TOTAL
	Value	Weight	Value	Weight	Value	Weight	
Dell	8	.4	10	.4	3	.2	7.8
Compac	10	.4	8	.4	4	.2	8
Merton	7	.4	8	.4	9	.2	7.8

Figure 9-3. Attribute criteria for personal computer purchase decisions.

2. The **conjunctive model** assumes that buyers base decisions on criteria that satisfy a set of minimum attribute levels. For example, given the values in Figure 9-3, if the human resources manager insisted that the personal computer her firm purchased have a memory capacity of at least 8 and a speed of at least 9, only the Compac model would remain in the choice set. A good illustration of the conjunctive model at work is a typical shopper buying products in a supermarket, with minimum standards required for each choice.

3. The **disjunctive model** assumes an either/or decision, based on high attribute levels. For example, the manager might decide she will not recommend purchase of personal computers unless each has either a cost value of 7 or a memory value of 8, in which case all three models will remain in the choice set.

4. The **lexicographic model** assumes people evaluate purchases on the basis of the most salient attributes (that is, attributes people are most likely to think of) and, in case of a tie, will shift to the next most salient attribute. This model is sometimes offered to explain how people choose leaders, with salient charisma given greater weight than positions on issues.

DECISION MODEL STRATEGY IMPLICATIONS

An understanding of decision models people use to select products can suggest product/market strategies. For example, strategies employed by Merton planners might be based on these assumptions regarding attitudes of accountants in a prospective entry market. (1) Accountants use the disjunctive decision model, with the primary requirement that memory capacity achieve at least a 9 rating. (2) However, if a memory capacity of 9 is not available in any of the alternative choices, processing speed of at least 9 will serve as a substitute. (3) Of the three attributes considered important, portability is the least important.

Referring again to Figure 9-3, it can be seen that, given these assumptions and perceptions, both the Compac and Merton brands, with their perceived values of 8 for memory, are summarily eliminated from the accountants' choice set.

Here are some strategies Merton planners might consider to get the MM back into the choice set:

- **Real repositioning:** Assuming that the accountants' perceptions are correct, improve the MM's memory so it achieves the desired 9 rating.

- **Psychological repositioning:** Assuming that the MM really is the equal of Dell in memory capacity, alter the perceptions of accountants to recognize this fact, perhaps through a promotional campaign featuring a point-by-point assessment of the three models.

- **Competitive depositioning:** This strategy would assume that the 10-rating on memory capacity achieved by Dell is an inaccurate perception—that it is really an 8 like the other two brands—and hence the buyer should go to the second criterion, speed, in which case only the Compac remains in the choice set.

- **Stressing neglected attributes:** This strategy would bypass attributes in which the MM was disadvantaged to focus on attributes in which it held an advantage (for example, the software package accompanying each computer). This attribute would be promoted as much more important than the others.

- **Altering importance weights:** If the preceding campaign succeeded in persuading prospective buyers that the "neglected attribute" was more important than processing speed and memory capacity in motivating a decision to buy, it would have achieved this objective by increasing the relative weight assigned to this attribute.

- **Shifting buyer's ideals:** This strategy implies the use of a highly persuasive "cosmic statement" to shift buyer focus from specific issues to a generalized ideal (for example, "No U.S. involvement in foreign wars!").

THE DECISION TO PURCHASE

Figure 9-4 depicts the relationship between the alternative evaluation stage just examined and the critical purchase-decision stage. Assume that, thanks to an effective "altering attribute weights" promotion strategy, the Merton MM attains the top rank in many accountants' choice sets (A) so that they now express an intention to purchase MM computer systems (B). At this point, two variables—attitudes of others and unanticipated situational factors—can still intervene to prevent the purchase of an MM. As much as possible, these variables should be anticipated in planning sales strategies for the MM.

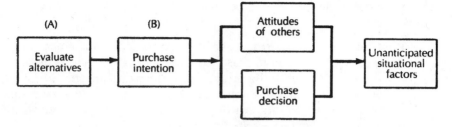

Figure 9-4. Purchase decision model.

- **Attitudes of others** can have a decided impact depending on the intensity of the negative attitude and the buyer's motivation to comply. For example, a partner at the accountant's firm might strongly recommend a less expensive alternative to the MM.

- **Unanticipated situational factors** can heavily influence buyer decisions. For example, perceived risk that the MM might not perform as expected might persuade the buyer to postpone this purchase while gathering more information and settling on a safe name brand computer.

POST-PURCHASE BEHAVIOR

Even after the purchase is made, the decision-making process is not over. This final stage focuses on the psychological responses of buyers to their purchase decisions. An understanding of these post-purchase responses is important to marketers in that they influence the likelihood that buyers will repurchase products and/or encourage others to purchase the product. These issues can be effectively addressed in promotion campaigns directed toward people who have already purchased the product, based on an understanding of the buyer's psychological response to the purchase and subsequent post-purchase reactions.

- **Psychological response:** According to Leon Festinger[2], all purchase decisions produce some degree of dissonance, which measures the gap between buyer expectations and product performance. For example, largely because of the time, effort, and expense involved in purchasing an MM, an accountant will probably have high expectations for its performance, and will likely perceive that it is not performing up to these expectations. This dissatisfaction, or **cognitive dissonance,** will likely lead to coping behavior, such as another search for information to reinforce the purchase decision. Alternately, the buyer might react to this dissonance by actually mag-

---

2 Leon Festinger, *A Theory of Cognitive Dissonance* (Stanford, CA: Stanford University Press, 1957).

nifying the gap between expectation and performance and begin to criticize the MM in public and privately.

- **Post-purchase reactions:** A satisfied customer is much more likely to recommend and repurchase the product; a dissatisfied customer is more likely to return the product or reduce dissonance by seeking confirming information. Public reactions might include legal action seeking redress directly from the firm or complaints to private or government agencies; private reactions could include boycotting the product or warning others against its use.

To address these anticipated post-purchase reactions, Merton planners devised a promotional strategy targeted toward target market members after they had purchased MM systems. Among other things, each buyer received a congratulatory telegram reinforcing the wisdom of the decision to purchase the MM and highlighting reliability, service, and state-of-the-art software associated with the system. Merton planners also solicited comments from owners, satisfied and unsatisfied, and followed up in various ways. Customer service representatives contacted dissatisfied buyers to eliminate the cause of dissatisfaction; comments from satisfied buyers were fed into the MIS database for analysis in designing future MM offerings.

INTERNATIONAL PERSPECTIVE

The essential task of marketers seeking to penetrate global markets is to first identify social-cultural values that predispose purchase of the product class or brand being marketed and then to identify countries with a sufficiently large proportion of these predisposing values to be considered a worthwhile target market. Finally, they need to build marketing mixes to attract target market members.

This is easier said than done, however. Developing information on consumer buying behavior is almost always more difficult in heterogeneous global markets than in the comparatively homogeneous domestic market. Differences in language, cultures, economies, and legal and political systems, as well as deficiencies of marketing research tools and techniques (discussed in Chapter 6) create sizeable problems in access, reliability, and validity of data—especially data pertaining to inter- and intrapersonal influences like reference groups, motives, and attitudes.

Exporters, in particular, face extensive problem-solving situations, with customers generally less familiar with their products, with fewer standards against which to base a purchase decision, and with these decisions often made in the context of dramatically different cultural values.

In Japan, for example, cultural values stressing the importance of cooperation, interdependence, and loyalty to the organization would require a different marketing appeal for MM systems than would cultural values in, for example, Poland, the Czech Republic, and Hungary, where a newly emerging class of free-market entrepreneurs aspires to values of their counterparts in Western Europe, while rejecting values of the communist command economies they helped overthrow.

In responding to these situations, marketers must understand what program modifications will be needed (language, taboo avoidance, and the like) consistent with cultural differences. They must also understand which risks (performance, financial, social, and so on) influence the decision-making process in different cultural contexts, and how these risks can be addressed (for example, offering an unusually strong warranty or money-back guarantee). Global Focus 9-1 shows how an understanding of the nature and needs of different markets helped in marketing ostrich meat in domestic and international markets.

GLOBAL FOCUS 9-1

Ostrich Rancher Looks to Feather His Nest in Overseas Markets

As general manager and vice president of Zion View Ostrich Ranch in St. George, Utah, Rick White oversees a ten-person, 250-acre operation that raises ostriches for meat and other products. The meat is marketed through specialty meat distributors and grocery stores, which order thousands of pounds a week.

"The biggest advantage of eating ostrich is that it is 98 percent fat-free and makes for a tasty and healthful meal, without the high fat content in beef or the potential for salmonella poisoning," White says.

To reinforce this point, the ranch's promotional literature describes ostrich as "A versatile red meat with mildly beefy flavor that makes a flexible addition to any menu."

"We've had great success here in the United States for different reasons," says White, citing the growing popularity of low-fat ostrich meat being sold in retail and health food stores.

"In addition, ostrich is a favorite of the lobster tail crowd who patronize pricey 'white tablecloth' restaurants, and of patrons who enjoy dining on unique foods like venison," he says.

Zion View first entered the domestic marketplace with ostrich meat in 1995, and began to tap the Japanese and European markets in 1996 as part of its long-term strategic marketing plan.

"One of the major appeals for doing business in Japan and Europe is that people spend more time dining at fine restaurants in those countries than in the United States," he says. "So obviously we are concentrating heavily on those marketing segments."

The Japanese and Europeans, like Americans, are becoming more conscious about their eating habits and are looking to reduce fat intake without diminishing the overall dining experience. "Ostrich is healthy eating without the sacrifice in taste," says White.

Source: Curtice K. Cultice, "Where's the Beef?," *Business America,* U.S. Department of Commerce, October 1996.

WHEN MARKETING PROGRAMS CAN BE STANDARDIZED

Somewhat offsetting these problems in social-cultural diversity is a growing recognition of the universality of much consumer behavior, especially among countries that have achieved higher levels of development. For example, one survey of 100 senior executives of leading multinationals in consumer package goods industries found that two thirds of total marketing programs—including product, price, distribution, and promotion components—were highly standardized, that is, practically identical from country to country. In promotion, the marketing mix area most responsive to differing cross-cultural characteristics and needs, study findings showed that almost three quarters of advertising messages had been standardized.

CHAPTER PERSPECTIVE

An understanding of consumer behavior is critical to successful strategic marketing planning, helping to define target markets, develop and implement marketing mix strategies, measure market potential, forecast sales, and control marketing effectiveness. While especially important in global markets, information on consumer markets, constrained by differences among nations, is also difficult to generate and process. A systematic approach for addressing these difficulties involves identifying and measuring the impact of inter- and intrapersonal variables (for example, peer groups, lifestyles, motives, and attitudes) on consumer behavior during each stage of the buyer decision-making process, from problem recognition through postpurchase evaluation.

KNOW THE CONCEPTS
TERMS FOR STUDY

Age-based groups
Altering importance weights
Aspirational groups
Attitude
Behavioral sciences
Buyer's black box
Cognitive dissonance
Commercial sources
Competitive depositioning
Consumer behavior
Decision-making process
Demographic variables
Disassociative groups
Environmental stimuli
Family-based groups
Family life cycle
Family of orientation
Family of procreation
Financial risk
Gender-based groups
Information search
Interpersonal variables
Intrapersonal variables

Learning
Lifestyle
Marketing stimuli
Maslow's hierarchy
Membership groups
Motives
Motivational research
Perception
Performance risk
Personal information sources
Personality
Physical risk
Post-purchase behavior
Problem recognition
Psychological repositioning
Psychological risk
Psychographics
Purchase decision
Real repositioning
Reference groups
Shifting buyer's ideals
Social risk
Stressing neglected attributes

MATCHUP EXERCISES

1. Match the promotional campaign outcome in the second column with the group that most influenced this outcome listed in the first column.

1. aspirational group

2. disassociative group

a. Campbell Soup stresses convenience in promoting soup to mothers in Poland, where 98 percent of soups are home-made.

b. Levi Strauss features Iowa teenagers in advertising its jeans in Indonesia.

3. families of orientation

    c. Dial soap achieves global success with its "Aren't you glad you use Dial" standardized campaign.

4. gender-based groups

    d. Harley-Davidson improves its product and image to attract a new market in Japan—young managers who don't want oil spilled on their Gucci loafers.

2. Match the campaign strategy in the second column with the associated purchase risk in the first column.

1. performance risk

    a. Perrier mineral water promoted itself as being served in the best restaurants.

2. psychological risk

    b. General Mills' Toy Group's European subsidiary, launching its G.I. Joe product line, has to change its commercials in Germany and Belgium, which ban advertising with violent or military themes.

3. financial risk

    c. Zippo lighters offer an unconditional money-back guarantee.

4. social risk

    d. The Rich Lumber Company of Beardstown, Illinois, ships a British contractor a trial container of kitchen cabinet doors to quality-test for six months.

3. Match the researcher's name in the first column with the significant finding in the second column.

1. Abraham Maslow

    a. distinct characteristics and product needs of people in different social classes

2. Leon Festinger

    b. the nature of the gap separating a buyer's expectation and perception of a product's performance

3. Richard Coleman

    c. human needs can be categorized in terms of physiological and psychological criteria

4. Match the stage of the buying decision process in the first column with the situation described in the second column.

1. problem recognition

    a. Winter work pressures are getting to you. Maybe it's time for a nice vacation to Florida or Hawaii.

2. information search

    b. You have in mind a specific price for a vacation package to either Florida or Hawaii.

3. evaluation of alternatives

    c. You check the Internet for the best prices and vacation package offerings.

4. post-purchase behavior

    d. Somehow, after your vacation in Hawaii is over, you still don't feel that you got the best deal.

QUESTIONS FOR REVIEW AND DISCUSSION

1. In the context of the strategic marketing planning process, explain the importance of an understanding of consumer behavior concepts and processes.

2. Discuss how motives, perceptions, and attitudes might combine to activate the purchase of a Merton MM system by a manager in an accounting firm intent on achieving partner status. What would be the general role of marketing in this process?

3. Describe how the components of the black box model might explain the impulse purchase of a *People* magazine at a supermarket checkout counter.

4. Describe how each of the following reference groups might have been instrumental in the success of a political party in a presidential election: membership, aspirational, disassociative.

5. Discuss, in terms of the factors that determine the strength of group influence on individual behavior, why pressure to succeed in college might be greater on the children of a family of Vietnamese immigrants than on children in a typical suburban American family.

6. At which level of Maslow's hierarchy of needs are the following messages directed?

- "Warning: Smoking can be dangerous to your health"
- "Don't leave home without it" (American Express)
- "Reach out and touch someone" (AT&T)
- "Be all that you can be" (U.S. Army)

ANSWERS
MATCHUPS

1. 1b, 2c, 3a, 4d
2. 1c, 2b, 3d, 4a
3. 1c, 2b, 3a
4. 1a, 2c, 3b, 4d

QUESTIONS FOR REVIEW AND DISCUSSION

1. The strategic marketing planning process involves identifying and defining target markets and matching marketing mix offerings to the nature and needs of these markets. This matching process is done in the context of a company mission, business and marketing objectives that derive from this mission, and strategies based on a researched understanding of how company strengths and weaknesses relate to marketplace threats and opportunities. In terms of this definition of the SMP process, everything—missions, objectives, marketing mix offerings, strategies—begins with and depends on an understanding of consumer behavior including prospective customer needs, what products and services the company can profitably market to meet these needs, and how these products and services can best be positioned.

2. A motive is a stimulated need that an individual seeks to satisfy; a perception is the process by which people derive meaning from the selection, organization, and interpretation of stimuli; and an attitude is a tendency to act in a consistent way toward products or classes of products. An example might illustrate how these three variables come together to activate an accountant's purchase of a Merton MM system. First, we understand that the accountant is motivated to achieve partner status (the unsatisfied, stimulated need). Furthermore, he or she might perceive (1) that an intensive training program might help to achieve this goal and (2) that the MM computer system, with associated training hardware, is the best such training system available. These perceptions will help condition an attitude tending toward the purchase of the MM system. The role of marketing in this process is to activate motives (for example, the unfulfilled need to achieve partner status), condition perceptions toward products that will satisfy unfulfilled needs, and, in so doing, also condition favorable attitudes (and actions) toward these products.

3. The marketing stimulus was the magazine itself, which might have featured an article capable of filling your social need to read about a well-publicized celebrity. Your response to the influence of these marketing and internal stimuli—the purchase of the magazine—results from your mind's information-processing activities.

4. Volunteers for the candidate were brought together in membership groups (Young Republicans or Democrats, for example), to plan in-home presentations to elicit support for the candidate. Meanwhile, the candidate was effectively excoriating disassociative groups ("those crazy big spenders") while associating his or her position with groups reflecting the party platform.

5. The Vietnamese family would probably be more cohesive because its members have suffered privation together and face, together, new pressures in an alien environment. Also, by tradition, members of this family tend to be "other directed" in that they exhibit a disciplined obedience to the wishes of parents and grandparents. Finally, the product in this case—a college education—is highly visible in terms of the many successful people with whom the Vietnamese family associates, directly or indirectly.

6. Each of these promotional messages may be directed to groups occupying more than one level of Maslow's hierarchy; however, the most likely target levels are:

- "Warning: Smoking can be . . . ," safety and security
- "Don't leave home . . . ," safety and security
- "Reach out . . . ," belonging
- "Be all that you can . . . ," self-fulfillment

10

ORGANIZATIONAL MARKETS AND BUYING BEHAVIOR

OVERVIEW

. The organizational market is composed mainly of manufacturers, trade industries, governments, and institutions, all defined and classified in the government's Standard Industrial Classification (SIC) system. It is much larger than the consumer market, involving many more transactions, and twice as many dollars. Demand patterns characterizing organizational markets include greater concentration geographically and by industry, direct purchasing, demand derived largely from consumer market demand, dramatic demand fluctuations, elastic then inelastic demand curves, and reciprocity arrangements. Buying practices are much more sophisticated than in consumer markets, involving buying centers, buyclasses, buyphases, and systematic procedures for evaluating vendors and values.

COMPONENTS OF THE ORGANIZATIONAL MARKET

The organizational market comprises the industrial producer market, the reseller market, the government market, and the institutional market. The following discussion covers characteristics of each market of concern to marketing planners, including relative size, demand patterns, products purchased, and purchasing policies and practices.

THE INDUSTRIAL PRODUCER MARKET

This market consists of individuals and organizations that acquire goods and services used, directly or indirectly, in the production of other products and services that are sold, rented, or otherwise supplied to others. Included are manufacturing firms, farmers and other resource industries, construction contractors, and providers of such services as transportation, public utilities, finance, insurance, and real estate. This market is typically the largest and most diverse of all the organizational market aggregates, frequently offering the largest sales and profit potential and the most formidable competitive challenges.

Figure 10-1, which shows the transactions involved in purchasing a single MM computer system, also shows reasons why the industrial producer market is typically the largest of all the aggregates, organizational or consumer. Note that the consumer market is involved in only one of the five transactional areas in which products are bought and sold, whereas the industrial producer and trade industries markets are each involved in two. In terms of the U.S. market, this translates into total annual sales of $3.5 trillion worth of goods and services in the industrial producer market, and $3 trillion worth of goods and services in the trade industries market, a total almost three times that of the total buying power of the entire consumer market. In terms of the value added by manufacturing—or the difference between the price charged by manufacturers and the cost of their inputs—the industrial producer market contributes about $1 trillion.

INDUSTRIAL MARKETS DIFFER FROM CONSUMER MARKETS

Industrial markets differ from consumer markets in terms of products purchased, demand patterns, and purchasing practices. For illustrative purposes, we will refer to a German automobile manufacturer.

This automobile manufacturer buys millions of marks worth of products and services in the course of a typical year, but practically all can be classified into four broad product categories:

RAW MATERIAL PROCESSOR	MERTON CONSUMER PRODUCTS DIV.	WHOLESALER	RETAILER	CONSUMER
BUYS: Copper, plastics, silicon Equipment Labor Energy	BUYS: Wire Plastic forms chip circuits Equipment Labor Energy	BUYS: Personal computers Space Equipment Labor Energy	BUYS: Personal computers Space Equipment Labor Energy	BUYS: Personal computer
SELLS: Wire, plastic forms etc.	SELLS: Personal computers	SELLS: Personal computers	SELLS: Personal computers	

Figure 10–1. Organizational market transactions in producing one product.

- **Long-lived capital goods** depreciated over time, including heavy equipment and installations;

- **Short-lived accessory items,** like tools and office machines, that don't become part of the finished product;

- **Expense items,** including raw materials used in production processes, and components, such as tires and small motors, that become part of the finished automobiles (original equipment, or OEM, items);

- **Supplies,** including maintenance, repair, and operating (MRO) items, like brooms, nails, and paper clips that don't go into the final product.

Marketing mix attributes of these products are discussed in Chapter 13.

SIC CATEGORIES DEFINE INDUSTRIES AND TRADES

The federal government's Standard Industrial Classification system, which precisely defines individual industries and trade within the total organizational market, is an invaluable tool for planning and controlling marketing plans. Under the SIC system, two-digit code numbers are assigned to each of ten broad industry categories (see column 2, Table 10-1). For example, the Merton Company's industrial products division falls within the category of "Electrical machinery, equipment, and supplies," which is assigned the code number 36. That category is part of the broad "manufacturing" industry, whose two-digit codes range from 20 to 39.

Within each industry classification, subindustries are further identified and defined with a third code digit. For example, within the 36 SIC category, the addition of a third digit 7 (367) more precisely defines the industry as "electronic components." For certain industries, four-, five-, and even seven-digit SIC codes are assigned. The SIC code number 3679, for example, identifies firms that manufacture electronics products primarily marketed to the appliance and computer industries, and more precisely defines the Merton Company's industrial products division.

The *Standard Industrial Classification Manual,* also published by the government, further defines each coded industry in terms of the products or services it produces and the processes and products used in these production activities. Other information on SIC-coded industries, such as size and sales potential characteristics, is available from a number of different government publications, such as the *Census of Manufacturers* and the *Census of Retailing and Wholesaling,* and from trade associations, business publications, state industrial directories, and private firms like McGraw Hill and Dun & Bradstreet.

Table 10–1. Organizational Market Categories

Functional Category	SIC Category	Size Categories		Employees per Organization
		No. of Organizations	No. of Employees	
INDUSTRIAL PRODUCERS				
Agriculture, forestry, fishing	01–09	3,486,000	3,571,000	1
Mining	10–14	181,000	1,028,000	6
Construction	15–17	1,412,000	5,756,000	4
Manufacturing	20–39	569,000	20,286,000	36
Transportation, Utilities	40–49	570,000	6,552,000	11
Finance, insurance, real estate	60–67	2,179,000	6,270,000	3
Services	70–89	4,777,000	30,090,000	6
TOTAL		13,174,000	73,553,000	6
TRADE INDUSTRIES				
Wholesalers	50–51	383,000	4,120,000	11
Retailers	52–59	1,855,000	16,638,000	9
TOTAL		2,238,000	20,758,000	9
GOVERNMENTS				
Federal	91–97	1	2,862,000	
State		50	3,747,000	
Local		82,290	9,324,000	
TOTAL		82,341	15,933,000	
OVERALL TOTALS		15,494,341	110,244,000	8

Source: U.S. Bureau of the Census, *Statistical Abstract of the United States: 1992,* 112th ed. (Washington, DC: U.S. Government Printing Office).

The SIC code system, through the vast amount of information it gathers, organizes, and presents, offers marketing managers clearly identified, defined, and presegmented markets. Thus, for example, the marketing manager for Merton's industrial products division would have easy access to information about the five three-digit industries that generate more than 80 percent of the division's sales and profits. This information is summarized in Table 10-2.

This summarized information, derived from a useful Labor Department publication called *County Business Patterns,* enables the marketing manager to know how many employees are in each industry in a single state in Merton's territory, as well as how much they get paid (columns 3 and

Table 10–2. SIC Analysis of Five Key Industries

(1) Code	(2) Industry	(3) No. of Employees	(4) Payrolls (000)	(5) Total Reporting Units	(6) No. of Reporting Units by Employee Class		
					8-49	58-99	100 +
361	Electric distribution products	6820	12,841	30	16	5	9
364	Lighting and wiring devices	5840	11,178	41	32	3	6
365	Radio, television equipment	1078	2,000	15	10	1	4
366	Communication equipment	669	1,090	10	7	2	1
367	Electronic components	7302	11,560	61	41	10	10

4). These are useful measures of the size and buying power of each industry. The two final columns in the table also provide useful information on the degree of concentration in each industry. For example, there are relatively few small firms in the 361 industry (where nine of thirty firms each employ more than 100 employees), and many more such firms in the 364 industry, where only six of forty-one firms employ more than 100 employees.

This readily accessible information from *County Business Patterns* can then be supplemented with more detailed information from Merton's own sales records and from other government publications, trade journals, and associations serving the 36 industry. The marketing manager can then develop, implement, and control marketing plans and programs based on the needs and characteristics of industries within the entire target market. (In Chapter 11, we will illustrate how SIC data are used to develop data on sales potential to start the strategic planning process.)

DEMAND PATTERNS CHARACTERIZING INDUSTRIAL MARKETS

When compared to demand patterns in consumer markets, demand patterns in industrial markets tend to be more concentrated, more direct, more dependent on demand patterns in other markets, more elastic initially and inelastic subsequently, and more likely to be dependent on purchases of related products and reciprocal arrangements.

• *CONCENTRATED DEMAND*

When compared to demand in consumer markets, demand in industrial markets is much more concentrated geographically and by industry—with fewer, larger manufacturing plants in related industries located in areas close to such resources as transportation, skilled workers, and power.

Industrial demand is also concentrated by purchasing practices, with most purchasing offices for large manufacturers concentrated in large metropolitan areas. Finally, demand concentration is displayed in a disproportionate relationship between size and productivity, with a relatively small number of plants, consistent with Pareto's principle, employing most of the production employees and generating most of the value added by manufacturing.

This high degree of concentration affects key aspects of the seller company's marketing mix. For example, it is easier to communicate with customers and prospects—the "promotion" aspect—and product distribution channels tend to be shorter than for final customers.

• *DIRECT PURCHASING*

Industrial buyers are more likely to purchase products directly from manufacturers, and in larger quantities, than are consumers. This is particularly true for products that are complex and expensive, like factory automation equipment used by automobile manufacturers.

• *DERIVED DEMAND*

Demand for industrial products derives largely from demand for consumer goods. For example, if MM systems sell well among managers and professionals—ultimate consumers—the producers of MM systems components will also do well.

• *FLUCTUATING DEMAND*

Small changes in consumer demand can lever much larger changes in industrial demand. To illustrate, assume demand for a popular minivan introduced by the auto manufacturer exceeds the firm's capacity to produce them. The company must then either build, or otherwise acquire, new plant facilities to handle this excess demand and anticipated future demand. This will result in sizeable purchases of industrial goods and services to accommodate demand that might only be slightly more than anticipated. Conversely, sales of this minivan might drop, say, 5 percent below expectations, but as a result the manufacturer might cut back purchases of OEM items more than 50 percent, relying on inventory until conditions improve. The disproportionate change in industrial demand caused by changes in consumer demand is called the **accelerator principle.**

• *ELASTIC DEMAND INITIALLY, INELASTIC DEMAND SUBSEQUENTLY*

Because many suppliers are actively competing on price for contracts, industrial demand can be extremely elastic during the early negotiation stage of the purchasing process, with demand increasing substantially with small decreases in competitive prices. Once contracts are negotiated, however, demand is inelastic in that demand for many industrial products is not influenced by short-run price changes. For example, assume that the automobile manufacturer contracts to purchase 1,000,000 fuses at a cost of $.15 per fuse, and streams them into the production of its automobiles. If the price of the fuses then drops to $.13 apiece, the company will not purchase additional quantities of fuses because the cost of storing them would exceed the small savings. Nor is the manufacturer likely to renegotiate its contract with the fuse manufacturer if a competitor comes in with the $.13 price; it would be too expensively disruptive to change suppliers in midstream. Of course, if the competitor's price were appreciably less—say, $.10 per fuse, where big cost savings resulted—the automobile manufacturer might change suppliers.

• *JOINT DEMAND*

Frequently, demand for some industrial products is related to demand for other industrial products. For example, if the automobile manufacturer has delivery problems with fuse boxes, it will probably cut back on its purchases of fuses.

• *RECIPROCAL ARRANGEMENTS*

Frequently, industrial buyers will select as suppliers firms that also purchase their products. For example, the automobile manufacturer might agree to purchase its fuses from a large electronics firm that agrees to specify the manufacturer's automobiles for its automobile fleet. In the United States, both the Federal Trade Commision (FTC) and the Justice Department forbid such reciprocity arrangements if it can be proved they unfairly shut out competition. If a competitor can prove that a reciprocity arrangement overrode considerations of price, quality, and service, the arrangement could be voided.

THE INDUSTRIAL BUYING PROCESS

Largely because of the costs, risks, and opportunities associated with the industrial buying function, it is frequently viewed as an important profit center, where the investment in goods and services purchased can be managed and controlled to improve the firm's profits and competitive posture. With this emphasis on profitability, many modern purchasing departments have evolved along lines similar to those of marketing departments, integrating functions—such as traffic, production scheduling, warehousing and inventory control—not traditionally associated with core procurement functions.

This broadened perception of the procurement function as an integrated, professionalized profit center, combined with the application of modern management techniques and controls in implementing this function, can spell opportunity for marketers who understand and can relate to these trends.

THE BUYING CENTER CONCEPT

The increasingly complex and professional nature of the procurement function has led to the development of the buying center concept, defined as all individuals and groups that participate in the purchase decision process because they share common risks and goals arising from buying decisions. Membership in buying centers varies with the cost and complexity associated with buying situations, or **buyclass categories.** These are classified as straight rebuy, modified rebuy, and new task situations.

- **Straight rebuy situations** involve purchases of a routine, repetitive nature, such as office supplies or inexpensive plant maintenance items. Such products require no modifications and are generally purchased on a regular basis from suppliers on the customer's list.

- **Modified rebuy situations** are essentially straight rebuy situations that have been taken out of this category by a change in price or specification. For example, a competitor might offer the present MM customer a similar system at a considerably lower cost.

- **New task situations** involve products never purchased before, thus entailing a higher degree of cost and risk than is usually associated with straight or modified rebuy situations (for example, purchasing expensive MM systems for the first time). These situations typically involve a larger number of people and a greater need for product information focusing on product specifications, price limits, delivery, service, payment terms, order quantities, and vendor acceptability standards.

Understanding how a company's products are perceived in terms of these buyclass categories can help salespeople recognize competitive threats and opportunities and do a more creative job of serving customer needs. Here are some of these threat/opportunity situations:

- **Threat:** A competitor tries to transform a straight rebuy situation involving an MM system into a modified rebuy or new task situation involving a system claimed to be superior.

- **Opportunity:** The salesperson turns a competitive straight rebuy situation into a modified rebuy situation favoring the MM system.

- **Opportunity:** The salesperson creates new task situations for MM systems by creating request-for-proposal situations in which she dramatizes savings and efficiencies.

ROLES OF BUYING CENTER MEMBERS

Understanding and responding to buyclass situations also requires an understanding of the various roles assumed by buying center members involved in these situations. For example, in preparing her presentation in behalf of the MM electronic training and development system, the salesperson dealt with:

- A gatekeeper who controls the information flow: In this case, the gatekeeper was a chief procurement officer who assessed her concept and decided whether, and in what form, it warranted further consideration.

- Two influentials: In the form of EDP and T&D (Training and Development) managers, the influentials were enthusiastic about installation of the new system and helped developed specifications for the system.

- A decider: In the form of the human resources manager, the decider made the final decision as to whether the system would be purchased and from what supplier.

- A buyer: The salesperson negotiated details of the sale with the buyer.

- The user: The T&D manager responsible for the operation of the system is the one who identified the need for the system in the first place.

In modified rebuy and new task situations, planning the sales presentation typically involves anticipating which roles will be supportive and hostile to the purchase decision, and how they will interact.

In the case of simple, inexpensive straight rebuy products, major influences motivating favorable purchase decisions are usually personal in nature, often based on social friendships between buyer and seller. As products become more complex and costly, however, industrial salespeople must deal with more people assuming more roles, and with more customer concerns in a variety of areas. Typical economic concerns, for example, focus on cost-benefit relationships, product and supplier reliability, and product guarantees and warranties. Environmental concerns focus on the likelihood of materials shortages, competitive advantages, and technological obsolescence. Organizational concerns focus on the compatibility of products with the firm's systems and procedures.

BUYPHASE ACTIVITIES

In addition to classifying product procurement situations into buyclasses, modern materials management departments and salespeople calling on these departments also classify procurement activities into **buyphases,** which they relate to each buyclass situation. Table 10-3 outlines such buyclass activities typically associated with each buyclass situation to provide guidelines for covering each situation efficiently and productively.

Table 10–3. Buyphase Activities Related to Buyclass Situations

STAGES OF THE BUYING PROCESS (BUYPHASES)	BUYING SITUATIONS (BUYCLASSES)		
	New Task	Modified Rebuy	Straight Rebuy
1. Problem recognition	Yes	Maybe	No
2. General need description	Yes	Maybe	No
3. Product specification	Yes	Yes	Yes
4. Supplier search	Yes	Maybe	No
5. Proposal solicitation	Yes	Maybe	No
6. Supplier selection	Yes	Maybe	No
7. Order routine specification	Yes	Maybe	No
8. Performance review	Yes	Yes	Yes

Source: Adapted from Patrick J. Robinson, Charles W. Faris, and Yocam Wind, *Industrial Buying and Creative Marketing* (Boston: Allyn & Bacon, 1967), p. 14.

Buyphase activities, all of which would probably come into play in a new task situation, entail first recognizing a problem (such as the need for more efficient training and development methods) and then describing the need in terms of performance standards to be achieved in addressing this problem.

Subsequent steps would involve translating product needs into product specifications and then embarking on a supplier search for the vendor best able to meet these specifications. Here—and, later, in the performance review stage—buying center members make use of formal **vendor analysis** tools and procedures that assess a supplier's performance against standards in such areas as price, delivery times, back orders, and attention to special requests. Proposals solicited from vendors would be the basis of a final supplier selection, which at Merton used the vendor analysis rating scale depicted in Figure 10-2 showing how a selected vendor achieved a score of 3.6 in terms of criteria the buyer considered most important.

ATTRIBUTES	RATING SCALE				
	Unacceptable (0)	Poor (1)	Fair (2)	Good (3)	Excellent (4)
Technical and production capabilities					x
Financial strength				x	
Product reliability					x
Delivery reliability				x	
Service capability					x

4 + 3 + 4 + 3 + 4 = 18

Average score:
18/5 = 3.6

Figure 10–2. Vendor analysis rating scale evaluation of performance of Merton's industrial division.

The final two steps of the buyphase process involve the following activities:

- **Order routine specification:** The purchasing agent on the buying team writes the final order for the supplier (or suppliers) selected to develop the new system. Covered in this order are technical specifications for system components, delivery times, performance standards, costs, and warranties.

- **Performance review:** This final buyphase stage encompasses procedures for monitoring the supplier performance to ensure compliance with the contract. Essentially, performance is evaluated against criteria used during the supplier selection stage to review proposals.

As shown in Table 10-3, the number of buyphase stages involved varies with the buyclass situation, with only product specification (stage 3) and performance review (stage 8) typically involved in a straight rebuy situation.

BUYPHASES FROM THE SELLER'S PERSPECTIVE

An effective industrial salesperson can recognize, and often create, buyphase stages and become actively involved in each stage. For example, during the buyphase stages leading up to the purchase of the MM system, the salesperson helped buying team members recognize and describe the problem (stages 1 and 2), design the system to help solve the problem (stage 3), and establish standards for supplier acceptability (stage 4), which she knew Merton could meet. During stage 5, she prepared a proposal that was as much a sales as a technical document, and that helped ensure Merton's selection during stage 6. In effect, she was working as a member of the manufacturer's buying team, helping to define and solve problems and ensuring that specifications drawn up would include Merton's products.

Throughout these buyphase stages, the salesperson made creative use of **value analysis,** a set of principles and tools that aid buyers in measuring value. A typical value analysis examines each component of a purchase with the aim of either deleting or replacing each with a more cost-effective substitute. A variant on value analysis, called customer value analysis, combines vendor and value analysis tools to help salespeople build closer relationships with customers. For example, the Merton salesperson would begin the process by first identifying major attributes that customers value and the level of performance desired in each of these attribute areas (for example, if reliable deliveries was the attribute, the desired performance level might be back orders only 0.05 percent of the time). Then, customers rank both Merton and Merton's major competitors on an attribute-by-attribute basis, with the understanding that Merton will be competitive in all indicated areas and be monitored over time.

Another tool the Merton salesperson used in relating effectively with customers was **systems selling,** whereby firms find it more profitable to purchase an entire turnkey operation system rather than purchase and combine system components themselves. Often, these systems are purchased from more than a single vendor, who form a strategic alliance for this purpose. For sellers, **systems buying** represents an opportunity to create profitable modified rebuy and new task situations to help win and hold accounts by promoting groups of interlocking products. (Market Focus 10-1 shows how one company utilizes all these tools in effectively serving customers in a dynamic, highly competitive market.)

MARKET FOCUS 10-1

Building Markets by Building Partnerships

The Delfield Company of Mount Pleasant, Michigan, designs and produces more than 300 kitchen equipment products for the food services industry, including refrigerators, freezers, display cases, and cafeteria systems. Customers include schools, hotels, grocery stores, military installations, and fast food chains like Taco Bell, Burger King, Arby's, and Kentucky Fried Chicken (KFC).

The key to Delfield's success, reflected in its strong market position and unbroken record of growth, is a core strategy designed to create and maintain productive relationships with customers and suppliers alike. Implementing this core strategy are programs that provide employees with (1) the skills and resources to produce quality products and (2) the tools, including strategic alliances, vendor analysis, value analysis, and systems selling to adapt these products to customer needs.

There are few industries where these needs change faster than the fast food industry, where new competitors, new outlets, new market segments, and new menus are the norm. There are few suppliers better prepared to relate to these dynamic changes than Delfield, as illustrated by the way the firm helped KFC address a challenge involving a new concept in fast food delivery.

KFC's challenge derived from its need to set up operations in alternative restaurant sites, since competitors, and existing KFC outlets, had already occupied most of the prime locations for fast-food restaurants. The problem with these alternative outlets, including high-traffic areas such as stores, airports, and college student centers, was limited space: typically, KFC would need equipment capable of meeting all the needs of a full-sized restaurant in roughly a 100-square-foot space.

To address this challenge, Delfield first formed a strategic alliance with other vendors to help develop new compact kitchens to fit into the limited space available. Selected vendors were subject to a vendor analysis assessment that measured performance against standards relating to quality, delivery, price, and technological expertise.

After 7 months, Delfield engineers, working with KFC and vendor personnel, had assembled a prototype "Small is Beautiful" (SIB) kitchen unit that met specifications for cooking equipment, fryers, hoods, and ventilating systems for full-sized units within the mandated space constraints. Throughout this process, and after the units had been installed in alternative KFC locations, value analysis processes continued to modify the basic design of the SIB unit to make it more efficient, for instance, by adding components, extra handles, and magnetic latches instead of mechanical ones.

THE RESELLER MARKET

The reseller market consists mainly of retailers and wholesalers who purchase products to resell or rent to others at a profit. Sometimes these resale products are finished goods (like automobiles or appliances) that are marketed to consumers; in other instances, some processing or repackaging may take place, as when lumber dealers process carloads of lumber to the specifications of individual customers.

Significant differences in purchasing practices between industrial producers and resellers derive from the fact that the latter are primarily purchasing products and services to sell or rent to others, not to be used up in the production process. In effect, they are acting as purchasing agents for their customers.

For marketing managers, this difference means that their marketing campaigns should stress how their reseller customers can make more profit by reselling the producer's products or cut costs by reselling their other products more efficiently. MM systems, for example, used both of these appeals: they were promoted, first, as a profitable product for computer dealers to resell and, second, as an efficient way to train dealer employees in new trends and developments in computer/software technology.

Beyond this difference in basic appeal, however, reseller purchasing procedures are quite similar to those of producers. Similar to producer buying centers, for example, are reseller buying committees, whose members assume roles similar to buying center counterparts (gatekeepers, users, buyers, and so on), and who categorize procurement situations into buyclasses and buyphases to help buying committee members make more profitable purchasing decisions. Three types of reseller buyclass situations of interest to Merton's salespeople included (1) **new item situations,** where Merton had an opportunity to sell its products for resale on a "yes/no" basis; (2) **best vendor situations,** where Merton presented its offerings to a reseller customer as a potential supplier, sometimes agreeing to manufacture products that the reseller would sell under its own private brand name; and (3) **better terms situations,** where a reseller customer pressed Merton for better arrangements in such areas as volume discounts, credit extension, and promotional assistance.

In understanding and relating to these situations, Merton salespeople also had to understand the reseller's buying decision-making process and how this process applied in different buyclass situations. For example, what problems faced by the reseller triggered the search for new products to sell? And what standards did the prospective reseller customer apply to vendors and their products to solve these problems? According to a study by the A. C. Nielsen Company, the most important criteria motivating a reseller's decision to accept a new product include (1) evidence of customer acceptance; (2) advertising/promotion acceptance; (3) introductory terms and allowances; and (4) the reason the product was developed.

Reseller markets will be covered in greater detail in Chapter 19.

THE GOVERNMENT MARKET

The huge government component of the organizational market comprises all federal, state and local governments which, in 1999, consisted of more than 85,000 buying units that purchased more than $900 billion in goods and services. The federal government was responsible for purchasing more than 40 percent of this total.

From the perspective of Merton's industrial marketing manager, the fact that governments must respond to the will of the electorate has a number of significant implications. To ensure public review, many products are purchased through a mandatory bidding procedure, and governments often are required to accept the lowest bid. Contracts for products not easily described, or without effective competition, can be negotiated directly, but, in any case, the ability to write clear specifications and precisely identify costs is important to marketers interested in serving the government market. Also important is an understanding of the environmental, organizational, and interpersonal factors that influence government buying decisions. These are generally similar to those in the producer segment, except that government buying decisions are more likely to be influenced by noneconomic criteria such as the needs of depressed industries, the perceived need for weapons, or the mandates of policies favoring various constituencies, such as small businesses, the elderly, or protected industries. A tolerance for considerable paperwork involved in dealing with complex bureaucracies characterizing government purchasing practices is also helpful.

THE INSTITUTIONAL MARKET

Institutions are represented by a wide diversity of organizations, including churches, schools, libraries, hospitals, foundations, clinics, prisons, and not-for-profit organizations. This diversity is reflected in varied institutional procurement practices. Some institutions, subject to political and legal constraints, behave like government buyers. Other, private institutions, may employ buying practices characterizing those of industrial procurement buying centers. Regardless of these specific differences, however, institutional procurement practices in general display characteristics of organizational procurement practices that differentiate them from those in consumer markets. A consortium of hospitals, for example, would exhibit concentrated demand, direct purchasing (of drugs from producers, for example), derived demand (based on community health needs), fluctuating demand (an epidemic in the community could cause outsized needs for facilities), and inelastic demand once contracts are negotiated (contracts with HMOs and other suppliers would not be easily terminated).

Chapter 13 examines the role of institutions as sellers of services, which differs significantly from the selling of more tangible products.

INTERNATIONAL PERSPECTIVE

Marketers planning to enter or grow in overseas organizational markets should recognize, first, that they are not facing the homogeneous domestic organizational market, where demand patterns, purchasing practices, and product needs are all relatively predictable from region to region. In global organizational markets, all these characteristics will tend to differ, depending mainly on the stage of development of the country or region targeted.

For their purposes, Merton researchers found the following five-stage model most useful as a starting point for deciding where, when, and how to penetrate the international organizational market with their capital goods electronic equipment and installations. This model classifies countries according to economic variables found to define markets for Merton capital goods products in the United States, including population, gross domestic product, manufacturing as a percent of national income, infrastructure, and per-capita income. Of particular importance was a listing of industrial products purchased, and emphasis on such product attributes as service, quality, performance, and costs.

STAGES OF ECONOMIC DEVELOPMENT

• *PREINDUSTRIAL COUNTRIES*

With per-capita incomes under $500, preindustrial countries are characterized by high birth rates and low literacy rates, political instability, little industrialization, much agriculture and subsistence farming, and heavy reliance on foreign aid (for example, Somalia and Haiti during the early 1990s). Concentrated mainly in Africa, these countries represent limited markets for most products and are insignificant competitive threats. Most industrial products purchased are used in production and transportation of a country's basic resources, such as specialized, expensive construction equipment.

• *LESS-DEVELOPED COUNTRIES*

With per-capita incomes of under $2000, the less-developed countries are at the early stages of industrialization, with factories erected to supply growing domestic and export markets. With consumer markets expanding, these countries represent an increasing competitive threat as they mobilize cheap and highly motivated labor. Together with preindustrial nations, these countries, concentrated in Asia, possess two thirds of the world's population but less than 15 percent of world income. Industrial products purchased are used to develop primary manufacturing capabilities and process resources.

• *DEVELOPING COUNTRIES*

With per-capita incomes averaging about $4000, developing countries are moving rapidly from an agricultural to an urbanized industrial base. Good worker skills, high literacy rates, and significantly lower wage costs than in advanced countries make these countries formidable competitors in export markets. Examples include many Latin American countries such as Uruguay, Peru, Colombia, Chile, and Argentina. Growth of manufacturing facilities for non- and semidurable consumer products creates a demand for entire factories (new and used); associated OEM, MRO, capital, and expense products; construction and mining equipment; and motor vehicles and parts.

• *INDUSTRIALIZED COUNTRIES*

With per-capita incomes of about $9000, industrialized countries are major exporters of manufactured goods and investment funds. They trade goods among themselves and also export them to other economies (developing, post-industrial) for raw materials and finished goods. High wages, strong infrastructures, educated populations, and a large middle class make these countries rich markets for all kinds of goods, as well as formidable competitors in export markets. Taiwan and South Korea are examples; they are poised to leap to post-industrialized status. The main need for industrial goods relates to rapidly growing consumer demand and to production of specialized goods for world markets.

• *POST-INDUSTRIALIZED COUNTRIES*

With per-capita incomes in excess of $14,000, post-industrialized countries are distinguished by an increased importance of the service sector (which accounts for more than 75 percent of GNP in the United States); the key importance of information processing and exchange; and the ascendancy of knowledge over capital and intellectual technology over technology. Other distinguishing features include an orientation toward the future, the importance of interpersonal and intergroup relationships, and sources of innovation that are derived increasingly from the codification of theoretic knowledge rather than from random inventions. Examples are Japan, Germany, Sweden, and the United States and the strong demand for consulting services and electronic highway products representing the confluence of computer, telecommunications, and television technologies. The tendency to specialize in products for the world market creates opportunities for sales of products in which the country doesn't specialize.

KEY EXPORT INDUSTRIES GENERATE JOBS AND GROWTH

Planners for Merton's entry and growth in international markets also found helpful a report prepared by the U.S. Department of Commerce, as part of its National Export Strategy, that identified six industry sectors given high priority for export to "Big Emerging Markets" expected to "more than double their share of world exports, to 27 percent, by 2010."[1] These sectors were selected on the basis of (1) the potential of the industry for creating "a significant number of high-paying U.S. jobs," (2) growth prospects of the sector; (3) superior U.S. competitiveness in the sector, and (4) the extent to which government action, in concert with the private sector, can further improve U.S. global competitiveness. (Global Focus 10-1 illustrates the extent to which government agencies are prepared to support U.S. company initiatives to penetrate these markets.)

Table 10-4 identifies and defines these industry clusters in terms of (1) major component technologies comprising each, (2) present size and prospective growth prospects of each cluster in global markets, (3) key global markets for each cluster, and (4) major competitors for each cluster. Growth prospects for these six industry clusters are projected to range from 5 percent (for transportation and environmental technologies) to more than 8 percent for information, health and energy clusters.

---

1 *Business America, National Export Strategy,* Vol. 115, No. 9, October 1994.

Table 10-4. Six High Potential Industry Clusters

	Environmental Technologies	Information Technologies	Health Technologies
Major component technologies	Design and construction services; stationary and mobile source air pollution control; solid, hazardous waste management; contaminated site remediation.	Computer hardware and software; telecommunication services; electronic components; semiconductor manufacturing equipment; information services; satellites; computer network services.	Medical and dental devices and supplies; pharmaceutical, biotechnologic, and health care services.
Present status and growth prospects	The United States is the leader and largest producer and consumer of environmental goods and services, which produced more than $140 billion in revenue in 1995. Worldwide market for these services is expected to grow to over $400 billion by year 2000, with U.S. exports accounting for about 10 percent of total.	Small and medium-sized companies comprise bulk of industry in United States with annual exports of over $20 billion expected to more than double by year 2010. U.S. computer systems and packaged software firms control 75 percent of information technologies world market, which is expected to grow at an annual rate of 7 percent, reaching $300 billion by 2010.	United States is world's leader in terms of research, patents, and number of products brought to market, with health care management companies expanding globally. U.S. share of global medical device industry is 52 percent, 50 percent for pharmaceuticals, with U.S. exports expected to rise to over $14 billion by 2010 (over $9 billion to BEMs).
Major BEM markets	Demand for environmental technologies is forecast to increase an annual rate of 20 percent by year 2000 in BEMs in Asia (Indonesia, India, S. Korea, and Chinese Economic Area), and over 15 percent in Latin American BEMs (Argentina, Brazil, Mexico).	Roughly 26 percent of growth gain in international markets will come from exports to BEMs, including South Africa, Poland, India, China (stressing telecommunications), Brazil, South Korea, Mexico, South Africa, and Taiwan (computer hard- and software); and China (information services).	Key BEM markets for health technology products include Russia, South Africa, Central Asia, Mexico, and Eastern Europe.
Major competitors	Germany, Japan, France, and the United Kingdom are strongest competitors—Japan and Germany especially in air pollution control technologies; France and Britain in waste-water treatment. Germany is attempting to get its standards, practices, and testing protocols adopted by the EU.	Japanese have narrowed technological and market gaps in computer equipment by building a strong domestic base in semiconductors and other enabling technologies. However, rising challenges from U.S. and South Korean challengers are eroding this lead in high-volume devices like memory chips. In telecommunications satellites, United States has lead, but Europeans are catching up, with diversified R&D and production across the EU.	Although U.S. medical device and pharmaceutical industries maintain global leadership position, West European and Asian companies, especially in Germany and Japan, gained ground in last decade, especially in exploiting emerging markets in Eastern Europe and China.

Defined by BEM* Markets and Competitors

Transportation Technologies	Energy Technologies	Financial Services
Aerospace technologies, automotive industry, and transportation infrastructure, including airports, ports, road, and railroad projects.	Gas and oil field equipment and infrastructure; conventional and renewable energy power generation equipment, facilities, and services; infrastructure facilities; engineering and related services.	Commercial banks, investment banks, securities dealers, and insurance companies.

The U.S. aerospace industry leads all other industry sectors in exports and manufactured goods, with $45 billion in exports in 1995. In 1995, the automotive industry, which encourages the development of new products and advanced technologies, accounted for about 5 percent of total U.S. manufacturing employment. The United States remains the global leader in engineering, management, and financial talent for foreign transportation infrastructure, responsible for 40–50 percent of foreign construction work.

The United States is internationally competitive both in advanced petroleum and power generation equipment, with exports of newly made power generation equipment increasing from $4 billion to $8 billion between 1980 and 1996.

U.S. securities firms are world leaders in financial innovation and development of financial instruments for raising capital through debt and equity. Income from international activities of U.S. financial service firms is expected to double, from $8 billion in 1993 to $17 billion by 2010.

Aerospace technologies: Asian and Latin America represent biggest markets (China alone expected to need over $40 billion in new aircraft over next 20 years); *Automotive:* including light, commercial, and specialized vehicles and small and medium-sized parts manufacturers will see major growth in Latin America, India, East Europe, and South Korea; *Transportation Infrastructure:* Major growth throughout Asia, primarily airports, subway systems, rail and road projects.

BEMs are expected to account for two thirds of projected global growth in power generation equipment by 2010. China's electric power generation capacity is expected to increase by 55 percent by year 2000; Mexico's demand increased by 8 percent annually; OPEC countries will continue to be largest market for oil and gas field equipment; also countries with major oil and gas exploration operations (e.g., Russia, Indonesia, China, India, Mexico).

Recipients of private capital flows in 1996 were generally middle-income Asian and Latin American countries, especially China, India, and Indonesia. The markets of Mexico, Brazil, and Argentina led bond issuers, followed by Turkey and South Korea. China was the largest receiver of foreign direct investment and commercial credit in 1995.

European aerospace manufacturers, often government subsidized, have formed partnerships and alliances to spread risk and gain leverage from resources. European and Japanese automotive manufacturers offer challenging competition to U.S. manufacturers in mature, saturated markets.

Barriers to increasing exports include incompatibility of U.S. standards and technical specifications, competitive financing to foreign suppliers with government subsidies, and regional "Buy National" policies. Petroleum equipment manufacturers face strong international competition from strategic alliances forged between European suppliers.

Primarily, developed European and Asian nations engaged in exploiting growth potential in BEMs.

* Big Emerging Markets (BEMs) include the Chinese Economic Area (China, Taiwan, Hong Kong), Indonesia, India, South Korea, Mexico, Argentina, Brazil, South Africa, Poland, and Turkey.

GLOBAL FOCUS 10-1

SIVAM: Case Study in Successful Advocacy

Following intense advocacy efforts by the U.S. government, the government of Brazil selected a U.S. consortium—led by Raytheon—to build a $1.5 billion Amazon environmental surveillance and air traffic control system (SIVAM). SIVAM will provide Brazilian government agencies with the capability to collect and process the information required to protect the environment, combat illegal mining and drug trafficking, improve population and public health controls, and strengthen border security.

The selection of the Raytheon-led group of companies to produce the SIVAM project in the face of stiff competition from a European group of companies led by the French firm Thomson CSF was partially a result of:

- Personal support from President Clinton via a letter to President Franco of Brazil;

- Support by our embassy in Brasilia, including the Ambassador, Deputy Chief of Mission, and US&FCS staff;

- Active monitoring by key senior officials, through the TPCC Advocacy Network, of the status of the bidding process;

- Advocacy letters from Ex-Im Bank Chairman Brody, TDA Director Grandmaison, Environmental Protection Agency Administrator Brower, Federal Aviation Administration Administrator Hinson, National Oceanic and Atmospheric Administration Under Secretary Baker, and members of Congress;

- Assistance from the Ex-Im Bank in developing a package competitive with the French government package, and additional financing by OPIC.

Source: Business America: National Export Strategy. Annual Report to the United States Congress, Vol. 115, No. 9, October 1994, p. 22.

DEMAND PATTERNS IN GLOBAL MARKETS

Particularly in industrialized and post-industrialized countries, demand patterns are generally similar to those discussed earlier in domestic organizational markets: concentrated, direct, derived, fluctuating, elastic then inelastic, reciprocal, and jointly dependent on sales of other products.

Differences among countries in these areas generally relate to unique conditions prevailing in different regions of the world. For example, industry concentration, a condition that makes marketing more efficient in organizational markets, tends to exist on a national scale in global markets, with fewer larger manufacturing plants in related industries located in countries close to such resources as transportation, skilled workers, and power. Some examples: in Italy, the world-leading footwear industry is concentrated within a 100-mile area in northern Italy; some 300 firms produce cutlery in one German town, making it a world center of that industry; most of the world's racing cars, including almost all the Indianapolis 500 racers, are built in a region north of London.

According to Porter,[2] this concentration among industries in industrial and post-industrial countries creates "hotbeds of competition" that help these industries overcome formidable obstacles and spur innovation:

> The health of such clusters is the key to the economic vigor of countries. . . . Most nations rely on a few dozen industrial clusters and a few hundred companies to provide most of their exports, raise productivity and improve national living standards.

Reciprocity arrangements also tend to proliferate much more in global than in domestic markets. With Japanese *kieretso* systems of interlocking manufacturers, distributors, and financial agencies, for example, these arrangements are not only common but also institutionalized, often making it difficult for offshore firms to compete.

Possibly the most prevalent form of reciprocity in global markets are **offsets,** a form of countertrade that mandates various forms of business activities as a condition of purchase. Typically, they obligate a seller of major purchases (for example, military hardware) to minimize any trade imbalance or other adverse impact caused by the outflow of currency required to pay for such purchases. Among the forms offsets take are licensing, subcontracting, or joint ventures. When Saudi Arabia purchases military aircraft from U.S. producers, the cost is usually offset through investments in the country's resources.

---

2 "Think Locally, Win Globally," *The Washington Post,* April 5, 1992; also Michael E. Porter, *The Competitive Advantage of Nations,* (New York: Free Press, 1990).

In countries that haven't reached this level of procurement sophistication, considerations involved in dealing with it—such as systematically relating product value to customer needs—can serve the seller well.

PURCHASING POLICIES AND PRACTICES IN GLOBAL MARKETS

Government policies and practices are responsible, in large measure, for the size, growth, competitiveness, and openness of many global markets in developed economies. Additionally, these governments invariably represent excellent markets themselves, with unique characteristics and purchasing practices that marketers should account for in strategic planning.

For firms selling industrial products in these global markets, it is important to recognize different conventions regarding specifications in working with customers to create sales. For example, margins of error allowed on specifications differ dramatically. Generally, in Europe and Japan, they are exact; if a beam is purchased to carry 20,000 pounds, that is the maximum weight it can carry. In the United States, the beam will usually have a sufficiently large safety factor built in to cover overload situations.

CHAPTER PERSPECTIVE

The organizational market, composed of industrial producers, resellers, governments, and institutions, exhibits procurement practices that distinguish it from consumer markets, including greater concentration, greater likelihood that products will be purchased directly from manufacturer, demand derived from demand in end consumer markets, dramatic fluctuations in demand, inelastic demand patterns once contracts are signed, and reciprocity arrangements. The modern perception of the organizational procurement function as a profit center has given rise to the formation of buying centers—in which individuals sharing common risks and goals participate in procurement decisions—as well as procedures for ensuring the "best buy." These procedures feature categorizing buying situations (straight rebuy, modified rebuy, new task), buyphase activities (problem recognition, supplier selection, performance review, and the like), and buying roles (gatekeepers, buyers, users, etc.), and then relating them to each other so as to make the most efficient, productive use of both the seller and the buyer. Participation as an effective member of the customer's buying center team involves an understanding of vendor and value analysis procedures, an ability to negotiate effectively, and a desire to help customers recognize and solve problems.

KNOW THE CONCEPTS
TERMS FOR STUDY

Accelerator principle
Accessory items
Best vendor situation
Better terms situation
Buyclasses
Buyer
Buying center
Buyphases
Capital items
Concentrated demand
Decider
Derived demand
Direct purchasing
Elastic/inelastic demand
Expense items
Fluctuating demand
Gatekeeper
Government market
Industrial producer market
Influentials
Institutional market
Joint demand
Modified rebuy

MRO items
New item situation
New task situation
OEM items
Offsets
Organizational market
Performance review
Problem recognition
Product specification
Profit center
Proposal solicitation
Reciprocal arrangements
Reseller market
SIC
Straight rebuy
Supplier search
Supplies
Systems buying/selling
Turnkey operations
Users
Value analysis
Vendor analysis

MATCHUP EXERCISES

1. Match the industrial product in the second column with the product category listed in the first column.

1. capital items

   a. At Goodyear's R&D center in Akron, computerized workstations test tire durability, traction, fuel efficiency, and compatibility with new car designs.

2. expense items

   b. A division of Textron makes gas turbine engines for the M1 tank.

3. MRO items

   c. Schaffer Eaton sells pens and paper products to law and accounting firms.

4. OEM items

    d. E-Z-Go makes utility vehicles used in factory materials handling operations.

2. Match the types of organizational market transactions in the first column with the situations described in the second column.

1. modified rebuy

    a. Rosegate Technology, a Cincinnati-based distributor of used equipment, enlists help of Russian physicians to upgrade ultrasound equipment in Russian hospitals.

2. new task

    b. Crystal International Corporation of New Orleans receives another order for its popular hot sauce from its Jordanian distributor.

3. straight rebuy

    c. Allied Signal Corporation of Morristown, New Jersey, sells turbochargers, filters, and other automotive aftermarket products to Mexican carriers to help them conform to new NAFTA-mandated truck emissions standards.

3. Match the roles involved in the industrial buying process in the first column with the situation described in the second column pertaining to efforts by the Toys "R" Us Corporation to construct retail outlets in Japan.

1. gatekeeper

    a. Japanese consumers complain about exorbitantly high prices they must pay for toys, largely because of the Large Store law, which effectively protects politically powerful small Japanese storekeepers from large retailers.

2. decider

    b. Following the law, the Japanese Ministry of trade and industry (MITI) often manages to stall incursions into the Japanese market by large retailers, even local ones.

3. buyers

c. By 1990, under pressure from the U.S. government and Japanese consumers, MITI changes the Large Store law to permit larger discount retailers to compete in Japan. However, local councils, composed of consumers, merchants, and professionals, often erect barriers to large discounters.

4. influentials

d. By 1995, Toys "R" Us had 20 outlets in Japan, each generating at least $15 million.

QUESTIONS FOR REVIEW AND DISCUSSION

1. Discuss the difference between organizational and consumer markets with respect to number of transactions and number of products/services involved in these transactions. How would these differences complicate the job of penetrating global organizational (as opposed to consumer) target markets?

2. In the three years following the signing of the NAFTA pact, Panamax, Inc., of San Rafael, California, experienced a 1000 percent increase in sales to Mexican distributors of surge protectors used primarily with personal computers and accessories, although sales to end-user consumers increased by only half this amount. Explain how derived demand and the accelerator principle might have accounted for this dramatic increase in demand, and for the equally dramatic decrease in demand when the peso collapsed in early 1994 and again in 1995.

3. Following up on question 2, describe how concentrated demand, direct purchases, and reciprocal arrangements might have characterized Panamax's successful entry into the Mexican market.

4. In 1986, the Finnish Air Force (FAF) decided to modernize its fighter fleet by replacing the aging Swedish-made Drakens and Soviet-made MIG 21s that comprised this fleet. In 1992, after protracted negotiations, the Finnish government selected the McDonnell Douglas (MDC) Hornet over a number of competitive models from Sweden, France, and the United States. At the onset of these negotiations, MDC, which wasn't among the aircraft companies invited to submit proposals, figured it had only a 5 percent chance of closing the deal but decided the size of the contract made it worth the effort. The $2 billion deal finally signed involved delivery of 57 F/A-18 Cs and 7 F/A-18 Ds between 1995 and 2000. Representing the Finnish government in these negotiations were the following agencies: (1) the Ministry of Defense, which, work-

ing with the FAF general staff, determined criteria for selection (specifications, delivery dates, prices) and made final purchase decisions, but turned most of the actual negotiating over to (2) the Ministry of Trade and Industry, assisted by a (3) Technical Working Group. Also involved in negotiations was (4) the Finnish Offset Committee, which was composed of technical specialists and representatives of business and government who determined offset commitments by the winning bidder.

a. Speculate on (1) the roles of the Finnish agencies and committees involved in these negotiations during the six buyphases of the organizational buying process and (2) MDC's role during these buyphases. (Note: MDC's group was called the F-18 Team.)

b. Discuss buyer roles that might have been assumed by members of Finnish government negotiating agencies and committees that the F-18 Team could relate to.

5. Discuss how the following products would have been involved in the manufacture of the F/A-18s discussed in question 4: expense items, capital items, MRO items, OEM items.

6. The Second Chance Company of Central Lake, Michigan, markets bullet-resistant vests to foreign countries through a network of native police and military personnel. Discuss how, on a given day, Second Chance representatives might encounter straight rebuy, modified rebuy, and new task transactions. How would the degree of buyer involvement, and the approach of Second Chance sales personnel, differ with each type of transaction?

ANSWERS
MATCHUPS

1. 1a, 2c, 3d, 4b
2. 1a, 2c, 3b
3. 1b, 2d, 3a, 4c

QUESTIONS FOR REVIEW AND DISCUSSION

1. Because industrial producer and trade organizational markets are intermediaries between the producers of raw materials and ultimate consumers that purchase products made from these raw materials, there are many more transactions, products, and dollars involved in organizational than in consumer markets. For example, the process of making a single pair of shoes for a consumer involves multiple transactions among hide tanners, shoe manufacturers, wholesalers, and retailers in-

volving a diversity of products and services. Reflecting all these transactions, aggregate purchasing power among these industrial producer and trade organizational markets, at least in developing, industrialized, and post-industrialized countries, is invariably much greater than that of consumer markets (in industrialized and post-industrialized countries, usually more than three times greater). This size, diversity, and complexity of the organizational market usually makes it much more challenging and expensive to penetrate than the consumer market in itself and suggests a rationale for bypassing the organizational market in global markets if feasible.

2. Derived demand means that demand for a product derives from the needs of ultimate customers—in this case, consumers in the Mexican market who used the surge protectors with their personal computers and accessories. When sales of these products increased sharply, Mexican wholesalers handling them ordered much larger amounts for their inventories from Panamax, in anticipation of a continued profitable growth of this market (many also ordered products from other suppliers to build facilities to handle this inventory). However, when the value of the peso dropped sharply in 1994 and again in 1995, throwing Mexico into a recession in which many U.S. imports became prohibitively expensive, many of these same Mexican distributors who earlier overbought surge protectors now stopped ordering them completely, as a means of reducing now-excessive inventory levels. Thus, purchases, in relation to actual consumer demand, were accelerated at each end of this buying cycle, consistent with the accelerator principle.

3. Although ultimate, end-user demand for Panamax surge protectors was diverse and geographically widespread, the number of distributors (primarily, three large chains of consumer electronics retailers) that had to be contacted directly to reach this market was concentrated both as to number and location (e.g., buyers in Mexico City and environs were responsible for more than 50 percent of sales volume). Reciprocal arrangements might have taken the form of various offsets, such as might relate to co-production, licensing, subcontracting, investment/technology development, export development, and tourism development in Mexico.

4a. The first buyphase stage of the process—problem recognition—would probably have been the responsibility of the general staff of the Finnish Air Force. The next two stages—preparing general need descriptions and product specifications—would probably have been the responsibility of the Ministry of Defense, working with the FAF general staff. Because the actual negotiating was delegated to the Ministry of Trade and Industry, this group would be responsible for the next three stages—supplier search, proposal solicitation, and supplier selection. During these buyphases, these groups would be working closely with the Finnish Offset Committee to determine countertrade requirements incorporated into the contract (in the final contract, MDC was obligated to complete an offset program by the year 2002 through a number of elements, including marketing assistance, export development, technology transfer, team purchases, and investment financing). Final approval of the selected firm would be made by the Ministry of Defense. The final two stages—order routine specification and performance review—would be performed by the FAF after the deal was closed.

MDC's role during these buyphases was to continually be ready and able to help the customer with information and assistance. Toward this end, MCD was the only company considered that actually set up a full-time office in Helsinki and was involved with all the constituencies in a full range of activities, such as setting up tests, helping to write specifications, and performing background research. Naturally, most of these activities were focused on the F-18 as the aircraft best suited to Finland's needs.

4b. Possible gatekeepers, controlling the flow of information, would include, primarily, the Ministries of Defense and Trade and Industry. Influentials, who could help persuade the negotiators to favor MDC over competitors, might include members of the Finnish parliament, and high-ranking officers of the Ministries of Defense and Trade and Industry. The main decider was the Ministry of Defense although all involved agencies made key decisions in such areas as supplier selection, specifications, and offsets. The Finnish government (through its purchasing office) was the buyer of the aircraft, and the FAF was the user.

5. Expense items are short lived goods and services charged off against revenues as used; they include raw materials, component materials, and fabricated parts that are relatively inexpensive on a per-unit basis (for example, wiring, batteries, and small motors used in the F-18). Capital items are goods used in the production process that do not become part of the final product, including expensive, long-lived installations and accessory equipment such as punch presses and wind tunnels used in manufacturing F-18s. MRO items could be any product—including expense and capital items—used in operating the plant or maintaining and repairing plant equipment. Examples would include lathes, paint, fork-lift trucks, brooms, and polishing cloths. OEM items would include any products used as original equipment in the F-18s, such as tires and batteries.

6. In a straight rebuy situation, a buyer would routinely reorder the same Second Chance vests previously ordered; in a modified rebuy situation, the buyer would specify Second Chance vests with some change in price or other specification (for example, the firm might want a lower price for the same vests or be willing to pay the same price for an upgraded model). In any event, some degree of negotiation would be indicated, thus taking this situation out of the routine. A new task situation would entail purchasing bullet-resistant vests for the first time, thus entailing a higher degree of cost and risk in which considerable decision making is undertaken by more decision participants seeking more information on alternative products and suppliers, product specifications, price limits, delivery terms and times, service, payment terms, acceptable suppliers, and the supplier under consideration (Second Chance). Because different decision participants (users, buyers, influencers) can influence each decision, Second Chance salespeople seek to provide product information and other assistance to as many key buying influences as possible. In straight rebuy situations, the salesperson's role is negligible or nonexistent; in modified rebuy situations, where a prospective customer wants to modify product specifications, terms, prices, or suppliers, "out" salespeople are often provided with an opportunity to gain new business by making a better offer.

11

MARKET SEGMENTATION, TARGETING, AND POSITIONING STRATEGIES

OVERVIEW

Market segments are groups of high-potential prospective customers with common characteristics and needs that distinguish them from other high-potential market segments. Identifying, defining, and targeting these groups helps marketers improve all aspects of the strategic marketing planning process, including devising attractive marketing mix offerings, formulating segmentation and product positioning strategies for efficiently reaching target markets, and controlling overall plan effectiveness.

TARGET MARKETING IMPROVES MARKET PLANNING

In previous chapters, we examined intra- and interpersonal variables that influence buying decisions among members of consumer and organizational markets, the dynamics of this process, and marketing strategies for favorably shaping buying decisions. In this chapter, we build on this background and offer a systematic approach for segmenting large market aggregates into smaller groups of customers, called **target markets,** each of which differs from the others in terms of its response to marketing mix offerings. To illustrate, Procter and Gamble has identified six different market segments for Crest toothpaste, based on age and ethnic differences (for example, children, Latinos, African-Americans), and has developed appeals to each segment using different promotion, distribution, and product positioning strategies.

Most products sold in consumer and organizational markets lend themselves to a segmentation strategy, which is basic to formulating, implementing, and controlling strategic marketing plans. An important advantage of a segmentation strategy is its consistency with the **Pareto effect,** named after the nineteenth-century economist Vilfredo Pareto who concluded that a large proportion of wealth is controlled by a small percent of the population. As applied to segmentation strategy, a relatively small proportion of total potential customers will typically purchase a disproportionately large share of product. Figure 11-1 shows this relationship, often called the 80/20 principle, among consumers of beer. Note that only 32 percent of the entire population drinks all the beer consumed, with 16 percent of the population responsible for almost 90 percent of beer consumption. Included among many other products for which this general pattern holds are cereals, shampoo, paper towels, dog food, soaps and detergents, and industrial metals—MRO and OEM products.

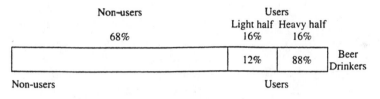

Figure 11–1. Beer consumption pattern in the United States.

From the marketer's perspective, this disproportionate market size/purchase potential relationship offers a diversity of pluses in the strategic planning process. First, economies and efficiencies derive from tapping most of the buying power in a given market by targeting a small percent of the market's population. Additionally, by specifying target customers and their needs, a segmentation strategy helps marketers position products and create marketing mixes responsive to these needs, enhancing customer loyalty and competitive posture.

An effective segmentation strategy also helps to measure overall market size (covered in Chapter 12); recognize, and respond to, competitive threats; and budget and control marketing performance. In sum, an effective segmentation strategy leads to the selection of the most attractive combination of markets and products, and to the strategic elements best calculated to bring them together.

SEGMENTATION STRATEGY OPTIONS

Essential to any segmentation strategy are decisions defining how many market segments will be encompassed by the firm's marketing program and how boundaries for these segments will be established. At one extreme, the marketer might elect to consider all actual or prospective customers as comprising a single market and design a single offering to satisfy needs in this single market. At the other extreme, the marketing manager might consider each customer a unique, discrete market in itself, and devise distinctive offerings to appeal to each. An example of this is large airplane manufacturers (Lockheed, Boeing) serving a relatively small number of large airlines (Lufthansa, United, Qantas).

Along this spectrum from total to individual target market segments, three segmentation strategies can be identified: undifferentiated (mass marketing), differentiated (target marketing), and concentrated (product differentiated or niche marketing). Here is how Merton might employ each of them.

• *UNDIFFERENTIATED*

An **undifferentiated,** or mass marketing, strategy is generally employed in situations where all prospective buyers have the same MAD-R characteristics, the product is new with no competition, and resources are sufficient to undertake the mass production and marketing initiatives required to serve this mass market.

Using an undifferentiated strategy, Merton would view all segments comprising its market as a single market and promote its products to this market with the same marketing mix. This would save the company production and promotion costs, but would make its offerings vulnerable to offerings of competitive firms targeting specific segments of this market.

• *DIFFERENTIATED*

Using a **differentiated** strategy, Merton would promote many products with different marketing mixes tailored to the wants and needs of diverse market segments. By providing increased satisfaction to each of many target market segments, a firm can often produce more sales, and profits, than its undifferentiated competitors that aim a single marketing mix at the entire market. However, differentiated marketing also increases costs to the extent that product and promotion efforts cannot be planned and implemented on a mass production basis.

• *CONCENTRATED*

Using a **concentrated** strategy (also called niche marketing), Merton would focus its efforts on profitably satisfying one market segment such as the accountant market. This strategy appeals to firms that offer highly specialized goods and services and lack the resources of competitors to adopt undifferentiated or differentiated strategies. Risks implicit in this strategy derive from the firm's ties to a single segment, which might lose purchasing power or succumb to competitive appeals. This second risk was illustrated by Netscape's 1997 suit against Microsoft, in which Netscape's concentrated strategy for marketing its browser software encountered the massive legal and competitive resources of one of the world's most highly capitalized differentiated marketing organizations.

Micromarketing is a fast-growing, more narrowly focused version of concentrated niche marketing that targets prospective customers on a local basis, such as zip codes or geographic lifestyle characteristics. An example would be the warehouse-size price club operations, which sell at retail to customers preselected on the basis of such criteria as occupation and union membership. Another version of concentrated marketing, customized marketing, adapts product and marketing programs to the needs and wants of specified target markets, as illustrated by the approach of such online marketers of computers and accessories as Gateway and Packard Bell.

CRITERIA THAT DEFINE WORTHWHILE SEGMENTS

In working to identify, define, and prioritize worthwhile target market segments for its MM systems and to decide on the most appropriate segmentation strategy to reach these segments, Merton marketing planners applied five criteria designed to identify the optimum number of market segments beyond which overall profits will begin to decline: (1) substantial, (2) homogeneous within, (3) heterogeneous with respect to other segments, (4) accessible, and (5) operational.

To illustrate these criteria, consider one segment of Merton's overall market: lawyers. Beginning with "Administrative and Government Law" to "Worker's Compensation," there are at least three dozen recognized legal specializations for which Merton could develop computer software packages. Some—like "Corporation," "Divorce and Family Law," and "General Practice"—were large practices; others—like "Computer Law," "Entertainment Law," and "Landlord and Tenant Law"—were small, but growing.

To qualify as a segment of Merton's target market, the prospective segment would first have to be sufficiently large—substantial—to justify the effort and expense of developing a discrete marketing mix, including software design, distribution, and promotional programs geared to member needs. Then, its members would have to be sufficiently homogeneous with respect to MAD-R criteria that define them as a market segment: they can afford MM systems (money), have the authority and desire to use them, and will respond similarly to the same marketing mix offering.

Additionally, members of sufficiently substantial, homogeneous markets should be sufficiently different from other prospective groups—heterogeneous—to justify treatment as a discrete entity; for example, environmental lawyers would require completely different software programs, and promotional appeals, than corporate lawyers.

Particularly important is the fourth criterion—accessibility—meaning that the segment, no matter how desirable, could be profitably reached by Merton communication and distribution programs.

Finally, the segment should be operational to the extent that characteristics of the segment—such as size, purchasing power, and basic needs—can be measured. For example, without reliable measurements of key dimensions of its lawyer target markets—income, size, needs, and the like—it would be impossible for Merton to devise marketing mix offerings attractive to these segments.

Note that these five segmentation criteria can be viewed as either qualifying or determining in nature, an important distinction when devising a segmentation strategy. **Qualifying criteria** are the same for all market segments. For example, all segments of the legal profession served in Merton's market were sufficiently substantial and accessible to justify developing offerings to meet their needs. Also, the needs of all these target market members can be measured and used to develop these offerings, so the "operational" criterion is met. However, each segment also possesses **determining characteristics** that distinguish it from other segments (for example, "homogeneous within" and "heterogeneous without" software needs), and these characteristics will determine how Merton's offering will differ from offerings designed for other segments of the legal market.

BASES FOR SEGMENTING MARKETS

Larger market aggregates may be subdivided into smaller target markets on the basis of geographic, demographic, psychographic, and behavioristic criteria.

• *GEOGRAPHIC CRITERIA*

Geographic criteria focus on the location of prospective target markets and distinguishing characteristics associated with each location. Marketing managers can focus on a single area, a few areas, or many areas, depending on such considerations as the size of each geographic area and the cost of serving it. If more than one area is selected, offerings may be tailored to different natures and needs among these areas. For example, Merton's training software for chefs was keyed to cuisine and cultural differences in different regions of the country.

• *DEMOGRAPHIC CRITERIA*

Demographic criteria refer to such state-of-being measures as age, sex, family size, family life cycle stage, income, occupation, and nationality. All can be used to identify and define target markets, and to develop offerings attractive to each segment. Examples of these criteria include the following:

Table 11-1. Using Demographic Criteria to Define Target Markets

Variable	Possible Segments	Products
Age	child, adult, senior citizen	toys, Medigap insurance
Sex	male, female	cosmetics, sporting equipment
Family size	1, 2, 3, 4 or more	packaged soup, minivans
Occupation	professional and technical, managers, clerical, sales, students, retired, unemployed	work shoes, MM computer systems
Nationality	American, British, Italian, Japanese	ethnic foods, movies

• *PSYCHOGRAPHIC CRITERIA*

Psychographic criteria are "state of mind" variables that have a direct influence on buyer behavior. They include social class, values, personality, and lifestyle, as measured by such instruments as AIO (Attitude, Interest, Opinion) surveys that ask consumers to agree or disagree with a series of statements describing various activities, interests, and opinions. Data emerging from these surveys allows researchers to develop lifestyle profiles from which marketers can develop marketing strategies that fit each profile. Illustrative of how marketers use these psychographic profiles for strategic planning is the four distinct psychographic groups identified among Generation X consumers, including cynical disdainers (pessimistic and cynical about their prospects); traditional materialists (more optimistic); hippies revisited (longing for lifestyles and values of the 1960s); and fifties machos (conservatives who resist accepting equal gender roles and multiculturism). Conceptually related to AIO surveys are VALS (values and lifestyles) surveys, developed by the SRI International research and consulting firm, that categorize consumers by opinions about social issues as they relate to buying behavior. For example, one of eight psychographic groups into which the VALS 2 survey categorizes consumers profiles Strivers as "image conscious, limited discretionary incomes, carry credit balances and spend on clothing and personal-care products."

• *BEHAVIORISTIC CRITERIA*

Behavioristic criteria define target market groups in terms of how market members behave, as consumers, toward a seller's offering, for example, how frequently they use it, how loyal they are toward it, and what benefits they seek from it. These criteria are useful both in identifying determining dimensions of a target segment and in devising marketing mixes to appeal to defined segments.

Here are some behavioristic variables Merton planners used to identify target markets and design attractive offerings for prospective Merton target segments in the legal profession.

OCCASIONS

Market segments can be identified in terms of occasions when its members get the idea to actually buy or use the product. For example, the planners identified periods during the year when tax accountants would have the most use for MM systems, and timed promotional programs to coincide with these periods.

BENEFITS SOUGHT

This unusually effective base for behavior segmentation focuses on benefits to which market segments will respond favorably. For example, among tax attorneys, Merton planners found that the major benefit desired in tax and financial planning /training systems was the timeliness of content. This and other desired benefits were incorporated into products and promotions designed for each group.

USER STATUS

Frequently, market segments can be defined and cultivated based on the extent to which segment members use the product. Merton planners, for example, developed profiles of groups that were not interested in their systems (non-users); groups that had purchased Merton planning /training systems in the past and then purchased another brand (ex-users); and groups that relied exclusively on Merton MM systems (regular users). Analyses of these profiles provided insights into the size and characteristics of prospective target market segments, and strategies to attract or keep worthwhile customer groups.

USAGE RATE

Many products sold in consumer and organizational markets can be defined in terms of the relatively small percent of the population that purchases a disproportionate quantity of that product. Merton planners found that, in their training programs, three legal practices—divorce and family law, corporate law, and tax law—purchased more than 80 percent of Merton systems sold. Analyses of reasons for this concentration suggested strategies for maintaining the loyalty of these segments and attracting other practices to MM systems.

LOYALTY STATUS

This behavioristic measure focuses on degrees of product loyalty as defined by usage patterns. For example, the following profiles of MM users were used in positioning, pricing, and promoting MM systems to different legal practices:

- Hard core loyals repurchased Merton computers and associated Merton software.

- Soft core loyals purchased many different computers and software systems in addition to Merton systems.

- Switchers were generally loyal to Merton computer systems but were willing to switch brands if a better offer was made.

BUYER READINESS

At any point, actual and prospective buyers may be in different stages of readiness to purchase products or services. With respect to MM systems, some might be completely unaware of their features and benefits; others may be aware, but not especially interested; still others may be informed, others interested, and others eagerly desiring to purchase a Merton MM system. Segmenting markets in terms of these buyer-readiness stages can provide useful cues for positioning and promoting products. For example, in different markets, any of these responses to the Merton MM—from unawareness to desire—might be anticipated and responded to in planning promotional programs and positioning MM systems.

EVALUATING AND USING SEGMENTATION BASES

In general, demographic and geographic criteria are not as useful as psychographic or behavioristic variables in determining what actually motivates people to buy products, and in devising appealing marketing mixes based on this understanding. For example, knowledge of a woman's motives for purchasing a particular brand of perfume or of the benefits she expects from this perfume would be considerably more useful in promoting this perfume than the demographic fact of her gender or the geographic fact that she lives in Houston. However useful, these demographic and geographic criteria must be incorporated into the mix if only to qualify prospective customers (Can they afford the product? Are they accessible?).

The key to successful segmentation, discussed next, is to group significant criteria variables—demographic, psychographic, and the like—into clusters that maximize within-group similarities and between-group differences, while suggesting strategies for melding marketing mix components.

IDENTIFYING AND DEFINING MARKET SEGMENTS

We will now demonstrate a procedure for identifying, defining, and prioritizing worthwhile market segments as used by Merton in qualifying markets for its planning /training software systems.

SELECT PRODUCT/MARKET AREA

The first step in the process involved determining which target markets would be best served from Merton's portfolio of planning /training systems. Even though, conceivably, a full range of Merton computers and software could be marketed, the initial decision was to go with the two markets that had proven most profitable—accounting and legal firms—and MM models, with associated software, that served these markets.

QUALIFY PROSPECTIVE MARKETS

The first series of segmentation criteria was designed to qualify market segments deserving of further study. These qualifying criteria, including such geographic and demographic factors as location, population size and makeup, and per capita income, were then applied to markets outside of Merton's immediate trading area to identify worthwhile new markets (accessible, substantial, operative, and so on), competitive conditions in these markets, and market growth trends.

DETERMINE WORTHWHILE TARGET MARKETS

After qualifying segmentation criteria had been applied to identify worthwhile new markets for Merton systems, product-related determining criteria were applied to help develop offerings attractive to these markets. Included in this multi-attribute segmentation process were demographic (occupation, education, and the like), psychographic (lifestyle, personality) and behavioristic (benefits, purchase occasion, and the like) criteria that tended to define product acceptance and profit potential.

PROFILE AND PRIORITIZE SEGMENTS

This final step in the process involved briefly profiling each segment in terms of the cluster of segmentation variables characteristic of each, and listing these profiled segments in priority order according to three factors relating to purchase of MM systems: sales potential, prospective return on investment, and ease of market entry.

CHOOSING A SEGMENTATION STRATEGY IN THE CONSUMER MARKET

After identifying, defining, and prioritizing prospectively profitable market segments, Merton planners faced the problem of choosing a suitable segmentation strategy for markets selected for entry. Table 11-2 shows some considerations involved in the selection of the three possible strategies discussed earlier in this chapter—undifferentiated, concentrated, and differentiated.

Table 11–2. Segementation Strategies Related to Product/Market Characteristics

Product/Market Characteristics	Segmentation Strategy Options		
	Undifferentiated	Concentrated	Differentiated
Company resources	Sufficient	Limited	Sufficient
Product homogeneity	Homogeneous (e.g., steel)	Capable of being differentiated	Capable of being differentiated
Product life cycle stage	Introductory stage	Introductory stage	Mature stage
Market homogeneity	If buyers have same MAD-R characteristics	Buyer groups have different MAD-R characteristics	Buyer groups have different MAD-R characteristics
Competitive strategies		Competitors practice undifferentiated strategies	Competitors practice undifferentiated strategies

Based on this matrix data, for example, the planners would select an undifferentiated mass marketing strategy in situations where all buyers had the same MAD-R characteristics (for example, if the only really substantial market in the territory was made up of tax accountants); the product was new to the market, with no competition; and Merton resources were sufficient to undertake the mass production and marketing initiatives required to serve this mass market. Or, without sufficient resources to undertake this undifferentiated strategy, Merton might embark on a concentrated niche marketing strategy, focusing on a single target market.

Then, as conditions change (for example, as multiple profitable markets, with diverse product needs, are identified, along with a changed competitive environment characterizing more mature life cycle stages), a differentiated strategy might be implemented.

CHOOSING A SEGMENTATION STRATEGY IN THE ORGANIZATIONAL MARKET

Many of the same criteria used to segment consumer markets can be used to segment producer and reseller components of organizational markets, including geographic bases and such behavioral bases as benefits sought, user status, usage rate, loyalty status, and readiness stage. As shown in Table 11-3, a number of other criteria also come into play relating to industrial consumer demographics, operating characteristics, purchasing approaches, situational factors, and personal characteristics.

Table 11–3. Major Segmentation Variables for Industrial Markets

Demographic
> *Industry:* Which industries that buy this product should we focus on?
> *Company size:* What size companies should we focus on?
> *Location:* What geographical areas should we focus on?

Operating variables
> *Technology:* What customer technologies should we focus on?
> *User/non-user status:* Should we focus on heavy, medium, or light users or non-users?
> *Customer capabilities:* Should we focus on customers needing many services or few services?

Purchasing approaches
> *Purchasing function organization:* Should we focus on companies with highly centralized or decentralized purchasing organizations?
> *Power structure:* Should we focus on companies that are engineering dominated, financially dominated, or marketing dominated?
> *Nature of existing relationships:* Should we focus on companies with which we already have strong relationships or simply go after the most desirable companies?
> *General purchase policies:* Should we focus on companies that prefer leasing? Service contracts? Systems purchases? Sealed bidding?
> *Purchasing criteria:* Should we focus on companies that are seeking quality? Service? Price?

Situational factors
   Urgency: Should we focus on companies that need quick and sudden delivery or service?
   Specific application: Should we focus on certain applications of our product rather than all applications?
   Size of order: Should we focus on large or small orders?
Personal characteristics
   Buyer-seller similarity: Should we focus on companies whose people and values are similar to ours?
   Attitudes toward risk: Should we focus on risk taking or risk avoiding customers?
   Loyalty: Should we focus on companies that show high loyalty to their suppliers?

Source: Adapted from Thomas V. Bonoma and Benson P. Shapiro, *Segmenting the Industrial Market* (Lexington, MA; Lexington Books, 1983).

Frequently, as with consumer segmentation strategies, criteria can be combined, as illustrated in the Figure 11-2 flowchart showing options for a manufacturer of chip circuits. Three potential markets include (1) resellers who will sell the chips to retailers, who will sell them to electronics hobbyists; (2) manufacturing firms that will use the chips as original equipment in products they manufacture (such as laptop computers); and (3) manufacturing firms that will use the chips in machinery (for example, robotics and computers) that will be used in production and maintenance operations. In terms of customer size, planners determined that the most lucrative market was businesses that will use the chips for OEM applications, which was more than twice as large as the next largest category. Subsequent analyses identified industries with the greatest demand for the chips, as well as benefits desired and readiness stages.

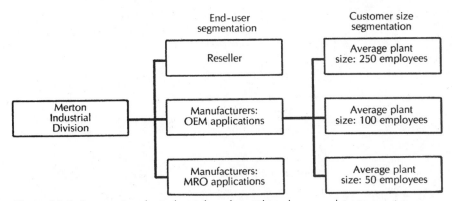

Figure 11-2. Segmenting the industrial market with end-user and customer size segmentation.

MARKET POSITIONING: FIND A SAFE NICHE

After the market for the product has been segmented and a segmentation strategy decided upon, marketers must decide what positions the product can most profitably occupy in each selected segment. The product position concept is an extension of the brand image concept, defined as the sum of perceptions, favorable or unfavorable, about attributes of a product based on consumers' experience and knowledge of the product. In brief, a product's position is its brand image with respect to competing products—the way the product is competitively defined by consumers on key attributes.

The three-dimensional **perceptual map** in Figure 11-3 illustrates an approach for deciding on a product positioning strategy in defined target market segments. This map assumes three major attributes of concern to managing partners in law firms in selecting computer systems for professional personnel: timeliness, in that software content reflects current developments in such areas as tax and environmental law; efficiency, in that the material can be conveyed quickly and effectively to extremely busy, costly attorneys; and cost of the systems.

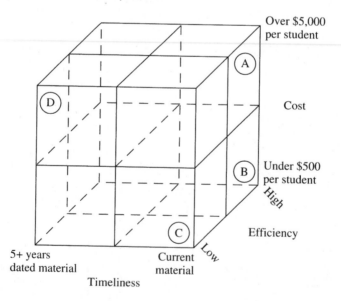

Figure 11-3. Perceptual map helps determine positioning strategies.

Given these criteria, the Merton MM might be positioned as perceived by consumers in the (A) quadrant of the map, as extremely efficient, timely, and costly. This perceptual map also assumes that competitors are already positioned in two other map quadrants, say, low cost, timely, and efficient (B), and low cost, timely, and less efficient (C).

Here are some guidelines for deciding where to position a product in terms of perceived important attributes and in relation to other competitors.

The product should be positioned in an unoccupied quadrant if:

- There are a sufficient number of buyers to justify the position (not too likely in the unoccupied low efficiency, high cost, low timeliness portion of unoccupied quadrant D).

- The position is feasible (consistent with the firm's mission, affordable, and technologically doable).

The product should be positioned in a quadrant occupied by competitors if:

- The preceding conditions for positioning the product in an unoccupied quadrant prevail.

- The product can be made (or be perceived to be) superior to competitive offerings.

INTERNATIONAL PERSPECTIVE

In international markets, approaches and techniques applicable to domestic markets also apply for segmenting markets, defining target markets, and devising positioning and marketing mix strategies attractive to these markets. However, because of significant geographic, demographic, economic, political, and cultural differences between and among foreign countries, international markets often present problems in applying these approaches and techniques. One problem is the difficulty in generating primary and secondary data to identify and prioritize qualifying and determining criteria due to things like language barriers (in Switzerland, for example, three different languages—German, French, and Italian—are spoken in three contiguous areas) and the lack of reliable primary and secondary information sources.

This problem of a paucity of sources of valid, reliable information on which to build segmentation, targeting, and positioning strategies leads to a problem of effectively applying information that is generated. For example, should qualifying or determining criteria predominate in identifying and defining markets? Are segment size, potential, and composition sufficient to justify differentiated or concentrated strategies? Should a standardized, undifferentiated strategy of using the same marketing mix across borders be implemented in preference to more expensive differentiated or concentrated strategies?

Although daunting, these problems in probing global markets can be overcome. In industrialized countries—especially English speaking, politically stable countries with favorable cultural and technological conditions and attitudes toward trade—problems in implementing effective targeting and positioning strategies are no more daunting than in the domestic market. And even in less-developed countries, local marketing firms and sources can usually be retained to cope with these problems.

As examples, Table 11-4 shows how psychographic segmentation was used to identify and define target markets for soft drinks in Australia. Figure 11-4 shows how market gridding was used to identify worthwhile global entry markets for Merton systems.

Table 11–4. Using Psychographic Segmentation to Identify and Define Markets

Soft Drink Brand	AIO Profile Related Positively to Brand	AIO Profile Related Negatively to Brand
Solo	Adventure seeker, extrovert, Australian chauvinist	Economic conservative, social conservative, authoritarian
Swing	Cynic, extrovert, social conservative	Family cohesion, critical consumer, Australian conservative
Tab	Family cohesion, thrifty consumer, critical consumer	Cynic, extrovert, social conservative

PSYCHOGRAPHIC SEGMENTATION

Note that most of the AIO profile characteristics that predict a favorable response to one soft drink also predict an unfavorable response to others, an important finding in positioning (or repositioning) a soft drink brand to appeal to a defined market segment or in developing a marketing mix to support this positioning strategy.

MARKET GRIDDING

Merton planners used a market gridding approach that showed the cumulative impact of a cluster of three segmentation variables—GNP growth rate, per-capita income growth rate, and specific country—on the attractiveness of these countries as entry markets.

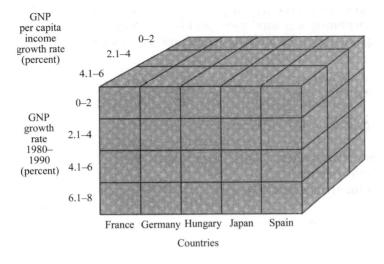

Figure 11-4. Segmentation of international market by three variables.

Given the opportunities depicted in perceptual maps and market grids profiling global markets, and the difficulty experienced in effectively positioning MM systems in cluttered quadrants of the domestic market, Merton planners looked forward to positioning the systems in less cluttered international target market segments. Global Focus 11-1 illustrates this process of building an effective international marketing strategy around a strong product position.

GLOBAL FOCUS 11-1

Nonalcoholic Wine Exporter Toasts World Markets

As owner of San Francisco-based Creative Juices (CJ), Lori Foster is marketing her nonalcoholic wine substitutes to users in the United States and most recently in Europe.

"Our wine substitute is superior to other wine imitations because of its exemplary taste," she says. "This is because our product never has any alcoholic content to begin with—all the other nonalcoholic wines on the market are actually wines with the alcohol removed."

Taking the alcohol out of wine requires a heating process that also destroys the original flavor of the wine, says Foster. "Our wine is never fermented," she says, "so you get the original flavor of our Chardonnay and Zinfandel grapes without the alcohol."

Creative Juices distributes most of its wines under the private labels of large chain stores, high-end gift stores, and catalogs. Major market segments include upper-level high schoolers who wish to enjoy the drinking experience without the consequences of alcoholic beverages, and adults seeking health benefits associated with reduced alcohol consumption.

Structuring her marketing strategy around its position as the nonalcoholic wine with an exemplary taste, Foster achieved profitable growth in the U.S. domestic market and hadn't really considered export markets until she heard about "Women in Trade" missions to Amsterdam and London in fall 1966.

Foster signed up and was one of twenty-two business women to participate. "My biggest surprise in Amsterdam was finding out how willing they were to try a new product," she says. "I showed a bottle to the Amsterdam distributor, and he actually grabbed it out of my hand and ran to show his friends."

As a result of the trade mission, Foster ultimately won a contract to supply Creative Juices to a grocery store chain in Amsterdam. "Through the stores, we sold 1500 cases of our wine substitute in just two weeks," says Foster, who credits the healthy Dutch lifestyle for her product's wide appeal in that country.

Creative Juices is also exploring opportunities with major airlines and restaurants, and the United Arab Emirates, Canada, and Asia have expressed interest.

Source: Curtice K. Coultice, "Bottoms Up," *Business America,* U.S. Department of Commerce, October 1966, pp. 25–27.

CHAPTER PERSPECTIVE

Identifying and defining profitable, high-potential target markets can upgrade all aspects of the strategic marketing process, including devising attractive marketing mixes, evolving strategies for bringing mixes and markets together, and controlling marketing effectiveness. The market segmentation process involves the systematic application of geographic, demographic, psychographic, and behavioristic criteria to identify customer groups that meet the standards defining productive target markets (substantial, homogeneous within, heterogeneous without, accessible, and operational). An important by-product of the segmentation process is information on how to position products in selected segments and the most appropriate segmentation strategy (undifferentiated, concentrated, differentiated) for penetrating entry.

KNOW THE CONCEPTS
TERMS FOR STUDY

Behavioristic bases
Benefits segmentation
Brand image
Buyer readiness stage
Concentrated strategy
Demographic bases
Determining criteria
Differentiated strategy
End-user segmentation
Geographic bases
Heterogeneous segments
Homogeneous segments
Loyalty status segmentation
Market gridding
Mass marketing

Micromarketing
Occasions segmentation
Pareto effect
Perceptual map
Positioning
Psychographic bases
Qualifying criteria
Segment size criteria
Segmentation bases
Segmentation strategies
Target marketing
Undifferentiated strategy
Usage rate segmentation
User status segmentation

MATCHUP EXERCISES

1. Match up the customer characteristic in the second column with the organizational segmentation variable in the first column.

   1. demographic
   2. operational

   3. purchasing

   4. personal

   5. situational

   a. Customer leases all its vehicles.
   b. Customer maintains strong working relationships with suppliers.
   c. Customer insists on prompt deliveries.
   d. Customer relies on supplier servicing capability.
   e. Customer employs 200 production workers in main plant.

2. Colgate Palmolive is launching its "Plus" toothbrush into the German marketplace. Match up the concepts pertaining to how this product will be positioned and promoted, which are listed in the first column, with their definitions in the second column.

1. attribute	a. have higher than average level of oral care involvement
2. position	b. as perceived as more effective in removing plaque and tartar when compared to Oral B Indicator and Advanced Design Reach (competitors)
3. perceptual map	c. superior brushing by cleaning teeth and caring for gums
4. target market	d. has rippled bristles

3. Match up the consumer market segmentation variable in the first column with the characteristic of a typical buyer of a Merton Mighty Mind in the accounting profession in the second column.

1. psychographic	a. has an active social life, which he mixes with business activities
2. behavioristic	b. makes sure he has the most state-of-the-art software
3. geographic	c. male, in his early thirties
4. demographic	d. works for a large Tokyo public accounting firm as a manager, with expectations of soon becoming a partner

4. Match the segmentation strategy in the first column with the product/ market strategy in the second column.

1. concentrated	a. Early in its history, Coca-Cola markets a single, Classic Coke, version of its soft drink to the world.
2. undifferentiated	b. Later in its history, Coca-Cola develops a group of soft drinks (Tab, Sprite, Diet Coke) for the diet drink market.
3. differentiated	c. Also later, Coca-Cola develops soft drinks and other products to appeal to diverse market segments.

QUESTIONS FOR REVIEW AND DISCUSSION

1. In terms of the four MAD-R characteristics that combine to define a market, why would none of the following groups of high school graduates qualify as a market for a rigorous education at the Massachusetts Institute of Technology (MIT)?

	SAT Score	Availability of Funds	Interest in Attending MIT	Interest in Enrolling Elsewhere
Group A	High	High	Low	High
Group B	High	Low	High	Low
Group C	Low	High	High	Low

2. In terms of the five criteria for defining a market, speculate on why an Italian restaurant that goes into business in New York's "Little Italy" goes out of business just as quickly.

3. Describe how five segmentation bases might have been used to identify and define markets and develop marketing mix offerings for these products:

   • The Lincoln Signature Series Town Car

   • General Electric Power Saver air conditioners

   • Johnny Walker Scotch whiskey

   • A $10,000-per-person New Year's Eve party featuring a flight to Paris on Virgin airlines for a gourmet meal

4. Explain the difference between qualifying and determining dimensions in terms of the selection of a spouse.

5. Describe conditions under which it would be worthwhile for a new delicatessen to start operations in a town that already has two delicatessens.

6. Identify the significant differences in segmentation approach between consumer and industrial markets.

7. Textron Inc., the Providence, Rhode Island, conglomerate, follows a deliberate strategy of targeting both government and consumer segments in marketing its lines of aerospace technology and commercial and financial products and services. In so doing, it aims to achieve the flexibility that some of its behemoth competitors are denied (for example, the Northrup Corporation realizes 91 percent of its sales from government contracts). This diversification strategy also dictates different marketing strategies for products and services in Textron's product portfolio (undifferentiated, concentrated, differentiated). Which strategy would you recommend for each of the following products, and why? (1) Gas turbine engines for M-1 tanks; (2) Schaeffer pens and paper products; (3) E-Z-Go golf carts.

ANSWERS

MATCHUPS

1. 1e, 2d, 3a, 4b, 5c

2. 1d, 2c, 3b, 4a

3. 1a, 2b, 3d, 4c

4. 1b, 2a, 3c

QUESTIONS FOR DISCUSSION AND REVIEW

1.

	SAT Score	Availability of Funds	Desire to Attend MIT	Desire to Enroll Elsewhere	Market Members Lack
Group A	High	High	Low	High	response, desire
Group B	High	Low	High	Low	money
Group C	Low	High	High	Low	authority

2. Speculative reasons for the failure of the Italian restaurant follow: (1) the market was not sufficiently large, since most residents of Little Italy did not consider Italian food an attraction or felt they could get superior meals in their own homes; (2) the market was not operational to the extent that it was difficult to measure the attitudes of market members, especially those unwilling to admit that they were tired of Italian food; (3) the offering was not considered sufficiently heterogeneous with respect to the many other Italian restaurants in Little Italy; (4) since the offering was not perceived as different (heterogeneous), a homogeneous target market group that perceived it as different could not be identified; (5) the restaurant was generally inaccessible to its real homogeneous target market: tourists who generally restricted their visits to Little Italy to less obscure locations.

3. Demographic criteria might be used to develop income and occupational profiles of typical Lincoln Town Car buyers; psychographic criteria, in the form of attitude-interest-opinion survey responses, might be used to develop lifestyle profiles, and behavioristic criteria might be used to profile prospective customers in terms of benefits desired and buyer readiness stage. The same criteria could be applied to define market segments and marketing mix components for Johnny Walker Scotch. In addition to these criteria, geographic base criteria would also be applied to determine the location of market segments most in need of the General Electric air conditioner.

As to the $10,000-per-person New Year's Eve party, the relatively small, select group that could afford to attend this event—or would even want to—would have behavioristic characteristics (such as benefits desired, user status), psychographic characteristics (age, income, family life cycle), that could effectively be used in defining the segment and developing an attractive offering.

4. Depending on the individuals' standards and values, qualifying dimensions for a spouse could include such demographic features as gender, age, occupation, and income. Determining dimensions might then distinguish the prospective spouse from other prospects on the basis of attitude-interest-opinion lifestyle characteristics and religious and political beliefs.

5. The following conditions might justify this decision: (1) there is a sufficient number of people in the town to use the services of this deli; (2) the new deli has the management and marketing expertise to operate profitably; (3) the new deli can position itself so as to be viewed as superior to its competitors in key attribute areas (for example, the quality and size of pastrami sandwiches).

6. In segmenting industrial markets, greater emphasis is placed on geographic and behavioristic segmentation. Segmentation bases more likely to be used in segmenting industrial markets include the type of industry, the company size, and the end-use of its products. The product itself is capable of being differentiated into different models to meet differing buyer needs, and the company can achieve economies, and the benefits of a strong market position.

7. (1) For the M-1 tank engines, conditions indicate an undifferentiated strategy, wherein the marketer goes after the entire market with a single offering: the product is homogeneous, to government specifications; the market is also homogeneous as to its needs; and the company has sufficient resources to implement this strategy. (2) For Schaeffer pens and paper products, a differentiated strategy is indicated, whereby the company would design different offerings (such as ballpoint and luxury pens) for several different target market segments (business offices, students, etc.). (3) For the E-Z-Go golf cart, a concentrated strategy is indicated, whereby the company goes after a large share of one or a few submarkets such as golf courses instead of after a small share of a large market. The product itself is capable of being differentiated into different models to meet differing buyer needs, and the company can achieve economies and the benefits of a strong market position.

12
MEASURING MARKET AND SALES POTENTIAL

OVERVIEW

Forecasts of the nature and extent of potential demand in defined market segments underpin all aspects of the strategic planning process, including establishing realistic marketing objectives, allocating resources to achieve these objectives, monitoring elements of the external environment, and keeping marketing efforts on track.

Market forecasts typically encompass measures of national, industry, and company sales in consumer and organizational markets along time, area, and product dimensions. Specific quantitative and qualitative forecasting techniques employed include correlation, time series, market factor, chain ratio, total market demand, market buildup, and surveys of experts, salesforce, and buyer intentions.

FORECASTS PROJECT MARKET AND SALES POTENTIAL

In Chapter 11, we examined strategies for identifying, defining, and prioritizing worthwhile consumer and organizational segments and positioning products to competitive advantage in these segments. Now, in this chapter, we examine strategies and techniques for forecasting market and sales potential in these target market segments. For illustrative purposes, we will refer again to the industrial and consumer products divisions of the Merton Electronics Company. As background, we will discuss:

- Differences between market and sales potential, and the value for marketing managers of forecasting each;

- Dimensions along which market and sales potential are forecast;

- Characteristics of market/sales potential in terms of (1) money/authority/desire/access criteria and (2) the relationship between marketing efforts and demand levels.

HOW MARKET AND SALES POTENTIALS DIFFER

Market potential is the prospective volume of a specific good or service that would be bought by a defined customer group over a specific time period in a defined geographic area and marketing environment and under a defined level and mix of industry marketing effort. **Sales potential** is the prospective proportion of market potential for a specific good or service that could be purchased from a specific seller, like Merton. Market potential is what consumer and organizational markets could purchase from all sellers; sales potential is what could be purchased from an individual seller.

A **forecast** is what the seller projects market or sales potential volume to be, usually stated in monetary or product units. **Market share** is the percentage of market potential that the seller actually gets. For example, if market potential for the Merton MM is $20,000,000 in a given market segment (i.e., what customers could purchase from all sellers), and Merton is only getting $2,000,000 of this potential, then its market share is 10 percent.

FORECASTS HELP PLAN AND ACHIEVE MARKETING GOALS

To illustrate the value of market/sales potential forecasts in the marketing planning process, assume that Merton marketing management is developing forecasts of marketing and sales potential for MM systems in the accountant target market in various presently uncovered territories. The following information can help Merton marketers.

• *MONITOR THE EXTERNAL ENVIRONMENT*

For example, a reliable forecast of sales and profits can take into account such environmental factors as the effect of the economy on purchasing power; political roadblocks to successful market entry; technological factors that will help to manufacture and market MMs; and the scope of competitive initiatives.

• *ESTABLISH REALISTIC SALES AND PROFIT OBJECTIVES*

Estimates of dollar potential of target market segments are necessary for budgeting marketing effort and dollars to achieve a desired level of sales and profits. Setting these goals begins the strategic planning process.

- ### *ALLOCATE RESOURCES TO ACHIEVE THESE ESTABLISHED OBJECTIVES*

Understanding the nature, needs, and dollar potential in a target market segment provides information on which to base goal-oriented resource allocation decisions in such areas as new product decisions, production scheduling, financial planning, inventory planning, distribution, pricing strategies, and promotional campaigns.

- ### *CONTROL MARKETING EFFORTS*

Market forecasts are basic to setting standards against which to measure actual performance. If marketing efforts result in sales or profits that are excessively above or below these standards, appropriate measures can be taken to bring actual figures back in line with projected expectations.

FORECASTING DIMENSIONS: TIME, SPACE, AND PRODUCTS

As shown in Figure 12-1, market and sales potential can be forecast along many different dimensions. Along the **area dimension,** for example, Merton's marketing planners might want to measure the sales potential of a single large customer, or all the customers in a given territory or region, in the entire domestic market, or in the entire global market.

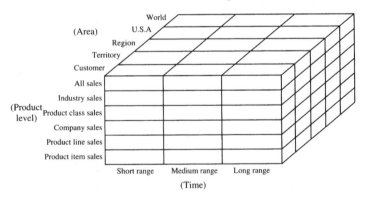

Figure 12–1. Product/space/time dimensions identify ninety categories.

Along the **product level dimension,** the marketing planners might want to know what demand is for MM systems designed for one professional group (product item), all computer system models Merton markets to professional groups (product class), or all the diverse consumer electronics products Merton makes and markets (product line). Merton planners might also want to know how the company is doing in relation to its competition, so industry sales will also be forecast. Additionally, they might want to know about how Merton's sales, and sales of its competitors, are doing as compared to sales of all products in this country and globally, so these forecasts will also be made.

Along the **time level dimension,** any of these product/area level forecasts might be made for a short-range period (up to one year); a medium-range period (one to three years); or a long-range period (more than three years).

FORECASTING CRITERIA: MONEY, AUTHORITY, DESIRE, AND ACCESS

Using the MM as an example, Figures 12-2(a) and (b) show some of the components into which market and sales potential can be divided and used to set goals and formulate strategies. The basis for these divisions are the criteria that define markets in general: money, authority, desire, and access.

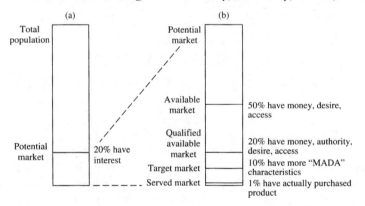

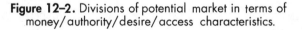

Figure 12–2. Divisions of potential market in terms of money/authority/desire/access characteristics.

Figure 12-2(a) depicts the two basic components of a market:

1. **Total population,** composed of all the people in a given country who may or may not be interested in buying a Merton MM system.

2. **Potential market,** composed of people among the total population who profess some level of interest in procuring an MM system.

Figure 12-2(b) begins with the 20 percent of the total market that represents the potential market for MMs and further defines and delimits this market. Thus, of this potential market, only 50 percent constitute its **available market,** which is made up of people who are interested in, can afford, and have access to MM systems. Assuming, however, that Merton is only interested in selling MM systems to accredited professionals such as lawyers and accountants, its **qualified available market** (20 percent of the potential market) would be limited to people who possess these credentials.

The **target market** is composed of that 50 percent of the qualified available market that Merton decides most justifies cultivation, and the **penetrated market** is composed of that 10 percent of target market members who have actually purchased Merton MM systems.

Viewing markets in terms of these categories is a useful starting point for planning marketing strategies. For example, forecasts depicting the nature and scope of these market segments might show Merton planners that a given target market isn't being effectively penetrated (10 percent of the potential market might be considered too small) and suggest initiatives, such as a more innovative, intensive promotion program, for converting target market members into members of the served market. Or, Merton might decide to lower its accreditation requirement to increase the size of the qualified available market, change its marketing mix to attract more members of the available market, or include more professional groups to increase the size of the potential market.

RELATIONSHIPS BETWEEN MARKETING EFFORT AND DEMAND

Figure 12-3 depicts another useful aspect of the forecasting process—the relationship between marketing effort and demand. On this model, the horizontal axis shows different possible levels of marketing expenditure in a given time period, and the vertical axis shows demand levels associated with each expenditure level. Point Q^0, the **market minimum,** represents sales volume that would result without any expenditures. For example, word-of-mouth promotion alone would result in the sale of some MM systems. Greater expenditures would yield more sales and push the sales response curve (that is, the extent to which sales change with expenditure changes) closer to the market potential line, which represents what all prospective customers could purchase of these products. The distance between the market minimum (Q^0) and **market potential** (Q^1) shows the overall **marketing sensitivity of demand.** If the distance is great, the market is capable of greater growth (it is highly expandable) and will be more likely to respond to marketing expenditures than if the distance is small. The market for innovative new products, or existing products introduced as new to markets, is usually more expandable and responsive to marketing efforts than existing products in domestic markets.

Forecast data, combined with primary and secondary source data analyzing sales by product and territory, can profile these characteristics in a given market. For example, in two adjacent territories, forecast and sales analysis

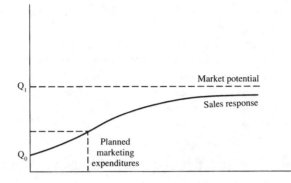

Figure 12–3. Sale responses as a function of planned expenditures.

data might define each as having approximately equal target, served, and qualified available markets; one territory, however, might be considerably more expandable than the other, and hence justify greater marketing expenditure to realize this increased potential.

THE THREE-STEP DIRECT FORECASTING APPROACH

Although marketers are typically most interested in measuring short-range potential for product classes in defined, targeted territories, these figures become more meaningful when compared to forecasted figures for the national economy as a whole, and the firm's industry as one component of this economy.

To illustrate the usefulness of these three forecast levels—national, industry, company—assume a situation in which the Merton MM proves to be a commercial success and attracts other competitors with similar electronic offerings. Also assume that, in an upcoming year, Merton forecasts a 10 percent increase in MM sales. If the actual increase is only 5 percent, does this indicate subpar performance in implementing Merton's marketing plan, and the need to revise this plan? Perhaps so, if industry forecasts show that Merton MM sales are losing market share to competitors. However, forecasts of industry performance in general might indicate that, in spite of its five-point sales decline, Merton is actually picking up market share in a recessive economic environment. The point is that the significance of Merton's forecast can best be understood, and acted upon, in a broader context of general economic and industry forecasts.

Generally, national economic forecasts are available from a number of sources listed in Chapter 7, including government publications, industry associations, trade magazines, banks, and private research organizations. From these sources, marketers can usually find a single forecast, or combination of forecasts, that have worked well in the past to forecast trends and developments.

Many of these organizations also prepare sales forecasts for specific industries. Unfortunately, these forecasts are usually made for broad business categories—services, steel, housing, and electronics for example—rather than for specific submarket categories such as notebook computer or tax accountant markets. Thus, marketers need to look to their own forecasting tools and techniques to generate useful, focused forecasts.

FORECASTS RELY ON NUMBERS, JUDGMENT, OR BOTH

In general, approaches for forecasting industry and product sales potential can be categorized as either quantitative or judgmental in nature.

Quantitative techniques rely primarily on sales volume and other numbers (such as disposable income), which are generated in the past and presumed to have predictive value into the future. In the specific quantitative techniques discussed next, these numbers are added, multiplied, and/or related to other figures in developing projections.

Judgmental techniques rely on the judgment of people presumed to have a special knowledge of the impact of different variables on sales. Salespeople, for example, or prospective customers, would presumably have a first-hand knowledge of how customers and markets will respond to a firm's products, and the environmental factors influencing these responses.

QUANTITATIVE AND JUDGMENTAL FORECASTING TECHNIQUES

In this section, we examine quantitative and judgmental techniques used to forecast market and sales potential in consumer and organizational markets.

Quantitative techniques for forecasting consumer markets include input-output, correlation, market factor index, chain ratio, and total market demand analyses to convert market potential figures into sales potential figures for specific products in specific areas.

• *INPUT-OUTPUT ANALYSES*

Input-output analyses show resources utilized by different industries for a given output as well as the interdependence of economic sectors.

Through the use of input-output tables, now published for all industrialized countries, production (output) of one sector is shown as the demand (input) for other sectors. For example, steel output becomes input for such sectors as automobile and airframe manufacturers, households, government, and the foreign sector. Using these tables for the U.S. domestic market, Merton analysts developed a profile of input-output features of the consumer electronics market, which was then matched to similar profiles of prospective entry markets where timely, reliable profiles existed.

• *CORRELATION ANALYSES*

This technique measures the degree of association (correlation) between potential sales of a product and a market factor that has closely paralleled sales of this product in the past. Typically, this market factor is a measurement of economic activity, called a **leading series,** which changes in the same direction but ahead of product sales being measured. For example, historical experience showed Merton researchers that consumer disposable income correlated closely with MM sales in Merton's domestic market and had been projected into the future with unusual accuracy by a number of private and government economists. In a typical year, the consensus among these forecasters was that disposable income would increase by 5 percent. Since total domestic sales of MM systems had been $20 million the previous year, Merton researchers projected MM sales at $20,100,000 for the coming year.

Two other correlates of particular value in identifying growth potential are indices of income elasticity and production growth:

- **Coefficients of income elasticity** correlate prospective purchases with increases, or decreases, in income. As discussed in the Chapter 4 section on Engel's law, purchases of certain categories of products, like recreation and education, increase at a faster rate than do increases in income. For example, if purchases of MM systems increase by 1.2 percent for each 1 percent income increase, the income coefficient of elasticity for this product is 1.20, a figure that can be projected into the near term and correlated with forecasted sales of MMs.

- **Production growth trends,** especially useful as an indicator of sales potential for any product or service required in manufacturing processes, is usually adjusted to include imported products used in production processes and to subtract inventories of finished goods.

There are two major limitations of correlation analyses:

1. They require a lengthy sales history to develop relationships—at least 20 quarters of sales records.

2. They are expensive and time-consuming, invariably requiring computerized databases and often beyond the skills of researchers.

• *MARKET FACTOR INDEX*

The **market factor index** technique was used as a check on the correlation analysis to develop data on overall MM sales potential. In Merton's experience, the **buying power index** formula, published each year by *Sales and Marketing Management* magazine in its *Survey of Buying Power,* had accurately reflected sales of MM systems among professional groups in Merton's domestic market. This formula is based on three weighted factors: an area's share of the nation's disposable personal income (y_i), retail sales (r_i), and population (p_i). Hence, the formula for buying power is

$$B_i = 0.5y_i + 0.3r_i + 0.2p_i$$

In one segment of Merton's domestic market, for example, the respective y, r, and p shares of national totals were 0.06, 0.08, and 0.07; hence, this area could account for 0.068 of total potential demand for MM systems (0.5 $\times$ 0.06 + 0.3 $\times$ 0.08 + 0.2 $\times$ 0.07) = 0.068. Thus, if national demand for MM systems was estimated to be, say, $30,000,000, demand in this segment would be estimated at $2,040,000 ($30,000,000 $\times$ 0.068).

• *CHAIN RATIO*

The **chain ratio** technique involves multiplying a base number, such as total number of buyers in a market, by various qualifying criteria that refine this base number to reflect specific characteristics of submarkets under study. For example, in Merton's domestic trading area, researchers estimated a total of 100,000 accounting professionals with interest in and access to MM system purchases—the potential market. Of this total, however, only 30 percent were estimated to have the disposable income to afford an MM system. Thus, Merton's qualified available market consists of 30,000 accountants (100,000 $\times$ 0.30).

• *TOTAL MARKET DEMAND*

The **total market demand** approach builds up to a total market demand figure Q by multiplying total number of buyers n by the quantity q purchased by the average buyer and the price p of an average unit. Thus, for example, starting with the 30,000 accountants figure emerging from the chain ratio calculation, and assuming that one in ten of these accountants would purchase an MM system at an average cost of $3000, Merton estimated its sales potential in this area to be $9,000,000 ($Q = 30,000 \times 0.10 \times \$3000$).

ORGANIZATIONAL MARKET FORECASTING STRATEGIES

In forecasting sales of MM systems to large professional legal and accounting firms in its domestic organizational market, Merton's most commonly used forecasting approaches were market buildup and time series analyses.

• *MARKET BUILDUP*

The market buildup approach involved building up to total potential figures for an entire trading area by adding together potential figures for specific industries in this area. Here, SIC categories, discussed in Chapter 9, proved useful to categorize individual target market industries for further study. For example, here is how Merton arrived at market potential estimates for MM systems in two target segments of the organizational market—accounting (SIC 7658) and law firms (SIC 7617)—in one territory in the firm's domestic market.

SIC Code	# of Employees	# of Firms	Potential Sales per Employee ($)	Market Potential ($)
7658	20,000	250	500	10,000,000
7617	15,000	200	400	6,000,000

This analysis shows that, based on surveys of a sampling of the accounting and law firm populations, market potential (what these firms could purchase from all suppliers of computer systems) was $16,000,000. This figure assumes that each of the 20,000 accountants in 250 accounting firms would purchase, on average, $500 worth of computer systems, and each of the 15,000 lawyers would purchase an average of $400.

Market Focus 12-1 illustrates a market buildup approach, particularly applicable to consumer markets, that replaces SIC codes with postal zip codes.

MARKET FOCUS 12-1

Building Forecasts and Market Plans on Zip Codes and Census Data

Geodemographic analysis (GA), an approach that links census data, lifestyle patterns, and postal zip codes, offers marketers a tool for refining estimates of market potential and identifying areas in which to concentrate marketing efforts. Used with different databases, GA is currently used for prioritizing market segments for a full range of products and services, notably food, clothing, and furniture.

To illustrate how GA works, consider how the Seventh Day Adventist religious denomination identifies the best zip code areas in which to recruit new members. Operating under the assumption that they will have the best chance to attract new members in new markets from zip code areas similar to those that contain most current members, church recruiters first code present Seventh Day Adventists into forty zip code clusters, each appropriately labeled in terms of a dominant defining characteristic (for example, "Hispanic mix" and "blue-blood estates"). Then, a concentration index for each cluster is determined by dividing the percentage of Adventists in the cluster by the percentage of the total population represented by the group and multiplying the result by 100. For example, if a particular defined group in a zip-coded cluster represents 10 percent of all Adventists, but only 2 percent of the U.S. population, it would have a concentration index of 500.

Next, clusters are prioritized according to the size of the concentration index, with zip-coded areas exceeding 100 targeted for focused marketing programs, including door-to-door recruiting, direct mail campaigns, and the opening of new Seventh Day Adventist churches.

Source: The North American Division Marketing Program, Vol. I: Profiling Adventist Members and Baptisms, 1986.

• *TIME SERIES ANALYSES*

This approach assumes that changes in sales levels in previous periods (the time series) can be used as a basis for predicting sales in the future. In Merton's domestic market, these changes generally reflected four components:

1. A **long-term trend T,** reflecting an underlying pattern of sales found by fitting a straight or curved line through past sales;

2. An **intermediate-term cycle C,** reflecting cyclic changes in economic or competitive activity, depicted by wavelike changes in the trend line;

3. A **season component S,** reflecting any recurrent weekly, monthly, or quarterly changes in sales patterns;

4. An **erratic events E** component, reflecting unexpected events (strikes, floods, fads, and the like) that might influence sales.

In using time series analyses to forecast sales volume in domestic markets, Merton marketers had sufficient data to compile trend, cycle, and seasonal components, to which they added a figure reflecting their best assessment of the nature and likelihood of possible erratic events. For example, in a year when the possibility of government initiatives in worldwide economic and military conflicts was expected to have an impact on the economy for better or worse, Merton projected a 10 percent sales increase T, to which was added another 5 percent resulting from an anticipated cyclic growth spurt C. Another 5 percent was added for spring and fall seasons—typically the busiest in Merton's year S and, finally, the total forecasted figure was reduced by 5 percent as the anticipated result of unusually high budget cutbacks in the public sector.

JUDGMENTAL FORECASTING TECHNIQUES

Groups whose judgment is typically solicited in preparing judgmental forecasts include experts, salespeople, and prospective customers. Here is how each group was used in compiling sales forecasts for MM systems in Merton's domestic market.

• *SURVEY OF EXPERT OPINION*

This approach relies on the opinion of people with presumed knowledge of different variables affecting sales. Merton's own executives, with their "big picture" understanding of various environmental influences, might constitute one such group; another might be a trade association of manufacturers of computer systems, or publications serving Merton's professional target markets, which gather and disseminate statistics from many sources, including manufacturers, sellers, and government researchers.

In developing such expert information from Merton executives, researchers made use of the **Delphi technique,** whereby estimates of future sales were sent back to the people who originally submitted these estimates until a consensus figure emerged. For example, one estimate ranged, initially, from a predicted sales decline of 6 percent to a predicted increase of 12 percent. These estimates were ranked, with supporting rationales, and returned to the executives with requests that they state their agreements and disagreements with the rank order and rationales, make any desired changes in their initial projections, and return the estimates. After several rounds, a consensus figure projecting a 4 percent increase emerged.

• *SURVEY OF BUYER INTENTIONS*

Using independent marketing research firms to maintain anonymity, Merton had a number of surveys of customers and prospects conducted to determine the likelihood that firms would purchase MM systems in general, and Merton systems in particular. A typical survey instrument used in these probes, the **purchase probability scale,** uses rating scale probabilities of from 0.00 (no chance) through 0.50 (fair chance) to 1.00 (certain) to measure purchase intentions. Among many domestic organizations that publish forecasts of buyer purchase intentions, the Survey Research Center of the University of Michigan, with its consumer sentiment measure, is probably the best known.

• *COMPOSITE SALESFORCE OPINION*

Similar to the survey of expert opinion, this approach bases sales forecasts on the opinion of salespeople. Logically, salespeople, closer to happenings in the marketplace, should be able to provide reliable estimates, although it is frequently argued that they lack a "big picture" overview of factors affecting sales. It is also argued that salespeople might have incentives to estimate low (for example, to get a lower quota) or, conversely, that the optimistic nature of the sales personality might encourage high estimates.

INTERNATIONAL PERSPECTIVE

Reliable forecasts are generally more difficult to come by in international markets than in domestic markets for such reasons as differing economic, political, and cultural changes within short timeframes and lack of valid, reliable secondary data on which to base forecasts.

JUDGMENTAL FORECASTING IN GLOBAL MARKETS

In general, judgmental (qualitative) forecasts are easier than quantitative forecasts to implement because they don't require as much objective secondary data. Often, firms will implement a judgmental forecast as a relatively inexpensive way to get a feel for an entry market before committing resources to a large scale, possibly futile, marketing effort. Such forecasts also often produce data to implement more sophisticated quantitative forecasting methods (for example, finding effective leading indicators for correlation analyses, or qualifying criteria to adjust chain ratio figures).

Obviously, polling salesforce opinion is not feasible if the firm has no salesforce in a prospective entry market, but sometimes salespeople from other firms can be polled, especially when an association or publication generates information from salespeople on market prospects.

Whether conducted in domestic or foreign markets, all of these judgmental techniques lend themselves to two techniques designed to improve accuracy and validity of findings while keeping costs low:

- **Focus group panels** (discussed in Chapter 7) are usually composed of eight to twelve members of a knowledgeable group (customers, salespeople, executives) who discuss, in an in-depth, free-wheeling manner, products, markets, threats, and opportunities.

- The **Delphi technique,** discussed earlier, is usually conducted with groups of between twenty to thirty participants.

QUANTITATIVE FORECASTING IN GLOBAL MARKETS

By way of addressing limitations endemic to quantitative forecasting approaches in global markets, marketers interested in entering or expanding in global markets generally employ two approaches different from those employed in domestic markets: (1) they modify these direct forecasting approaches, and/or (2) they rely on analogy approaches to measure market variables.

MODIFYING DIRECT APPROACHES

All the direct quantitative forecasting approaches discussed earlier—correlation, chain ratio, market buildup, and the like—require considerable amounts of valid, reliable secondary data from many sources. Just defining the nature and scope of a potential market to be forecast, for example, mandates demographic and psychographic information on size, location, needs, and income of discrete market segments. Deeper probes of these markets requires information on things like production trends, retail sales, disposable income, income elasticity, and competitive activity.

In modern industrialized and post-industrialized countries, much of the same information, from similar sources (government bureaus, trade associations, publications) is available that is available to researchers in the United States. Typically, however, this information is tabulated in different ways (for example, England, Germany, and the United States each measures gross domestic product in different ways), and these differences must be accounted for in using this information for forecasting purposes.

In using quantitative forecasting techniques in foreign markets, it's often possible to substitute information that is available for information that isn't. For example, if projected disposable personal income has proven to be a reliable indicator of buying intentions of a given group in the domestic market, but it is not available in the foreign market under study, then possibly just average income can serve as a substitute. In organizational markets, where SIC data is not generally available, Harmonized Commodity Classification figures can be used as surrogate data in market forecasting.

The notion of substituting one element for another is the key premise underpinning analogy approaches to market forecasting, discussed next, and illustrated by Global Focus 12-1.

GLOBAL FOCUS 12-1

Analogy Forecasts Help Build Lakewood's World Market for Chopsticks

Searching for new global markets and business opportunities, Ian Ward, president of Lakewood Forest Products in Hibbing, Minnesota, discovered an unmet need for chopsticks in the Orient, where the chopsticks industry was generally fragmented, technologically backward, and lacking in natural resources (for example, there were 450 chopsticks factories in Japan alone, serving a market demand for 130 million pairs of disposable wooden chopsticks per day). Ward perceived that his plant in Hibbing was ideally positioned to serve this market: the decline of mining in the area had created an excellent labor pool and a regional desire for new industry; Hibbing had an abundance of unmarred aspen wood ideal for making chopsticks; and Ward himself had the financing and production know-how (with the help of sophisticated equipment purchased from Denmark) to create an automated production line with a capacity of up to 7 million chopsticks a day. With a unit manufacturing cost of $.03, and a unit selling price of $.057, Ward had no trouble preselling his first 5 years' output to Japan, earning a pretax profit of $4.7 million in 1989, his first year.

At this point, Ward began exploring other opportunities in the global marketplace, using a variety of forecasting techniques. For example, in Taiwan, with a state of socioeconomic development similar to that of Japan, an estimate by analogy approach proved most effective in estimating potential for Lakewood chopsticks. In substance, potential per-capita consumption of the chopsticks would be assumed to be the same in Taiwan as in Japan. In the case of China, with its state of socioeconomic development well behind Japan's, a time displacement approach proved most appropriate. Thus, chopstick usage in Japan, at a point in its history when the country was on a socioeconomic level with China, was found to approximate China's per-capita consumption, and consumption projections for future sales in China were based on assumptions regarding the time required to reach Japan's present socioeconomic status. With respect to the U.S. population of Oriental descent (and assuming a latent interest among this population to use traditional eating implements), an "analogy among similar products" approach proved most productive. That is, the number of knives and forks purchased on a per-capita basis in this community might serve as a surrogate estimate for the number of chopsticks that could be purchased.

ANALOGY FORECASTING APPROACHES

In general, the **estimate by analogy** approach assumes that demand develops in much the same way in different countries and can be measured with the same indices used in the country that serves as the basis of the analogy. A variant on the estimate by analogy approach, called the time displacement approach, assumes a different kind of analogy between countries that are dissimilar in terms of growth stage and other defining variables. Specifically, this approach assumes an analogy between stages of development in both countries, and the time each stage is reached. Thus, for example, this approach might assume that the Mexican professional market for MMs will achieve parity with the U.S. market, say, in ten years, and a sales projection line can be drawn based on the assumption that demand growth will follow the same pattern as in the United States.

Still another variant on the estimate by analogy approach assumes an analogy between similar products. For example, Japanese consumption of beef, sugar, liquor, and dairy products grew, between 1972 and 1992, at a rate closely paralleling that in the United States in an earlier period. This growth rate also closely paralleled the relative growth of per-capita income in the two countries. Thus, marketers could base forecasts of sales of these products, and similar products (such as other sweeteners or foodstuffs) in Japan on projections of per-capita income growth in the United States.

The prospective flaw in all analogy approaches is the assumption of similarity. In the Mexican example, other factors, unique to Mexico, might be dominant in determining product purchases. Also, it is at least possible—perhaps likely—that technological and social factors might permit the country to leapfrog previous development stages in the United States, helping Mexico achieve parity in fewer than ten years. And there might be enough differences among similar products to significantly change demand patterns of each.

Given these constraints, it's important, when applying analogy approaches, to know the needs a product serves domestically before similar needs and potential can be measured in foreign markets. It is also important to have a sufficiently long historical record of the bridging variable, or variables, to ensure the validity and reliability of these indices. For example, if per-capita income growth serves as a reliable indicator of sales of dairy products in both Japan and the United States for ten consecutive years, then its validity, reliability, and usefulness as a forecasting tool for these products can probably be assumed.

GAP ANALYSIS SCANS AND COMPARES

After estimates of market or sales potential are made in given domestic or international markets, **gap analysis** is a useful technique for putting these figures into meaningful perspective. This is done by comparing gaps in a number of areas and taking appropriate action based on this understanding. As examples, consider gaps between: (1) sales forecasts for countries A, B, C, and D; (2) sales forecasts and forecasts of market potential; and (3) sales forecasts for product A and competitive products B, C, and D. In situations where these gaps are significantly large, further investigation is usually indicated to identify, and rectify, their cause, which may be due to a number of factors, including customer attitudes, competitive initiatives, promotional failures, product (or price) inadequacies, or distribution failures.

CHAPTER PERSPECTIVE

Valid, reliable market and sales forecasts, in both consumer and organizational markets, are basic to formulating and implementing strategic marketing plans, including setting objectives, assigning resources, and controlling marketing effectiveness. Sales and marketing forecasts can be conducted to encompass at least ninety possible combinations of area, space, and time dimensions in consumer and organizational markets and are usually developed in the broader context of industry forecasts and forecasts for the economy as a whole. The specific segment of the market being forecast (potential, available, served), based on money/authority/desire/access criteria, helps determine the specific forecasting techniques used. Quantitative and judgmental techniques are generally combined in generating forecast data, with the number used dependent on such variables as data availability and cost constraints. Direct methods for generating sales and market forecasts in domestic markets include input-output and correlation analyses, chain ratio and total market demand techniques, and surveys of expert, salesforce, and customer opinion. In generating forecasts for the global marketplace, various analogy approaches are typically used. All are based on the assumption that there are measurable similarities between the home country, serving as the basis of the analogy, and the foreign country, where various dimensions of sales and markets are being forecast.

KNOW THE CONCEPTS
TERMS FOR STUDY

Analogy approaches
Available market
Buying power index
Chain ratio technique
Coefficient of income elasticity
Company sales potential
Correlation analysis
Delphi technique
Expandable demand
Focus groups
Forecasting dimensions
Gap analysis
Input-output analysis
Judgmental techniques
Leading indicator
Market buildup method
Market factor index method

Market forecast
Market potential
Market share
Marketing sensitivity of demand
Penetrated market
Potential market
Production growth trends
Purchase probability scale
Qualified available market
Quantitative methods
Salesforce opinion
Sales response function
Survey of buyer intentions
Survey of expert opinion
Time displacement approach
Time series projection
Total market demand

MATCHUP EXERCISES

1. Match up the market component in the first column with the situation
that best describes it in the second column.

1. potential market

    a. These people are most likely to want to take a cruise on the Holland-America Line.

2. target market

    b. These people have already taken a cruise on the Holland-America Line.

3. served market

    c. These people would like to take a cruise on the Holland-America line, if circumstances permit.

4. qualified available market

    d. These people would like to take a cruise on the Holland-America line, can afford to, and have access to a port of departure.

2. Match up the quantitative forecasting technique in the first column with
the example in the second column.

1. coefficient of income elasticity   a. Increases in disposable income and retail sales should push sales of Merton Mighty Minds up by 20 percent this quarter.

2. market factor index technique   b. As disposable income increases by 1 percent, jewelry sales increase by 1.5 percent.

3. chain ratio   c. Eighty percent of automobile buyers in Taiwan can't afford a BMW; among the remainder, one in ten will purchase a BMW within the next five years.

4. correlation analysis   d. There is a strong positive relationship between annual precipitation in the Ukraine and the amount of wheat purchased abroad.

5. time displacement   e. China is alleged to have stolen the secret of miniaturizing warhead components from the United States, gaining them about ten years of technological development when compared to the United States.

3. Match up the qualitative forecast technique in the first column with the defining situation in the second column.

1. Delphi technique   a. have "big picture" understanding of market forces

2. survey of expert opinion   b. purchase probability scale

3. survey of buyer intentions   c. summarizes and resubmits estimates

4. composite salesforce opinion   d. closer to the customer

QUESTIONS FOR REVIEW AND DISCUSSION

1. Explain the relationship among demand levels, marketing expenditures, and marketing forecasts.

2. How does a reliable forecast assist in the marketing planning effort?

3. Assume that the following conditions occur before the Christmas buying season: (1) the Toys 'R' Us chain underestimates demand for an electronic fad toy; (2) The Foot Locker shoe store chain overestimates demand for a well-advertised tennis sneaker. Identify two costs associated with each situation that could have an adverse impact on short- and long-range profits for each store.

4. In terms of the space-product-time context in which marketing forecasts are made, how would you define the following forecasting situations facing the chairman of the Republican Party, who would like to
know:

- How the party in general will fare during the first decade of the twenty-first century in attracting voters;

- How the party's presidential candidate will fare in the next election;

- How the party's slate of senatorial candidates will fare in this year's
election;

- Whether one of the party's star candidates will upset a well-
entrenched incumbent in this year's Massachusetts gubernatorial
election.

5. A large multinational manufacturer of sporting equipment is undertak-
ing a sales forecast for 2001 in one of five industrialized Latin American
countries where total sales of the firm's golf clubs totaled $50,000,000
in 2000. Using market factor index and chain ratio forecasting techniques, estimate the sales of the manufacturer's golf clubs in this country given the following data:

- This country has 0.09 percent of total income of the five countries,
0.12 percent of retail sales generated in these countries, and 0.15
percent of the total population of the five countries.

- This country has 800,000 golfers, of which 20 percent will purchase
(or receive as a gift) a new set of golf clubs during the coming year.
One in ten of this group will buy or receive a set of the manufacturer's golf clubs paying, on average, $400.

From your answers, what can you conclude about when and why to
meld a number of forecasting techniques to arrive at sales forecasts?
How might two judgmental forecasts be used to supplement these
quantitative forecasts?

6. In terms of marketing control, what is a gap analysis and how might
such an analysis be used by the multinational sporting goods manufacturer (question 5) after developing forecasts in the five industrialized
countries that comprise the company's Latin American market? How
might these concepts be involved in implementing activities emerging
from this analysis: potential market, penetrated market, qualified market, available market?

7. Describe the difference between the potential market, the qualified
available market, the target market, and the penetrated market for pro-

fessional courses marketed by Merton's Speech Recognition (SR) software division.

8. Assume that Merton's industrial electronics division is attempting to estimate potential for its Moonchip in a new territory and has the following facts and figures to go on based on its experience with the Moonchip in other territories: 50 percent of its Moonchip sales are in the SIC 3661 industry (telephone/telegraph equipment) and the SIC 3662 industry (radio and TV equipment). SIC 3661, with a total of 1500 employees in firms served by Merton, purchased $75,000 worth of Moonchips; SIC 3662, with 2000 employees in served firms, purchased $200,000 worth. In the new territory, SIC 3661 firms employ 1200, and SIC 3662 firms employ 1000. What do you estimate the sales potential for Moonchips to be in the new territory?

ANSWERS

MATCHUP EXERCISES

1. 1c, 2a, 3b, 4d
2. 1b, 2a, 3c, 4d, 5e
3. 1c, 2a, 3b, 4d

QUESTIONS FOR REVIEW AND DISCUSSION

1. The amount a firm spends in marketing a product will determine the point at which market potential is transformed into sales dollars for this product. At one extreme, some sales will probably result from no expenditures at all; at the other extreme, a point will be reached beyond which each additional dollar invested in marketing effort will produce less than a dollar's return in sales. Between these extremes, valid and reliable sales forecasts indicate the extent to which sales, in units or dollars, will increase with incremental increases in marketing expenditures.

2. A sales forecast indicates the amount of sales, or the sales response, that a firm can expect to generate given a planned level of marketing expenditure. This forecast also indicates the amount of sales, stated as shares of market, that competitors will generate in this product market. Strategic marketing planning involves, essentially, identifying market opportunities and projecting goals and plans that will make productive use of the firm's resources to achieve these opportunities against the efforts of competitors to do the same thing. Thus, an effective sales forecast is basic to the marketing planning effort in that it helps define the opportunity, the competitive share of market, and the planned level of expenditure needed to achieve this opportunity.

3. Costs associated with underestimated demand include the cost of lost sales—and the profits to be made from these sales—and the possible cost of future sales resulting from a loss of customer goodwill. Costs associated with overestimated demand include the cost of carrying excess inventory and the cost, later, of reducing the price of the inventory to move it off the shelves.

4.

	Space	Product	Time
The party in general	country	company	long range
The presidential candidate	country	item	medium range
The slate of candidates	country	class	short range
The star candidate	territory	item	short range

5. Using the market factor index forecasting technique, estimated 2001 sales for the firm's golf clubs in this country will be $5,500,000:

$$0.5 \times 0.09 + 0.3 \times 0.12 + 0.2 \times 0.15 = 0.111, \text{ multiplied by } \$50,000,000$$
$$\text{Total five-country sales} = \$5,500,000$$

Using the chain ratio forecasting technique, estimated 2001 sales will be $6,400,000:

800,000 golfers
×   .20 will buy (or receive) a set of golf clubs
160,000

×   .10 will buy manufacturer's clubs
16,000 golfers × $400 per golfer = $6,400,000 sales

    The dollar difference between the two estimates—almost a million dollars—suggests that the data from this country that forecasters have to work with (percentages in the market factor index formula that reflect the situation in the United States) is not overly reliable, and that additional forecasting techniques should probably be added to the mix. Two judgmental techniques that might be added include (1) a survey of buyer intentions, in which a sampling of golf club buyers such as pro shops and sporting goods distributors are asked to estimate their probable purchases of the manufacturer's golf clubs, based on their understanding of market conditions in this country, and (2) a survey of expert opinion, in which knowledgeable people such as company marketing executives and editors of golf magazines are surveyed, perhaps using the Delphi technique to reach a consensus. Possibly, in using this technique, the estimates from the quantitative methods used ($5,500,000 and $6,400,000) could be the parameters for the original estimates.

6. In global marketing terms, a gap analysis is a tool for comparing a company's performance in different countries in order to calculate how well the company is doing in each, and then to take appropriate action when actual performance doesn't meet expectations (marketing control). In the case of the sporting goods manufacturer, for example, assume that actual sales in three of the five Latin American countries for which forecasts were prepared closely adhered to forecasted figures. In the fourth country, however, sales were dramatically lower than forecast, and in the fifth country, they were dramatically higher. These "gaps" between performance and expectations suggest some action by marketing management. In the case of the fourth country, management may have found out what went wrong and done something about it (such as revising the forecast for next year, or changing the marketing mix to reflect marketplace realities). In the case of the fifth country, management may have found out what went right in this country so that they could effectively apply it to the other countries. In general, approaches used would entail the following strategies: (1) increasing the size of the potential market penetrated and/or (2) expanding the size of the qualified market or the available market (for example, by changing qualifying standards).

7. The potential market would include all consumers with some level of interest in purchasing Merton's SR software. The qualified potential would supplement this interest with sufficient income and qualifications to take these courses. In addition, members of the qualified potential market would have access to sellers of SR software. The target market is the portion of the qualified available market Merton decides to pursue, and the penetrated market is that portion of the target market who have actually taken SR courses.

8. Answer: $320,000. Calculations: $50 per employee in the 3661 industry; $100 per employee in the 3662 industry; therefore, in the new territory, with employment of 1200 and 1000, respectively, total sales forecasted will be $160,000 in these industries; however, this is only half of Merton's anticipated sales in this territory. Therefore: $320,000.

13

PRODUCT PLANNING I: PRODUCT/MARKET GROWTH STRATEGIES

OVERVIEW

Products and services largely determine a firm's customers, its competitors, its allocation of resources, and its supportive price/place/promotion marketing mix elements. Existing and new products can be defined in terms of objective features, extended features, benefits, and marketing mix implications in both consumer and organizational markets. Products move through different stages of the product life cycle, with each stage dictating different marketing mix strategies. These strategies are also influenced by characteristics of products that lend themselves to various degrees of adaptation, from standardized to customized plans, where marketing mix elements change to accommodate the nature and needs of specific markets. As products move from local to global status, leverage benefits accrue, including economies of scale and transferability of skills and resources.

PRODUCTS DEFINE CUSTOMERS, COMPETITORS, AND MARKETING MIX

To this point, we have examined strategic marketing planning processes whereby marketers (1) understand and account for favorable and unfavorable environmental influences on prospective markets and (2) identify, define, and measure target market segments consistent with company missions, objectives, and resources.

In the next eight chapters, we focus on the four components of the marketing mix—product, price, promotion, and distribution—that marketers combine to achieve company objectives by satisfying market needs.

We start with the product component as the dominant marketing mix element. To a large extent, products define the firm's business, including its customers, competitors, resource requirements, and supportive distribution, pricing, and promotion strategies. This chapter categorizes products in a number of ways that help to segment markets and formulate marketing strategies, including (1) actual, augmented, and core products; (2) consumer and industrial products; (3) products and services; and (4) local, multinational, international, and global products. We will also discuss the importance of new products in successful entry/growth strategies and how product life cycle models help shape and guide these strategies.

PRODUCTS DEFINED: BUNDLES OF SATISFACTIONS

Products are broadly defined as anything offered for attention, acquisition, use, or consumption that are capable of satisfying needs. This satisfaction can derive from a tangible product, like a bar of soap, or from a service, like a good haircut, or from a symbolic idea, like a political slogan. From the marketing manager's perspective, they are all products in that they can all be marketed to provide need-fulfilling satisfactions.

Figure 13-1 shows how a marketing manager might view the need-fulfilling satisfactions his or her firm's products offer along a broad spectrum from highly tangible pure goods to highly intangible psychic satisfactions. The largest segment of goods along this spectrum represents some combination of goods and services. A tire, for example, is a pure good, although its purchase price may also include the service of installing and balancing it. The Merton Mighty Mind system illustrates products along this spectrum. At the "goods" extreme is the computer with accompanying accessories and software that allow it to be used in a diversity of applications, such as computer-assisted design, spreadsheet analyses, and online training and development (T&D) sessions. The T&D software represents a combination of tangible goods (CD-ROMs) and services (lectures carried on the CD-ROMs). Intangible ideas are represented by the content of the lectures.

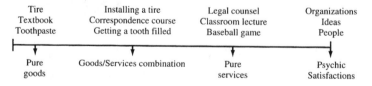

Tire	Installing a tire	Legal counsel	Organizations
Textbook	Correspondence course	Classroom lecture	Ideas
Toothpaste	Getting a tooth filled	Baseball game	People
Pure goods	Goods/Services combination	Pure services	Psychic Satisfactions

Figure 13–1. The goods-services spectrum.

In addition to being defined in terms of their location on this tangible-intangible spectrum, products can be defined in terms of attributes exhibited at any point on this spectrum. On the uppermost level is the

actual product, defined in terms of such intrinsic features as quality level, taste, size, price, styling, color, efficiency in use, brand, and packaging.

Next, a level down is the **augmented product,** which encompasses the tangible elements of the product as well as an accompanying cluster of image and service features. The augmented MM, for example, would include software programs, instructions for use, guarantees and warrantees, maintenance agreements, brand name associations, and promptness of service. To the consumer, the augmented product is part of the total product, with augmented features often used to distinguish otherwise similar products. For example, the simple fact that a wine was produced in France or an automobile was manufactured in Germany might be sufficient augmentation to distinguish these products for consumers.

For marketers, a key product management decision is determining how, and how far, to augment the product. Frequently, this decision entails examining buyer consumption patterns as they relate to the product, including where, when, why, how, and by whom it was purchased.

Finally, another level down is the **core product,** defined in terms of benefits it offers or problems it solves for the buyer. For example, MM T&D software, as a core product, might be defined as a convenient way to increase productivity and earning power of professionals. To the extent that marketers sell benefits, they generally focus on the core product in developing marketing strategies. Here are some examples.

- "In the factory we make cosmetics, in the drugstore we sell hope" (Charles Revson of Revlon).

- "One million quarter-inch drills were sold not because people wanted quarter-inch drills, but because they wanted quarter-inch holes" (Theodore Levitt, Harvard professor).

CONSUMER / INDUSTRIAL PRODUCTS DEFINED

Another way to define products that helps in developing product/market strategies is in terms of the nature and needs of consumers and industrial buyers. Tables 13-1 and 13-2 summarize classes and categories of products purchased in each market, buying behaviors typically displayed by consumer and industrial buyers with respect to these products, and marketing mix implications of interest to marketing planners.

Table 13–1. Consumer Products: Buyer Behavior and Marketing Mix Attributes

Consumer Product Classifications	Examples	Buying Behavior	Marketing Mix Attributes			
			Product	Price	Place	Promotion
CONVENIENCE Inexpensive habit or impulse purchases; little service or selling costs • Staples • Impulse • Emergency	food, drug items TV Guide, candy bar umbrellas	Purchases often planned in store, based on "best buys" Fast, unplanned purchases; based on strong felt need Purchased when need great; little shopping done	Branding, packaging, labeling important to encourage impulse purchases, inform buyers	Low unit price for staples, impulse goods; higher for emergency goods	Carried by many outlets; impulse goods in highly conspicuous locations, near checkout counters; emergency items often carried as "fill in" items	Mass market advertising main element in promotion mix
SHOPPING Products perceived as worth time and effort to compare with competition • Homogeneous (perceived basically the same) • Heterogeneous (perceived as different)	certain sizes, types of refrigerators, TV sets; relatively expensive supermarket items (coffee, butter), furniture, cameras, clothing	Looks for lowest price Compare on basis of preconceived quality standards, features	Extended product attributes (installation, credit, follow-up, delivery, services) developed; wide assortments needed to satisfy individual tastes	Usually cost more than convenience goods	Location convenience stressed	Homogeneous products stress extended product feature (service, quality); heterogeneous competitive features, benefits; personal selling key part of mix
SPECIALTY Perceived as worth a special trip	Mercedes automobiles, Gucci boots, Cabbage Patch dolls	Buyer wants a specific product; no comparison required; will expend considerable time and effort to acquire	Brand identification important, also extended product attributes like service, packaging; product line extension decisions important	Unique product characteristics, brand name associations permit high price	Location of outlets, rather than number, most important	Stresses unique product attributes and associations; advertising appeals and media decisions reflect product image; personal selling important
UNSOUGHT Customers don't want product, or are unaware they can purchase it	New unsought: 500 channel cable TV; smoke detectors Known unsought: life insurance, encyclopedias	Need exists, but buyer not motivated to satisfy it No product search	Extended product attributes (service, guarantees) important	Must be competitive to overcome buyer resistance, but high enough to cover selling costs	Unsought status requires many outlets, often inhouse presentations	Require strong emphasis on all elements of promotion mix, especially advanced personal selling methods; benefits rather than features emphasized

Table 13-2. Industrial Products: Buyer Behavior and Marketing Mix Attributes

Industrial Product Classifications	Examples	Buying Behavior	Marketing Mix Attributes			
			Product	Price	Place	Promotion
INSTALLATIONS Long-lived capital goods depreciated over time	Buildings (used) Buildings (new) Fixed equipment customized standardize	Motives primarily economic (return on investment) multiple, high-level buying influences; negotiation with vendors important	Purchase expense and risk often makes leasing more attractive than buying; form of product doesn't change; very low consumption rate	High per-unit price; demand tends to be inelastic, especially during economic upswings with attractive ROI; otherwise, competition on bid basis	Usually purchased directly from manufacturer	Indirect promotion (advertising, publicity) much less important than personal selling; can be focused in centralized market, but to meet needs of individual buyer
ACCESSORY EQUIPMENT Short-lived items that don't become part of finished product	Tools, equipment for production, office activities (portable drills, typewriters, etc.)	Many more potential customers, but fewer buying center influences than for installations; small order size	More standardized than installations; leasing attractive in some target markets; engineering services less important	Medium per-unit price; demand tends to become more elastic as equipment become more standardized	Market geographically dispersed, so use more middlemen	More use of the indirect promotion (especially sales promotion)
RAW MATERIALS Unprocessed expense items that enter production process	Natural and nurtured resources (crude oil, iron ore, lumber); also farm products	Low-level decision making; supply continuity, cost efficiency key motives; prefer sorted, graded products; may encourage contract purchasing to control supply	Perishable, seasonal, not expandable in short run	Often depends on supply, which is difficult to adjust to demand; generally, inelastic for industry, elastic for individual firms	Constant demand, seasonal production mean emphasis on storage, transportation, grading; dispersed producers, centralized buyers mean large, centralized distributors vertical integration	Products difficult to differentiate, so direct selling important component of promotion mix
COMPONENTS Expense items that require more processing than raw materials; also enter production process	Parts (finished or nearly finished, ready for assembly); tires, small motors Materials (need further processing) wire, yarn, iron	Modified rebuy or new task situation if components are important, expensive; straight rebuy for standards economic needs (price, availability, quality, important); usually many backup sources	Highly rapid consumption puts emphasis on service and continuity	Industry demand derived and basically inelastic, but elastic for individual firms, with price a key factor in mix; unit price low	Many suppliers create competitive market conditions	OEM, and after markets, especially attractive
SUPPLIES MRO items; don't become part of final product	Paint, nails, brooms, nuts, paper clips, lubricating oils	Require backup sources; usually straight rebuy, with few buying influences, little shopping; may negotiate contracts to create straight rebuy situation; reciprocity often expected	Branding important to make buying easier; packaging for easy storage; rapid consumption puts emphasis on reliability; should offer full line	Unit prices very low; highly elastic demand in short run	Many suppliers create competitive conditions	Media advertising, sales promotion support direct selling efforts
SERVICES • Maintenance and repair • Business advisory	Painting, machinery repair, janitorial Management consulting, accounting	Frequently purchased on contract or retainer basis, often handled internally	Brand associations, product quality, service	Demand often inelastic if unique product; otherwise, wide range of prices possible through negotiation	Difficult to expand distribution; importance of location varies with amount of customer contact	Personal selling dominant for highly personalized service; referrals important; advertising more important as service becomes less personal

CONSUMER PRODUCTS

In consumer markets, products are defined in terms of life span and the buying behavior of shoppers toward them.

• *LIFE SPAN*

Products that are consumed in one or a few uses, such as paper clips or candy bars, are called nondurable goods; tangible actual products that survive many uses, such as furniture or heavy appliances, are called durable goods.

• *BUYING BEHAVIOR OF SHOPPERS*

Convenience goods are purchased often, quickly, and with little comparison or effort. Shopping goods involve product comparisons on such bases as quality, price, style, and suitability. Specialty goods possess unique attributes for which a significant group of buyers will make a special effort. These shopping characteristics, in turn, determine marketing mix emphasis for each product type. For example, the often-impulsive nature of convenience goods purchases stresses the place element to make sure that these products are available and visible, whereas the brand insistence status of specialty goods emphasizes promoting the product brand name.

INDUSTRIAL PRODUCTS

From the marketing planner's perspective, industrial products are typically categorized in terms of how they are used in productive processes, as defined in terms of the people who purchase them. As noted in Chapter 10, this buying behavior differs appreciably from buying behavior in consumer markets. For example, demand for industrial products typically derives from demand for consumer products, is more inelastic, fluctuates more, and is characterized by more concentrated buying by more people. Industrial buying situations are categorized as straight rebuy, modified rebuy, and new task.

Certain kinds of industrial goods, such as raw materials and components, become a part of the finished product, whereas others, such as installations and supplies, become part of the maintenance, repair, and operating activities involved in getting products produced.

Buying behavior toward industrial products, and the use made of these products, largely determines marketing mix responses toward different product categories. For example, expensive installations, depreciated over time, typically require high-level expenditure authorization and participation by groups of buying influentials. To reach these influentials, emphasis is usually placed on personal selling and service in the marketing mix. With less expensive products, purchased routinely in straight rebuy situations, emphasis is likely to be on price, especially with products that are hard to differentiate.

THE BURGEONING GLOBAL GROWTH OF SERVICES

Services are activities, benefits, or satisfactions that are offered for rent or sale and that are essentially intangible and do not result in the ownership of anything.

Expenditures for services during the past decade increased to the point where they represented approximately three quarters of the U.S. gross domestic product, and nearly 80 percent of all jobs, in 1999. Data processing, management consulting, accounting /finance, and engineering / architectural services were among the fastest growing fields.

A major impetus for this burgeoning growth of the services sector has been the deregulation of service industries, beginning in the United States in the late 1960s. Since then, this movement toward deregulation of services by governments and service associations has spread throughout industrial nations, exposing them to free market competitive forces. Major service industries affected include transportation, banking, telecommunications, and professional markets for the Merton MM, such as health care, law, and accounting. More competition has led to lower prices, which increases demand, new service entrants, and an accelerating search for new markets.

Other stimulants to the worldwide growth of service industries include advances in computer and telecommunication technology leading to faster transmission of information and resources and the horizontal integration of service-related industries into new growth industries, envisioned in the United States by the Telecommunications Act of 1996, designed to define and guide the effective integration of entertainment, cable TV, telecommunications, and internet technologies.

CHARACTERISTICS OF SERVICES DEFINE APPLICATIONS AND STRATEGIES

Services can be viewed from a number of perspectives that help to identify unique problems in marketing them and strategies to address these problems.

First, services can be viewed in terms of their relationship to more tangible products. Often, services augment, and differentiate, tangible products, and vice versa. In the airline industry, for example, the consideration that secures the sale of airplanes to airlines could be follow-up maintenance services offered. However, once the sale is secured, a number of other services—hotel reservations, car rentals, and the like—will be dependent on the dependable functioning of tangible airplanes.

Services can also compete with tangible products (leasing versus buying an automobile for example) or with other services, such as car rental services, which are clamoring for airline traveler dollars.

Often, the key to competitive success is recognizing these relationships between intangible services and tangible products. For example, what services can be dropped, or added, to enhance the appeal of a product or service in a given market?

SERVICES CLASSIFIED BY CUSTOMERS, CONTENT, AND CHARACTERISTICS

Services can also be viewed in terms of types of customers served, with service firms like Young and Rubicam (advertising) and Deloitte & Touche (accounting) serving the organizational market and service firms like Club Med, Thomas Cook, and Hilton Hotels serving the consumer market.

Still another way to classify services is in terms of the extent to which they combine tangible and intangible elements. For example, a visit to a doctor's office may have a 5 percent goods content—say, a stethoscope—and a 95 percent nongoods content—say, the doctor's diagnosis and your feeling of satisfaction that you're in good shape. A janitorial service, at the other extreme, might be 80 percent goods content (mops, pails, and the like)—and only 20 percent nongoods (a clean workplace). Services with a relatively high goods content are often classified as equipment based, whereas less tangible, nongoods services are classified as people based.

From the perspective of the marketer interested in segmenting and entering new markets, perhaps the most productive way to classify and define services—especially people-based services offered by consultants, writers, teachers, accountants and other professionals—is in terms of attributes that differentiate services from more tangible products. Table 13-3 highlights these differences and how they influence marketing mixes.

Table 13–3. Services: Characteristics and Marketing Mix Attributes

Service Characteristics	As Compared to More Tangible Products	Examples	Marketing Mix Attributes			
			Product	Price	Place	Promotion
Intangibility	More difficult to taste, feel, see, or otherwise sample before using	Quality of a haircut, audit, or advertising campaign	Build, sustain quality image and track record; tangible symbols in brand names (Merrill Lynch's bull)	Strong track record, quality image can justify high price; some services are indirect pricing to avoid issue (e.g., commissions)	Tangible aspects of service environment stressed (inflight meals, magazines in dentist's office, etc.)	"Image" advertising, spokesperson testimonials, free trials, referrals, and personal selling important to document expected benefits
Inseparability	More difficult to separate from person or image of seller	Psychiatrists, doctors, lawyers	Brand name associations with seller image (H&R Block)	Highly personal service fees often negotiated (accountants, real estate brokers); strong seller image; often commands high fees	Channel opportunities restricted for highly personal services, encouraging direct-run operations (Jacoby and Myers) or franchises (H&R Block, McDonald's)	Promotion focuses on quality of service personnel (Club Med associates, reliable airline pilots), often using service personnel as spokespersons (H&R Block, bank presidents)
Variability • in use	Number of users more likely to change from time to time	Resort seasons, rush-hour train schedules	Often incorporate tangible equipment (e.g., automatic teller machines) to spread usage to off periods	Wide range of negotiated prices possible	Important that service have supplies when needed	Media schedules must conform to service use periods; promotion encourages off-peak use
• in quality	Quality of use experience more likely to change from time to time	Boring baseball games, 2-hour flight delay	Work to achieve, maintain high quality levels; often modify to relate to new needs	Must often price higher in peak seasons to recoup off-peak costs	Location can enhance "quality" image (Saks Fifth Avenue)	Emphasizes quality experiences (an exciting world series)
Perishability	Must often be consumed while being produced; difficult to keep in inventory	Physical examination, television air time	Customize service to meet needs of customer at time of use (Burger King, hamburger)	Emphasis on a variety of pricing incentives (seasonal, cash, quantity discounts, etc.) to ensure commitment to use	Service must be made efficiently accessible to customer when needed	Promotes special incentives to commit to service use (e.g., tangible rewards for buying airline, magazine subscriptions)
Labor intensity	Services are generally more dependent on quality, ability of personnel; difficult to achieve economy of scale, learning curve benefits	Physical examination, ocean cruise, income tax preparation	Important to select, motivate, and train service personnel for high productivity	Tends to push up price for services, since labor is typically the highest cost component	Service must be located for convenient access by staff members	Service employees encouraged to play active role in selling services, are often used in promotion, (e.g., Avon Lady, Lawn Doctor)
Legal, ethical barriers	Higher standards mandated and policed by service industry itself and/or governmental regulatory bodies	American Association of Advertising Agencies, Securities and Exchange Commission, utility regulatory boards	High codes of ethical behavior, especially for personnel services (drug tests for police, renew panels for doctors)	Concern for legislative response often important in determining prices (e.g., medical services prices (utilities) determined by regulatory bodies	Personalized merchandising services (door-to-door, direct mail, selling) frequently subject to fraud and subsequent legal constraints	In regulated services, tends to be defensive in nature, anticipating regulatory curbs (e.g., a politician's apology, a utility's rate increase justification); advertising even considered unethical in some fields (law, physician)

To illustrate these attributes, consider some of the problems faced by a sports team in marketing its services. Because this service is perishable, it can't be kept in inventory; a rained-out game is usually lost income. Because this service is variable, benefits will vary from game to game, ranging from boring to highly exciting. Because this service is intangible, there is no way to guarantee specific benefits from attending a game (if the home team loses, it might be an acutely distressing experience). Labor intensity is another problem, especially when most of the laborers are getting six-figure incomes, making it difficult to cut costs and raise profits through economies of scale and learning curve efficiencies. Because services are more inseparable from their providers than tangible products, provider-client interaction is a special feature of services marketing, with athletes often expected to serve as role models for customers.

In addition to these differences, many professionals, such as doctors and lawyers, face legal and ethical constraints that frequently make them more vulnerable to penalties for self-promotion or malpractice.

These characteristics of services have a number of implications for marketers. For example, the variability of services puts a strong emphasis on quality control—in medicine, the law, and other professions—to ensure more favorable outcomes. And the fact that services are difficult to separate from their providers means that they don't lend themselves to standardization strategies, although this human factor does provide opportunities to differentiate services.

Another sizeable challenge in marketing services derives from their intangible variability, which means that they are often statistically invisible, with information regarding income generated, jobs created, and activities undertaken difficult or impossible to come by. This low profile maintained by services also makes them a relatively easy target for governmental regulations, often made by agencies unconcerned with broader policy concerns.

SEGMENTATION IMPLICATIONS

Categorizing products and services in terms of uses, characteristics, and buyer behavior is an excellent basis for segmenting markets and for determining marketing mix emphasis. For example, the marketing manager for a large insurance company can define market segments in terms of its "unsought" status: what age, income, and attitude characteristics do people have in common that make this product unsought? Similarly, market segment profiles can be derived from characteristics of people who perceive products as shopping, specialty, new task, straight rebuy, and so forth. A management consultant interested in introducing her expertise into international markets can tailor product, price, and promotional strategies to reflect the inseparability, labor intensity, and intangibility of her services. In devising segmentation and marketing mix strategies, marketers should be aware that the same product or service can be viewed differently by different customer groups. For example, a package of computer software sold to consumers might be perceived as a convenience good by members of the computer "hacker" segment, and as a shopping good by a member of the new owner segment. In the industrial market, the same software might be used to activate a production line in an MRO application, or, among professional people, be perceived as an administrative tool.

PRODUCT LIFE CYCLES HELP PLAN STRATEGIES

The Product Life Cycle (PLC) model assumes that products successfully introduced into competitive markets go through a predictable cycle, over time, consisting of introduction, growth, maturity, and decline stages, with each stage posing threats and opportunities that marketers must address to maintain product profitability (Figure 13-2). Table 13-4 lists typical threats, opportunities, and responses characterizing each stage of the PLC.

In introducing new products to the MM Systems line, Merton planners used the PLC in conjunction with product diffusion and adaptation models (discussed next), to anticipate threats and opportunities during each PLC stage, identify and define target markets, and formulate marketing mix offerings attractive to these markets.

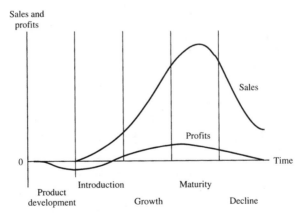

Figure 13–2. Sales and profits over stages of product life cycle.

PLC CHARACTERISTICS

Depending on a diversity of considerations—including kind and amount of competition, level of user benefit, marketing effort expended, and sophistication of the product's technology—PLC length can vary dramatically.

Table 13–4. Threats, Opportunities, and Marketing Mix Responses Characterizing Each PLC Stage

	Stage in Life Cycle			
Characteristics	Introduction	Growth	Maturity	Decline
Marketing objective	Attract innovators and opinion leaders to a new product	Expand distribution and product line	Maintain diffential advantage	(a) Cut back (b) revive (c) terminate
Industry sales	Increasing	Rapidly increasing	Stable	Decreasing
Competition	None or small	Some	Many	Few
Industry profits	Negative	Increasing	Decreasing	Decreasing
Profit margins	Low	High	Decreasing	Decreasing
Customers	Innovators	Affluent mass market	Mass market	Laggards
Product mix	One basic model	Expanding line	Full product line	Best sellers
Distribution	Depends on product	Expanding number of outlets	Expanding number of outlets	Decreasing number of outlets
Pricing	Depends on product	Greater range of prices	Full line of prices	Selected prices
Promotion	Informative	Persuasive	Competitive	Informative

For example, costly, complex technology kept color television in the introductory stage of the PLC for more than a decade. At the other extreme, a number of simple, inexpensive, aggressively marketed fad products, like pet rocks and Hoola Hoops, traversed all the stages of their cycles in fewer than two years. Market life cycles, which follow the same introduction-growth-maturity-decline stages that PLCs follow, is another important consideration. For example, depending on the stage of market development, a product can be in different life cycle stages in different countries, suggesting different strategic responses in each.

TYPICAL PLC STAGES

Following are descriptions of typical situations and responses during each PLC stage, assuming a product perceived as new succeeds in an entry market and transverses all the PLC stages.

• *INTRODUCTION*

The main objective of this stage is to build sales for the product, frequently at the cost of profits. Although competition is limited—or in the case of a major innovation, nonexistent—profit margins are low because:

- The initial market isn't sufficiently large to generate sales volume and economies of scale required for profitable operations;

- Production and marketing costs, on a per-unit basis, are usually higher than they will be during subsequent stages, reflecting the high costs of gaining momentum.

Because costs are high, usually only one model of the product is sold during this stage. For a convenience item, like a new magazine, distribution is extensive, through many dealers; for expensive shopping or specialty items, like automobiles, it is usually selective or exclusive, through few dealers. Depending mainly on product type, the product may have a high status price or a low mass market price.

Promotion generally aims to make prospects aware of the product and to inform them of its features and benefits. Product trial is encouraged through coupons, samples, or invitations to try the product.

• *GROWTH*

The main marketing objective during this stage is to expand distribution and range of product alternatives. Primary demand for the product class increases rapidly as more firms enter a highly attractive market with substantial untapped potential. Unit profits increase because members of an expanding market are willing to pay higher prices for the still-limited quantity of products available. To accommodate the needs of this fast-growing market, modified versions of the product are offered (such as MM's programs for additional professional groups). Additionally, distribution is expanded, price ranges are offered, and mass promotion becomes more persuasive, focusing on competitive features and benefits.

• *MATURITY*

This stage is characterized by intense competition, and sales stabilize as the market becomes saturated with firms eager to capitalize on still sizeable demand. The main marketing objective of the firm is to maintain its differential advantage, and profits associated with this advantage, through more product models and features, lower prices, more service options, and more innovative promotion. As discounting becomes popular, total industry and unit prices begin to decline. As the best target markets become saturated, other, less attractive market segments become the focus of marketing efforts. A full product line is made available, sold through many outlets at different prices.

• *DECLINE*

Demand decreases during this stage because customers are fewer and other products are more attractive. Sellers now face three alternatives: (1) cut back on marketing programs, the number of products marketed, distributors, and promotion used; (2) revive the product by repositioning, repackaging, or otherwise remarketing it; or (3) terminate the product. As industry sales decline, the product mix concentrates more on the best selling products, most productive distributors, and most effective pricing and promotion strategies.

DIFFUSION AND ADOPTION PROCESS MODELS SUPPLEMENT PLC

Diffusion and adoption process models are conceptually similar to the PLC model in that they track the sales experience of new products over time. Unlike the PLC, however, these models focus on the people who buy products, rather than on the products themselves. In so doing, they help planners profile the buying behavior of different classes of consumers—from individuals to large groups—and formulate marketing strategies based on these profiles.

• *THE DIFFUSION PROCESS MODEL DESCRIBES GROUP BUYING BEHAVIOR*

According to the diffusion process model (Figure 13-3, page 333), a sequence of five adopter groups purchase products over time, ranging from innovators to laggards. Each of these groups is defined in terms of its percentage of the buying population (e.g., the early and late majority groups comprise 68 percent of this population), and in terms of demographic, psychographic, and media characteristics. For example, one researcher describes early adopters as:

> . . . younger in age, with higher social status, a more favorable financial position, more specialized operations, and a different type of mental ability from later adopters . . . (they) utilize information sources that are more impersonal and cosmopolite, and are in closer contact with the origin of new ideas. . . .[1]

---

1 Everett M. Rogers, *Diffusion of Innovations* (New York: Free Press, 1983), p. 192.

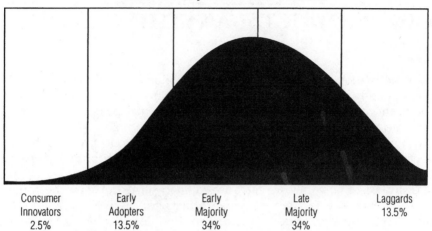

Time of Adoption of New Product

| Consumer Innovators 2.5% | Early Adopters 13.5% | Early Majority 34% | Late Majority 34% | Laggards 13.5% |

Figure 13-3. Categories of adopters based on times of adoption.

• *THE CONSUMER ADOPTION PROCESS MODEL DESCRIBES INDIVIDUAL BUYING BEHAVIOR*

The consumer adoption process model focuses on perceptions and decisions made by individuals who become regular buyers of a product. As with the diffusion model, Merton planners were interested in moving people through the stages of the model as quickly as possible. The stages of the consumer adoption process can be classified as:

1. **Awareness:** The consumer learns of the new product, but lacks information about it.

2. **Interest:** Potential buyers are stimulated to seek information about the new product.

3. **Evaluation:** They consider whether likely benefits of the new product justify trial.

4. **Trial:** They make trial purchases to improve their original estimate of the new product's value.

5. **Adoption:** They decide to use the new product regularly.

In moving potential buyers through the adoption process, Merton planners used tactics appropriate to each stage. For example, they enhanced the evaluation and trial of new professional software programs by offering free trials to prospective buyers and offered free use of Merton computers to induce prospects from trial to adoption stages.

NEW PRODUCTS: ANYTHING THAT'S NEW

From the marketer's perspective, a new product is anything perceived as new, including a major or minor invention or innovation, or a slight or major modification of an existing product. The product may be new to the market, or just to the company that introduces it into the market.

In the U.S. domestic market, about 70 percent of new products brought to market are product modifications, 20 percent are minor innovations, and 10 percent are major innovations.

Regardless of how they are categorized, many firms consider the continuing, systematic development of new products critical to growth and profitability in competitive markets. These firms find new products an invaluable way to achieve diverse corporate objectives, such as matching competitors, completing product lines, meeting sales and profit objectives, and utilizing excess capacity.

Other firms shun new product development, assuming, instead, a "follow the leader" posture in relation to new product pathfinder firms like Microsoft, GE, 3M, and Gillette. Reasons cited for their reluctance include fragmented markets, which produce lower sales and profits from smaller segments; a shortage of new product ideas resulting from a shortage of new technologies; shorter product life spans to earn back investments; accelerating costs of new product development; and lack of capital to meet these costs.

Perhaps the main reason for reluctance to enter the new products sweepstakes pertains to the high odds against success. A recent study of 700 firms by the Conference Board showed that only one in seven new product concepts see the commercial light of day, and that one third of these commercialized products never return a profit. The failure rate among industrial products is about 20 percent; it is between 15 and 20 percent for services, and 40 about percent for consumer products.

ORGANIZING FOR NEW PRODUCT DEVELOPMENT

The four most common structures for developing new products include the following:

- A **brand manager structure** wherein a single manager assumes responsibility for new product development, in addition to determining objectives, defining target markets, and devising marketing mix strategies for a single product or a product line.

- A **new product committee,** which is composed of top managers from key functional areas who meet periodically to screen new product ideas and then return to their regular positions.

- **Venture teams,** which are composed of managers from different functional areas with authority to plan and carry out new product ventures, independent of other functional departments.

- A **new product department,** which is composed of specialists in all areas of product development—research, finance, production, marketing—responsible for all stages of the new product development process, from idea generation to commercialization.

In a multiproduct, multicountry company, the enormous number of possible new products, combined with the huge number of information sources, suggests the latter organizational option: a full-time new product unit. According to one study,[2] there is a strong correlation between functionally organized firms with new product departments and the speed of introducing new products abroad: 40 percent of innovations from such firms went abroad in two years or less, compared with 6 percent of innovations that went abroad in functionally organized firms lacking such new product departments.

NEW PRODUCT DEPARTMENT FUNCTIONS

Typically, new product departments carry out the following steps in the new product development process: (1) idea generation, (2) idea screening, (3) concept development and testing, (4) marketing strategy development, (5) business analysis, (6) product development, (7) test marketing, and (8) commercialization. Here is how the Merton new product department followed these steps in developing new products in the MM Systems line.

• *IDEA GENERATION*
This step in the process entails both sources of new ideas, and methods for generating these ideas.

- **Idea sources:** These include customers, suppliers, competitors, salespeople, distributors, agents, subsidiary executives, home office executives, internal reports, and actual observation. Table 13-5 shows percentages of new product ideas from these sources in consumer and industrial markets. At Merton, information from these sources was systematically gathered and organized into the firm's

---

2 William Davidson and Philippe Haspaslegh, "Shaping a Global Product Organization," *Harvard Business Review,* Vol. 59, March–April 1982, pp. 69–76.

MIS database (discussed in Chapter 6) and then channeled to relevant screening and decision centers.

Table 13–5. Sources of New Product Ideas

Source	Industrial Products (%)	Consumer Products (%)	Total (%)
Research & development	24.3	13.9	20.8
Internal other than research and development	36.2	31.6	34.6
User suggestions, complaints	15.8	12.7	14.7
Formal research user needs	10.5	17.7	13.0
Analysis competitor products	27.0	38.0	30.7
Analysis published information	7.9	11.4	9.1
Suggestions from suppliers	12.5	3.8	9.5

Source: Leigh Lawton and David Parasuraman, "So You Want Your New Product Planning To Be Productive" *Business Horizons,* December 1980.

- **Generating Ideas:** Supplementing Merton's systematic procedures for gathering new product ideas were techniques for transforming these ideas into product concepts. Two of these techniques— product analysis and brainstorming—involved, first, systematically assessing a diversity of competitive personal computer systems to identify key features and benefits that produced market success. Then, during brainstorming sessions, department members were brought together to generate ideas in a freewheeling environment in which criticism was discouraged and participants were encouraged to "piggyback" on the ideas of others. All ideas were recorded, with the realization that few, if any, would emerge from the next stage of the process.

• IDEA SCREENING

The purpose of this second step of the process is to reduce ideas generated during the first step to the few worth further consideration. In so doing, department members set out to avoid "drop" errors, whereby a product with real potential gets dropped from consideration (for example, both IBM and Kodak dropped the Xerox copy technology), and "go" errors, whereby a firm decides to go with a product that later fails (among history's biggest product flops are Ford's Edsel, Dupont's Corfam, Polaroid's Polavision, RCA's Videodisk, the SONY Betamax, IBM's PCjr, New Coke, and Nutrasweet's Simpless fat substitute).

Basic to Merton's screening process was a checklist, covering economic considerations (such as investment required and profit potential), market criteria (such as prospective competition, size of market potential, and availability of distribution channels), and product characteristics (such as its fit with existing product line and production capabilities, and its anticipated product life). In addition to providing a quantitative index of success by giving weights to each criteria area and scores to each product concept in each attribute area, this checklist also pointed out areas where action could be taken to improve success chances. For example, if the product scored low in the area of "promotable features," design changes could be undertaken to remedy this shortcoming.

After the new product concept emerging from this checklist analysis was written up on a standard form containing estimates regarding its market, competition, strengths and shortcomings, development costs, and profit return, it moved to the next stage of the process.

• *CONCEPT DEVELOPMENT AND TESTING*

This third step of the new product development process sets out to further develop product ideas into product concepts, defined in terms meaningful to prospective consumers. The general approach is to develop the initial idea into alternate product concepts and to evaluate the relative attractiveness of each concept by presenting an elaborated version of each, with descriptive copy and illustrations, to consumer focus groups who responded to questions like: Does this product meet a real need? Does it offer significant benefits over competitive offerings? How would you improve it? What should it cost? What is the likelihood that you would buy it?

• *MARKETING STRATEGY DEVELOPMENT*

If the new product concept survives to this step, it has been developed and tested to the point where a marketing strategy could be formulated. The statement elaborating this strategy, which would be the model for the marketing plan formulated later if the product were to be commercialized, typically contains sections describing: (1) the product, the market for the product, and the competitive environment in which it will be launched; (2) the planned marketing mix strategy in support of the product launch; (3) long-range marketing mix strategies and sales/profit projections; and (4) proposed schedules and budgets.

• *BUSINESS ANALYSIS*

During this step in the new product development process, assumptions and projections of previous steps are exposed to the harsh light of economic analysis. Key questions are asked: What size investment will we require to launch and sustain this product? At what rate will sales, costs, and profits grow? Will anticipated return on investment be sufficient to justify this investment over other less risky alternatives? What will be the effect of the growth of this product on other products in our line? Tools and techniques used to address these questions included breakeven, cash flow, and return on investment analyses.

• *PRODUCT DEVELOPMENT*

During previous steps, the proposed new product had undergone a series of changes, from a word picture, to "paper prototype" drawings, to actual product mockups.

During this stage of the process, the Merton research and development department was charged with developing prototypes of the product that would embody all the attributes of the final product and could be used to determine its commercial feasibility. The cost of this step exceeded the combined cost of the previous steps, but produced prototypes that could be tested functionally, under laboratory conditions, to get feedback from prospective buying influences (such as professionals who would later be customers for models of MM systems). For example, could the product be improved? How? Were promotional claims believable and persuasive? Was price consistent with perceived value? How did this product compare with competitive offerings?

• *TEST MARKETING*

This step of the process involves introducing the new product offering into a real-life environment, such as two test market cities, and then measuring the relative impact of various marketing mix combinations under experimental conditions described in Chapter 8. Typically, however, this step is omitted as excessively expensive and competitively risky. In testing Merton product concepts, test market studies were replaced by consumer panels that helped produce desired degrees of secrecy, reliability, and validity of research findings.

• *COMMERCIALIZATION*

This final step of the new product development process is invariably the most costly, involving outlays for full-scale production and marketing investments that can exceed $200 million in commercial markets. To improve the odds of successfully marketing a new product in a new country, Merton focused on four decision areas:

- **Where to launch the product,** with the decision based on a thorough analysis of environmental threats and opportunities and market compatibility in the prospective entry market.

- **At whom to launch,** with the decision based on an understanding of the nature, needs, present size, and growth potential of prospective target markets.

- **When to launch,** with decisions based on an understanding of when target market needs would be greatest and competitive responses most manageable.

- **How to launch,** with decisions based on data showing how much to spend for the new product launch, and how these funds should be allocated among the four components of the marketing mix.

All these areas of concern were documented in a marketing plan that helped coordinate and control marketing efforts supporting the new product launch.

INTERNATIONAL PERSPECTIVE

Most of the concepts pertaining to product planning in the domestic market that are discussed in this chapter also apply in international markets. Consumer and industrial products and services are defined similarly (convenience, shopping, accessories, components) and are characterized by similar buyer behavior and marketing mix supports. Also similar are the purposes and stages of product life cycles and the new product development process.

In the broader context of global markets, however, these basic concepts also take on broader meanings: an overlay of product categories supplementing the product categories of products in domestic markets; an expanded definition of the product life cycle; and additional considerations shaping the new product development process. These broader meanings, in turn, influence the way products in international markets are designed, developed, and marketed.

CATEGORIZING PRODUCTS IN INTERNATIONAL MARKETS

In addition to categorizing global products and services in terms of characteristics, uses, and buyer behavior, Keegan[3] suggests the following categories for defining them in terms of their marketability, and marketing mix support calculated to ensure the success of product/market growth strategies.

- **Local products** are products that are perceived as having potential only in a single market. Example: Certain types of clothing—saris and kilts—worn in specific countries.

- **Multinational products** are products adapted to the perceived unique characteristics of national markets. Example: Electrical appli-

3 Warren J. Keegan, *Global Marketing Management,* 6th ed. Englewood Cliffs, New Jersey: Prentice Hall, 1994.

ances designed to accommodate power facilities in different countries.

- **International products** are products perceived as having potential for extension into a number of national markets (e.g., McDonald's fast food restaurant chain).

- **Global products** are international products that have achieved global status; these include world brands such as Marlboro cigarettes, Exxon oil, and Coca-Cola. In general, global products employ the same positioning and marketing mix strategies in all countries, with small modifications to meet local culture and competitive requirements.

GLOBAL PRODUCT BENEFITS

As products move from local to global status, benefits multiply. Sales volume increases to the point where expensive regional and national headquarters offices are justified. Economies of scale and learning curve savings accrue. The firm's products are able to maintain a single, unified brand image that helps introduce new products and generates sales, particularly among the increasing number of customers who travel across borders.

Additionally, global or international status creates opportunities for international leverage through comparative analysis.

- **International leverage** assumes that excellence and experience in one area of the global landscape—production, R&D, marketing—can be transferred to other areas.

- **Comparative analysis** assumes an experience record for a product in one or more markets, and the ability to find market comparability in either the same or displaced time. For example, sales and profit growth of MM systems in Canada might be compared with sales and profit growth in a similar U.S. market to pinpoint areas where performance in one or the other country is markedly above or below the other and to examine why these discrepancies exist. Or, comparative analysis might be undertaken in the "displaced" Mexican market, which, it might be assumed, would achieve parity with the U.S. market in the foreseeable future, with plans and projections based on this assumption.

STANDARDIZED VS. CUSTOMIZED PLANS

If an important task of global marketers is determining the most effective status for products in international markets—local, multinational, international, global—an important, related issue is the extent to which product or service offerings will have to be adapted to the nature and needs of the different markets they will be entering. Global brands like Coca-Cola, Honda, and Marlboro can employ a marketing mix that is essentially the same worldwide—a **standardized plan** with only minor changes to account for local differences in such areas as language and legal requirements. A product that lends itself to a standardized plan reaps many of the advantages noted previously, such as centralized economies of scale and the benefits of comparative analysis.

Other products might require sizeable changes in product design or other marketing mix elements to achieve success in international markets. These **customized plans** are usually costlier than standardized plans, although they do usually provide such benefits as faster responses to local competitive challenges and the development of managers with international marketing skills.

Forces like economic integration and the increased sophistication of communication technologies are moving markets toward greater unification, lending these markets to standardized marketing plans. For most products, however, standardized plans aren't feasible, as evidenced by a study of 174 consumer packaged goods, which showed that only one in ten was exported without significant modification, with an average of 4.1 changes made in such areas as brand name, product features, packaging, labeling, and user instructions.[4]

As illustrated in Global Focus 13-1, failure to modify products/services to meet local market needs can have expensive consequences.

GLOBAL FOCUS 13-1

When Product Plans Go Awry

Two examples illustrate what happens when well-laid product plans fail to account for customers, competitors, cultures, and conditions in entry markets.

---

4 John S. Hill and Richard R. Still, "Adapting Products to LDC Tastes," *Harvard Business Review,* Vol. 62 (March–April 1984), pp. 92–101.

1. When Wal-Mart opened its first store in Argentina in 1995, it assumed the rising tide of globalization that was spreading American cultural values throughout South America would ensure success for its team of American managers and the same basic American store model that made Wal-Mart the largest general merchandise retailer in the world. Four years, and four overhauls of management later, when Wal-Mart finally eked out a profit, the size of Wal-Mart's miscalculation was reflected in the size of the huge losses the store racked up (meanwhile, the French chain Carrefour—the world's second largest general merchandiser and Wal-Mart's main competition in Argentina—continued to rack up record sales and profits). Merchandise miscalculations included featuring American steaks like T-bones instead of the rib strips and tail rumps that Argentines prefer; cosmetic counters filled with bright-colored rouge and lipstick instead of the softer, natural colors Argentine women prefer; clothing sizes that didn't account for the fact that Argentines are on average a bit smaller than Americans; jewelry counters emphasizing diamonds, emeralds, and sapphires when Argentine women prefer wearing gold and silver; and tools and appliances wired for 110-volt electric power when the standard throughout Argentina is 220. Other miscalculations included store aisles much too narrow to accommodate the greater traffic patterns in Argentina, and carpeting that wore out rapidly.

2. During the April–June 1993 quarter—normally the second-best of the year—the Euro-Disney theme park in France lost a disastrous $87 million, while stock values plunged 20 percent. Key reasons include misjudged economic trends (for example, higher-than-expected interest rates made Disney's $3.7 billion of debt very expensive, and the European recession hit recreation spending particularly hard) and misjudged cultural environments (for example, Disney's Puritanical codes—stipulating alcohol-free restaurants and undergarments to be worn by women employees—were anathema to the insouciant French, who were also less willing than other nationals to wait on long lines or to change lunch hours to conform to American schedules). Interestingly, the same values resoundingly rejected in France were resoundingly successful in Disney Japan, where more visitors traipsed through the theme park in five years than traipsed through the original Disneyland theme park in 35 years.

REASONS FOR MODIFYING PRODUCTS

Key reasons for customizing offerings pertain to the nature and needs of customers, markets, countries, competitors, and the exporting company.

• *CUSTOMER CHARACTERISTICS AND NEEDS*

The degree of cultural grounding in an entry market can strongly influence the need to adapt a product. For example, in Muslim countries strongly grounded in cultural taboos against alcohol and pork products, products containing these ingredients would obviously have to be adapted to conform to these taboos. In general, consumer nondurable products have the highest sensitivity to cultural tastes and constraints and are most likely to require adaptation. Consumer durables such as cameras and home electronics products are less sensitive to cultural grounding, and industrial products such as steel and chemicals and high-tech products such as scientific and medical equipment are the least sensitive.

In addition to cultural characteristics, customer physical characteristics can also mandate adaptive changes. For example, racial characteristics (skin pigmentation, height, and so on) mandate adaptation of products relating to these characteristics (for example, skin care products and room furniture).

• *ECONOMIC DEVELOPMENT*

For reasons discussed in Chapter 5, the general stage and state of a country's economic development can mandate an adaptation strategy. For example, products might be packaged to conform to family size and income (for example, four- instead of six-packs and family-sized food packages).

• *POLITICAL AND LEGAL CONSIDERATIONS*

For a variety of reasons covered in Chapter 5, countries erect tariff and nontariff barriers to certain imports that usually lead to product adaptation by exporters. For example, by simply changing the stated purpose of a wrench, one firm succeeded in relegating it to a much lower tariff classification. Sweden bans all aerosol sprays, Japan requires testing of all pharmaceuticals in their laboratories, and French law mandates that all product-related presentations (labels, instructions, promotion, and the like) be in the French language.

• *PRODUCT CHARACTERISTICS AND COMPONENTS*

Fayerweather[5] suggests five product characteristics useful as criteria defining the need for, and nature of, adaptation required to expand into additional markets: primary functional purpose, secondary functional purpose, durability and quality, method of operation, and maintenance. Following is how Merton marketing planners used these criteria to define adaptation needs of MM systems in countries where economic, political, and cultural environments would permit entry.

---

5 John Fayerweather, *International Business Management: A Conceptual Framework* (New York: McGraw-Hill, 1969).

1. **Primary functional purpose:** In its domestic market, the MM's primary purpose was to help educate professional people quickly, effectively, and economically, providing an interactive online learning format and access to vast databases. Foreign markets that needed professional education programs represented potential for MM systems.

2. **Secondary functional purpose:** Each MM system, and associated software, was also capable of performing computational and analytic tasks more typical of personal computer applications. To the extent that foreign markets had no need for professional education programs, they might have need for the benefits provided by these more traditional applications.

3. **Durability and quality:** How could MM systems be expected to hold up in different foreign environments? Would servicing the systems be a problem? If so, would service be available? If available, at what cost? (In high-pay countries, for example, the market for home appliances costing less than $40 is limited because it's too expensive to repair them.) Can Merton afford to improve product durability and quality to the point where service needs are not an issue?

4. **Maintenance:** If service was available at a competitive cost, was it of consistently high quality to accommodate the diverse, sophisticated maintenance needs of MM's users?

5. **Method of operation:** Were technological conditions in the prospective entry country consistent with MM operations? For example, would it be possible to access the internet? Were voltage and cycle requirements in the country consistent with MM operations?

• *COMPETITIVE CONDITIONS*

A company will often find, or create, a niche for itself in international markets by an adaptation strategy that differentiates its offering from those of competitors.

• *COMPANY CONSIDERATIONS*

Some firms mandate specific first-year return-on-investment (ROI) levels that an entry strategy must achieve, which can lead to product adaptation strategies to bring first-year costs in line with this profit objective.

PRODUCT/MARKET ADAPTATION STRATEGIES

The four product/market strategies depicted in Figure 13-4 for bringing product/service offerings into line with criteria discussed earlier, focus on the two dominant, most expensive elements of the marketing mix—the product and the communication campaign—and range from a standardized plan involving only small changes in product and promotion to a customized plan for radically changing both.

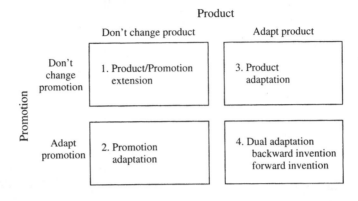

Figure 13–4. International product/promotion strategies.

• *PRODUCT-COMMUNICATIONS EXTENSION*

A product is marketed in a foreign market with the same product and promotional appeals used in the home market. This straight extension has been a success in some cases and a disaster in others. As examples, Kellogg cereals, Heineken beer, and Pepsi Cola are all successfully sold in about the same form worldwide. But Philip Morris couldn't sell U.S.-style blended cigarettes in many markets that prefer straight cigarettes; General Foods couldn't sell powdered Jell-O in the British market, which prefers a cake form; and Philips only sold its coffee makers in Japan when it reduced their size to fit smaller Japanese kitchens.

• *PRODUCT EXTENSION. COMMUNICATIONS ADAPTATION*

The same product fills a need or serves a purpose that is different in different global markets. For example, American outboard motors are used for recreational purposes in the home market but for commercial fishing in the Oriental market. Here, the communications campaign supporting the product, including basic appeals and media, is adapted to the differing nature and needs of the global market, incurring costs for revising communication programs to reflect local conditions.

• *PRODUCT ADAPTATION. COMMUNICATIONS EXTENSION*

Differing local-use conditions mandate changes in the product while the communication strategy remains essentially unchanged. Examples of this strategy, which is the most frequently used of all in global marketing, include (1) IBM adapting its worldwide personal computer lines to meet local needs, which mandated 20 different keyboards in Europe alone, and (2) Exxon reformulating its gas for different weather conditions in different countries. In both situations, the company communication strategy was essentially unchanged; for example, Exxon's "Put a Tiger in Your Tank" appeal is used universally.

• *DUAL ADAPTATION*

Both the product and the promotion strategy are adapted to local market needs. This strategy represents a combination of the preceding two strategies and is illustrated by Hallmark's greeting card strategy in Europe. There, people are used to writing individual messages on cards rather than having the messages written for them as they are on cards sold in the United States. The result is different products with different communication appeals.

An extreme example of dual adaptation, product invention, can take the following two forms:

- **Backward invention,** typically used when introducing products in less-developed parts of the world, involves simplifying the product back to an earlier stage of its development. For example, NCR sells large numbers of its reintroduced crank cash registers in the Orient and Latin America.

- **Forward invention,** occurs when a firm designs new products to meet new needs in global markets. For example, Anton/Bauer, a small Connecticut company, developed a portable power system that addresses the problem of different power availabilities around the world, ranging from 50 to 230 volts and 50 to 60 cycles. Composed of batteries and chargers, the system "reads" the type of power plugged into and adjusts accordingly. Also, Procter & Gamble developed Ariel laundry detergent for the European market, where washload requirements (soaking time, water temperature, load size, and the like) differ from country to country.

Forward invention is generally considered to be the riskiest, costliest, and most time-consuming of all the product-market strategies, but it can pay off in the highest profits and, often, gain the firm worldwide recognition.

THE FAST-GROWING GLOBAL SERVICES SECTOR

Although the preceding discussion about global product categories, benefits, and marketing mix strategies applies to services as well as to more tangible consumer and industrial products, it should be noted that services in global markets present unique opportunities and problems that mandate unique marketing strategies.

Services represent the fastest growing sector of world trade, accounting for about 30 percent of world trade in 1996 and, among industrialized nations, about 65 percent of trade with each other. Services play a paramount role among U.S. exports, with service trade surpluses helping to reduce our massive annual trade deficits by about one third.

A major impetus for the burgeoning growth of the services sector has been the deregulation of service industries, beginning in the United States in the late 1960s. Since then, this movement toward deregulation of services by governments and service associations has spread throughout industrial nations, exposing them to free-market competitive forces. Major service industries affected include transportation, banking, telecommunications, and professional markets such as health care, law, and accounting. More competition has led to lower prices, which increases demand, new service entrants in global markets, and an accelerated search for new markets.

Other stimulants to the worldwide growth of service industries include advances in computer and telecommunication technology leading to faster transmission of information and resources and the horizontal integration of service-related industries into new growth industries, such as those that integrate cable TV, telecommunications, and internet technologies.

CHARACTERISTICS OF SERVICES DEFINE MARKET PROBLEMS AND STRATEGIES

Services can also compete with tangible products (for example, leasing versus buying an automobile) or with other services, such as car rental services clamoring for airline traveler dollars.

Often, the key to competitive success in marketing services in international markets is recognizing relationships between intangible services and tangible products (for example, between a leasing service and the tangible automobiles it leases). These relationships are likely to change across borders (for example, what services can be dropped, or added, to enhance the appeal of a tangible product offering in a given market?).

Marketing managers should also recognize problems these relationships create in international markets. For instance, a single export license is required for the sale of a tangible product (such as a turnkey production line or a fleet of vehicles) in a host country, but such licenses are often required every time the home-country seller services the product. This means that service contracts can be held hostage to political conditions in the host country.

INTERNATIONAL PRODUCT LIFE CYCLES HELP PLAN STRATEGIES

When innovative products like MM systems move from local to global status, accruing benefits discussed earlier as they move (leverage, learning curve, economies of scale, and the like), they also typically move through the stages of two product life cycles. The first PLC characterizes the domestic market and was discussed earlier in this chapter. The second is the international PLC model, which puts a different interpretation on each of the four stages (introduction, growth, maturity, decline) of the domestic PLC. According to this model, the location of production of these products shifts internationally at different stages for competitive and cost reasons. During the introduction stage, production occurs only in the home country. Then, during subsequent stages, production moves to other developed countries and then to less-developed countries, still usually controlled by the original firm. Between the stage when the product is introduced and its decline, it faces increasing competition and becomes more price sensitive and standardized. The company producing the product requires more capital to finance global ventures and, eventually, becomes a net importer.

As with the domestic PLC model, each stage of the international PLC suggests marketing mix strategies appropriate to various product/market situations, including identifying threats and opportunities, targeting markets, and formulating marketing mixes. These strategies are also influenced by characteristics of products that lend themselves to various degrees of adaptation, from standardized to customized plans, with associated adaptation strategies.

Regardless of the stage of global development, the accelerating pace of product introductions, abetted by the increasing ability of nations (like India and the Philippines) with low production costs and pools of skilled workers to replicate products more quickly and cheaply, have shortened PLCs in global markets and made product introductions more expensive and risky. Whereas these introductions could previously be spread out over years, firms must now prepare for PLCs that can be measured in months or less.

In international markets, then, where initial investment required to introduce products is typically greater and payback longer and riskier than in domestic markets, the message of the PLC is to generally avoid introducing products that will have short life cycle curves, such as fad or fashion-oriented products, products that can't be differentiated from competitive products, or high-tech products with insufficient backup.

INTRODUCING NEW PRODUCTS INTO GLOBAL MARKETS

In international markets, the most characteristic type of new product is an existing product already marketed by the company and introduced for the first time into a selected national market. The least common, and most risky, type of new product introduction is that of a product that is new to the company and to the foreign market. Regardless of how it is defined, new product introductions often represent the best way to gain early access to the best target markets and distribution channels.

ORGANIZING FOR GLOBAL NEW PRODUCT DEVELOPMENT

Recently, there has been a pronounced trend to supplement centrally directed new product development departments toward the use of foreign-based resources to help multinational firms compete more effectively. As firms like Asea Brown Boveri and the Dutch electronics giant Philips have discovered, funding product development in worldwide business units rather than in centralized business laboratories offers a number of benefits, including greater awareness of and access to technological developments in local and global markets, faster technology transfer from parent to subsidiary, and the development of new products expressly for selected global markets. Occasionally, an idea for a new product emerges when global scanning indicates sudden demand spurts for products in specific nations, indicating potential that can be transferred to other nations.

CHAPTER PERSPECTIVE

In domestic markets, how consumer and organizational products and services are defined (for example, tangible, intangible, unsought, accessories) helps define target market behavior toward them and marketing mix strategies attractive to these target markets. Guiding and supporting these product/market strategies are product life cycle projections and new product development processes that follow the product from initial idea generation to final commercialization. In international markets, the status of a product as local, international, multinational, or global largely defines the degree to which marketing mix supports will be standardized or customized. The risk and cost of introducing new products into foreign markets can be mitigated through an understanding of international leverage and comparative analysis techniques, the workings of the international product life cycle, and new product planning processes as applied in foreign markets.

KNOW THE CONCEPTS
TERMS FOR STUDY

Accessory equipment
Actual products
Augmented product
Backward invention
Brand manager
Commercialization
Comparative analysis
Components
Consumer products
Convenience goods
Core products
Customized plans
Dual adaptation
Forward invention
Global products
Industrial products

International leverage
International products
Local products
Multinational products
New product committee
New product development strategies
Product adaptation strategies
Product life cycle
Products
Services
Shopping products
Specialty goods
Standardized plans
Supplies
Unsought goods

MATCHUP EXERCISES

1. Match up the product concept in the first column with the descriptor in the second column.

   1. nondurable
   2. augmented
   3. core
   4. durable

   a. the warranty accompanying Black & Decker drill presses
   b. a drill press
   c. the holes made by the drill press
   d. the paper clip attached to the product warranty

2. Match the product categories in the first column with the products in the second column.

   1. convenience
   2. supplies
   3. shopping
   4. components

   a. you need a new refrigerator
   b. what you use to sweep the factory floor and paint the walls
   c. the motor in the refrigerator
   d. the escalator that takes you to the refrigerators

5. installations

e. purchasing a copy of *The National Enquirer* at the checkout counter

3. Match the stage of the new product development process in the first column with the descriptor in the second column.

1. concept development & testing

a. Let's brainstorm this.

2. idea generation

3. idea screening

4. business analysis

b. That's a goofy idea!

c. Well then, how about this one?

d. With a good promotion push, it should sell.

5. marketing strategy development

e. It may sell, but no way will it generate enough profits.

4. Match the global product/communication strategy in the first column with the situation described in the second column.

1. product-communication extension

a. American bicycles are positioned for recreation in the United States but for basic transportation in China.

2. product extension, communication adaptation

b. No additional R&D, manufacturing, or promotional expenses are incurred.

3. product adaptation, communication extension

c. General Foods recognizes that the British drink coffee with milk and the French drink it black.

4. dual adaptation

d. Gas formulations change, but Exxon's "Tiger in Your Tank" stays the same.

5. Match up the PLC stage in the first column with the situations summarized in the second column.

1. introduction

2. growth

a. fewer competitors, outlets, sales

b. stable sales, lower margins, less competition

3. maturity

c. expanding lines, outlets, sales, price ranges

4. decline

d. informative promotion, innovative customers, increasing sales

QUESTIONS FOR REVIEW AND DISCUSSION

1. How would you define Club Med and Windows 2000 in terms of core, actual, and augmented dimensions? Which dimension would be most important in positioning, promoting, and pricing each?

2. Anderson Consulting, the largest consulting firm in the world, generates more than 65 percent of its gross revenues from services abroad. In terms of characteristics of services that distinguish them from more tangible products, discuss problems you, as a partner in this firm, would face in opening an office in Japan.

3. Following up on question 2, assume that, after two years of operation, and unlike most other Anderson offices in Oriental countries, Anderson's Japanese office still isn't generating a profit. Discuss how use of international leverage and comparative analysis might address this problem.

4. The Ray-O-Vac Company, producer of batteries and other consumer goods for global markets, plans to announce the development of a new, more powerful battery for powering vehicles. In terms of Fayerweather's criteria, describe considerations that Ray-O-Vac marketers will have to account for in building this new battery into a high-leverage global product.

5. Discuss the nature and role of promotional expenditures at each stage of the product life cycle for a new line of high-resolution television sets that are one-eighth inch thick and hang on the wall like a poster.

6. Could the eight stages of the new product development process be applied as effectively in generating, developing, and commercializing ideas for new services or, at the extreme end of the tangibility spectrum, new ideas?

7. Speculate on why seven out of ten new products introduced into consumer markets are product modifications.

ANSWERS

MATCHUP EXERCISES

1. 1d, 2a, 3c, 4b
2. 1e, 2b, 3a, 4c, 5d
3. 1c, 2a, 3b, 4e, 5d
4. 1b, 2a, 3d, 4c
5. 1d, 2c, 3b, 4a

QUESTIONS FOR REVIEW AND DISCUSSION

1. Each core dimension would be defined in terms of problem-solving services or the benefits it offers. For example, and depending on the market segment attracted to each, Club Med's core dimension benefits

might include finding a mate, acquiring a lovely tan, expanding cultural horizons, or just getting away from all that snow. Core benefits of Windows 2000 might include professional advancement, more productive employment of time and money, or expansion of social and learning experiences through access to the internet. Actual product dimensions would define each in terms of quality level, features, styling, brand name, and packaging. In the case of Club Med, for example, these dimensions would cover aspects like the comfort of accommodations, reliability of tour guides, cost, and other components of the vacation package including side trips whereas for Windows 2000 they would encompass things like cost, ease of operation, associations of the Microsoft brand, and programs included in the software. The augmented dimension for both would include additional services and benefits including money-back warranties if not satisfied, lessons in the use of Windows, and a toll-free telephone number to call for additional information.

Even though actual, core, and augmented product features would probably all be used to position, promote, and price the Club Med and Windows 2000 offerings (for example, promotion for Club Med would include information on prices, destinations, and accommodations), core benefits are what buyers are ultimately paying for. Hence, from the marketer's point of view, these benefits—the lovely tan, the adventures on the internet—would probably be of most use.

2. As distinguished from products, services tend to be less tangible and more variable, perishable, and labor intensive. They are also more likely to face legal and ethical barriers and to be inseparable from the provider. The labor-intensive aspect of this consulting service suggests that it would be difficult, and expensive, to recruit the professionals required to staff this new office and that these costs would be difficult to reduce through economies of scale. Meanwhile, because your consulting services are perishable and can't be kept in inventory, there would be no way to recoup losses while the office was generating billings through expensive personal contact work with prospective clients, often involving taking engagements at discounted fees. And because of the variability of services, and professional ethics involved in client relations, it would be impossible (and unethical) to promise prospective clients specific benefits, further diluting the persuasive impact of your new business presentations. Inseparability of your services from their providers probably means your consultants are going to have to spend a lot of nonbillable time developing personal relations with clients and prospects.

3. International leverage implies that a firm engaged in global marketing can transfer success factors from one country to another, including systems, strategies, services, and personnel. Comparative analysis is the process that facilitates this transfer. For example, other profitable An-

derson offices similar in tenure, scope, objectives, and markets served might be compared to the Japanese office to identify success factors that might succeed in making the Japanese office profitable.

4. In terms of primary functional purpose, the battery market potential would first be assessed in terms of primary applications for which they were developed, and where in the world these applications existed. With respect to secondary functional purpose, additional, secondary applications for the batteries would then be researched, with market potential figures upgraded in terms of where these applications existed. For example, although designed for vehicles, possibly the batteries could be used in power plants in developing countries with little access to centralized energy sources. In terms of durability and quality, the batteries would be tested against conditions under which they would be used throughout the world, including arctic and tropical climates. The maintenance requirements for the batteries would be assessed against maintenance resources in prospective global entry markets. Finally, the method of operation analysis would aim to determine if conditions and facilities existed in prospective entry markets (for example, for recharging the batteries) to properly maintain the batteries. Based on these analyses, and feasible modifications that could be made to the batteries consistent with uncovered needs, Ray-O-Vac marketers could begin product modification strategies to transform the new batteries into global products.

5. During the introductory stage of this product's life cycle, advertising and publicity would perform an essentially pioneering role, attempting to make innovator and early adopter groups aware of, and informed about, the new TV technology, and building primary demand for the product's class. Sales promotion would also be stressed to encourage early trial, and personal selling to get distributors interested. During the growth stage, with competition much more aggressive, the focus would be on building selective demand for the product itself, rather than for the product class. Advertising and publicity continue to be important, but sales promotion is reduced because fewer incentives to buy the product class are required. During the maturity stage, when competition increases appreciably, sales promotion becomes important again in the promotion mix; firms that have achieved a leadership position engage in reminder advertising; others pursue highly aggressive persuasive advertising. During the final, decline stage, reminder advertising continues to prevail; publicity and sales promotion is downgraded or eliminated; and salespeople give the product minimum attention.

6. The eight stages of the new product development process could be applied to new services or new ideas quite easily. To illustrate, envision a situation where a group of politicians meet to hammer out a platform for a candidate for high office (the "product" who will communicate the ideas in the platform). Ideas would be generated during a brain-

storming session (Balance the budget? Introduce a flat tax? Install a "pro-life" plank in the platform?) and then screened for consistency with larger party missions and goals. Next, they would be developed and tested among a sample of the electorate (probably using staff pollsters). Successful ideas would be transformed into a marketing strategy including media advertising, publicity, and speaking engagements and subjected to cost-benefit economic scrutiny during the business analysis stage, to determine if the expected additional votes resulting from this strategy are worth the additional tangible and intangible costs. Then they would be further developed, test marketed (for example, during local primary elections), and finally commercialized during introduction into the rough and tumble of the actual campaign.

7. Diversification strategies that entail changes in both markets and products tend to be riskier than either market development strategies, which involve existing products sold in new segments, or product development strategies, which involve new products sold in existing segments. And penetration strategies, in which existing products are marketed more aggressively in existing segments, are usually the least risky of all strategic options. In this context, major and minor product innovations are more likely to represent higher risk diversification or product/market development strategies than product modifications, which are usually part of penetration strategies. Safer product modification strategies also make sense in terms of trends that work against new product success, such as higher developmental costs, a shortage of capital, less profitable market segments, and a shortage of new technologies that spawn new product ideas in many fields.

14

PRODUCT PLANNING II: PRODUCT DESIGN AND DEVELOPMENT STRATEGIES

OVERVIEW

In both domestic and global markets, the goal of product planning is the same: developing products and marketing strategies that will meet customer needs and company objectives in such areas of concern as product design, branding, quality, safety, service, packaging, and labeling.

PRODUCT PLANNING MEETS CUSTOMER NEEDS, COMPANY GOALS

In Chapter 13, we began our discussion of the four elements of the marketing mix by defining categories and characteristics of products and services and illustrating a systematic approach to create, evaluate, and commercialize new products. This approach employed concepts from three models that describe product/market dynamics: the product life cycle model, and models describing product adaptation and diffusion processes.

In this chapter, we continue our discussion of the product component of the marketing mix with an examination of planning considerations calculated to help achieve and maintain profitability in domestic and international markets. These considerations pertain to product design, branding, quality, service, safety, packaging, labeling, lines, and mixes.

PRODUCT PLANNING IN CONTEXT

Product planning does not take place in a vacuum. Most successful products reflect an understanding of how the product will be used, by whom, and in what kind of competitive, economic, technological, cultural, and political climate. Uninformed product planning, beginning with the basic design of the product, can doom an otherwise successful product concept.

PRODUCT DESIGN: A CRUCIAL DECISION

Often the most crucial decisions affecting the success of products sold in competitive markets pertain to characteristics of tangible products and augmented extensions of these products.

TANGIBLE PRODUCT DESIGN CHARACTERISTICS

Design characteristics of tangible products, defined in terms of such intrinsic attributes as taste, price, style, size, and color, are conditioned mainly by customer preferences, costs, and compatibility.

• *CUSTOMER PREFERENCES*

What customers want and expect in products has to be the main consideration in product design and can only be ignored at the sellers' peril. In recent years, for example, the number of lawsuits filed against U.S. manufacturers has skyrocketed, largely reflecting growing public concern for product safety, and for legislation supporting this concern. Safety features (and product liability insurance) are now integral components of modern product design strategies.

• *COST*

The cost to make and market a product puts a floor under the price charged, and can be the main determinant of the product's competitiveness and profitability. Key considerations, in addition to the cost of designing to suit customer preferences, include the cost of labor and materials used in its production and the cost of marketing the product.

• *COMPATIBILITY*

Products must be designed to be compatible with the environment in which they will be used. Different climates, different measurement systems, and different power and broadcast systems are but a few of the environmental constraints that can affect product design.

AUGMENTED PRODUCT DESIGN CONSIDERATIONS

In addition to design characteristics of the tangible product, a complete product planning effort would encompass design characteristics of the augmented product, encompassing both tangible product features and accompanying image and service features. Included among these features would be brand name, quality, safety, and service levels, packaging and labeling characteristics, and decisions pertaining to length and width of product lines and mixes.

PRODUCT BRANDS: DEFINITIONS, BENEFITS, AND STRATEGIES

A brand is a name, term, sign, symbol, design, or combination thereof that identifies and helps to differentiate and control products and services of a single seller, such as Honda or Ford, or a group of sellers, such as the National Fluid Milk Processor Promotion Board. Brands can be local, national, regional, or worldwide in scope.

A brand name is that part of the brand that can be spoken; the Prudential Insurance Company is an example. A brand mark is that part of the brand that can be recognized, but is not utterable; an example is Prudential's Rock of Gibraltar brand mark. A trademark is a brand name or mark that is given legal protection; for example, the Xerox trademark can only be legally used by the Xerox Corporation. A copyright is legal protection given literary, musical, or artistic works so that they can only be published or sold by the copyright holder.

BRANDING BENEFITS BUYERS, SELLERS, AND SOCIETY

Illustrative of how branding benefits buyers, sellers, and society at large is a situation that existed in the former Union of Soviet Socialist Republics (USSR), a command economy that mandated centralized control of production and distribution, with few of the niceties of competitive free markets. Under this system, most color television sets for the (then) far-flung Soviet empire were produced in two huge factory complexes. Unfortunately, the Soviet population quickly and painfully recognized that the output of one of the complexes was unfit for human consumption; practically everything that could go wrong with a color television set did, with the promptness of breakdowns contrasting sharply to the length of time required for repairs. Because there was no easy way to distinguish between the output of the two factories, the public stopped buying color television sets, throwing the industry into chaos.

Now contrast this situation with an analogous situation in competitive markets where companies brand their products. From the buyer's viewpoint, the brand name makes it easy to identify and shop for the brand that will meet the buyer's needs and standards. (It will also make it easier to shop for the new products this branded manufacturer offers.) Because the seller has put its corporate reputation on the line with its brand name, a consistent level of product quality is ensured. The strength of this brand name, and its associations of quality and unique product values, makes it easier for the seller to control product pricing and promotion. These associations can also help to build a strong corporate image for all the seller's product lines, attracting a loyal, profitable group of target customers and facilitating the successful introduction of new products under the brand name. Branding also helps sellers segment markets. For example, the color TV manufacturer can offer different lines of TVs to attract different benefit-seeking segments.

Finally, branding benefits society at large. A successful branded product encourages other firms to improve on this success. Thus, branding stimulates competition, innovation, and continuing product improvement, in addition to making shopping more efficient and maintaining product quality. Indicative of the enormous psychological power of brands is a study of American consumer goods showing, on average, that the #1 brand in a category earns a 20 percent return, the #2 brand earns a 5 percent return, and the rest lose money.[1]

BRAND SPONSORSHIP STRATEGIES

Brand sponsorship strategies available to sellers include a manufacturer's brand, a private brand, or a generic brand. A manufacturer's, or national, brand is assigned by the manufacturer of the product, such as Hellman's mayonnaise. A private, or dealer, brand is assigned by the wholesaler or retailer of a product, such as Ann Page brand mayonnaise (A&P). Generic brands are plainly marked as such. Dealers see generic brands as a way to increase profits by saving on advertising, packaging, and other costs associated with manufacturer and private brands.

Frequently, a seller opts for more than one branding strategy. For example, the Whirlpool Corporation manufactures products under its own brand name and under Sears' private brand name (Kenmore).

Competition for supermarket shelf space between manufacturer's brands and private brands is a fast-growing trend in both domestic and international markets that is especially troubling to manufacturers, who must frequently make unwanted concessions to dealers.

---

1 "The Year of the Brand," *Economist,* December 24, 1988.

BRAND NAME STRATEGIES

The following four brand name strategies were considered by department members in devising brand names for products in the MM systems line:

- **An individual brand name strategy.** A brand name is applied to each product in the line and the company name is deemphasized. An example is Procter & Gamble's product line (Tide, Cheer, Folger's, Crest). The advantages are that brands can be targeted to specific markets, failure of one brand doesn't endanger others, and more individual brands occupy more shelf space. On the other hand, a strong companywide image is often sacrificed, as are mass production and marketing economies.

- **Separate family names for different categories of products.** For example, Sears has a family brand name for appliances (Kenmore) and another family brand name for tools (Craftsman). The advantages of separate family names are that it is easier to implement a brand extension strategy of launching new or modified products under a successful brand name, there is less expenditure on research to identify successful brand names, and there is less cost for promoting brand name recognition and preference.

- **A blanket family name for all products.** Examples include General Electric and Heinz 57 product lines. Generally, there are the same benefits as for the separate-family-names strategy.

- **A company brand name combined with an individual brand name.** Kellogg's Rice Krispies is an example. One advantage is that it is easier to launch new products under the company brand, while targeting markets under individual brand names.

Deciding which of these brand name strategies, or combinations thereof, to implement depends on product/market conditions in which products are introduced and commercialized. For example, if a firm's product mix lends itself to segmentation, an individual brand name strategy might be most appropriate. If a firm sells most of its products in a few markets, a blanket family name might be more appropriate. However, if a firm's product lines differ appreciably—such as Swift and Company's Premium brand hams and Vigoro fertilizer—a family brand name might not be able to stretch far enough, and a combination family/individual brand name strategy might be more appropriate.

CHOOSING EFFECTIVE BRAND NAMES

At Merton, the following five-step process was used to select effective brand names for new products introduced into the global marketplace.

• *ESTABLISH BRAND NAME CRITERIA*

Primary criteria against which prospective brand names were assessed included compatibility with customer perceptions, the image desired for the product, and the product's marketing mix. In the case of the MM systems line, for example, planners wanted a name that suggested a high-tech image that would lend itself to product promotions. Beyond that, the brand name should be distinctive; suggest product features and benefits; be relatively easy to recognize, recall, and pronounce; and be applicable to other products added to the line.

• *CREATE A LIST OF POTENTIAL BRAND NAMES*

Primary sources include names of products already in the mix, the name a private label dealer gives the product, a name licensed from a firm that holds a trademark on it, or any of a variety of original names, including initials (IBM, CBS), invented names (Kleenex, Exxon), numbers (Century 21), mythological characters (Samsonite luggage), personal names (Ford), geographical names (Southwestern Bell), dictionary names (Whirlpool appliances), foreign names (Nestlé), and word combinations (Head and Shoulders shampoo).

• *SCREEN THE LIST TO SELECT THE MOST APPROPRIATE FOR FURTHER TESTING*

Here, planners referred to the original selection criteria.

• *OBTAIN CONSUMER REACTIONS TO THE REMAINING NAMES*

This step involved informal surveys and focus group interviews with Merton staff and prospective buyers of MM systems.

• *CONDUCT A TRADEMARK SEARCH*

A multinational firm must register trademarks in every country in which it markets its products, a process that can be time consuming and expensive. In order to be legally protected, a trademark must adhere just to the product, its package, or label; can't imply characteristics the product doesn't possess and must not be confused with other trademarks. Once registered, a trademark gives the firm exclusive use of a "word, symbol, combination of letters or numbers, or other devices, such as distinctive packaging" for as long as the trademarked product is marketed. However, a brand name can become generic public property by becoming too popular, as happened to brand names like aspirin, linoleum, and nylon, and is threatening to happen to brand names like Xerox and Kleenex.

BRAND LEVERAGING STRATEGIES

Brand names that achieve market success can be leveraged to achieve additional market share and profits, sometimes to dramatic extremes. Three of these leveraging strategies—brand extension, brand licensing, and co-branding—were all employed by Merton planners once the Mighty Mind brand name had achieved brand insistence status for some MM systems products. (As the ultimate stage in brand loyalty, achieved by few firms, brand insistence means customers refuse to accept alternatives and search extensively for the product. It follows the brand preference stage, when customers will choose the brand over competitors' brands if it is available, and the leveraging potential of the brand name is much less than during the brand insistence stage. During the first brand recognition stage of brand loyalty, the leveraging potential of a brand name is practically nil.)

- **Brand extension** means attaching a popular brand name to a new product in an unrelated product category in the hope of obtaining new customers in new markets. Examples of successful brand extension strategies include BIC disposable shavers to BIC disposable lighters, Barbie dolls to Barbie games, and Lipton tea to Lipton soup mixes. Unsuccessful brand extension strategies include Harley-Davidson bikes to Harley-Davidson cigarettes, Levi jeans to Levi business wear, and Jack Daniel's bourbon to Jack Daniel's charcoal briquettes.

- **Brand licensing** is a variant on brand extension that involves a firm accepting payments from other firms to use the seller's brand name. Royalties are typically between 4 and 8 percent of wholesale revenues generated by the licensed product.

- **Co-branding** joins two strong brand names for a single product. Perhaps the most ubiquitous example of this strategy is the proliferation of credit cards that partner the card issuer brand with a strong product brand name. More than 13 million people have the General Motors Master Card.

GLOBAL USE PATTERNS DEFINE QUALITY LEVELS

Defined in terms of user perceptions, and applicable to national, private, and generic brands, quality is the rated ability of the product to perform its functions through such objective and subjective attributes as durability, safety, reliability, appearance, ease of operation, and service.

The trend toward greater emphasis on quality in products is summarized in Figure 14-1, which shows that, even though superior quality increases profitability only slightly over high quality, low quality hurts profits substantially, and profits increase appreciably between "average" and "high" quality levels. However, circumstances can change these conclusions. For example, if all competitors in an entry market deliver high quality, lowering quality to offer a lower price might be a quick path to profits.

Figure 14–1. Relationship between quality levels and profitability.

DETERMINING BRAND QUALITY

Sellers have three options available in deciding the level of quality to be built into their products: (1) continually upgrade quality; (2) maintain the existing level of quality; or (3) reduce quality, usually in response to rising costs or in the expectation of higher profits.

WEBER'S LAW HELPS DEFINE QUALITY LEVELS

In general, if quality is raised, sellers hope buyers will recognize the change; if quality is lowered, they hope buyers won't notice. A useful way to determine how much to raise, or lower, brand quality is to apply Weber's law, named after the nineteenth-century German scientist Ernst Weber, who discovered that the just-noticeable-difference of a stimuli was an amount relative to the size of the stimuli that precedes it. Weber's law maintains that K, or the just-noticeable-difference (jnd), is a constant that varies over the senses and can be determined as follows:

$$K = \Delta I/I$$

where ΔI equals the smallest increase in stimulus intensity that will be perceived as different from the existing intensity, and I equals the existing stimulus intensity.

For example, would it be worth the more expensive technology for Merton to improve the visual resolution of the Mighty Mind by 10 percent? Possibly, if focus group research indicated the average K of prospective buyers to be 8 percent, over which level they would notice a change in visual resolution.

On the other hand, if K—the level at which prospects would notice this change in visual resolution—was 11 percent, the change wouldn't be noticed and probably shouldn't be made. Weber's law is applicable in many other marketing situations, such as determining how much to raise or lower a price, or when people will notice changes in color or noise intensity in promotional campaigns.

OVERLOOKED SERVICE OPPORTUNITIES

Along with product quality, quality of customer service is assuming increased importance as a competitive tool, and many firms have established customer service departments to address customer needs and complaints. The importance of service in competitive international markets is highlighted by a recent survey of international users of heavy construction equipment, which showed that, next to the manufacturer's reputation, quick delivery of parts was the most important criterion for selecting a supplier.

This survey also revealed major customer complaints, all relating to the service function: orders are delayed, credit memo notices aren't sent, guarantees and warranties aren't honored, returns and allowances aren't sufficient, after-sales service is ignored, and damaged parts aren't replaced. Market Focus 14-1 illustrates the importance of service in achieving marketing goals.

MARKET FOCUS 14-1

The Increasing Importance of Service in Competitive Markets

The experience of three companies illustrates the importance of service as a key variable in competing effectively.

- **The Hutchinson Technological Corporation, Hutchinson, Minnesota.** According to Rick Penn, director of sales and marketing, "high quality service is as important as high quality products in meeting or exceeding customer requirements." Toward this objective, Hutchinson, a manufacturer of computer and medical components, has implemented a "Service Plus" program to systematize employee and customer feedback and measure customer satisfaction. For example, results of a recent survey showed a rating of at least 82 percent in the areas of quality, frequency of contact, delivery, and price. The firm maintains a quality control laboratory in Asia to measure and test returned parts from Asian customers "on the spot."

- **Royal Dental Manufacturing, Everett, Washington.** According to Harold Tai, CEO, exports account for more than 20 percent of Royal Dental's total sales of dental chairs and doctor stools, sold through dealers mainly to customers in Eastern Europe, Russia, Saudi Arabia, China, and Korea. "We are doing particularly well in Poland, " says Tai, "thanks to ongoing economic privatization efforts that have helped modernize dental care and generate demand for the latest in dental equipment." Even though U.S. dental technology, internationally recognized for quality standards, is a large part of the reason for Royal Dental's success, Tai gives equal credit to the firm's service program. "We maintain fast, efficient communication with our dealers and customers, through mail, fax, and U.S. Department of Commerce-sponsored shows in such countries as China, Pakistan, and India; additionally, our dealers worldwide send their technicians to our factory for training in use of our equipment, so they can better serve dentists and health care professionals who purchase and operate our equipment."

- **Paper Machinery Corporation, Milwaukee, Wisconsin.** As the world's primary source of converting machinery for the production of paper products, Paper Machinery, in 1996, supplied approximately 40 percent of the worldwide export market for paper cup and container forming machines, with major markets in China, Japan, Europe, and South America and major marketing efforts currently focused on East European nations and the Commonwealth of Independent States. During the decade leading up to 1996, the 185-employee firm increased its gross earnings nearly fivefold. According to Donald Baumgartner, president, the key to the firm's continued profitable growth is service: "No customer in any of the 40 countries we serve is more than a local phone call away from a service call. We even routinely call on customers who don't call us just to make sure our machinery is working properly."

Source: Business America, U.S. Department of Commerce, March 1996, pp. 22–23.

FULFILLING CUSTOMER SERVICE NEEDS

Primary service decisions in both domestic and global markets pertain to (1) services included in the service mix and (2) level of service to offer. Both of these questions can be addressed by systematically analyzing customer needs, competitive offerings, and company resources. Merton, for example, conducted a survey that prioritized customer service needs with respect to MM systems, with "good warranty coverage," "prompt deliveries," and "low service cost" heading the list in one entry market.

Survey findings also listed the following as least important service attributes in this market: "convenient servicing locations," "returns and allowances," and "replacement guarantee."

Then, having identified the most and least important service attributes, Merton conducted surveys to determine (1) the level of service customer firms were presently receiving from firms competing with Merton and (2) the level of service Merton could afford to offer.

Service mix and service level decisions were then based on data from these surveys. For example, although "good warranty coverage" was the most desired service attribute, none of Merton's competitors in this entry market offered the level desired by customers, so Merton designed a warranty slightly superior to that offered by its main competitor in this market.

Figure 14-2 shows the approach used by Merton to monitor its service mix. The vertical dimension ranks these attributes from extremely to slightly important, whereas the horizontal axis rates how effectively service needs of MM buyers were met. Note, for example, that the two most important service attributes—good warranty coverage and low service cost—are positioned in Quadrant II, with its "keep up the good work" mandate. The third important attribute—"prompt deliveries"—is positioned in Quadrant I, where the mandate is to "concentrate here." The three least important attributes are positioned in Quadrant III, but this didn't overly concern Merton planners since this was the Low Priority area.

PRODUCT PACKAGING DECISIONS RESPOND TO ENVIRONMENTAL NEEDS

As with decisions relating to product branding, quality, and service, product packaging decisions can strongly influence customer responses to the product, and all marketing mix elements supporting the product.

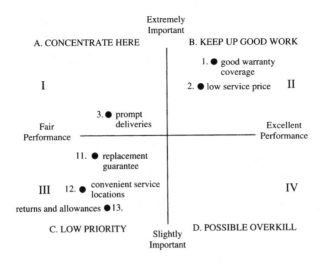

Figure 14–2. Approach for measuring and controlling service effectiveness.

In arriving at packaging decisions for MM systems and parts in international entry nations, Merton accounted for the following packaging objectives relating to Merton marketing objectives and conditions in these nations.

• *CONTAIN AND PROTECT THE PRODUCT*

The package in which a product is exported usually is composed of three separate packages: the immediate product container, called the primary package; the package containing the primary package, called the secondary package; and the package used to transport and store a number of secondary packages, called the shipping package. Materials available to contain and protect products include paperboard, plastic, metal, glass, styrofoam, and cellophane. (A major protective packaging innovation of the 1990s was asceptic containers for milk and fruit drinks. The Swedish Company Tetra Pak International converted 40 percent of milk sales in Western Europe to its asceptic packaging system, which keeps perishables fresh, without refrigeration, for five months.)

• *ENCOURAGE PRODUCT USE*

Jumbo detergent packages and six-packs of soda are examples of package designs that encourage greater use of the product, as do packaging features that make it easier to use the product, such as boil-in bags, flip-top beer cans, and software packages for MM courses, which are easy to file and retrieve.

• *IDENTIFY AND PROMOTE THE PRODUCT*

Package design can facilitate communication on two levels:

- The **information** level, by identifying the brand and providing ingredients (or components) and directions;

- The **promotional** level, by differentiating the product from competing products with a sales message highlighting features and benefits.

Key packaging decisions addressed by Merton planners in this area include: Where should instructions appear on the package? What informational message and promotional "image" should the package convey? Will promotional inserts be needed? How can package aesthetics—size, color, and shape—be tailored to the promotional message?

• *NEW PRODUCT PLANNING*

A package design can reinforce the image of the product as new (such as depicting a new cereal), or can be, in itself, what is "new" in the product, such as toothpaste pump dispensers or microwaveable containers for frozen dinners. Typical concerns pertaining to this objective include the size, color, shapes, and other visual and written messages that will best communicate "newness." Will a family packaging policy, with every package the same (e.g., Campbell Soup) make it difficult to implement this objective?

• *CHANNEL COOPERATION*

Package design can help address needs of wholesalers, retailers, and other channel members by making it easier for them to handle, store, and display products; mark prices and control inventory; and ensure reasonably long shelf life. Key questions in developing packages that take distributor needs into account include: Are there traditional packaging practices expected by dealers? What are competitors' packaging practices? Will the distributor expect features (such as Universal Product and Optical Character Recognition Codes that allow electronic scanners to enter product/price information into a database) that help to improve inventory control and customer service? Do company packages exhibit an adverse environmental impact, or additional customer cost, that would not be acceptable in the entry country?

LABELING DECISIONS SUPPLEMENT PACKAGING DECISIONS

The main function of a label is to provide information about the packaged product, or about the seller of the product. The label itself may be printed as part of the package itself or on a tag affixed to the product.

Labeling decisions typically involve three kinds of labels:

- **Grade labels** announce product quality with letters (Grade A), numbers (#1), or conditions ("choice");

- **Informative labels** focus on the care, use, and preparation of the product ("This side up");

- **Descriptive labels** explain important characteristics or benefits ("23 percent more coffee").

In general, labeling decisions supplement packaging decisions in helping to encourage product use, promote communication, segment markets, and plan new products. Labels can also play an important role in responding to social and legal considerations. For example, open dating indicates the expected shelf life of the product to avoid spoilage. Nutritional labels disclose amounts of nutrients, fat, sodium, and calories in processed foods. Unit pricing allows customers to compare values among competing brands by stating prices in terms of basic units, like ounces or pints.

PRODUCT LINE AND MIX STRATEGIES

A product line consists of related products with similar features, markets, and/or end use applications. The MM systems product line, for example, is composed of computers of various degrees of size and sophistication, with associated software tailored to the needs of different market segments. Taken together, all of Merton's product lines, including its lines of computer accessories marketed to organizational markets, constitute its **product mix.**

Product line decisions facing Merton planners included:

- **Product line length decisions** pertaining to the number of products included in the line (generally, products are added as long as they contribute to profits and don't cannibalize sales and profits from existing products);

- **Product line stretching decisions** pertaining to products added to an existing line to attract less profitable markets (downward stretch), more profitable markets (upward stretch), or both (two-way stretch);

- **Product line filling decisions** focusing on plugging gaps in an existing line, usually to gain additional sales or profits, utilize excess capacity, or respond to competitive initiatives or dealer needs;

- **Product line featuring decisions** pertaining to which products to feature in promotional campaigns.

Product mix decisions facing Merton planners in different markets included:

- **Mix width decisions,** pertaining to how many different lines Merton would market (as with product line length decisions, generally dependent on profitability of new lines, consistency with company mission, and danger of cannibalizing sales from other lines);

- **Mix consistency,** pertaining to how closely related the firm's products are in terms of common end uses, distribution outlets, price ranges, and markets served.

A consistent mix of product lines is particularly important in international markets, where such factors as high entry costs and limited communication and distribution channels often limit profit opportunities. Mix consistency can offset these limitations by helping firms concentrate production and marketing efforts, achieve scale economies, and create strong brand images and relations with distributors.

Product life cycle positions for Merton's product lines and mixes often suggested which of these decisions were appropriate. For example, if products in the firm's mix were situated primarily in the highly competitive growth stage, line stretching and filling decisions might be indicated to meet these threats. Mix width and consistency decisions might also be made in response to competitive PLC environments, with products added or modified during growth periods, and pruned and narrowed during periods of decline. For individual products comprising the MM line, three strategies in particular were appropriate during later PLC stages, when competition became more intense, and markets and profits began to decline.

- **Repositioning strategies** involved use of advertising and promotion campaigns to create changed consumer perceptions of the product, as when Merton opted to change its blue chip image to accommodate its line of less expensive computer systems geared to the needs of less affluent target markets. The danger of such a strategy is the possibility of losing, or confusing, the firm's main market.

- **Product life extension strategies** entail one or more of the following tactical options: new uses for the product; new product features or benefits; new classes of customers for present product; increased product usage; and/or a changed marketing strategy. All these options came into play when Merton, late in MM's life cycle in the domestic market, redesigned and repositioned this product to serve new groups of customers in global markets.

- **Product deletion strategies** involve removing products from the line when they are no longer profitable. They include (1) a **continuation strategy** of continuing to market the product until it must be dropped; (2) a **milking strategy** of cutting back marketing expenses to maintain profits during the decline PLC stage; and (3) a

concentrated strategy of aiming all marketing efforts at the strongest existing segment, and phasing out all others.

A danger in milking and concentration deletion strategies is that they will be applied prematurely, without regard to the impact on the rest of the line (or mix) and without fully considering possibilities in repositioning and product life extension strategies.

INTERNATIONAL PERSPECTIVE

Whether product planning takes place in domestic or global markets, most basic considerations and approaches pertaining to product design, branding, quality, service, labeling, and packaging are the same. In global markets, however, additional considerations in these areas derive from environmental conditions and constraints not generally applicable in domestic markets.

We examine these considerations in this section, along with the problem of product counterfeiting, and appropriate responses to different manifestations of this problem.

PRODUCT DESIGN IN GLOBAL MARKETS

As noted earlier in this chapter, two key product design determinants include cost and compatibility with the environments in which the products will be used.

In global markets, cost is usually the dominant consideration in determining product design features, as well as the product's competitiveness and profitability. Key variables, in addition to the cost of designing to suit customer preferences and of labor and materials (which can be appreciably lower in foreign countries), include costs for transporting products and hurdling tariff and other barriers erected in the entry country. (These costs, and their impact on prices and other marketing mix variables, are discussed in Chapter 15.)

Product design for global markets must also account for environments in which the products will be used. Different climates, different measurement systems (the United States is the only nonmetric country in the world), and different power and broadcast systems are but a few of the environmental constraints that can affect product design. Of particular importance to designers of American products are product standards mandated by individual countries and regional economic communities. For example, with the European Economic Area (EEA) agreement in force as of January 1994, design requirements must be met in order to sell many categories of products—including toys, construction products, pressure vessels, gas appliances, medical devices, telecommunications equipment, and machinery—in eighteen European countries.

In addition to these national and supranational standards, Richard Robinson[2] suggests consideration of the following nine key environmental factors and product design changes deriving from each.

Environmental Factor in Entry Country	Design Change
Low level of technical skills	Product simplification
High labor cost	Automation or manualization
Low literacy level	Remarking and simplification
Low income level	Quality and price change of product
High interest rates	Quality, price change (investment in high quality not financially desirable)
Low maintenance level	Change in tolerance, simplification
Climatic differences	Product adaptation
Isolation (maintenance and repair difficult, expensive)	Product simplification, improved reliability
Different standards	Recalibration, resizing

Global Focus 14-1 describes product failures and successes attributable to the design features that reflected differing global environments.

GLOBAL FOCUS 14-1

Learning from Product Design Successes and Failures

The following examples highlight the importance of designing products compatible with customer preferences, cost constraints, and competitive conditions in global entry markets.

- **Parking Solutions,** a small family manufacturer of Redondo Beach, California, overcame competition from 17 Japanese manufacturers in selling its automobile parking lifts to Tech Corporation of Hiroshima. A company spokesman described the parking lifts of Japanese manufacturers as "overengineered and overpriced." The Japanese liked the American lifts because they are simply designed, easy to operate, and less costly.

---

2 Richard Robinson, *International Business Management* (Hinsdale, IL: Dryden Press, 1985).

- **Kryptonite Corporation** of Canton, Massachusetts, got a sales boost in its Asian market when it received the award for outstanding design and function of a bicycle lock by the Japanese Design and Promotion Organization.

- **The Olivetti Company** discovered that its modern, award winning, lightweight typewriter, enormously successful in Europe, couldn't compete against heavy, bulky typewriters designed and sold in the United States. Olivetti was forced to adapt its typewriter design (on display in the Museum of Modern Art) to preferences of American consumers.

Source: Business America, World Trade Week 1993 Edition.

BRANDING PRODUCTS IN GLOBAL MARKETS

Few U.S. brands get beyond the national level. Indeed, with the exception of a few global brands such as Coca-Cola and Levi's jeans, the majority of U.S. brands achieve more than 80 percent of sales from the domestic market, with most of the rest coming from culturally similar markets.

Even when a product or service succeeds in global markets, it can rarely afford the luxury of a standardized plan, with only very minor marketing mix changes to account for small differences among different foreign markets. Rather, they perforce use customized plans, requiring sizeable changes in product design and other marketing mix elements.

An effective global branding strategy can change this. In international markets, the brand is one of the easiest aspects of the offering to standardize and can help standardize other products in the line and marketing mix elements (e.g, price, quality, promotion). Standardized products and brands do not necessarily go together; for example, it's possible to have a standardized brand name on a local product (e.g., a German beer brand brewed in the United States), or vice versa (an American appliance with a local brand name in a foreign country).

NAMING BRANDS IN GLOBAL MARKETS

A key consideration in naming brands in global markets is the extent to which the name translates easily into the language of prospective foreign customers, without unanticipated negative connotations. (Here are some examples of these embarrassing language blunders: Coke, in Chinese, translates to "bite the wax tadpole"; the Chevrolet Nova translates into Spanish as "it doesn't go"; Sunbeam's Mist-Stick hair curling iron translates in German to "manure wand.")

Another important consideration in naming products in international markets derives from stereotyped attitudes or country-of-origin effects toward foreign products that can help or hinder marketing efforts. One study, for example, showed the following quality scores assigned by Germans to their products and those of other countries: German, 54; British, 30; Dutch, 24; French, 16; Belgian, 8; Italian, 2. Among Italians, who were listed last in terms of German perceptions, assigned quality scores were: German, 37; Dutch, 25; Italian, 24; British, 10; French, −1. Another study showed that the "Made in U.S.A." label had lost ground appreciably in global perceptions to the "Made in Japan" label. National perceptions of the products of other nations should probably be taken into consideration when planning all aspects of the marketing mix strategy, particularly a brand name that advertises the product's derivation. In Germany, for example, the Maxwell House brand, along with its "great American coffee" slogan, proved to be a turnoff when it was found Germans have about as much respect for American coffee as they have for American beer. In another situation, a Brazilian manufacturer of sensitive oil drilling equipment overcame negative stereotypes of Brazilian products in Mexico by first exporting components of the equipment to Switzerland, where they were assembled and stamped "Made in Switzerland." Facing these negative stereotypes, a successful branding strategy often uses local names or well-known local brands to contribute to a national identity. Alternately, if the country's products are favorably perceived in an entry country—as is the case with many imported beers in the United States—the brand should probably reflect this fact ("Becks—The most popular beer in Germany").

QUALITY IN GLOBAL MARKETS

In international markets, desired degree of product quality is invariably relative to use patterns and standards in the country where the product is marketed. For example, DuPont adopted ISO 9000 standards (a set of technical standards chosen by the European Union to encourage manufacturing and service organizations to implement sound quality procedures) after losing a big order to an ISO-certified British firm. Alternately, high quality by standards in developed countries may represent unnecessary cost in less-developed countries.

A strong emphasis on quality among consumers in North America is evidenced by demand for product quality in Japanese automobiles and electronics and in European automobiles, clothing, and food. A number of domestic companies are catering to this growing interest in quality, illustrated by Ford's "Quality is Job 1" promotion campaign. In international markets, quality is also growing as a key criterion for product purchase, especially for products where quality differences are not easy to perceive, such as refrigerators or color TV sets. A study by the PIMS group (Profit Impact of Marketing Strategies), for example, concluded that companies that innovate and deliver quality achieve higher rates of return in both mature and stagnant markets. These companies also avoid the unprofitable trap of competing on the basis of commodity or undifferentiated items.

PRODUCT COUNTERFEITING THREATENS GLOBAL TRADE

Counterfeit products, defined as goods bearing an unauthorized representation of a trademark, patented invention, or copyrighted work, are reaching a magnitude where they seriously threaten to disrupt international trading patterns. Hardest hit are the products of innovative, fast-growing industries (computer software, pharmaceuticals, entertainment) and highly visible consumer goods brands (Polo, Gucci, Izod). The fact that these tend to be major categories of U.S. exports helps explain the estimated $70 billion U.S. companies lose each year because of product counterfeiting and other infringement of intellectual property. (Worldwide, the International Chamber of Commerce estimates the trade in counterfeit goods at 5 percent of total world trade.)

From the perspective of an American exporter, responses to product counterfeiting depend primarily on where the firm's products are being counterfeited and sold. Of counterfeit goods, 75 percent are produced outside the United States, with China, Brazil, Korea, India, and Taiwan the major offenders. If these products are sold in the country of origin, infringement actions are usually brought under the laws of that country. In 1995, for example, an intellectual property agreement was reached with China, under threat of sanctions, to close down a number of factories in business only to counterfeit American products.

Products counterfeited abroad and sold in the United States should be stopped at the customs barrier, although lack of personnel and the increasingly high-tech character of counterfeit products makes enforcement difficult. Problems involving the 25 percent of counterfeit products that are either made in this country or imported and labeled here are best resolved through infringement actions brought in U.S. federal courts.

Although there is no such thing as an international patent, trademark, or copyright, some protection exists under such international treaties and agreements as the Paris Convention for the Protection of Industrial Property, the Patent Cooperation Treaty, the Berne Convention for the Protection of Literary and Artistic Works, and the Universal Copyright Convention, as well as regional patent and trademark offices.

PACKAGING AND LABELING PRODUCTS IN GLOBAL MARKETS

In deciding on materials to include in packages designed to maintain and protect MM systems that were shipped, unloaded, and stored in international markets, planners took into account extra handling and longer transportation needs, and protection against climate conditions (humidity, excess heat, and the like) that would otherwise adversely affect product shelf life.

With large shipments, containerization was used, whereby shipping packages containing MM systems were put in sturdy containers that were sealed until delivered, thereby reducing damage and pilferage. Pilferage was also discouraged by using only shipping codes on outside packaging whenever feasible.

In foreign markets, conditions peculiar to specific countries will often dictate package design, such as where lack of refrigeration or income suggest a quantity less than six-packs.

As with any promotional message, color can play an important role in packaging to gain attention and help shape the product's image. For example, research indicates that African nations prefer bold colors, and that, in industrialized countries, silver is associated with luxury, black with quality, and white with generic products. Illustrative of the impact of color in promotion is the experience of Pepsi Cola in Southeast Asia, where market share was lost because consumers associated Pepsi's light blue promotional color with death and mourning.

In labeling products for export, it's important to observe the importer's language requirements, such as bilinguality requirements for Canada (French and English), Belgium (French and Flemish), and Finland (Finnish and Swedish).

CHAPTER PERSPECTIVE

Basic product planning concepts are the same in domestic and international markets: products must be designed, branded, packaged and labeled, and cost-benefit decisions made pertaining to levels of service and quality associated with the augmented product. Additionally, product line and mix strategies must be formulated to ensure that the needs of customers and distributors are profitably met. In the complex global market, however, a diversity of factors make these decisions, and strategies emerging from them, more critical and difficult.

KNOW THE CONCEPTS
TERMS FOR STUDY

Blanket family name
Brand
Brand mark
Co-branding
Company/individual brand name
Copyright
Country-of-origin effects
Forward extension
Generic brands
Individual brand names
Labeling
Licensing
Manufacturer's brand
Open dating
Package aesthetics

Packaging
Private brand
Product compatibility
Product deletion strategy
Product design
Product life extension strategy
Product line strategies
Product mix strategies
Product planning
Quality
Repositioning strategies
Separate family names
Trademark
Unit pricing
Weber's law

MATCHUP EXERCISES

1. Match up the branding strategy in the first column with the descriptor in the second column.

1. manufacturer's brand
2. blanket family name
3. generic brands
4. family/individual brands
5. private brands

a. one name for two or more products
b. obtains most sales for most product categories
c. emphasizes products, not names
d. names designated by distributors
e. Chrysler Dodge, Dodge Aires

2. Match the product attribute in the first column with the appropriate planning consideration in the second column.

1. branding
2. quality
3. service
4. packaging

a. Will greater product use be encouraged?
b. Individual, family, or both?
c. Increase level above the jnd.
d. Profits increase most between "average" and "high" levels.

3. Match up the product line/mix strategy in the first column with a key strategy objective in the second column.

1. product line length	a. plug gaps
2. product line stretching	b. add related lines
3. product line filling	c. attract new markets
4. product mix consistency	d. add profitable products
5. product mix width	e. add profitable lines

QUESTIONS FOR REVIEW AND DISCUSSION

1. In terms of criteria for effective brand names, analyze and assess the expensive name change from Bank Americard to VISA.

2. By the year 2002, Campbell Soup wants half of company revenues to come from outside domestic markets, up from 30 percent in 1995, with Asia—and China in particular—targeted as the area with the greatest growth potential. In China, most of the competition will come from homemade soup. To counter this competition, Campbell plans to keep prices attractive, promote its products on convenience, and make extensive use of local ingredients in its soups (drawing the line, however, on dog and shark fin soups). How will the strength of Campbell's brand name, worldwide, help Campbell achieve its goal? How will it motivate Chinese buyers to select Campbell soups over alternatives? And how will it benefit the Chinese economy, as it moves haltingly toward a free-market model?

3. How would you categorize the brand names "Merton Mighty Mind" (for computers) and "Merton Moon Chip" (for chip circuits)? What alternative categories might have been selected? Why (or why not) is this category preferable? Why (or why not) does it meet criteria for an effective brand name?

4. Describe how Weber's law might have been employed with respect to all components of the marketing mix (product, price, place, promotion) for a service that purchases unsold space on airlines and ocean lines at sizeable discounts and then sells it to the traveling public at a discount from the retail price that still permits the firm to make a profit. Travel agencies will receive a commission for selling the tickets, which will be promoted primarily over the Internet and in advertisements in travel sections of Sunday newspapers.

5. A study of Canadian buyers of industrial equipment ranked service elements in the following order of importance: (1) delivery reliability; (2) prompt quotations; (3) technical advice; (4) prompt discount credits; (5) after-sales service; (6) sales representation; (7) ease of contact; and (8) replacement guarantee. Given these priorities, what advice would you offer a Canadian distributor whose service level profile looks like this:

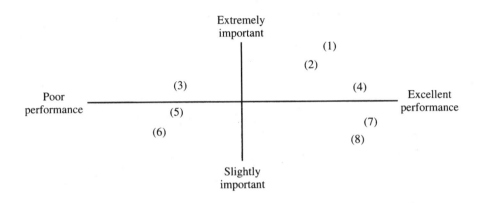

6. Describe two typical packaging objectives performed by each of these packages:

- Wine in pop-top containers;

- L'Eggs Pantyhose in an egg-shaped package;

- A shipping carton that converts into a compartmentalized display rack for light bulbs.

- WD-40 rust inhibitor available in 8- or 12-ounce cans and 55 gallon-drums.

7. Discuss how and why the Merton Mighty Mind computer system, over the course of its life span, might use the following strategies: product line stretching, product mix consistency, product life extension.

8. The Apple Computer Company has seen virtually all its lines of computers and computer software counterfeited, with about 70 percent of faked merchandise made and marketed outside the United States, and 20 percent either manufactured in this country or imported into this country and labeled here. Suggest a strategy that Apple might use to effectively combat this unauthorized representation of their inventions, copyrights, and trademarks.

ANSWERS

MATCHUP EXERCISES

1. 1b, 2a, 3c, 4e, 5d

2. 1b, 2d, 3c, 4a

3. 1d, 2c, 3a, 4b, 5e

QUESTIONS FOR REVIEW AND DISCUSSION

1. Compared to the original Bank Americard brand name, the VISA brand is distinctive, short, easy to recognize and remember, suggests something about product benefits (a visa to the exciting lifestyles portrayed in its commercials), and doesn't have negative connotations in foreign languages.

2. Campbell's strong brand name, strongly promoted in global markets, will provide benefits for customers, the company, and the economy. For example, using the Chinese entry market as an example, prospective customers will benefit from a brand name and its promotional-induced associations, that they can relate to their wants and needs and quickly identify when shopping. The Campbell Soup Company will benefit in that they can focus their promotional efforts on a single product name, thus achieving benefits of standardization, as well as benefits from being able to maintain price and production levels consistent with Campbell's strong, positive brand image. A well-promoted brand name will also help Campbell introduce dozens of new soups in this market under this name, knowing that prospective customers will bring to these new products the same positive associations they have for present Campbell products. And this desire to build a loyal customer base will serve as an incentive for Campbell to maintain high levels of product quality. Branding will also help Campbell segment its China market, with different branded product lines (for example, Hungry Man and Ranchero) for different market segments. Finally, Campbell's branding strategy will benefit the Chinese economy to the extent that competitors are motivated to innovate in improving their products and marketing campaigns to emulate Campbell's success, as well as to help to improve shopping efficiency and maintain product quality.

3. The names "Merton Mighty Mind" and "Merton Moon Chip" illustrate the company-brand-name-combined-with-individual-brand-name category. Alternative categories that might have been selected include a blanket family name (Merton computers and Merton chip circuits) and separate family names (Mighty Mind computers and Moon Chip circuits). One advantage of the company-individual brand name combination is that new products can be launched under the company (Merton) brand, while markets can be targeted under the individual brand name. Also, unlike the situation with individual brand names, a strong, focused, companywide product image can be maintained. With respect to the criteria for effective brand names, these brands seem to meet them: they suggest the high-tech nature of the products (the Moon Chips were used on lunar space probes), as well as the product benefits, are relatively easy to recognize, recall, and pronounce; and can be applied to other products added to each line.

4. Product: The routes chosen for travel discounts would have to be perceived as sufficiently attractive. Place: The discount offered travel agents would have to be sufficiently large to justify their administering the service. Price: The discount offered prospective customers would have to be perceived as sufficiently large to attract target market members. Promotion: Newspaper and Internet ads would have to be perceived as sufficiently intrusive to attract the attention of prospective customers.

5. This service profile indicates that the firm's customers are not well served by the firm's outside salesforce, with generally poor performance ratings for "technical advice," "after-sales service," and "sales representation." After the order is placed, however, customers are well served, with high ratings for "reliability," "prompt quotations," and "prompt discount credits." Indeed, customers might be too well served, perhaps to compensate for the lack of effective salespeople, since the relatively unimportant attributes "ease of contact" and "replacement guarantee" are also highly regarded. According to this analysis, the firm should probably work harder on training its salespeople to do a more creative, conscientious job of selling its products, while perhaps achieving savings by cutting back on its guarantees.

6. The following matrix lists major packaging objectives fulfilled by each package. Actually, an argument could be made that each package, to some extent, furthers all the objectives.

	Contain product	Encourage use	Communicate	Plan new products	Channel cooperation
Wine in pop-up containers		X		X	
L'Eggs Pantyhose			X		X
Convertible shipping carton	X		X		X
Rust inhibitor containers		X		X	X

7. Product line stretching would be used, probably during growth and maturity life cycle stages, to attract new market segments to the line of thin TV sets—downward stretch with cheaper models for less profitable markets, upward stretch for more profitable models, two-way stretch for markets at both ends. Product mix consistency considerations would help ensure that new lines (for example, a line of CD ROMs) were consistent with the firm's product mix in terms of common end uses, distribution outlets, price ranges, markets served, and promotion programs to reach these markets. For example, if the firm has a standardized promotion program to reach many global markets, a new line added to the mix should probably also fit within this standardization. Product life extension strategies, employed during maturity and decline stages of the life cycle, would focus on new uses for the product (for example, as a component in a modularized entertainment center), new product features or benefits, new classes of customers for the product, and increasing product usage.

8. For counterfeiting initiated in the United States, Apple has had considerable success through infringement actions brought in federal courts. For counterfeiting initiated outside the United States, but conducted in this country (imported fakes are assembled or marketed here), Apple supplements federal court infringement actions by cooperating with the Customs Bureau to stop smuggling of fakes into this country. In addressing the problem of fakes made and marketed overseas, Apple uses a full range of corrective options, including legislative action, bilateral and multilateral negotiations with and among offending countries, private actions taken with other companies in Apple's field, and individual actions (such as staged raids with local authorities, or bringing offenders into the Apple family by converting them to legitimate licensees), thus giving them a profit stake in apprehending other offenders.

15
ESTABLISHING PRICING OBJECTIVES AND POLICIES

OVERVIEW

Of all marketing mix elements, price is the most flexible and typically has the greatest direct impact on customer perceptions, sales, and profits.

Setting productive prices is a complex, challenging task that involves the establishment of realistic objectives, as well as policies, strategies, and tactics designed to achieve these objectives. Considerations involved in the price planning process include accounting for the nature and behavior of costs, customers, and competitors, as well as economic, legal, and political constraints on pricing.

PRICING OBJECTIVES DEFINE POLICIES AND STRATEGIES

In this chapter, we continue our examination of marketing mix elements with a discussion of the price planning process whereby global marketers arrive at pricing objectives, policies, strategies, and tactics. An example involving Merton's planned entry of MM systems into a new market illustrates relationships among these four concepts.

An objective of this entry might be to achieve a 20 percent share of this market within two years. This objective, in turn, might define a set of pricing policy guidelines indicating a penetration pricing strategy of pricing MM systems below competitive levels. This strategy, in turn, would entail a number of tactics such as raising or lowering prices in response to competitive initiatives.

This process of devising and implementing pricing strategies to achieve profit objectives involves a sophisticated understanding of such variables as the behavior of costs, demand patterns of customers, and responses of competitors.

In examining these variables, we begin with a discussion of the importance of price, which refers to both monetary and nonmonetary exchanges of goods and services, in terms of its impact on sales, profits, markets, and other marketing mix elements. Then we examine the first two stages of the price-planning process: establishing pricing objectives and policies through the systematic analysis of data on products, costs, markets, competitors, and other uncontrollables. In Chapter 16, we examine pricing strategies and tactics that emerge from these objectives and policies.

PRICES INFLUENCE SALES, PROFITS, AND MARKETING MIXES

To illustrate the critical role of prices in generating sales, profits, and marketing mix values, we will make some assumptions about the price of an MM system being introduced into a new foreign market, and consumer responses to this product.

Assume, first, that Merton's costs to make and market each system are $900, but that it decides to price each at $2000. Also assume that most prospective customers perceive the combination of values comprising each system to be only worth $1100, so sales are disappointing until Merton lowers its price closer to this $1100 market price.

Now assume a different scenario. In an effort to penetrate this new market quickly, Merton prices the MM system at a level equal to its actual costs—and below competitor's prices—at $900 per unit. The firm anticipates that this price will increase sales and generate economies of scale (that is lower procurement, production, and marketing costs associated with mass production economies and efficiencies) that will soon begin to generate big profits.

At this lower price, however, prospective customers perceive the MM system to be a cheap version of competitive systems, subject to expensive breakdowns, so sales increases are again disappointing. Realizing its miscalculation, Merton planners raise the MM's price up toward the $1100 price that customers perceive the units are worth and discover, to their delight, that sales and profits increase with each incremental increase.

This example illustrates a number of characteristics of the important, complex price component of the marketing mix. It is certainly the most flexible of marketing mix elements, subject to change on very short notice. It is also the only marketing mix element that produces revenues; the other elements represent costs. In the opinion of most marketing executives responding to a number of surveys, it is also the most important marketing mix element, due to the diverse, complex considerations that must be factored into a typical price, including customers, competition, costs, and governmental interventions.

Beyond these general characteristics, this example illustrates the direct, specific influence price can have on consumer perceptions, sales revenues flowing from these perceptions, and profits flowing from sales revenues.

To illustrate the dramatic impact of prices on profits, consider one of the price increases Merton makes that doesn't also increase costs: from $1000 to $1100. Note that this 10 percent price increase (100/1000) levers a 100 percent increase in profits—from $100 to $200.

PRICES SUPPORT MARKETING MIX ELEMENTS

Since a product's price helps position the product offering, communicate its tangible and intangible values, determine how and where it will be distributed, and even define its target markets, price planning is invariably done in conjunction with product, place, and promotion planning.

In the case of MM systems, for example, special price incentives were offered to distributors to encourage them to carry the MM line; quality differences between MM systems and competitive systems were reflected in price differences; and selection of appeals and media for promoting MM systems reflected this price-quality relationship. Thus, just as price can enhance customer perceptions, sales, and profits, it can also enhance the effectiveness of marketing mix elements in achieving marketing goals.

This relationship among price, marketing objectives, and other marketing mix elements will become clearer as we examine the approach used by Merton planners to arrive at profitable price policies and strategies for the MM systems product line.

PRICING VIEWED AS A MARKETING FUNCTION

In general, firms interested in penetrating competitive markets are well advised to view pricing as a marketing, rather than an accounting, function. This marketing perception of pricing is especially applicable to multiline firms serving consumer markets, where price planners consider such factors as demand patterns, cost behaviors, legal constraints, product and product life cycle characteristics, competitive initiatives and responses, discounts and allowances offered distributors, and degree of flexibility available.

A key positive objective of effective price planning is to enhance profit return; a key negative objective is to avoid three major pricing failures: (1) failure to relate prices to needs and perceptions of target market members; (2) failure to properly integrate prices with other marketing mix elements; and (3) failure to modify pricing policies and strategies to match changing competitive environments.

This isn't to say that a simple cost-plus accounting approach to price planning isn't ever appropriate. In some situations, cost is the only real consideration, with competition and customer response largely immaterial. For example, large public utilities set prices on a cost-plus basis to achieve targeted profit returns acceptable to regulatory boards.

ESTABLISHING PRICING OBJECTIVES, POLICIES, AND STRATEGIES

At Merton, however, pricing of its computer systems and components was invariably perceived as a marketing function in both domestic and global markets. Reflecting this perception, the following approach was used to establish pricing objectives, policies, and strategies.

• *ESTABLISH PRICING OBJECTIVES*

Typically, pricing objectives are based on the following external and internal considerations:

- **External considerations:** How customers perceive the offering, costs involved in delivering the offering to customers, and prices of competitive offerings.

- **Internal considerations:** Company mission, and business objectives deriving from this mission (for example, Merton's expensive, blue-chip image), company resources (for example, financial, marketing, and manufacturing), and the nature of the product (for example, easy to distinguish from competitive models).

Based on an assessment of these and related considerations, price planning typically sets out to achieve one or more of the following objectives:

TARGETED RETURNS

Targeted return objectives, used by both distributors and manufacturers, specify a percentage dollar return on either sales or investment. For example, retailers and wholesalers set a percentage markup on sales large enough to cover anticipated operating costs plus a desired profit. Target return on investment pricing refers to the practice of pegging a price at a level that achieves a specified after-tax return on invested capital. Common ROI targets are typically between 10 and 30 percent after taxes, with lower returns usually set in response to competition, higher returns when little competition is anticipated.

In larger multinational and global companies, a target return on investment objective simplifies measuring and controlling the performance of many divisions and departments, all of which use capital. It can also simplify the pricing process. Over time many firms learn that their investments have earned a certain average rate of return, which becomes the target rate desired for new product introductions. This emphasis on mandated profit return, however, can obscure other important factors affecting pricing decisions and is often cited as a reason for the lackluster performance of some firms against companies willing to sacrifice short-term profits for larger long-run profits.

MARKET SHARE LEADERSHIP

Market share leadership goals usually forego initial profits for larger, long-range profits by pricing products below the market to achieve a strong market position. In this entrenched leadership position, firms benefit from mass market economies of scale, whereas competitors (for example, Pepsi versus Coca-Cola or Goodrich versus Goodyear) are forced to play a more expensive game of catch-up. Leader firms are also better positioned to increase prices, later, to make up for early low prices.

PRODUCT QUALITY LEADERSHIP

Product quality leadership objectives typically require high introductory prices to connote product quality to target market members. Customer perceptions are a key consideration in achieving this objective. If the product's prestige image drops below its high price, sales and profits will also drop.

OTHER PRICING OBJECTIVES

Other objectives that pricing strategies and tactics can help achieve include (1) helping to sell other products (e.g., a supermarket's low price for Perdue chickens attracts customers who pay higher prices for other products) and (2) helping to survive (for example, in the face of too much capacity or competition or too few customers, an airline's "Super Saver" ticket prices, while not profitable, at least ensure a sufficiently large number of passengers and dollars to cover fuel costs and flight personnel salaries).

• *UNDERSTAND DEMAND BEHAVIOR*

Market Focus 15-1 illustrates the importance of consumer perceptions as a determinant of value, overriding considerations of cost and inherent quality.

MARKET FOCUS 15-1

How Customer Perceptions Define Quality and Price

A 1991 survey by *Popular Mechanics* found that many U.S. car buyers say they would rather buy American than Japanese if the cars were similar. What happens when indeed the Japanese and American cars are not only similar but identical?

The Plymouth Lazer and the Mitsubishi Eclipse are identical sports coupes built by Diamondstar Motors (a 50-50 partnership between Chrysler and Mitsubishi). Whatever the nameplate, the car sold for $11,000 for a basic model, around $17,500 for a souped-up version, in 1991. Sales, however, were not the same. In 1990, Chrysler's 3000 dealers sold 40,000 Lasers whereas Mitsubishi's 500 dealers sold 50,000 Eclipses. That astounding difference says a lot about the image problem facing American-made cars. "People perceive the Japanese car to be of better quality. It is a lot easier to sell than a Laser," says Ira Rosenberg, the owner of adjoining Plymouth and Mitsubishi dealerships in Crystal Lake, Illinois.

Source: John Harris, "Advantage, Mitsubishi," *Forbes,* March 18, 1991, p.100.

Basic to an understanding of pricing policies and strategies best calculated to achieve pricing objectives is an understanding of how these consumer perceptions manifest themselves in demand curve behavior. If, for example, prospective customers perceived an MM system to be unique and necessary, then Merton price planners might adopt a strategy of pricing them well in excess of what it actually takes to make and market them. Alternately, if MM systems are perceived as no different from competitive makes, such a pricing strategy could kill the MM's competitive chances.

To illustrate the relationship between customer perceptions of product values and prices, assume the demand schedules shown in Figure 15-1 as depicting relationships between price and demand for MM systems. Note that the demand pattern for MM systems depicted in this schedule slopes upward from (P^1, Q^1), through (P^2, Q^2), to point (P^3, Q^1). Thus, up to point (P^2, Q^2), demand for the MM actually increases, even though its price is also increasing. Even at point (P^3, Q^1), where price is three times as high as at point (P^1, Q^1), demand is still at least as strong.

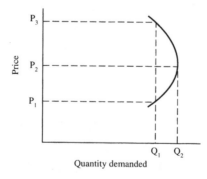

Figure 15–1. Demand schedule for MM systems.

Economists express this relationship between price and quantity sold in terms of **elasticity coefficients** that result from dividing the percentage change in quantity by the percentage change in price:

$$\text{Elasticity coefficient } E = \frac{\%\ \text{change in } Q}{\%\ \text{change in } P}$$

Inelastic demand schedules, as illustrated in the preceding example, are reflected in a coefficient of less than 1 (for example, an increase in price doesn't result in a proportional decrease in sales). Inelastic demand characterizes products that people want and that have few substitutes, for which buyers do not readily notice a higher price, or find such a price justified. A doctor's bill, for example, might fit these criteria. From the perspective of a price planner, such a desirable demand pattern suggests high profit potential through higher prices without declining sales.

Products with many substitutes not perceived as necessities exhibit an **elastic demand pattern,** where the elasticity coefficient is greater than 1, and lower prices are favored. For example, with the advent of sub-$1000 computers (a percentage decrease in P), sales increased dramatically to the point where they accounted for half of all U.S. computer sales by 1999.

Another important variable in determining the price of a product is the amount of this product that a seller is willing or able to make available at different prices (see the supply curve). For example, at low, unprofitable prices, Merton would probably make fewer MMs available than at high, profitable prices, although eventually a limit on the amount Merton could make available would be reached, regardless of price.

When a demand curve, like DE in Figure 15-2, is superimposed on a supply curve AB, an equilibrium point (F) is reached at which the quantity and price sellers are willing to offer equal the quantity and price buyers are willing to accept. This is the product's market price.

• *UNDERSTAND COMPETITIVE PRICES*

Since all marketing-oriented pricing policies and strategies assume that product prices will be pegged in relation to competitive price levels, understanding competitive prices is a necessary step in the price-planning process.

In cases where Merton planned to introduce MM systems into markets where no competition existed, information on competitive prices had to be deduced or envisioned. Surveys among prospective customers and focus group interviews provided useful clues as to the worth consumers placed on MM product/service values (as well as data on which to develop demand schedules described earlier in this chapter). Supplementing these surveys and interviews, Merton planners also used the substitute method, involving careful analyses of products similar to the product being introduced. For example, in one prospective entry market, average per student cost of professional training was used as a surrogate for purchases of MM systems featuring professional training software.

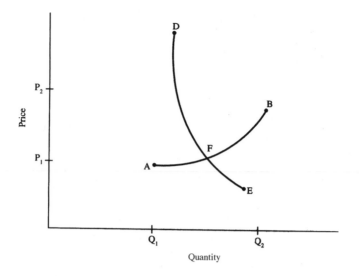

Figure 15–2. Equilibrium of supply and demand.

• *UNDERSTAND COST BEHAVIOR*

Price planning in all markets must also account for the following kinds of costs involved in making and marketing products:

- **Fixed costs (FC),** such as rent, taxes, and executive salaries, remain constant regardless of how many product units are produced.

- **Average fixed costs (AFC)** are fixed costs divided by the number of units produced. The more MMs produced, the less the average fixed cost assigned to each MM. For example, if it costs $1,000,000 in fixed costs to set up production for the MM, and 10,000 are produced, each would be allocated an average of $100 in fixed costs.

- **A variable cost (VC)** is a cost directly related to production; when production stops, so do these costs. Material costs or sales commissions are examples of variable costs, which can be controlled in the short run by simply changing the level of production.

- **Average variable cost (AVC)** is total variable cost divided by number of units produced. Usually high for the first few units produced, AVC decreases as production increases owing to various economies of scale. For example, after a time, production workers would learn to assemble more MMs per hour, and salespeople could sell more in a given day. Eventually, however, a point would be reached where AVC would begin to move up as existing facilities reached capacity and new facilities (a new factory, for example) would be required.

- **Total cost (TC)** is the sum of total fixed and variable costs for a specific quantity produced.

- **Average total cost (ATC)** is total cost divided by number of units produced.

- **Marginal cost (MC)** is the cost of producing each additional unit and indicates the minimum extra revenue that should be generated by each additional unit. It is usually equal to the variable cost of producing the last unit.

The interrelationships among these costs is graphically displayed in Figure 15-3, which shows how each changes with changes in quantities produced. Note that all these costs drop over the quantity output range and then begin to rise at different quantity levels. Also note that marginal cost per unit begins to rise at a lower level of output than average variable cost and then intersects AVC and ATC curves from below at their low points and then rises rapidly. (The fact that AVC and ATC are averaged over many units keeps their rise gradual; marginal cost, the same as variable cost per unit, rises rapidly because it is assigned to a single unit.) For pricing purposes, the marginal cost per unit is the most important cost because this is the extra cost revenues must cover. Thus, to optimize profits in manufacturing, the firm should produce that level of output where marginal cost is just less than or equal to marginal revenue (the revenue brought in by the last unit sold). All units produced up to this point have been profitable, and the accumulated profits represent the most the company can expect to make on the product.

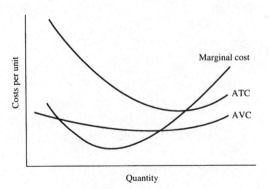

Figure 15-3. How unit costs change as quantity increases.

Figure 15-4 shows another important cost consideration for establishing prices over the product life cycle. Although cost curves trend upward in the short range, these curves trend downward over the long range, as production experience (the learning curve) and more efficient production equipment and methods lock into place.

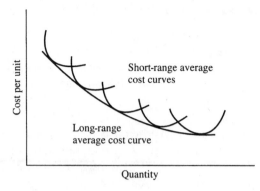

Figure 15–4. Long-range cost curves curve downward.

HOW POLITICAL / LEGAL CLIMATES AFFECT PRICING

In Chapters 4 and 5, we examined a diversity of government policies, statutes, and regulations that restrain or encourage trade. As they relate to pricing, these initiatives have a direct impact on two areas: (1) transfer pricing; and (2) pricing legislation that mandates when, where, and how prices can be changed or maintained.

TRANSFER PRICING

Transfer pricing refers to the price charged for moving goods among profit centers (any part of an organization to which revenues and controllable costs can be assigned, such as a department or distribution center). In setting these prices, planners must decide whether they should encompass only costs directly associated with making the product, or include other, indirect costs such as overhead and a profit margin. In the domestic market, a producer like Merton generally designs transfer pricing policies that motivate divisional managers to achieve divisional goals while contributing to overall company goals. For example, if Merton's transportation cost for transferring MMs to subsidiary A on the West Coast is twice what it is for East Coast subsidiary B, an adjustment will be made to make the transfer price paid by each comparable, and competitive, in each marketplace. Implicit in this arrangement is the assumption that each subsidiary, by being able to price the MMs competitively, will be motivated to sell sufficient quantities to compensate for adjustments to the transfer price.

PRICING LEGISLATION

Pricing legislation generally encompasses laws and regulations in the following areas that influence prices to both ultimate and intermediate customers over the course of product life cycles.

• *PRICE CONTROLS*

Price controls, either mandated by legislative processes or encouraged by legislated policies, typically result from combinations in restraint of trade between and among manufacturers and distributors that are tolerated much more in foreign than in domestic markets. In the domestic market, price fixing, in collusion with competitors, is illegal except when carried out under government supervision, such as in regulated transportation industries.

• *PRICE DISCRIMINATION*

Price discrimination, or offering different prices to buyers at the same trade level (for example, all wholesalers of MMs in the same sales volume category) is illegal in the United States under the Robinson-Patman Act (1936) unless price differences are (1) cost justified (for example, by economies a manufacturer realizes by selling in larger quantities to larger customers), (2) made in a good faith attempt to meet lower competitive prices, or (3) not harmful to competitors.

• *PRICE INCREASES*

Price increases in the domestic market are generally unregulated, except for public utilities, with companies free to raise prices at will.

• *COMPETITIVE PRICING TACTICS*

Other areas of pricing legislation pertain to pricing tactics that tend to restrain trade, including: (1) resale price maintenance, or the illegal requirement by manufacturers that dealers charge specified resale prices; (2) minimum pricing legislation, requiring that sellers not sell below cost in an intent to destroy competition; and (3) deceptive pricing legislation, which forbids, among other things, false claims that prices were reduced from former levels, and unverified claims that a firm's price is lower than other prices in the trading area. Predatory pricing, in which an incumbent firm apparently tries to drive out newer, smaller rivals with aggressive pricing, is difficult to prove because federal law requires demonstrating that the alleged predator prices below an appropriate measure of its average cost and that it had a reasonable expectation of recouping its losses.

INTERNATIONAL PERSPECTIVE

The complex task of pricing products in domestic markets is further comp-licated in global markets, where an array of economic, logistical, political, cultural, and legal considerations must be accounted for. In international markets, these pricing considerations focus mainly on issues pertaining to cost behavior, transfer pricing, currency valuations, escrow requirements, dumping regulations, and price legislation.

HOW COST CONSIDERATIONS AFFECT GLOBAL PRICING DECISIONS

In highly competitive international markets, an understanding of the nature and behavior of costs associated with making and marketing products at dif-ferent price and demand levels is important for establishing initial prices and modifying these prices over the product life cycle.

In general, export-related costs fall into three categories: (1) costs of mod-ifying the product offering for global markets; (2) costs for operating the export function (personnel, marketing research, shipping and insurance, overseas promotional costs, foreign communication costs etc.); and (3) entry costs (tariffs, taxes, commercial, political, and foreign exchange risks).

Table 15-1 illustrates the extent of price escalation that can occur in ex-porting a product that retails for $12 in the domestic market. Four different scenarios are offered, all including a CIF (cost + insurance + freight) and a 20 percent tariff on the CIF cost. Beyond this common cost, additional costs are added for each scenario for things like a value-added tax, an im-porter's margin, and various margins for distributors. Note that the least costly scenario increases the domestic retail price by 70 percent; the most costly increases it by 275 percent.

Because exporter costs tend to appreciate dramatically over their domes-tic counterparts, an effective cost accounting system is a must for identifying and applying all costs involved in making, marketing, and moving products into and through global channels. Without an understanding of the nature and extent of these costs, marketers can't determine the profit conse-quences of prices pegged at, above, or below competitive prices, nor can they accurately find ways to bring costs in line with those of advantaged competitors.

Table 15-1. Export Price Escalation

International Marketing Channel Elements and Cost Factors	Domestic Wholesale-Retail Channel	Case 1 Same as Domestic with Direct Wholesale Import CIF/Tariff	Case 2 Same as Case 1 with Foreign Importer Added to Channel	Case 3 Sames as Case 2 with VAT Added	Case 4 Same as Case 3 with Local Foreign Jobber Added to Channel
Manufacturer's net price	6.00	6.00	6.00	6.00	6.00
+Insurance and shipping cost (CIF)	—	2.50	2.50	2.50	2.50
=Landed cost (CIF value)	—	8.50	8.50	8.50	8.50
+Tariff (20% on CIF value)	—	1.70	1.70	1.70	1.70
=Importer's cost (CIF value + tariff)	—	10.20	10.20	10.20	10.20
+Importer's margin (25% on cost)	—	—	2.55	2.55	2.55
+VAT (16% on full cost plus margin)	—	—	—	2.04	2.04
=Wholesaler's cost (=importer's price)	6.00	10.20	12.75	14.79	14.79
+Wholesaler's margin (33⅓% on cost)	2.00	3.40	4.25	4.93	4.93
+VAT (16% on margin)	—	—	—	.79	.79
=Local foreign jobber's cost (=wholesale price)	—	—	—	—	20.51
+Jobber's margin (33⅓% on cost)	—	—	—	—	6.84
+VAT (16% on margin)	—	—	—	—	1.09
=Retailer's cost (= wholesale or jobber price)	8.00	13.60	17.00	20.51	28.44
+Retailer's margin (50% on cost)	4.00	6.80	8.50	10.26	14.22
+VAT (16% on margin)	—	—	—	1.64	2.28
=Retail price (what consumer pays)	12.00	20.40	25.50	32.41	44.94
Percentage price escalation over domestic		70%	113%	170%	275%
Percentage price escalation over Case 1			25%	59%	120%
Percentage price escalation over Case 2				27%	76%
Percentage price escalation over Case 3					39%

Bringing Escalating Global Costs in Line

Following are some of the approaches a company might explore to reduce escalating costs for such factors as international transportation and distributors in entry countries demanding special price concessions:

- Search the firm's international manufacturing system to identify potentially lower cost sources of materials and methods;

- Audit the exiting distribution system to identify less costly alternative intermediaries, or greater efficiencies and economies in physical distribution systems and procedures;

- Make use of other marketing mix elements; for example, design a simplified, but suitable, version of the product to sell at a competitive price, or modify the product offering to bring it in under a lower tariff classification (it's often possible to get a lower classification—called a **duty drawback**—by importing components and materials used in the manufacture of the exported product from the importing country). It might also be possible to develop a promotional campaign to persuade target market members that the higher price is justified in terms of benefits to them not otherwise available (for example, AT&T's campaign to convince prospective users that superior quality and service justify the higher rates they pay).

TRANSFER PRICING AND TAX-TARIFF GAMES

In domestic markets, transfer pricing, as noted earlier, typically applies to goods shipped among divisions of the same company, with limited objectives—usually to help managers compete more effectively on price and achieve divisional sales and profit goals—and little legal exposure.

In the global marketplace, however, a new set of considerations enters into transfer pricing formulas because of differential tax and tariff constraints. To illustrate, assume country A has a moderately high tariff, but a low tax rate on exports, whereas country B has a slightly lower tariff but an extremely high tax rate on exports. In this situation, it might profit an exporter to charge a lower transfer price to its country A affiliate, assuming that the high profits realized would be taxed at a much lower rate than in country B, where the high transfer price might eliminate any profits to be taxed. And profits from country A would more than offset higher tariffs charged there. This was the reasoning of Hoffman LaRoche, which charged its low-tax Italian subsidiary only $22 a kilo for librium, while charging its high-tax British subsidiary $925 per kilo, effectively eliminating any profits to be taxed.

Hoffman LaRoche's experience illustrates one important reason why companies are generally trending away from this accounting game of balancing tax and tariff consequences in pegging transfer prices. The British government—which, like all governments, has the right to reallocate income and expenses—sued the company for back taxes and won. All industrialized countries now carefully review situations where transfer pricing seems based primarily on tax/tariff tradeoffs (Section 482 of the U.S. tax code is devoted in its entirety to the subject), and just the idea of the expense and bother entailed in defending this practice is sufficient to deter many companies. Global Focus 15-1 examines how governments are acting—and companies reacting—with respect to legal and legislative initiatives designed to curb transfer pricing abuses.

GLOBAL FOCUS 15-1

PENALIZING TRANSFER PRICING ABUSES: ACTIONS AND REACTIONS

The U.S. Internal Revenue Service (IRS) has begun to look more closely at transfer pricing on sales of goods and services among subsidiaries or between subsidiaries and the parent company. It has filed claims against hundreds of companies in recent years, claiming that multinational companies too often manipulate intracompany pricing to minimize their worldwide tax bills. Experts calculate that foreign-based multinationals evade at least $20 billion in U.S. taxes. Other countries have also strengthened their review systems. Japan has created specific transfer pricing legislation that penalizes marketers for not providing information in time to meet deadlines set by the government. German tax authorities are carefully checking intracompany charges to deem their appropriateness.

In its biggest known victory, the IRS made its case that Japan's Toyota had been systematically overcharging its U.S. subsidiary for years on most of the cars, trucks, and parts sold in the United States. What would have been profits in the United States were now accrued in Japan. Toyota denied improprieties but agreed to a reported $1–billion settlement.

Increasing communication among tax authorities is having a dramatic effect and will continue to accelerate, especially with the trend toward shifting profits. Historically, transfer pricing from the point of view of a U.S. company meant the shifting of income out of the United States, but with the corporate tax rate at 34 percent, many U.S. multinationals must be prepared to justify transfer pricing on two or more fronts.

> The entire tax equation has become more complicated because of changes in customs duties. In many countries, revenues from customs and indirect taxes are greater than revenue from corporate taxes. Authorities will zealously guard the income stream from customs taxes, and marketers could find gains on income taxes erased by losses on customs taxes.
>
> *Source:* "Pricing Yourself into a Market," *Business Asia,* December 21, 1992, p. 1.

Another deterrent to transfer pricing abuses is the trend, fostered by economic communities, toward global equalization of tax rates; still another deterrent is the realization that motivation and resource allocation benefits of transfer pricing based on competitive market conditions usually offset benefits from playing tax/tariff games. (As an example of how such manipulations can distort normal marketing processes, the manager of a foreign affiliate kept receiving big bonuses for extraordinary profit performance until his firm realized his profits were largely a byproduct of the firm's policy of charging artificially low transfer prices into, and high transfer prices out of, his country.)

CURRENCY VALUATION THREATS AND OPPORTUNITIES

Currency valuations include both devaluation and revaluations of a country's currency. **Devaluation** means reducing the value of a country's currency relative to currencies of other countries. For example, if the number of Japanese yen required to purchase an American dollar—and products financed by dollars—falls from 200 to 100, then that is the extent to which the dollar has been devalued in Japan. The effect of devaluation is the same as reducing prices of exported products by the amount of the devaluation, although prices in the home country aren't affected.

Another effect is to increase sales of devalued products in foreign countries, and productivity, investment, and employment at home. The devaluing country's balance of payments is also usually improved, as the value of exports exceeds the value of imports.

Still another effect of devaluation is to increase the cost of products sold in the devaluing country, now priced in more expensive foreign currency. Indeed, to the extent that products exported from the devaluing country include foreign-made components, devalued prices will be increased. For example, American computers sold in Japan in the early 1990s, when the dollar was devalued versus the yen, were less of a price bargain if they contained more expensive Japanese microchips.

Revaluation is devaluation in reverse; instead of decreasing in value relative to the currencies of other countries, the value of a country's currency increases. Thus, exports become more expensive and less competitive, and the advantages of devaluation turn into disadvantages: sales and productivity decline, and the balance of payments tilts against the revaluing country.

Marketers on the wrong side of a currency valuation change—for example, competing in an importing country against the devalued products of an exporter, or in a foreign devaluing country with revalued prices—face difficult pricing decisions. If the marketed product has a strong, safe competitive position, it might be possible to pass the revalued price increase on to the customer. Otherwise, options include sourcing from the devaluing country (as the Honda automobile company did when, in 1993, it announced that 90 percent of its automobile parts would be manufactured in the United States), absorbing cost increases by reducing prices to meet devalued competition, and/or reducing marketing and operating costs.

Beginning in the mid-1980s, when the U.S. dollar began a long decline against many worldwide currencies, researchers got a good idea of how countries actually do respond on either side of the devaluation equation:

- U.S. exporters, whose products were now less expensive in importing countries, generally lowered foreign-currency-denominated prices to improve their competitive positions;

- Foreign manufacturers (such as Japan) have, on average, absorbed about half of the decline in the trading value of their currencies.

Other strategies employed by countries facing the competition of a devalued currency include: (1) change to markets where a better exchange ratio exists (for example, Germany refocuses sales of Mercedes and BMWs from the United States to Japan); (2) push products that are generally immune to the competitive effects of devaluation (for example, U.S. oil field service companies sell in the Mid- and Far East regardless of currency value fluctuations); or (3) set up manufacturing operations in the devaluing country (for example, Honda in the United States).

To illustrate other strategies to protect companies against adverse exchange rate fluctuations, assume an exchange rate of $1 = 2.10 German Marks (DM), and that a German exporter to the United States agrees to accept $250,000, to be paid in 90 days, for a shipment of computer parts, valued at 525,000 DM ($250,000 × 2.10). However, in 90 days, the value of the dollar has dropped to 2 DM, meaning the German exporter loses 50,000 DM on the deal ($250,000 × 2).

One protective strategy the German exporter could have used would have been to quote prices in German currency, thereby insuring receipt of the dollar equivalent of 525,000 DM at the end of 90 days. Because this tactic passes the risk of devaluation to the buyer, however, it isn't always possible.

Some foreign governments insist on quotations in their own currencies, and many foreign buyers have the leverage to mandate these quotations.

Another protective strategy is for the exporter to insist on shorter terms when negotiating with countries with a history of shaky currencies. In this case, if the German seller had insisted on payment in 15 instead of 90 days, there would probably be less likelihood that the dollar would have devaluated by the amount it did.

Still another protective strategy for companies exporting to countries with fluttering exchange rates is through the **forward exchange market** whereby, for a premium, a bank guarantees that an exporter will be paid at an agreed upon exchange rate. In the preceding example, regardless of the fluctuation of the dollar versus the DM, the German exporter would be paid at the $1 = 2.10 DM exchange rate at the end of 90 days. Of course, if the value at that time was $1 = 2.20 DM, the exporter would swallow the loss.

ESCROW REQUIREMENTS TIE UP EARNING POTENTIAL

Escrow requirements typically require exporters to tie up money that would otherwise be earning income as the price of doing business in a foreign country. Consider the following examples.

- **Cash deposit requirements** mandating that an exporter has to tie up funds, equal to a percent of anticipated profits in an importing country, for a specified time period.

- **Profit transfer rules,** which restrict conditions under which profits may be transferred out of the country.

In both these situations, transfer pricing manipulation can be a way of reducing deposit requirements or transferring profits out of the country.

DUMPING: HARD TO DEFINE AND PROVE

Dumping is defined by the U.S. Congress as "unfair price cutting having as its objective the injury, destruction, or prevention of the establishment of American industry" and includes price differentials resulting from sales of imports on the U.S. market at prices either below those of comparable domestic goods or below those in the producing country. Thus, for example, Japan could be penalized for dumping motorcycles in the United States if it could be proven that they cost consumers less here then they cost

Japanese consumers, or were priced lower than comparable American motorcycles. Sometimes, a dumping charge is the unintended result of a firm's attempt to manipulate transfer payments in its favor, or respond to an unfavorable currency devaluation in a foreign market. More likely, a firm will dump products to achieve a larger, faster share of a foreign market or to remove excess inventory and maintain price stability in its home market.

What makes dumping difficult to prove is generating evidence, in the face of shifting currency valuations, that the product did, indeed, cost more in the home country or, in the face of the exporters' efforts to differentiate their products, that there is anything comparable in the importing country. Additionally, both price discrimination and injury must be proven. (The International Trade Commission did find the Japanese firms of Honda and Kawasaki guilty of dumping motorcycles on the U.S. marketplace and imposed a special five-year tariff, between 1983 and 1988, that began at 45 percent.)

The GATT definition of dumping is less expansive, defining the practice as selling the product in a member importing country at a price less than the price at which it left the exporting country. "Comparable product" prices in the importing country aren't an issue.

Some dumping is continuous—for example, government-subsidized farm products sold on international markets for less than in the domestic market—and some is sporadic. Sporadic dumping tends to be more disruptive because it is difficult to anticipate and plan for. Some firms, to avoid the penalties of dumping without sacrificing the benefits, make nonprice arrangements with affiliates and distributors as incentives to flood their markets. For example, generous discounts or credit extension arrangements can have the same effect as a generous price reduction on the open market.

PRICING LEGISLATION

Pricing legislation and regulations pertaining to price controls, price discrimination, and price increases are much more likely to influence price planning in offshore than in domestic markets.

• *PRICE CONTROLS*

Price controls, mandated by legislative processes, are much more common in foreign than in domestic markets. Sometimes, surplus production of such raw materials as coffee, oil, tin, and rubber motivates these controls; often, they are imposed in an effort to control a runaway inflation or to redress a shortage of foreign exchange. Frequently, they result from combinations in restraint of trade between and among foreign manufacturers and wholesalers that are tolerated much more in foreign than in domestic markets. (In the domestic market, price fixing, in collusion with competitors, is illegal except when carried out under the supervision of a government agency, such as in regulated transportation industries.)

Recognizing the threat represented by these foreign combinations and cartels to American trade, Congress passed the Webb-Pomerene Act in 1918, which helps U.S. exporters compete with large European cartels by combining to share costs of export operations to reap common rewards. The act exempts companies in these "Webb-Pomerene" associations from the normal strictures of antitrust legislation and enforcement. As of 1992, only 22 Webb-Pomerene associations actively existed, accounting for less than 2 percent of U.S. exports and casting doubt as to their general efficacy. A better strategy for contesting the effects of price controls is through petitioning regulatory authorities. Generally, arguments for relief from price controls demonstrate that the petitioning firm isn't achieving sufficient return on investment to justify continued investment and production.

• *PRICE DISCRIMINATION*

Price discrimination, or offering different prices to buyers at the same trade level (for example, all wholesalers of MMs in the same sales volume category) is illegal in the United States but not in many other countries. Thus, arrangements with channel members to gain competitive advantage through price incentives are often more feasible in these countries (a universally legal form of price discrimination is discussed in Chapter 16).

• *PRICE INCREASES*

Price increases in the domestic market are generally unregulated, except for public utilities, with companies free to raise prices at will. This isn't always the case in global markets, and firms should look for exceptions in planning pricing strategies.

Other areas of pricing legislation, discussed earlier, that companies should investigate in planning global pricing strategies pertain to: (1) resale price maintenance, or the requirement that dealers charge specified resale prices; (2) minimum pricing legislation, requiring that sellers not sell below cost in an intent to destroy competition; and (3) deceptive pricing legislation, which forbids false claims that prices were reduced from former levels and unverified claims that a firm's price is lower than other prices in the trading area. Generally, legislation and regulations in these areas in foreign markets is less codified and restrictive than in the U.S. domestic market.

CHAPTER PERSPECTIVE

The price of a product influences how customers perceive it, how profitable it will be, and how it should be positioned, promoted, and distributed. The complex challenge of pegging the "best" prices for different segments of markets entails formulating productive pricing objectives, policies, and strategies and implies a sophisticated understanding of how costs, customers, competitors, and legislatures behave.

KNOW THE CONCEPTS
TERMS FOR STUDY

Cost behavior

Cost curves

Currency valuations

Demand schedule

Devaluation

Dumping

Elasticity coefficients

Escrow requirements

Exchange rates

Forward exchange market

Marginal cost

Market price

Market share leadership

Price controls

Price discrimination

Price escalation

Price increases

Price legislation

Pricing objectives

Pricing policies

Pricing strategies

Product quality leadership

Revaluation

Supply-demand

Target return objectives

Transfer pricing

MATCHUP EXERCISES

1. Match up the price-related marketing objectives in the first column with the corporate actions in the second column.

1. market share leadership	a. During market doldrums, automobile dealers price below cost and offer large rebates.
2. survival	b. Mercedes Benz, however, refuses to cut its price.
3. product quality leadership	c. Anticipating economic doldrums during good times, appliance dealers stop discounting.
4. current profit maximization	d. Fuji achieves a strong market position by pricing its photographic equipment below the market price.

2. Match up the price-type in the first column with the quote in the second column.

1. market price	a. "If we can get $100 apiece for these cellular phones, we'll market half a million of them."
2. inelastic price	b. "I know he charges $300 an hour, but he's worth it."

3. transfer price

   c. "We'll charge our Japanese subsidiary $40 a liter."

4. devalued price

   d. "We'll give Wal-Mart a bigger discount than we give K-Mart because we need their business more."

5. discriminatory price

   e. "Better stock up—French wine will never be this cheap again."

3. Match up the cost-type in the first column with the descriptor in the second column.

1. fixed costs

   a. total cost divided by number of units sold

2. variable costs

   b. what it costs to produce that last widget

3. average total cost

   c. remains constant no matter how many units are produced

4. marginal cost

   d. directly related to production and marketing

QUESTIONS FOR REVIEW AND DISCUSSION

1. A three-part exercise based on the assumption that you are going into business for the summer selling submarine sandwiches from a roadside stand.

a. Using the formula $S = P \times U$ (Sales volume = Price × Number of units sold), what is your sales volume if you sell 1000 submarines during the month of July at a cost of $2 per sub?

b. Using the formula $NP = S - CGS - E$ (Net profit = Sales volume − Cost of goods sold − Expenses), how much profit will you make if the ingredients in each sandwich cost $1, and your total expenses for the season (mainly expenses involved in selling and delivering the subs) totaled $500?

c. Assume that there was such a demand for your subs that you discovered you could increase the price of each to $2.20 without losing sales. By what percentage would your net profits have increased if this had been the price throughout the season?

2. What do the exercises in question 1 say about the role of price in influencing consumer perceptions, sales, profits, and other marketing mix elements?

3. Hewlett-Packard, a $16 billion company that produces technical products for business and dominates the high-quality, high-price end of the hand calculator market, achieves competitive advantage in selected markets based on customer perceptions of unique, high-value products worth their high price. Presently, Hewlett-Packard, with a workforce of 15,000 in Asia and sales of $3 billion, is embarking on market growth strategies in Japan and Malasia. Discuss the relationship between Hewlett-Packard's high quality/price image and the following aspects of its market growth strategy: (1) target market selection; (2) product/place/promotion elements of its marketing mix.

4. On the accompanying graph, identify the following depicting supply-demand relationships defining the entry of Merton Mighty Mind computer systems into a selected market: line DE, line AB, point F. What are the strategic implications of this information to Merton's marketing manager?

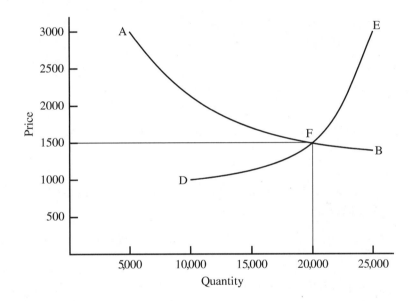

5. The following table shows price escalation generated in shipping 1908 cases of assorted chemicals, weighing 35,000 pounds, from Kansas City to Encarnacion, Paraguay. Note that the price of the shipment has more than doubled in transit. Discuss three ways in which the final retail price might be made more competitive.

Item			As a Percentage of F.O.B. Price
F.O.B. Kansas City		$10,090	100%
Freight to New Orleans	$ 110		
Freight to Encarnación, Paraguay	1,897		
Counselor invoices	21		
Forwarding fee	8		
Insurance ($19,000 value)	383		
Port charge	434		
Documentation	3		
Total shipping charges		2,856	28
C.I.F. value		$12,946	
Duty (20% on C.I.F. value)		2,584	26
Distributor markup (10%)		1,547	15
Dealer markup (25%)		4,289	43
Total retail price		$21,384	212%

6. Define the following costs involved in printing a newspaper:

- The cost of renting the printing plant;

- The cost of extra paper and dyes purchased to print an "extra" edition of the newspaper;

- The cost of producing the last newspaper comprising the "Extra" edition;

- The sum of all costs divided by the number of newspapers produced.

Which of these costs defines the point at which additional copies produced will no longer produce a profit? How does price fit into this equation?

7. Motorola, the world's fourth largest semiconductor manufacturer, opened a multi-million-dollar chip manufacturing plant in Hong Kong, in expectation of supplying the entire $16 billion Pacific rim market for semiconductors by the year 2002. Interpret the long-range cost curve, below, in terms of what it depicts and how it will affect Motorola's pricing strategy for its semiconductors.

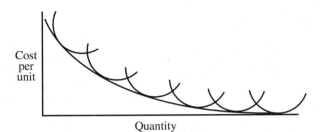

Cost
per
unit

Quantity

8. In selling its semiconductors to its Asian customers, would it be more desirable if the exchange rate of the U.S. dollar falls, or rises, against that of the Oriental currency? What measures could Motorola take to protect itself against the less desirable situation?

ANSWERS
MATCHUP EXERCISES

1. 1d, 2a, 3b, 4c
2. 1a, 2b, 3c, 4e, 5d
3. 1c, 2d, 3a, 4b

QUESTIONS FOR REVIEW AND DISCUSSION

1. a. Sales volume = $2 × 1000 = $2000
   b. Net profit = $2000 − $1000 − $500 = $500
   c. Net profit increase = $2200 − $1000 − 500 = $700 ($200 more)
$$\frac{\$\ 200}{\$\ 500} = 40\%$$

2. The fact that the price of the subs could be raised without lowering sales shows that customers perceived product values to be worth more than the $2.00 price you charged for each sub. The perception of the subs' price/quality relationship was sufficient to generate sales for your entire output. However, although price can influence sales, its impact on profits can be dramatic, as shown by the 40 percent profit increase when price was increased by 10 percent. Continued high demand at this higher price reflects consumer perceptions of all marketing mix elements comprising the sub offering, including its flavor (product), the location of your stand (place), and how you advertise your subs.

3. As it relates to target market selection, Hewlett-Packard's high-price/high-quality strategy focuses marketing efforts on small selected markets whose members can afford H-P's unique, high-value products. Target marketing at H-P also involves continual monitoring of market members to measure customer satisfaction (John Young, H-P's former CEO, notes that nine of ten customers who rank themselves highly satisfied purchase from H-P again, a highly profitable result in light of Young's estimates that it costs five times as much to gain as to keep a customer). With respect to the relationship between H-P's high price and the other marketing mix elements, here are some effects. Product: Research and development, advanced product design, and "zero defects" quality control help H-P maintain a quality level perceived to justify its pricing strategy. In its move to expand its Asian market, for example, H-P, since 1991, has streamlined its manufacturing, project management, and design capabilities in Asia. Place: To a much lesser extent than is the case with lower-end price competitors, H-P's products are most likely to be sold directly to customers, rather than through mass market outlets; this personalized service is considered a part of the price customers are paying for H-P products. Promotion: Although H-P does not centralize advertising strategy or implementation—delegating most product-related advertising to overseas business units who are encouraged to be guided by local trends and cultures—all promotion campaigns are constrained by companywide identification and design standards that reflect H-P's high-quality/high-price image.

4. Line DE on the graph is a supply curve that depicts the quantity of MM computer systems that Merton would be prepared to make available at different prices. For example, at the $3000 price (point E), Merton would be willing to reorder its production priorities and resources among its various product lines to make 25,000 units available (note that this isn't many more than the 24,000 units Merton would be willing to make available at the profitable $2500 price, at which level of production the firm begins to run out of capacity and resources to produce more units). AB is a demand curve, indicating the number of MM systems customers would be willing to purchase at different price levels. At a $3000 price (point A), Merton's research indicates that only 8000 customers would buy Mighty Mind systems, for an overall sales volume of $24,000,000. Then, as the price gets lower, more customers purchase MM systems, with the number reaching 20,000 at the $1500 price, for an overall sales volume of $30,000,000. The fact that sales volume increases as price is lowered—at least up to a point—indicates that demand for MMs in this particular market is elastic. In another market, where the MM is perceived as both unique and necessary, demand might exhibit an inelastic pattern, where sales volume increases as the MM's price increases. Point F, where supply and demand curves intersect, is called the equilibrium point, or market price, where what people will buy just equals what the seller is willing to offer. From a marketer's perspective, understanding supply-demand relationships is critically important in devising product, price, place, and promotion marketing mix

strategies. For example, if supply-demand analyses showed Merton's marketing manager that the MM exhibited an inelastic demand curve, she would price it high to optimize profit return and base positioning and promotion strategies on this high-price/high-quality image. In any event, she would avoid the mistake of pricing the MM too high for the market (point E) or too low (point D).

5. Three ways whereby the retail price of this shipment of assorted chemicals might be made more competitive at its destination include any or all of the following: (1) begin with a lower price at F.O.B. Kansas City. This could be done if the seller uses a marginal pricing strategy—assuming fixed costs have already been captured in marketing these chemicals in the U.S. domestic market—and/or relinquishes a portion of desired profit in Paraguay in order to compete more effectively; (2) source portions of this order (for example, the containers for the chemicals, or components in the chemical mix) from Paraguay, which might appreciably reduce the high duty on the chemicals; and (3) change to less costly distribution channels, if available.

6. Rental cost is a fixed cost; the extra paper and dye are variable costs; the cost of producing the last newspaper is the marginal cost; the sum of all costs divided by the number of newspapers produced is average total cost. Marginal cost defines the point beyond which additional copies produced will no longer produce a profit; to recoup costs, revenues from this last newspaper produced must equal marginal cost. As long as marginal revenue (the additional sales volume produced by each additional newspaper run off) exceeds marginal cost (the cost of producing each additional newspaper), each newspaper produced will add to profits. Profits will be greatest where marginal cost and revenue are equal, when output equals the total profit on all newspapers produced to this point. The price to be charged for the newspaper can be induced by working back from desired profits, costs, and the planned newspaper run to reach this point.

7. The long-range cost curve depicted shows that short-range average cost curves comprising long-range costs tend to decline and then increase and that the long-range curve just declines. The short-range curves decline because learning curve efficiencies and economies of scale combine to push costs downward; the reason they then increase is because a point is eventually reached where Motorola will incur new costs (to build additional production capacity) that exceed learning curve and scale savings. However, because each short-range cost curve is lower than its predecessor, the aggregate long-range cost curve trends downward, meaning that, in spite of temporary dislocations, Motorola can afford to lower its prices over time. Personal computers, video cameras, and videocassette recorders are but a few examples of products whose prices have decreased dramatically as costs decreased and competition increased.

8. Assuming its products for export were manufactured in the domestic market, it would be more beneficial for Motorola if the exchange rate of the U.S. dollar fell against that of foreign currencies. This would mean, for example, that German marks or Japanese yen could purchase more dollars, and more products priced in dollars. For Motorola, this would mean it could afford to lower its prices below those of competitors in these countries, possibly achieving a competitive edge without sacrificing profits, because it would still be getting the same number of dollars. To protect itself from situations where the value of the dollar rises against foreign currencies, meaning it would have to lower its price to remain competitive, Motorola might use the services of the Forward Exchange Market to ensure payment in noninflated dollars or to negotiate shorter payment terms so that currency revaluations could be anticipated and countered.

16

FORMULATING PRICING STRATEGIES AND TACTICS

OVERVIEW

Pricing strategies, from cost to demand based, reflect economic and competitive climates in which prices are pegged. Supporting these basic strategies are price modification strategies that recognize differences among customers in such areas as functions performed, quantities purchased, and time of purchase and payment. In addition to setting prices, price planning involves determining terms of sale and payment and changing prices in response to competitive challenges.

PRICING STRATEGIES HELP ACHIEVE MARKETING GOALS

In Chapter 15, we examined major considerations involved in arriving at productive, profit-oriented objectives and policies that help define pricing strategies and tactics calculated to help achieve them. We also examined characteristics of markets pertaining to costs, customers, competitors, and legislation that make price planning such a difficult, complex challenge.

In this chapter, we examine a variety of price strategies employed to achieve diverse marketing goals in diverse competitive climates. We begin with cost-based pricing strategies appropriate to monopolistic and oligopolistic markets and then move on to demand- and competition-based strategies appropriate to competitive free markets. Also examined are product mix pricing strategies that deal with groups of products and product change strategies that focus on reasons and means for raising or lowering prices.

PRICING OPTIONS RESPOND TO MARKET CHALLENGES

Companies that set prices in consumer and organizational markets have a number of options over the course of a product's life cycle:

- Set cost-based prices that add a predetermined profit to computed costs;

- Set demand-based prices that link prices to consumer preferences and channel needs;

- Set competition-based prices that stress competitive prices over demand and cost considerations;

- Set product mix prices that deal with products in groups, rather than individually.

Other options include product modification and product change prices that alter prices in response to environmental challenges, such as the need to satisfy distributors or suddenly raise or lower prices.

One key point as background to this examination of pricing strategies and tactics is that titles given to these strategies are not exclusive. Thus, a cost-based strategy suggests an emphasis on cost, but doesn't preclude consideration of demand or competitive considerations. Similarly, demand- and competitive-based strategies do not exclude other factors that influence pricing strategies.

COST-BASED STRATEGIES: ROI, MARKUPS, AND BREAKEVENS

Cost-based pricing strategies, including cost-plus, markup, and breakeven pricing, are most used by companies that face little or no competition.

• *COST-PLUS PRICING*

Cost-plus pricing, the simplest method of cost-based pricing, merely adds a predetermined profit to costs. This strategy is largely used by monopolies with no competitors, such as power and light utilities and products sufficiently unique or prestigious to dominate their market. For example, in determining the price for MM systems in such markets, Merton first estimated the number of systems it would be able to sell in a certain price range over a specified time period and then added total variable and fixed costs (TVC and TFC) to total desired profit. Price was then obtained by dividing this amount by the number of systems to be produced. Thus,

$$Price = \frac{TFC + TVC + Projected\ profit}{Units\ produced}$$

To illustrate, if sales of 5000 units were projected for a given market, and Merton desired a profit of $500,000, the price of each system, given the following total fixed and variable costs, would be

$$\frac{\$1,500,000 + \$3,000,000 + \$500,000}{5000} = \$1000$$

Two problems exist with cost-plus pricing. First, it assumes that fixed and variable costs can be separated out and assigned to specific products, which often proves to be a problem. Second, it assumes that consumer demand patterns and competitive responses to prices are largely irrelevant, which doesn't always prove to be the case.

• *MARKUP PRICING*

Markup pricing, a form of cost-plus pricing, is used mainly by wholesalers and retailers, who often carry thousands of products and couldn't possibly analyze demand and competitive factors for each. A simple formula for determining product markup pegs the final price of the product equal to the purchase cost to the company divided by 1.0 minus the desired markup percentage. For example, assuming a retailer purchases an MM for $1000 and desires a markup of 40 percent, then

$$\$1000/(1 - 0.40) = \$1000/0.60 = \$1666$$

The size of a distributor's markup depends on a variety of factors including industry practices, manufacturer's list price, inventory turnover desired, effort required to compete successfully, and other available discounts discussed later in this chapter. Typically, distributors using markup pricing take consumer demand into account by dropping products that don't sell at the desired markup.

• *BREAKEVEN-POINT PRICING*

Breakeven-point pricing considers both cost and market demand to identify the point at which the firm begins to get its money back on a product. In essence, this breakeven point is the point at which total revenues (units sold times price per unit) equals total fixed and variable costs.

Breakeven points can be computed in terms of units or sales dollars:

$$\text{Breakeven point (units)} = \frac{\text{Total fixed costs}}{\text{Price} - \text{Variable costs (per unit)}}$$

$$\text{Breakeven point (sales dollars)} = 1 - \frac{\dfrac{\text{Total fixed costs}}{\text{Variable costs (per unit)}}}{\text{Price}}$$

For example, assume that Merton plans to sell MM systems in a foreign market for $1000, with $1,500,000 in fixed costs assigned to its production, and $600 in variable costs assigned to each system sold. In units, the breakeven point would be 3750 or $1,500,000 /($1000 − $600); in dollars, it would be $3,750,000 or $1,500,000 /[1 − (600/1000)]. Beyond this breakeven point, income generated represents profits. If Merton research indicates that it can easily exceed this point, it should launch the MM.

Breakeven analyses, although useful as a rough indicator of the relationship between costs, revenues, and prices, is subject to a number of limitations when used as the sole measure of these relationships. For example, it assumes that fixed costs can be precisely assigned to specific products—when many shared fixed costs can't be—and that variable costs can be clearly identified—when many semivariable costs can't be. Also, many breakeven analyses assume that total cost lines continue to rise linearly when they are much more likely to assume erratic configurations due to things like experience curves and sudden rises in costs as capacity is reached and new facilities are required.

• *ROI PRICING*

Return on investment pricing, also called target return pricing, measures total investment in a product—which, in the case of a new product like the first MM system, includes sizeable up-front costs in addition to current fixed and variable costs—and then sets a price that will earn a predetermined profit return on this investment. Target pricing is practiced mainly by capital-intensive firms, such as aircraft manufacturers and public utilities. The method for setting prices under ROI is

$$\text{Price} = AVC + \frac{TFC}{PV} + \frac{(ROI)\ (I)}{PV}$$

where AVC = average variable cost, TFC = total fixed cost, PV = planned volume, and I = investment.

For example, during the MM's growth period in a highly favorable foreign market, each system was priced at a level that would produce a 10 percent profit return on investment. Thus,

$$\$2300 = \$600 + \$5,000,000/3000 + 0.10\ (\$1,000,000)/3000$$

Since the demand curve indicated that 3000 MMs would be sold in one target market at the $2300 price, this became the MM's price. Like other forms of cost-based pricing, an ROI pricing strategy assumes that planned sales volume will actually be achieved at the derived price. This assumption worked well for global firms like Kodak, IBM, and Toyota until the early 1990s, when economic and competitive pressures frequently made it impossible to price products to achieve ROI goals.

OLIGOPOLISTIC STRATEGIES: COPY CATS AND KINKED DEMAND

An oligopoly consists of a few firms—generally, but not necessarily, large ones—that comprise most of an industry's sales. In the United States, oligopolistic industries produce automobiles, cigarettes, turbines, breakfast cereals, and refrigerators. In its early stage of growth in the U.S. market, the Merton MM systems division, with a few other large competitors, also found itself in an oligopolistic market climate.

In this oligopolistic climate, a few sellers are highly sensitive to each other's marketing and pricing strategies, giving rise to the kinked demand curve shown in Figure 16-1. Note that all competitors are pricing their products at point A on this curve. The rationale for this copy-cat pricing strategy is that if one competitor lowers its price to point B, all the other competitors will follow, thus largely canceling out the advantage of the lowered price, with demand barely increasing. On the other hand, if one firm increases its price to point C, none of the other competitors will follow, and this firm will rapidly lose sales to its lower-priced competitors.

Note two characteristics of this oligopolistic pricing strategy. First, unlike monopolistic, cost-based strategies, it must also account for buyer and competitor behavior. Thus, although Merton used breakeven and ROI analyses to arrive at a kinked price point, this point was now determined more by how buyers and competitors would respond than by predetermined profit goals. Second, unlike previous cost-based strategies, this oligopolistic

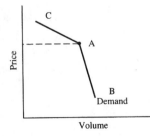

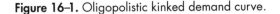

Figure 16–1. Oligopolistic kinked demand curve.

strategy no longer aims to optimize profits, but simply to satisfy what all competitors agree, at least implicitly, are reasonable profit goals.

DEMAND-BASED PRICE STRATEGIES: SKIM OR PENETRATE?

To this point, our focus has been on pricing strategies appropriate to environmental climates in which competitors are monopolistically nonexistent or oligopolistically cozy with each other. In the real world, however, firms don't typically enter or grow in such markets; sooner or later, if the product is capable of attracting a market, it will also attract competitors. And competitors rise or fall based on their ability to relate to demand patterns in their markets.

Anticipating this demand-based competitive climate, Merton price planners usually faced two strategic options: penetrate or skim the market.

PENETRATION STRATEGY

A market penetration strategy would suggest a low introductory price in this market, perhaps even lower than the cost of producing MMs. The objective of this low price would be to stimulate market growth by grabbing market share from existing or prospective competitors. Achieving a dominant share of a target market usually produces long-term benefits that easily compensate for short-term profit losses. For one thing, it's difficult to knock leader companies off their top rung; firms like Coca-Cola, Lipton Tea, Goodyear Tires, Life Savers and Quaker Oats have all been leaders in global markets for more than 80 years. For another, a position of leadership usually ensures economies of scale in making and marketing products that make it easier to generate profits and control prices—including raising prices more easily than can the catch-up playing competition.

In considering a penetration strategy, price planners should also recognize conditions under which such a strategy is most likely to succeed. Usually required is a large, expandable, price-sensitive target market, and the possibility of economies of scale, with per-unit production and distribution costs decreasing with sales increases. Additionally, the lower price should effectively discourage competition and not invite charges of violating price legislation or regulations.

SKIMMING STRATEGY

Much safer, from a legal/political perspective, is a price skimming policy, with prices pegged high to lure the comparatively small target market more attracted to the quality, uniqueness, and usefulness of the MM than to its price. Then, after sales to this primary target market begin to fall off, the MM's price would be lowered to attract members of the next target market down the line, and so on. A skimming price is appropriate if the product isn't attracting excessive competition, if a high price helps support a quality image, if there are a sufficiently large number of target market members willing to pay this price, and if a positive short-term return on investment is mandated. Other factors supporting a skimming pricing strategy include limited production facilities and the need to work weaknesses out of manufacturing/marketing processes.

PRICE-QUALITY STRATEGIES

Figure 16-2 shows a range of demand-based pricing strategies based on consumer perceptions of the relationship between a product's quality and its price. For example, a product perceived as both high in quality and high in price—a Mercedes-Benz automobile for example—would be perceived as a "premium" product, whereas a similar high-quality product, priced low, would be perceived as a "superb value." Understanding consumer perceptions of a product along this spectrum can be a helpful starting point for planning marketing mix strategies for either reinforcing a product's present price-quality niche (for example, many premium fashion products don't even mention price in their promotions) or finding a more profitable niche (for example, the "Planet Hollywood" restaurant chain, generally perceived as "overcharging" and "ripoff," attempts to reposition itself as "premium" by improving the quality of the cuisine).

	PRICE		
	High	Medium	Low
High	Premium	Penetration	Superb value
Medium	Overcharging	Average value	Good value
Low	Ripoff	Poor value	Cheap value

QUALITY

Figure 16–2. Price quality pricing strategies.

PRICE DISCRIMINATION FAVORS DIFFERENT SEGMENTS

Discriminatory pricing, a demand-based strategy appropriate in both consumer and organizational markets, is defined as the legally sanctioned practice of selling a product at two or more prices that do not reflect a proportional difference in costs. Conditions favorable to discrimination include the following situations:

- Different segments of the market (accountants, doctors, lawyers, and so on) must show different intensities of demand;

- One segment won't undersell the product to the segment paying a higher price;

- Cost required to police price discrimination doesn't exceed the extra revenues produced by discriminating;

- Price discrimination doesn't breed ill-will;

- Discrimination doesn't violate legal prescriptions (summarized in Chapter 15).

FORMS OF PRICE DISCRIMINATION

A familiar form of price discrimination is place discrimination, in which, for example, a customer at a football or soccer game pays more for a seat at midfield than in the end zone, although the cost of installing each seat is the same.

Other forms of discriminatory pricing include customer, time, and product price discrimination. Following are examples of each implemented in pricing MM systems:

- **Customer discrimination** was used when Merton charged professionals working for large firms less than self-employed professionals for MM systems—a strategy analogous to corporate discounts offered by airlines and car rental companies.

- **Time discrimination** was used when Merton increased the price of MM systems during periods of peak demand, usually after the summer months, with vacations over and company training programs starting up again.

- **Product discrimination** was used when Merton charged more for software training programs that were in high demand, even though the actual cost of producing and marketing all programs was essentially the same.

PROMOTIONAL PRICING ATTRACTS MARKET SEGMENTS

Merton's demand-based promotional pricing strategy for MM systems involved pricing them below list, or even below cost, in order to achieve larger sales or profit goals. For example, it was not unusual for MM's distributors to discount the price of MM customized software during special sales campaigns designed to increase sales of MM computers. The overall increase in sales and profits easily compensated for smaller profits on the software.

At the peak of its maturity stage, as competition among computer system producers became intense and differences among the systems became more difficult to perceive, Merton also used cash rebates as an incentive for end users to purchase the systems and for distributors to push them. This incentive allowed Merton to retain its original price and the premium image associated with this price.

EXPECTED PROFIT STRATEGIES CONTROL BIDDING

Another demand-based strategy, employed by Merton in the organizational market, was expected profit pricing. Table 16-1 shows how this approach, used mainly in response to requests for bids by large prospective customers, worked in a sealed bid Merton submitted to a large accounting firm for an order of 1000 MM systems.

Table 16–1. Highest Expected Value Determines Selected Bid

Company Bid	Company Profit	Estimated Success Probability	Expected Profit
$ 600,000	$ 20,000	.70	$14,000
800,000	220,000	.30	66,000
1,000,000	420,000	.05	21,000
1,200,000	620,000	.01	6,200

At the time this bid was made, Merton had managed to reduce its costs for making and marketing each MM system to $580. Thus, if it were to charge $600 for each MM, for a total bid price of $600,000, it would make a total profit of $20,000. At this low bid price, collective management wisdom and past experience indicated that Merton had a 70 percent chance of getting the order, so the expected profit from this $600,000 bid was $14,000 (.70 × $20,000). Other expected values of bids of $800, $1000, and $1200 per MM, following the same approach, indicated that a bid of $800,000, with a 30 percent chance of succeeding, generated the highest expected profit— $66,000—so that was Merton's bid.

PRODUCT LINE PRICING STRATEGIES

Unless a product is introduced as a discrete entity in itself, pricing considerations and concerns are usually dictated by perceptions of products as components of larger product mixes and product lines. For example, the Merton
MM line of computers and associated software was part of a mix of electronic
products and components for consumer and organizational markets. In this
broader context, three demand-based strategies were used to help achieve
marketing objectives: price lining, optional pricing, and captive pricing.

PRICE LINING: RANGES DEFINE QUALITY

When Merton introduced a more sophisticated MM system to its existing
product line, many of the analyses required to peg a price for this product
had already been made in pricing other MMs in the line; for example, price
planners already knew what profit margin the new product would be expected to generate, and what kind of product image it should reflect.

Pricing the new MM in this product line context, the planners' main concern focused on cost differences between this model and others in the line,
prices that competing firms charged for similar MM models, and assessments of the new model by prospective customers.

Also guiding their planning were considerations pertaining to establishing
price differentials among products within the line of MMs. They realized,
for example, that price points should be spaced far enough apart so customers would perceive functional and quality differences among different models; otherwise, customers would simply buy the lowest priced model. They
also realized that prices should be spaced farther apart at higher levels,
where consumer demand becomes more inelastic. Thus, the deluxe MM
model at the top of the line was priced at $400 more than the next most
expensive MM, which was priced only $300 above the lowest priced unit.

From the viewpoint of Merton and its distributors, price lining offered a
number of benefits. An assortment of MM models could be offered to attract
many market segments, and members of these segments could be encouraged to trade up, thus increasing sales and profits. Also, a broad product
line, with models throughout the price range, is a strong deterrent to competitors.

OPTIONAL PRICING MAKES STANDARDS OPTIONS

Under an optional pricing strategy, companies face the problem of which
components and accessories to offer as options and which to offer as stan-

dards. For example, an auto manufacturer can attract customers with a stripped-down model at a very attractive price and then sell up to more attractive, option-loaded models. This was General Motors' normal pricing strategy until the early 1980s when, in response to Japanese automakers, it included in its sticker price many useful items previously sold only as options.

CAPTIVE PRICING: HIGHER AFTERPRICES

Under a captive pricing strategy, firms produce products that must be used with the main product and that influence the price of both products and overall profitability. A camera manufacturer, for example, might set a low price for cameras, and a higher-than-market price for the film used with the camera, thus making up with film profits what is lost in camera profits. This strategy proved effective for Merton when, in highly competitive, price sensitive markets, it could lower prices on its MM models while concurrently increasing prices on customized software to take up some of the profit slack.

PRICE MODIFICATION STRATEGIES MEET DISTRIBUTORS' NEEDS

Merton's early success in marketing MM systems in domestic markets soon translated into strong demand among retailers and wholesalers to carry Merton product lines. Before this demand among intermediary customers developed, however, Merton, with no track record to attract distributors, implemented the following price modification strategies, consisting of discounts and allowances designed to reduce risk and improve income for distributors willing to stock and market MM systems.

- **Functional discounts,** also called trade discounts, are offered by manufacturers to trade channel members in return for performing such distribution functions as buying, stocking, selling, market research, and credit extension.

- **Quantity discounts** are offered to customers who purchase merchandise in larger than normal quantities. Merton offered distributors higher than average discounts to compensate them for additional costs for carrying excess inventory.

- **Cash discounts** are price reductions offered to customers as an incentive to pay bills on time. For example, a discount of 2/10, net 20, means that payment is due within 20 days, but the buyer can deduct 2 percent from the bill if it is paid within 10 days.

- **Allowances** are reductions from the list price covering periodic or unanticipated contingencies such as a special promotion or the failure of the product to sell. For example, recognizing early distributor perceptions that MM systems might not sell in certain markets, Merton offered unusually generous return allowances to distributors: a full refund on their purchase price, less 10 percent to cover shipping and handling charges. Promotional allowances were also generous, with Merton contributing two dollars for every dollar contributed by a distributor.

GEOGRAPHIC PRICING INCENTIVES

In addition to a generous schedule of discounts and allowances, Merton also offered generous geographic pricing incentives to its distributors to help them compete more effectively. Among such incentives offered distributors were the following:

- Under a **free on board (FOB) origin pricing** strategy, merchandise shipped to distributors would be placed free on board a carrier, following which title and responsibility would pass on to the distributor, who would pay the freight from that point on. An advantage of this approach is its basic fairness; each distributor pays its fair share based on its distance from the manufacturer. However, excessively high costs borne by distant distributors can put them at a competitive disadvantage vis-à-vis distributors paying lower freight costs.

- A **uniform delivered pricing (UDP)** strategy allowed Merton to charge the same freight rate to all customers regardless of their location. This rate was sufficiently high to cover the seller's shipping costs, but sufficiently low to allow individual dealers to compete effectively on price.

- Under **zone pricing,** features of both FOB and UDP are combined into a strategy that features two or more zones wherein all distributors in a given zone pay the same rate. For example, all distributors west of the Mississippi might pay a freight rate higher than that paid by distributors east of the Mississippi, but not as high as they would pay under FOB pricing. Since this approach is an amalgam of both FOB and UDP, its pros and cons are also an amalgam of these strategies: it's not as fair as FOB, but it is fairer than UDP; it allows distributors to keep prices at competitive levels, but not as effectively as with UDP.

- **Basing point pricing** takes into account the location of a firm's most lucrative domestic and foreign markets and places a "basing point" at the center of each area, which becomes a low rate zone.

For example, if France represented the market with the largest potential in Europe for Merton products, Paris might become the base point for lowest freight rates, which would then increase in areas of lesser potential.

- Under **freight absorption pricing,** Merton would absorb all, or most, of the freight cost to buyers. This strategy is typically employed as the strongest geographic pricing incentive for distributors to take on a product, but it can create an unacceptable profit drain to the seller.

Considering the pros and cons of these pricing options in terms of marketing goals for MM systems, Merton price planners decided on a basing point strategy whereby distributors in Merton's five highest potential trading areas would pay a relatively low freight rate, which would increase in areas of lesser potential.

PRICE CHANGE STRATEGIES: WHEN AND HOW

Whether perceived as a discrete entity, or as part of larger product mixes or lines, a product that successfully competes in global markets will sooner or later have to have its price changed (for example, lowered to meet competitive challenges or raised to reflect favorable supply-demand conditions in the marketplace).

• *CUTTING PRICES*

Typical reasons for cutting a price generally prevailed during the late maturity and decline stages of MM systems in most markets; falling market share had produced excess capacity and the need to generate sales to remove this excess. Another key reason for cutting prices was illustrated by price reductions of MM models during Merton's introductory stage in competitive markets—a drive to achieve a position of market leadership, with the economies of scale associated with this position.

• *RAISING PRICES*

As noted in Chapter 15, a relatively small price increase can lever dramatic profit increases, assuming demand doesn't decrease appreciably as a consequence of this increase. Although price increases are almost always more difficult to implement than price decreases, they can often be justified for the following reasons:

- Unexpectedly high demand for the product justifies increasing a price perceived as too low.

- Cost inflation forces all manufacturers in a field to raise prices more or less simultaneously.

- Unbundling of services often provides a justification for increasing the price of individual services. For example, the tax division of a large accounting firm might unbundle financial planning services, which are easier to "value price" in terms of customer perceptions than are routine tax compliance activities, which are billed at a lower hourly rate.

- Discounts, allowances, rebates, and other price adjustment arrangements can justify increases in the product's price.

- Use of escalator clauses, with built-in contractual assurances that an agreed-upon profit will be realized, often permits price increases in negotiating government contracts.

ANTICIPATING REACTIONS TO PRICE CHANGES

Planners should anticipate potentially adverse responses to a product price change by customers and competitors and should help ensure that they are favorable. For example, when Merton raised the price of MM systems in certain foreign markets, the firm sent out promotional messages stressing that this increase was evidence of the MM's quality and value and that, as such, it might soon be unobtainable even at the new, higher price. Similarly, when Merton lowered the price of MMs during competitive and maturity stages, promotion addressed possible perceptions that the product was about to be replaced by a later version, or that the price would come down even farther if customers just waited it out.

INTERNATIONAL PERSPECTIVE

In international markets, the same factors that shape pricing strategies and tactics in domestic markets apply, including competitive conditions, cost structures, demand patterns, and company objectives. However, three characteristics unique to global markets complicate the task of actually applying these factors:

• *EXPORT-RELATED COSTS*

As noted in Chapter 15, an exporter must account for a number of unique export-related costs in setting prices or preparing quotations. In addition to costs for modifying the product for foreign markets, these costs include operational costs for the export function and costs incurred in entering foreign markets (tariffs, taxes, currency risks etc.). Another cost frequently incurred by U.S. exporters is that of distributors in industrialized foreign countries, who frequently expect higher percentage markups than do domestic distributors to compensate for generally less efficient operations.

• *CROSS-COUNTRY DIFFERENCES*

Multinational and global firms that price products in different countries— such as those comprising the European Union—must adopt pricing strategies and tactics to different cultural, political, economic, and financial climates, typically resulting in a range of prices, from cost- to demand-based, in these countries.

• *GRAY MARKETS*

Currency valuation discrepancies are a key difference among countries that don't generally characterize homogeneous domestic markets and that give rise to the risk of gray markets, or parallel importation.

To illustrate the nature and potentially debilitating effects of gray markets, assume that Merton sells its MM systems in all fourteen countries comprising the EU, where the dearth of trade barriers makes it relatively easy to move products across borders. Among these EU countries, currency valuation differences mean that prices for products sold in Southern European countries like Spain and Portugal are almost invariably lower than the prices of identical products sold in Northern European countries like Norway and Germany. Often, this price discrepancy will be sufficient to stimulate entrepreneurs to profitably sell MM systems purchased in Southern European countries at prices below Merton's lowest prices in Northern European countries, effectively short-circuiting Merton's distribution network and marketing programs in these countries.

Worldwide, the effect of gray markets, which are generally considered legal, can be daunting for a whole range of products, from inexpensive candy bars to expensive capital equipment. For example, many products made and sold in Japan are so expensive—thanks to high taxes, the high value of the yen, and government incentives to export these products—that it is often profitable for Japanese marketers to go to Los Angeles to buy export versions of Japanese-made products.

ADDRESSING GLOBAL PRICING PROBLEMS

In successfully addressing problems brought on by price escalation and cross-country differences in markets and currency valuations, price planners focus on tight control and coordination of prices, proper organization of the pricing function, and strategic initiatives appropriate to global markets.

• CONTROLLING AND COORDINATING GLOBAL PRICES

Because improperly pegged prices can have a strong impact on profitability, price planners continually monitor prices and the marketing mix context in which pricing strategies emerge in global markets. Pricing strategies and tactics are then implemented on the basis of this information. For example, pricing strategies implemented to counter the emergence of gray markets include introducing low-cost brands (for example, in high-price countries like Norway and Germany) to make parallel importation unprofitable, or subsidizing higher price maintenance programs in low-price countries from profits in high-price countries.

• ORGANIZING FOR GLOBAL PRICING

The need for a "big picture" understanding of prices across many different countries suggests the need for centralized control of the pricing function to identify areas where prices are not responding to the nature and needs of specific markets, or price differences are stimulating the growth of gray markets. Also of concern are legalistic issues affecting pricing in global markets (for example, setting artificially low prices to mitigate the emergence of gray markets can bring on charges of dumping or predatory pricing).

However, a strong centralized control over global pricing sacrifices the benefits of decentralized input to react quickly to local market conditions. Studies have shown that most multinationals do allow their subsidiaries considerable freedom in setting prices, subject to centralized control in well-defined situations.

• IMPLEMENTING EFFECTIVE GLOBAL PRICING STRATEGIES

Key strategies implemented by multinational and global firms to relate prices to competitive, economic, and legal conditions in global markets include marginal cost, market hold, optional pricing, and price modification strategies.

- **Marginal cost pricing** disregards fixed costs for making and marketing products when pricing these products for global markets, assuming these costs have already been captured in the domestic market. Thus, the base product price is the marginal cost of producing and marketing it for export, a strategy that can often effectively offset price escalation.

- **Market hold pricing** is a demand-based pricing strategy designed to hold a company's share of market in the face of unfavorable exchange rates. In the early 1980s, for example, when the dollar appreciated against most other currencies, American companies based prices on the competitive situation in each market and the ability of customers to pay rather than on U.S. prices translated into foreign currencies at current exchange rates. As noted in Chapter 15, most companies facing depreciated currencies in competitive markets follow this strategy of relating prices to demand, to the extent that they absorb, on average, 50 percent of the effective resulting price increase.

- **Optional pricing** decisions can also offer practical legal benefits in global markets. For example, by including as part of an automobile accessory a tool that had previously been sold separately, the manufacturer bypasses the relatively high tariff on that tool and acquires immunity from antidumping regulations by making the product no longer comparable to competing goods in the target market.

• *PRICE MODIFICATION STRATEGIES*

Whether a firm adopts a cost- or demand-based strategy, an important additional component will be price modification strategies that define conditions under which ownership will pass from seller to buyer—terms of sale—and under which payment will be made from buyer to seller—terms of payment.

In global markets, terms of sale and payment can vary in degree of their attractiveness to buyer and seller and can affect, favorably or unfavorably, the profitability of transactions for either party. To the extent that they favor the buyer, they represent potent competitive tools for persuading market intermediaries to carry products and end-user or consumer customers to buy them. The examples in Global Focus 16.1 highlight the importance of relating terms of sale and payment to customer needs, and accounting for the effects of these terms on profitability.

GLOBAL TERMS OF SALE

The global terms of sale, called **Incoterms,** which are discussed here, define degrees of responsibility assumed by buyers and sellers in transporting goods from point of origin to final destination. These terms were adopted by the International Chamber of Commerce (ICC) and went into effect in 1990. They indicate the point from which ownership of exported goods passes from buyer to seller, ranging from ex-works with most risk and cost assumed by the buyer, to delivered duty paid, where this obligation is assumed by the seller.

- **Ex-works (EXW)** means charges for transporting the goods are assumed by the buyer at the point (the mine, factory, or warehouse) from which the order originates.

- **Free carrier (FCA)** means the seller is responsible for loading goods into the means of transportation at a designated inland shipping point; the buyer is responsible for all subsequent risks and expenses.

- **Free alongside ship (FAS)** means the exporter assumes charges for delivering the goods alongside a vessel at the port, including unloading and wharfage. Loading, ocean transportation, and insurance are left to the buyer.

- **Free on board (FOB)** means the seller's price covers all expenses up to and including delivery of goods on an overseas vessel provided by or for the buyer.

- **Cost and freight (CFR)** means the seller's price includes the cost of transportation to a named overseas port of import. The cost of insurance and the choice of insurer are left to the buyer. With a CIF provision in a quote, the seller's price includes all cost, insurance, and freight to the point of debarkation from a vessel or aircraft.

- **Delivered duty paid (DDP)** means the seller delivers the goods, with import duties paid, right to the buyer's facility. With delivered duty unpaid, destination customs duty and taxes are paid by the buyer.

Increasingly, sellers are moving toward freight absorption terms, usually on a CFR or DDP basis, as being in their best economic interest. As a sales tool, such a strategy allows the seller to offer foreign buyers an easily understood delivered cost, and cuts down on expensive administrative procedures for buyers. Such a strategy also offers opportunities for sellers to negotiate volume discounts on purchases of transportation services and to maintain control of product quality and service, ensuring arrival to the buyer in good condition.

GLOBAL FOCUS 16-1

Different Companies, Different Price Strategies

The complexity of export pricing, and its impact on profits, is illustrated by different approaches to price modification taken by different companies.

- Baughman, a division of Fuqua Industries, manufactures steel grain storage silos and related equipment and has traditionally exported approximately 30 percent of its sales. Baughman's products are of high quality, and pricing has not often been an active element of the marketing mix. The firm's export sales terms consist of an irrevocable confirmed letter of credit in U.S. dollars with no provisions for fluctuating exchange rates.

Export and domestic prices are identical before exporting costs are added. However, Baughman will make concessions to this policy to secure strategically important sales.

- Ray-O-Vac, a producer of batteries and other consumer goods, has been exporting successfully since the 1950s. Exports account for 20 percent of total business, and major markets include Europe, the Far East, and Japan. These markets are entered through wholly-owned subsidiaries that are treated as cost or profit centers. Competitive pressures demand flexible pricing, and discounts are often granted to gain market share. Branch managers may adjust prices on a day-to-day basis to counter exchange rate fluctuations.

- During a four-year period, Hart-Carter International exported $12 million worth of agricultural machinery to more than 90 countries without a single default. The firm's policy with respect to new customers is to utilize a credit form of payment, whereby the firm presents proof of shipment to a U.S. bank in which the foreign customer has established credit, receiving payment the day goods are shipped. Later, as the firm gains experience with new customers, they reduce credit requirements, even placing many on an open account basis. Almost without exception, these open accounts pay within 30 days.

- Richard Winter, owner of Schummel Novelty Products of Englewood, Colorado, offers this caution for exporters: "In international financing, be careful to prepare letters of credit properly. Once you do so, there is hardly any risk, but when they are improperly prepared, you hear horror stories." Even with his background in law and accounting, Winter still has all his firm's letters of credit checked by a banker and the president of Schummel's freight forwarding company.

Source: "Stories of Exporting Success," *Business America,* October 1993 and June 1994.

GLOBAL TERMS OF PAYMENT

In global markets, payments usually flow from buyer to seller along a spectrum of arrangements—from cash in advance to consignment—that become progressively less beneficial from the seller's perspective and more beneficial to the buyer. Considerations involved in deciding which arrangement best meets the needs of both seller and buyer include the customer's credit rating, industry practices, the amount of payment, the relative strength of buyer and seller, and the seller's capacity for financing global transactions.

Following are characteristics and relative benefits of each approach:

• *CASH DEPOSITS IN ADVANCE*

Exporter requests payment in cash, in whole or part, in advance of shipment. Cash deposits in advance are typically used when exchange restrictions in destination country, or doubtful customer creditworthiness, render payments slow or speculative. The volume of international trade handled this way is small.

• *EXPORT LETTER OF CREDIT (LOC)*

If irrevocable and confirmed by a bank in the exporting country, the LOC affords the exporter the best protection next to cash in advance in obtaining payment. The LOC eliminates the possibility of cancellation of the order before payment, protects the exporter from exchange restrictions in the destination country, and ensures payment on presentation of such shipping documents as a full set of bills of lading in negotiable form, parcel post receipts, and consular invoices. LOCs can be revolving or nonrevolving, can help ensure financing, and can give importer "float."

• *DOLLAR (OR FOREIGN CURRENCY) DRAFTS*

Usually drawn on a bank for immediate payment or for acceptance 30, 60, or 90 days after sight or date and accompanied by shipping documents to the bank holding the draft, this form of finance also offers protection against currency restrictions and customer credit risk. With either sight or time draft, the buyer can extend the credit period by avoiding receipt of goods.

• *OPEN ACCOUNT*

No written evidence of debt, or any guarantee of payment exists. The open account is common in trade among European Union countries, and in other situations where exchange controls are minimal and exporters have good relations with creditworthy customers, or are selling to branches or subsidiaries. A major objection to open account sales in international trade is the possibility of litigation with no written confirmation of debt; usually, bad debts are easier to avoid than rectify.

• *CONSIGNMENT SALES*

In countries with free ports or free trade zones, consigned merchandise can often be placed under bonded warehouse control in the name of a foreign bank, with partial lots released against regular payment terms when sales are generated. The merchandise is not cleared through customs until the sale has been completed. Like open account sales, no tangible obligation is created, leading to potential legal complications.

CHAPTER PERSPECTIVE

Basic pricing strategies, designed to follow pricing policies in achieving marketing objectives, reflect the economic/competitive climate in which they are pegged, from purely cost-based strategies in monopolistic markets to demand-based strategies in competitive climates. For example, over the course of a product's life cycle in a selected foreign market, a company might begin with cost-based breakeven and ROI pricing strategies, then, as demand and competition grow, adopt skimming, penetration, and eventually holding pricing strategies. Supplementing these basic strategies would be a number of tactically oriented price modification strategies governing terms of sale and payment, designed to attract customers and intermediaries while achieving profit goals. A key price planning decision throughout the product life cycle is when and how to raise or lower prices.

KNOW THE CONCEPTS
TERMS FOR STUDY

Allowances	Letter of credit
Basing point pricing	Marginal cost pricing
Breakeven-point pricing	Market holding price
Captive pricing	Markup pricing
Cash discount	Oligopolistic pricing
Competitive pricing strategies	Open account
CIF	Optional pricing
Consignment selling	Penetration price
Cross-country differences	Price change strategies
Cost-plus pricing	Price discrimination
Dollar drafts	Price lining
Expected profit pricing	Price modification strategies
Export-related costs	ROI pricing
Freight absorption pricing	Skimming price
Freight forwarders	Target return pricing
Functional discount	Terms of payment
Gray markets	Terms of sale
Incoterms	Uniform delivered pricing strategy
Kinked demand	Zone pricing

MATCHUP EXERCISES

1. Match up the cost-based pricing strategy in the first column with the descriptor in the second column.

1. breakeven	a. Purchase cost/0.60
2. a 40 percent markup	b. Total revenues = Total costs
3. cost-plus price	c. price at the kink
4. ROI	d. price that earns a predetermined profit
5. oligopolistic price	e. Costs + Projected profit/ Projected sales

2. Match up the demand-based prices in the first column with the descriptors in the second column.

1. promotional pricing	a. Merton Mighty Mind computers will be discounted by 20 percent.
2. captive pricing	b. The cost of training and development software used with MMs will be increased by 10 percent.
3. penetration pricing	c. Of course, senior citizens will be given the usual 10 percent discount.
4. price discrimination	d. We need a large, expandable, price-sensitive market, and probable economies of scale.
5. expected profit pricing	e. We estimate that we have a 50 percent chance of getting the order if it's priced at $800,000.

3. Match up the price modification terms in the first column with the descriptors in the second column.

1. ex-works	a. no written evidence of debt
2. DDP	b. firm charges same rate for all customers
3. open account	c. most risk and cost assumed by buyer
4. UDP	d. most risk and cost assumed by seller
5. 2/10 net EOM	e. must pay by the end of the month

QUESTIONS FOR REVIEW AND DISCUSSION

1. In terms of conditions favoring either a penetration or a skimming price strategy, discuss the pricing strategy most appropriate for (1) an eminent Harvard professor retained to help East European governments establish free-market economic policies and programs, and (2) McDonald's aggressive push into the French market in the late 1980s, primarily because France was the only major country where McDonald's lagged behind Burger King.

2. HCR, a woman-owned firm based in Rochester, New York, was recently awarded a contract to conduct a year-long feasibility study on health care in the Republic of Tatarstan, Russia. Assume that, in preparing your proposal for conducting this study, you anticipated the following costs in U.S. dollars: professional amenities (renting and furnishing an office, hiring secretarial help, and the like), $36,000; 150 billable hours a month, at $50 an hour; $10 an hour profit. Using the cost-plus formula, determine the hourly fee you listed in your proposal.

3. Viracom, U.S.A. of Owatonna, Minnesota, a maker of tempered, heat-strengthened, laminated, insulated, coated security glass, set its sights on exporting in 1987 and, since, has seen its export department increase from one to ten people, with 70 percent of exports going to Pacific Rim countries. A typical Asian Viracom service facility requires $20,000 in specialized equipment, and two installation specialists paid at the U.S. equivalent of $15 an hour, with customers charged $25 an hour for their services. Using the breakeven formula, determine the number of hours it will take to break even on Viracom's investment in this equipment and in these specialists.

4. Discuss how foreign competition in differentiated oligopolistic markets (autos, cameras, cereals, and so on) can change the situation from that depicted in diagram A to that depicted in diagram B.

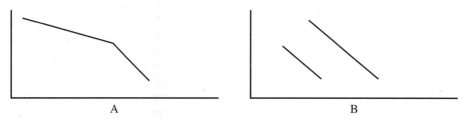

A   B

5. In terms of conditions that favor price discrimination, why would it be difficult to implement such a policy during a Bruce Springsteen concert tour?

6. Describe how Foremost-McKesson, a large international drug wholesaler, might make use of discounts and allowances to enhance its own profitability and that of its retailer customers (pharmacists and drug stores).

7. Given the following data, which bid should the company make?

Company Bid ($)	Company Profit ($)	Estimated Success Probability
5,000	1,000	.80
10,000	2,200	.40
20,000	3,500	.20

ANSWERS
MATCHUP EXERCISES

1. 1b, 2a, 3e, 4d, 5c

2. 1a, 2b, 3d, 4c, 5e

3. 1c, 2d, 3a, 4b, 5e

QUESTIONS FOR REVIEW AND DISCUSSION

1. For the American consultant, conditions favor a skimming strategy; there is little chance that a high price will generate excessive competition because the consultant's credentials and knowledge are unique. Also, there is a large market, potentially made up of Russia and all the satellite nations comprising the ex-Soviet Union. Additionally, a high price will reinforce the aura of preeminence so important to the trust and confidence of the consultant's clients. McDonald's, on the other hand, would employ a penetration pricing strategy: it achieves large economies of scale through the high volume brought on by low prices, thanks to its production line food preparation methods. Additionally, if it increases its price, it will not be able to attract volume from Burger King and other fast food French restaurant chains in an expanding, price-sensitive market.

2.
$$\frac{\text{TFC} + \text{TVC} + \text{Projected profit}}{\text{Units produced}} = \frac{\$36,000 + (1800 \text{ hr} \times \$50) + \$1800}{12 \times 150 \text{ hr/mo}}$$
$$= \$80/\text{hr}$$

3. $\dfrac{\$20,000}{\$25 - \$15} = 2000 \text{ hours}$

4. Diagram A depicts the "kink point" at which a few large firms that dominate an oligopolistic industry tacitly agree to set prices. If a competitor prices below this point, the other competitors will follow, thus eliminating the competitive benefit of a lowered price, with demand barely increasing. And if one firm increases its price, none of the others will follow, so the firm will rapidly lose its sales to its few lower-priced competitors. However, aggressive competition from offshore firms (for example, Japanese automakers competing in the United States) can transform this oligopolistic environment to one of monopolistic competition, with kink points replaced by demand curves, and successful firms push their curves to the right as customer preferences are based more on nonprice features.

5. Of the four forms of price discrimination, the most likely form practiced at a Bruce Springsteen concert would be place discrimination, with locations close to the performer costing considerably more than those farther away. Time discrimination probably wouldn't be practiced because the concert would only be given at one time in each city visited. Customer discrimination probably wouldn't be practiced except, perhaps, for attendees selected by Mr. Springsteen, since attendees would be mostly from the same market segment (for example, few seniors or children). Also, product discrimination wouldn't apply because Mr. Springsteen doesn't come in different models.

Ticket scalping could also make price discrimination difficult, to the extent that it violates three conditions required for effective discrimination: one group shouldn't be encouraged to sell lower priced tickets at higher prices to other groups, the seller shouldn't incur excessive costs in policing price discrimination, and discrimination shouldn't generate ill will, which large-scale scalping does.

6. Foremost-McKesson could help improve the profitability of its retailer customers through a series of discounts and allowances to improve sales and reduce costs. For example, promotional allowances would help retailers finance sales programs to improve revenues, while retailer costs would be reduced through functional discounts for performing such activities as stocking and delivering merchandise, cash discounts for paying bills on time, and quantity discounts for buying and stocking in larger, more economical quantities.

7. The company should put in a bid of $10,000, which produces the largest expected profit ($2200 × .40 = $880).

17

PROMOTION PLANNING I: INDIRECT PROMOTION

OVERVIEW

The promotion element of the marketing mix, consisting of two-way communication designed to inform, remind, or persuade, combines with other marketing mix elements to create more efficient marketing processes and mutually satisfactory exchanges. Planning promotional campaigns entails, initially, establishing objectives based on an assessment of marketing communication opportunities and the need to modify the marketing mix elements. Then, indirect and direct elements of the promotion mix—advertising, publicity, sales promotion, and personal selling—are combined to optimize the effectiveness of each, and the final promotion plan is documented with budgets and timetables.

PROMOTION MIX ELEMENTS INFORM, PERSUADE, OR REMIND

This chapter deals with the promotion mix, a component of the marketing mix that involves communication with customers and prospects to inform, persuade, or remind them about a company's goods, services, image, or impact on society.

Promotion mix elements encompass indirect advertising, sales promotion, word-of-mouth and publicity/public relations communications that support direct personal selling communication, as when a Merton salesperson attempts to persuade a prospect to purchase a Mighty Mind computer system.

WHAT PROMOTIONAL PEOPLE DO

Promotional campaigns can be directed toward consumers or businesses; may be commercial or noncommercial; may be product or nonproduct oriented; and may encompass local, regional, national, or international markets.

The task of the marketing manager is to blend and focus indirect and direct elements of the promotion mix so that they reinforce each other and the other marketing mix elements. A product or service that is designed, priced, and distributed to meet the needs of clearly defined target customers is only as successful as the promotional support it receives.

A MODEL OF THE COMMUNICATION PROCESS

Figure 17-1 incorporates the main features common among recent models of the communication process, and illustrates the stages through which a message passes as it flows from the sender, or source, to the receiver, or audience. Before we can send a letter to a friend, for example, our mental images have to be converted into a form that will be understood by our friend and that can be transmitted, via words or other symbols, so we write them down, or encode them. Merton Electronics combined printed copy with color illustrations to create an image that target market members would hopefully understand and respond to.

The next stage, transmitting the message through a media channel, requires that we affix postage and mail our letter. Merton's messages, including information on the company name and image and differential advan-

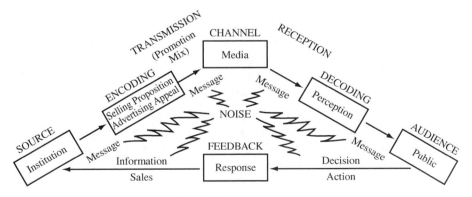

Figure 17-1. The marketing communications process.

tages of MM systems, were transmitted through various media, including direct mail, newspapers, and magazines.

At the other end of the channel, our friend receives and opens the mail. In Merton's communications, the audience for its promotional messages usually is composed of members of its target market. It is obvious, but important, to recognize that the audience at the receiving end must be able to decode the message from the form in which it was received. Encoding and decoding depend on a common frame of reference.

Because communication requires effort, expense, and time, most messages are sent with the expectation of some kind of response, or feedback. From your friend, this response might be an answer to your letter or no answer; from the audience for Merton's message, it might be to buy or not to buy an MM system, or perhaps to develop a more favorable attitude toward Merton and its line of products, with the likelihood of purchase some time in the future.

Every stage of the communication process is vulnerable to interference from noise, which can be internal or external. Internal noise might be distracting thoughts. External noise usually occurs in physical forms such as electrical interference in a television or radio transmission. It is all other messages distractingly clamoring for attention, such as the many advertisements that surround Merton print advertisements.

PLANNING PRODUCTIVE PROMOTION PROGRAMS

An effective promotion program generally has three outcomes:

- The promotional message reaches the intended audience;

- The message is understood by this audience;

- The message stimulates recipients to take a desired action (e.g., buy, try, or distribute the product).

The following seven-step approach is designed to achieve these outcomes: (1) assess marketing communication opportunities; (2) select communication channels; (3) establish objectives; (4) determine promotion mix; (5) develop the promotional message; (6) develop the promotion budget; (7) determine campaign effectiveness.

STEP 1. ASSESS MARKETING COMMUNICATION OPPORTUNITIES

This first step of the promotion planning process involves an understanding of the nature and needs of target markets, the environments that shape these needs, and what company and product attributes can most profitably be communicated to these markets. In addition to potential buyers of the company's products, this audience could include current users, deciders, and influencers among individuals, groups, or the public. For example, Merton planners would profile target markets in terms of uses and benefits expected from MM systems and economic and cultural characteristics that would help determine effective promotional appeals.

STEP 2: SELECT COMMUNICATION CHANNELS

At this point in the promotion planning process, sufficient information about markets, products, and environments will have been generated to arrive at decisions as to what channels will be required through which to launch and maintain a promotional campaign. Communication channels are of two broad types: personal and nonpersonal. Personal channels involve two or more people communicating directly with each other face to face, through the mails, or over the telephone and present opportunities to personalize the message and receive feedback. A personal sales presentation for an MM system illustrates three types of personal communication channels: the Merton salesperson would be an advocate channel; an expert on computerized training systems that the salesperson cites during a sales presentation would be an expert channel; and the recommendation of a satisfied user of MM systems to a friend at a meeting of training directors would be a social channel. Merton promotion programs for MM systems were designed to reach all these channels.

Nonpersonal communication channels transmit messages without personal contact or interaction. In the main, these messages come through the following paid media: print (newspapers, magazines, direct mail), broadcast (radio, television), electronic (audiotape, videotape, videodisc), and display (billboards, signs, posters). In addition to these media, nonpersonal communication channels include: (1) publicity, or nonpaid messages about products in print or electronic media; (2) atmospheres, or "packaged environments" that create or reinforce a buyer's plan to purchase a product (such as viewing rooms where prospective customers could sample MM software); and (3) "events" designed to communicate promotional messages to target customers (such as MM displays at conferences of training directors).

Guiding Merton's efforts to coordinate promotional strategies designed to reach both personal and nonpersonal channels were research findings by Katz and Lazersfeld[1] that indicated the horizontal nature of opinion leadership. As shown in Figure 17-2, these findings indicate that communications flow in a two-step process, from opinion leaders to peers, and not vertically from higher to lower socioeconomic levels. A key implication of these findings is that people get most of their information from members of their own social class, and that mass communication messages are more efficiently directed toward opinion leaders who will carry the message to others.

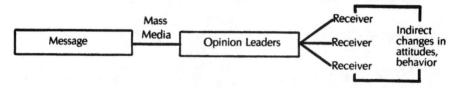

Figure 17–2. Katz-Lazersfeld two-stage communication model.

STEP 3: ESTABLISH OBJECTIVES

Unlike marketing objectives, which typically pertain to quantified measures like sales, profits, or share of market, most promotional objectives are stated in terms of long- or short-term behaviors by people exposed to promotional communication.

For example, MM systems might have a succession of such behavioral objectives assigned to supportive promotion over the course of its life cycle. Initially, a key objective might be to make people **aware** of the product; then, when awareness is achieved, **comprehension** of product benefits might be the promotional objective (brand acceptance), followed by **conviction** (brand preference), **desire** (brand insistence), and **action** (brand trial or purchase). **Satisfaction** after purchase might be the final objective.

Whatever promotional objective or objectives are projected for a campaign, it should be clearly stated, measurable, and appropriate to the stage of market development. For example, a clearly stated action objective to "increase sales by 15 percent next year" would hardly be realistic if most prospective customers were not even aware of the product.

STEP 4: DETERMINE PROMOTION MIX

This step involves allocating resources among sales promotion, advertising, publicity, and personal selling. Key considerations in allocation deci-

---

1 Elihu Katz and Paul Lazersfeld, *Personal Influence* (New York: Free Press, 1955); also Elihu Katz, "The Two-Step Flow of Communications: An Up-to-Date Report on a Hypothesis," *Public Opinion Quarterly,* Spring 1957, pp. 61–78.

sions include characteristics of each promotional tool, the nature and life cycle stage of the product being promoted, and planned distribution strategies. Figure 17-3 shows the relative importance of promotion tools in consumer and industrial markets, which also applies in developed global markets.

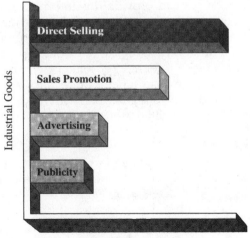

Figure 17–3. Relative importance of promotion tools in consumer versus industrial markets.

• *CHARACTERISTICS OF PROMOTION MIX COMPONENTS*

Here is how promotion mix allocation decisions were made for MM systems, given the following characteristics of promotion mix components.

SALES PROMOTION

Sales promotion includes short-term, one-time incentives to distributors or customers designed to reinforce other components of the promotion and marketing mixes and stimulate sales (for example, coupons, contests, samples, games, trade shows).

ADVERTISING

Advertising is short- or long-term nonpersonal communication by an identified sponsor through diverse media. Its objectives include to inform (new products, new product uses), to persuade (buy the product, change brands, request more information), and/or to remind (of product's existence, where to buy it). Major advertising media are characterized as print (newspapers, magazines) or electronic (television, radio). Business and trade journals, the main media used by international marketers, can be global, regional, or country-specific in scope, and horizontal (catering to functions across industries, such as purchasing or industrial distribution) or vertical (catering to a single industry like chemical engineering) in content. Some journals, such as *Business Week* and the *Wall Street Journal* are standard sources worldwide. Information on print media circulation and rates is available from the Standard Rate and Data Service (SR&D), which publishes a complete list of international publications, as well as circulation audit information similar to that generated for the U.S. market. For areas not covered by SR&D, publishers and local representatives can provide this information.

Another popular advertising medium among firms entering global markets is direct marketing, primarily direct mail and catalog marketing. Direct mail, which includes letters, ads, samples, and foldouts sent to prospects on mailing lists, permits high target-market selectivity, can be personalized, is flexible, and allows easy measurement of results. Although cost-per-thousand-people (CPM) reached is higher than with magazines or electronic media, people reached are usually better prospects.

CATALOG MARKETING

Catalog marketing involves mailing catalogs to a select list of customers, or making them available in stores, to make the seller's name known, generate requests for information, stimulate orders, and serve as reminders between orders. Advantages and disadvantages are basically the same as for direct mail. Among global companies that use catalog marketing as a key element of their promotion mixes are Avon, L. L. Bean, and Walt Disney, which send out millions of catalogs worldwide promoting everything from panty hose to videotapes. Catalogs are particularly effective in promoting organizational and high-tech products requiring the service of specialists.

PUBLICITY

Publicity is short-term, nonpaid, nonpersonal communication about products and people in print or electronic media. Because it is presented in an editorial format, readers tend to perceive it as more believable than advertising. Significant opportunities for publicity involve portraying global firms as good citizens, in introducing new products, and in anticipating and countering criticism.

PERSONAL SELLING

Personal selling involves face-to-face sales presentations among intermediaries, customers, and prospects. It can generate long- and short-term personal relationships that add persuasive conviction to sales presentations that relate products and services to buyer needs. Chapter 18 covers roles of salespeople and sales managers in coordinating with other marketing mix elements to generate revenues and profits.

• *HOW MERTON MELDS PROMOTION MIX ELEMENTS*

During the introductory stage of the MM systems' life cycle, advertising in professional journals was designed to create product awareness among prospective users, and publicity was used to help transform this awareness into comprehension and conviction.

Advertising and publicity were also placed in journals sent to prospective distributors to encourage them to handle the line, supplemented with special presentations at trade shows (where, for example, Merton retained a hospitality room and promoted its presence via a direct mail campaign for selected buyer and distributor prospects).

Merton's initial emphasis on lining up distributors for MM systems was consistent with its **push distribution strategy,** designed to push MM systems through channels; the promotion campaign aimed at prospective users was a **pull distribution strategy,** designed to build consumer demand so that they would ask distributors for the product.

As awareness, comprehension, and conviction objectives were achieved among distributors and prospective MM buyers, and the MM entered the growth stage of its product life cycle, proportionately more resources were allocated to the personal selling promotion mix element, with the efforts of salespeople now made more efficient and productive by the awareness, comprehension, conviction, and word-of-mouth promotion engendered by advertising and publicity campaigns. Further enhancing personal selling efforts, and the effectiveness of other promotion- and marketing-mix elements, were sales promotion tools. Examples of these tools included contests to encourage greater productivity among distributors, MM displays at trade shows, and catalogs that MM sales representatives left with prospective buyers.

STEP 5: DEVELOP THE PROMOTIONAL MESSAGE

Focus in this area is on the content, or appeal, and the structure, format, and source of the message. The **appeal** is the reason that the audience should take the action requested—the benefit that they will derive. It is "the one best thing to say about the product"—the Unique Selling Proposition (USP). It may be rational, emotional, or moral, and it is an important device in positioning the offering against competition. Message **structure** is concerned with whether the communicator should draw a conclusion or leave that to the audience and whether to mention shortcomings along with benefits. The **message format** includes such decisions as the headline, copy, color, and illustrations to use with a print ad, or the script, sound, and camera angles to use with electronic media. The final consideration in message design, the source, considers the credibility of the spokesperson. Credibility is enhanced by expertise, trustworthiness, and likeability.

In successful promotional campaigns, appeal and execution always work together; for example, the macho appeal of Levi Strauss jeans is executed using Western cowboy models, music, and themes in its promotion.

STEP 6: DEVELOP THE PROMOTION BUDGET

After decisions regarding the promotion campaign standardization and implementation have been made, a total promotion budget can be prepared. This involves determining cost breakdowns per territory and among promotion mix elements. Typical approaches for allocating dollars among these entities are affordability, percent of sales, and competitive parity, which all assume that external influences (how much is available, how much was sold, how much do competitors spend) dictate promotional allocations. Although these approaches are all applicable in certain situations and can be used as a check in most situations, the most effective approach is generally the objective-and-task approach, which first determines what must be done to achieve promotional objectives and then estimates what this will cost.

STEP 7: DETERMINE CAMPAIGN EFFECTIVENESS

After marketing communication tasks are assigned, the promotion plan is formalized in a written document including a situation analysis, copy platform, and timetables for the effective integration of promotion mix elements with other elements of the marketing mix. Also included in this plan are the means for measuring its effectiveness once it is implemented, in terms of how actual performance measures up to planned objectives. This typically involves asking the target audience whether they recognize or recall specific advertising messages, what points they recall, how they felt about the message, and previous and current attitudes toward the company and product. Also included would be behavioral measures of audience response such as how many people bought the product, liked it, and talked about it to others.

INTERNATIONAL PERSPECTIVE

Whether planning promotional campaigns in domestic or global markets, the same basic concepts and approaches apply. For example, the communication model (sources encoding messages sent through noisy media to targeted audiences that generate measurable feedback) guides the steps of the basic process for developing global promotional campaigns (assess opportunities, select channels, establish objectives, determine promotion mix, develop message and budget, and measure effectiveness).

Beyond these general similarities, however, environmental differences between domestic and foreign markets change the way promotional concepts and approaches are applied in international markets. This section examines these environmental differences, the problems they present, and how these problems are addressed in planning and implementing global promotional campaigns.

ADVERTISING AROUND THE WORLD

Led by Japan, worldwide advertising expenditures—the largest component of the indirect promotion mix—have increased, on average, more than 10 percent per annum over the past decade. In 1999, total annual worldwide advertising expenditures, outside the United States, was more than $180 billion. Leading global advertisers were Unilever, Procter & Gamble, Nissan, and Nestlé. The United States, with global advertising expenditures in excess of $100 billion, spent more than three times as much on advertising as the next five countries (Japan, United Kingdom, Germany, Canada, and France) combined. Although worldwide per-capita advertising expenditures average $55, U.S. per-capita expenditures are over $500, and many countries (including Switzerland, Finland, Norway, Canada, and Australia) average over $200 per capita. The lowest per-capita expenditures are in Africa and Asia.

The quality of international advertising is generally very high; advertising agencies are as good as those in the United States, and preeminent in some media, such as cinema and poster advertising.

GLOBAL PROMOTION PLANNING PROBLEMS

In international markets, members of many distinct target markets respond to promotional messages that are often subject to strong cultural and legal constraints, in environments where promotional resources are frequently inadequate or nonexistent.

CULTURAL CONSTRAINTS

Illustrative of cultural differences affecting promotional planning in foreign markets was a macho campaign for Levi Strauss jeans using Western cowboy models, themes, and music. In countries without a common "old West" heritage, however, this appeal didn't have nearly the impact as in the domestic market. In Japan, for example, where Levi's Western execution barely budged market share, brand awareness, and ad recall figures, the campaign was changed to capitalize on the Japanese fascination with American movie stars, who endorsed Levi's jeans. Brand awareness soared to 75 percent; advertising awareness was 65 percent.

The experience of Levi Strauss illustrates some of the problems in transferring domestic appeals and executions from domestic to foreign markets. Different languages and perceptual frameworks among foreign customers cause different interpretations of promotional messages, as illustrated by these examples:[2]

- Coors beer's message—"Get loose with Coors"—did not fare too well in Japan, where it translated to "Get the runs with Coors."

- In Latin countries, the Chevrolet Nova (renamed the Caribe) translated into "no go"; Ford's Fiera into "ugly old woman"; and Evitol shampoo into "dandruff contraceptive."

- The color white denotes purity in Europe and death in Asia.

- Coca-Cola's "Coke adds life" theme in Japanese translates to "Coke brings your ancestors back from the dead."

Other problems in translating appeals to foreign countries derive from the sheer diversity of languages (in Israel, fifty different languages are spoken), which represent nightmare problems for translators; high illiteracy rates, which put a premium on visual promotional communication; and culture/subculture differences (in Hong Kong, there are ten distinct patterns

2 Marty Westerman, "Death of the Frito Bandito," *American Demographics,* March 1989, pp. 28–32.

of eating breakfast among youth, the elderly, and urban and suburban residents) that must be accounted for in tailoring appeals to local needs and perceptions. Even the nature of advertising copy can pose problems in translating basic appeals, with the abstract, terse writing characterizing American advertising difficult to translate into other foreign grammars.

LEGAL CONSTRAINTS

Laws that restrict the amount spent on advertising, media used, product advertised, and type of copy and illustrations acceptable represent another constraint on standardized promotion campaigns in many countries. For example, in Germany, use of comparative terminology ("We're the best!") is illegal; in Italy, it's illegal to use many common words like "deodorant" and "perspiration"; in Kuwait, only 32 minutes a day is allocated for TV commercials; in Britain, the Monopolies Commission forbids advertising that might help to create a monopoly (prompting the commission to throw certain P&G commercials off the air); in Austria, taxes on the media (radio, television, cinema) in different states range from 10 to 30 percent of billing. In other countries, many items can't be promoted in the media, including candy, dancing, cigarettes, alcohol, chocolate, airlines, and contests.

MEDIA/MEASUREMENT CONSTRAINTS

In devising promotion mixes for the global market, Merton faced an additional concern not generally faced in its domestic market: the lack of available media. Even when markets are similar in demographic characteristics, media situations can vary dramatically. For example, television advertising barely exists in the Nordic countries; in other countries, there is a dearth of print media—magazines and newspapers—serving target markets. In others, too many publications serve too many market segments to get effective coverage.

Another consideration constraining media choices is cost. For example, advertising agency compensation arrangements and media prices differ dramatically from country to country, with one study showing a range of from $1.58 in Belgium to $5.91 in Italy to reach 1000 readers.

Still another constraint on media allocations is coverage. Given media limitations, it's often practically impossible to reach certain target markets; if they can be reached, it's often prohibitively expensive. How effectively are media reaching target markets? It's frequently impossible to find out. Most industrialized countries have organizations like the Audit Bureau of Circulations (ABC) to audit print media circulations, but often their findings are inaccurate and unreliable.

Even if circulation can be measured, there is generally a dearth of demographic and psychographic marketing data (age, income, attitudes, preferences, and the like) on consumers to flesh out these figures.

GUIDELINES FOR SUCCESSFUL GLOBAL PROMOTIONS

In the face of constraints in global markets, promotion planners are well advised to follow guidelines of successful marketers, including focusing on productive elements of the global promotion mix, working toward standardization, and considering a rollout approach.

FOCUS ON PRODUCTIVE MIX ELEMENTS

As compared to the domestic market, most elements of the promotion mix in global markets—notably advertising, public relations, sales promotion, and direct marketing—are generally more difficult and expensive to successfully implement in global markets.

One exception is trade promotions. Trade shows, in particular, offer marketers many more opportunities to achieve promotional goals in foreign than in domestic markets, with more than 8000 shows held worldwide each year, transacting more than $25 billion in business.[3] (In Europe, for example, trade shows and fairs have been a tradition for almost 1000 years, and individual European distributors and manufacturers attend, on average, more than nine a year.)

For Merton, advantages of participating in trade shows as a means to successfully penetrate global markets included introducing, demonstrating, and promoting MM systems; finding intermediaries to help make and market these products (for example, distributors, bankers, investors, government officials); sizing up the competition in prospective target markets; and generating feedback on marketing effectiveness. To help realize these benefits, Merton set specific goals (for example, number of sales leads or prospective distributors) and implemented follow-up procedures.

Possibly the largest drawback of trade show participation is the cost, although this can be mitigated by attending expositions where tickets are sold to offset exhibitor costs or by sharing expenses with distributors, representatives, or even competitors.

Another way to mitigate trade show costs is to participate in events sponsored by the U.S. Department of Commerce or exhibit at U.S. trade centers or export development offices. Global Focus 17-1 shows how one company, with assistance from the Department of Commerce, builds its entire international marketing program around overseas trade shows.

---

3 Echo Montgomery Garrett, "Trade Shows," *World Trade,* December, 1993, pp. 88–89.

GLOBAL FOCUS 17-1

Overseas Trade Shows Enhance Direct Selling

Dugal Corporation of Miami, Florida, has built its international marketing program around overseas trade shows. The small, family-owned company exports all its products, consisting of a complete line of European-style fashion jewelry. David Poniman, executive vice president, and his wife, Joanna, president and chief designer of the jewelry, go to twenty trade shows a year in Europe, Southeast Asia, the Middle East, and South and Central America. They spend only one week of each month, on average, in their Miami headquarters.

David Poniman explains, "We arrange to attend two or more trade shows in a region during a foreign trip to make the best use of our time and to keep our costs down. While there, we visit with distributors with whom we had previously established a business relationship. We always arrive in a city a day or two before a trade show and stay a day or two afterward."

The U.S. Export Assistance Center in Miami, operated by the U.S. Department of Commerce and other federal agencies, helps the Ponimans make even more efficient use of their time. The Center alerts commercial officers in U.S. Embassies by electronic mail that they are coming so they can receive a briefing and advice on any problems they may face in the country. Poniman considers U.S. sponsorship of exhibits at trade shows valuable because it lends prestige to an exhibition and commands greater attention from business people in the host country.

Trade shows tie in well with Dugal's way of doing business, which is direct selling—the firm has no sales agents. The Ponimans meet distributors face-to-face and make deals on the spot. "Customers appreciate not having to rely on pictures," Poniman said. "They can see the jewelry and feel it and decide on that basis whether they like it."

The personal contact gives Joanna Poniman an opportunity to observe the reactions of customers in different countries to the jewelry so that she can modify it to suit their tastes.

Source: Business America, Vol. 115, No. 6, June 1994, p 10.

WORK TOWARD A STANDARDIZATION STRATEGY

A standardized promotional campaign conveys essentially the same message, by essentially the same means, in all markets. For example, Exxon's message of power, conveyed by the "Tiger in Your Tank" slogan, is applied globally. As compared to a campaign that is modified to the nature and needs of each country, a standardized campaign usually generates considerable savings through centralization. Fewer agencies, domestic or foreign, need be used, and there is less expense, effort, and duplication in such areas as copy, artwork, media, and research. Standardized campaigns are also easier to control—allowing comparisons of similar creative executions in different venues—and offer more opportunities for creative leverage because the effect of promotional innovations can be measured from similar bases. Additionally, standardized campaigns benefit from the overlap of readership, listeners, and viewers in contiguous countries (the magazine *Paris Match,* for example, has readers in Belgium, Switzerland, Luxembourg, Germany, Italy, and Holland). Another argument favoring standardized campaigns is the notion that differences between attitudes and needs of people in different countries are diminishing, and they are more likely to respond to a single campaign. Studies of the feasibility and applicability of standardized campaigns seem to generally agree on these conclusions:

- Certain products, by their very nature, have universal appeal that lends itself to standardized promotion campaigns (for example, Swiss watches, Italian designer clothes, Scotch whiskey, and frequently purchased, low-cost, mass-marketed items like cigarettes and colas).

- Buyer motivation patterns are the key determinant of when a standardized campaign is feasible. If people buy similar products for different reasons, the campaign should be modified; if they react similarly to the same promotional stimuli, the campaign should probably be standardized.

- Promotion campaigns directed toward business markets are generally easier to standardize than campaigns directed toward consumer markets because buyer motives, products, and product uses tend to be more uniform.

Given the problems of standardizing promotional campaigns in global markets, it's not surprising that a survey of 50 experienced advertising executives concluded that only strong buying appeals (such as "top quality" and "low price") can be transferred more than 50 percent of the time to foreign markets, and that creative executions of these appeals translate effectively less than 25 percent of the time. Most of these same executives also agree that, despite these difficulties, it's worth the effort to work toward standardization of promotion—and products—because of cost savings, control, and creative leverage benefits. For example, Pepsico uses four basic commercials, worldwide, to communicate product appeals, with each foreign appeal a modification of the basic setting of people having fun at a party or on the beach to reflect music preferences, racial characteristics, and the general physical environment of North America, South America, Europe, Africa, and Asia.

The Pepsico campaign is an example of the pattern standardization approach that allows some degree of campaign modification to meet local conditions. Typically, multinational firms that employ this strategy develop a prototype promotional campaign at their headquarters, which is delivered to foreign subsidiaries who are given considerable leeway to adapt the creative expression to local conditions.

CONSIDER A ROLLOUT APPROACH

In general, promotion campaigns in foreign markets—especially in competitive environments and during early stages of the campaign—are more expensive than those in domestic markets, often leading to decisions to scale back initial plans by focusing on one or two key markets. For example, European liquor marketers concentrate promotional efforts in the United States and Britain, where volume consumption is greatest.

CHAPTER PERSPECTIVE

Planning promotional programs involves integrating and interpreting promotion mix elements—including advertising, sales promotion, publicity, and personal selling—in terms of diverse needs, perceptions, and environmental constraints. Key decision areas include setting objectives, standardizing campaigns, selecting media channels, devising persuasive appeals, formulating promotional budgets, and measuring campaign effectiveness.

KNOW THE CONCEPTS
TERMS FOR STUDY

Advertising
Advertising appeal
Audit Bureau of Circulation
Awareness
Business/trade journals
Conviction
Catalogs
Decoding
Direct mail
Direct promotion
Electronic media
Encoding
Indirect promotion
Medium
Message

Message format
Personal selling
Print media
Promotion budget
Promotion mix
Publicity
Public relations
Pull strategy
Push strategy
Sales promotion
Trade fairs
Trade missions
Unique selling proposition
Word of mouth

MATCHUP EXERCISES

1. Match the communication process component in the second column with the activity involved in Kellogg's advertising campaign promoting Rice Krispies in Japan, which appears in the first column:

   1. Instead of "snap, crackle, pop," which the Japanese find hard to pronounce, the Rice Krispies critters are scripted to say "patchy, pitchy, putchy."

      a. media

   2. Research indicates that, just as in the United States, Japanese homemakers are the primary target market for the Rice Krispies advertising campaign.

      b. audience

   3. The Rice Krispies critters are portrayed primarily in family magazines read by target market members.

      c. feedback

4. Post campaign research indicates that the Rice Krispies campaign was primarily instrumental in increasing sales above planned expectations.

        d. encoding

2. In 1998, the Tupperware Corporation conducted more than 15 million Tupperware parties in more than 100 foreign countries. From just one of these parties, match up the selling activity in the first column with the behavioral outcome it is calculated to produce, which appears in the second column.

1. awareness	a. Tupperware sales representative explains product features and benefits to party participants.
2. comprehension	b. Sales representative demonstrates how product features and benefits make product superior to alternate means of storing food.
3. conviction	c. Party participants receive invitations to Tupperware party, including incentives to attend.
4. desire	d. Sales representative shows how product features and benefits can solve storage problems facing participants, saving money, improving nutrition, and making them more appreciated by family members.
5. action	e. Sales representative concentrates on using the peer pressure of the group to get all participants to commit to a purchase of Tupperware products.

3. Match the promotion mix component in the first column with the second column descriptor.

1. advertising	a. nonpaid, nonpersonal presentations
2. publicity	b. most important in marketing industrial goods; less important in marketing consumer goods
3. sales promotion	c. short-term incentives to buy or distribute product

4. direct selling	d. most important in marketing consumer goods; less important in marketing industrial goods

4. Match up the approach for preparing a promotion budget in the first column with the descriptor comments in the second column.

1. affordable	a. "Sales dictate ad expenditures, not vice versa."
2. percent of sales	b. "We'll spend what we've got left over after we've covered our other costs."
3. competitive parity	c. "Here's what we'll have to do, and here's what it will cost."
4. objective and task	d. "The way to keep up is to spend what they spend."

QUESTIONS FOR REVIEW AND DISCUSSION

1. Judith Sans of Atlanta, Georgia, began marketing her natural cosmetics and skin care products overseas in 1985, when she joined a trade mission to the Far East to meet representatives of foreign businesses. Her firm now sells in more than twenty countries, with exports accounting for more than 50 percent of total sales volume in 1995. Promotion for Ms. Sans' product line is strongly associated with healthy, natural lifestyles, including proper dietary and exercise regimens. What advertising, publicity, and sales promotion tools might she combine to market a new skin care addition to her product line?

2. Referring to the Judith Sans effort in question 1, discuss problems she might face in getting her promotional message before members of a target market in a country that is less developed than the domestic market.

3. Identify three personal communication channels that might have been used by SmithKline Beecham to market its new medication Avandia, positioned as "a new treatment for type 2 diabetes" designed to "strengthen your body's own ability to control blood sugar."

4. Track through each of the stages of the marketing communications model as it might be applied to introduce a new Merton Mighty Mind laptop computer.

5. When the Xerox Corporation introduced its new line of copiers (Models 1020, 1035, 1045, and 1075) for different segments of the global business market, its promotion campaign combined local and international media to carry a creative theme built around a symbol chosen to convey the endurance of the product line: the marathon ("Finally, there's a copier that's as rugged as it is compact. Introducing the Xerox 1020 Marathon copier . . . "). Speculate on considerations in the first five steps of the campaign planning process that might have produced this campaign.

ANSWERS

MATCHUP EXERCISES

1. 1d, 2b, 3a, 4c

2. 1c, 2a, 3b, 4d, 5e

3. 1d, 2a, 3c, 4b

4. 1b, 2a, 3d, 4c

QUESTIONS FOR REVIEW AND DISCUSSION

1. The market for natural products—including organically grown fruits and vegetables, drinks, and body care products—is substantial and growing worldwide. Use your imagination to add to the following list:

Advertising:	ads in health magazines; commercials on radio programs about healthy lifestyles; mailings to cosmeticians on leased mailing lists; mailings to health publication subscriber lists.
Sales promotion:	samples or trial sizes in counter displays; booths at trade fairs; cents-off coupons.
Publicity:	press kits to newspapers and radio stations explaining features and benefits of the new product.

2. Problems faced by Sans in getting her "healthy lifestyle" message before members of her target market would probably begin with identification of this target market, and definition of market needs as they relate to this product. Strong cultural differences, and lack of demographic and socioeconomic data to help interpret these differences, might make market analysis a daunting job. And even when these target markets are identified and defined, Sans will probably face equally daunting problems in reaching them, given the less-developed state of available media. For example, will timely mailing lists be available, directed toward markets (for example, cosmeticians) she hopes to influence? Will electronic (radio, television) and print (newspapers, magazines) media be available targeted to user or distributor target markets? If so, will these media be affordable, in terms of CPM criteria? And even if afford-able media are available, will there be any reliable way to measure their relative efficacy in reaching markets and achieving promotion goals?

3. A SmithKline Beecham salesperson calling on doctors to persuade them to prescribe Avandia for patients with type 2 diabetes would be an ex-ample of an advocate channel. The head of the research team that de-veloped Avandia and best understands its benefits and limitations would be an expert channel. Doctors who have successfully prescribed Avandia and recommend it to other doctors at a consortium of diabetes specialists would be examples of social channels. All these channels would probably be targets of Beecham's promotional campaign.

4. With the customer-user in mind, and based on survey research identify-ing the nature and needs of various target markets, Merton's advertising department should:

   • Translate the new product's features into customer-perceived bene-fits (for example, enough memory to support popular spreadsheet programs, high-resolution monochrome monitor for less eyestrain, ability to run all available software) and then encode the most impor-tant or unique benefit into the advertising appeal ("The FULL-MEMORY computer that lets you do serious work anywhere.")

   • Transmit this message through selected media representing the communications channel (for example, computer magazines). When the message is received it must be decoded. Therefore, along with the jargon of the computer buff, the advertiser should provide a translation, in everyday language, to help broaden the market for the new computer to include serious computer novices. Its content will be perceived by each member of the audience in terms of that member's unique life experience, attitudes, wants, and needs.

   Throughout the process, noise can be expected (for example, other ads and editorial matter competing for the reader's attention), but its negative effects can be minimized by an attention-getting layout; com-pelling, carefully worded copy; and repetition.

   The success of the communication can be estimated from the amount of feedback in terms of desired response like dealer inquiries, user inquiries, and sales.

5. The first step of the campaign planning process—assessing marketing communication opportunities—would involve Xerox planners in an analysis of the nature and needs of different target markets, defined geographically, demographically, and behavioristically (for example, product specifiers or users in small businesses in Germany or Spain). This analysis would also examine how products in the Marathon line would best meet these needs, as well as the cultural, economic, and political conditions in each market that would influence the campaign.

The second step in the planning process—determining degree of standardization/adaptation needed—would rely on data derived from the first step to make any necessary modifications in the planned campaign. Thus, even though the Marathon theme will characterize all campaigns in all markets, the cultural, legal, and language differences among countries might mandate some changes in individual cases, such as constraints against "boastful" or comparative advertising, or words that might be offensive in certain countries.

The third step—analyzing marketing communication resources—would involve Xerox planners in cost-benefit analyses to determine projected costs of the campaign and the probable return on campaign expenditures. For example, research into different media costs in different markets might indicate that existing resources won't be able to cover a broad-based global campaign, leading to a decision to "roll out" the campaign, starting with the most potentially profitable markets.

The fourth step—establish objectives—will be implemented using data already developed on the nature and needs of markets, and resource constraints in reaching these markets. Because promotional objectives focus on desired behaviors—ranging from awareness to action—the main emphasis here will be on measuring and pitching presentations toward perceptual states in each market (for example, in markets where prospective buyers or influencers are aware of, and favorably disposed toward, Xerox products, presentations might focus more on achieving conviction and desired behaviors).

The fifth step—determining the promotion mix—will focus on allocating resources among advertising, publicity, sales promotion, and direct selling elements of the marketing mix, now and in the future. For example, during the introductory stage of the Marathon introduction, emphasis might be on sales promotion (especially trade shows and demonstrations) and publicity (such as writeups in business and technical journals to generate awareness and comprehension). Then, advertising and direct marketing might be emphasized as part of push strategies to persuade distributors to handle the line, and pull strategies to persuade end-users to specify Xerox Marathon products.

Sales promotion would also be emphasized, in the form of catalogs, price lists, demonstration models, and other incentives for distributors and buyers to buy the copiers. Direct selling might now be emphasized to capitalize on all the good spade work done by earlier promotion efforts to generate leads and get prospective buyers in a state where they desire the product and are ready to act by trying or buying it.

18

PROMOTION PLANNING II: SALES AND SALES MANAGEMENT

OVERVIEW

Different categories of salespeople—ranging from passive order takers to creative order getters—are engaged in the only direct profit-producing activity of the enterprise: personal selling. A productive order getter typically integrates elements of marketing and promotion mixes into his or her presentation, which begins with preapproach research and ends with the final close and post-sale follow-up. Continuing concerns of sales managers include recruiting, selecting, motivating, evaluating, and compensating salespeople, tasks that become considerably more challenging in global markets.

PERSONAL SELLING: EXPENSIVE AND PROFITABLE

This chapter examines the personal selling function, which is the only component of the promotion mix that generates revenues and customer feedback directly attributable to it. It is also the most expensive component of the promotion mix: for example, while the average firm budgets between 1 and 3 percent of costs for advertising, sales expenses average between 10 and 15 percent. When multiplied by the 15 million people engaged in sales in the United States, it also becomes the largest promotional macroexpense.

THE ULTIMATE GOAL IS THE ULTIMATE SALE

Because the ultimate focus of all promotion and marketing mix activities is on the ultimate sale, that is where this chapter will begin. Then, using a single sales call as an illustrative point of departure, we will examine different types of selling; reasons and benefits for entering the selling profession; activities and challenges involved in managing the salesforce; and recent trends toward automating the selling function.

ANATOMY OF A SALES CALL

Eric Sandham, a salesman for a large distributor of consumer and business-to-business electronic systems, specializes in the sale of Merton MM training systems. Although Sandham sells to a broad range of professions, his area of specialization—based on his educational and experiential background—is in the professional accounting field.

Because Sandham is a typical professional salesperson, the average cost of each of his calls, including his salary, commission, bonuses, benefits, and sales management costs attributable to him will average about $115—and only one in three such calls will produce any revenue. However, Sandham is selling in an environment where personal selling is likely to pay off: his customers are geographically concentrated, individual orders are typically large, he is selling technically complex goods and services (MS training and development systems for large staffs that are continually updated), and the products he sells move through short channels (that is, one level or, in the case of insurance or encyclopedia salespeople, zero levels).

The particular call we will examine is on the training director of a multi-branch accounting firm, which, in addition to an audit department, has tax accounting and financial planning departments. Figure 18-1 shows the steps leading up to this call, the call itself, and follow up. A number of studies have shown that time and effort expended during the early steps of this process—prospecting, qualifying, planning, and preparation—leads to faster closings and larger orders during later stages of the process.

PROSPECTING AND QUALIFYING

Sandham's primary source of sales leads was his own company, which provided him information from primary and secondary sources (for example, past sales records, census data, and data from the Internet) on the number, size, and location of accounting firms in his territory, past purchases, and

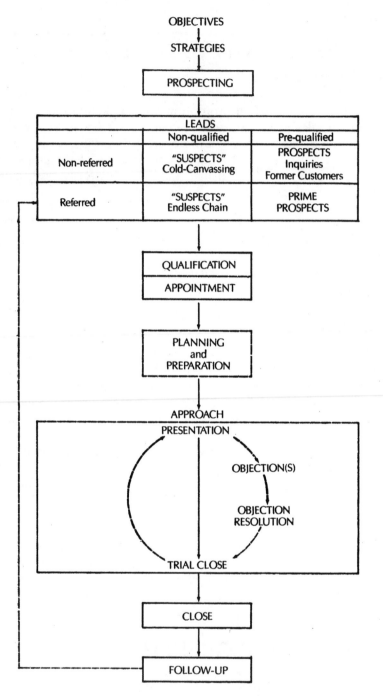

Provided courtesy of Roy C. Brown, 1985

Figure 18–1. The creative sales process.

names of buying influences. Sandham supplemented this information with information from other sources, including accounting associations he belonged to, accountants attending seminars he had conducted, articles in accounting journals, and cold canvassing calls made on accounting firms, either over the telephone or in person. However, Sandham's best sources of sales leads were existing satisfied customers for MM training systems, who also provided potent endorsements when, later, these leads turned into sales calls (Sandham, who disliked cold canvassing, was reassured by a study showing that one customer referral was worth twelve cold calls).

Indeed, it was a satisfied customer who provided Sandham with the sales lead for the call he was planning, at an accounting firm that had only recently achieved a level of growth sufficient to justify a formal training department. The new manager of this new department, Nancy Knipscher, had recently been promoted to this position from the firm's tax department.

However, the mere fact that this firm seemed like a prospective customer didn't necessarily make it so. Based on his own experience, and the collective experience of his firm's sales force, Sandham had established certain threshhold criteria to qualify the customer as worth the effort and expense of planning and carrying out sales calls. These qualifying criteria generally followed the MADR formula discussed in Chapter 1 (the prospect should be able to afford the product, have the authority to purchase it, need the product, and respond positively to the sales message). As a minimum, for example, the prospect firm should have a formal training department, at least a dozen staff members in need of training, and a minimum level of sales volume.

THE APPOINTMENT

After qualifying the firm as a viable prospect, Sandham called Knipscher's office and, after a few unsuccessful attempts, got through to her to request an appointment. He explained that he recognized that she was new in her position and that he could perhaps provide her with information on state-of-the-art training and development techniques and equipment that would help make her new job easier and more productive. They also agreed that the main purpose of his first call would be to develop information on which subsequent-call presentations would be based.

Sandham also sent Knipscher a personal letter thanking her for providing him with this opportunity, and including some promotional materials, such as articles and advertisements, to pre-sell her on MM systems.

PLANNING AND PREPARATION

During these steps in the selling process, Sandham aimed, first, to learn as much as possible about the prospect company and then prepare a presentation based on this knowledge. For Sandham, planning involved first answering questions like: What are this firm's training needs? Who will be involved in the purchase decision? (As noted in Chapter 10, a number of people in an organization, such as gatekeepers, buyers, and users, can all influence a decision like this.) What is the buying "style" of the person most responsible for the purchase decision? (Is he or she action oriented? Fact and detail oriented? Oriented toward social relationships? A big-thinking visionary?) Who are this firm's main competitors? Which of Merton's competitors does the firm buy from? What are their policies regarding salespeople? What objections is my presentation likely to incur?

Based on answers to these and related questions, Sandham built a presentation scenario in writing that covered (1) the greeting and impression to be made, (2) features and benefits of MM systems to stress, (3) the benefit used to obtain the appointment, enlarged and supplemented with others to overcome anticipated objections, (4) image-creating words and phrases to bolster key points, and (5) specific questions Sandham would ask to learn Knipscher's needs and flush out objections.

THE APPROACH

The approach, or initial contact, has other objectives in addition to need identification, such as reducing the prospect's tension, encouraging trust, and creating interest in the product or service. Using the information he had gathered and the presentation scenario he had prepared, Sandham began to develop a relationship with Knipscher. His general appearance, dress, and physical movements were calculated to create a favorable first impression. His greeting was sincere, natural, and accompanied by a smile and eye contact. His handshake appeared to be spontaneous.

After preliminary pleasantries, Sandham began asking questions to determine Knipscher's needs. These needs are usually either organizational (finance, image, performance, and the like) or personal (ego, status, and the like). His questions were open-ended, designed to elicit Knipscher's true opinions and feelings, regardless of whether favorable or unfavorable to MM systems. These probing, open-ended questions were used throughout Sandham's presentation to learn Knipscher's wants, needs, and attitudes, which would all be accounted for in Sandham's subsequent presentations.

THE PRESENTATION

In general, presentations can be categorized as follows:

- The **structured,** or formula, **approach,** is sometimes referred to as a canned presentation. It is based on the stimulus-response theory, which asserts that when subjected to certain stimuli, the prospect will respond with Pavlovian predictability. This approach is used by inexperienced part-time salespeople and some kinds of door-to-door selling. Built around the product's best selling points, this approach generally ignores the customer's real needs.

- The **need satisfaction approach** is based on the notion that all purchasing is need based or problem solving. It encompasses these steps: (1) determine the prospect's perceived problem; (2) obtain the prospect's confirmation of the problem; and (3) offer a solution to the problem. The drawback to this approach is the time, cost, and effort needed for intensive sales training and the presentation itself.

- The **hybrid approach** combines the structured approach of stressing key selling points with the need-satisfaction approach of identifying the prospect's needs to customize the presentation specifically to the individual customer. This was Sandham's approach, and the preferred approach for professional salespeople.

During his presentation, Sandham manifested the following techniques applicable to effective sales presentations in general:

- If the salesperson is not sensitive to the possibility that the prospect might be ready to order, and becomes involved in a lengthy, gratuitous presentation, he or she may unknowingly "buy back" the product because the prospect has time to wonder about the features and whether a better price might not be available from the competition. During every sales presentation, Sandham kept in mind the ABC motto—"Always be closing."

- Sandham viewed his presentation as "show and tell," with as much emphasis on the show as the tell. Hence, documentation—in the form of company literature, testimonials, Web sites, independent reports, and magazine articles—and product demonstrations, such as videotapes of selected training programs, were important components of his presentation.

- On each visit subsequent to his initial need-identification call, Sandham began by restating what had been agreed on during the previous call to bring the prospect up to the proper mental and emotional stage.

HANDLING OBJECTIONS

Sandham welcomed objections during his presentations because they could be viewed as disguised requests for more information and showed that the prospect was listening and interested. After the objection was addressed, Sandham often attempted a trial close, which, if successful, led to the final close. If not successful, the presentation resumed.

In handling objections, Sandham followed these guidelines:

- **Hear the prospect out.** Although Sandham had usually heard the objection dozens of times, the prospect hadn't voiced it before and deserved the courtesy of polite attention. By being a sympathetic listener, the salesperson learns what the prospect knows and is therefore at an advantage because the prospect does not know what information the salesperson has. In addition, by allowing the prospect to discharge pent-up feelings, the salesperson will receive a better ear because the prospect won't be tuning out the salesperson's comments.

- **Repeat the objection,** letting the prospect know that the objection was understood.

- **Question the objection,** to encourage the prospect to amplify it, giving more information that can be used to answer the objection.

- **Answer the objection.** When the objection has been answered, obtain acknowledgment from the prospect with a comment like "does that answer that?" and wait for agreement before proceeding.

Some objections may be common with certain products. These can be anticipated by the salesperson during the presentation.

THE CLOSE

An effective close is the goal of the presentation, the purpose of the sales training, and the reason for the sales presentation that sets it up. Considering this importance, it is surprising how few salespeople move for the **close**—to ask for the sale (studies show that salespeople do not ask customers to buy in approximately 70 percent of all sales calls). The reason most often advanced is the salesperson's fear of rejection. More likely, it is insufficient training and drilling in closing techniques. The prospect has more objections than the salesperson has closes!

A common resistance to a close is "I want to think it over." This is usually just a delaying tactic to give the prospect an opportunity to shop for a lower price. Given this opportunity, some other salesperson will cash in on the work of the first because the prospect has already bought the concept. Therefore, the salesperson must try to close. The response might be, "Why certainly. I agree that such a decision deserves every consideration. But just to clarify my thinking, what is it you want to think over? Is it the integrity of my company? Benefit A that we agreed on? Benefit B?" The prospect will likely reply "No" to each of these questions and struggle to think of something to think over. After listing each benefit agreed on, in effect providing a summary of benefits, and having the prospect admit to not knowing what he or she wanted to think over, the salesperson can ask if it is the cost, and the prospect will probably eagerly agree. By getting the prospect to specify how much too much is, the salesperson can add up the savings associated with purchasing the product, subtract the losses from not using it, divide the cost over the expected payback period, and show how its use will multiply efficiency, performance, and any other pertinent benefit.

FOLLOW-UP

Follow-up refers to the recontact of a customer. It may be a telephone call to check if material was delivered or to provide additional information. Whatever the reason, it is an indication to the customer that the salesperson cares and did not forget. If the product or service is expensive and regularly used, then follow-up after the sale is of utmost importance. Follow-up can benefit the salesperson in several ways:

- **Reinforcement of sale.** If there is a complaint, timely follow-up may be able to resolve it and prevent cancellation of the order and return of the merchandise.

- **Referred leads.** We have seen the value of referred leads. Those received from a satisfied customer are best because they are given with enthusiasm.

- **Repeat business.** Really successful sales professionals cultivate customers like a cash crop, following up sales with inquiries about how the product is performing. This keeps them in touch so that when a new model comes out, they improve the odds of closing another sale.

- **Add-on business.** The representative who keeps in touch will have the best opportunity of selling accessories to upgrade the product purchased and to recommend when the product should be replaced.

TYPES OF SELLING

There are basically three types of jobs in the sales field:

- **Order getters,** like Sandham, are engaged in creative selling, in the sense that they are creating customers by identifying needs and solving problems in an authoritative, persuasive manner. These salespeople are found in all industries, but especially where products must be adapted to individual customer needs, such as high-tech MM systems. These professional salespeople may be assigned a variety of titles, such as account executive, sales consultant, or sales representative. A highly skilled version of the order getter is the national account manager, who calls on headquarters sites of key customers, makes formal presentations, develops strategic plans for top-level executives, and assists in all product decisions at that level. An example would be if Sandham were to call on a single account in the accounting field—say, Deloitte Touche's New York City headquarters—obviating the need for Merton salespeople to call on this firm's far-flung offices.

- **Support salespeople** are specialists who support order getters in a number of ways. Often, they will team up with an order getter like Sandham to assist with the technical aspects of sales presentations. Other support salespeople may set up product displays in the customer's business with the customer's permission. Still others complete and follow up on order processing or perform related tasks to free the salesperson to spend more time in creative selling. One such task, performed by missionary salespeople, is to identify worthwhile prospects and provide them with sufficient information to ease the path of order getters who close the sale.

- **Order takers** are responders. Merchandise is bought from them rather than sold by them. Examples of order takers include retail clerks, delivery route persons, and inside sales/customer service personnel who receive telephoned orders. If a retail store in which the order-taker rings up and packages purchased items is oriented toward personal service, the salesperson can act as an order getter, identifying needs, helping with merchandise selection, and practicing suggestion selling (for example, a tie to match the suit).

- **Telemarketers** utilize the telephone for selling, prospecting, or following up with customers. Outbound telemarketers use the telephone to call customers; inbound telemarketers (also called inside salespeople) respond to customers calling to place orders. These firms often employ toll-free numbers as a convenience for customers.

CAREERS IN SELLING

The outdated portrayal of salespeople as glad-handing con artists has unfortunately tainted a profession that is not only challenging and rewarding but also vital to the well-being of companies and the country. Sandham's call suggests some of the personal satisfactions: the intellectual and emotional reward of facing new problems and helping customers, flexible schedules, opportunities for travel and socializing, and limited supervision.

Also, compensation for salesmen is quite high. In 1999, the salary for a sales trainee averaged $24,290, which, with costs for travel and entertainment, increased to $34,790 for the beginning sales representative. For experienced sales executives, salaries range from $50,000 to more than $200,000 per year, according to surveys conducted by the American Marketing Association.

Further, the outlook for employment places the sales profession among the fastest growing fields, expected to grow by 24 percent by 2005, according to the U.S. Department of Labor.

SALES MANAGERS MANAGE PEOPLE

Sales management refers to the management of sales personnel, not the management of sales. Like all managers, the sales manager delegates responsibility and commensurate authority to others to multiply his or her effectiveness. However, there are some basic differences between supervising a field salesforce and managing an internal department. One is the geographic dispersion of the salesforce, precluding much face-to-face communication and complicating the process of communication and supervision.

Another is the main requirement of the creative selling job, to satisfy the customer. Thus, the sales manager's people are also working for a second boss, a fact that can lead to problems when, for example, the customer demands a low price that Merton can't afford to allow. Also, salesmen's hours can be long, and their work is often frustrating, with many other departments (billing, credit, shipping, promotion, and the like) influencing their activities, and many tasks (meeting objectives, servicing old accounts while bringing in new accounts, developing product knowledge, conducting effective sales presentations, and handling the paperwork associated with selling, among others) to be accomplished.

In addition to managing these often difficult-to-manage salespeople, the sales manager also has myriad other responsibilities, including planning, budgeting, forecasting, and designing the salesforce.

PLANNING

The planning task of the sales manager is conceptually the same as that of the marketing manager, involving the establishment of mission-related objectives based on a "SWOT" understanding of strengths, weaknesses, opportunities, and threats. Salesforce objectives include developing new business, selling, servicing, information gathering, and protecting the territory against inroads from competition. These objectives, which guide the formulation of sales strategies, should be developed in conjunction with the sales-force.

An important component of the sales planning process is the preparation of contingency plans that take into account unpredictable, uncontrollable influences, such as changes in economic, legal, or regulatory environments, that can affect sales performance. The planing framework should incorporate several premises, including a worst-case scenario.

FORECASTING

The whole organization looks to the sales manager's input to the forecast of what and how much can be expected to be sold. In a manufacturing operation, capacity, raw materials, components, labor, and space requirements are derived from the forecast. If it is too optimistic, the company has to bear the high cost of excessive inventories and the bad publicity from laying off surplus staff. If the forecast is low, the firm doesn't have the capacity to fill all the orders received. In this case, not only these orders but also many customers are lost, along with the money to get them to order, and all the future business they represent.

Recognizing the importance of forecasts, Merton marketers put special emphasis on getting them right, using breakdown and top-down techniques discussed in Chapter 12 and relying especially on input from inside and outside salespeople and sales management.

BUDGETING

Like all department heads, the sales manager develops a budget. For the sales department, this includes costs of administration, training, and expenses associated with selling, such as travel, meals, entertainment, vehicles, communications, sales meetings, shows and exhibits, and memberships.

SALESFORCE DESIGN

Major emphasis in this area was on how the salesforce would be structured, and what strategies would be implemented, to achieve the mission-related objectives established during the planning stage.

SALESFORCE STRUCTURE

The salesforce structure may be based on geography (territorial), product, customer type, or a combination of these. For example, Merton's sales manager could assign members of the salesforce to territories where potential sales volume justified this expense, or he could specialize the salesforce by product group (MM systems, Merton manufacturing components, and the like), or he could specialize the salesforce by customer types (for example, Sandham's focus on accounting professionals). At Merton's regional offices, a combination structure was used, with every sales associate cross-trained to understand all the product offerings.

SALESFORCE STRATEGY

Merton's sales managers, as part of their jobs, were responsible for holding periodic strategy sessions at which sales associates, based on their understanding of Merton new product introductions, changing needs and demographic characteristics of the market, and environmental changes (especially competitive initiatives) affecting market growth and profitability, agreed on strategic and tactical responses. For example, at these informal get-togethers, sales associates aired new objections they had heard from customers and discussed ways of overcoming them.

SALESFORCE MANAGEMENT

In general, the main focus of the sales manager's efforts was on recruiting, selecting, training, developing, directing, controlling, motivating, evaluating, and compensating productive sales associates.

RECRUITING AND SELECTING SALESPEOPLE

The objective of recruiting is to have a pool of applicants large enough to provide a sufficient number of persons with standards that meet the selection criteria, thus ensuring the recruiter the opportunity for critical selection. Because they bring to the job formal training in marketing, accounting, computers, the sciences, and other disciplines, college graduates are often recruited for sales training.

But recruiting costs money and takes time. Many sales jobs are filled through the hidden job market, when the sales manager calls some business acquaintances and asks where some good people might be found. There is always a certain amount of flux and good people changing jobs. If the opportunity is made sufficiently attractive, the job can be filled and is never advertised. Contacts and networking are the best ways to tap the hidden job market.

Hiring people whose objectives mesh with the organization's can reduce turnover, the greatest single personnel cost in industry today. Whenever an employee exits the company, the investment in orientation and training is lost along with the employee's future potential. When a salesperson leaves, a territory temporarily receives inadequate coverage, which not only reduces revenue due to lost orders but jeopardizes customer relations. If competition moves in, not only are orders lost, but customers are also lost, and customers are worth both the investment in direct and indirect promotion and the future business that will not be generated. Selection of salespeople is typically done after the recruit's personal history, aptitude, and intelligence test results have satisfied predetermined criteria. Ultimately, selection is based on interviews with sales executives who have unique experience to judge an applicant's potential contribution. It is important to be honest and realistic with recruits regarding promotion paths and potential earnings. A rosy picture painted to attract an outstanding candidate sows the seeds of disappointment and early departure.

TRAINING AND DEVELOPMENT

By increasing the employee's productivity and resultant earnings, training and development increase job satisfaction and reduce turnover. Training usually covers these areas:

- **Company orientation:** Because the salesperson will be representing the company, company orientation is important. Also, the representative needs to know whom to call for a customer with a technical problem, an inquiry about a credit line, or information from a specialist.

- **Product knowledge:** The salesperson is the expert on the product and must be thoroughly versed in product features and derivative benefits.

- **Selling approaches and techniques:** These are discussed earlier in this chapter.

- **Nonselling activities:** These activities include servicing, forecasting, sampling, handling complaints, and helping customers understand company credit and billing policies.

- **Market knowledge:** This area includes potentials, trends, and competitive activity. Some of this will be learned in the field. The salesperson, as eyes and ears of the company, will be reporting market conditions via daily call reports. Not the least of this knowledge is getting to know the customer's problems and viewpoint.

Development is a continuous process of renewing basics and introducing the salesforce to new products and applications. The latter is important in that it gives the representative an excuse to recontact customers and sell those who want the latest features.

DIRECTING AND CONTROLLING

Directing and controlling a far-flung group of ambitious, independent, creative, customer-oriented producers is a challenge. One of the reasons people enter sales is to be their "own boss," within limits. Unfortunately, the number of people who have the ability to set priorities and manage their time efficiently could be much larger. Since the advantage of personal selling over indirect forms of promotion is physical presence and the ability to overcome objections and close, a salesperson works most productively when with the client. But under normal conditions, the typical salesperson has time to make only six calls per day. Since Friday afternoon isn't too productive because some customers leave work early, many representatives do their paperwork then, leaving four-plus days per week to make calls. Subtract three weeks for vacation, seven holidays, time spent at development and sales meetings, storm days, sick days, and personal business, and it becomes obvious that the salesperson must make productive use of what time is available.

Prioritizing customers into key, medium, and small accounts helps to make more efficient use of time. Establishing call norms for these customer targets and specifying that, say, a minimum of 20 percent of new business should be added each year, guides the representative in territory planning and gives the sales manager a yardstick against which to measure performance.

MOTIVATION

It is particularly important in sales to counteract demotivating forces such as overdemanding customers, aggressive competition, fear of failure, and insecurity and, at the other extreme, a windfall such as very high commission income. Motivation cannot be generated from the outside—it is an inner drive. There are no universal motivators—ideally, each individual should have his or her own motivation mix, based on individual career paths. The components of that mix can be categorized as direct and indirect incentives. **Direct incentives** include:

- **Creating an organizational environment** in which participation and communication are encouraged.

- **Setting quotas** that are achievable by a majority of the salesforce with a moderate amount of extra effort. It is better to have a salesforce of enthusiastic winners than disappointed losers. Furthermore, since their sales are too low to achieve quota this period, some losers may decide to let orders from customers who are not in a rush accumulate until the next period, creating cash flow peaks and valleys.

- **Providing recognition, awards, and other nonmonetary incentives.**

Indirect incentives include **contests,** which have to be carefully planned so that they do not result in an effect opposite to that planned. For example, a contest to generate business during an off-peak period might be based on total volume of orders written during that period. If rules are not clear, or if there are insufficient controls, some salespeople might explain to key accounts that they need orders to win a contest and get the customer to anticipate future requirements and place orders early, with the understanding that shipment and billing will be delayed. This creates peaks and valleys in business volume instead of smoothing them.

EVALUATION

The sales manager's evaluation of the salesforce will typically consist of both informal and formal approaches.

- **Informal assessment** may be based on call reports, a work plan or territory marketing plan, and field trips with the representative to visit key accounts.

- **Formal reviews** are characterized by comparisons with other salespersons and past performance in such areas as productivity and cost control.

COMPENSATION

Compensation should fairly reflect sales objectives. If the emphasis is on service, and management wants to maintain strong control, straight salary is usually paid. If sales volume is most important, and profit margins are critical, straight commission is a popular arrangement. Most professional salespeople with a good product or service prefer straight commission arrangements, usually with a draw (repaid from commissions), under which they can often earn more than the company president.

Combination plans can be structured to achieve a desired balance of advantages of different compensation plans (for example, 50 percent guaranteed salary and 50 percent commission). The package can be further modified by offering a bonus based on a predetermined performance level over a defined period of time. A problem with bonuses is that they are too often regarded as a benefit, and if total performance expectations are not realized and the bonus is not paid, it can hurt morale and affect performance.

SALESFORCE AUTOMATION

Eric Sandham, whose sales call illustrated the sales presentation process, also illustrates a major trend in selling—Salesforce Automation (SFA) or the application of new technologies to make personal selling and sales management more efficient and cost effective. Among the benefits of SFA are improved sales presentations and product launches; lower selling, print, and training costs; and more attentive customer service. SFA tools include pagers, portable fax machines, notebook computers, software programs, cellular phones, and voice and electronic mail.

For example, in planning calls, Sandham uses a software package in his laptop computer that identifies prospective accounts in his territory and routes calls on these accounts for efficient coverage. This computer, hooked into Merton's MIS database, also provides information regarding the sales potential of prospective accounts, and the needs and sales history of existing customers. Other software packages assist Sandham in preparing and making presentations, organizing prospect lists, and making follow-up calls. Spreadsheets help customers optimize purchase expenditures, and Web sites cover product features and benefits (Internet marketing is covered in Chapter 21).

Supplementing his laptop, Sandham uses his cellular phone and portable fax to communicate with customers and Merton office personnel for a variety of reasons, such as making appointments, getting price approvals, confirming delivery dates, solving customer problems, and getting up-to-date information on products and prospects.

Sandham's sales manager also has many uses for these electronic vehicles, including spreadsheet programs for processing sales data, communicating with sales representatives, and preparing and presenting sales meetings.

INTERNATIONAL PERSPECTIVE

Both salespeople and sales managers, as key components of the promotion mix, face problems in global markets they rarely face in the domestic market.

Sales presentations, for example, are generally subject to the same cultural and legal restraints, discussed in Chapter 17, that affect advertising and other indirect promotional appeals. Language barriers in particular can present extreme communication problems in the face-to-face context, as highlighted by Global Focus 18-1.

GLOBAL FOCUS 18-1

Block Those Language Blunders!

Many U.S. multinationals have had difficulty crossing the language barrier, with results ranging from mild embarrassment to outright failure. Seemingly innocuous brand names and advertising phrases can take on unintended or hidden meanings when translated into other languages. Careless translations can make a marketer look downright foolish to foreign consumers, as shown by these classic language blunders:

- When Coca-Cola first marketed Coke in China in 1929, it developed a group of Chinese characters that sounded like the product name but translated to mean "bite the wax tadpole." Today, the characters translate as "happiness in the mouth."

- Several car makers have had problems when their brand names crashed into the language barrier. The Chevrolet Nova translated into Spanish as *no va*—"it doesn't go." GM changed the name to Caribe, and sales increased. Ford introduced its Fiera truck only to discover that the name means "ugly old woman" in Spanish. And it introduced its Comet car in Mexico as the Caliente—slang for "streetwalker." Rolls Royce avoided the name Silver Mist in German markets, where "mist" means "manure." Sunbeam, however, discovered the Germans had little use for a "manure wand" when it entered this market with its Mist Stick.

- Advertsing themes often lose—or gain—something in the translation. The Coors beer slogan, "get loose with Coors," came out in Spanish as "get the runs with Coors." Coca-Cola's "Coke adds life" theme in Japanese translated into "Coke brings your ancestors back from the dead."

Such classic boo-boos are soon discovered and corrected, and they may result in little more than embarrassment for the marketer. But countless other more subtle blunders may go undetected and damage performance in less obvious ways. The multinational company must carefully screen its brand names and advertising messages to guard against those that might damage sales, make it look silly, or offend its customers.

Source: David A. Ricks, "Products that Crashed into the Language Barrier," *Business and Society Review,* Spring 1983, pp. 46–50.

Other barriers to effective face-to-face communication include different perceptual frameworks, and laws and regulations affecting message and media selection. Additionally, salespeople often face the problem of inadequate sources from which to research customer needs and build persuasive presentations.

SALES MANAGEMENT CHALLENGES IN GLOBAL MARKETS

In addition to communication problems facing their salesforces, which they must help them address, sales managers representing U.S. companies abroad also face a diversity of personnel management problems unique to foreign markets.

The variety of roles, status, and tenure among salespeople engaged in international marketing activities, added to the diversity of cultures they are likely to encounter, presents problems in personnel management hardly imagined in the domestic market. Exacerbating these problems is the comparative lack of intercultural competence among U.S. firms competing in global markets, where lack of foreign language and international business skills costs millions in inefficient management, weak negotiations, and lost sales.

From the sales manager's perspective, these general considerations present a number of practical problems in recruiting, selecting, training, motivating, and compensating salesforce members. The following summaries of these problems also offer guidelines for addressing them consistent with global environmental constraints, status of the salesperson (expatriate or national), and goals of sales personnel and employers.

• *RECRUITING*

This critical first step of the process, designed to attract a pool of attractive candidates from which to select employees, begins with formal job descriptions that consider long- and short-range company goals and needs and requirements indigenous to specific countries. These descriptions should also spell out advantages and disadvantages of the foreign position in terms of prospective employee needs and goals. In addition to traditional domestic personnel sources (current salespeople, employment agencies, job ads, and the like), global recruiters should consider foreign students attending domestic colleges; other companies selling in foreign markets; foreign expatriates who want to go home; and acquisition, or joint venture arrangements, with foreign companies and their pools of prospective employees.

• SELECTION

Recruiting will attract applicants from which the company must select the best, a procedure that can vary from a single informal interview to lengthy interviewing and testing of such measures as sales aptitude, analytical and organizational skills, and personality traits. Regardless of procedure, of key importance are such personal attributes related to foreign assignments as intelligence, ambition, appearance, speaking ability, sales and business background, sensitivity toward other cultural differences, interpersonal communication skills with host country contacts, the ability to make decisions and work independently without home office support, knowledge in many areas relating to a new cultural environment, and a favorable outlook toward an international assignment.

Given the difficulty, importance, and cost of selecting expatriate employees, many companies are including employee families as part of the selection process, especially in light of evidence that unsuccessful family adjustment is the main reason for expatriate dissatisfaction. Interviews with family members frequently reveal unexpected antagonisms toward potentially painful adjustments to new foods, languages, cultural values, schools, friends, and status.

Many of these attributes—such as the ability to adopt to a foreign culture or speak the language—can be assumed when a company is recruiting and selecting host-country nationals to work in the host country, but selection procedures should be at least as rigorous, especially in light of stringent laws protecting host-country worker rights in most European, Oriental, and less-developed countries (in Venezuela, for example, a terminated employee national is legally entitled to one month's severance pay and 15 day's salary for every month of service exceeding eight months, plus an additional 15 day's pay for each year employed, plus a mandate that he or she be replaced by another national, at the same salary, within 30 days).

• TRAINING

In addition to content of programs that train sales personnel in domestic markets (for example, objectives, products, and markets; product features and benefits; competitor characteristics and strategies; customer needs, motives, habits; effective sales presentations), programs designed to train expatriates to work in foreign markets include content on developing cultural skills, as well as learning about the customs, values, social, and political institutions of the host country. Objectives of a typical intercultural program include abilities and skills required to (1) communicate verbally and nonverbally and convey a positive regard and sincere interest in people and their culture, (2) tolerate ambiguity and cope with cultural differences and frustration, (3) display empathy for other peoples' needs and differences from their viewpoint, and (4) be nonjudgmental regarding the values and standards of others.

Training programs for host-country nationals are similar to domestic programs, emphasizing the company, its products and markets, technical information, and selling methods. Because both expatriates and nationals tend to cling to their own attitudes and behavior, an important goal of both programs is to establish an open-minded ability to see things from the perspective of others. Continuation training is generally more important in global than in domestic training programs because of lack of routine contact with the home office.

• *MOTIVATION*

The overall goal of most motivation programs—to persuade employees to blend personal objectives with company objectives—is difficult enough to achieve in the domestic market, where marketing jobs frequently involve hard work, long hours, travel away from home, aggressive competitors, and, especially, isolation from associates.

To boost morale and encourage people to work at their best level in the face of these obstacles, management typically relies on the motivational force of: (1) an organizational climate that encourages participation and communication, holds marketing people in high esteem, and rewards outstanding performance; (2) quotas, or standards, that are achievable with a moderate amount of extra effort; and (3) both monetary and nonmonetary incentives (bonuses, meetings, honors, and opportunities to meet with "company brass").

In international markets, however, these traditional motivational methods don't always work. For example, the very nature of an expatriate's situation isolates him or her from other company personnel. Cultural differences can also affect motivation method effectiveness; for example, in Japan, a tradition of paternalism, collectivism, lifetime employment, and seniority can render recognition for individual performance acutely embarrassing to an employee who doesn't want to appear different from his or her peers. Similarly, in countries with the fatalistic philosophy that Allah is responsible for all achievement, it is often difficult to reward individual enterprise effectively.

Management should take these differences into account in developing motivational plans in international markets where, given the high cost of turnover and low morale, they can be even more important than in the domestic market. Of particular importance is making criteria for promotion and other rewards clear and following through quickly and fairly.

• *COMPENSATION*

Especially in managing international personnel, compensation plans can be used to reward, recruit, develop, motivate, and retain personnel, although they tend to get unwieldy if they try to do too much.

Before deciding on the mix of goals a compensation plan will aim to achieve, the manager should consider how circumstances in global markets will modify these objectives. For example, in high-tax countries, more emphasis is often placed on liberal expense accounts and fringe benefits, which can account for up to 60 percent of salary in a high-tax country like France. Another circumstance involves differences in compensation between expatriate and "home" personnel working for the same company. If the group receiving the lesser amount feels aggrieved and mistreated, it can be reflected in performance and turnover costs. And there will be differences: short-term expatriate assignments usually involve payment of overseas premiums, all excess expenses, and allowances for tax differences. Longer expatriate assignments can include home-leave benefits and travel allowances for spouses and children, often exceeding the base salary. (One study showed that fringe benefit costs for a base salary of $40,000, over a three-year period, ranged from $138,300 in Canada to $427,000 in Nigeria.) Indeed, sometimes the amount paid to expatriates to persuade them to take a foreign assignment can make it difficult to repatriate them back to a much higher cost of living in the home country.

CHAPTER PERSPECTIVE

The personal selling function is the most expensive component of the promotion mix and the only one that generates direct revenues and feedback from customers. Professional salespeople are order getters who are often supported by technical and missionary salespeople and order-taking inside salespeople, usually in selling expensive, technically complex products in business and consumer markets. Professional selling careers offer a variety of benefits, including the intrinsic reward of helping customers, good compensation, limited supervision, and interesting, responsible work. In preparing need-oriented customer presentations, professional salespeople integrate other promotion mix elements into a process that involves prospecting, qualifying, identifying needs, handling objections, closing sales, and initiating follow-up. In addition to sales compensation, most of the high cost of the selling function is generated by the sales management function, involving such activities as forecasting, budgeting, and recruiting, selecting, motivating, directing, evaluating, and compensating salespeople. All these management tasks become much more difficult in foreign markets, where cultural and legal differences create problems in all areas of sales and sales management. Mitigating, somewhat, these communication problems and costs is Salesforce Automation or the application of new technologies to the sales process.

KNOW THE CONCEPTS
TERMS FOR STUDY

Approach
Budgeting
Close
Cold canvassing
Compensation
Creative selling
Follow-up
Forecasting
Handling objections
Incentives
Need satisfaction presentation

Order getters
Order takers
Personal selling
Planning presentations
Prospecting
Qualifying
Salesforce automation (SFA)
Salesforce design
Salesforce management
Structured approach
Telemarketing

MATCHUP EXERCISES

1. Match up the activity in the second column with the stage of the sales process listed in the first column.

1. prospecting
2. qualifying
3. approach

4. presentation

5. close

a. Wear a smile and a shoeshine.
b. Check prospect's potential.
c. Summarize benefits; ask for order.
d. Show how your service will solve customer's problem.
e. Ask customer for referrals.

2. Match up the benefits in the second column with the sales activities in the first column.

1. handling objections

2. forecast
3. follow-up
4. directing/controlling

a. helps salesperson use time more effectively
b. opportunity for add-on business
c. helps relate resources to sales
d. shows that prospect is interested and wants more information

3. Match up the type of selling in the first column with the statement in the second column.

1. order getter

2. missionary salesperson

a. This drill press will give you twice as many holes at half the cost.
b. How many of your employees are engaged in manufacturing?

3. suggestion selling

4. telephone salesperson

c. What would you like to drink with your cheeseburger?

d. You have been selected for an all-expense-paid trip to Hawaii!

4. Match up the sales management activity in the first column with the outcome in the second column.

1. budgeting

2. recruiting
3. motivating

4. compensating

a. Costs keep pace with unexpected changes in sales volume.
b. Builds large pool of applicants.
c. Sales reps don't feel it will be impossible to achieve their quotas.
d. Airing of complaints is encouraged.

QUESTIONS FOR REVIEW AND DISCUSSION

1. This excerpt of a want ad appeared in the "Sales Opportunities" section of a large metropolitan newspaper:

INTERNET ENGINEERING SALES REPRESENTATIVE
$150K

Network Strategies is an Internet engineering company, which specializes in e-commerce solutions to Fortune 100 companies. Our core competencies are in protocol analysis and Cisco router training for biz-to-biz e-commerce, VPNs & streaming video. The candidate will be responsible for cultivating existing and opening new accounts. We are seeking an energetic individual w/the ability to handle multitasks in an entrepreneural environment. 3-5 yrs exp in sales w/a proven track record of meeting or exceeding financial targets.

What does this advertisement suggest about the benefits of a position as a professional salesperson?

2. You are just starting a job selling photographic supplies and accessories to retailers. Describe how you would prospect for leads.

3. Design a reporting system that will provide you with a record of customer status (activity and when last purchased) and product sales.

4. What preparation should be done prior to contacting a referred lead?

ANSWERS
MATCHUP EXERCISES

1. 1c, 2b, 3a, 4d, 5c

2. 1d, 2c, 3b, 4a

3. 1a, 2b, 3c, 4d

4. 1a, 2b, 3d, 4c

QUESTIONS FOR REVIEW AND DISCUSSION

1. Benefits include helping customers, good compensation, travel opportunities, limited supervision, increasing responsibilities, and a high-visibility career track.

2. In a local library, look through the Yellow Pages of telephone books that cover your territory and jot down the names, addresses, and telephone numbers of each photography store. Note names of proprietors, store specialties, and branches if given. Don't overlook photo departments in larger stores, and commercial photographers. Try to obtain a list of any associations, and of stores that buy as a group. As you travel through your territory, be on the lookout for new stores that might not have been listed in the telephone directories. Ask your customers about competition.

3. The simplest system would be a 3 × 5 card file, or a loose leaf ledger. Use one card or page for each customer. Note the date of each sales call and what was purchased. Keep a running subtotal.

On a separate spreadsheet, preferably a multicolumnar accounting worksheet, head a separate column for each product you sell with the name of the item and its unit price. As sales are made, write the customer name at the left of the items purchased in the proper columns. Weekly, subtotal the columns and "cross foot" the rows. This will provide you with sales by customer and sales by product.

More sophisticated, electronic spreadsheet systems are available from business supply houses, or your vendor may have a system they prefer you use.

4. If it is a referred lead, make sure that you have the name of the referrer correct and that you have obtained as much information from the referrer as you can. Determine what additional information you need to qualify the prospect and list the questions to be asked to obtain it. Based on what you know about the prospect, think about his or her problem(s) and how your product or service can help. Plan what you are going to say when you telephone, remembering that the purpose of the call is to get an appointment to see qualified prospects. Work on the phrasing of the first few sentences to create a favorable first impression and lead into your qualification questions. Anticipate and write down the replies that could be made to each question and what you will say in return. Add to this list with each telephone call and revise your replies until you have the wording that works best. As you continue to make calls, your experience and feel for the situation will result in an improving "batting average" of appointments, which will improve your confidence and enthusiasm.

19

DISTRIBUTION PLANNING I: CHANNEL STRATEGY

OVERVIEW

Distribution is generally the most differentiated and least understood of all marketing mix components; it is also the component least susceptible to change and most likely to block a successful entry strategy in global markets, where channels lengthen and logistics problems multiply. Efficient channel and logistics strategies begin with an understanding of available channel structures, flows, functions, values, and costs as they relate to customer needs and company objectives and resources.

DISTRIBUTION PLANNING MOVES GOODS THROUGH CHANNELS

The fourth, or place, component of the marketing mix entails distribution planning designed to implement marketing plans by getting the right product or service to the right place, in the right form, at the right price, to the right customers at the right time. It is also, frequently, the component that has the most direct, decisive influence on other marketing mix components. For example, Merton's selection of a channel (for example, agents or brokers) to introduce its MM systems into a new market will help determine the MM's price (which must account for distribution costs discussed in Chapter 16), its promotion program (which will involve supporting distributor promotion efforts and working with distributor salespeople), and the product itself (which must be attractive and profitable to the distributor and fit into an existing product line).

Distribution planning involves systematic analysis and decision making pertaining to the movement of materials and final goods from producers to consumers. These decisions encompass channel selection and control, as well as the four elements of the physical distribution process: transportation, warehousing, inventory management, and order processing. Key goals of the distribution planning process include integrating the elements of the physical distribution process with each other, with selected channels, and with the product/price/promotion elements of the marketing mix.

In this chapter, we focus on the first stage of the distribution planning process: designing, finding, and managing distribution channel systems that best meet a diversity of selection criteria, such as customer needs, product characteristics, and company resources and objectives. We begin with an overview of types of channels available, functions they perform, flows they facilitate, decisions they make, costs they incur, and benefits they provide. Then we examine considerations and criteria involved in designing and managing efficient channel systems. In Chapter 20, we examine logistics considerations controlling the flow of products into, through, and out of channels between maker and customer.

CHANNEL FUNCTIONS ENHANCE MARKETING COST EFFECTIVENESS

Distribution channels are defined as individuals and organizations, also called intermediaries, that help get materials and finished products from producers to consumers. Worldwide, they are among the most varied of all marketing mix elements, the least understood and controlled by marketing management, and the most likely to block a company's entry into global markets. Channels can vary in length (number of intermediaries used), depending on the functions the manufacturer needs to have performed and the feasibility of delegating these functions to others.

At one extreme the manufacturer assumes all distribution functions, including contacting customers, matching products to customer needs, promoting products, physically distributing the products, and financing sales. At the other extreme, practically all these functions are delegated to various kinds of distributors, including wholesalers, retailers, agents, and brokers.

In Merton's domestic market, for example, stocking distributors provide a number of functions that combine to make marketing MM systems a lot more efficient and inexpensive than if Merton salespeople sold MM systems directly to customers. For one thing, these distributors are better equipped than a single company would be to locate and contact the tens of thousands of prospective MM customers and to match MM systems to their needs. In addition to saving Merton the expense of hiring and managing a huge salesforce, these distributors also provide a number of other useful functions: they promote Merton products on the local level, assume risks of financing the purchase of MM systems by extending credit to their customers, feed back useful research to Merton planners on changing needs and product applications in their territories, and assume a large part of the cost of storing and moving MM systems out to customer premises. From the all-important perspective of the customer, these functions combine to get the right products to them at the right time, from the right place, in the right form.

CHANNEL NETWORKS IN CONSUMER AND INDUSTRIAL MARKETS

In planning distribution networks for the MM line in both domestic and global markets, Merton planners first had to decide what external distribution channels, if any, to use. Then, if it is decided to use external intermediaries, subsequent decisions would pertain to types of channel intermediaries to use (retailers or wholesalers, for example) and elements of physical distribution needed to ensure that Merton products moved efficiently and profitably to customers. (Chapter 20 examines global logistics considerations that address physical distribution processes.)

Figure 19-1 illustrates channels commonly used to distribute consumer and industrial products.

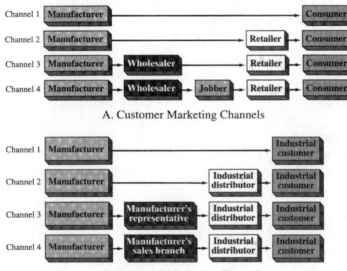

A. Customer Marketing Channels

B. Industrial Marketing Channels

Figure 19–1. Consumer and industrial marketing channels.

• *CONSUMER PRODUCTS*

Figure 19-1A shows the main channels of distribution for consumer products. Channel 1 consists of a manufacturer selling directly to consumers, as when Fuller Brush or Avon sells products door-to-door or L. L. Bean sells through direct catalog sales. Channel 2 contains one distribution level, as when large retailers like Sears, IKEA, and Wal-Mart sell cameras, furniture, and other products that they buy directly from manufacturers. Channel 3 contains two distribution levels, as when small manufacturers of food, drugs, and other products sell to wholesalers, who then sell to retailers, who then sell to consumers. Channel 4 contains three distribution levels, as when jobbers in the meat-packing industry buy from wholesalers and sell to smaller retailers, who sell to consumers.

• *INDUSTRIAL PRODUCTS*

Figure 19-1B shows the main channels for distributing industrial products. A manufacturer can use its own salesforce to sell directly to industrial customers (Channel 1), or it can sell to industrial distributors who sell to industrial customers (Channel 2), or it can sell through manufacturer's representatives or its own sales branches to industrial distributors, who sell to industrial customers (Channels 3 and 4).

CHANNEL FLOWS INFLUENCE CHANNEL CHOICE

From the perspective of a marketing planner assessing channel options in domestic and global markets, an understanding of channel flows is a good starting point for weighing costs and benefits of each option. As illustrated in Figure 19-2 (see page 487), these flows, which connect the intermediaries in a channel, encompass goods, ownership, payment, information, and promotional materials.

Here is how Merton planners envisioned that these flows would affect the distribution of MM systems and choice of channel strategies in diverse markets.

- **Physical flow:** Suppliers ship parts to Merton, which are then assembled into Merton systems distributed through various intermediaries farther down the line.

- **Title flow:** Merton buys parts and then assembles and sells MM systems; thus, the ownership passes from suppliers to Merton and then to dealers and finally to the consumer. Sometimes Merton assumes the risk of resale by offering merchandise on consignment, delaying payment from the dealer—and passage of ownership—until the product is sold.

- **Information flow:** If products are to succeed, each link on the chain must adjust according to information provided by other channel members.

- **Promotion flow:** Merton receives promotional materials from suppliers for parts it needs and then promotes its products and services

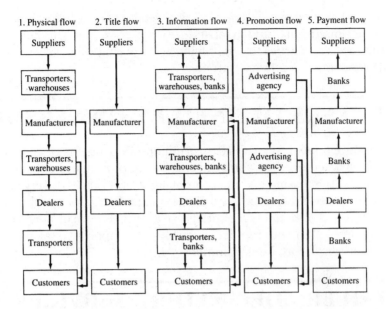

Figure 19–2. Marketing flows emphasize complexity of channels.

to dealers that carry and promote MM systems to prospective customers.

- **Payment flow:** This is a backwards flow, where money passes from customer to intermediary to Merton to Merton's suppliers to pay for goods delivered, using payment methods discussed in Chapter 16 (open account, consignment, letters of credit, and so on).

Note that the more cluttered a channel is with intermediaries, the more complex, costly, and risky become these flows. For example, products can get lost, stolen, or damaged with long physical flows; cash flows can get dammed with long payment flows, and communications can get distorted and delayed with long information and promotion flows. Assessing the relative value of a channel then becomes a matter of balancing the cost of these flows against the value of functions distributors can perform for sellers.

RETAILERS AND WHOLESALERS

More than 90 percent of all goods sold in developed countries move through wholesale and/or retail channels, so it behooves marketers formulating a channel strategy to understand characteristics, costs, and benefits of each, and how they can be linked together to achieve various marketing objectives.

In the next section, we describe types of retailers and wholesalers as they exist in the United States and in most developed countries. This next section also examines approaches for identifying and working effectively with retailers, wholesalers, and other intermediaries.

RETAILERS DEFINED BY OWNERSHIP

By ownership, retailers are classified as either independents or chains. A retail chain, characterized by common ownership of multiple units, engages in centralized purchasing and decision making, and is able to serve a large, dispersed market because of specialization, standardization, and elaborate control systems. Although accounting for a relatively small percentage of outlets in developed countries, retail chains are responsible for more than half of total retail store sales volume.

RETAILERS DEFINED BY SERVICES AND FACILITIES

To stay in business, retailers must offer location, price, service, convenience, and product assortment features while keeping costs down. The features each stresses will determine the nature of the retail operation.

Following are predominant types of store and nonstore retailers and the mix of features each employs to implement its marketing strategy.

STORE RETAILERS

• *CONVENIENCE STORES*
Convenience stores provide convenience in the form of long hours and locations close to residential areas. They are food-oriented and cater to emergency purchases. Prices are higher, selection is limited, and the stores are basically self-service; 7-Eleven is an example of this kind of retailer.

• *SPECIALTY STORES*
Specialty stores focus on product depth rather than width. For example, Blockbuster Video outlets carry a narrow product line (videotapes) and a depth of film categories and titles. Typical product lines carried include apparel, gourmet foods, appliances, toys, electronics, and sportswear. Salespeople are generally knowledgeable, and prices are relatively high. Hours and location must be convenient enough to draw some impulse shoppers, but depth of product offerings provides the main draw.

• *DEPARTMENT STORES*

Department stores are organized into separate departments for purposes of buying, promotion, service, and control. They feature a high degree of product assortment, including fashion apparel, furniture, home furnishings, and appliances. Because they must serve large numbers of customers to turn over their large inventory, department stores are centrally located and offer convenient hours. Pricing varies according to store image.

• *FULL-LINE DISCOUNT STORES*

Full-line discount stores, like K-Mart and Wal-Mart, are department stores with low prices, relatively broad merchandise assortments, brand name products, low-rent locations, wide aisles, self-service, many merchandise displays, and less emphasis on credit sales.

• *CATALOG SHOWROOMS*

Catalog showrooms offer deep discounts on high-ticket, name-brand products and even less service than discount stores offer. Customers must often wait in line to examine, or pick up, merchandise selected from catalogs. Credit and return policies are limited, location is often inconvenient, and facilities are spare.

• *SUPERMARKETS*

Supermarkets are relatively large, low-margin, low-price, high-volume, self-service operations with convenient locations and hours, and a wide selection of groceries, meat, fish, prepared foods, household products, and produce.

• *SUPERSTORES*

Superstores combine the food and product assortment of supermarkets with that of department, or sometimes specialty, stores. Products carried include garden supplies, TVs, clothing, wine, boutique items, books, banking and dry cleaning services, bakery products, household appliances, and a full line of supermarket items. They typically occupy about twice the 15,000 to 20,000 square feet of supermarkets and generate more than twice the $6 million of average annual supermarket sales.

• *COMBINATION STORES*

Combination stores combine food/grocery and general merchandise sales in one facility, with general merchandise providing 30 to 40 percent of overall sales. Combination stores go farther than superstores in appealing to one-stop shopping, typically occupying between 50,000 and 200,000 square feet. Size and customer volume allow these retailers to operate more efficiently, increasing impulse purchases and size of average transaction (often selling products in bulk quantities). Prices are often discounted, generally reasonable, for low-profit food items and higher-profit general merchandise.

A **hypermarket** is a variant on the combination store that integrates a supermarket and a discount department store and occupies at least 60,000 square feet. Europe has about 2500 hypermarkets; the United States has about 1500. Other forms of low-price store retailing showing appreciable recent growth include limited-line and warehouse food stores, off-price chains, discount drug stores, factory outlet stores, and flea markets. All are characterized by few customer services, low prices, and plain store fixtures.

NONSTORE RETAILERS

• *SERVICE BUSINESSES*

Service businesses, like movie theaters, banks, taxi companies, hospitals, and health clubs provide a product that is a service.

• *VENDING MACHINES*

Vending machines use coin or card-operated machinery to dispense goods and services, such as soda, food, cigarettes, video games, and airline life insurance. Advantages include around-the-clock sale, and no need for sales personnel. Disadvantages include risks of pilferage, damage, and high maintenance costs.

• *DIRECT MARKETING*

Direct marketing includes mail order catalogs, direct response advertising, direct mail, telemarketing, and television shopping, as discussed in Chapter 17.

TYPES OF WHOLESALERS

There are three principal types of wholesalers: merchant-wholesalers, agents/brokers, and manufacturer-wholesalers.

MERCHANT-WHOLESALERS

Merchant-wholesalers are independently-owned operations that buy and take possession of goods for future resale. They represent the largest group of wholesalers, accounting for more than 50 percent of sales in developed markets. This group is further divided into full-service and limited-service wholesalers.

• *FULL-SERVICE WHOLESALERS*

Full-service wholesalers buy merchandise; maintain inventory: provide trade credit; store and deliver merchandise; offer research, management, and promotional assistance; and service customers with sales personnel. This model is common in the pharmaceutical, grocery, and hardware industries. As examples, **General merchandise (fill-in) wholesalers** carry a wide assortment of products (such as hardware, apparel, and drugs) for retailers, but they don't offer much depth within any product line. **Specialty merchandise (limited line) wholesalers** carry an extensive assortment within a limited product range (for example, health and frozen foods) and offer a broad range of functions. **Rack jobbers** set up displays on racks or shelves and sell their merchandise—usually heavily advertised, branded products (for example, health and beauty aids, stationery, toys)—on consignment. **Franchise wholesalers** service independent retailer affiliates, such as hardware and auto parts suppliers, who use a standardized storefront design, business format, name, and purchase system. **Industrial distributors** sell to producers rather than retailers. They may carry a broad range of merchandise (such as ball bearings, power tools, and motors), a general line, or a specialty line. They perform a full range of wholesaler services, including inventory, credit, and delivery, for their customers.

• *LIMITED-SERVICE WHOLESALERS*

Limited-service wholesalers do not provide the full range of functions provided by full-service wholesalers. A **drop shipper,** for example, takes an order, finds a company to fill it, takes title to merchandise, but does not maintain inventory; **Cash-and-carry wholesalers** provide no credit, delivery, merchandising, or promotional assistance; have no salesforce; and don't aid in marketing research or planning. They are, however, important for "fill-in" items (such as auto parts) or perishable goods (such as fruit), have low prices, and offer immediate product availability. **Truck wholesalers** carry semiperishable merchandise (bread or milk, for example) and simultaneously sell and deliver along a regular sales route. **Mail-order wholesalers** maintain no salesforce, relying on catalogs to get attention for their products, which retailers may order and receive by mail.

BROKERS AND AGENTS

Brokers and agents work for commissions or fees, provide trained salesforces, and help manufacturers expand sales. This form of wholesaling does not involve ownership of goods and limits the amount of service offered. Brokers are employed as needed to bring buyers and sellers to terms. Although paid by the seller, they are useful to both because of their knowledge of market conditions and their ability to negotiate. Agents are permanent, independent salespeople who represent either the buyer or the seller. They may represent more than one manufacturer, which removes the need to invest in a salesforce. There are several different kinds of agents.

• *MANUFACTURERS' AGENTS*

Manufacturers' agents represent two or more firms carrying complementary, noncompeting items. By selling many different products, these agents make it economically feasible to cover geographically scattered markets. Small manufacturers may have only one product represented by agents, which gets wider exposure by being grouped with others. Manufacturers' agents work on commission, do not offer credit, carry limited inventory, and have little to say about pricing and promotion.

• *SELLING AGENTS*

Selling agents, although also independent, handle a manufacturer's entire product line. This, too, saves the manufacturer from maintaining a salesforce. The selling agent negotiates terms of pricing, delivery, and credit and may perform other wholesaler functions except ownership of goods. Selling agents are prevalent among small manufacturers.

• *PURCHASING AGENTS*

Purchasing agents work for the buyer, choosing and often warehousing and shipping suitable merchandise to the retail outlets served.

• *COMMISSION MERCHANTS*

Commission merchants are common in agriculture. They take goods on consignment, sell them, and keep a portion of the proceeds as a commission.

MANUFACTURER-WHOLESALERS

Manufacturer-wholesalers are owned and operated by manufacturers with sales volume that justifies such an investment. These operations consist of sales branches that warehouse and sell goods and sales offices that are limited to arranging for merchandise distribution.

RETAILER AND WHOLESALER MARKETING DECISIONS

Understanding marketing decisions made by retailers and wholesalers in such areas as target market selection and product, place, price, and promotion strategies can help tailor marketing mix programs that will attract and maintain productive distribution relations.

• *TARGET MARKET SELECTION*

For both wholesalers and retailers, all decisions regarding products, distribution, price, and promotion follow this initial decision. Both attempt to narrow prospective markets to the most profitable segments. Using such demographic data as age, income, and geographic location of profitable prospect groups, retailers tailor product offerings, prices, store location, and store atmosphere to attract these groups.

Wholesalers use retailer characteristics to identify profitable target markets. Will they serve large or small retailers? Variety stores or specialty stores? Those in need of quick delivery? Backup service? Financing? Answers to these questions determine the nature of wholesale operations.

• *PRODUCT ASSORTMENT AND SERVICE*

Here are some of the questions addressed by retailers in deciding on product assortments. Should a wide variety of products be stocked, or only a few lines, with a depth of products within each? Should high-quality or lower priced goods be emphasized? Additionally, intangibles such as service and the atmosphere in which products are presented are considered. Customers buying quality merchandise expect quality service and a posh store atmosphere.

Wholesalers are usually expected to carry a large assortment of products to meet retailers' immediate needs. Because wholesalers generally pay for the goods they stock, however, carrying a large inventory is expensive, and the tendency is to pare lines down to the most profitable products, without losing retail customers. Retailers' desire for services such as credit and delivery must also be considered in attempting to find a balance between serving customers and maintaining profitability.

• *PLACE*

A number of options are open to retailers in selecting a location. An isolated location may be fine for a discount store or catalog showroom, where price advantages will impel customers to go out of their way to shop. Specialty stores and service businesses may choose to locate in an unplanned central business district, with its heavy foot traffic. In neighborhood or regional shopping centers (shopping malls), a planned mix of stores benefits all retailers.

Wholesalers mimic low-end retailers in their choice of location. For them, a functional building in a low-rent, low-tax neighborhood is ideal. Key considerations include proximity to manufacturers, retailers, or major connecting highways. Money spent on improving facilities is usually directed at increasing efficiency, such as by computerizing or automating warehouses.

• *PRICE*

For retailers, price decisions depend on product decisions. A high-quality product line will require higher prices; a strategy that rests on quick turnover of stock points to lower pricing. High overhead resulting from liberal customer services and "atmosphere" will raise prices. Still, the key to profitability is intelligent buying, with an understanding of the price that can reasonably be charged for the goods. Retailers often employ creative pricing policies, where underpriced items draw customers who then buy more profitable products. Or products are overpriced initially because a percentage of stock will sell at that price, with markdowns made later.

Wholesalers, like retailers, operate under a "buy low, sell high" law of profitability. However, if wholesalers can find appropriate merchandise at low prices, the price break will usually be passed on to retailers to encourage volume buying or to attract new customers.

• *PROMOTION*

Retailers vary greatly in the types and degree of promotion they use to attract customers. A funeral home would never advertise that its prices were "insane"; an out-of-the-way discount store would never rely on word-of-mouth advertising. As with all other marketing decisions, target market determines promotional strategy.

Because image counts less, and because they perform a straightforward service, wholesalers advertise little. Some wholesalers do employ salesforces, however, and find it wise to promote themselves to retailers in other ways.

VMS STRUCTURES AID CHANNEL COOPERATION

Manufacturers, wholesalers, retailers, and other channel intermediaries interact in many ways to get the distribution job done. But each member is dissimilar from the others, with its own immediate interests uppermost. Although each channel member benefits individually when the whole system works well, competitive pressures often prevent individual members from behaving to benefit the group. For example, dealers might pressure suppliers for pricing arrangements that eliminate profits for other channel members, or suppliers might do the same to dealers.

Vertical marketing systems (VMSs) are arrangements among channel members that help mitigate these pressures and ensure cooperation. In these arrangements, the producer, wholesaler, and retailer function as a unified system, reducing conflict to a minimum. There are various types of VMSs:

• *CORPORATE VMS*

A corporate VMS combines successive stages of production and distribution under single ownership. For example, Sears, a retailer, has equity in many manufacturers that supply its products, whereas Sherwin-Williams, a manufacturer, owns more than 2000 retail outlets.

• *CONTRACTUAL VMS*

A contractual VMS is composed of independent channel members that join together for mutual benefit. In the producer-wholesaler-retailer model, there are three possible combinations:

- **Producer-wholesaler:** This may take the form of a franchise operation, where the manufacturer licenses the wholesaler to distribute the product. Coca-Cola, for example, licenses bottlers worldwide to process its syrup concentrates into soda, which is then sold to independent retailers.

- **Producer-retailer:** This arrangement also usually consists of a franchising operation, where the producer gives the retailer the right to sell its products in return for the retailer's meeting producer-imposed conditions. The automobile industry, with its system of dealerships, is an example of this type of VMS. Service industries, too, often use this approach. For example, restaurant and motel chains are often made up of individually licensed and owned retail operations.

- **Retailer-wholesaler:** These systems are split into those controlled by the retailer and those controlled by the wholesaler. In wholesaler-sponsored voluntary chains, independent retailers are encouraged to band together to order large quantities from the wholesaler, who passes on price advantages otherwise available only to large chains. The producer and wholesaler benefit from larger orders, and the retailer benefits from lower prices. Retailer-controlled systems are called cooperatives, in which retailers join together to create their own wholesaling operation. Co-op members buy from the jointly-owned wholesaler and share in the profits it generates.

• *ADMINISTERED VMS*

An administered VMS is based on the size and power of one of the channel members. IBM, for example, can command greater cooperation and support from resellers through its potent market presence.

VMS ALTERNATIVES: HORIZONTAL AND MULTICHANNEL SYSTEMS

Horizontal marketing systems encourage cooperation among channel members through combinations of companies on the same channel level. By working together either temporarily or permanently, companies can combine capital, production capabilities, or marketing resources to achieve more than any company working alone. Two examples follow:

- H&R Block and Hyatt Legal Services formed a joint venture in which Hyatt gains market penetration for its legal clinics by renting space and office facilities in H&R Block's tax preparation offices. Block benefits from renting its facilities, which would otherwise have a highly seasonal pattern.

- A number of savings banks locate office facilities and automated teller machines in supermarkets to gain quick market entry at low cost. The supermarkets benefit by offering in-store banking convenience to customers.

Multichannel marketing systems achieve cooperation and increased sales by setting up two or more marketing channels to reach one or more market segments. For example, McDonald's sells through a network of independent franchisees but owns a third of its outlets.

GOOD DISTRIBUTOR AGREEMENTS FACILITATE GOOD COMMUNICATIONS

Approaches for implementing productive, two-way communication include distributor advisory councils and personal visits among the partner firms. Invariably, however, these initiatives are no better than the basic agreements between the principal and intermediaries on which they are based. In general, these agreements should cover a specific time period (usually one or two years), with a trial period of between three and six months for new distributors. Other areas provided for include products covered, geographic boundaries, other distribution methods allowed, methods of payment (including terms of sale), currencies used, functions and responsibilities of intermediaries, credit and shipment terms and procedures, information each partner is entitled to, and means of communicating this information.

Beyond these specific content considerations, here are some general guidelines for preparing productive, protective distributor agreements:

- Be specific in defining performance. For example, use phrases like "Agent agrees to sell a minimum of ten MM systems every quarter."

- Be specific in defining consequences of nonperformance. For example, "agent will transfer to principal all legitimate property, including trademarks, patents, company name, and lists of customers and contacts."

- Be specific as to what law will govern contract disputes. If feasible, specify U.S. common law, rather than the harsher civil law characterizing most other world jurisdictions.

- Be specific as to what forum will adjudicate disputes. Almost invariably, from the principal's perspective, arbitration or conciliation are preferable to civil law courts.

- Finally, be specific as to the language in which contract clauses will be interpreted. Even if written in the language of the agent or distributor, consider interpreting the contract in the language of the principal.

INTERNATIONAL PERSPECTIVE

This section examines the nature and scope of distribution systems in global markets, problems an exporter like Merton might face in achieving market share through these systems, and strategies for addressing these problems.

GLOBAL DISTRIBUTION SYSTEMS

In global markets, distribution systems are generally similar to those in domestic markets: types of wholesalers (agents, brokers, drop shippers, and the like) and retailers (department stores, discount stores, and the like) are similar, as are flows among channel members (physical, title, informational, and the like), conflicts between them, and strategies for managing channel members to distribute products to consumer and organizational markets.

What makes the task of an exporter like Merton challenging in evolving channel strategies in global markets, however, are not these general similarities, but specific differences among channels in scope and structure. Often, in global markets, exporters like Merton have no choice but to assume most, or all, distribution functions; in underdeveloped countries, for example, channels similar to those in domestic markets usually don't exist. Or, if they do exist in more developed countries, channel management might not be willing to distribute the exporter's product for a variety of reasons.

Structural differences characterizing distribution systems in global markets present other challenges to exporters. For example, Japanese **kieretsu** systems link importers, producers, distributors, and retailers, either through banks or trading companies, into distribution systems that combine features of vertical, horizontal, and multichannel systems. Frequently, these systems—perhaps best illustrated by the Mitsubishi kieretsu that includes 150 companies—create barriers to the successful penetration of an entry market by foreign "outsiders." Similar barriers are created by monopoly distribution systems characterizing many of the command economies of former communist-bloc countries and some developed countries, such as for the distribution of alcoholic spirits in Sweden and Finland.

Even if an exporter can get distribution for a product line in a developed foreign market, the likelihood is that delegated functions—particularly selling, promotion, and matching functions—will not be performed as effectively as in domestic distribution channels.

GUIDELINES FOR EFFECTIVE GLOBAL CHANNEL STRATEGIES

In addressing problems faced in setting up profitable distribution channels in overseas markets, Merton management employed a careful, staged strategy of first retaining effective facilitating intermediaries and then working with these agencies to design, select, and manage global channels.

RETAINING EFFECTIVE FACILITATING INTERMEDIARIES

One way for a firm—especially smaller firms without experience or expertise in penetrating global markets—to address costly problems in exporting products to foreign markets is to retain the services of an export management company (EMC) or an export trading company (ETC). EMCs are usually small domestic firms that serve either as agents or distributors for several exporting firms. The marketing services they perform for their clients depend mainly on whether they function as agents or distributors. As agents, the EMCs earn commissions, don't handle or take title to goods, and operate under formal or informal contracts that specify exclusivity agreements, price arrangements, promotional payments, and sales quotas. As distributors, EMCs purchase and take title to products from client companies, provide a fuller range of marketing services, and assume the trading risk.

An export trading company, based on a concept originated by European trading houses in the seventeenth century and brought to fruition in Japan in the twentieth century (where, in 1996, nine trading companies acted as intermediaries for about half of Japan's exports and two thirds of its imports), received a strong growth impetus in the United States with passage in 1982 of the Export Trading Company Act. Under this act, a wide variety of structures were permitted for ETCs to help them match the Japanese kieretso model. For example, antitrust regulations were relaxed to permit competing companies to form joint ventures, and banks were permitted to participate in ETCs to allow better access to capital and easier receipt of title to goods. Today, modern ETCs perform a diversity of functions for exporting and importing clients, including assistance in: (1) selecting competent distributors; (2) arranging for financing, insurance, and export documentation for trade transactions; (3) developing marketing plans; (4) researching and developing new products; (5) establishing personal contact with foreign buyers; (6) handling countertrade requirements; (7) evaluating credit risks of foreign buyers; (8) organizing promotion at foreign shows; (9) arranging for foreign packaging and marking; (10) preparing training programs, advertising, and promotion for use in foreign markets.

Because Merton management believed the company would retain more control over the export process by working with an EMC than if they were to sell their products outright to an ETC, this was the option decided upon, with the selection criteria based on the ETC's track record in representing product lines similar to Merton's.

DESIGNING AND SELECTING PROFITABLE GLOBAL CHANNELS

Channel design decisions pertain to kinds of intermediaries that comprise channel systems and how these intermediaries are linked to connect producers and customers in the most efficient and effective manner.

In general, exporters and their facilitating intermediaries face two decisions in designing distribution systems to serve global markets. The first decision pertains to which of three distribution systems the exporter will employ:

- **Indirect exporting** involves dealing with another U.S.-based firm, such as an EMC or ETC, that serves as a sales intermediary, saving the exporter the cost of setting up its own channels.

- **Direct exporting** involves either selling directly to foreign customers or through local representatives that sell directly to customers.

- **Integrated distribution** involves an investment in the foreign intermediaries to sell products in one or more global markets.

Global Focus 19-1 illustrate how U.S. firms achieved distribution in foreign markets using these strategies.

GLOBAL FOCUS 19-1

Direct and Indirect Selling: Exporters Go Both Ways

There are two basic distribution approaches in exporting: direct and indirect selling.

In direct selling, the U.S. firm deals with foreign importers and is usually responsible for shipping the products overseas. However, direct selling may include utilizing the services of foreign sales representatives or agents. In the indirect method, the U.S. firm relies on another firm that acts as a sales intermediary and normally will assume responsibility for marketing and shipping the products overseas. The decision to market products directly or indirectly should be made on the basis of a number of key considerations, including the size of the firm, the nature of its products, previous export experience, and business conditions in the selected overseas markets.

The following export success stories show the application of these considerations.

- **Second Chance Body Armor, Inc.,** of Central Lake, Michigan, sells its specialized line of bullet-resistant vests to foreign countries through a network of native experts in police and military work who help the forty-five-employee firm secure contracts with official agencies in their countries.

- **Gamble Brothers** of Louisville, Kentucky, obtained an agent in the United Kingdom who found a strong demand for the firm's wood kitchen cabinet components. From that point, sales blossomed in Ireland, Spain, the Benelux countries, and Greece.

- **Hallmark Sales Corporation** of Houston, Texas, a wholesale exporter of industrial equipment and supplies, hired employees fluent in Spanish to keep in direct contact with customers from offices the firm set up in Mexico and Argentina.

- **SAS Institute, Inc.,** of Cary, North Carolina, maintains a network of wholly-owned subsidiaries in Canada, Europe, and the Asia / Pacific region. This strategy allows the company to adapt its products to particular markets effectively, because the subsidiaries are staffed almost exclusively with nationals with an understanding of local culture and business practices.

- **H.F. Henderson Industries** of West Caldwell, New Jersey, chooses to sell its automatic weighing machines directly to foreign customers rather than through overseas agents or distributors. For that reason, the firm emphasizes travel and a willingness to adapt to language and cultural differences. Henry Henderson, Jr., president, has made seven trips to China, where he has socialized with the Chinese and learned their ways of doing business. He has also traveled to Australia, South Korea, Hong Kong, France, Russia, Switzerland, Austria, Hungary, Italy, Finland, and Brazil, among other countries.

- The **Ohmart Corporation** of Cincinnati, Ohio, took the opposite tack of building a strong organization of international sales representatives. The 130-employee manufacturer of industrial process measurement and control systems has chosen, as representatives, experienced engineers capable of presenting technical data to customers' technical staffs.

Source: Business America, World Trade Week, 1993 Edition, Vol. 114, No. 9, pp. 4–5.

The second decision confronts exporters that decide on a strategy of integrated distribution. Specifically, should selected intermediaries be distributors or agents? As noted earlier, distributors are usually organized along product lines, purchase and take title to goods, provide a complete marketing service, and are more independent than agents, who operate on a commission basis and don't usually physically handle the goods.

Figure 19-3 provides a classification of retailers that link up with these distributors trading internationally. These retailers have been assigned into clusters in terms of geographic trading presence, and by their preferred mode of entry ("high cost/ high control" suggests company-controlled outlets; "low cost/ low control" suggests franchise outlets).

CHANNEL SELECTION CRITERIA

Consideration of the following list of interactive factors will help marketers relate channel opportunities to company objectives and resources in designing new global channel systems or modifying existing systems.

• *COMPANY OBJECTIVES*

Particularly in areas of desired market share and profit return, company objectives can have a strong influence on the nature and design of channel systems. For example, a strong competitive presence needed to quickly develop market share in a territory might indicate a distribution system including joint ventures and strongly motivated stocking distributors.

• *CUSTOMER CHARACTERISTICS*

Understanding the nature and scope of target markets, and the needs and behavior of target market members, is a logical starting point for identifying distributors to serve these markets. Start with a broad view of relevant demographic factors and then focus on specifics that will help identify and profile desired distributors.

For example, how does your prospective foreign target market compare with known domestic markets in terms of such criteria as age, income, and education level? What are product information needs of market members? How price sensitive are they? How important are quality and service values? What are the buying habits of target market members: how do they usually purchase the product or service marketed, and from whom? How do they

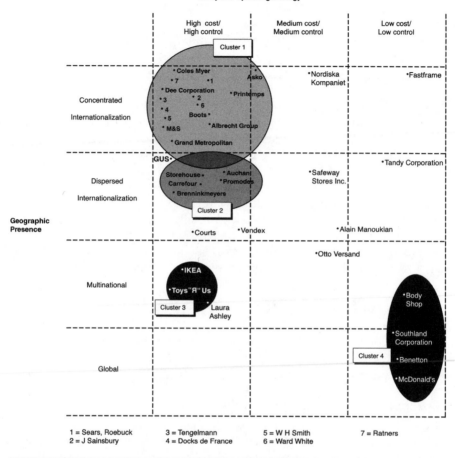

Entry and Operating Strategy

Figure axes and content:

- Horizontal axis (Entry and Operating Strategy): High cost/High control | Medium cost/Medium control | Low cost/Low control
- Vertical axis (Geographic Presence): Concentrated Internationalization | Dispersed Internationalization | Multinational | Global

Cluster 1:
- Coles Myer
- 7, 1
- Dee Corporation
- 3, 2
- 6
- 4
- 5, Boots
- M&S, Albrecht Group
- Grand Metropolitan
- Asko
- Printemps
- Nordiska Kompaniet
- Fastframe

Cluster 2:
- GUS
- Storehouse, Auchan
- Carrefour, Promodes
- Brenninkmeyers
- Safeway Stores Inc.
- Tandy Corporation
- Courts, Vendex
- Alain Manoukian

Cluster 3:
- Otto Versand
- IKEA
- Toys "Я" Us
- Laura Ashley

Cluster 4:
- Body Shop
- Southland Corporation
- Benetton
- McDonald's

1 = Sears, Roebuck 3 = Tengelmann 5 = W H Smith 7 = Ratners
2 = J Sainsbury 4 = Docks de France 6 = Ward White

Note: Cluster 1—cautious internationalists; cluster 2—emboldened internationalists; cluster 3—aggressive internationalists; cluster 4—world powers. Source: Alan D. Treadgold, "The Developing Internationalisation of Retailing," *International Journal of Retail & Distribution Management* 18 (1990): 10.

Figure 19–3. A typology of international retailers.

respond to different selling approaches? If feasible, actually interview prospective customers (including distributors, who are also customers).

In general, the larger a target market, the greater the need for distributors, regardless of the stage of a country's market development. If market size is in the millions, retail distribution and direct marketing channels for consumer products are usually required; if the market is characterized by many low-volume retailers, wholesalers are almost certainly needed to service them.

• *PRODUCT CHARACTERISTICS*

Frequently, product characteristics are the single most important consideration in identifying worthwhile global channels. Some key concerns are noted here. How standardized is the product? (Will distributors have to customize it to meet customer needs?) Is it expensive? (Products with a high unit price, such as MM systems, are often sold through shorter, more direct channels because selling price is a small percentage of total price, and such products usually require specialized selling expertise.) How perishable is the product? (Perishable products usually require fewer, and more specialized, channel members to get them to market quickly.) How bulky is the product? (Bulky products call for channel arrangements that minimize shipping distances.)

• *THE COMPETITIVE CLIMATE*

Exporters entering highly competitive entry markets face the problem of differentiating their product or service to attract both end customers and distributors. A potent brand name, or attractive, patented feature, or significant price advantage are possibilities. However, even this might not be enough to attract distributors who, worldwide, usually aren't interested in taking on new or untested products; they want to represent products for which demand has already been created. Even if the distributor does agree to represent the product, it doesn't guarantee that the distributor will exert the sales effort to increase demand.

Facing these conditions—a highly competitive market and low distributor motivation to take on, or push, a product line—exporters have two options:

- Provide additional incentives for distributors to take on and push the line (for example, payments for performance, guaranteed gross margins, or subsidizing the cost of promotional programs supporting the product).

- Bypass outside intermediaries to set up their own distribution channels, with the future option of signing up distributors when the product, by its share of market growth, has proven itself.

• *CHANNEL CHARACTERISTICS*

Channel structures and functions in international markets might differ from those in domestic markets in ways that could affect channel selection and design. For example, in global markets, retailers and wholesalers generally expect more financial and sales support from their suppliers and are more likely to demand full acceptance of returns.

Another key variable is the coverage offered by existing channels. Specifically, are channels available to cover target market territories? And with the kind of coverage desired (for example, intensive, selective, or exclusive)?

• *LEGAL-POLITICAL REALITIES*

Channel design decisions usually culminate in legal commitments with outside distributors—wholesalers, agents, brokers, and the like—that can be extremely difficult to change or terminate. In many countries in Europe and Latin America, laws and regulations governing channel relationships tend to be much harsher than U.S. laws with respect to agency/principal relations, often viewing termination of an agent as a matter of national concern rather than as a private matter among individuals. Exacerbating these contractual problems is the fact that, in many foreign and legal jurisdictions, "sales agents" and "distributors" are not defined, legally, as they are in the United States. In the United States, a distributor is an independent business that represents a number of competing companies; abroad, many distributors not only stock for the local market but also represent a single manufacturer, functioning as both distributor and exclusive sales representative. Not carrying competing products, this distributor will expect exclusivity and many other contractual prerequisites not normally expected by U.S. distributors.

Also, in such jurisdictions, agents are given the power of attorney, meaning they can legally bind principals to contract and expose them to legal and economic risk. In some Latin American countries, this economic risk for canceling a contract can equal five times annual gross profits, plus the value of the agent's investment, plus many additional payments. Often, these indemnities increase with the time the contract is in force and include compensation for the increased value of the market created.

In some countries, channel design decisions can also be shaped by legislation requiring that foreign firms be represented only by distributors that are 100 percent locally owned, or, in a few cases, legislation that totally prohibits the use of dealers in order to protect consumers from abuses attributed to them.

• *FINANCIAL IMPLICATIONS*

Three areas of financial concern to exporters engaged in establishing or modifying distribution channels in international markets include:

- **Capital requirements** to set up a desired channel system, covering such accounts as beginning inventories, preferential loans, construction, staffing, and training costs.

- **Continuing costs** for maintaining channels once established, which are a function of a number of factors, including stage of the life cycle of the product and distributor relationship, the relative power of the principal vis-à-vis intermediaries, and functions (selling, materials handling, and so on) performed by each.

- **Risk,** which is also a function of many factors, including the stability of a market's currency, the strength of the relationship among principal and intermediaries, and the extent to which they share risk in contractual relationships.

FINDING DISTRIBUTORS IN INTERNATIONAL MARKETS

Before embarking on a search for distributors to help market products or services in established or entry global markets, the principal should first gather information, covering considerations discussed earlier, pertaining to how threats and opportunities in distribution climates can best be shaped to match the principal's goals and resources. This information will help define components of effective distribution systems and negotiate these systems into being.

For informed principals, there are so many domestic and foreign private and government sources of information on available distributors, that the biggest initial problem is often where to start. One excellent starting point is the Trade Promotion Coordinating Committee (1-800-872-8723), an interagency group tasked with the development and coordination of U.S. export programs. This committee directs inquirers to sources of up-to-date information on types and names of distributors in prospective entry markets and arranges contacts with those of particular interest. Two services of the U.S. Commerce Department—the Agent/Distributor Service and the World Traders Data Report—locate and profile foreign firms interested in export proposals submitted by U.S. firms.

Private sources of information on distribution availabilities in global markets include country and regional business directories, published worldwide, or domestic lists, which categorize distributors by country and line of business and that can be ordered from Dun & Bradstreet, Reuben H. Donnelly, McGraw-Hill, Kelly's Directory, and Johnson Publishing. Principals can also solicit information from facilitating agencies—such as banks, advertising agencies, and shipping lines—or take a more direct role and solicit information and applicants at major trade fairs.

MANAGING CHANNELS IN INTERNATIONAL MARKETS

Finding and selecting distributors in international markets and motivating them to team up to profitably market products or services is only the beginning of a complex, dynamic partnership that must be effectively managed to produce mutual long-term benefits. For this partnership to work in the face of cultural, logistical, operational, and legal constraints in global markets, effective two-way communication among the partners is key in order to effectively convey goals, implement marketing plans, and resolve conflicts.

Approaches for implementing these communications include distributor advisory councils, personal visits among the partner firms, and, most importantly, productive, protective distributor agreements. Content considerations of such agreements were noted earlier, including guidelines for defining performance and consequences for nonperformance, adjudicating disputes, and the law and language in which agreement provisions will be interpreted.

CHAPTER PERSPECTIVE

The distribution planning process entails designing channels and physical distribution systems for moving products from manufacturers to ultimate consumers or users efficiently and economically. For exporters, longer channels, more complex channel flows, and problems in attracting distributors and setting up physical distribution systems can create costly roadblocks to successful market entry. Total costs and total systems approaches for integrating all elements of the distribution process help level the competitive playing field.

KNOW THE CONCEPTS
TERMS FOR STUDY

Administered VMS	Horizontal marketing system
Agent	Indirect exporting
Broker	Intermediaries
Channels	Integrated distribution
Channel management	Kieretsu
Channel flows	Merchant wholesalers
Channel functions	Multichannel marketing system
Contractual VMS	Nonstore retailer
Corporate VMS	Retailer
Direct exporting	Retailing functions
Distribution planning	Store retailer
Export management company	Vertical marketing system
Export Trading Company Act	Wholesaler
Export trading company	Wholesaler function

MATCHUP EXERCISES

1. Match up the number of levels in the distribution channel described in the first column with the activity described in the second column.

1. zero level
2. one level
3. two level

4. three level

a. A Tupperware party.
b. Ikea holds a furniture sale.
c. Wholesalers sell beef to jobbers, who sell to small retailers.
d. Mattel sells toys to wholesalers, who sell to retailers.

2. Match up the distributor category in the first column with the column descriptor in the second.

1. selling agents
2. manufacturers' agents

3. nonstore retailer

4. store retailer

a. 7-Eleven
b. market manufacturer's entire output
c. represent two or more firms making complementary product lines
d. the Bijou motion picture theater

3. Match up the concern in the first column with the decision area in the second column.

1. target market selection
2. location
3. product assortment
4. price

5. promotion

a. How wide? How deep?
b. Fast turnover or quality image?
c. Customer wants and needs
d. Proximity to customers and transportation
e. Upscale, downscale, or midscale?

4. Match up the descriptor in the first column with the channel flow in the second column.

1. payment
2. information
3. promotion

4. ownership

a. sales trends by product line
b. the only backwards flow
c. done by suppliers, dealers, and producers
d. consignment delays

5. Match up the forms of channel integration in the first column with the distributors in the second.

1. contractual VMS

2. corporate VMS

a. Sears obtains 50 percent of goods it sells from companies it partly or wholly owns.
b. Ford licenses independent dealers to sell its cars.

3. administered VMS

4. Horizontal Marketing System

c. Pillsbury and Kraft Foods cooperate to advertise and sell products to retailers.

d. Campbell Soup's size and power command cooperation from retailers.

QUESTIONS FOR REVIEW AND DISCUSSION

1. Distinguish between intermediaries and facilitating agencies in terms of the basic role of each in moving products from producer to consumer. Why are decisions pertaining to the proper melding of intermediaries and facilitating agencies important in devising and implementing marketing plans?

2. In 1996, overseas sales, resulting from more than 14 million Tupperware parties in more than 100 foreign countries, generated 85 percent of the Tupperware Corporation's $1.40 billion in total revenues. In terms of key considerations involved in deciding number of channel levels, why do you suppose Tupperware management chose a zero-level channel in preference to multilevel channels? (Note: Your answer should also apply to other global zero-level channel users like Avon Home Products and Electrolux vacuum cleaners.)

3. In the 1970s, about 200 distributors handled about half of all pharmaceutical products distributed worldwide, with manufacturers distributing the rest directly. By the early 1990s, fewer than 125 distributors handled 65 percent, with McKesson far and away the largest distributor. Explain, in terms of channel flows, how this trend toward larger wholesalers, and less direct distribution, might have come about.

4. Describe what kinds of channel structures (vertical, horizontal, multichannel) are implicit in the following product/market situation: Sherwin Williams, the world's largest paint producer, distributes paint through more than 1700 company-owned and independent paint stores, mass merchandisers, wholesale distributors, and, for some products, direct selling.

5. In terms of functions performed by distributors, discuss reasons why IBM sold its company-owned product centers and opted to distribute its products only through independent channel members and sales personnel.

ANSWERS
MATCHUP EXERCISES

1. 1a, 2b, 3d, 4c
2. 1b, 2c, 3d, 4a
3. 1c, 2d, 3a, 4b, 5e
4. 1b, 2a, 3c, 4d
5. 1b, 2a, 3d, 4c

QUESTIONS FOR REVIEW AND DISCUSSION

1. Facilitating agencies, such as advertising agencies, banks, and transportation companies, assist in the performance of distribution functions but neither take title to goods nor negotiate purchases or sales; some intermediaries, such as brokers and sales agents, search for customers and may negotiate on behalf of the producer, but they do not take title to the goods. Other intermediaries, such as wholesalers and retailers, buy, take title to, and resell the merchandise. The manner in which intermediaries and facilitating agencies are melded in designing distribution channels is among the most crucial decisions facing management, in that it intimately affects all other marketing decisions. For example, pricing depends on kinds of distributors used and costs entailed in moving products through channels; advertising and selling decisions depend on training and motivation needed by distributors; and the critical ability to reach and efficiently serve target markets is invariably a function of channel strategies.

2. Tupperware's decision to employ a zero-level channel was justified in terms of organizational goals and resources, as well as the fact that the nature of the firm's products and markets lent themselves to this approach. For example, the firm manufactures a broad range of products, all of which lend themselves to demonstrations in a direct selling format (door to door, office to office, home sales parties). Also, because there is such a large market for Tupperware products—practically every household worldwide—the company can capitalize on economies of scale that are usually generated by multilevel channels. Given these conditions, Tupperware management, which has the resources to recruit, train, and manage an international salesforce, decided its return on its investment in this salesforce, which included discounts and commissions it would otherwise have to pay distributors, made the zero-channel option the best "opportunity cost" of all channel alternatives. An additional benefit was the degree of control a zero-level channel

gives Tupperware. The firm can hire, train, motivate, and compensate salespeople to their specifications and know they will only sell Tupperware products.

3. Just as mass marketing can create manufacturing economies of scale for producers, it can also create distribution economies of scale for wholesalers, which tend to foster centralization and more efficient flows among channel intermediaries. For example, McKesson, in performing the information flow, provides suppliers with tailor-made reports showing detailed sales, inventory, and marketing research data, including best-shelf placement for pharmaceutical products, and major illnesses and allergies requiring medical and pharmaceutical attention. Using this information and its sizeable resources, McKesson is also better positioned to promote and sell its suppliers' products (promotion flow) and to make sure proper assortments and quantities of pharmaceutical products are stocked and transported throughout the channel (physical distribution). With all these distributional values available, along with the steady predictable sales volume represented and the risk reduction that results when distributors take title to and pay for merchandise (title and payment flows), it is probably understandable that the trend is away from direct selling in the pharmaceutical field.

4. Sherwin Williams' company-owned outlets would be an example of a corporate vertical marketing system. When paired with independent paint stores, it is an example of multichannel distribution. It is also an example of horizontal integration to the extent that Sherwin Williams purchased other paint companies and now uses their channels in addition to its own.

5. A distribution network with a broad range of electronic product lines supplementing the IBM line and serving a broad diversity of consumer and organizational target markets—such as the Computerland and Prodigy networks—would have a larger base of prospective customers to contact and a broader base of products to match to the needs of these prospects. Additionally, this deeper product/market base would provide the foundation for more useful marketing research feedback, and a more productive response to promotional efforts supporting IBM's product line. Finally, this independent distribution network would be better able to move IBM's products to customers because this is their essential business, just as making electronic business machines is IBM's essential business. Another plus: IBM is now sharing much of the financial risk with distributors—such as the risk of no-pay customers or another PCjr. debacle.

20
DISTRIBUTION PLANNING II: LOGISTICS SYSTEMS

OVERVIEW

Logistics entails the coordination and control of materials management and physical distribution functions—including packaging, transportation, storage, order processing, and inventory management—that combine to move products between producers and customers. Guiding this effort are total systems and total cost concepts that view logistics systems as a single integrated entity, with decisions in one functional area, such as transportation, affecting decisions in all other functional areas to keep overall costs as low as possible consistent with customer needs, competitive offerings, and company objectives. Dramatic differences between domestic and international markets in materials management and physical distribution challenges can generate equally dramatic cost-benefit outcomes when the global logistics function is properly managed.

LOGISTICS: GETTING PRODUCTS TO CUSTOMERS

Concurrently with distribution planning efforts to design channel systems consistent with customer needs, competitive climates, and company resources, marketing planners are also focusing on logistics issues involved in moving goods into and through these channels. These logistics issues often represent the largest deterrent to successful marketing programs, especially when markets entered are highly competitive and channel availabilities are limited.

The logistics function melds together a variety of activities—including packaging, transportation, storage, inventory control, and order processing—to coordinate and control two subfunctions: materials management, which focuses on the timely arrival of raw materials, parts, and supplies into and through the firm, and physical distribution, which focuses on the movement of the firm's finished products to its customers.

The importance of logistics in marketing planning can be measured by a number of costly concerns: transportation and storage costs, number of intermediaries involved in logistics processes, transactions among these intermediaries, freight rates and packaging / labeling requirements, inadequate storage and materials handling facilities, slow- or nonmoving inventory, and cumbersome, inefficient order processing.

Another measure of the importance of logistics is the growing appreciation for the "team" concept among producers, suppliers, customers, and other channel members in the areas of performance, quality, and timing. Manifestations of this jointness of purpose include **just-in-time (JIT)** inventory systems, which reduce inventory carrying costs by ordering more frequently and in lower quantities; **quick response (QR)** inventory systems, under which suppliers and distributors cooperate to reduce retail inventory while providing a merchandise supply that more closely addresses buying patterns of consumers; and **early supplier involvement (ESI)** for better planning and product movement. Properly implemented, these strategic logistical tools can create competitive advantages and savings in an area where large savings are still possible, given that logistics costs typically comprise between 15 and 30 percent of the total cost of a completed order. Market Focus 20-1 illustrates the nature and benefits of this team concept to all members of the distribution chain.

MARKET FOCUS 20-1

Distributors as Strategic Business Partners

"We treat our worldwide distributors as customers and also as strategic business partners," says Peter J. Rogers, Jr., Director of Marketing Systems for MICROS Systems, Inc., of Beltsville, Maryland. The 450-employee firm makes point-of-sale systems, a modern form of cash register, for hotels, restaurants, cruise ships, casinos, theme parks, and stadiums.

"Our market niche is the hospitality business—hospitality knows no national boundaries," Rogers said. "We have incorporated the concept of hospitality into the way we operate, which means we are very much customer-focused."

He continued, "Our philosophy of pleasing our customers is fundamental to our success in exporting, as well as in domestic sales, and it applies not only to our distributors but to end users of our equipment. We place a high value on the teamwork approach. Before we pick distributors or hire employees, we make it clear that the company's goal is to serve customers. Our distributors are strategic partners in the sense that they are a key piece of our business strategy, of giving our customers assurance that they have strong backup in sales and marketing, technical assistance, and software programming and development.

MICROS Systems, which was established in 1977, has 50 distributors and six overseas subsidiaries—two in the United Kingdom and one each in France, Germany, Switzerland, and Spain. It has an office in Frankfurt, Germany, to support its operations in Europe, the Middle East, and Africa, and an office in Singapore to support operations in Asia and the Pacific rim. Today, MICROS Systems exports 28 percent of its products.

To give the best service in foreign countries, MICROS Systems has a policy of hiring nationals for its support operations. Rogers explained, "Because they understand the culture, we think they are best able to help us grow in their countries."

Typically, MICROS Systems sells its equipment to distributors, who add value by modifying the equipment for local conditions, such as installing the database in a foreign language. The distributor may then sell the equipment to a hotel, which has access to an effective locally-based sales and service staff, which in turn is backed up by MICROS Systems corporate headquarters.

Source: "Stories of Exporting Success," *Business America,* Vol. 115, No. 6, June 1994, p. 8.

TOTAL SYSTEMS AND TOTAL COSTS DEFINE LOGISTICS GOALS

Two interrelated concepts combine to help guide logistics planners: total systems and total costs.

• *TOTAL SYSTEMS*

The total systems concept views materials management and physical distribution functions, including packaging, order processing, inventory control, warehousing, and transportation, as an integrated whole instead of as a group of discrete entities. Under total systems, decisions in one area influence decisions in other areas. For example, a warehouse location decision will influence the selection of transportation methods and the amount of inventory stocked by retailers served by the warehouse.

• *TOTAL COST*

The total cost approach to logistical management offers a means of integrating materials management and physical distribution functions, using statistical and mathematical techniques, so as to provide a set of alternatives that optimize cost/profit relationships in the entire logistical system. This doesn't mean that costs in each area—warehousing, transportation, order processing, and the like—are necessarily low, but that overall logistical costs are as low as possible consistent with customer needs, company objectives, and competitive offerings. For example, the Armour Pharmaceutical Company determined that high air freight costs to serve its market lowered inventory carrying and warehousing costs, and, by increasing average order size, lowered order-processing costs. The sum of these costs was the lowest of all alternatives examined, each of which entailed lower transportation costs.

Implicit in both total systems and total cost concepts is the notion of tradeoffs within and among logistical functions. For example, within the inventory management function, more money spent to place orders means less money spent to carry ordered goods in inventory. Among functions, more money spent for proper packaging lowers transportation, storage, order processing, and overall logistics costs to optimize overall systems efficiency.

PLANNING COST-EFFICIENT LOGISTICS SYSTEMS

To illustrate how logistics planning can design and coordinate materials management and physical distribution systems that achieve benefits of total cost and total systems concepts, we will first examine the costs entailed in the following functions and the beneficial tradeoffs within each and among all to reduce these costs.

• *PACKAGING*

In integrating packaging decisions with other components of physical distribution and marketing mixes, Merton planners realized that a number of tradeoffs would be necessary. For example, materials selected to contain and protect the product might interfere with other packaging objectives, such as encouraging product use. Or, a feature designed to encourage product use might discourage efficient handling and storage. This is what happened in the case of the new easy-pour containers for motor oil, which occupied considerably more storage space than the traditional metal can they replaced.

In addition to these tradeoffs, the Merton marketing team also considered typical criticisms of packaging, which usually derive from the potentially adverse environmental impact of certain kinds of packages, and increasing costs to consumers of unfunctional package features. For example, throwaway bottles, which contribute to environmental pollution, also use three times as much energy to produce as returnable bottles, a cost usually passed on to the consumer.

• TRANSPORTATION

Transportation costs—including tangible carrier costs and less tangible costs involved in pricing products, delivery performance, condition of shipped goods, and customer satisfaction—are usually the highest of all functional logistics costs. In selecting carriers most consistent with total cost-systems concepts, Merton logistics planners assessed the relative merits of the following transportation modes.

AIR SHIPPING

Although the fastest growing of all transportation modes—with volume almost tripling between 1980 and 1996—total volume of airfreight in relation to total shipment volume in global markets is small: only one percent of volume and 20 percent of value. It is the most expensive of all transportation modes and fairly undependable because of constantly changing air schedules. Use of air transport may remove the need for extra warehouses because of its ability to span long distances quickly. High value, high density, perishable, and emergency goods dominate air shipments. Among the factors making air transport an attractive transport alternative are better ground facilities, containerization, and the ability to transport bulky cargoes on jumbo planes.

RAILROADS

The most popular worldwide transportation mode, railroads specialize in transporting large, heavy shipments over long distances. For shipments of a carload or more, they are comparatively inexpensive and provide good speed and reliability. Rail service is a good choice for shipments of lumber, coal, and agricultural products. Three trends have improved transporting capabilities of railroads: new shipping techniques and equipment to handle special categories of goods, more operating flexibility due to deregulation, and mergers to improve efficiency.

WATER

Transport by ships and barges is second only to railroads as the most popular mode of transportation worldwide. It is relatively inexpensive, but it is slow and unreliable due to its dependence on the weather. Because ships can only go where there is water, delivery areas are limited. Waterways in the domestic market are used mainly to transport low-value, high-bulk items, such as coal, grain, and cement.

TRUCKS

Because they can go anywhere, as opposed to trains that follow the rails, ships that follow the waterways, and airplanes that follow air routes, trucks are the transportation of choice when flexibility is at a premium. Truck transportation is also fast and dependable, but because trucks are limited by their size to smaller cargoes, it is not as economical as rail or water.

PIPELINES

The Alaska Pipeline is perhaps the best-known example of this kind of transportation, transporting more than 2 billion cubic feet of natural gas per day to the continental United States. There are no stops or alternate routes on pipelines, and only fluid products (gases, liquids, or semiliquids) can be transported. For them, pipelines provide cheap, reliable transportation.

In deciding which modes to use to transport Merton products to different destinations, Merton planners balanced considerations of time, cost, and reliability. In one situation, for example, they decided trucks would be the best mode to transport MM systems to cross-country distributors. Though rail would be cheaper, they feared damage would be higher in the large carload quantities required. Besides, warehouse destinations were not directly on rail lines, and there would be extra cost to transport them from the train to the warehouse. Although air service would be even quicker, the added cost did not justify the benefit in this case.

• STORAGE

Types of storage facilities available in the domestic market include private warehouses, already in business to serve target markets, or space rented in public warehouses, or company-owned warehousing facilities. Consistent with the total systems concept, Merton planners were attracted to distribution centers designed to move goods rather than just store them as is done in storage warehouses. These large, highly automated and computerized centers receive goods, take orders, control inventory, and deliver filled orders to customers quickly and efficiently.

Basic storage issues facing logistics planners include type, or types, of stocking locations to use, and where they should be located. The approach for addressing these issues involves an analysis of markets, products and competitive climates to measure costs versus benefits of maintaining storage facilities. For example, in a highly competitive market, where product applications, such as production line components, mandate reliably fast deliveries, distribution centers able to rapidly process and deliver orders might be a competitive necessity. Other, less critical products might be stocked at fewer, less localized warehouses.

• ORDER PROCESSING

Merton's challenge here was to get customer orders, which begin the physical distribution function, processed and filled quickly and accurately.

Typically, when a customer order is received, order processing involves: (1) determining customer credit standing and product availability; (2) issuing a shipping order and invoice, copies of which are sent to the customer and various departments; (3) noting the decrease in inventory; and (4) ordering new stock, when needed. If the quantity ordered isn't in stock, it is back ordered.

In integrating Merton order processing systems with systems of wholesalers in its distribution channels, Merton subsidized, where necessary, computerized systems initiated by electronic point of sale (EPOS) terminals. Resembling cash registers and connected to centralized EPOS terminals in distribution centers, the EPOS system recorded each sale and automatically sent an order to the distributor when inventory fell below levels determined through inventory control procedures.

In planning this integrated order processing system—which, in turn, was integrated with other elements of materials management and physical distribution systems—planners were quite cognizant of the tradeoff between cost (EPOS was quite expensive) and the value of order-processing timeliness and accuracy to customers.

• INVENTORY MANAGEMENT

Three key inventory management formulas define quantities of goods that should be maintained in inventory, when these quantities should be replenished, and how much should be ordered when they are replenished: the reorder point formula, the economic order quantity (EOQ) formula, and the average inventory formula. We will assume that these formulas are being applied by a distributor who is ordering MM systems from a Merton assembly plant for distribution to retailers of computer systems.

BALANCING COSTS AGAINST CUSTOMERS

All three formulas begin with the notion that Merton, ideally, would like to respond 100 percent to customer demand for MM systems by filling every order placed. They realize, however, that items in stock incur a diversity of carrying costs—including insurance, interest, warehouse utilities, obsolescence, and damage—so carrying enough inventory to fill all orders would incur excessive costs. On the other hand, carrying insufficient levels of stock could decrease sales and profits as customers switch to other sellers who can fill orders more reliably. The challenge, then, is to balance costs and potential profits.

• THE REORDER POINT FORMULA

The first formula for achieving this balance between costs and profits—the reorder point formula—ensures that there will be sufficient merchandise in inventory to fill customer orders often enough to keep them satisfied. Here is how this formula was applied by Merton's distributor to ensure that customer orders are filled 90 percent of the time:

Order lead time	×	Usage rate	+	Safety stock	=	Reorder point
6 days	×	2 MMs per day	+	5 MMs	=	17 MMs

Note that, after a distributor places an order for MM systems, it will take an expected six days (order lead time) for the order to arrive. During this period, the distributor will sell, on average, two MMs each day. To account for the odd day when the distributor sells more than two MMs (say, six), a safety stock of five MMs is kept as a backup. Thus, when the inventory level gets down to seventeen MMs (the reorder point), an order should be put in through the distributor's EPOS system for a sufficient quantity of MM systems to take care of customer needs while waiting for the order to arrive.

• *THE EOQ FORMULA*

The economic order quantity formula shows the quantity of stock to reorder when the reorder point (seventeen MMs) is reached. As quantities ordered increase, economies of scale lower the cost of ordering each individual item. For example, one purchase order, costing $20 to process, can be used to order 1 or 1000 MMs; obviously, if 1000 are ordered for inventory, ordering costs per unit ordered will be quite low. However, each item ordered incurs carrying costs (noted earlier), so if 1000 MMs were ordered, these costs would far exceed ordering cost savings.

The EOQ formula shows the tradeoff point (the quantity ordered) at which ordering and carrying costs are equal (Figure 20-1). This also happens to be the lowest total cost for ordering the item.

$$EOQ = \frac{2\,SO}{iP}$$

Where S = annual quantity sold in units, O = cost of placing an order, i = carrying cost, as a percent of selling price, and P = price per unit.

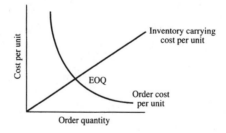

Figure 20–1. EOQ is point at which ordering and carrying costs intersect.

For example, assume the following figures for the distributor ordering MM systems: S is 500, O is $20, i is 20 percent, and P (the price of each MM) is $2000. Plugging these figures into the EOQ formula produces a figure of 7; that is, the distributor should reorder seven MMs each time the reorder point of seventeen MMs (determined by the first formula) is reached. Since annual quantity sold is 500, seventy-one orders will be placed over the course of the year.

• THE AVERAGE INVENTORY FORMULA

The third formula employed by the Merton distributor used data from the first two formulas to determine average inventory size (the average amount of MM systems in inventory at any given time). This formula is:

$$AI = \frac{OQ}{2 + ss}$$

Average inventory (AI) is the amount of inventory ordered each time OQ (from the EOQ formula) divided by 2 and added to the safety stock (also used in the reorder point formula). Thus, assuming that the Merton distributor maintains a safety stock of 5, average inventory would be rounded off 8 (7/2 + 5). Average inventory is especially useful as a basis of comparison with inventory management results of other competitors. For example, an excessively high average inventory figure might suggest that the distributor's carrying costs are too high.

TRADEOFFS AMONG LOGISTICS FUNCTIONS OPTIMIZE COSTS

Viewing these logistical functions from a total systems/cost perspective, Merton planners could implement a number of tradeoffs to reduce overall logistics costs while making the entire logistics system work more efficiently. For example, setting up sourcing and production facilities, although expensive, might be cost effective when compared to costs incurred in transporting MM systems to distant markets. Other tradeoffs might involve altering transportation modes, improving order transmittal procedures (direct computer-order entry, for example), and locating storage facilities in low-cost areas.

INTERNATIONAL PERSPECTIVE

In this section, we examine differences in the logistical environment that distinguish global from domestic markets, including higher transportation and storage costs brought on by longer distances traveled via diverse transportation modes; more intermediaries involved in logistics processes; transactions among these intermediaries in different currencies and exchange

rates; diverse border-crossing regulations and customs inspections protocols; humidity, pilferage, and breakage problems; differing packaging /
labeling requirements; inadequate docking and materials handling facilities;
and red tape involved in acquiring marine insurance, licenses, and other
documents required by exporting and importing nations.

We will first examine the interrelated, usually adverse, repercussions these
differences have on transportation, storage, inventory, and order-processing
functions. Then, we will examine tradeoffs that exporting companies like
Merton make within and among these functions to achieve total cost/
systems goals, as well as the support and organizational systems they use
to plan and implement these tradeoffs.

TRANSPORTATION CONSIDERATIONS AND CONSTRAINTS

The same modes of transportation available to shippers in domestic markets
are available to those in global markets, but with a strong difference in
modes emphasized. This change in emphasis generally favors air and water
transportation to carry products through channels to customers in global
markets, based mainly on considerations pertaining to time, cost, and reliability.

• *TRANSIT TIME*

Transit time is often the major consideration in global transport decisions,
in that faster, more frequent deliveries can lever dramatic savings in inventory size, need for overseas depots, and capital availability. Faster deliveries
can also generate a competitive advantage when just-in-time inventory policies are an issue or when shipping perishable and emergency products. Fast
transportation in global markets, however, is expensive, and subject to analysis to determine if justified by prospective savings.

• *COST*

Cost is generally highest, on a per-item basis, for shipping products via
airfreight, with ocean transport next. However, even high per-item costs are
subject to a number of variables in global markets, such as favorable exchange rates, supply-demand patterns, and the monopoly power of individual carriers. Viewed in a broad logistical context, even extremely high
transport costs can be justified for a number of reasons, as when savings
exceed these costs, or customers will pay for fast service, or the product
itself (for example, diamonds) can absorb high transport costs.

• *RELIABILITY*

As with transit time, transit reliability can generate savings in competitive
benefits. For example, if Merton distributors in Japan know that ordered

merchandise will arrive on the day expected, they can maintain lower, cheaper safety stocks in inventory and be able to competitively fulfill customer needs.

TRANSPORTATION MODES AND PREFERENCES

Based on considerations of time, cost, and reliability, Merton logistics planners focused on the relative merits of the following transportation modes in implementing strategic plans to enter and grow in foreign markets. Two of these modes—air and water—were rarely used in Merton's domestic market.

• *RAILROADS*

As in domestic markets, railroads are the most popular mode of transportation in foreign markets, providing good speed, economy and reliability in transporting carload-size shipments over long distances. Railroad transport is especially popular in advanced countries like Japan, France, and Germany, where "bullet" trains are making railroads competitive with airlines.

• *AIR SHIPPING*

High-value, high-density, perishable, and emergency goods dominate air shipments in global markets. The most expensive of all transportation modes, air shipments are also used when a firm is testing, or beginning operations, in a new country or is aggressively expanding operations in an existing market. Among the factors making air transport an attractive transport alternative are better ground facilities, containerization, and the ability to transport bulky cargoes on jumbo planes.

• *WATER*

In international markets, a number of ocean shipping options are available, including: (1) liner service, which carries cargo and passengers on established, scheduled routes; (2) bulk service, which provides contractual services for individual voyages, or for long time periods; and (3) tramp service, available for irregular routes and scheduled only on demand. Ocean carrier services can also be categorized by type of cargo carried, including: (1) break-bulk cargo vessels, useful for oversized and unusual cargoes; (2) container ships that carry standardized containers to facilitate loading, unloading, and intermodal transfers; (3) Roll-on-roll-off (RORO) vessels that ferry loaded trucks to their destinations; and (4) lighter aboard ship (LASH) vessels that ferry loaded barges to destinations, where they can operate on inland waterways.

Regardless of the water transportation option a shipper chooses, particular attention should be paid to how shipboard cargo is packaged. Packaging in international markets is strongly influenced by a passage in the U.S. Carriage of Goods by Sea Act that states: "Neither the carrier nor the ship shall be responsible for loss or damage arising from insufficiency of packing." A related consideration, illustrated in Figure 20-2, relates to stress hazards facing products in global markets; breakage from these hazards, combined with pilferage and theft losses, actually exceed losses caused by fire, sinkings, and collision of vessels.

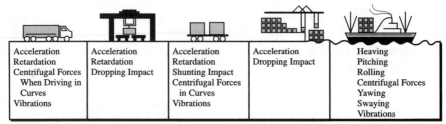

Acceleration	Acceleration	Acceleration	Acceleration	Heaving
Retardation	Retardation	Retardation	Dropping Impact	Pitching
Centrifugal Forces	Dropping Impact	Shunting Impact		Rolling
When Driving in		Centrifugal Forces		Centrifugal Forces
Curves		in Curves		Yawing
Vibrations		Vibrations		Swaying
				Vibrations

Note: Each transportation mode exerts a different set of stresses and strains on containerized cargoes. The most commonly overlooked are those associated with ocean transport.
Source: Reprinted with permission from *Handling and Shipping Management,* September 1980 issue, p. 47; David Greenfield, *Perfect Packing for Export.* Copyright © 1980, Penton Publishing, Cleveland, OH.

Figure 20–2. Stresses in intermodal movement.

To help ensure that these hazards are avoided, and that merchandise arrives at ultimate destinations in safe, maintainable, presentable condition, logistics planners should design product packaging to account for diverse threats and opportunities, including climate changes, nature and quality of port and inland transportation facilities, weight (especially when freight rates or duties are based on it), and special packaging instructions mandated by the importing country or company.

One solution to packaging problems in global markets is **intermodal containers**—large metal boxes that fit on trucks, ships, railroad cars, and airplanes and offer safety from pilferage and damage. A container of oil rig parts, for example, can be loaded in Tulsa, go by truck and train to Kansas City, and then get loaded on a ship to Saudi Arabia.

As with other modes of transportation, costs for water transportation can often be reduced through leverage achieved when the exporter joins an association of shippers.

TRANSPORTATION TRADEOFFS

Illustrative of the tradeoffs that exporters make among transportation modes in global markets is a method called "sea-air" transport. This method combines ships (usually the cheapest transportation mode) and airplanes (usually the fastest and most reliable mode) to avoid the two extremes of high cost and long shipping delays. For example, many Japanese shippers send Europe-bound cargo by ship to the U.S. West Coast; from there, the cargo is flown to its final destination in Europe. By combining the two modes, the trip takes about two weeks, as opposed to four or five weeks with an all-water route, and the cost is about half of an all-air route. A growing practice among Japanese and European shippers sending goods to South America is to sail to U.S. ports and then fly South from there. Ocean carriers from Japan unload at the port of Los Angeles and either fly on from there or truck the cargo to Miami. From the growing sea-air port of Miami, the cargo proceeds by air to destinations such as Brazil. An all-water route from Japan to South America can take a month, whereas sea-air takes about eleven days. Certain types of cargo, such as perishables and bulky items, have to be shipped solely one way or the other, so sea-air is not for everyone.

The key to the success of sea-air are facilities at transfer points. First, a short and easy commute is needed between the dock and airport. Second is the ability to quickly offload from one transport mode and onload to a second as smoothly and quickly as possible. A third vital feature is committed port authorities who can help minimize customs, paperwork, and other red tape associated with international transportation. A fourth is the willingness of local transportation providers to prioritize designated sea-air cargo. When all these features are brought together, the utilization of sea and air can make for a happy ending.[1]

STORAGE FACILITY AVAILABILITY AND QUALITY

Unfortunately, availability of storage facilities abroad, and quality standards of those that exist, might not meet the needs of exporting firms, confronting planners with the problem of long-term, large-scale investment in such facilities and the need to justify this investment in terms of the profit potential of the market.

Strategies for reducing the cost of locating storage facilities abroad include capitalizing on differentials in factor endowments and making use of foreign trade zones.

- **Factor endowment differentials,** such as costs for labor and capital, often exist between adjoining countries to the advantage of locating storage and distribution facilities. For example, the *maquiladora* program between the United States and Mexico permits firms to carry out labor-intensive operations in Mexico while sourcing raw materials and components from the United States, free of Mexican tariffs. Semifinished or assembled products then shipped to the U.S. are assessed only for the foreign labor component.

---

1 "Sea-Air: Cheap and Fast," *Global Trade,* February 1992, pp. 16–18.

- **Foreign trade zones** are special areas, outside the customs territory of the country in which they are located, that can be used for warehousing, packaging, inspecting, labeling, exhibiting, assembling, fabricating, or transshiping without the burden of duties. Trade zones are located at major ports of entry and inland locations near major production facilities and provide exporting firms like Merton with benefits that easily offset any increased factor costs. For example, an exporting firm setting up operations in one of China's special economic trade zones receives substantial tax incentives, pays low taxes and prices for land and labor, and achieves "made in" status for products assembled in these zones.

ORDER PROCESSING IN GLOBAL MARKETS

Mainly because of additional intermediaries in the distribution chain between Merton's domestic manufacturing facilities and ultimate customers in foreign markets—including channels, freight forwarders, customs agents, brokers, and banks—order-processing paperwork and costs increased dramatically. When these costs are added to higher transportation and storage costs, the impact on inventory size and cost in global markets can be appreciable, as the following analysis shows. (Note: In international markets, all costs are figured after taxes, to account for the influence of different tax policies.)

HOW LOGISTICS FUNCTIONS AFFECT INVENTORY IN GLOBAL MARKETS

Assume the following changes in the numbers plugged into the three inventory management formulas discussed earlier resulting from Merton's attempt to penetrate the Indonesian market. These numbers, which might apply to a single distributor in Indonesia, are probably conservative; for example, lead time could easily grow to more than fifty days.

• *REORDER POINT FORMULA*

1. Order lead time has been extended from six to twenty-four days because of longer distances, more channel intermediaries and facilitators to deal with, administrative and customs delays, materials handling and physical distribution delays (special packing for transit, poor inland transit, and the like).

2. Sales average two MM systems per day; however,

3. Safety stock requirements double, from five MM systems to ten systems, largely because of (1) inconsistency of deliveries resulting from transport of shipments among different transportation modes and (2) less predictable sales patterns in a new global market as compared to the domestic market.

Given these changes, the reorder point now changes from seventeen to fifty-eight MM systems; that is, when inventory reaches the level of fifty-eight MM systems, more inventory will be ordered (24 days × 2 MM systems sold each day + 10 MMs in the safety stock).

• *ECONOMIC ORDER POINT FORMULA*

1. Annual quantity sold (S) is still 500 units.

2. Cost of placing an order (O) increases from $20 to $40, mainly as a result of additional paperwork and red tape involved in dealing with more intermediaries and facilitators, over longer distances, to place and expedite orders.

3. The price of each MM system (P) increases from $2000 in the domestic market to $3000 in this new foreign market, primarily to cover additional logistical costs involved in transporting the MM systems to Indonesia, as well as the start-up marketing costs involved in aggressively entering this new market.

4. Inventory carrying cost as a percent of the $3000 selling price remains at 20 percent.

Although the numbers plugged into the EOQ formula as applied in the Indonesian market have changed appreciably, the actual economic quantity of MM systems to order when the reorder point (58) is reached only increases from seven to eight. The size of the average inventory in Indochina, however, now increases from eight MM systems to fourteen systems, along with a dramatic increase in the costs of carrying this inventory.

INVENTORY AS AN INFLATION HEDGE

Beyond the formulas that help determine inventory size, reorder points, and quantities to reorder, another consideration affecting inventory policy in global markets pertains to currency exchange fluctuations. For example, in situations where a host country's currency is about to be devalued, increasing inventory will reduce the exporter's exposure to devaluation losses that would result from holding cash. Similarly, large inventories can provide a hedge against high inflation rates in that, unlike cash, its price can be increased in tandem with inflation rates. In such circumstances, the exporter must assess the tradeoff costs of maintaining larger inventories versus the exchange rate savings from hedging against inflation or devaluation.

COORDINATING TRANSPORTATION

By way of addressing the myriad logistics (in addition to pricing, promotion, and product design/development) problems they anticipated in attempting to enter and grow in the global marketplace, Merton planners had no hesitation in retaining the services of outside specialists, including freight forwarders and contract logistics specialists.

INTERNATIONAL FREIGHT FORWARDERS

Because a single shipment through channels to a foreign customer will probably involve a combination of transportation modes, Merton planners utilized international freight forwarders, specialized firms that act as agents for international marketers. In consolidating shipments and moving cargoes to overseas destinations, freight forwarders advise marketers on shipping documentation and packing costs, prepare necessary documents, and book necessary space aboard carriers. Freight forwarders offer economies of scale because carload rates are much lower than less-than-carload rates. They also provide traffic management services, such as selecting the most reasonable transportation modes.

CONTRACT LOGISTICS SPECIALISTS

A growing preference among global firms, adopted by about one third of Fortune 500 companies, is contract logistics, whereby logistical management is contracted out to third-party logistics providers with specialized logistics experience and expertise. Services offered by these providers range widely, from purely consultive services based on proprietary systems and databases, through subcontracting out portions of the logistical task, to use of their own assets to perform a complete logistics service. A key benefit of contracting out the logistics function to full-service providers in foreign markets is the ability to take advantage of an in-place network of channels and facilities able to start up and maintain materials management and physical distribution activities in unfamiliar markets. Global Focus 20-1 highlights benefits that can derive from such a full-service contractual arrangement.

GLOBAL FOCUS 20-1

How BLS Simplified NSC's Delivery Problem

Today, information moves around the world in a blink of an eye, and semiconductors are instrumental in making this happen. Increasingly, producers of semiconductors recognize that their product itself needs to move from producer to consumer nearly as fast.

One company that attempts to do just that is National Semiconductor Corporation (NSC) located in California. The firm realized that, to allow greater speed of delivery, its global supply network needed an overhaul. The old logistical network of decentralized control was a tangle of unnecessary interchanges, propped up by forty-four different international freight forwarders and eighteen different air carriers. "The complexity of it all wasn't allowing consistent service," comments Kevin Phillips, NSC director of worldwide logistics.

National Semiconductor wanted to change its five- to eighteen-day delivery time and offer a two-day delivery guarantee. The key factor in the strategy was the recruitment of a third-party logistics firm to provide valuable expertise as well as needed infrastructure. NSC turned to Federal Express's Business Logistics Services (BLS) as a partner. Explains Philips, "Our company competes on technology; we cannot compete on logistics; Federal's core competency is delivery; it can do what we can't." BLS was able to provide National Semiconductor with a formidable logistics network by granting access to 420 aircraft, 1869 worldwide facilities, more than 100,000 computer terminals, 31,000 surface vehicles, and an infrastructure with more than 90,000 employees. Phillips views NSC's partnership with Federal as "using the experts who spend billions on logistics."

Source: Macro Logistics for Microprocessors," *Distribution,* April 1993, pp. 66–72.

MANAGING THE LOGISTICS FUNCTION

Two general options are available to exporters in managing the logistics function: do it yourself, or let someone else do it for you. If the first option is selected, two other possibilities present themselves:

- Under a centralized framework, both local and headquarters management would report to a single person at headquarters with authority for coordinating and controlling logistics activities. This framework, which helps achieve cohesion, fast decision making, and economies of scale, is especially effective when the objective is rapid growth in global markets. A potential drawback is the ill will that can arise when local managers are appraised and rewarded on the basis of performance they do not control.

- Under a decentralized framework, subsidiaries are perceived as profit centers, with managers given authority and responsibility to develop and implement marketing plans and programs. This framework works best when the firm serves many diverse global markets. Among the advantages of this model are better training and satisfaction of local managers and the ability to adapt to local conditions. However, some benefits of centralization are lost; these benefits include coordinating diverse marketing plans and achieving quantity transportation discounts.

CHAPTER PERSPECTIVE

This chapter examines the logistical function in international markets, encompassing such materials management and physical distribution functions as packaging, transportation, storage, order processing, and inventory control. Particularly in global markets, with longer transportation routes and more intermediaries to deal with, the high cost of logistical activities is usually the single largest deterrent to successful market entry. Guided by total systems and total cost concepts, logistics managers help transform these high costs into sizable savings by treating discrete logistics functions as components of a single system, with tradeoffs within and among them to generate optimal efficiencies at minimal cost. This chapter also examined situations in which centralized, decentralized, or third-party approaches for managing the logistics function were appropriate.

KNOW THE CONCEPTS
TERMS FOR STUDY

Average inventory formula
Carriage of Goods by Sea Act

Carriers
Contract logistics

Economic order quantity (EOQ)   Order cycle
Electronic data interchange   Order processing
   (EDI)   Packaging
Electronic point of sale (EPOS)   Physical distribution
Factor endowment differentials   Reorder point
Just in time (JIT)   Storage
Logistics management   Total costs
Intermodal containers   Total systems
Inventory management   Tradeoffs
Materials management   Transportation modes

MATCHUP EXERCISES

1. Match up the first-column concept with the second-column descriptor.
   1. global logistics
   2. materials management
   3. physical distribution
   4. logistics management

   a. timely arrival of goods into and through the firm
   b. movement of finished parts to customers
   c. flow of products into, through, and out of international companies
   d. coordination of materials management and physical distribution

2. Match up the concepts in the second column with the logistics functions in the first column.
   1. packaging   a. EPOS
   2. order processing   b. RORO
   3. inventory management c. EOQ
   4. transportation   d. Carriage of Goods by Sea Act

3. Match up the inventory management concept in the second column with the descriptor in the first column.
   1. the inventory level that   a. EOQ
      triggers another order
   2. the amount ordered   b. RP
      when this level is reached
   3. the time between when the   c. order cycle
      order is placed and when
      the ordered goods arrive
   4. making sure inventory arrives   d. JIT
      at precisely the time it is needed

QUESTIONS FOR REVIEW AND DISCUSSION

1. Differences between distribution systems in the United States and Russia are striking. For example, in the United States in 1996, 40 percent of all shipments were delivered under quick response just-in-time conditions, with distribution costs representing about 10 percent of sales. In Russia, however, quick response is often no response, and costs of this sluggish distribution are about 300 percent higher than they are in the United States. In terms of logistical concepts, discuss reasons for this cost-effectiveness disparity.

2. One logistical system that does work well in Russia is that comprising McDonald's enterprise. From a joint venture agreement signed in 1988 (the largest ever between a food company and the then Soviet Union), this enterprise, by 1993, constituted the largest McDonald's restaurant in the world—employing over 1000 people and serving 50,000 people daily—and a 10,000 square-meter food production and distribution center. Located in the Moscow suburb of Solntsevo, the distribution center supplied the restaurant located in the center of Moscow and was itself supplied by farmers throughout Russia who had contracted to provide quality food supplies, including beef, onions, fruit, lettuce, pickles, milk, flour, butter, and a variety of potatoes needed to make McDonald's famous french fries. At full capacity, the meat line produces 10,000 patties per hour, and the bakery line turns out over 14,000 buns per hour. Storage space at the center holds 3000 tons of potatoes, and the pie line produces 5000 pies per hour. As with restaurants in the McDonald's chain built in Russia after 1993, the original Moscow restaurant accepted only rubles.

   In terms of the McDonald's enterprise, define the following concepts: physical distribution, materials management, logistics management, total systems, total cost.

3. Which mode of transportation would you judge to be most appropriate for the following products and why:

   - Kegs of beer for a fraternity party;

   - The late Jacqueline Kennedy's personal effects, auctioned off in New York;

   - Oil from Saudi Arabia to the United States.

4. Here are three inventory management problems, the first involving reorder points, the second concerning economic order quantities, and the third regarding average inventory size:

   - Reorder point: Assume that a distributor of consumer electronics products sells, on average, five computer modems a day; desires a safety stock of twenty modems; and realizes that it will require, on average, twenty days for an order of modems to arrive from the manufacturer. How many modems will remain in inventory when an order is placed?

- Economic order quantity: Assume that the annual demand for modems is 1000 units, the ordering cost per unit is $25, and the inventory carrying costs are 25 percent of the $100 selling price of each modem. What is the amount to be ordered when the reorder point (above) is reached? How many orders would be placed in a year?

- Average inventory size: Given the preceding facts and figures, what is this firm's average inventory of modems?

ANSWERS
MATCHUP EXERCISES

1. 1c, 2a, 3b, 4d
2. 1d, 2a, 3c, 4b
3. 1b, 2a, 3c, 4d

QUESTIONS FOR REVIEW AND DISCUSSION

1. The root cause of this disparity traces largely to seventy years of centralized command economy stress on productivity, whereas the means for distributing this output—such as advertising agencies, banks, and wholesale and retail outlets—were generally perceived as lecherous, unproductive intermediaries. As a result, distribution in Russia is primitive at best, with poor supply lines and use of warehouse space, insufficient distribution and service centers, inadequate transportation facilities, and archaic inventory management systems. What was generally ignored in Marxist central planning is the value of the place/time/possession utilities created by an efficient logistics system. Thus, for example, if you purchase a digital watch battery in a supermarket, you get the proper battery, in a convenient location, when you need it, for a reasonable price. In creating these utilities, the distribution system also performs a number of functions, often better than they could be performed by the producer, such as finding customers, matching products to customer needs, grading and storing products, financing purchases, and developing first-hand marketing information. Actually, an efficient distribution system with a diversity of channels and intermediaries usually reduces the price we pay for products, as evidenced by a comparison of prices for similar products in economies with strong, mature logistical systems and those with weak, archaic systems.

2. Physical distribution encompasses the broad range of functions involved in the efficient delivery of foods from Russian farmers to the production/distribution center and from the center to the restaurant, including packaging, transportation, order processing, inventory management, and storage. Materials management encompasses systems, procedures, and controls to ensure that these functions work together efficiently in moving raw materials (potatoes, lettuce) and finished goods (Big Macs) to designated places, at designated times, in proper condition. Logistics management entails the initial planning of physical distribution and materials management systems and activities, following total systems and total cost concepts. The total systems concept would view all physical distribution functions as a single integrated entity, with decisions in any one area affecting decisions in all other areas. For example, the decision to transport raw materials from the farms to the processing center, and from the processing center to the McDonald's restaurant, in the fastest, most expensive way possible, consistent with just-in-time mandates, might dramatically improve the functioning of order processing, storage, and inventory management functions. The related total cost concept identifies a set of alternatives that optimize cost-benefit relationships. For example, in the example just given (large investments in transportation and state-of-the-art order processing and inventory management functions), total benefits in terms of zero-wastage of products, and rapid preparation, presentation, and purchase of menu items, might easily justify this expense.

3. Kegs of beer: Transport by truck because they require flexibility in delivery and are traveling a short distance.
Jackie O's effects: Transport by air because they are high in value and low in bulk.
Oil: Transport by pipeline and water transport because it isn't solid and must move a long distance.

4. Reorder point:
Order lead time × Usage rate + Safety stock = Reorder point
20 × 5 + 20 = 20

Economic order quantity:
$$EOQ = \frac{2\,(1000)(25)}{(0.25)(100)} = 500 = 22$$

Average inventory: AI = OQ/2 + ss = 22.5 + 20 = 43

21 MARKETING ON THE INTERNET

OVERVIEW

Internet marketing can dramatically improve all aspects of the strategic marketing planning process, including identifying and defining target market segments, building marketing mixes, setting marketing objectives, implementing marketing programs, and measuring performance. Key to effective Internet marketing are Web sites that achieve profit objectives by communicating interactively with a firm's publics along the World Wide Web.

HOW INTERNET MARKETING EVOLVED

The history of Internet marketing began roughly in the mid 1950s, when companies first began to make extensive use of computers to perform accounting tasks, payroll processing, and production planning. Next, companies began to develop private networks that allowed them to interchange purchase orders, shipping instructions, reorder forms, and other information among departments and distribution channels worldwide.

Then, in the early 1970s, two early versions of the Internet were created. The first, called ARPANET (Advanced Research Projects Agency Network) was created by the U.S. Department of Defense to provide secure communications among organizations involved in defense-related research. The second, called the NSFNet (National Science Foundation Network), was established to enable researchers and academics in nondefense fields to use a network similar to ARPANET. NSFNet became the model for the Internet.

Finally, four interrelated developments brought together these public and private networks into the modern Internet, which today encompasses data networks set up by organizations, the World Wide Web, e-mail, and many proprietory networks. First, the World Wide Web was created by an Oxford-educated physicist, Tim Berners-Lee, while working at a physics laboratory outside Geneva, Switzerland. Second, businesses developed their electronic commerce intranets, which connect computers within a company, and extranets, which connect computers within the firm to computers outside the firm and with the Internet. Third, network servers, or hubs, that interface with the Internet for businesses and individuals achieved levels of growth necessary to allow the fast and diverse connections needed for effective communication. Fourth, the number of customers with access to the Internet through a personal computer or Web TV device grew large enough to be commercially viable.

The dramatic growth of Internet communication in the United States—where, at the turn of the century, U.S. companies like Amazon.com, Yahoo, Cisco, IBM, Microsoft, and Sun Microsystems collected 85 percent of revenues and represented 95 percent of stock market value of Internet companies—was stimulated by a variety of causes characterizing the entrepreneurial climate in the United States: venture capital financing, close ties between business and universities, a deregulated business environment, flexible labor markets, and a culture that celebrates risk-taking and getting very rich, very fast.

THE GROWTH OF INTERNET MARKETING

Internet marketing, or e-commerce, includes all activities of a firm between manufacturers, intermediaries, customers, and other publics that use the Internet to help exchange products. The business-to-business market is the largest segment of Internet marketing, with commerce totaling more than $50 billion in the year 2000 and representing more than two thirds of the total Internet activity. Today, more than 95 percent of large businesses have Internet sites, with about two thirds of this total using a site for sales activity, and almost half reporting that the site is profitable.

Among consumers, use of the Internet has been doubling every 18 months to the point where, in the year 2000, there were more than 87 million Internet users, either connected at work or home, in North America. This is about half the size of the world market. Of this total, about 50 million were online buyers, representing more than one quarter of all Americans 14 or older.

Figure 21-1 profiles the changing demographic face of Internet users in the United States, and Figure 21-2 summarizes reasons why consumers use the Internet.

	Started Using Net	In Past Year	More Than a Year
	Percent of all Net users	46	53
Percent of users who are:	Male	48	55
	Female	52	45
Age:	18–29	25	30
	30–49	52	50
	50–64	16	15
	65+	4	4
Income:	$50,000+	35	45
	$30,000–49,000	23	22
	Under $30,000	23	16
Education	College graduate	29	46
	Some college	32	30
	High school graduate	33	19
	Less than high school	6	3
Use Net for:	Work	24	30
	Pleasure	52	39
	Mix	22	31

Source: Pew Research Center, 1998 telephone survey, www.people-press.org/tech98sum.htm

Figure 21–1. Changing demographics of Internet users.

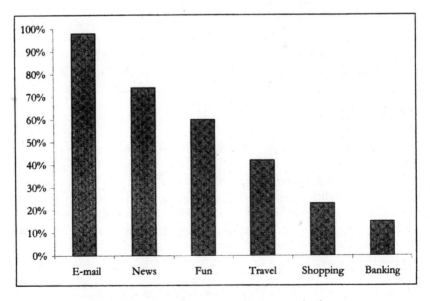

Figure 21–2. Reasons why consumers use the Internet.

INTERNET MARKETING AIDS STRATEGIC PLANNING

Internet marketing improves all the components of the strategic marketing planning process, from setting marketing objectives through defining target markets and building marketing mixes that reflect the nature and needs of these markets to planning, implementing, and controlling strategic plans that bring together markets and marketing mixes. Because the Internet needs only a server to be connected, all firms, from the smallest to the largest, can compete on a relatively level playing field.

These benefits of Internet marketing derive mainly from four types of Web sites through which most commerce and communication take place: company/brand sites, information sites, selling sites, and service sites. Market Focus 21-1 shows how these sites interact to efficiently achieve customer and company objectives in marketing new and used cars. An analysis of these interactions defines the following Internet components. The **Internet** itself is a worldwide network of interconnected computer networks that carry data and exchange information. **Intranets** connect computers within a business together (for example, the network of computers connecting the selling Web sites to the automobile dealers that subscribe to these sites). The **World Wide Web** (or Web) is a collection of hyperlinked documents (not computers) that use a common protocol; the illustrated information about new and used cars carried on each selling site, along with banner headlines (called hypertext) linking each selling site to other sites. The Webmaster is responsible for maintaining and upgrading each selling site.

MARKET FOCUS 21-1

How to Buy a Car over the Internet

Illustrative of how Internet marketing works for both buyers and sellers, and how it differs from more traditional marketing methods, is the process involved in purchasing an automobile over the Internet. Conceptually, this process also applies to the purchase of practically any other product or service imaginable, from a local supermarket order to a world cruise.

The prospective buyer, perhaps wishing to avoid the bother and frustration of hard-sell pressures and haggling negotiations at traditional dealer showrooms, might decide, instead, to visit a virtual dealer showroom on an Internet site.

Two such showroom types are available: a dealer referral site, the most popular, and an online buying site. Both types provide information to help shoppers make informed choices, and the means to purchase the automobile chosen. However, the first site-type—represented by referral sites like autoweb.com and autobytel.com—entails a short visit to the dealer after a bid is accepted to wrap up purchase paperwork and drive the car away. The second site-type—represented by sites like CarsDirect.com and InvoiceDealers.com—eliminates the need for the visit to the dealer by arranging for delivery of the car to the buyer's home or office.

Both sites earn the bulk of their income from referrals to local automobile dealers, some of which sign up with more than one site. Most of the rest of the site's income comes from selling advertising on their sites, the sale of after-market products to buyers and, in a few cases, fees charged to dealers or buyers. All Web sites try to engage shoppers in conversations with each other or with the site itself, as a means of exposing them to advertising and eliciting useful information—including rave reviews, horror stories, and personal preferences about autos and accessories.

A typical showroom page on an auto Web site will include these features:

- Illustrations of new and used cars, often in dramatized contexts like 3D surround video, supplemented by legible tables for specifications.

- Comparisons of new and/or used cars, or different makes or models of the same type of vehicle (vans, sport utility vehicles, and the like).

- Feedback from satisfied and unsatisfied customers.

- Information on costs of options, loans, and leases, usually in a format that takes into account different situations (duplicated options, longer or shorter lease terms, different insurance coverages, and the like) and provides links to dealer referral and financing sites.

By way of making visits to dealer referral or online buying sites more productive, the shopper might first consult a reference site, such as the Kelley Blue Book site (kbb.com) or the Yahoo site (autos.yahoo.com), for information about prices, options, reviews, and trade-in values for new and used cars. These reference sites also often include message boards, chat rooms, and links to financing or dealers.

In using referral, online buying, or reference sites, shoppers typically answer questions about the type of vehicle they are looking for and provide information, including their phone numbers, to help consummate the transaction. Usually, the shopper's bid will be supplied to a number of participating dealers in a prescribed geographic area, and the buyer will get a call from the dealer quoting a price the same day. In most cases, the dealer promises to stand by the price quoted online.

Buyers benefit from the speed, convenience, and economy of buying cars online, with the assurance that their buying decisions are based on objective information and that they get a good price. Dealers can afford to sell at a lower price because the cost of the sale is less, involving less time and paperwork.

INTERNET SITES SELL, SERVICE, AND INFORM

Most Internet activity relating to strategic marketing planning objectives and activities is implemented on company/brand, information, selling and service sites. These sites will form the context for a discussion of how Merton Electronics used the Internet to penetrate the global marketplace.

• *COMPANY/BRAND SITES*

These sites are directly informational, and indirectly promotional. The Coca-Cola Web site is an illustrative example. This site consists of twelve sections, including three international sites, that explain the company's history, mission, and products; allow visitors to interact with company spokespeople; provide information to Coke memorabilia collectors; provide links to sports and entertainment providers; and offer puzzles and word games. None of these sites actively sell Coke products, but, collectively, enhance brand equity and promote purchases of Coke products through other outlets.

• *INFORMATION SITES*

This type of site relies on member loyalty to generate revenue through advertising or subscription rates. An example of such a site is the *Wall Street Journal* interactive site (www.WSJ.com), which generates fees from subscribers who read up-to-the-minute financial information and *WSJ* articles and advertisers whose banner headlines promote related financial products. This site also provides links that allow subscribers to track markets and investments, and research financial products and markets. Additionally, this site's affiliate program allows other businesses to integrate this site into their sites, with the *WSJ* paying them a fee for any subscriptions that result from click throughs (a process whereby a prospect "clicks through" to purchase from the host site's banner advertisement).

Another type of information site, represented by the Yahoo! search engine, helps Internet surfers find information they seek. Search engines like this generate revenue by selling banner advertising, which is segmented according to the type of search being conducted. For example, a request for information on corporate training programs might bring up a banner advertisement for Merton Electronics. In addition to the search feature on the Yahoo! site, users can bid on products at auction, get up-to-date news, build a virtual store online, or join a virtual community that shares information among members.

• *SELLING SITES*

Amazon.com is a good example of a selling site (virtual stores that allow customers to buy products over the internet). The Amazon.com site sells more than five million books, CDs, audiobooks, DVDs, computer games, and related products to customers in more than 160 countries worldwide. At this site, visitors can search for books or CDs by author, title, artist, or key word; can get recommendations for further reading based on profiles of what other readers with similar tastes read; read reviews by the media or by other readers; or link to a site that recommends music and other products.

Like Amazon.com, most selling sites are designed to move consumers through multiple stages of the decision-making process (as discussed in Chapter 9). The Daimler Chrysler site, for example: (1) asks questions, the answers to which help prospects screen themselves to identify individual needs relating to ownership of an automobile (problem recognition); (2) provides information on Daimler Chrysler offerings (for example, the Jeep Grand Cherokee) relating to these identified needs (information search); and (3) compares features and benefits of different makes and models in the buyer's choice set (alternative evaluation). After the shopper chooses make and model, he or she can get a quote on the price of the car from dealers participating in the site (purchase). Post-purchase evaluation is manifest in the service site, discussed next.

Direct catalog marketers such as L. L. Bean (llbean.com) use selling sites extensively, mainly because of the lower costs of presenting catalogs online versus printing and mailing costs associated with direct mailing to consumers.

• *SERVICE SITES*

The Wells Fargo service site is a good example of characteristics and benefits of these sites. On a basic level, their ATMs (Automated Teller Machines), which simplify financial transactions with customers, allow banks to extend banking hours to twenty-four hours a day without the need for additional personnel and, by including ATMs in retail establishments, to expand geographically without having to build additional branches.

On the Internet level, Wells Fargo's interactive online service site allows customers to access account balances, review transaction histories, buy and sell securities, transfer funds between accounts, pay bills, and apply for lines of credit and home equity loans. Savings on telephone and personnel charges from customers requesting balance information was sufficient to subsidize their entire Web site.

Federal Express is another excellent example of savings possible through a well-designed service Web site. The FedEx Web site, which helps customers interactively track packages from initial shipping to destination, saves the company about $125,000 a month in telephone charges and support personnel who were previously required to answer customer questions about the whereabouts of packages.

THE WELL-DESIGNED WEB SITE

Like any well-designed promotional campaign, a well-designed Web site should have the prospective customer in mind. This means that the site should attract the prospect to it and do a persuasive job of interacting with the prospect once he or she arrives there.

Creating a desire to visit a particular site can be aided by marketing the site through other media—print advertising, TV commercials, newsletters, and the like—and by giving the site a brand name and image that creates its own promotion (for example, the IWon.com site that offers a lottery prize of up to $1 million for visiting it). Good site design avoids the tendency to "copycat" other sites, or to give the site an obscure, irrelevant name. The site name should be registered with more than one browser (or portal) and should be promoted thereon.

Once attracted to the site, the prospect should be encouraged to interact in a mutually productive manner. This means the site should pique the customer's interest by providing information of interest, as the Coca-Cola site, discussed earlier, does with its array of special sections aimed at diverse interests, including traders, mystery lovers, sports enthusiasts, and word game players all over the world. This interesting information should be updated regularly, to prevent staleness and encourage return visits. It should also be sufficiently rewarding to encourage the prospect to provide information of use in identifying individual and group needs and in designing product offerings that meet these needs. Without this interaction, the main purpose of e-commerce Web sites is defeated.

Whatever its primary goal—selling, service, information—a well-designed Web site should also perform a number of secondary services. For example, a selling site designed primarily to sell products and services can also provide public relations information on its history and goals, and a site primarily designed to provide service or disseminate information should have a sales message, if only indirectly. To help achieve these multiple objectives, all site-types—selling, service, brand, information—should seek hyperlinks with other, related products. For example, a selling or information site promoting financial products might feature banner headlines promoting discount subscriptions to financial journals.

Beyond these customer-oriented features, some basic considerations applicable to all sites include registering the domain name, copyrighting the site, and seeking permission for trademarked or copyrighted material.

HOW INTERNET MARKETING HELPS BUILD MARKETS

At the time marketers at Merton Electronics began to implement strategic plans to expand into international markets, Merton had already implemented an Internet marketing system that was as pervasive a component of its corporate mission as its product/market strategic plans or the societal marketing concept that guided these plans. This Internet system encompassed all operational areas involved in making and marketing Merton products and systems, including integrating channels of supply and distribution, optimizing production economies and efficiencies, automating the sales force, identifying and defining target markets, and devising product/price/promotion/distribution marketing mixes attractive to these markets.

Merton's use of Internet marketing to help penetrate the British market early in the twenty-first century illustrates uses and benefits of Internet marketing. The two Web sites that formed the core of Merton's Internet system, and the marketing strategies this system helped implement, included the following sites:

- A company/brand Web site that encompassed background information on Merton (history, mission, financial statements, and the like), with special emphasis on features and benefits of Merton systems. Also included were interactive sections that encouraged browsers to answer questions to pinpoint their training and development needs, and that allowed viewers to screen selected excerpts from Merton training programs targeted to these needs. Another section made recommendations for training materials on a broader scale, including software and equipment from firms other than Merton, some of which advertised on Merton's site. Also recommended were dealers (along with Web site names) from which MM systems could be purchased.

- A selling site for Merton products sold to organizational buyers—buyers that purchased in sufficiently large quantities to justify bypassing distributors and purchasing directly from Merton. As with its company/brand site, this site encouraged interaction with prospective customers to solicit information regarding training needs, specific systems that best met these needs, the size of the training program that would be implemented, and the prospect's ability to pay for it.

- A for-profit learning Web site that offered a full range of online courses for accrediting or maintaining accreditation for business and professional people.

- Connections to online hubs, like America Online and Microsoft Network, are expensive, usually over $1 million. For its connection to America Online, however, Merton (along with 400 other e-commerce partners) gained access to 25 million subscribers.

- Connections to Web portals like Yahoo!, Excite, and Lycos, cost considerably less than the hub connection (for example, $15,000 for a 3-month slot with Yahoo!), and are excellent sources of click-throughs. Web portals typically bunch companies, and encourage customers to shop merchandise, not specific sellers: Merton would be bunched with other companies selling training and development systems.

- Connections to related Web sites related to training and development products and systems (including service, selling and brand sites) cost considerably less than hub or portal sites, and can even represent a source of revenue when the banner headlines of other companies appear on Merton's site.

Costs involved in activating these and other sites (for example, a site for servicing failed Merton products and systems) included connections to on-line hubs, Web portals, and related sites.

INTERNET MARKETING STARTS WITH SUPPLIERS AND DISTRIBUTORS

Initially, Merton's buying center used its Internet access to identify and evaluate suppliers of parts and equipment for the company's industrial and MM systems divisions. Information elicited included specifications, delivery times, and prices of MRO and OEM products and equipment for Merton production facilities in England. Suppliers and licensees selected were then integrated into Merton's distribution system via its intranet system, which encompassed logistical systems for efficiently and economically processing orders and managing inventory. Also selected via Internet and intranet processes were English distributors for Merton products, systems, and services.

Turning from suppliers and distributors to customers and prospective customers, Merton promoted its Web sites along with its products and services through direct mail and print media campaigns. Special incentives to visit, and interact with, Merton's brand and selling sites included profiles of suggested career options based on self-administered aptitude/interest tests, and Merton courses the visitor might take to achieve various business and professional goals.

BENEFITS OF INTERNET MARKETING

In committing companywide to Internet marketing, Merton also committed to dramatic departures from traditional marketing strategies and approaches. These differences, in turn, highlighted benefits of Internet marketing that affected all components of the strategic marketing planning process, especially identifying and defining target markets and building marketing mixes attractive to these markets.

FINDING MARKETS ON THE INTERNET

The pull-oriented nature of Internet marketing, with customers selecting and defining themselves by clicking on and interacting with Merton's Web sites, supplemented or replaced many traditional marketing research tools and techniques (for example, focus groups and telephone surveys), used by Merton marketers to identify and define target markets. This information, voluntarily revealed, allowed Merton to build profiles of target markets featuring the most useful kind of geographic/demographic/psychographic/behavioristic data for crafting persuasive marketing mixes.

CRAFTING MARKETING MIXES FROM INTERNET DATA

In all four marketing mix areas—product, promotion, place, and price—traditional marketing approaches were enhanced by Internet marketing.

• *PRODUCT*

Product design and development strategies differed in that Internet interaction produced a constant stream of information regarding current, often changing, wants and needs about Merton's product lines, and the lines of its competitors. This dynamic data source, and the resultant need to match products to needs, produced a greater focus on reformulating and customizing products and systems. It also helped build stronger relationships among Merton's production, marketing, procurement, and finance functions.

• **PROMOTION**

Both direct and indirect promotional strategies were affected by Merton's commitment to Internet marketing. The main effect of the Internet on direct promotion was to improve performance during all stages of the creative selling process. For example, here is how Internet selling helped Eric Sandham improve the quality of sales presentations he prepared, as discussed in Chapter 18.

During the prospecting and qualifying stages, Sandham referred to databases and Web sites to develop such information on prospect companies as products produced, financial viability, size and growth record, which would help him decide if calls were justified, and what needs could be met by Merton products. These databases and Web sites would also be referenced during the planning/preparation stages, along with search engines and participation in chat room discussions. During customer contact stages—including the approach, the presentation, handling objections and closing—Web sites would be used to supplement his presentation, providing graphic illustrations of Merton systems, visually addressing objections, and providing navigation pathways through Web sites customized to customer needs. E-mail inquiries and individualized offers (for example, new training software) would implement the follow-up stage.

Indirect promotion was affected in diverse ways, with Internet advertising supplementing traditional print and electronic media, which now promoted Merton's Web site in addition to the firm's products and services. (Illustrative of the emphasis firms place on promoting their Internet sites was the remarkable number of commercials for such sites during the 2000 Super Bowl game—17 such commercials.) Economies and efficiencies were also achieved in this area by publishing, and continually updating, Merton catalogs and direct mailings online.

• **PLACE**

As compared to more traditional approaches, the largest savings in time and dollars were achieved in the distribution function, along the full length of the distribution chain. Initially, the Internet made possible fast evaluation of suppliers and distributors in new territories. Then, in managing logistics in these territories, Internet and intranet systems facilitated automated systems for ordering, reordering, and invoicing. Because the Internet facilitated better matching of inventory to customer needs, just-in-time inventory management procedures were facilitated so that defect-free parts and materials were delivered for Merton production processes just when needed, as were Merton products and systems to its customers. As a result, costs associated with inventory management—such as for interest, storage, and obsolescence—were dramatically reduced.

• *PRICING*

Changes from traditional marketing approaches brought on by Internet marketing produced dramatic savings for Merton in many areas, including: (1) more efficient, productive relations with supplier and distributor channel members; (2) direct sales presentations and indirect promotional activities; (3) marketing research to define the nature and needs of target markets; (4) product design and development strategies reflecting documented customer needs and preferences; and (5) customer service and follow-up. These savings, achieved while improving marketing functions, gave Merton much greater flexibility in pricing its products than competitors without an integrated Internet strategy.

All of these benefits of Internet marketing—the level competitive field it provided; better, faster identification of target markets; and economies and efficiencies in all marketing mix areas—combined to help Merton achieve a rapid, successful penetration of the English market and, subsequently, other European and Asian markets. The changes from traditional marketing approaches and methods represented by Internet marketing also produced profound changes in other components of the firm's strategic marketing planning processes, including the objectives it now set for itself, and the standards and controls for measuring performance.

CHAPTER PERSPECTIVE

The dramatic growth of Internet marketing, consisting of internets, intranets, and extranets that facilitate interactive communication among businesses, customers, and other publics along the World Wide Web, is producing equally dramatic changes in traditional marketing approaches. Well-designed Web sites that sell, service, and inform are helping to level the competitive playing field while generating economies and efficiencies in all areas of the strategic marketing planning process, from identifying target markets to energizing product development, promotion, distribution, and pricing strategies to meet the defined needs of these markets.

KNOW THE CONCEPTS
TERMS FOR STUDY

Banner headlines
Click through
Company/brand sites
E-commerce
E-mail
Extranets
Host site
Hubs
Hypertext
Hyperlinks
Information sites
Internets

Internet marketing
Intranets
Online buying
Portals
Reference sites
Search engines
Selling sites
Servers
Service sites
Webmaster
WWW (World Wide Web)

MATCHUP EXERCISES

1. Match the company name in the first column with the descriptor in the second column.
   1. Yahoo!
   2. Federal Express
   3. America Online

   a. server
   b. Webmaster
   c. search engine

2. Match the activity in the first column with the result in the second column.
   1. banner advertising
   2. clicking through
   3. preference questionnaires

   a. links Web sites together
   b. active involvement
   c. information exchange

3. Match the term in the first column with the descriptor in the second column.
   1. Internet

   2. extranet

   3. Web

   a. a collection of linked documents that use a common protocol
   b. a network of interconnected computer networks
   c. a network that connects computers outside firm to intranet at the firm

4. Match the Web site function in the first column with the descriptor in the second column.

1. brand
   a. *Sports Illustrated's* Web site gives you the latest scores.

2. selling
   b. The "Shop Here" section of Tide's Web site directs you to retailers of Ricky Rudd collectibles.

3. information
   c. FedEx's Webmaster tracks your package.

4. service
   d. You order shirts for Dad through L. L. Bean's site.

QUESTIONS FOR REVIEW AND DISCUSSION

1. The domestic travel market is expected to more than double between 2000 and 2005. Discuss how Internet marketing can exploit this growth in terms of the stages of the buyer decision process (covered in Chapter 9). The following five questions refer to this situation: Assume that you have sufficient financing to start up a Web site designed to provide on-line retailers with an opportunity to improve profitability by offering extended warranties to their customers to supplement warranties that already exist on these products.

2. What companies, performing what functions, would you have to persuade to participate in this venture?

3. How might you promote your Web site to encourage people to refer to your site?

4. How would you profit from your Web site?

5. What costs will you incur in operating your Web site?

6. How do the following terms apply in this situation: selling site, service site, information site, brand site, intranet, extranet, click through, banner headline.

ANSWERS
MATCHUP EXERCISES

1. 1c, 2b, 3a
2. 1b, 2c, 3a
3. 1b, 2c, 3a
4. 1b, 2d, 3a, 4c

QUESTIONS FOR REVIEW AND DISCUSSION

1. The buyer decision-making process, as discussed in Chapter 9, entails 5 stages: problem recognition, information search, alternative evaluation, purchase decision, and post-purchase behavior. Online travel services account for buyer behavior in all these stages: for example, banner headlines relating to travel might point up a problem the buyer faces (he or she needs a vacation); comparative information on a travel information site, with which the buyer interacts to define his or her vacation needs, might assist in seeking information on vacation alternatives, and comparing different travel packages as to costs and accommodations; the purchase decision of a specific vacation package is facilitated by the ease of making this purchase; and post-purchase evaluation is facilitated in that the vacation sites are continually available to the buyer, and he or she can express, interactively, satisfaction, or lack of same, with the vacation package chosen.

2. As Webmaster, your primary customers would be retailers of products that lend themselves to warranty protection (appliances, personal electronics, expensive watches, and the like); another group would be companies that would repair these products when warranties go into effect; still another group might be insurance companies that traditionally underwrite product warranties.

3. Your primary customers—the retailer group—would probably do most of your promotion for you in recommending your Web site for purchasing extended warranties to their customers. You would most likely promote your site, and your warranties, in print and electronic media vehicles referred to by potential customers. For potential retailer customers, your appeal would be the profit that extended warranties produce (retailers typically earn profits of between 30 and 75 percent on such warranties), and the fact that such warranties will give them a post-purchase association with buyers that can lead to future sales and service profits. As an incentive to view your site, you might offer end-users consumer services relating to warranties, such as warranty information on branded products and a breakdown history of these products to help buyers make better selections. Another selling point would be an offer to register all of the buyer's warranties on your Web site automatically, including warranties not purchased through your site. With this information, end-users can keep track of their warranties and stay informed of warranty benefits.

4. Your Web site would produce at least four sources of income: commissions from each of the groups participating in your Web site—retailers, repair shops, and underwriters—who will generate extra sales volume themselves from participation, as well as companies that advertise on your site. (For example, appliance manufacturers and issuers of warranties that can assume your site will be viewed by many in your targeted audience interested in purchasing, and getting coverage for, appliances.) If your site becomes popular enough, you might even be able to charge subscription rates for portions of it, such as your report on product breakdown rates.

5. Costs include up-front costs involved in setting up your site, lining up Web site participants, and administering the whole process of selling the extended warranties to end-users. Additionally, processing repair claims will be very high, and probably preclude profits for years. (One Web site, Amazon.com, considered by investors to be one of the most successful business ventures in history, didn't make a profit for its first four years.) To illustrate the scope of this task, one online warranty company, WarrantyNow, had to sign up 60,000 repair companies in the United States before getting started. Other continuing expenses would involve maintaining and updating your site, and promoting it on other Web sites and other media.

6. A selling site would be the section of your Web site from which the end-user purchases the extended warranty; a service site would be the section through which the end-user applies for warranty coverage when the product breaks down; the information site would be the site to which the end-user refers (and possibly subscribes) to get information on the breakdown history of an appliance that, say, he or she is considering purchasing; and a brand site might be a site of one of the large insurance companies that underwrites your extended warranties, explaining things like its history, mission, and array of products and services it offers. The intranet would be the connection of computers among you and your Web-site partners used in your operations, whereas, the extranet would be the network of computers external to your intranet that feeds your business (for example, between end-user customers and retailers). To click through is what a customer does, perhaps in response to a banner headline on another Web site, to arrive at your site and perhaps subscribe to or purchase your service, and a banner headline is what a company interested in reaching members of your market might run across the top of your site.

GENERAL INDEX

INTERNATIONAL MARKETING INDEX

NAME AND COMPANY INDEX